Wrightslaw:
Special Education Law

Peter W. D. Wright

Pamela Darr Wright

Harbor House Law Press

Hartfield, Virginia 23071

Wrightslaw: Special Education Law
By Peter W. D. Wright and Pamela Darr Wright

Library of Congress Cataloging-in-Publication Data
    Wright, Peter W. D. and Pamela Darr Wright
      Wrightslaw: Special Education Law / 1st ed.
      p.   cm.
      Includes bibiliographical references and index.
      ISBN 1-892320-03-7
      1. Legal reference – special education – United States.   I. Title
      2. Special education – parent participation – United States.
      Library of Congress Catalog Card Number: 99-90349

Printing History

    Harbor House Law Press issues new printings and new editions to keep our books current. New printings include technical corrections and minor changes. New editions include major revisions of text and/or changes in law. We offer a Recycling Policy to help you stay up-to-date on the latest legal information. For more information about our Recyling Policy, check the pages after the Index.
    First Edition   November 1999
    Third Printing   May 2000

When You Use a Self-Help Law Book

    Law is always changing and evolving. The information contained in this book is general information and may or may not reflect current legal developments. This book is designed to provide general information in regard to the subject matter covered. It is sold with the understanding that the publisher and author are not engaged in rendering legal or other professional services. For legal advice about a specific set of facts, you should consult with an attorney.

Disclaimer

    Every effort has been made to make this book as complete and accurate as possible. However, there **may be mistakes** both typographical and in content. Therefore, this text should be used as a general guide only and not as the ultimate source of information about special education law.
    The purpose of this book is to educate and inform. The authors and Harbor House Publications shall have neither liability nor responsibility to any person or entity with respect to any loss or damage caused, or alleged to be caused, directly or indirectly, by the information contained in this book. If you do not wish to be bound by the above, you may return this book to the publisher for a full refund. Every effort has been made to ensure that no copyrighted material has been used without permission. The authors regret any oversights that may have occurred and are happy to rectify them in future printings of this book.

Bulk Purchases

    Harbor House Law Press books are available at quantity discounts for bulk purchases, academic sales or textbook adoptions. For information, contact **Harbor House Law Press,** P. O. Box 480, Hartfield VA 23071. Please provide the title of the book, ISBN number, quantity, how the book will be used, and date needed.
    Toll Free Phone Orders: (877) LAW IDEA or (877) 529-4332.
    Toll Free Fax Orders: (800) 863-5348.
    Internet Orders: Order on the **Wrightslaw store** at http://www.wrightslaw.com

What People Are Saying About
Wrightslaw: Special Education Law

Wrightslaw: Special Education Law is a remarkable tool . . . you never lose sight of the real beneficiaries of these laws - the students and their families.

To borrow a phrase, I would advise parents "Don't leave home for a meeting at your child's school without it." *Rosa Hagin, Ph.D., Learning Disabilities Association of America*

Wrightslaw: Special Education Law clarifies special education law in an educator-friendly manner. Anyone who teaches courses in special education at the post-secondary level will find **Wrightslaw: Special Education Law** to be an invaluable resource.

Administrators and educators in every school should have access to the timely information included in each chapter. -- *Quentin L. Griffey, Ph.D., Chair and Professor of Special Education, Pfeiffer University*

Wrightslaw: Special Education Law is straightforward and direct in style but infused with empathy and passion for children and youth with disabilities, their educational welfare, and their rights under special education law. -- *Jamie Ruppman, educational advocate and mother of two sons with disabilities.*

Excellent guide. Well organized. . . . stresses the need to use researched-based methods. Regular and special educators need to equate the terms "appropriate" and "research-based." Nice job! -- *Bill Matthew, Ph.D. Director of Special Education, Delano, CA*

The laws, regulations, cases - and Pete's comments on legal interpretations of special education law - all in **Wrightslaw: Special Education Law**! This comprehensive book takes the guesswork out of finding answers to the most common questions that plague parents and advocates. -- *Patricia Howey, Special Education Consultant and Advocate*

Your concise, practical commentaries on specific sections of the law and regulations should help parents see where they have been and where they should be going with regard to their children's education.

As an attorney and advocate, I found **Wrightslaw: Special Education Law** helpful in reducing the cacophony about IDEA into a useful framework. Thanks, Pete! -- *Joanne Simon, Esq.*

The concise, clear descriptions of what the law means will be of value to every interested individual, from parents to university professors. -- *Douglas Carnine, Ph.D., National Center to Improve the Tools of Educators*

Thank you for taking this confusing, complex information and making it user friendly for the parent of a disabled child and informative for the most proficient advocate. So many questions are answered . . . you are absolutely right when you advise parents to read the statute, the regulations, and case law. -- *Sandra Britt, Immediate Past President, Learning Disabilities Association of America*

Extremely well done, balanced and useful. I recommend that parents read the Individuals with Disabilities Act with your section overviews. It is like taking a mini-course on the law at one's own pace.

Wrightslaw: Special Education Law is an important contribution to understanding special education law and how to use it more effectively. -- *William F. Byrne, Esq.*

Wrightslaw: Special Education Law is written and organized in a way that provides lay persons and professionals with the information and understanding needed to effectively advocate for students with disabilities. -- *Rebecca Felton, Ph.D., Educational Consultant*

Acknowledgments

We are indebted to the Internet.

This journey began on November 9, 1993, after the U. S. Supreme Court issued the *Carter* decision.

Our phone was ringing continuously. From all parts of the country, parents were calling about special education problems. We were struck by the fact that the legal and factual issues in these cases were similar, without regard to the location of the caller or nature of the child's disability. We wrote some articles about legal issues and mailed these articles and the *Carter* decision to the callers.

One day, we picked up a voice mail message from **Hal Meyer**, a member of the Ch.A.D.D. Board of Directors. Hal had questions about the *Carter* case and asked us to write an article about the case for the ADD Forum on CompuServe.

The ADD Forum was an incredible resource. Members uploaded research, articles, book chapters, and other information to the Libraries. This information helped thousands of people.

The ADD Forum was also a community of people, many of whom became friends. Through the ADD Forum, we met **Thom Hartmann, Janie Bowman, Sue Burgess**, and **Dave deBronkart**. With Janie, we co-authored the "Letter to the Stranger" which was first published on the ADD Forum and is a classic in the field of special education advocacy. Later, the "Letter to the Stranger" and other memorabilia from the ADD Forum were permanently archived at the Smithsonian Institute.

We realized that we needed to write a book about special education law. We decided that the ideal book would include the law, regulations, cases, and information about tactics and strategy. This book would be a working manual for parents, advocates, and attorneys. We didn't know where to start such an ambitious project.

We are indebted to **Roger Habeck** of Chester, Virginia. Roger is a brilliant individual who also possesses an extraordinary amount of common sense. Roger gave us answers and vision. Under his guidance, we developed a manuscript that fulfilled this vision - but was nearly 1,000 pages long. Roger sent us to the next person to whom we are indebted - our editor.

Valerie O'Brian carefully reviewed the enormous manuscript. Tactfully, Valerie explained that we were trying to accomplish too much. We had written three books, not one. Valerie told us to start over, from the beginning. She advised us to focus on the tactics and strategy book or the law book of statutes, regulations and cases.

Since the Individuals with Disabilities Education Act of 1997 had been amended, we decided to focus on the law book. Soon, the proposed special education regulations were released. We waited for the final regulations so we could include them in the book. Time passed. The regulations were delayed again and again.

We talked to **Janie Bowman** of Olympia, Washington about our plans. Janie gave us some excellent advice: "Get a website up before your book is published!" We built our website and called it "The Special Ed Advocate." Over time, the site became known as "**Wrightslaw**." (http://www.wrightslaw.com)

Wrightslaw is now the premier website about special education law and advocacy on the Internet. Wrightslaw allows us to discuss issues with parents, attorneys, advocates, educators, psychologists and school administrators. We are deeply indebted to Janie for her encouragement and good advice.

At 6:30 a.m., Friday, March 12, 1999, the U. S. Department of Education published the special education regulations. Two hours later, the regulations were up at the Wrightslaw site.

The "Wrightslaw" website has become an important part of our identity. For this reason, we decided to include "Wrightslaw" in the title of this book.

We turned our attention back to The Law Book. We consulted with our Internet community of friends about the book. We received encouragement and help from so many people and are unable to list them all. We know some only by their email addresses.

We want to acknowledge and thank the following persons who provided helpful comments, insight, recommendations, and good advice.

Quentin L. Griffey, Professor of special education from North Carolina
Sandra Britt from Mississippi, past-president of the Learning Disabilities Association of America
Bill Laviano, Attorney in Connecticut and South Carolina
Doug Carnine, Professor and Director of National Center to Improve the Tools of Educators, Oregon
Jim Rosenfeld, Attorney and founder of the EdLaw Center in Florida
Jo Anne Simon, Attorney in New York City
Bill Matthew, Director of Special Education of a California school district
Pat Howey, Educational Consultant and Advocate in Indiana
Jamie Ruppman, Educational Consultant and Advocate in Virginia
Rebecca H. Felton, Educational Consultant in North Carolina
William F. Byrne, Attorney in West Virginia
Thom Hartmann from Vermont, author of **Attention Deficit Disorder: A Different Perception** and Sysop of the ADD Forum

We offer special thanks to **John O. Willis**, school psychologist in New Hampshire. John spent many hours going through the manuscript, and made dozens of excellent suggestions that we have incorporated into **Wrightslaw: Special Education Law**.

Mike Cody and **Brandy Salmons** designed the cover of **Wrightslaw: Special Education Law**.

We give thanks to **Debra Pratt**, our incredibly competent and resourceful office manager.

Finally, we want to thank **Shannon Carter** and her parents, **Emory and Elaine Carter**.

Dedication

We dedicate this book to our parents, **Virginia Bowen Darr**, **Robert William Darr**, **Penelope Ladd Wright** and **Thomas W. D. Wright**. From these remarkable people, we inherited our passion and commitment to make the world a better place for all children.

We also dedicate this book to our children, **Hillary Bowen Nobles**, **Damon W. D. Wright**, **Stephanie Rich Wright**, and **Jason Daniel Wright** who are carrying on the legacy.

Finally, we dedicate this book to **Roger Saunders** and **Diana Hanbury King** who taught Peter how to read, write, spell and do arithmetic.

CONTENTS

SECTION FOUR - FAMILY EDUCATIONAL RIGHTS AND PRIVACY ACT (FERPA)

SECTION FIVE: CASELAW

CHAPTER 1
WHY THIS BOOK?

Special education law is complicated and confusing. What does the law say about evaluations and reevaluations, test procedures, and eligibility decisions? What does the law say about Individualized Educational Programs (IEPs) and IEP teams? Goals, objectives and benchmarks? Transition plans? Least restrictive environment and inclusion?

What does the law say about discipline? Positive behavioral intervention plans and interim alternative placements? Manifestation Review Hearings?

What does the law say about educational progress? Tuition reimbursement and parent notice? Independent educational evaluations? Mediation?

Wrightslaw: Special Education Law will help you find the answers to your questions in the statutes, regulations, and caselaw.

Who Should Read This Book

If you are the parent of a child with a disability, you represent your child's interests in securing an appropriate special education program. To be an effective advocate for your child, you need to understand your rights and responsibilities under the special education laws.

If you are like most **teachers** and **service providers** to children with disabilities, you have received confusing and conflicting information about the special education laws. This information may be inaccurate or incomplete. If you work in the field of education, you need to know what the laws say.

If you are an **attorney or advocate** who represents children with disabilities, you need the statutes, regulations and landmark Supreme Court cases close at hand. In **Wrightslaw: Special Education Law**, your main legal references are in one volume.

Law evolves and changes, regardless of the statute and regulations. Congress may pass a new bill tomorrow that changes a portion of the law. A judicial interpretation that is accepted today will change tomorrow, next week, or next year after a legal precedent or conflicting statute. **This is the nature of law.**

Who Are "Special Education" Children?

More than five million children receive special education services under the Individuals with Disabilities Education Act (IDEA). Who are these children?

The largest group - about 2.5 million children - have learning disabilities. Other children have speech/language disorders, communication disorders, autistic spectrum disorders, non-verbal learning disabilities, and attention deficit disorders. Some children have visual impairments, hearing impairments, mobility problems, cerebral palsy, brain injuries and mental retardation.

Millions more handicapped children are protected from discrimination by Section 504 of the Rehabilitation Act.

In 1997, the Individuals with Disabilities Education Act was reauthorized. During the reauthorization process, Congress received research about special education outcomes. Congress found that special education "has been impeded by low expectations, and an insufficient focus on applying replicable research on proven methods of teaching and learning for children with disabilities." (See 20 U.S.C. 1400(c)(4))

Congress concluded that special education should be made more effective by "having high expectations for such children and ensuring their access to the general curriculum to the maximum extent possible." Congress strengthened the role of parents and urged school districts to use "prereferral interventions instead of waiting until children fail or are labeled." (See 20 U.S.C. 1400 (c))

How This Book is Organized

Wrightslaw: Special Education Law is organized into five sections. **Section One** focuses on **law** and **special education law.** In Chapter 1, you learn how this book is organized. Chapter 2 includes a review of law and explains the process of legal change. Chapter 3 includes a brief history of public education, special education, and early education law from *Brown v. Board of Education* to *Public Law 94-142.*

Section Two is about special education and the Individuals with Disabilities Education Act. Chapter 4 contains an overview of the **Individuals with Disabilities Education Act of 1997.** In Chapter 5, you'll find the full text of the **Individuals with Disabilities Education Act of 1997,** a comprehensive analysis of the statute, and suggestions about how to secure appropriate services for the child. Chapter 6 includes the IDEA regulations including the new Appendix A.

Section Three is about **civil rights and discrimination** as it relates to handicapped children. Handicapped children are entitled to protection from discrimination under the civil rights statutes. Chapter 7 includes an overview of **Section 504 of the Rehabilitation Act.** In Chapter 8, you'll find pertinent text from Section 504 of the Rehabilitation Act. The implementing regulations for Section 504 are in Chapter 9.

Section Four is about **records and confidentiality.** The privacy of educational records is governed by the **Family Educational Records Privacy Act (FERPA).** Under FERPA, schools must honor parental requests to inspect and review their child's educational records within strict timelines. Chapter 10 contains an overview of FERPA. Chapter 11 includes the text of the FERPA statute. The FERPA regulations are in Chapter 12.

Section Five is about **caselaw.** Chapter 13 is an overview of special education decisions by the United States Supreme Court. Chapter 14 is a casebook that includes the landmark Supreme Court decisions in *Rowley* (1982), *Burlington* (1985), *Honig* (1988), *Carter* (1993), and *Cedar Rapids* (1999).

Tips To Help You Use This Book

The statutes and regulations in this book are set in Garamond Book font. Wrightslaw's explanations, analyses, and tips that are in Helvetica font and preceded by a large arrow like this ➡ are **not** part of the statute. We used **bold type** to emphasize certain words and phrases in the statute. Look at the example below. The statute begins with **(A) In General.** The explanation begins with ➡ **IDEA AND FAPE.**

> **(A) In General** - The term '**child with a disability**' means a child-
> (i) with mental retardation, hearing impairments (including deafness), speech or language impairments, visual impairments (including blindness), serious emotional disturbance (hereinafter referred to as 'emotional disturbance'), orthopedic impairments, autism, traumatic brain injury, other health impairments, or specific learning disabilities; and
> (ii) **who, by reason thereof, needs special education and related services.**

> ➡ **IDEA AND FAPE**
> IDEA confers a right to a free appropriate public education (FAPE). The IDEA child is entitled to an IEP [as described in 20 U.S.C. §1414(d)] and special education that confers educational benefit. All children with disabilities are protected under Section 504. It is important for parents to understand that if their child does not receive services under IDEA, the child does not have IDEA procedural protections.

References

When references to other works are cited, the full bibliographic citation is at the end of the chapter.

Contact Us

What did you like about **Wrightslaw: Special Education Law?** What did you dislike about **Wrightslaw: Special Education Law?** How can we improve this book so it meets your needs? Send your ideas, thoughts and comments about how we can improve **Wrightslaw: Special Education Law** to: **Harbor House Law Press,** P. O. Box 480, Hartfield VA 23071. (877) 529-4332 or (877) LAW-IDEA

CHAPTER 2

OVERVIEW OF LAW

There are four types of law: federal and state constitutions, statutes, administrative rules and regulations, and case law.

Constitutional Law

The United States Constitution outlines the structure of the federal government. All laws passed must agree with the principles and rights set forth in the Constitution. The first ten amendments to the Constitution are called the Bill of Rights. The Bill of Rights is the source of the most fundamental rights – freedom of speech and religion, right to a jury trial, protection against unreasonable searches and seizures. These Amendments were added to the Constitution to protect citizens against interference from the federal government.

Federal Statutes

Statutes are laws that are passed by federal, state and local legislatures. Federal statutes are passed by the United States Congress and signed into law by the President. Federal statutes are organized by subject, indexed, and published in the United States Code by Title number. Title 20 is about Education.

References to law are called **citations**. Legal citations are written in a standardized form describing exactly where the statute is located. Citations to federal statutes include the title for the U.S. Code and the section number.

The Individuals with Disabilities Education Act is a federal statute. The statute is in Title 20 of the United States Code, beginning at Section 1400. The legal citation is 20 U.S.C. § 1400, *et. seq.* § is legal shorthand for symbol and is made by two S's superimposed. The term "*et. seq.*" means at Section 1400 and continuing thereafter.

Section 504 of the Rehabilitation Act is a federal statute. Section 504 is in the Rehabilitation Act of 1973 which is codified in Title 29 of the United States Code at Section 794 and is cited as 29 U. S. C. § 794. "Congressional Findings and Purpose" are in Section 701. "Definitions" are in Section 705.

The Family Educational and Privacy Rights Act is a federal statute. The FERPA statute is in Title 20 of the United States Code at Section 1232.

Federal Regulations

The purpose of regulations is to clarify and explain the statute. Although regulations give force and effect to a statute, they must also be consistent with the statute. Regulations have the same power as the statute. An Appendix to a regulation is a part of a regulation and may or may not have the same force and effect as a regulation, depending on the context. Regulations are published in the Code of Federal Regulations or C.F.R. Before Regulations are published in the Code of Federal Regulations, they are published in the Federal Register (F.R.) which is issued daily.

Title 20 of the U. S. Code requires the U. S. Department of Education to develop and publish the IDEA regulations. The IDEA regulations are in Volume 34, Part 300 of the Code of Federal Regulations. The legal citation for the IDEA regulations is 34 C.F.R. §. The first IDEA regulation is "Purpose" which is at 300.1. The legal citation for "Purpose" is 34 C.F.R. § 300.1.

Appendix A is part of the special education regulations. Appendix A provides additional guidance about IEPs, the involvement of the child's parents, transition, and the child's participation in state and district-wide assessments of achievement in a Question and Answer format. In the former statute, the comparable regulation was Appendix C.

The Section 504 regulations are in Volume 34, Part 104 of the Code of Federal Regulations (C.F.R.). The legal citation for the Section 504 regulations is 34 C.F.R. §. The first Section 504 regulation is "Purpose" which is at 104.1. The legal citation for "Purpose" is 34 C.F.R. § 104.1.

The FERPA regulations are in Volume 34, Part 99 of the Code of Federal Regulations (C.F.R.). The legal citation for the FERPA regulations is 34 C.F.R. §. The first FERPA regulation is "To Which educational agencies or institutions do these regulations apply?" The legal citation for this regulation is 34 C.F.R § 99.1.

State Law and Regulations

State constitutions establish the structure of state government. States must develop special education statutes and regulations that are consistent with the United States Code (U.S.C.) and the Code of Federal Regulations (C.F.R.). State statutes and regulations may provide more special education rights than the corresponding federal law but states may not take away rights that are provided by federal law.

Legislative Intent

Statutory and regulatory law are based on legislative intent. In many cases, the legal interpretation of a law, the meaning of a specific section, or the meaning of a particular word will be influenced by the use of "may" instead of "shall," or even the location of a semicolon.

Sometimes, one word in a statute will lead to extensive litigation. In the area of special education law, the word "appropriate" has been litigated extensively. After more than twenty years of case law, "appropriate" has many interpretations that vary considerably from one set of facts to another.

Sometimes, members of Congress are unable to agree on the wording of a proposed statute. To keep a bill from dying in committee, the legislators will often agree to vague compromise wording. Because Courts must interpret the meaning of a word or phrase in the context of the statute, it is not surprising that courts often arrive at different conclusions.

When you read decisions by the U. S. Supreme Court, you will see that the Justices often include a discussion of legislative intent and legislative history in their decisions. Through this process, vague, ambiguous words and terms receive more precise legal definitions.

The legislative history of the Individuals with Disabilities Education Act is in the *United States Code Congressional and Administrative News 1975* beginning at page 1425 (U.S.C.C.A.N. 1975, p. 1425).

To learn about the purpose of Section 504, read "Congressional Findings and Purpose" in Section 701 (included in this book).

Judicial Interpretations

It is not unusual for one court to interpret a word, phrase, or code section differently from another court, even when facts are similar. This process leads to more interpretations and more litigation. Over time, a "majority rule" usually develops as courts agree on the same interpretation. A "minority rule" also develops.

If a clear majority rule does not develop, the legal issue will become more confusing and diverse. A U. S. Court of Appeals may issue a ruling in a case that controls the lower courts.

Sometimes, two or more U. S. Courts of Appeal issue rulings that are in direct conflict with each other. This is called a "split among circuits." When a split occurs, Congress may amend the law or the U. S. Supreme Court may issue a decision that clarifies the issue. Legal issues that result in a "split among circuits" have the highest probability of being accepted for review by the U. S. Supreme Court.

Caselaw

Caselaw is the body of law that evolves in state and federal courts. Hearing decisions in special education cases can be appealed to state or federal court. Decisions issued by state court judges can be appealed to higher state courts. In most states, the highest state court is the state's Supreme Court.

For example, a New York trial judge's interpretation of the special education statute will be governed by earlier rulings by the Supreme Court of New York. However, New York state court judges are not bound by opinions issued by state court judges from other states.

Decisions by U. S. District Court judges can be appealed to the U. S. Court of Appeals for that geographical area. District Court judges are bound by interpretations and rulings from their Courts of Appeals. New York is in the Second Circuit. U. S. District Court judges in New York must follow rulings from the Second Circuit Court of Appeals. California is in the Ninth Circuit. U. S. District judges in California must follow rulings from the Ninth Circuit.

Interpretations of the federal statute by U. S. District Courts are binding on state court trial judges. However, decisions from a U. S. District Court in New York are not binding on state court or Federal court judges in California. Decisions from a U. S. District Court in California are not binding on state or Federal judges in New York or other states.

When the U. S. Supreme Court issues a ruling, all state and federal courts must follow the ruling.

How Caselaw Evolves

Often, the facts of a case will cause the hearing officer, review officer, or judge to want to rule in one direction, even if this ruling is contrary to existing caselaw. In this situation, the decision-maker may find that the unique facts in this case create an exception to the general caselaw. These decisions cause the body of law to grow, expand, and change.

After the U. S. Supreme Court issues a ruling, Congress will sometimes enact a new law that has the effect of overruling the Supreme Court's decision. The new statute will become the law.

Different Interpretations

Law is always subject to different interpretations. Attorneys interpret the law differently, depending on their perspectives. Judges interpret the law differently. Most articles about special education law provide an overview of the statute. These interpretations of law are little more than one person's opinion. When you read the statute and the regulations, you will develop your interpretation of the law and the impact it is likely to have on you.

How to Research the Law

To learn about the law, you must study the statutes, regulations, and caselaw. When you have a question about a legal issue, read the statute about the issue, then read the regulation that discusses the issue. You should then re-read the statute and re-read the regulation.

You may need to read the comments about the regulation that are in the Federal Register. The Code of Federal Regulations does not include all the comments that are in the Federal Register.

Next, read the cases that have interpreted the issue. Read the earlier interpretations first, before you tackle more recent interpretations.

If the case was appealed, read the decision that was appealed and reversed, or appealed and affirmed. When you read the earlier law, you will see how the law is evolving.

For every position taken by one court that a legal issue is clear black letter law, you can be sure that another court has taken the opposite position while asserting that their ruling is black letter law.

Black is white, white is black. Truth is in shades of gray. This is the nature of law.

Recommended Reading

Elias, Stephen and Susan Levinkind. (1997) *Legal Research: How to Find and Understand the Law.* (Berkely: Nolo Press)

Bergman, Paul and Sara J. Berman-Barrett. (1998) *Represent Yourself in Court : How to Prepare and Try a Winning Case.* (Berkely, CA: Nolo Press)

This page intentionally left blank.

CHAPTER 3
A SHORT HISTORY OF SPECIAL EDUCATION LAW

To understand the battles being fought today for children with disabilities, it is important to understand the history and traditions associated with public schools and special education.

Common Schools Teach Common Values

During the last century, waves of poor, non-English speaking, Catholic and Jewish immigrants poured into the United States. Citizens were afraid that these new immigrants would bring class hatreds, religious intolerance, crime, and violence to America. Social and political leaders searched for ways to "reach down into the lower portions of the population and teach children to share the values, ideals and controls help by the rest of society." (Church, 81)

An educational reformer named Horace Mann proposed a solution to these social problems. He recommended that communities establish common schools funded by tax dollars. He believed that when children from different social, religious and economic backgrounds were educated together, they would learn to accept and respect each other. Common schools taught common values that included self-discipline and tolerance for others. These common schools would socialize children, improve interpersonal relationships, and improve social conditions. (Cremin, 183-194)

Early Special Education Programs

The first special education programs were delinquency prevention programs for "at risk" children who lived in urban slums. Urban school districts designed manual training classes as a supplement to their general education programs. By 1890, hundreds of thousands of children were learning carpentry, metal work, sewing, cooking and drawing in manual classes. Children were also taught social values in these classes.

> Manual training was a way of teaching children industriousness, and clearing up their character problems . . . the appeal of this training was the belief that it would attract children to school, especially poor children, so their morals could be reshaped . . . Manual training would teach children to be industrious and prevent the idleness that accounted for the increasing crime rate . . . it could teach self discipline and will power. (Cremin, 220-222)

Early special education programs also focused on the "moral training" of African-American children. (Cremin, 192-226) When the Individuals with Disabilities Act was reauthorized:

> In 1997, Congress found that poor African-American children continue to be over-represented in special education classes:
> (8) (A) Greater efforts are needed to prevent the intensification of problems connected with **mislabeling and high dropout rates among minority children with disabilities.**
> (B) More minority children continue to be served in special education than would be expected from the percentage of minority students in the general school population.
> (C) **Poor African-American children** are **2.3** times more likely to be identified by their teacher as having **mental retardation** than their white counterpart. (20 U.S.C. §1400)

Compulsory Attendance Laws

For public schools to succeed in the mission of socializing children, all children had to attend school. Poor children attended school sporadically, quit early, or didn't enter school at all. Public school authorities lobbied their legislatures for compulsory school attendance laws. Compulsory attendance laws gave school officials the power to prosecute parents legally if they failed to send their children to school. (Sperry, et. al., 139-145; Cremin; *Brown v. Board of Education*, 347 U.S. 483 (1954))

Handicapped Children Excluded

Until 1975, handicapped children were often excluded from school. When allowed to attend, children with many different disabilities were often lumped together in generic special education classes. Because schools segregated children with disabilities from "normal" children, special education classes were often held in undesirable, out-of-the-way places like trailers and school basements.

Despite compulsory attendance laws, most states allowed school authorities to exclude children if they believed that the child would not benefit from education or if the child's presence would be disruptive to others, i.e., to non-disabled children and teachers. In 1958, the Illinois Supreme Court held that compulsory education laws did not apply to children with mental impairments. Until 1969, it was a crime in North Carolina for a parent to try to enroll a handicapped child in public school after the child had been excluded. (Weber, "Statutory Background")

Brown v. Board of Education, 347 U.S. 483 (1954)

In 1954, the U.S. Supreme Court issued a landmark civil rights decision in *Brown v. Board of Education*, 347 U.S. 483 (1954). In *Brown*, school children from four states argued that segregated public schools were inherently unequal and deprived them of equal protection of the laws. The Supreme Court found that African-American children had the right to equal educational opportunities and that segregated schools "have no place in the field of public education." The court wrote that:

> Today, education is perhaps the most important function of state and local governments. Compulsory school attendance laws and the great expenditures for education both demonstrate our recognition of the importance of education to our democratic society. It is required in the performance of our most basic public responsibilities, even service in the armed forces. It is the very foundation of good citizenship. Today it is a principal instrument in awakening the child to cultural values, in preparing him for later professional training, and in helping him to adjust normally to his environment. In these days, it is doubtful that any child may reasonably be expected to succeed in life if he is denied the opportunity of an education. Such an opportunity, where the state has undertaken to provide it, is a right which must be made available to all on equal terms.

> We come then to the question presented: Does segregation of children in public schools solely on the basis of race, even though the physical facilities and other "tangible" factors may be equal, deprive the children of the minority group of equal educational opportunities? We believe that it does.

In *Brown*, the Supreme Court described the emotional impact that segregation has on children, especially when segregation "has the sanction of the law:"

> To separate them from others of similar age and qualifications solely because of their race generates a feeling of inferiority as to their status in the community that may affect their hearts and minds in a way unlikely ever to be undone. The effect of this separation on their educational opportunities was well stated by a finding in the Kansas case by a court which nevertheless felt compelled to rule against the Negro plaintiffs:

> Segregation of white and colored children in public schools has a detrimental effect upon the colored children. The impact is greater when it has the sanction of the law; for the policy of separating the races is usually interpreted as denoting the inferiority of the negro group. A sense of inferiority affects the motivation of a child to learn. Segregation with the sanction of law, therefore, has a tendency to [retard] the educational and mental development of negro children and to deprive them of some of the benefits they would receive in a racially integrated school system.

After the decision in *Brown*, parents of children with disabilities began to bring lawsuits against their school districts for excluding or segregating children with disabilities. The parents argued that by excluding these children, schools were discriminating against the children because of their disabilities.

P.A.R.C. and Mills

During the early 1970s, two cases were catalysts in special education law: *Pennsylvania Assn. for Retarded Children v. Commonwealth* 334 F. Supp. 1257 (E.D. Pa. 1971) and 343 F. Supp. 279 (E. D. Pa. 1972) and *Mills v. Board of Education of District of Columbia*, 348 F. Supp. 866 (D. DC 1972).

P.A.R.C. dealt with the exclusion of mentally retarded children from public schools. *Mills* involved the practice of suspending, expelling and excluding "exceptional" children from the District of Columbia public schools.

In *Mills*, the Court found that:

> The genesis of this case is found (1) in the failure of the District of Columbia to provide publicly supported education and training to plaintiffs and other "'exceptional'" children, members of their class, and (2) the excluding, suspending, expelling, reassigning and transferring of "exceptional" children from regular public school classes without affording them due process of law.

In May, 1972, legislation was introduced in Congress after several:

> ... landmark court cases establishing in law the right to education for all handicapped children ... In 1954, the Supreme Court of the United States (in *Brown v. Board of Education*) established the principle that all children be guaranteed equal educational opportunity. The Court stated "In these days, it is doubtful that any child may reasonably be expected to succeed in life if he is denied the opportunity of an education. Such an opportunity ... is a right which must be made available to all on equal terms." (At 1430 in the legislative history.)

Congressional Findings

Millions of "Invisible Children"

Congress launched an investigation into the status of children with handicaps and disabilities. They found that millions of children were not receiving an appropriate education:

> Yet, the most recent statistics provided by the Bureau of Education for the Handicapped estimated that of the more than 8 million children ... with handicapping conditions requiring special education and related services, only 3.9 million such children are receiving an appropriate education. 1.75 million handicapped children are receiving **no educational services at all**, and 2.5 million handicapped children are receiving **an inappropriate education.** (At 1432)

Social and Economic Costs

Congress described the social and economic costs of failing to educate disabled children:

> The long-range implications of these statistics are that public agencies and taxpayers will spend billions of dollars over the lifetimes of these individuals to maintain such persons as dependents and in a minimally acceptable lifestyle. With proper education services, many would be able to become **productive citizens, contributing to society** instead of being forced to remain burdens. Others, through such services, would increase their **independence**, thus reducing their dependence on society. (At 1433)

> There is no pride in being forced to receive economic assistance. Not only does this have negative effects upon the handicapped person, but it has far-reaching effects for such person's family. (At 1433)

> Providing educational services will ensure against persons needlessly being forced into institutional settings. One need only look at public residential institutions to find thousands of persons whose families are no longer able to care for them and who themselves have received no educational services. Billions of dollars are expended each year to maintain persons in these subhuman conditions ... (At 1433)

Parents of handicapped children all too frequently are not able to advocate the rights of their children because they have been **erroneously led to believe** that their children will not be able to lead meaningful lives . . . It should not . . . be necessary for parents throughout the country to continue utilizing the courts to assure themselves a remedy . . . (At 1433)

Public Law 94-142

On November 19, 1975, Public Law 94-142 was enacted into law. Public Law 94-142 was called the Education for All Handicapped Children Act of 1975. When the law was reauthorized in 1990, it was renamed the Individuals with Disabilities Education Act (IDEA).

By passing Public Law 94-142, Congress intended that all handicapped children would "have a right to education, and to establish a process by which State and local educational agencies may be held **accountable** for providing educational services for all handicapped children." (U.S.C.C.A.N. 1975 p.1427)

The Individuals with Disabilities Education Act is in the United States Code, Volume 20 U.S.C. § 1400. The regulations are in the Code of Federal Regulations, Volume 34, beginning at Part 300. The legislative history of the law is in the *United States Code Congressional and Administrative News 1975* beginning at page 1425 (U.S.C.C.A.N. 1975, p. 1425).

The term "handicapped" was used in Public Law 94-142. The term "handicapped" was replaced by the term "child with a disability" in the statute and regulations.

Board of Education v. Rowley, 458 U.S. 176 (1982)

In 1982, the U. S. Supreme Court issued the first decision in a special education case in *Board of Education v. Rowley, 458 U.S. 176*. The decision includes a comprehensive analysis of the evolution of special education law. This is an excellent source of information and should be read carefully by the student who is doing research about special education law. The analysis begins in the text of the decision and continues into the footnotes. (The *Rowley* decision is the caselaw section of **Wrightslaw: Special Education Law**)

References

Church, Robert L. (1976) *Education in the United States.* (New York: The Free Press)

Cremin, Lawrence A. (1967) *The Transformation of the School: Progressivism in American Education, 1876-1957* (New York: Knopf)

Sperry, David, Philip T. K. Daniel, Dixie Snow Huefner, E. Gordon Gee. (1998) *Education Law and the Public Schools: A Compendium.* (Norwood, MA: Christopher-Gordon Publishers, Inc.)

Weber, Mark. (1992) *Special Education Law and Litigation Treatise* (Horsham, PA: LRP Publications, Inc.)

United States Code Congressional and Administrative News 1975 (U.S.C.C.A.N. 1975)

CHAPTER 4

OVERVIEW OF
THE INDIVIDUALS WITH DISABILITIES EDUCATION ACT OF 1997

The Individuals with Disabilities Education Act is in the United States Code (U.S.C.) at Volume 20, beginning at Section 1401. This book is based on the United States Code although it does include references to various Sections within the Act. The Individuals with Disabilities Education Act of 1997 is divided into four parts.

The U. S. Department of Education is responsible for issuing the special education regulations. The IDEA Regulations are published in Volume 34 of the Code of Federal Regulations (C.F.R.), beginning at Section 300. Appendix A to the Regulations includes 40 questions and answers about IEPs and transition services.

The regulations about early intervention programs for very young children is in Volume 34 of the Code of Federal Regulations beginning at Section 303.

Parents, advocates, attorneys, and educators will refer most often to Part A and Part B, Sections 1400, 1401, 1412, 1414, and 1415 and the corresponding regulations that relate to these sections.

Part A: General Provisions, Definitions and Other Issues

Part A is titled "General Provisions, Definitions and Other Issues" and begins with "Congressional Findings and Purpose." Part A is very important because it discusses the purpose of the special education law. Part A also includes definitions of terms that are used in the statute.

Part B: Assistance for Education of All Children with Disabilities

Part B is titled "Assistance for Education of All Children with Disabilities" and includes funding, state plans, evaluations, eligibility, due process, discipline and other areas relating to direct services. Section 1414 is about evaluations, eligibility, and IEPs. Section 1415 describes the procedural safeguards for children and their parents, including the requirement about "Prior Written Notice," Mediation, Due Process Procedures, "stay put," and discipline issues. Section 1419 includes procedural information about grants to states that have preschool programs for children as young as two years of age.

Part C: Infants and Toddlers with Disabilities

Part C is "Infants and Toddlers with Disabilities" and begins with "Findings and Policy" at Section 1431. The term "at-risk infant or toddler" is defined as an individual under 3 years of age who would be at risk of experiencing a substantial developmental delay if early intervention services were not provided. Part C requires a comprehensive child find system and individual family service plans (ISFP) that are similar to IEPs in Part B.

Part D: National Activities to Improve Education of Children with Disabilities

Special education methods and techniques are often criticized for not being based on research and best practices. At the beginning of the IDEA statutue is this statement from Congress:

> However, the implementation of this Act has been impeded by low expectations, and an insufficient focus on applying replicable research on proven methods of teaching and learning for children with disabilities." 20 U.S.C. § 1400(c)(4)

Part D focuses on the need to improve special education programs, preparing personnel, disseminating information, supporting research, and applying research findings to education. Part D is called "National Activities to Improve Education of Children with Disabilities" and includes two subparts. Subpart One is "State Program Improvement Grants for Children with Disabilities." Subpart Two is "Coordinated Research, Personnel Preparation, Technical Assistance, Support, and Dissemination of Information."

Definition: IDEA Child

What is the definition of a child who requires special education services under IDEA? The United States Code, i.e., the Individuals with Disabilities Education Act of 1997, at 20 U.S.C. § 1401(3) explains that a 'child with a disability' means a child-

(i) with mental retardation, hearing impairments (including deafness), speech or language impairments, visual impairments (including blindness), serious emotional disturbance (hereinafter referred to as 'emotional disturbance'), orthopedic impairments, autism, traumatic brain injury, other health impairments, or specific learning disabilities; and
(ii) who, by reason thereof, needs special education and related services.

The key term is "who, by reason thereof, needs special education and related services." What is the legal definition of special education?

Definition: IDEA Special Education

At 20 U.S.C. § 1401(25), the law defines special education:

The term **'special education'** means specially designed instruction, at no cost to parents, to meet the unique needs of a child with a disability, including -
(A) instruction conducted in the classroom, in the home, in hospitals and institutions, and in other settings; and
(B) instruction in physical education.

The law is clear that special education is not limited to traditional special education classes. Special education should include a range of services designed to meet the unique needs of children with disabilities. Special education may include "instruction conducted in the classroom," intensive structured programs in residential facilities, one-to-one tutoring, remediation, and 40+ hour programs of Applied Behavioral Analysis (ABA) therapy for young autistic children.

The term **"free appropriate public education"** means "special education and related services that . . . are provided in conformity with (an) individualized education program (which is) . . . a written statement . . . that includes a statement of the child's present levels of educational performance . . . measurable annual goals, including benchmarks or short-term objectives, . . . a statement of the special education and related services and supplementary aids and services to be provided to the child, or on behalf of the child and . . . for school personnel . . ." 20 U.S.C. § 1414(d)(1)(A)

The child's special education program must be reviewed at least once a year. An appropriate special education program provides the child with educational benefit so the child may become an independent functioning member of society.

Summary

The Individuals with Disabilities Education Act (IDEA) requires public schools to locate and identify children with disabilities who may be in need of specialized education. These children will "have available to them a free appropriate public education that emphasizes special education and related services designed to meet their unique needs and prepare them for employment and independent living; (and) . . . to ensure that the rights of children with disabilities and parents of such children are protected . . ." 20 U.S.C. § 1401(d)

The statute includes specific requirements about eligibility for services, components of the Individualized Educational Program (IEP), IEP team members, review of the child's IEP, prior written notice, members of eligibility and IEP teams, and comprehensive procedural requirements related to disputes and complaints.

Remember - law is always changing and evolving. To understand the law, you need to read the statute, the regulations, and cases that have interpreted the statute and regulations.

CHAPTER 5
THE INDIVIDUALS WITH DISABILITIES EDUCATION ACT

SECTION HEADINGS

PART A - GENERAL PROVISIONS, DEFINITIONS AND OTHER ISSUES

PART C - INFANTS AND TODDLERS WITH DISABILITIES

CHAPTER 2 - IMPROVING EARLY INTERVENTION, EDUCATIONAL, AND TRANSITIONAL SERVICES AND RESULTS FOR CHILDREN WITH DISABILITIES THROUGH COORDINATED TECHNICAL ASSISTANCE, SUPPORT, AND DISSEMINATION OF INFORMATION

THE INDIVIDUALS WITH DISABILITIES EDUCATION ACT

Part A - General Provisions, Definitions and Other Issues

➡ **OVERVIEW OF PART A**

Part A includes Sections 1400 through 1406. Part A includes information about the purpose of special education and definitions of many terms that are used in the statute.

20 U.S.C. §1400 - Congressional Findings and Purpose
20 U.S.C. §1401 - Definitions
20 U.S.C. §1402 - Office of Special Education Programs
20 U.S.C. §1403 - Abrogation of State Sovereign Immunity
20 U.S.C. §1404 - Acquisition of Equipment; Construction or Alteration of Facilities
20 U.S.C. §1405 - Employment of Individuals with Disabilities
20 U.S.C. §1406 - Requirements for Prescribing Regulations

20 U.S.C. - §1400 Congressional Findings and Purpose

➡ **SECTION OVERVIEW**

This section provides the history, findings, and purpose of the Individuals with Disabilities Education Act and is the **most important section** of this book. If you are unsure about the purpose and intent of a code section in the statute or regulation, return to Section 1400, especially 1400(d), which will help you understand the statute in context. The U. S. Supreme Court discusses the purpose of the statute when they issue rulings in cases. Lawyers, parents, and educators often agonize over the meaning of a word or phrase but have not read this section. Section 1400 is the key to understanding the special education statute. **Reminder:** Comments in this typeface that are preceded by an arrow ➡ are by the author and are not part of the law.

(a) SHORT TITLE. This Act may be cited as the 'Individuals with Disabilities Education Act.'

(b) TABLE OF CONTENTS. The table of contents for this Act is as follows:

Part A - General Provisions. (Sections 1400 through 1406)
Part B - Assistance for Education of All Children with Disabilities. (Sections 1411 through 1419)
Part C - Infants and Toddlers with Disabilities. (Sections 1431 through 1445)
Part D - National Activities to Improve Education of Children with Disabilities. (Sections 1451 through 1487)

(c) FINDINGS.

(1) Disability is a natural part of the human experience and in no way diminishes the right of individuals to participate in or contribute to society. **Improving educational results** for children with disabilities **is an essential element of our national policy** of ensuring **equality of opportunity, full participation, independent living,** and **economic self-sufficiency** for individuals with disabilities.

(2) Before the date of the enactment of the Education for All Handicapped Children Act of 1975 (Public Law 94 142)-

(A) the special educational needs of children with disabilities were not being fully met;

(B) **more than one-half** of the children with disabilities in the United States did not receive appropriate educational services that would enable such children to have full equality of opportunity;

(C) **1,000,000 children with disabilities** in the United States were **excluded entirely from the public school system** and did not go through the educational process with their peers;

(D) there were many children with disabilities throughout the United States participating in regular school programs whose disabilities prevented such children from having a successful educational experience because their **disabilities were undetected**; and

(E) because of the **lack of adequate services** within the public school system, families were often forced to find services outside the public school system, often at great distance from their residence and at their own expense.

(3) Since the enactment and implementation of the Education for All Handicapped Children Act of 1975, this Act has been successful in ensuring children with disabilities and the families of such children **access to a free appropriate public education** and in improving educational results for children with disabilities.

> ➡ **BEFORE PUBLIC LAW 94-142, ONE MILLION CHILDREN EXCLUDED FROM SCHOOL**
> When Congress passed the original special education statute, more than one million children with disabilities were barred from attending public schools. Congress found that these children were denied "access" to an education without due process of law. Congress included an elaborate system of legal checks and balances in the law called "procedural safeguards" to protect the rights of children and their parents. The original law focused on access to an education and due process of law. Today, most children with disabilities are allowed to attend school. The Individuals with Disabilities Education Act of 1997 maintains the goals of access and due process while focusing on accountability and improved outcomes.

(4) However, the implementation of this Act has been **impeded by low expectations, and an insufficient focus on applying replicable research on proven methods of teaching and learning** for children with disabilities.

> ➡ **SPECIAL EDUCATION SHOULD BE RESEARCH-BASED**
> The amended IDEA emphasizes accountability and results. To improve results, the law stresses the need to use "proven methods of teaching and learning" that are based on "replicable research." These are important terms. Although children with disabilities are entitled to a special education that is individualized and tailored to their unique needs, many children do not receive these individualized services. Often, decisions about the services children will receive are dictated by the district's service delivery system. The revised IDEA says that children with disabilities will "be involved in and progress in the general curriculum" to the maximum extent possible. Children with disabilities will be tested on state and district standardized tests. These changes focus on accountability and improved results. Litigation will target special education programs that are not research-based and school districts that fail to use effective educational practices.

(5) Over 20 years of research and experience has demonstrated that **the education of children with disabilities can be made more effective** by-

(A) having **high expectations** for such children and ensuring their **access in the general curriculum** to the maximum extent possible;

> ➡ **TWENTY YEARS OF RESEARCH RARELY USED BY PUBLIC SCHOOLS**
> Litigation will target special education programs with low expectations. Although most children with disabilities benefit from remediation or direct instruction administered one-to-one or in very small, homogeneous groups, many special education programs provide no individualized remediation. In an appropriate remediation program, a trained teacher actively teaches the child skills, i.e., how to read, write, spell, do arithmetic. If children with disabilities are taught basic academic skills, most can be educated successfully in regular education classrooms.
> Many IEPs offer modifications and accommodations that are designed to make things easier for the child by lowering the bar. Modified programs may provide a crutch for the child, instead of teaching skills. In some circumstances, modifications and accommodations are appropriate, i.e., teaching the child techniques that help the child overcome a problem. Section 504 plans usually include modifications and accommodations. One purpose of special education is to promote "economic self-sufficiency for individuals with disabilities." If children with disabilities do not learn how to read, write, spell, and do arithmetic, they will not have the skills they need for "economic self sufficiency."

(B) **strengthening the role of parents** and ensuring that families of such children have meaningful opportunities to participate in the education of their children at school **and at home**;

➡ **ROLE OF PARENTS STRENGTHENED**
The amended law strengthened the role of parents. School districts must encourage parents to take an active role in the children's education. Parents are full members of eligibility, IEP and placement teams.

(C) coordinating this Act with other local, educational service agency, State, and Federal school improvement efforts in order to ensure that such children benefit from such efforts and that **special education can become a service for such children rather than a place where they are sent**;

➡ **PLACEMENT DRIVES SERVICES, ILLEGALLY**
More litigation is focusing on placement decisions and how placement decisions are made. Many schools districts design "one-size-fits-all" special education programs and "shoehorn" special needs children into these programs. Many inappropriate placement decisions are fueled by administrative convenience. "One-size-fits-all" programs do not meet the unique needs of children with disabilities, as the law requires.

(D) providing appropriate **special education and related services and aids and supports in the regular classroom** to such children, whenever appropriate;

➡ **NATIONAL INSTITUTES OF HEALTH: SPECIAL EDUCATION FAILS**
When the re-authorization of IDEA was being debated in Congress, many legislators expressed concerns about special education outcomes. They wanted to know if the billions of dollars going into special education was money well spent. Congress ordered the National Institutes of Health to conduct studies on special education outcomes. During the 1997 re-authorization, Congress received results from the NIH longitudinal studies. According to these studies and other research, special education often fails to teach children the basic skills they need to function independently after they leave school.

➡ **SPECIAL EDUCATION MOVES INTO REGULAR EDUCATION CLASSROOMS**
With mounting evidence that special education was failing, the revised law shifts special education into regular education classes. With the proliferation of inclusion and "collaborative" teaching models, more children with disabilities will receive special education in regular classes. As disabled children are placed in regular education classes, many questions arise.
Will regular education teachers receive the training, supervision and support they need to teach children with disabilities? Will regular education teachers have higher standards, lower standards, or equal standards for children with disabilities? Will these children be taught how to read, write, spell and do arithmetic? Will children with disabilities become burdens to regular classroom teachers? Will these children receive intensive one-to-one tutoring by qualified specialists? Or, will these children be shifted to untrained classroom aides. Will the push for higher standards cause more students with disabilities to be retained? Will there be a backlash from parents who believe that students without disabilities are being distracted or held back by the students with disabilities in their classes?

(E) supporting **high-quality, intensive professional development** for all personnel who work with such children in order to ensure that they have the **skills and knowledge** necessary to enable them-

(i) to meet developmental goals and, to the maximum extent possible, those **challenging expectations** that have been **established for all children**; and
(ii) to be prepared to lead productive, independent, adult lives, to the maximum extent possible;

➡ **PRODUCTIVE LIVES**

The goal of special education is to prepare children with disabilities to lead productive, independent lives as adults, to the maximum extent possible.

(F) providing incentives for whole-school approaches and **pre-referral intervention to reduce the need to label children as disabled** in order to address their learning needs; and

➡ **INTERVENE BEFORE REFERRAL TO SPECIAL EDUCATION**

Some school districts do not provide children with specialized educational services until after the child is failing. For many disabled children, the neurological "window of opportunity" to learn begins to close during elementary school. Late remediation is more difficult and carries a high price tag, emotionally and economically. Instead of waiting until children can be "labeled," schools should provide early intervention services. If children receive appropriate early intervention services, many will not need labels or special education. With the present system, children often fall behind, receive a "label," are placed in special education where they are **not** taught the skills they need to learn.

Families and friends need to pressure their state and local school boards to provide intensive, remedial reading, writing, and math services to all children who need these services. These remedial services should be in addition to the special education services provided to identified children.

(G) focusing resources on teaching and learning while reducing paperwork and requirements that do not assist in improving educational results.

➡ **RELIEF FROM PAPERWORK**

Special education teachers are being buried under mountains of paperwork. Most of this paperwork serves no useful purpose, but takes hours of instructional time away from children who need specialized instruction.

(6) While states, local education agencies, and educational service agencies are responsible for providing an education for all children with disabilities, it is in the national interest that the Federal Government have a role in assisting State and local efforts to educate children with disabilities in order to improve results for such children and to ensure equal protection of the law.

(7) (A) The Federal Government must be responsive to the growing needs of **an increasingly diverse society**. A more equitable allocation of resources is essential for the Federal Government to meet its responsibility to provide **an equal educational opportunity for all individuals**.

(B) America's **racial profile** is rapidly changing. Between 1980 and 1990, the rate of increase in the population for white Americans was 6 percent, while the rate of increase for racial and ethnic minorities was much higher: 53 percent for Hispanics, 13.2 percent for African-Americans, and 107.8 percent for Asians.

(C) By the year 2000, this Nation will have 275,000,000 people, nearly one of every three of whom will be either African-American, Hispanic, Asian-American, or American Indian.

(D) Taken together as a group, **minority children** are comprising an ever larger percentage of public school students. Large-city school populations are overwhelmingly minority, for example: for fall 1993, the figure for Miami was 84 percent; Chicago, 89 percent; Philadelphia, 78 percent; Baltimore, 84 percent; Houston, 88 percent; and Los Angeles, 88 percent.

(E) Recruitment efforts within special education must focus on bringing larger numbers of minorities into the profession in order to provide appropriate practitioner knowledge, role models, and sufficient manpower to address the clearly changing demography of special education.

(F) The **limited English proficient population is the fastest growing in our Nation**, and the growth is occurring in many parts of our Nation. In the Nation's 2 largest school districts, limited English students make up almost half of all students initially entering school at the kindergarten level. Studies have documented apparent discrepancies in the levels of referral and placement of limited English proficient children in special education.

➡ **NEEDS OF "LIMITED ENGLISH PROFICIENT" (LEP) STUDENTS**
The Department of Education analyzed the process of referral, assessment, and services for students from non-English language backgrounds. They found that school districts often place limited English proficient (LEP) children in pre-existing special education programs that are not designed to meet these children's needs. School districts need to develop appropriate remediation programs for children with limited English proficiency.

(8) (A) Greater efforts are needed to prevent the intensification of problems connected with **mislabeling and high dropout rates among minority children with disabilities**.

(B) More minority children continue to be served in special education than would be expected from the percentage of minority students in the general school population.

(C) **Poor African-American children** are **2.3** times more likely to be identified by their teachers as having **mental retardation** than their white counterparts.

(D) Although African-Americans represent 16 percent of elementary and secondary enrollments, they constitute 21 percent of total enrollments in special education.

(E) The **drop-out rate is 68 percent higher for minorities** than for whites.

(F) **More than 50 percent of minority students** in large cities **drop out** of school.

(9) (A) The opportunity for full participation in awards for grants and contracts; boards of organizations receiving funds under this Act; and peer review panels; and training of professionals in the area of special education by minority individuals, organizations, and historically black colleges and universities is essential if we are to obtain greater success in the education of minority children with disabilities.

(B) In 1993, of the 915,000 college and university professors, 4.9 percent were African-American and 2.4 percent were Hispanic. Of the 2,940,000 teachers, pre-kindergarten through high school, 6.8 percent were African-American and 4.1 percent were Hispanic.

(C) Students from **minority groups** comprise more than 50 percent of K - 12 public school enrollment in seven States, yet minority enrollment in teacher training programs is less than 15 percent in all but six States.

(D) As the **number of African-American and Hispanic students in special education increases**, the **number** of **minority teachers** and related service personnel produced in our colleges and universities **continues to decrease**.

(E) **Ten years ago**, 12 percent of the United States teaching force in public elementary and secondary schools were members of a minority group. Minorities comprised 21 percent of the national population at that time and were clearly underrepresented then among employed teachers. **Today**, the elementary and secondary **teaching force is 13 percent minority**, while one-third of the students in public schools are minority children.

(F) As recently as 1991, historically black colleges and universities enrolled 44 percent of the African-American teacher trainees in the Nation. However, in 1993, historically black colleges and universities received only 4 percent of the discretionary funds for special education and related services personnel training under this Act.

(G) While African-American students constitute 28 percent of total enrollment in special education, only 11.2 percent of individuals enrolled in preservice training programs for special education are African-American.

(H) In 1986-87, of the degrees conferred in education at the B.A., M.A., and Ph.D. levels, only 6, 8, and 8 percent, respectively, were awarded to African-American or Hispanic students.

(10) Minorities and under-served persons are **socially disadvantaged because of the lack of opportunities** in training and educational programs, undergirded by the practices in the private sector that impede their full participation in the mainstream of society.

➡️ **MINORITIES OFTEN MISLABELED, DROP-OUT**
Given the emphasis in Sections 7, 8, 9, and 10, school districts should expect close scrutiny during audits and investigations by the U. S. Department of Education and the Office for Civil Rights (OCR). OCR is analyzing special education services provided to minority children and children with limited English proficiency.

(d) PURPOSES - The purposes of this title are-

(1)

(A) to ensure that all children with disabilities have available to them a free appropriate public education that emphasizes special education and related services **designed to meet their unique needs and prepare them for employment and independent living;**

(B) to ensure that the **rights of children with disabilities and parents** of such children **are protected**; and

(C) to assist States, localities, educational service agencies, and Federal agencies to provide for the education of all children with disabilities;

(2) to assist States in the implementation of a statewide, comprehensive, coordinated, multidisciplinary, interagency system of **early intervention services for infants and toddlers** with disabilities and their families;

(3) to ensure that **educators and parents** have the necessary **tools to improve educational results** for children with disabilities by supporting systemic-change activities; **coordinated research** and **personnel preparation**; coordinated technical assistance, dissemination, and support; and technology development and media services; and

(4) **to assess, and ensure the effectiveness of, efforts to educate children with disabilities**.

20 U.S.C. §1401 - Definitions

➡️ **SECTION OVERVIEW**
When in doubt about the meaning of a term or phrase, check this section for definitions of key terms (i.e., FAPE, IEP, LD, transition, etc.). The definitions section will often take you to the code section that will answer your questions .

(1) ASSISTIVE TECHNOLOGY DEVICE - The term 'assistive technology device' means **any item, piece of equipment**, or **product system**, whether acquired commercially off the shelf, modified, or customized, that is **used to increase, maintain, or improve functional capabilities** of a child with a disability.

(2) ASSISTIVE TECHNOLOGY SERVICE - The term 'assistive technology service' means **any service** that directly assists a child with a disability in the selection, acquisition, or use of an assistive technology device. Such term includes-

(A) the evaluation of the needs of such child, including a **functional evaluation of the child in the child's customary environment;**

➡ **HOME IS A "CUSTOMARY ENVIRONMENT" FOR CHILDREN**
Assistive technology service may include a functional evaluation of the child in the home.

(B) purchasing, leasing, or otherwise providing for the acquisition of assistive technology devices by such child;

(C) selecting, designing, fitting, customizing, adapting, applying, maintaining, repairing, or replacing of assistive technology devices;

(D) coordinating and using other **therapies**, **interventions**, or **services** with assistive technology devices, such as those associated with existing education and rehabilitation plans and programs;

(E) training or technical assistance for such child, or, where appropriate, the family of such child; and

(F) **training or technical assistance for professionals** (including individuals providing education and rehabilitation services), **employers**, or **other individuals** who provide services to, employ, or **are otherwise substantially involved in the major life functions of such child.**

➡ **ASSISTIVE TECHNOLOGY (A.T.) INCREASES INDEPENDENCE**
Technology allows people with disabilities to be more independent. Children who cannot write are using dictation software to communicate their thoughts and ideas. Smart machines read text to visually impaired children. Children who cannot speak are using computerized speaking machines. Congress intends disabled children to use technology devices and services to increase, maintain, and improve their ability to function independently in school and out of school.

(3) CHILD WITH A DISABILITY -

(A) In General - The term '**child with a disability**' means a child-

(i) with mental retardation, hearing impairments (including deafness), speech or language impairments, visual impairments (including blindness), serious emotional disturbance (hereinafter referred to as 'emotional disturbance'), orthopedic impairments, autism, traumatic brain injury, other health impairments, or specific learning disabilities; and
(ii) **who, by reason thereof, needs special education and related services.**

➡ **DISABILITY DOES NOT MEAN ELIGIBILITY FOR SPECIAL EDUCATION**
Having a disability does not automatically qualify a child for services under IDEA. A child may have a disability but not be eligible for special education and related services. The key phrase is "who, by reason thereof, needs special education and related services." Read the definition of "special education" (see below). If the child has a disability but does not need special education services, the child will not qualify for special education and related services under IDEA. If the child has a disability but does not need special education and related services under IDEA, the child may be entitled to protections under Section 504 of the Rehabilitation Act. Section 504 is a civil rights statute that protects individuals with disabilities from discrimination for reasons related to their disabilities.

➡ **UNDERSTANDING SECTION 504**
Section 504 is a civil rights statute that protects individuals with disabilities from discrimination. Section 504 children usually receive accommodations and modifications in Section 504 plans. A Section 504 plan should be a formal, written plan, not just a verbal agreement to help the child. The Section 504 child does not have a right to an individualized program (IEP) that is designed to meet the child's unique needs, from which the child receives educational benefit. Children with disabilities are protected under Section 504.

➡️ **IDEA AND FAPE**

IDEA confers the right to a free appropriate public education (FAPE). The IDEA child is entitled to an IEP [as described in 20 U.S.C. §1414(d)] and special education that confers educational benefit. It is important for parents to understand that if their child does not receive services under IDEA, the child does not have IDEA procedural protections.

(B) Child aged 3 through 9 - The term 'child with a disability' for a child aged 3 through 9 may, at the **discretion of the State and the local educational agency**, include a child -

(i) **experiencing developmental delays**, as defined by the State and as measured by appropriate diagnostic instruments and procedures, in one or more of the following areas: physical development, cognitive development, communication development, social or emotional development, or adaptive development; and
(ii) who, by reason thereof, **needs special education and related services**.

➡️ **CATCH-ALL SECTION FOR CHILDREN WITH DELAYS, NOT OTHERWISE ELIGIBLE**

School districts should provide special education services to very young children with delays who have not been classified. If a child between the ages of three to nine has a delay but does not qualify under Section 1401(3)(a)(i), this section opens the door to special education. Requiring schools to provide services to young children with developmental delays attempts to address these children's needs for early intervention services. Part C of IDEA focuses on the educational needs of very young children with disabilities.

➡️ **ELIGIBILITY DISPUTES**

What can parents do if the district claims their child is not eligible for services? What can parents do if they disagree with the school's definition or classification of the child's disability? If the child has a developmental delay, the child should be found eligible on this basis alone. Congress does not intend for schools to withhold special education services until children are old enough to be diagnosed with a specific disability, as defined in 20 U.S.C. §1401, and are damaged by this delay.

(4) EDUCATIONAL SERVICE AGENCY - The term 'educational service agency' -

(A) means a regional public multi-service agency -
(i) authorized by State law to develop, manage, and provide services or programs to local educational agencies; and
(ii) recognized as an administrative agency for purposes of the provision of special education and related services provided within public elementary and secondary schools of the State; and

(B) includes any other public institution or agency having administrative control and direction over a public elementary or secondary school.

(5) ELEMENTARY SCHOOL - The term 'elementary school' means a nonprofit institutional day or residential school that provides elementary education, as determined under State law.

(6) EQUIPMENT - The term 'equipment' includes -

(A) machinery, utilities, and built-in equipment and any necessary enclosures or structures to house such machinery, utilities, or equipment; and

(B) all other items necessary for the functioning of a particular facility as a facility for the provision of educational services, including items such as instructional equipment and necessary furniture; printed, published, and audio-visual instructional materials; telecommunications, sensory, and other technological aids and devices; and books, periodicals, documents, and other related materials.

(7) EXCESS COSTS - The term 'excess costs' means those costs that are in excess of the average annual per-student expenditure in a local educational agency during the preceding school year for an elementary or secondary school student, as may be appropriate, and which shall be computed after deducting -

    (A) amounts received -
        (i) under part B of this title;
        (ii) under part A of title I of the Elementary and Secondary Education Act of 1965; or
        (iii) under part A of title VII of that Act; and

    (B) any State or local funds expended for programs that would qualify for assistance under any of those parts.

(8) FREE APPROPRIATE PUBLIC EDUCATION - The term 'free appropriate public education' means special education and related services that-

    (A) have been provided at public expense, under public supervision and direction, and without charge;

    (B) meet the standards of the State educational agency;

    (C) include an appropriate preschool, elementary, or secondary school education in the State involved; and

    (D) are provided in conformity with the individualized education program required under section 1414(d).

> **➡ DEFINITION OF FAPE**
> FAPE is not clearly defined in the statute. The first U. S. Supreme Court decision to define FAPE was *Rowley*, which is included in the Caselaw section of this book. In *Rowley*, the Supreme Court ruled that FAPE is not the best program nor is it a program that maximizes benefit or learning.
> Parents must never say they want what is "best" for the child. Children are not entitled to the "best" education. Reports from private sector experts should never say "The best program for Johnny is . . ." or "Ideally, Johnny should receive . . . " If you use the word "best," this may ensure that Johnny will **not** receive this service or program. Use the term "appropriate" or "minimally appropriate" to describe the services Johnny needs.

(9) INDIAN - The term 'Indian' means an individual who is a member of an Indian tribe.

(10) INDIAN TRIBE - The term 'Indian tribe' means any Federal or State Indian tribe, band, rancheria, pueblo, colony, or community, including any Alaska Native village or regional village corporation (as defined in or established under the Alaska Native Claims Settlement Act).

(11) INDIVIDUALIZED EDUCATION PROGRAM -The term 'individualized education program' or 'IEP' means a written statement for each child with a disability that is developed, reviewed, and revised in accordance with section 1414(d).

> **➡ IEPs SHOULD BE REVIEWED OFTEN**
> The IEP is at the heart of most special education litigation. (See *Rowley*, *Burlington*, *Honig*, and *Carter* decisions in the Caselaw section of this book.) The child's IEP should be reviewed often to ensure that the child is making progress toward the annual goals and objectives.

(12) INDIVIDUALIZED FAMILY SERVICE PLAN - The term 'individualized family service plan' has the meaning given such term in section 1436.

(13) INFANT OR TODDLER WITH A DISABILITY - The term 'infant or toddler with a disability' has the meaning given such term in section 1432.

(14) INSTITUTION OF HIGHER EDUCATION - The term 'institution of higher education' -

(A) has the meaning given that term in section 1201(a) of the Higher Education Act of 1965; and

(B) also includes any community college receiving funding from the Secretary of the Interior under the Tribally Controlled Community College Assistance Act of 1978.

(15) LOCAL EDUCATIONAL AGENCY -

(A) The term 'local educational agency' means a public board of education or other public authority legally constituted within a State for either administrative control or direction of, or to perform a service function for, public elementary or secondary schools in a city, county, township, school district, or other political subdivision of a State, or for such combination of school districts or counties as are recognized in a State as an administrative agency for its public elementary or secondary schools.

(B) The term includes -
  (i) an educational service agency, as defined in paragraph (4); and
  (ii) any other public institution or agency having administrative control and direction of a public elementary or secondary school.

(C) The term includes an elementary or secondary school funded by the Bureau of Indian Affairs, but only to the extent that such inclusion makes the school eligible for programs for which specific eligibility is not provided to the school in another provision of law and the school does not have a student population that is smaller than the student population of the local educational agency

(16) NATIVE LANGUAGE - The term 'native language', when used with reference to an individual of limited English proficiency, means the language normally used by the individual, or in the case of a child, the language normally used by the parents of the child.

(17) NONPROFIT - The term 'nonprofit', as applied to a school, agency, organization, or institution, means a school, agency, organization, or institution owned and operated by one or more nonprofit corporations or associations no part of the net earnings of which inures, or may lawfully inure, to the benefit of any private shareholder or individual.

(18) OUTLYING AREA - The term 'outlying area' means the United States Virgin Islands, Guam, American Samoa, and the Commonwealth of the Northern Mariana Islands.

(19) PARENT - The term 'parent' -

(A) includes a legal guardian; and

(B) except as used in sections 1415(b)(2) and 1439(a)(5), includes an individual assigned under either of those sections to be a surrogate parent.

(20) PARENT ORGANIZATION - The term 'parent organization' has the meaning given that term in section 1482(g).

(21) PARENT TRAINING AND INFORMATION CENTER - The term 'parent training and information center' means a center assisted under section 1482 or 1483.

(22) RELATED SERVICES -The term 'related services' means **transportation**, and such **developmental, corrective, and other supportive services** (including speech-language pathology and audiology services, psychological services, physical and occupational therapy, recreation, including therapeutic recreation, social work services, counseling services, including rehabilitation counseling, orientation and mobility services, and medical services, except that such medical services shall be for diagnostic and evaluation purposes only) as may be **required to assist a child** with a disability **to benefit from special education**, and includes the **early identification and assessment of disabling conditions in children**.

➡️ **RELATED SERVICES SHOULD HELP CHILD BENEFIT FROM SPECIAL EDUCATION**
Related services are services that the child needs to benefit from special education. Compare this term to "supplementary aids and services" (below). Related services and supplementary services may include one-to-one tutoring or remediation in reading, writing, spelling and arithmetic skills. The child does not have to be placed in a special education class for tutoring or remediation. Transportation to school is included in this term.

(23) SECONDARY SCHOOL - The term 'secondary school' means a nonprofit institutional day or residential school that provides secondary education, as determined under State law, except that it does not include any education beyond grade 12.

(24) SECRETARY - The term 'Secretary' means the Secretary of Education.

(25) SPECIAL EDUCATION - The term 'special education' means **specially designed instruction**, at **no cost to parents, to meet the unique needs** of a child with a disability, including-

(A) instruction conducted in the classroom, **in the home**, in hospitals and institutions, and in other settings; and

(B) instruction in physical education.

➡️ **SPECIAL EDUCATION MEANS SPECIALIZED INSTRUCTION**
The key phrase is "specially designed instruction . . . to meet the unique needs . . ." Is the child receiving specially designed instruction? Is the child receiving modifications and accomodations so he or she has an equal opportunity to learn? Special education should include a range of services that are designed to meet the unique needs of individual children with disabilities. Special education includes one-to-one tutoring, remediation, and 40+ hour programs of Applied Behavioral Analysis (ABA) therapy.

(26) SPECIFIC LEARNING DISABILITY -

(A) In general - The term 'specific learning disability' means a disorder in one or more of the basic psychological processes involved in **understanding or in using language, spoken or written**, which disorder may manifest itself in imperfect ability to **listen, think, speak, read, write, spell, or do mathematical calculations**.

➡️ **THE LEGAL DEFINITION OF "SPECIFIC LEARNING DISABILITY"**
The amended IDEA did not change the legal definition of "specific learning disability." The legal definition of "specific learning disability" does not contain any reference to a "discrepancy" between the child's IQ and educational achievement test scores.
Some states use discrepancy formulas to decide whether children are eligible for special education services. When discrepancy formulas are used, there must be a specific statistical difference between the child's ability (as measured by an IQ test) and the child's achievement (as measured by educational achievement test scores). This "discrepancy" varies from state to state, and jurisdiction to jurisdiction. If a child moves to a jurisdictions or state that uses a larger discrepancy measure, the move may "cure" the child's disability.
Most states have clauses that allow eligibility teams to identify a child with a specific learning disability, even if the formula is not satisfied. The federal special education regulations do not allow the child's eligibility to be determined solely with a discrepancy formula. .

➡️ **PUBLIC LAW 94-142: NO REFERENCE TO A DISCREPANCY FORMULA**
Public Law 94-142 contained no reference a "discrepancy formula" that school districts or states should use to determine if a child with a learning disability is eligible for special education services. In 1977, the U. S. Department of Education placed the term "discrepancy" in the Code of Federal Regulations.

Experts from the National Institute of Child Health and Human Development (part of the National Institutes of Health) and the Learning Disabilities Association of America (LDAA) urged the U. S. Department of Education to eliminate discrepancy formulas in the identification of children with learning disabilities. Congress did not write a "discrepancy formula" into the original statute. It should not take an Act of Congress to remove the term from the regulations.

➡️ **WARNING: THE "MARK PENALTY"**
School psychologists use the "Mark Penalty" to describe situations in which the child's processing disorder depresses IQ and achievement, and may even eliminate the discrepancy between IQ and achievement scores. A discrepancy between ability and achievement should not be hidden or masked by the Mark Penalty. Falling IQ scores are a sign of an inappropriate education.

(B) Disorders included - Such term includes such conditions as **perceptual disabilities**, brain injury, minimal brain dysfunction, dyslexia, and developmental aphasia.

➡️ **PERCEPTUAL DISABILITIES ARE INCLUDED UNDER LD**
If there is no "severe discrepancy" between the child's intelligence and educational achievement test scores (as discussed above), but there is significant "scatter" between subtest scores, this suggests that the child may have a perceptual or processing disorder. If there is significant scatter, the general or full scale score on an IQ test may not be a valid estimate of the child's intelligence. Children with perceptual or processing disorders may be eligible for special education on this basis alone. The terms used to describe learning disabilities are those used in 1975, when Congress enacted Public Law 94-142. "Minimal brain dysfunction" is a term for "Attention Deficit Disorder" that was used by the American Psychiatric Association (APA) during the 1970's. Dyslexia is a language learning disability (i.e., reading, writing, spelling, math).

(C) Disorders not included - Such term does not include a learning problem that is primarily the result of visual, hearing, or motor disabilities, of mental retardation, of emotional disturbance, or of environmental, cultural, or economic disadvantage.

➡️ **LEARNING DISABILITIES: OFTEN DEFINED BY EXCLUSION**
"Learning disability" is a catch-all phrase. If a child has a disability that adversely affects educational performance, and the child is not retarded, does not have a visual, hearing or motor disability, is not emotionally disturbed, and is not negatively affected by environmental, cultural or economic disadvantages, the child has a learning disability. However, a child can have both mental retardation and a specific learning disability. The term "dyslexia" requires that specific criteria be met. For legal purposes, dyslexia is a type of learning disability that adversely affects educational performance which opens the door to specialized instruction under IDEA.

(27) STATE - The term 'State" means each of the 50 States, the District of Columbia, the Commonwealth of Puerto Rico, and each of the outlying areas.

(28) STATE EDUCATIONAL AGENCY - The term 'State educational agency' means the State board of education or other agency or officer primarily responsible for the State supervision of public elementary and secondary schools, or, if there is no such officer or agency, an officer or agency designated by the Governor or by State law.

(29) SUPPLEMENTARY AIDS AND SERVICES - The term 'supplementary aids and services' means, **aids**, **services**, and **other supports** that are provided in **regular education classes** or **other education-related settings** to enable children with disabilities to be educated with nondisabled children to the maximum extent appropriate in accordance with section 1412(a)(5).

➡️ **SUPPLEMENTARY SERVICES MEANS SERVICES FOR REGULAR CLASSROOM SUCCESS**
Related services are for special education. Supplementary services are for regular education. **Memory Trick**: "Related" is never regular. "Supplemental" is never special. Related services **and** supplementary services may include one-to-one tutoring and/or remediation in reading, writing, spelling, and arithmetic

skills. Children do not have to be placed in special education classes to receive these services. Go back and read the definition of "related services" in subsection 22 again.

Supplementary aids and services may be important to the outcome of a disciplinary proceeding. In a disciplinary hearing, the Hearing Officer must determine if the school district made "reasonable efforts to minimize the risk of harm in the child's current placement, including the use of supplementary aids and services." [See 20 U.S.C. §1415(k)(2)(C)]. These terms are important in disciplinary proceedings.

(30) TRANSITION SERVICES - The term 'transition services' means a coordinated set of activities for a student with a disability that-

(A) are designed within an **outcome-oriented process**, which promotes movement from school to **post-school activities**, including post-secondary education, vocational training, integrated employment (including supported employment), continuing and adult education, adult services, independent living, or community participation;

(B) are based on the individual student's needs, taking into account the student's preferences and interests; and

(c) include instruction, related services, community experiences, the development of employment and other post-school adult living objectives, and, when appropriate, acquisition of daily living skills and functional vocational evaluation.

➡ **TRANSITION SHOULD BE "OUTCOME-ORIENTED"**
The terms "outcome-oriented" and "post-school activities" mean that transition must have clear outcomes. Special education should teach children the skills they need to be independent and self-sufficient. For more about transition services, see Appendix A of the IDEA regulations.

20 U.S.C. §1402 - Office of Special Education Programs

(a) ESTABLISHMENT - There shall be, within the Office of Special Education and Rehabilitative Services in the Department of Education, an Office of Special Education Programs, which shall be the principal agency in such Department for administering and carrying out this Act and other programs and activities concerning the education of children with disabilities.

(b) DIRECTOR - The Office established under subsection (a) shall be headed by a Director who shall be selected by the Secretary and shall report directly to the Assistant Secretary for Special Education and Rehabilitative Services.

(c) VOLUNTARY AND UNCOMPENSATED SERVICES - Notwithstanding section 1342 of title 31, United States Code, the Secretary is authorized to accept voluntary and uncompensated services in furtherance of the purposes of this Act.

20 U.S.C. §1403 - Abrogation of State Sovereign Immunity

➡ **SECTION OVERVIEW**
This section establishes that the state can be sued for violations of IDEA.

(a) IN GENERAL - A State shall not be immune under the eleventh amendment to the Constitution of the United States from suit in Federal court for a violation of this Act.

(b) REMEDIES - In a suit against a State for a violation of this Act, remedies (including remedies both at law and in equity) are available for such a violation to the same extent as those remedies are available for such a violation in the suit against any public entity other than a State.

➡ **REMEDIES AT LAW AND IN EQUITY MAY MEAN RELIEF IN DOLLARS AND/OR SERVICES**
This section affirms that "Yes, you can sue the state."

(c) EFFECTIVE DATE - Subsections (a) and (b) apply with respect to violations that occur in whole or part after the date of the enactment of the Education of the Handicapped Act Amendments of 1990.

20 U.S.C. §1404 - Acquisition of Equipment; Construction or Alteration of Facilities

➡ **SECTION OVERVIEW**

Funds may be spent to acquire, construct and alter equipment, so long as other federal laws, including the ADA, are followed.

(a) IN GENERAL - If the Secretary determines that a program authorized under this Act would be improved by permitting program funds to be used to acquire appropriate equipment, or to construct new facilities or alter existing facilities, the Secretary is authorized to allow the use of those funds for those purposes.

(b) COMPLIANCE WITH CERTAIN REGULATIONS - Any construction of new facilities or alteration of existing facilities under subsection (a) shall comply with the requirements of -

(1) Appendix A of Part 36 of Title 28, Code of Federal Regulations (commonly known as the 'Americans with Disabilities Accessibility Guidelines for Buildings and Facilities'); or

(2) Appendix A of part 101-19.6 of title 41, Code of Federal Regulations (commonly known as the 'Uniform Federal Accessibility Standards').

20 U.S.C. §1405 - Employment of Individuals with Disabilities

The Secretary shall ensure that each recipient of assistance under this Act **makes positive efforts to employ and advance** in employment qualified individuals with disabilities in programs assisted under this Act.

20 U.S.C. §1406 - Requirements for Prescribing Regulations

➡ **SECTION OVERVIEW**

This section describes the process that the U. S. Department of Education shall follow when issuing regulations and policy letters and position statements.

(a) PUBLIC COMMENTS PERIOD - The Secretary shall provide a Public Comments period of at least 90 days on any regulation proposed under part B or part C of this Act on which an opportunity for public Comments is otherwise required by law.

(b) PROTECTIONS PROVIDED TO CHILDREN - The Secretary **may not implement**, or publish in final form, **any regulation** prescribed pursuant to this Act **that would procedurally or substantively lessen the protections provided to children with disabilities under this Act,** as embodied in regulations in effect on July 20, 1983 (particularly as such protections relate to parental consent to initial evaluation or initial placement in special education, least restrictive environment, related services, timelines, attendance of evaluation personnel at individualized education program meetings, or qualifications of personnel), except to the extent that such regulation reflects the clear and unequivocal intent of the Congress in legislation.

➡ **NEW REGULATIONS ARE SUBSERVIENT TO JULY 20, 1983 REGULATIONS**

The new Regulations may not lessen the protections offered by the former regulations, except where the revised statute clearly modifies the earlier law. A large body of case law is based on the original statute and regulations. This clause retains the validity of this case law.

Laws regulate conduct and behavior. Many states have regulations that require all localities to use a standard "Uniform Traffic Summons." The form and operating procedures that govern speeding tickets (Uniform Traffic Summons) are standardized. The sheriff's department, metropolitan police department, and highway patrol often use the same forms. If the state agency that is responsible for preparing and distributing these forms fails to provide them to law enforcement agencies, you will still receive a speeding ticket if you exceed the posted speed limit.

States often complain that the federal government does not provide them with sample forms and adequate guidance about the law. Local school districts often complain that the state does not provide them with adequate guidance or forms. The law is available for all to read. By using a word processor, anyone can develop forms.

(c) POLICY LETTERS AND STATEMENTS - The Secretary **may not**, through policy letters or other statements, establish a rule that is required for compliance with, and eligibility under, this part **without following** the requirements of section 553 of title 5, United States Code.

(d) CORRESPONDENCE FROM DEPARTMENT OF EDUCATION DESCRIBING INTERPRETATIONS OF THIS PART -

(1) **In General** - The Secretary **shall**, on a quarterly basis, **publish in the Federal Register**, and widely disseminate to interested entities through various additional forms of communication, **a list of correspondence** from the Department of Education received by individuals during the previous quarter that describes the interpretations of the Department of Education of this Act or the regulations implemented pursuant to this Act.

(2) **Additional Information** - For each item of correspondence published in a list under paragraph (1), the Secretary shall identify the topic addressed by the correspondence and shall include such other summary information as the Secretary determines to be appropriate.

> ➡ **KEEPING THE PUBLIC INFORMED**
> By publishing the U. S. Code, Code of Federal Regulations, and Federal Register on the Internet, the government attempts to ensure that citizens have access to law and regulations. The Department of Education does not release letters of interpretation on the Internet but publishes a "list" of these letters which has little meaning.

(e) ISSUES OF NATIONAL SIGNIFICANCE - If the **Secretary receives a written request regarding a policy, question, or interpretation** under part B of this Act, **and** determines that it raises an **issue of general interest** or applicability of national significance to the implementation of part B, the Secretary **shall-**

(1) include a statement to that effect in any written response;

(2) **widely disseminate** that response to State educational agencies, local educational agencies, parent and advocacy organizations, and other interested organizations, subject to applicable laws relating to confidentiality of information; and

(3) **not later than one year** after the date on which the Secretary responds to the written request, **issue written guidance** on such policy, question, or interpretation through such means as the Secretary determines to be appropriate and consistent with law, such as a policy memorandum, notice of interpretation, or notice of proposed rulemaking.

(f) EXPLANATION - Any written response by the Secretary under subsection (e) regarding a policy, question, or interpretation under part B of this Act shall include an explanation that the written response-

(1) is provided **as informal guidance and is not legally binding**; and

(2) represents the interpretation by the Department of Education of the applicable statutory or regulatory requirements in the context of the specific facts presented.

> ➡ **INTERPRETATIONS OF LAW MAY OR MAY NOT HAVE NATIONAL SIGNIFICANCE**
> If the Secretary does not deem that an interpretation in 20 U.S.C. 1406(d) has "national significance," this 1406(e) subsection does not apply. If a reply has "national significance," the Department of Education must issue a policy memorandum, notice of interpretation, or notice of proposed rulemaking. Administrative convenience may mean that few "written responses" raise issues of "general interest" or "national significance."

END OF PART A

Part B - Assistance for Education of All Children with Disabilities

➡ **OVERVIEW OF PART B**

Part B includes Sections 1411 through 1419. §1412 discusses services for students in private schools and unilateral placements by parents. Evaluations, eligibility, IEPs, and placement decisions are in §1414. Procedural safeguards, including mediation, due process, and discipline proceedings, are in §1415.

20 U.S.C. §1411 - Authorizations; Allotment; Use of Funds; Authorization of Appropriations
20 U.S.C. §1412 - State Eligibility
20 U.S.C. §1413 - Local Educational Agency Eligibility
20 U.S.C. §1414 - Evaluations, Eligibility, IEPs, & Placement
20 U.S.C. §1415 - Procedural Safeguards
20 U.S.C. §1416 - Withholding and Judicial Review
20 U.S.C. §1417 - Administration
20 U.S.C. §1418 - Program information
20 U.S.C. §1419 - Preschool Grants

20 U.S.C. §1411 – Authorizations; Allotment; Use of Funds; Authorization of Appropriations

➡ **SECTION OVERVIEW**

This section provides funding formulas, ratios, definitions, and requirements.

(a) GRANTS TO STATES -

(1) Purpose of Grants - The Secretary shall make grants to states and the outlying areas, and provide funds to the Secretary of the Interior, to assist them to provide special education and related services to children with disabilities in accordance with this part.

(2) Maximum Amounts -The **maximum amount** of the grant a State may receive under this section for any fiscal year is

(A) the number of children with disabilities in the State who are receiving special education and related services -

(i) aged 3 through 5 if the State is eligible for a grant under section 1419; and

(ii) aged 6 through 21; multiplied by

(B) 40 percent of the **average per-pupil expenditure** in public elementary and secondary schools in the United States.

(b) OUTLYING AREAS AND FREELY ASSOCIATED STATES -

(1) Funds Reserved - From the amount appropriated for any fiscal year under subsection (j), the Secretary shall reserve not more than one percent, which shall be used -

(A) to provide assistance to the outlying areas in accordance with their respective populations of individuals aged 3 through 21; and

(B) for fiscal years 1998 through 2001, to carry out the competition described in paragraph (2), except that the amount reserved to carry out that competition shall not exceed the amount reserved for fiscal year 1996 for the competition under part B of this Act described under the heading 'SPECIAL EDUCATION' in Public Law 104-134.

(2) Limitations for Freely Associated States -

(A) Competitive Grants - The Secretary shall use funds described in paragraph (1)(B) to award grants, on a competitive basis, to **Guam, American Samoa, the Commonwealth of the Northern Mariana Islands**, and the **freely associated States** to carry out the purposes of this part.

(B) Award Basis - The Secretary shall award grants under subparagraph (A) on a competitive basis, pursuant to the recommendations of the Pacific Region Educational Laboratory in Honolulu, Hawaii. Those recommendations shall be made by experts in the field of special education and related services.

(C) Assistance Requirements - Any freely associated State that wishes to receive funds under this part shall include, in its application for assistance -

(i) information demonstrating that it will meet all conditions that apply to States under this part;

(ii) an assurance that, notwithstanding any other provision of this part, it will use **those funds only for the direct provision of special education and related services** to children with disabilities and to enhance its capacity to make a free appropriate public education available to all children with disabilities;

(iii) the identity of the source and amount of funds, in addition to funds under this part, that it will make available to ensure that a free appropriate public education is available to all children with disabilities within its jurisdiction; and

(iv) such other information and assurances as the Secretary may require.

(D) Termination of Eligibility - Notwithstanding any other provision of law, the freely associated States **shall not** receive any funds under this part for any program year that begins **after** September 30, 2001.

(E) Administrative Costs - The Secretary may provide not more than five percent of the amount reserved for grants under this paragraph to pay the administrative costs of the Pacific Region Educational Laboratory under subparagraph (B).

(3) Limitation - An outlying area is not eligible for a competitive award under paragraph (2) unless it receives assistance under paragraph (1)(A).

(4) Special Rule - The provisions of Public Law 95-134, permitting the consolidation of grants by the outlying areas, shall not apply to funds provided to those areas or to the freely associated States under this section.

(5) Eligibility for Discretionary Programs - The freely associated States shall be eligible to receive assistance under subpart 2 of part D of this Act until September 30, 2001.

(6) Definition - As used in this subsection, the term 'freely associated States' means the Republic of the Marshall Islands, the Federated States of Micronesia, and the Republic of Palau.

(c) SECRETARY OF THE INTERIOR - From the amount appropriated for any fiscal year under subsection (j), the Secretary shall reserve 1.226 percent to provide assistance to the Secretary of the Interior in accordance with subsection (i).

(d) ALLOCATIONS TO STATES -

(1) In General - After reserving funds for studies and evaluations under section 1474(e), and for payments to the outlying areas and the Secretary of the Interior under subsections (b) and (c), the Secretary shall allocate the remaining amount among the States in accordance with paragraph (2) or subsection (e), as the case may be.

(2) Interim Formula - Except as provided in subsection (e), the Secretary shall allocate the amount described in paragraph (1) among the States in accordance with section 1411(a)(3), (4), and (5) and (b)(1), (2), and (3) of this Act, as in effect prior to the enactment of the Individuals with Disabilities Education Act Amendments of 1997, except that the determination of the number of children with disabilities receiving special education and related services under such section 1411(a)(3) may, at the State's discretion, be calculated as of the last Friday in October or as of December 1 of the fiscal year for which the funds are appropriated.

(e) PERMANENT FORMULA -

(1) Establishment of Base Year - The Secretary shall allocate the amount described in subsection (d)(1) among the States in accordance with this subsection for each fiscal year beginning with the first fiscal year for which the amount appropriated under subsection (j) is more than $4,924,672,200.

(2) Use of Base Year -

(A) Definition - As used in this subsection, the term 'base year' means the fiscal year preceding the first fiscal year in which this subsection applies.

(B) Special Rule for Use of Base Year Amount - If a State received any funds under this section for the base year on the basis of children aged 3 through 5, but does not make a free appropriate public education available to all children with disabilities aged 3 through 5 in the State in any subsequent fiscal year, the Secretary shall compute the State's base year amount, solely for the purpose of calculating the State's allocation in that subsequent year under paragraph (3) or (4), by subtracting the amount allocated to the State for the base year on the basis of those children.

(3) Increase in Funds - If the amount available for allocations to States under paragraph (1) is equal to or greater than the amount allocated to the States under this paragraph for the preceding fiscal year, those allocations shall be calculated as follows:

(A) (i) Except as provided in subparagraph (B), the Secretary shall -

(I) allocate to each State the amount it received for the base year;

(II) allocate 85 percent of any remaining funds to States on the basis of their relative populations of children aged 3 through 21 who are of the same age as children with disabilities for whom the state ensures the availability of a free appropriate public education under this part; and

(III) allocate 15 percent of those remaining funds to States on the basis of their relative populations of children described in subclause (II) who are living in poverty.

(ii) For the purpose of making grants under this paragraph, the Secretary shall use the most recent population data, including data on children living in poverty, that are available and satisfactory to the Secretary.

(B) Notwithstanding subparagraph (A), allocations under this paragraph shall be subject to the following:

(i) No State's allocation shall be less than its allocation for the preceding fiscal year.

(ii) No State's allocation shall be less than the greatest of -

(I) the sum of -

(aa) the amount it received for the base year; and

(bb) one third of one percent of the amount by which the amount appropriated under subsection (j) exceeds the amount appropriated under this section for the base year;

(II) the sum of -

(aa) the amount it received for the preceding fiscal year; and

(bb) that amount multiplied by the percentage by which the increase in the funds appropriated from the preceding fiscal year exceeds 1.5 percent; or

(III) the sum of -

(aa) the amount it received for the preceding fiscal year; and

(bb) that amount multiplied by 90 percent of the percentage increase in the amount appropriated from the preceding fiscal year.

(iii) Notwithstanding clause (ii), no State's allocation under this paragraph shall exceed the sum of -

(I) the amount it received for the preceding fiscal year; and

(II) that amount multiplied by the sum of 1.5 percent and the percentage increase in the amount appropriated.

(C) If the amount available for allocations under this paragraph is insufficient to pay those allocations in full, those allocations shall be ratably reduced, subject to subparagraph (B)(i).

(4) Decrease in Funds - If the amount available for allocations to States under paragraph (1) is less than the amount allocated to the States under this section for the preceding fiscal year, those allocations shall be calculated as follows:

(A) If the amount available for allocations is greater than the amount allocated to the States for the base year, each State shall be allocated the sum of -

(i) the amount it received for the base year; and

(ii) an amount that bears the same relation to any remaining funds as the increase the State received for the preceding fiscal year over the base year bears to the total of all such increases for all States.

(B)(i) If the amount available for allocations is equal to or less than the amount allocated to the States for the base year, each State shall be allocated the amount it received for the base year.

(ii) If the amount available is insufficient to make the allocations described in clause (i), those allocations shall be ratably reduced.

(f) S**TATE** L**EVEL** A**CTIVITIES** -

(1) General -
(A) Each State may retain not more than the amount described in subparagraph (B) for administration and other State-level activities in accordance with paragraphs (2) and (3).
(B) For each fiscal year, the Secretary shall determine and report to the State educational agency an amount that is 25 percent of the amount the State received under this section for fiscal year 1997, cumulatively adjusted by the Secretary for each succeeding fiscal year by the lesser of -
(i) the percentage increase, if any, from the preceding fiscal year in the State's allocation under this section; or
(ii) the rate of inflation, as measured by the percentage increase, if any, from the preceding fiscal year in the Consumer Price Index For All Urban Consumers, published by the Bureau of Labor Statistics of the Department of Labor.
(C) A State may use funds it retains under subparagraph (A) without regard to -
(i) the prohibition on commingling of funds in section 1412(a)(18)(B); and
(ii) the prohibition on supplanting other funds in section 1412(a)(18)(C).

(2) State Administration -
(A) For the purpose of administering this part, including section 1419 (including the coordination of activities under this part with, and providing technical assistance to, other programs that provide services to children with disabilities) -
(i) each State may use not more than twenty percent of the maximum amount it may retain under paragraph (1)(A) for any fiscal year or $500,000 (adjusted by the cumulative rate of inflation since fiscal year 1998, as measured by the percentage increase, if any, in the Consumer Price Index For All Urban Consumers, published by the Bureau of Labor Statistics of the Department of Labor), whichever is greater; and
(ii) each outlying area may use up to five percent of the amount it receives under this section for any fiscal year or $35,000, whichever is greater.
(B) Funds described in subparagraph (A) may also be used for the administration of part C of this Act, if the State educational agency is the lead agency for the State under that part.

(3) Other State-Level Activities - Each State shall use any funds it retains under paragraph (1) and does not use for administration under paragraph (2) for any of the following:
(A) Support and direct services, including technical assistance and personnel development and training.
(B) Administrative costs of monitoring and complaint investigation, but only to the extent that those costs exceed the costs incurred for those activities during fiscal year 1985.
(C) To establish and implement the mediation process required by section 1415(e), including providing for the costs of mediators and support personnel.
(D) To assist local educational agencies in meeting personnel shortages.
(E) To develop a State Improvement Plan under subpart 1 of part D.
(F) Activities at the State and local levels to meet the performance goals established by the State under section 1412(a)(16) and to support implementation of the State Improvement Plan under subpart 1 of part D if the State receives funds under that subpart.
(G) To supplement other amounts used to develop and implement a Statewide coordinated services system designed to improve results for children and families, including children with disabilities and their families, but not to exceed one percent of the amount received by the State under this section. This system shall be coordinated with and, to the extent appropriate, build on the system of coordinated services developed by the State under part C of this Act.
(H) For subgrants to local educational agencies for the purposes described in paragraph (4)(A).

(4)
(A) Subgrants to Local Educational Agencies for Capacity-Building and Improvement - In any fiscal year in which the percentage increase in the State's allocation under this section exceeds the rate of inflation (as measured by the percentage increase, if any, from the preceding fiscal year in the Consumer Price Index For All Urban Consumers, published by the Bureau of Labor Statistics of the Department of Labor), each State shall reserve, from its allocation under this section, the amount described in subparagraph (B) to make subgrants to local educational agencies, unless that

amount is less than $100,000, to assist them in providing direct services and in making systemic change to improve results for children with disabilities through one or more of the following:

(i) Direct services, including alternative programming for children who have been expelled from school, and services for children in correctional facilities, children enrolled in State-operated or State-supported schools, and children in charter schools.

(ii) Addressing needs or carrying out improvement strategies identified in the State's Improvement Plan under subpart 1 of part D.

(iii) Adopting promising practices, materials, and technology, based on knowledge derived from education research and other sources.

(iv) Establishing, expanding, or implementing interagency agreements and arrangements between local educational agencies and other agencies or organizations concerning the provision of services to children with disabilities and their families.

(v) Increasing cooperative problem-solving between parents and school personnel and promoting the use of alternative dispute resolution.

(B) Maximum Subgrant - For each fiscal year, the amount referred to in subparagraph (A) is

(i) the maximum amount the State was allowed to retain under paragraph (1)(A) for the prior fiscal year, or for fiscal year 1998, 25 percent of the State's allocation for fiscal year 1997 under this section; multiplied by

(ii) the difference between the percentage increase in the State's allocation under this section and the rate of inflation, as measured by the percentage increase, if any, from the preceding fiscal year in the Consumer Price Index For All Urban Consumers, published by the Bureau of Labor Statistics of the Department of Labor.

(5) Report on Use of Funds - As part of the information required to be submitted to the Secretary under section 1412, each State shall annually describe -

(A) how amounts retained under paragraph (1) will be used to meet the requirements of this part;

(B) how those amounts will be allocated among the activities described in paragraphs (2) and (3) to meet State priorities based on input from local educational agencies; and

(C) the percentage of those amounts, if any, that will be distributed to local educational agencies by formula.

(g) SUBGRANTS TO LOCAL EDUCATIONAL AGENCIES -

(1) Subgrants Required - Each State that receives a grant under this section for any fiscal year shall distribute any funds it does not retain under subsection (f) (**at least 75 percent of the grant funds**) to local educational agencies in the State that have established their eligibility under section 1413, and to State agencies that received funds under section 1414A(a) of this Act for fiscal year 1997, as then in effect, and have established their eligibility under section 1413, for use in accordance with this part.

(2) Allocations to Local Educational Agencies -

(A) Interim Procedure - For each fiscal year for which funds are allocated to States under subsection (d)(2), each State shall allocate funds under paragraph (1) in accordance with section 1411(d) of this Act, as in effect prior to the enactment of the Individuals with Disabilities Education Act Amendments of 1997.

(B) Permanent Procedure - For each fiscal year for which funds are allocated to States under subsection (e), each State shall allocate funds under paragraph (1) as follows:

(i) Base Payments - The State shall first award each agency described in paragraph (1) the amount that agency would have received under this section for the base year, as defined in subsection (e)(2)(A), if the State had distributed 75 percent of its grant for that year under section 1411(d), as then in effect.

(ii) Allocating of Remaining Funds - After making allocations under clause (i), the State shall -

(I) allocate 85 percent of any remaining funds to those agencies on the basis of the relative numbers of children enrolled in public and private elementary and secondary schools within the agency's jurisdiction; and

(II) allocate 15 percent of those remaining funds to those agencies in accordance with their relative numbers of children living in poverty, as determined by the State educational agency.

(3) Former Chapter 1 State Agencies -
    (A) To the extent necessary, the State -
        (i) shall use funds that are available under subsection (f)(1)(A) to ensure that each State agency that received fiscal year 1994 funds under subpart 2 of part D of chapter 1 of title I of the Elementary and Secondary Education Act of 1965 receives, from the combination of funds under subsection (f)(1)(A) and funds provided under paragraph (1) of this subsection, an amount equal to -
            (I) the number of children with disabilities, aged 6 through 21, to whom the agency was providing special education and related services on December 1 of the fiscal year for which the funds were appropriated, subject to the limitation in subparagraph (B); multiplied by
            (II) the per-child amount provided under such subpart for fiscal year 1994; and
        (ii) may use those funds to ensure that each local educational agency that received fiscal year 1994 funds under that subpart for children who had transferred from a State-operated or State-supported school or program assisted under that subpart receives, from the combination of funds available under subsection (f)(1)(A) and funds provided under paragraph (1) of this subsection, an amount for each such child, aged 3 through 21 to whom the agency was providing special education and related services on December 1 of the fiscal year for which the funds were appropriated, equal to the per-child amount the agency received under that subpart for fiscal year 1994.
    (B) The number of children counted under subparagraph (A)(i)(I) shall not exceed the number of children aged 3 through 21 for whom the agency received fiscal year 1994 funds under subpart 2 of part D of chapter 1 of title I of the Elementary and Secondary Education Act of 1965.

(4) Reallocation of Funds - If a State educational agency determines that a local educational agency is adequately providing a free appropriate public education to all children with disabilities residing in the area served by that agency with State and local funds, the State educational agency may reallocate any portion of the funds under this part that are not needed by that local agency to provide a free appropriate public education to other local educational agencies in the State that **are not adequately providing special education and related services** to all children with disabilities residing in the areas they serve.

(h) DEFINITIONS - For the purpose of this section -

    (1) the term '**average per-pupil expenditure** in public elementary and secondary schools in the United States' means -
        (A) without regard to the source of funds -
            (i) the aggregate current expenditures, during the second fiscal year preceding the fiscal year for which the determination is made (or, if satisfactory data for that year are not available, during the most recent preceding fiscal year for which satisfactory data are available) of all local educational agencies in the 50 States and the District of Columbia); plus
            (ii) any direct expenditures by the State for the operation of those agencies; divided by
        (B) the aggregate number of children in average daily attendance to whom those agencies provided free public education during that preceding year; and

    (2) the term 'State' means each of the 50 States, the District of Columbia, and the Commonwealth of Puerto Rico.

(i) USE OF AMOUNTS BY SECRETARY OF THE INTERIOR -

    (1) Provision of Amounts for Assistance -
        (A) In General - The Secretary of Education shall provide amounts to the Secretary of the Interior to meet the need for assistance for the education of children with disabilities on reservations aged 5 to 21, inclusive, enrolled in elementary and secondary schools for Indian children operated or funded by the Secretary of the Interior. The amount of such payment for any fiscal year shall be equal to 80 percent of the amount allotted under subsection (c) for that fiscal year.
        (B) Calculation of Number of Children - In the case of Indian students aged 3 to 5, inclusive, who are enrolled in programs affiliated with the Bureau of Indian Affairs (hereafter in this subsection referred to as 'BIA') schools and that

are required by the States in which such schools are located to attain or maintain State accreditation, and which schools have such accreditation prior to the date of enactment of the Individuals with Disabilities Education Act Amendments of 1991, the school shall be allowed to count those children for the purpose of distribution of the funds provided under this paragraph to the Secretary of the Interior. The Secretary of the Interior shall be responsible for meeting all of the requirements of this part for these children, in accordance with paragraph (2).

(C) Additional Requirement - With respect to all other children aged 3 to 21, inclusive, on reservations, the State educational agency shall be responsible for ensuring that all of the requirements of this part are implemented.

(2) Submission of Information - The Secretary of Education may provide the Secretary of the Interior amounts under paragraph (1) for a fiscal year only if the Secretary of the Interior submits to the Secretary of Education information that -

(A) demonstrates that the Department of the Interior meets the appropriate requirements, as determined by the Secretary of Education, of sections 1412 (including monitoring and evaluation activities) and 1413;

(B) includes a description of how the Secretary of the Interior will coordinate the provision of services under this part with local educational agencies, tribes and tribal organizations, and other private and Federal service providers;

(C) includes an assurance that there are public hearings, adequate notice of such hearings, and an opportunity for comment afforded to members of tribes, tribal governing bodies, and affected local school boards before the adoption of the policies, programs, and procedures described in subparagraph (A);

(D) includes an assurance that the Secretary of the Interior will provide such information as the Secretary of Education may require to comply with section 1418;

(E) includes an **assurance that the Secretary of the Interior and the Secretary of Health and Human Services have entered into a memorandum of agreement**, to be provided to the Secretary of Education, for the coordination of services, resources, and personnel between their respective Federal, State, and local offices and with State and local educational agencies and other entities to facilitate the provision of services to Indian children with disabilities residing on or near reservations (such agreement shall provide for the apportionment of responsibilities and costs including, but not limited to, child find, evaluation, diagnosis, remediation or therapeutic measures, and (where appropriate) equipment and medical or personal supplies as needed for a child to remain in school or a program); and

(F) includes an assurance that the Department of the Interior will cooperate with the Department of Education in its exercise of monitoring and oversight of this application, and any agreements entered into between the Secretary of the Interior and other entities under this part, and will fulfill its duties under this part. Section 1416(a) shall apply to the information described in this paragraph.

(3) Payments for Education and Services for Indian Children with Disabilities, Aged 3 Through 5 -

(A) In General - With funds appropriated under subsection (j), the Secretary of Education shall make payments to the Secretary of the Interior to be distributed to tribes or tribal organizations (as defined under section 4 of the Indian Self-Determination and Education Assistance Act) or consortia of the above to provide for the coordination of assistance for special education and related services for children with disabilities aged 3 through 5 on reservations served by elementary and secondary schools for Indian children operated or funded by the Department of the Interior. The amount of such payments under subparagraph (B) for any fiscal year shall be equal to 20 percent of the amount allotted under subsection (c).

(B) Distribution of Funds - The Secretary of the Interior shall distribute the total amount of the payment under subparagraph (A) by allocating to each tribe or tribal organization an amount based on the number of children with disabilities ages 3 through 5 residing on reservations as reported annually, divided by the total of those children served by all tribes or tribal organizations.

(C) Submission of Information - To receive a payment under this paragraph, the tribe or tribal organization shall submit such figures to the Secretary of the Interior as required to determine the amounts to be allocated under subparagraph (B). This information shall be compiled and submitted to the Secretary of Education.

(D) Use of Funds - The funds received by a tribe or tribal organization shall be used to assist in child find, screening, and other procedures for the early identification of children aged 3 through 5, parent training, and the provision of direct services. These activities may be carried out directly or through contracts or cooperative agreements with the BIA, local educational agencies, and other public or private nonprofit organizations. The tribe or tribal organization is encouraged to involve Indian parents in the development and implementation of these activities. The above entities shall, as appropriate, make referrals to local, State, or Federal entities for the provision of services or further diagnosis.

(E) Biennial Report - To be eligible to receive a grant pursuant to subparagraph (A), the tribe or tribal organization shall provide to the Secretary of the Interior a biennial report of activities undertaken under this paragraph, including the number of contracts and cooperative agreements entered into, the number of children contacted and receiving services for each year, and the estimated number of children needing services during the 2 years following the one in which the report is made. The Secretary of the Interior shall include a summary of this information on a biennial basis in the report to the Secretary of Education required under this subsection. The Secretary of Education may require any additional information from the Secretary of the Interior.

(F) Prohibitions - **None of the funds** allocated under this paragraph **may be used** by the Secretary of the Interior **for administrative purposes**, including child count and the provision of technical assistance.

(4) Plan for Coordination of Services - The Secretary of the Interior shall develop and implement a plan for the coordination of services for all Indian children with disabilities residing on reservations covered under this Act. Such plan shall provide for the coordination of services benefiting these children from whatever source, including tribes, the Indian Health Service, other BIA divisions, and other Federal agencies. In developing the plan, the Secretary of the Interior shall consult with all interested and involved parties. It shall be based on the needs of the children and the system best suited for meeting those needs, and may involve the establishment of cooperative agreements between the BIA, other Federal agencies, and other entities. The plan shall also be distributed upon request to States, State and local educational agencies, and other agencies providing services to infants, toddlers, and children with disabilities, to tribes, and to other interested parties.

(5) Establishment of Advisory Board - To meet the requirements of section 1412(a)(21), the Secretary of the Interior shall establish, not later than 6 months after the date of the enactment of the Individuals with Disabilities Education Act Amendments of 1997, under the BIA, an advisory board composed of individuals involved in or concerned with the education and provision of services to Indian infants, toddlers, children, and youth with disabilities, including Indians with disabilities, Indian parents or guardians of such children, teachers, service providers, State and local educational officials, representatives of tribes or tribal organizations, representatives from State Interagency Coordinating Councils under section 1441 in States having reservations, and other members representing the various divisions and entities of the BIA. The chairperson shall be selected by the Secretary of the Interior. The advisory board shall --

(A) assist in the coordination of services within the BIA and with other local, State, and Federal agencies in the provision of education for infants, toddlers, and children with disabilities;

(B) advise and assist the Secretary of the Interior in the performance of the Secretary's responsibilities described in this subsection;

(C) develop and recommend policies concerning effective - inter-and intra-agency collaboration, including modifications to regulations, and the elimination of barriers to - inter-and intra-agency programs and activities;

(D) provide assistance and disseminate information on best practices, effective program coordination strategies, and recommendations for improved educational programming for Indian infants, toddlers, and children with disabilities; and

(E) provide assistance in the preparation of information required under paragraph (2)(D).

(6) Annual Reports -

(A) In General - The advisory board established under paragraph (5) shall prepare and submit to the Secretary of the Interior and to the Congress an annual report containing a description of the activities of the advisory board for the preceding year.

(B) Availability - The Secretary of the Interior shall make available to the Secretary of Education the report described in subparagraph (A).

(j) AUTHORIZATION OF APPROPRIATIONS - For the purpose of carrying out this part, other than section 1419, there are authorized to be appropriated such sums as may be necessary.

20 U.S.C. §1412 - State Eligibility

➡ SECTION OVERVIEW

Secion 1412 provides an overview of the requirements of the statute. Skim through the headings before reading this section. Section 1412 includes Child Find, Least Restrictive Environment, services for children in private schools, unilateral private placements and tuition reimbursement, and the state's responsibility for educational programs for children with disabilities. Section 1412 mandates that expelled children are entitled to a free appropriate public education. This section requires children with disabilities to be included in State and district-wide assessments and requires states to establish advisory panels and that most members of these panel are individuals with disabilities or parents of children with disabilities.

(a) IN GENERAL - A State is eligible for assistance under this part for a fiscal year if the State demonstrates to the satisfaction of the Secretary that the State has in effect policies and procedures to ensure that it meets each of the following conditions:

(1) Free Appropriate Public Education -

(A) In General - A free appropriate public education is available to all children with disabilities residing in the State between the ages of 3 and 21, inclusive, including children with disabilities who have been suspended or expelled from school.

➡ EXPELLED CHILD HAS RIGHT TO FAPE

The law is clear. A child who receives services under IDEA is entitled to FAPE, even if the child has been suspended or expelled from school.

(B) Limitation - The obligation to make a free appropriate public education available to all children with disabilities does not apply with respect to children:

(i) **aged 3 through 5 and 18 through 21** in a State to the extent that its application to those children would be inconsistent with State law or practice, or the order of any court, respecting the provision of public education to children in those age ranges; and

(ii) **aged 18 through 21** to the extent that State law does not require that special education and related services under this part be provided to children with disabilities who, in the educational placement prior to their incarceration in an adult correctional facility:

(I) were not actually identified as being a child with a disability under section 1402(3) of this Act; or

(II) did not have an Individualized Education Program under this part.

(2) Full Educational Opportunity Goal - The State has established a goal of **providing full educational opportunity** to all children with disabilities **and a detailed timetable** for accomplishing that goal.

(3) Child Find -

(A) In General - **All** children with disabilities residing in the State, **including** children with disabilities attending private schools, regardless of the severity of their disabilities, and who are in need of special education and related services, **are identified, located, and evaluated** and a practical method is developed and implemented to determine which children with disabilities are currently receiving needed special education and related services.

➡ CHILD FIND FOR CHILDREN WHO ATTEND PRIVATE SCHOOLS

Under the re-authorized IDEA, Child Find requirements changed. Under the old law, all children with disabilities had to be "identified, located, and evaluated." The new law continues this requirement but adds that Child Find includes children who attend private schools. States must implement procedures to determine whether children who need special education services are actually receiving these services.

(B) Construction - **Nothing** in this Act **requires that children be classified by their disability** so long as each child who has a disability listed in section 1402 and who, by reason of that disability, needs special education and related services is regarded as a child with a disability under this part.

➡️ **CLASSIFICATION BY DISABILITY NOT REQUIRED**

It is not necessary to determine the exact nature of the child's disability before the child can receives special education services. Some school districts spend months evaluating the child before offering any special education services. During this time, the child is continuing to fall further behind. It is not necessary to classify the child's disability before providing an appropriate education.

(4) Individualized Education Program - An **individualized education program**, or an **individualized family service plan** that meets the requirements of section 1436(d), is developed, reviewed, and revised for each child with a disability in accordance with Section 1414(d).

(5) Least Restrictive Environment.

(A) In General - To the maximum extent appropriate, children with disabilities, including children in public or private institutions or other care facilities, are educated with children who are not disabled, and special classes, separate schooling, or other removal of children with disabilities from the regular educational environment occurs only when the nature or severity of the disability of a child is such that education in regular classes with the use of supplementary aids and services cannot be achieved satisfactorily.

➡️ **LEAST RESTRICTIVE v. MAINSTREAMING v. INCLUSION**

The definition of "least restrictive environment" is unchanged. "Mainstreaming" is written into the statute but "inclusion" is not. Judicial decisions that define "mainstreaming" and "least restrictive environment" (LRE) vary, even within the same state. Some school districts claim that the law requires them to mainstream all children with disabilities, even when children need individualized instruction that cannot be delivered in regular classrooms. In other districts, parents must fight to have their disabled child "included" in regular classes. The law attempts to takes a commonsense approach to the issue: children with disabilities should be mainstreamed "to the maximum extent appropriate." Children can be removed from regular classes if this is necessary for them to learn.

(B) Additional Requirement.

(i) In General - If the State uses a funding mechanism by which the State distributes State funds on the basis of the type of setting in which a child is served, the funding mechanism **does not** result in placements that violate the requirements of subparagraph (A).

(ii) Assurance - If the State does not have policies and procedures to ensure compliance with clause (i), the State shall provide the Secretary an assurance that it will revise the funding mechanism as soon as feasible to ensure that such mechanism does not result in such placements.

(6) Procedural Safeguards -

(A) In General - Children with disabilities and their parents are afforded the procedural safeguards required by section 1415.

(B) Additional Procedural Safeguards - Procedures to ensure that **testing and evaluation materials and procedures** utilized for the purposes of evaluation and placement of children with disabilities will be selected and administered so as **not to be racially or culturally discriminatory**. Such materials or procedures shall be provided and administered in the child's native language or mode of communication, unless it clearly is not feasible to do so, and **no single procedure shall be the sole criterion for determining an appropriate educational program** for a child.

➡️ **NON-DISCRIMINATORY TESTING MATERIALS**

The "additional procedural safeguards" about testing and evaluation materials are new. In "Findings" (Section 1400), Congress expressed concerns about mislabeling of minority children and over-representation of minority children in special education. The new requirement that "no single procedure shall be the sole criterion" attempts to correct this problem by requiring comprehensive evaluations of children.

Tests often measure the impact of the disability on the child's learning and performance. Assume that a child has auditory processing problems. The child is tested with standard intelligence and educational achievement tests. Portions of these tests are given orally. Will the child's scores on the oral tests provide accurate information about the child's abilities and acquired knowledge? Will the oral subtests measure the child's auditory processing problems? In this instance, the child's test scores may not provide an accurate picture of the child's abilities and knowledge but may actually measure the impact of the child's disability.

(7) Evaluation - Children with disabilities are evaluated in accordance with subsections (a) through (c) of section 1414.

(8) Confidentiality - Agencies in the State comply with section 1417(c) (relating to the confidentiality of records and information).

(9) Transition from Part C to Preschool Programs - Children participating in **early-intervention programs** assisted under Part C, and who will participate **in preschool programs** assisted under this part, **experience a smooth and effective transition to those preschool programs** in a manner consistent with section 1437(a)(8). **By the third birthday** of such a child, an individualized education program or, if consistent with sections 1414(d)(2)(B) and 1436(d), an individualized family service plan, has been developed and is being implemented for the child. The local educational agency will participate in transition planning conferences arranged by the designated lead agency under section 1437(a)(8).

(10) Children in Private Schools -
   (A) Children Enrolled in Private Schools by Their Parents -
   (i) In General - To the extent consistent with the number and location of children with disabilities in the State who are enrolled by their parents in private elementary and secondary schools, provision is made for the participation of those children in the program assisted or carried out under this part by providing for such children special education and related services in accordance with the following requirements, unless the Secretary has arranged for services to those children under subsection (f):
      (I) Amounts expended for the provision of those services by a local educational agency shall be equal to a proportionate amount of Federal funds made available under this part.
      (II) Such **services may be provided to children with disabilities on the premises of private, including parochial, schools**, to the extent consistent with law.
   (ii) Child-find Requirement - The requirements of paragraph (3) of this subsection (relating to child find) shall apply with respect to children with disabilities **in the State who are enrolled in private, including parochial,** elementary and secondary **schools**.

➡ **CHANGING CASELAW**
Caselaw about the need to provide special education in private schools is changing. Child Find clearly applies to children in private and parochial schools. Several courts have held that if the public school offers an appropriate program (FAPE), the school is not required to provide services to the child who is enrolled in a private program. [See Section (10)(C)(i) below] However, the amended IDEA also says that special education services **may** (not shall) be provided to children who attend private and parochial schools.

(B) Children Placed in, or Referred to, Private Schools by Public Agencies -
   (i) In General - Children with disabilities in private schools and facilities are provided special education and related services, in accordance with an individualized education program, at no cost to their parents, if such children are placed in, or referred to, such schools or facilities by the State or appropriate local educational agency as the means of carrying out the requirements of this part or any other applicable law requiring the provision of special education and related services to all children with disabilities within such State.
   (ii) Standards - In all cases described in clause (i), the State educational agency shall determine whether such schools and facilities meet standards that apply to State and local educational agencies and that **children so served have all the rights they would have if served by such agencies**.

(C) Payment for Education of Children Enrolled in Private Schools Without Consent of or Referral by the Public Agency.
➡ **WHEN COSTS AWARDED OR DENIED**
Parents who want to be reimbursed for educational expenses, including tuition and other educational expenses, must understand this section.

(i) In General - Subject to subparagraph (A), this part **does not** require a local educational agency to pay for special education and related services for a child with a disability at a private school or facility **if** that agency made a free appropriate public education available and the parents elected to place the child in such private school or facility.

(ii) Reimbursement for Private School Placement - If the parents of a child with a disability, who previously received special education and related services under the authority of a public agency, enroll the child in a private elementary or secondary school without the consent of or referral by the public agency, a court or a **hearing officer may require the agency to reimburse the parents** for the cost of that enrollment **if** the court or hearing officer finds that the agency **had not made a free appropriate public education available to the child in a timely manner prior to that enrollment**.

➡ **IF FAPE IS DENIED**

If parents remove the child from a public school program and place the child into a private program, they may be reimbursed for the costs of the private program **if** a hearing officer or court determines that the public school did not offer FAPE "in a timely manner."

(iii) Limitation on Reimbursement - The cost of reimbursement described in clause (ii) may be reduced or denied-

    (I) **if** --

        (aa) **at the most recent IEP meeting** that the parents attended prior to removal of the child from the public school, the parents did not inform the IEP team that they were rejecting the placement proposed by the public agency to provide a free appropriate public education to their child, including stating their concerns and their intent to enroll their child in a private school at public expense;

        or

        (bb) **10 business days** (including any holidays that occur on a business day) **prior to the removal of the child** from the public school, the parents did not give written notice to the public agency of the information described in division (aa);

    (II) if, prior to the parents' removal of the child from the public school, the public agency informed the parents, through the notice requirements described in section 1415(b)(7), of its **intent to evaluate the child** (including a statement of the purpose of the evaluation that was appropriate and reasonable), **but the parents did not make the child available for such evaluation**; or

    (III) upon a judicial finding of **unreasonableness** with respect to actions taken by the parents.

(iv) Exception - Notwithstanding the notice requirement in clause (iii)(I), the cost of reimbursement may not be reduced or denied for failure to provide such notice if

    (I) the parent is illiterate and cannot write in English;

    (II) compliance with clause (iii)(I) would likely result in physical or serious emotional harm to the child;

    (III) the school prevented the parent from providing such notice; or

    (IV) the parents had not received notice, pursuant to section 1415, of the notice requirement in clause (iii)(I).

➡ **SUMMARY**

School districts use this section to deny parental requests for reimbursement. Before taking steps to remove the child from a public school program, parents must understand this section. **To protect parental rights, parents must take several steps** -

1. At the **most recent IEP meeting**, before withdrawing the child from the public school program -

    A. You must state your concerns and

    B. You must state your intent to enroll your child in a private school at public expense;

or

2. **Ten business days** before withdrawing the child from the public school program, you must write a letter to the school in which

    A. You state your concerns and

    B. You state your intent to enroll your child in a private school at public expense.

TIP: Write this statement out before the meeting. During the meeting, make your statement orally and give a copy of the statement to the IEP team.

(11) State Educational Agency Responsible for General Supervision -

(A) In General - The State educational agency is responsible for ensuring that-

(i) the requirements of this part are met; and

(ii) all educational programs for children with disabilities in the State, including all such programs administered by any other State or local agency-

(I) are under the general supervision of individuals in the State who are responsible for educational programs for children with disabilities; and

(II) meet the educational standards of the State educational agency.

(B) Limitation - Subparagraph (A) **shall not limit the responsibility of agencies in the State** other than the State educational agency **to provide, or pay for some or all of the costs of, a free appropriate public education** for any child with a disability in the State.

(C) Exception - Notwithstanding subparagraphs (A) and (B), **the Governor** (or another individual pursuant to State law), consistent with State law, **may assign to any public agency in the State** the responsibility of ensuring that the requirements of this part are met with respect to children with disabilities who are convicted as adults under State law and incarcerated in adult prisons.

(12) Obligations Related to and Methods of Ensuring Services -

(A) Establishing Responsibility for Services - The Chief Executive Officer or designee of the officer shall ensure that an interagency agreement or other mechanism for interagency coordination is in effect between each public agency described in subparagraph (B) and the State educational agency, in order to ensure that all services described in subparagraph (B)(i) that are needed to ensure a free appropriate public education are provided, including the provision of such services during the pendency of any dispute under clause (iii). Such agreement or mechanism shall include the following:

(i) **Agency Financial Responsibility** - An identification of, or a method for defining, the financial responsibility of each agency for providing services described in subparagraph (B)(i) to ensure a free appropriate public education to children with disabilities, provided that the financial responsibility of each public agency described in subparagraph (B), including the State Medicaid agency and other public insurers of children with disabilities, shall precede the financial responsibility of the local educational agency (or the State agency responsible for developing the child's IEP).

(ii) **Conditions and Terms of Reimbursement** - The conditions, terms, and procedures under which a local educational agency shall be reimbursed by other agencies.

(iii) **Interagency Disputes** - Procedures for resolving interagency disputes (including procedures under which local educational agencies may initiate proceedings) under the agreement or other mechanism to secure reimbursement from other agencies or otherwise implement the provisions of the agreement or mechanism.

(iv) **Coordination of Services Procedures** - Policies and procedures for agencies to determine and identify the interagency coordination responsibilities of each agency to promote the coordination and timely and appropriate delivery of services described in subparagraph (B)(i).

(B) Obligation of Public Agency -

(i) **In General** - If any public agency other than an educational agency is otherwise obligated under Federal or State law, or assigned responsibility under State policy or pursuant to subparagraph (A), to provide or pay for any services that are also considered special education or related services (such as, but not limited to, services described in sections 1402(1) relating to assistive technology devices, 1402(2) relating to assistive technology services, 1402(22) relating to related services, 1402(29) relating to supplementary aids and services, and 1402(30) relating to transition services) that are necessary for ensuring a free appropriate public education to children with disabilities within the State, such public agency shall fulfill that obligation or responsibility, either directly or through contract or other arrangement.

➡ **WHEN OTHER PUBLIC AGENCIES ARE RESPONSIBLE FOR SERVICES**
When other public agencies are responsible for providing services, they must comply with this section. Because the statute focuses on the transition from school to work, state Departments of Vocational Rehabilitation may be responsible for services.

(ii) Reimbursement for Services by Public Agency - If a public agency other than an educational agency fails to provide or pay for the special education and related services described in clause (i), the local educational agency (or State agency responsible for developing the child's IEP) shall provide or pay for such services to the child. Such local educational agency or State agency may then claim reimbursement for the services from the public agency that failed to provide or pay for such services and such public agency shall reimburse the local educational agency or State agency pursuant to the terms of the interagency agreement or other mechanism described in subparagraph (A)(i) according to the procedures established in such agreement pursuant to subparagraph (A)(ii).

(C) Special Rule - The requirements of subparagraph (A) may be met through-

(i) State statute or regulation;

(ii) signed agreements between respective agency officials that clearly identify the responsibilities of each agency relating to the provision of services; or

(iii) other appropriate written methods as determined by the Chief Executive Officer of the State or designee of the officer.

(13) Procedural Requirements Relating to Local Educational Agency Eligibility - The State educational agency will not make a final determination that a local educational agency is not eligible for assistance under this part without first affording that agency reasonable notice and an opportunity for a hearing.

➡ **SEA SUPERVISION OF LEAs**
State educational agencies (SEAs) are responsible for ensuring that local educational agencies (LEAs) are eligible for assistance. Parents often complain that the state department of education does not supervise the local school district. State education staff often worked for local school districts before "moving up the ladder." Many SEA staff have friendships with former co-workers who continue to work for LEAs. These relationships may make it difficult for state employees to find local school districts out of compliance.

(14) Comprehensive System of Personnel Development - The State has in effect, consistent with the purposes of this Act and with section 1435(a)(8), a comprehensive system of personnel development that is designed to ensure an adequate supply of qualified special education, regular education, and related services personnel that meets the requirements for a State improvement plan relating to personnel development in subsections (b)(2)(B) and (c)(3)(D) of section 1453.

➡ **PERSONNEL DEVELOPMENT PROGRAMS**
The personnel development programs in many states are inadequate. Many LEAs and SEAs do not provide teachers with training in effective practices, proven methods of teaching and learning, or research-based educational techniques. Attorneys and advocates should read 20 U.S.C. §1453 about State Improvement Plans for Infants and Toddlers with Disabilities. State departments of education should hold LEAs accountable for the educational progress of children with disabilities and should address in-service and pre-service needs of school personnel.

(15) Personnel Standards -

(A) In General - The State educational agency has established and maintains standards to ensure that personnel necessary to carry out this part are appropriately and adequately prepared and trained.

(B) Standards Described - Such standards shall -

(i) be consistent with any State-approved or State-recognized certification, licensing, registration, or other comparable requirements that apply to the professional discipline in which those personnel are providing special education or related services;

(ii) to the extent the standards described in subparagraph (A) are not based on the highest requirements in the State applicable to a specific profession or discipline, the State is taking steps to require retraining or hiring of personnel that meet appropriate professional requirements in the State; and

(iii) allow paraprofessionals and assistants who are appropriately trained and supervised, in accordance with State law, regulations, or written policy, in meeting the requirements of this part to be used to assist in the provision of special education and related services to children with disabilities under this part.

(C) Policy - In implementing this paragraph, a State may adopt a policy that includes a requirement that local educational agencies in the State make an ongoing good-faith effort to recruit and hire appropriately and adequately trained personnel to provide special education and related services to children with disabilities, including, in a geographic area of the State where there is a shortage of such personnel, **the most qualified individuals available** who are making satisfactory progress toward completing applicable course work necessary to meet the standards described in subparagraph (B)(i), consistent with State law, and the steps described in subparagraph (B)(ii) within three years.

➡ **TRAINED STAFF**

There is a clear line of responsibility from state education agencies to local school districts. State education agencies can require local school districts to hire staff who are appropriately trained. Some states have strengthened their certification and licensing requirements for special education service providers. Other states have a generic certification that requires special educators to teach all children with disabilities.

(16) Performance Goals and Indicators - The State -

(A) has established goals for the performance of children with disabilities in the State that-

(i) will promote the purposes of this Act, as stated in section 1401(d); and

(ii) are consistent, to the maximum extent appropriate, with other goals and standards for children established by the State;

(B) has established performance indicators the State will use to assess progress toward achieving those goals that, at a minimum, address the performance of children with disabilities on assessments, drop-out rates, and graduation rates;

(C) will, every two years, report to the Secretary and the public on the progress of the State, and of children with disabilities in the State, toward meeting the goals established under subparagraph (A); and (D) based on its assessment of that progress, will revise its State improvement plan under subpart 1 of part D as may be needed to improve its performance, if the State receives assistance under that subpart.

(D) based on its assessment of that progress, will revise its State improvement plan under subpart 1 of part D as may be needed to improve its performance, if the State receives assistance under that subpart.

➡ **PERFORMANCE GOALS AND INDICATORS**

This section discusses the use of "performance indicators" to assess progress and, at a minimum, address performance in regard to the uniform statewide assessments, drop-out rates, and graduation rates. This section is also linked to grant approval criteria under Part D. See 20 U.S.C. § 1453(b)(1)

(17) Participation in Assessments -

(A) In General - Children with disabilities are included in general State and district-wide assessment programs, **with appropriate accommodations, where necessary**. As appropriate, the State or local educational agency-

(i) develops guidelines for the participation of children with disabilities in alternate assessments for those children who cannot participate in State and district-wide assessment programs; and

(ii) develops and, **beginning not later than July 1, 2000**, conducts those alternate assessments.

(B) Reports - The State educational agency makes available to the public, and reports to the public **with the same frequency and in the same detail** as it reports on the assessment of nondisabled children, the following:

(i) The number of children with disabilities participating in regular assessments.

(ii) The number of those children participating in alternate assessments.

(iii)

(I) The performance of those children on regular assessments (beginning not later than July 1, 1998) and on alternate assessments (not later than July 1, 2000), if doing so would be statistically sound and would not result in the disclosure of performance results identifiable to individual children.

(II) Data relating to the performance of children described under subclause (I) shall be disaggregated-

(aa) for assessments conducted after July 1, 1998; and

(bb) for assessments conducted before July 1, 1998, if the State is required to disaggregate such data prior to July 1, 1998.

➡ **ASSESSMENT MAY TRIGGER LITIGATION**

The requirements about assessing disabled children on state and district testing may lead parents to realize that the child is not benefiting from special education. Litigation may begin sooner when this part of the statute takes effect. The section may encourage schools to teach children with disabilities to read, write, spell, and solve arithmetic problems.

This emphasis on statewide assessments and drop-out rates relates to the purpose of special education which is to increase independence and self-sufficiency. Since the law was passed, federal and state governments have spent billions of dollars on programs that have not accomplished the goals of increasing independence and reducing dependency.

(18) Supplementation of State, Local, and Other Federal Funds -

(A) Expenditures - Funds paid to a State under this part will be expended in accordance with all the provisions of this part.

(B) Prohibition Against Commingling - Funds paid to a State under this part **will not be commingled** with State funds.

(C) Prohibition Against Supplantation and Conditions for Waiver by Secretary - Except as provided in section 1413, funds paid to a State under this part will be used to supplement the level of Federal, State, and local funds (including funds that are not under the direct control of State or local educational agencies) expended for special education and related services provided to children with disabilities under this part and in no case to supplant such Federal, State, and local funds, except that, where the State provides clear and convincing evidence that all children with disabilities have available to them a free appropriate public education, the Secretary may waive, in whole or in part, the requirements of this subparagraph if the Secretary concurs with the evidence provided by the State.

(19) Maintenance of State Financial Support -

(A) In General - The State does not reduce the amount of State financial support for special education and related services for children with disabilities, or otherwise made available because of the excess costs of educating those children, below the amount of that support for the preceding fiscal year.

(B) Reduction of Funds for Failure to Maintain Support - The Secretary shall reduce the allocation of funds under section 1411 for any fiscal year following the fiscal year in which the State fails to comply with the requirement of subparagraph (A) by the same amount by which the State fails to meet the requirement.

(C) Waivers for Exceptional or Uncontrollable Circumstances - The Secretary may waive the requirement of subparagraph (A) for a State, for one fiscal year at a time, if the Secretary determines that -

(i) granting a waiver would be equitable due to exceptional or uncontrollable circumstances such as a natural disaster or a precipitous and unforeseen decline in the financial resources of the State; or

(ii) the State meets the standard in paragraph (18)(C) of this section for a waiver of the requirement to supplement, and not to supplant, funds received under this part.

(D) Subsequent Years - If, for any year, a State fails to meet the requirement of subparagraph (A), including any year for which the State is granted a waiver under subparagraph (C), the financial support required of the State in future years under subparagraph (A) shall be the amount that would have been required in the absence of that failure and not the reduced level of the State's support.

(E) Regulations -

(i) The Secretary shall, by regulation, establish procedures (including objective criteria and consideration of the results of compliance reviews of the State conducted by the Secretary) for determining whether to grant a waiver under subparagraph (C)(ii).

(ii) The Secretary shall publish proposed regulations under clause (i) not later than 6 months after the date of the enactment of the Individuals with Disabilities Education Act Amendments of 1997, and shall issue final regulations under clause (i) not later than 1 year after such date of enactment.

(20) Public Participation - Prior to the adoption of any policies and procedures needed to comply with this section (including any amendments to such policies and procedures), the State ensures that there are public hearings, adequate notice of the hearings, and an opportunity for Comments available to the general public, including individuals with disabilities and parents of children with disabilities.

(21) State Advisory Panel -

(A) In General - The State has established and maintains an advisory panel for the purpose of providing policy guidance with respect to special education and related services for children with disabilities in the State.

(B) Membership - Such advisory panel shall consist of members appointed by the Governor, or any other official authorized under State law to make such appointments, that is representative of the State population and that is composed of individuals involved in, or concerned with, the education of children with disabilities, including-

(i) **parents of children with disabilities**;

(ii) **individuals with disabilities**;

(iii) **teachers**;

(iv) representatives of institutions of higher education that prepare special education and related services personnel;

(v) State and local education officials;

(vi) administrators of programs for children with disabilities;

(vii) representatives of other State agencies involved in the financing or delivery of related services to children with disabilities;

(viii) representatives of private schools and public charter schools;

(ix) at least one representative of a vocational, community, or business organization concerned with the provision of transition services to children with disabilities; and

(x) representatives from the State juvenile and adult corrections agencies.

(C) Special Rule - A majority of the members of the panel shall be individuals with disabilities or parents of children with disabilities.

➡ ADVISORY PANEL MEMBERS

Most advisory panel members shall be individuals with disabilities or parents of children with disabilities. Members shall include representatives from private and public charter schools, and from corrections agencies.

(D) Duties - The advisory panel shall -

(i) advise the State educational agency of unmet needs within the State in the education of children with disabilities;

(ii) Comments publicly on any rules or regulations proposed by the State regarding the education of children with disabilities;

(iii) advise the State educational agency in developing evaluations and reporting on data to the Secretary under section 1418;

(iv) advise the State educational agency in developing corrective action plans to address findings identified in Federal mnitoring reports under this part; and

(v) advise the State educational agency in developing and implementing policies relating to the coordination of services for children with disabilities.

(22) Suspension and Expulsion Rates -

(A) In General - The State educational agency examines data to determine if significant discrepancies are occurring in the rate of long-term suspensions and expulsions of children with disabilities-

(i) among local educational agencies in the State; or

(ii) compared to such rates for nondisabled children within such agencies.

(B) Review and Revision of Policies - If such discrepancies are occurring, the State educational agency reviews and, if appropriate, revises (or requires the affected State or local educational agency to revise) its policies, procedures, and practices relating to the development and implementation of IEPs, the use of behavioral interventions, and procedural safeguards, to ensure that such policies, procedures, and practices comply with this Act.

(b) State Educational Agency as Provider of Free Appropriate Public Education or Direct Services - If the State educational agency provides free appropriate public education to children with disabilities, or provides direct services to such children, such agency-

(1) shall comply with any additional requirements of section 1413(a), as if such agency were a local educational agency; and
(2) may use amounts that are otherwise available to such agency under this part to serve those children without regard to section 1413(a)(2)(A)(i) (relating to excess costs).

(c) Exception for Prior State Plans -

(1) In General - If a State has on file with the Secretary policies and procedures that demonstrate that such State meets any requirement of subsection (a), including any policies and procedures filed under this part as in effect before the effective date of the Individuals with Disabilities Education Act Amendments of 1997, the Secretary shall consider such State to have met such requirement for purposes of receiving a grant under this part.

(2) Modifications Made by State - Subject to paragraph (3), an application submitted by a State in accordance with this section shall remain in effect until the State submits to the Secretary such modifications as the State deems necessary. This section shall apply to a modification to an application to the same extent and in the same manner as this section applies to the original plan.

(3) Modifications Required by the Secretary - If, after the effective date of the Individuals with Disabilities Education Act Amendments of 1997, the provisions of this Act are amended (or the regulations developed to carry out this Act are amended), or there is a new interpretation of this Act by a Federal court or a State's highest court, or there is an official finding of noncompliance with Federal law or regulations, the Secretary may require a State to modify its application only to the extent necessary to ensure the State's compliance with this part.

(d) Approval by the Secretary.

(1) In General - If the Secretary determines that a State is eligible to receive a grant under this part, the Secretary shall notify the State of that determination.

(2) Notice and Hearing - The Secretary shall not make a final determination that a State is not eligible to receive a grant under this part until after providing the State -
(A) with reasonable notice; and
(B) with an opportunity for a hearing.

(e) Assistance Under Other Federal Programs - Nothing in this title permits a State to reduce medical and other assistance available, or to alter eligibility, under titles V and XIX of the Social Security Act with respect to the provision of a free appropriate public education for children with disabilities in the State.

(f) By-Pass for Children in Private Schools -

(1) In General - If, on the date of enactment of the Education of the Handicapped Act Amendments of 1983, a State educational agency is prohibited by law from providing for the participation in special programs of children with disabilities enrolled in private elementary and secondary schools as required by subsection (a)(10)(A), the Secretary shall, notwithstanding such provision of law, arrange for the provision of services to such children through arrangements which shall be subject to the requirements of such subsection.

(2) Payments -

(A) Determination of Amounts - If the Secretary arranges for services pursuant to this subsection, the Secretary, after consultation with the appropriate public and private school officials, shall pay to the provider of such services for a fiscal year an amount per child that does not exceed the amount determined by dividing -

(i) the total amount received by the State under this part for such fiscal year; by

(ii) the number of children with disabilities served in the prior year, as reported to the Secretary by the State under section 1418.

(B) Withholding of Certain Amounts - Pending final resolution of any investigation or complaint that could result in a determination under this subsection, the Secretary may withhold from the allocation of the affected State educational agency the amount the Secretary estimates would be necessary to pay the cost of services described in subparagraph (A).

(C) Period of Payments - The period under which payments are made under subparagraph (A) shall continue until the Secretary determines that there will no longer be any failure or inability on the part of the State educational agency to meet the requirements of subsection (a)(10)(A).

(3) Notice and Hearing -

(A) In General - The Secretary shall not take any final action under this subsection until the State educational agency affected by such action has had an opportunity, for at least 45 days after receiving written notice thereof, to submit written objections and to appear before the Secretary or the Secretary's designee to show cause why such action should not be taken.

(B) Review of Action - If a State educational agency is dissatisfied with the Secretary's final action after a proceeding under subparagraph (A), such agency may, not later than 60 days after notice of such action, file with the United States court of appeals for the circuit in which such State is located a petition for review of that action. A copy of the petition shall be forthwith transmitted by the clerk of the court to the Secretary. The Secretary thereupon shall file in the court the record of the proceedings on which the Secretary based the Secretary's action, as provided in section 2112 of title 28, United States Code.

(C) Review of Findings of Fact - The findings of fact by the Secretary, if supported by substantial evidence, shall be conclusive, but the court, for good cause shown, may remand the case to the Secretary to take further evidence, and the Secretary may thereupon make new or modified findings of fact and may modify the Secretary's previous action, and shall file in the court the record of the further proceedings. Such new or modified findings of fact shall likewise be conclusive if supported by substantial evidence.

(D) Jurisdiction of Court of Appeals, Review by United States Supreme Court - Upon the filing of a petition under subparagraph (B), the United States court of appeals shall have jurisdiction to affirm the action of the Secretary or to set it aside, in whole or in part. The judgment of the court shall be subject to review by the Supreme Court of the United States upon certiorari or certification as provided in section 1254 of title 28, United States Code.

20 U.S.C. §1413 - Local Educational Agency Eligibility

➡ **SECTION OVERVIEW**

This section includes information about personnel development, eligibility requirements, school-based improvement plans, and the provision of services by SEAs.

(a) IN GENERAL - A local educational agency is eligible for assistance under this part for a fiscal year if such agency demonstrates to the satisfaction of the State educational agency that it meets each of the following conditions:

(1) Consistency with State Policies - The local educational agency, in providing for the education of children with disabilities within its jurisdiction, has in effect policies, procedures, and programs that are consistent with the State policies and procedures established under section 1412.

(2) Use of Amounts -

(A) In General - Amounts provided to the local educational agency under this part shall be expended in accordance with the applicable provisions of this part and -

(i) shall be used only to pay the excess costs of providing special education and related services to children with disabilities;

(ii) shall be used to supplement State, local, and other Federal funds and not to supplant such funds; and

(iii) shall not be used, except as provided in subparagraphs (B) and (C), to reduce the level of expenditures for the education of children with disabilities made by the local educational agency from local funds below the level of those expenditures for the preceding fiscal year.

(B) Exception - Notwithstanding the restriction in subparagraph (A)(iii), a local educational agency may reduce the level of expenditures where such reduction is attributable to -

(i) the voluntary departure, by retirement or otherwise, or departure for just cause, of special education personnel;

(ii) a decrease in the enrollment of children with disabilities;

(iii) the termination of the obligation of the agency, consistent with this part, to provide a program of special education to a particular child with a disability that is an exceptionally costly program, as determined by the State educational agency, because the child -

(I) has left the jurisdiction of the agency;

(II) has reached the age at which the obligation of the agency to provide a free appropriate public education to the child has terminated; or

(III) no longer needs such program of special education; or

(iv) the termination of costly expenditures for long-term purchases, such as the acquisition of equipment or the construction of school facilities.

(C) Treatment of Federal Funds in Certain Fiscal Years -

(i) Notwithstanding clauses (ii) and (iii) of subparagraph (A), for any fiscal year for which amounts appropriated to carry out section 1411 exceeds $4,100,000,000, a local educational agency may treat as local funds, for the purpose of such clauses, up to 20 percent of the amount of funds it receives under this part that exceeds the amount it received under this part for the previous fiscal year.

(ii) Notwithstanding clause (i), if a State educational agency determines that a local educational agency is not meeting the requirements of this part, the State educational agency may prohibit the local educational agency from treating funds received under this part as local funds under clause (i) for any fiscal year, only if it is authorized to do so by the State constitution or a State statute.

(D) Schoolwide Programs Under Title I of the ESEA - Notwithstanding subparagraph (A) or any other provision of this part, a local educational agency may use funds received under this part for any fiscal year to carry out a schoolwide program under section 1114 of the Elementary and Secondary Education Act of 1965, except that the amount so used in any such program shall not exceed -

(i) the number of children with disabilities participating in the schoolwide program; multiplied by

(ii) (I) the amount received by the local educational agency under this part for that fiscal year; divided by

(II) the number of children with disabilities in the jurisdiction of that agency.

(3) Personnel Development - The local educational agency -

(A) shall ensure that **all personnel necessary to carry out this part are appropriately and adequately prepared**, consistent with the requirements of section 1453(c)(3)(D); and

(B) to the extent such agency determines appropriate, shall contribute to and use the comprehensive system of personnel development of the State established under section 1412(a)(14).

(4) Permissive Use of Funds - Notwithstanding paragraph (2)(A) or section 1412(a)(18)(B) (relating to commingled funds), funds provided to the local educational agency under this part may be used for the following activities:

(A) Services and Aids that Also Benefit Nondisabled Children - For the costs of special education and related services and supplementary aids and services provided in a regular class or other education-related setting to a child with a disability in accordance with the individualized education program of the child, **even if one or more nondisabled children benefit** from such services.

(B) Integrated and Coordinated Services System - To develop and implement a fully integrated and coordinated services system in accordance with subsection (f).

(5) Treatment of Charter Schools and Their Students - In carrying out this part with respect to charter schools that are public schools of the local educational agency, the local educational agency -

(A) serves children with disabilities attending those schools in the same manner as it serves children with disabilities in its other schools; and

(B) **provides funds** under this part to those schools **in the same manner** as it provides those funds to its other schools.

(6) Information for State Educational Agency - The local educational agency shall provide the State educational agency with information necessary to enable the State educational agency to carry out its duties under this part, including, with respect to paragraphs (16) and (17) of section 1412(a), information relating to the performance of children with disabilities participating in programs carried out under this part.

(7) Public Information - The local educational agency shall make available to parents of children with disabilities and to the general public all documents relating to the eligibility of such agency under this part.

(b) EXCEPTION FOR PRIOR LOCAL PLANS -

(1) In General - If a local educational agency or State agency has on file with the State educational agency policies and procedures that demonstrate that such local educational agency, or such State agency, as the case may be, meets any requirement of subsection (a), including any policies and procedures filed 45 under this part as in effect before the effective date of the Individuals with Disabilities Education Act Amendments of 1997, the State educational agency shall consider such local educational agency or State agency, as the case may be, to have met such requirement for purposes of receiving assistance under this part.

(2) Modification Made by Local Educational Agency - Subject to paragraph (3), an application submitted by a local educational agency in accordance with this section shall remain in effect until it submits to the State educational agency such modifications as the local educational agency deems necessary.

(3) Modifications Required by State Educational Agency - If, after the effective date of the Individuals with Disabilities Education Act Amendments of 1997, the provisions of this Act are amended (or the regulations developed to carry out this Act are amended), or there is a new interpretation of this Act by Federal or State courts, or there is an official finding of noncompliance with Federal or State law or regulations, the State educational agency may require a local educational agency to modify its application only to the extent necessary to ensure the local educational agency's compliance with this part or State law.

(c) NOTIFICATION OF LOCAL EDUCATIONAL AGENCY OR STATE AGENCY IN CASE OF INELIGIBILITY - If the State educational agency determines that a local educational agency or State agency is not eligible under this section, the State educational agency shall notify the local educational agency or State agency, as the case may be, of that determination and shall provide such local educational agency or State agency with reasonable notice and an opportunity for a hearing.

(d) LOCAL EDUCATIONAL AGENCY COMPLIANCE -

(1) In General - If the State educational agency, after reasonable notice and an opportunity for a hearing, finds that a local educational agency or State agency that has been determined to be eligible under this section is failing to comply with any requirement described in subsection (a), the State educational agency shall reduce or shall not provide any further payments to the local educational agency or State agency until the State educational agency is satisfied that the local educational agency or State agency, as the case may be, is complying with that requirement.

(2) Additional Requirement - Any State agency or local educational agency in receipt of a notice described in paragraph (1) shall, by means of public notice, take such measures as may be necessary to bring the pendency of an action pursuant to this subsection to the attention of the public within the jurisdiction of such agency.

(3) Consideration - In carrying out its responsibilities under paragraph (1), the State educational agency shall consider **any decision made in a hearing held under section 1415 that is adverse to the local educational agency** or State agency involved in that decision.

(e) JOINT ESTABLISHMENT OF ELIGIBILITY -

(1) Joint Establishment -
    (A) In General - A State educational agency may require a local educational agency to establish its eligibility jointly with another local educational agency if the State educational agency determines that the local educational agency would be ineligible under this section because the local educational agency would not be able to establish and maintain programs of sufficient size and scope to effectively meet the needs of children with disabilities.
    (B) Charter School Exception - A State educational agency may not require a charter school that is a local educational agency to jointly establish its eligibility under subparagraph (A) unless it is explicitly permitted to do so under the State's charter school statute.

(2) Amount of Payments - If a State educational agency requires the joint establishment of eligibility under paragraph (1), the total amount of funds made available to the affected local educational agencies shall be equal to the sum of the payments that each such local educational agency would have received under section 1411(g) if such agencies were eligible for such payments.

(3) Requirements - Local educational agencies that establish joint eligibility under this subsection shall -
    (A) adopt policies and procedures that are consistent with the State's policies and procedures under section 1412(a); and
    (B) be jointly responsible for implementing programs that receive assistance under this part.

(4) Requirements for Educational Service Agencies -
    (A) In General - If an educational service agency is required by State law to carry out programs under this part, the joint responsibilities given to local educational agencies under this subsection shall -
        (i) not apply to the administration and disbursement of any payments received by that educational service agency; and
        (ii) be carried out only by that educational service agency.
    (B) Additional Requirement - Notwithstanding any other provision of this subsection, an educational service agency shall provide for the education of children with disabilities in the least restrictive environment, as required by section 1412(a)(5).

(f) COORDINATED SERVICES SYSTEM -

(1) In General - A local educational agency may not use more than 5 percent of the amount such agency receives under this part for any fiscal year, in combination with other amounts (which shall include amounts other than education funds), to develop and implement a coordinated services system designed to improve results for children and families, including children with disabilities and their families.

(2) Activities - In implementing a coordinated services system under this subsection, a local educational agency may carry out activities that include -
    (A) improving the effectiveness and efficiency of service delivery, including developing strategies that promote accountability for results;
    (B) service coordination and case management that facilitates the linkage of individualized education programs under this part and individualized family service plans under part C with individualized service plans under multiple Federal and State programs, such as title I of the Rehabilitation Act of 1973 (vocational rehabilitation), title XIX of the Social Security Act (Medicaid), and title XVI of the Social Security Act (supplemental security income);

(C) developing and implementing interagency financing strategies for the provision of education, health, mental health, and social services, including transition services and related services under this Act; and

(D) inter-agency personnel development for individuals working on coordinated services.

(3) Coordination with Certain Projects Under Elementary and Secondary Education Act of 1965 - If a local educational agency is carrying out a coordinated services project under title XI of the Elementary and Secondary Education Act of 1965 and a coordinated services project under this part in the same schools, such agency shall use amounts under this subsection in accordance with the requirements of that title.

(g) SCHOOL BASED IMPROVEMENT PLAN -

(1) In General - Each local educational agency may, in accordance with paragraph (2), use funds made available under this part to permit a public school within the jurisdiction of the local educational agency to design, implement, and evaluate a school-based improvement plan that is consistent with the purposes described in section 1451(b) and that is designed to improve educational and transitional results for all children with disabilities and, as appropriate, for other children consistent with subparagraphs (A) and (B) of subsection (a)(4) in that public school.

(2) Authority -
(A) In General - A State educational agency may grant authority to a local educational agency to permit a public school described in paragraph (1) (through a school-based standing panel established under paragraph (4)(B)) to design, implement, and evaluate a school-based improvement plan described in paragraph (1) for a period not to exceed 3 years.
(B) Responsibility of Local Educational Agency - If a State educational agency grants the authority described in subparagraph (A), a local educational agency that is granted such authority shall have the sole responsibility of oversight of all activities relating to the design, implementation, and evaluation of any school-based improvement plan that a public school is permitted to design under this subsection.

(3) Plan Requirements - A school-based improvement plan described in paragraph (1) shall -
(A) be designed to be consistent with the purposes described in section 1451(b) and to improve educational and transitional results for all children with disabilities and, as appropriate, for other children consistent with subparagraphs (A) and (B) of subsection (a)(4), who attend the school for which the plan is designed and implemented;
(B) be designed, evaluated, and, as appropriate, implemented by a school-based standing panel established in accordance with paragraph (4)(B);
(C) include **goals and measurable indicators to assess the progress** of the public school in meeting such goals; and
(D) ensure that all children with disabilities receive the services described in the individualized education programs of such children.

(4) Responsibilities of the Local Educational Agency - A local educational agency that is granted authority under paragraph (2) to permit a public school to design, implement, and evaluate a school-based improvement plan shall -
(A) select each school under the jurisdiction of such agency that is eligible to design, implement, and evaluate such a plan;
(B) require each school selected under subparagraph (A), in accordance with criteria established by such local educational agency under subparagraph (C), to establish a school-based standing panel to carry out the duties described in paragraph (3)(B);
(C) establish -
(i) criteria that shall be used by such local educational agency in the selection of an eligible school under subparagraph (A);
(ii) criteria that shall be used by a public school selected under subparagraph (A) in the establishment of a school-based standing panel to carry out the duties described in paragraph (3)(B) and that shall ensure that the membership of such panel reflects the diversity of the community in which the public school is located and includes, at a mini-

mum

(I) parents of children with disabilities who attend such public school, including parents of children with disabilities from unserved and underserved populations, as appropriate;

(II) special education and general education teachers of such public school;

(III) special education and general education administrators, or the designee of such administrators, of such public school; and

(IV) related services providers who are responsible for providing services to the children with disabilities who attend such public school; and

(iii) criteria that shall be used by such local educational agency with respect to the distribution of funds under this part to carry out this subsection;

(D) disseminate the criteria established under subparagraph (C) to local school district personnel and local parent organizations within the jurisdiction of such local educational agency;

(E) require a public school that desires to design, implement, and evaluate a school-based improvement plan to submit an application at such time, in such manner, and accompanied by such information as such local educational agency shall reasonably require; and

(F) establish procedures for approval by such local educational agency of a school-based improvement plan designed under this subsection.

(5) Limitation - A school-based improvement plan described in paragraph (1) may be submitted to a local educational agency for approval only if a consensus with respect to any matter relating to the design, implementation, or evaluation of the goals of such plan is reached by the school-based standing panel that designed such plan.

(6) Additional Requirements -

(A) Parental Involvement - In carrying out the requirements of this subsection, a local educational agency shall ensure that the parents of children with disabilities are involved in the design, evaluation, and, where appropriate, implementation of school-based improvement plans in accordance with this subsection.

(B) Plan Approval - A local educational agency may approve a school-based improvement plan of a public school within the jurisdiction of such agency for a period of 3 years, if -

(i) the approval is consistent with the policies, procedures, and practices established by such local educational agency and in accordance with this subsection; and

(ii) a majority of parents of children who are members of the school-based standing panel, and a majority of other members of the school-based standing panel, that designed such plan agree in writing to such plan.

(7) Extension of Plan - If a public school within the jurisdiction of a local educational agency meets the applicable requirements and criteria described in paragraphs (3) and (4) at the expiration of the 3-year approval period described in paragraph (6)(B), such agency may approve a school-based improvement plan of such school for an additional 3-year period.

(h) DIRECT SERVICES BY THE STATE EDUCATIONAL AGENCY -

(1) In General - A State educational agency shall use the payments that would otherwise have been available to a local educational agency or to a State agency to provide special education and related services directly to children with disabilities residing in the area served by that local agency, or for whom that State agency is responsible, if the State educational agency determines that the local education agency or State agency, as the case may be -

(A) has not provided the information needed to establish the eligibility of such agency under this section;

(B) **is unable to establish and maintain programs of free appropriate public education** that meet the requirements of subsection (a);

(C) is unable or unwilling to be consolidated with one or more local educational agencies in order to establish and maintain such programs; or

(D) has one or more children with disabilities **who can best be served by a regional or State program or service-delivery system** designed to meet the needs of such children.

(2) Manner and Location of Education and Services - The State educational agency may provide special education and related services under paragraph (1) in such manner and at such locations (including regional or State centers) as the State agency considers appropriate. Such education and services shall be provided in accordance with this part.

(i) STATE AGENCY ELIGIBILITY - Any State agency that desires to receive a subgrant for any fiscal year under section 1411(g) shall demonstrate to the satisfaction of the State educational agency that -

(1) all children with disabilities who are participating in programs and projects funded under this part receive a free appropriate public education, and that those children and their parents are provided all the rights and procedural safeguards described in this part; and

(2) the agency meets such other conditions of this section as the Secretary determines to be appropriate.

(j) DISCIPLINARY INFORMATION -

The State may require that a local educational agency include in the records of a child with a disability a statement of any current or previous disciplinary action that has been taken against the child and transmit such statement to the same extent that such disciplinary information is included in, and transmitted with, the student records of nondisabled children. The statement may include a description of any behavior engaged in by the child that required disciplinary action, a description of the disciplinary action taken, and any other information that is relevant to the safety of the child and other individuals involved with the child. If the State adopts such a policy, and the child transfers from one school to another, the transmission of any of the child's records must include both the child's current individualized education program and any such statement of current or previous disciplinary action that has been taken against the child.

20 U. S. C. §1414 - Evaluations, Eligibility, IEPs, and Placements
➡ **SECTION OVERVIEW**
     This section includes evaluations, reevaluations, eligibility, IEPs and IEP teams and placements.

(a) EVALUATIONS AND REEVALUATIONS

(1) Initial Evaluations.
  (A) In General. A State educational agency, other State agency, or local educational agency shall conduct a full and in-dividual initial evaluation, in accordance with this paragraph and subsection (b), before the initial provision of special education and related services to a child with a disability under this part.
  (B) Procedures. Such initial evaluation shall consist of procedures-
    (i) to determine whether a child is a child with a disability (as defined in section 1402(3)); and
    (ii) to determine the educational needs of such child.
  (C) Parental Consent.
    (i) In General. The agency proposing to conduct an **initial evaluation** to determine if the child qualifies as a child with a disability as defined in section 1402(3)(A) or 1402(3)(B) **shall obtain an informed consent** from the parent of such child **before the evaluation** is conducted. **Parental consent for evaluation shall not be construed as consent for placement** for receipt of special education and related services.
    (ii) Refusal. If the parents of such child **refuse consent** for the evaluation, the agency may continue to pursue an evaluation by utilizing the mediation and due process procedures under section 1415, except to the extent inconsistent with State law relating to parental consent.

(2) Reevaluations. A local educational agency **shall ensure that a reevaluation** of each child with a disability is conducted-
  (A) if conditions warrant a reevaluation or **if the child's parent or teacher requests a reevaluation**, but **at least once every 3 years**; and
  (B) in accordance with subsections (b) and (c).

(b) EVALUATION PROCEDURES.

(1) Notice. The local educational agency **shall provide notice to the parents** of a child with a disability, in accordance with subsections (b)(3), (b)(4), and (c) of section 1415, that **describes any evaluation procedures** such agency proposes to conduct.

(2) Conduct of evaluation. In conducting the evaluation, the local educational agency **shall—**
  (A) use a variety of assessment tools and strategies to gather **relevant functional and developmental information, including information provided by the parent**, that may assist in determining whether the child is a child with a disability and the content of the child's individualized education program, including information related to enabling the **child to be involved in and progress in the general curriculum** or, for preschool children, to participate in appropriate activities;
  (B) not use any single procedure as the sole criterion for determining whether a child is a child with a disability **or** determining an appropriate educational program for the child; **and**
  (C) use technically sound instruments that may assess the relative contribution of cognitive and behavioral factors, in addition to physical or developmental factors.

(3) Additional requirements. Each local educational agency **shall ensure that-**
  (A) tests and other evaluation materials used to assess a child under this section-
    (i) are selected and administered so as not to be discriminatory on a racial or cultural basis; and
    (ii) are provided and **administered in the child's native language** or other mode of communication, unless it is clearly not feasible to do so; and

(B) any standardized tests that are given to the child -
   (i) have been **validated** for the specific purpose for which they are used;
   (ii) are administered by **trained and knowledgeable personnel**; and
   (iii) are administered in accordance **with any instructions** provided by the producer of such tests;
(C) the child is assessed in all areas of suspected disability; and
(D) assessment tools and strategies that provide **relevant information** that directly assists persons in determining the educational needs of the child are provided.

(4) Determination of eligibility. Upon completion of administration of tests and other evaluation materials-
   (A) the determination of whether the child is a child with a disability as defined in section 1402(3) shall be made by a **team of qualified professionals and the parent** of the child in accordance with paragraph (5); and
   (B) a copy of the evaluation report and the documentation of determination of eligibility **will be given to the parent**.

➡ **THE CHILD'S PARENT IS A MEMBER OF THE ELIGIBILITY TEAM**
   Decisions about eligibility must be made by a team that includes the child's parent. Previously, parents were often excluded from eligibility meetings. In changing the law, Congress made parents members of all decision-making teams. Parents are entitled to evaluation reports and documentation about how eligibility decisions are made.

(5) Special rule for eligibility determination. In making a determination of eligibility under paragraph (4)(A), a child shall not be determined to be a child with a disability if the determinant factor for such determination is lack of instruction in reading or math or limited English proficiency.

(c) ADDITIONAL REQUIREMENTS FOR EVALUATION AND REEVALUATIONS.

(1) Review of existing evaluation data. As part of an **initial evaluation** (if appropriate) and as part of **any reevaluation** under this section, the IEP Team described in subsection (d)(1)(B) and other qualified professionals, as appropriate, shall-
   (A) review existing evaluation data on the child, **including evaluations and information provided by the parents of the child**, current classroom-based assessments and observations, and teacher and related services providers observation; and

➡ **SCHOOL MUST CONSIDER INFORMATION FROM PRIVATE EVALUATIONS**
   The school must consider information from private sector evaluations provided by the parents.

(B) on the basis of that review, **and input from the child's parents**, identify what additional data, if any, are needed **to determine**-
   (i) whether the child has a particular category of disability, as described in section 1402(3), or, in case of a reevaluation of a child, whether the child continues to have such a disability;
   (ii) the **present levels of performance** and educational needs of the child;

➡ **PRESENT LEVELS OF PERFORMANCE**
   The term "present levels of performance" refers to the child's skills now, in the **present**. IEP teams often use outdated information from educational achievement tests to make decisions about services. When IEP teams use old test data, IEP decisions are often inappropriate.

   (iii) whether the child needs special education and related services, or in the case of a reevaluation of a child, whether the child continues to need special education and related services; and
   (iv) whether any **additions or modifications** to the special education and related services are needed to enable the child to meet **the measurable annual goals** set out in the individualized education program of the child and to participate, as appropriate, in the general curriculum.

➡ **PROGRESS TOWARD IEP GOALS SHOULD BE MEASURED WITH OBJECTIVE TESTS**

The child's progress toward IEP goals should be measured with objective tests, not by "teacher observations" and "teacher made tests." The teacher's subjective beliefs about the child's progress are not objective information.

Assume that your child's IEP includes a goal about keyboarding. Should the child's progress be measured by "teacher observation" at an "80%" success rate"? Should the child's progress be measured on timed tests in the number of words typed per minute, minus number of errors?

Assume that your child's IEP includes a goal of improving reading skills. Should your child"s progress be measured using teacher observations, with success defined as "80%"? Should your child's decoding skills improve from the 5.0 to the 6.0 grade level, as measured by the Woodcock Reading Mastery Test?

(2) Source of data. The local educational agency shall administer such tests and other evaluation materials as may be needed to produce the data identified by the IEP Team under paragraph (1)(B).

(3) Parental consent. Each local educational agency **shall** obtain **informed parental consent,** in accordance with subsection (a)(1)(C), **prior to conducting any reevaluation** of a child with a disability, except that such informed parent consent need not be obtained if the local educational agency can demonstrate that it had taken reasonable measures to obtain such consent and the child's parent has failed to respond.

(4) Requirements if additional data are not needed. If the IEP Team and other qualified professionals, as appropriate, determine that no additional data are needed to **determine whether the child continues** to be a child with a disability, the local educational agency-

(A) shall notify the child's parents of -

(i) that determination and **the reasons for it**; and

(ii) the **right** of such parents to **request an assessment** to determine whether the child continues to be a child with a disability; and

(B) shall not be required to conduct such an assessment unless requested to by the child's parents.

(5) Evaluations before change in eligibility. A local educational agency **shall** evaluate a child with a disability in accordance with this section **before** determining that the child is no longer a child with a disability.

(d) INDIVIDUALIZED EDUCATION PROGRAMS.

(1) Definitions. As used in this title:

(A) Individualized education program. The term 'individualized education program' or 'IEP' means a written statement for each child with a disability that is **developed, reviewed, and revised** in accordance with this section and that includes-

(i) a statement of the child's present levels of educational performance, including-

(I) how the child's disability affects the **child's involvement and progress in the general curriculum**; or

(II) for preschool children, as appropriate, how the disability affects the child's participation in appropriate activities;

(ii) a statement of measurable annual goals, including **benchmarks or short-term objectives**, related to -

(I) meeting the child's needs that result from the child's disability to enable the child to be involved in and progress in the general curriculum; and

(II) meeting each of the child's other educational needs that result from the child's disability;

(iii) a statement of the special education and related services and supplementary aids and services to be provided to the child, or on behalf of the child, and a statement of **the program modifications or supports for school personnel** that will be provided for the child-

(I) to advance appropriately toward attaining the annual goals;

(II) to be involved and progress in the general curriculum in accordance with clause (i) and to participate in extracurricular and other nonacademic activities; and

(III) to be educated and participate with other children with disabilities and nondisabled children in the activities described in this paragraph;

➡ PROGRAM MODIFICATIONS FOR STAFF
Program modifications and supports for school personnel can be written into the child's IEP.

(iv) an explanation of the extent, if any, to which the child will not participate with nondisabled children in the regular class and in the activities described in clause (iii);

➡ EXCLUSION
The IEP must explain the extent to which the child will be excluded from regular classes.

(v) (I) a statement of **any individual modifications** in the administration of **State or districtwide assessments of student achievement** that are needed in order for the child to participate in such assessment; and
  (II) if the IEP Team determines that the child will not participate in a particular State or districtwide assessment of student achievement (or part of such an assessment), a statement of
    (aa) why that assessment is not appropriate for the child; and
    (bb) how the child will be assessed;
(vi) the projected date for the beginning of the services and modifications described in clause (iii), and the anticipated **frequency, location, and duration** of those services and modifications;
(vii)
  (I) beginning **at age 14**, and updated annually, a **statement of the transition service needs** of the child under the applicable components of the child's IEP that focuses on the child's courses of study (such as participation in advanced-placement courses or a vocational education program);
  (II) beginning **at age 16** (or younger, if determined appropriate by the IEP Team), a statement of **needed transition services** for the child, including, when appropriate, a statement of the **interagency responsibilities** or any needed linkages; and
  (III) beginning **at least one year before the child reaches the age of majority** under State law, a statement that **the child has been informed of his or her rights** under this title, if any, that will transfer to the child on reaching the age of majority under section 1415(m); and
(viii) a statement of -
  (I) **how the child's progress toward the annual goals described in clause (ii) will be measured;** and
  (II) **how the child's parents will be regularly informed** (by such means as periodic report cards), at least as often as parents are informed of their nondisabled children's progress, of-
    (aa) their **child's progress toward the annual goals** described in clause (ii); and
    (bb) the extent to which that **progress is sufficient** to enable the child to achieve the goals by the end of the year.

➡ IEP OVERVIEW
IEP goals and objectives must be individualized to address the child's unique needs. IEP goals and objectives provide a way for parents and teachers to measure the child's progress. Educational progress can and should be measured objectively.

➡ IEP GOALS AND OBJECTIVES
IEP goals and objectives should be measureable and should enable the child to participate in the general curriculum. IEP goals and objectives should be linked to the child's present levels of performance, as measured by objective tests.

IEPs often provide modifications and accommodations instead of teaching skills. The child may receive books on tape but is not learning how to read, write, spell, or do math. As a parent, you should insist that your child receive the remediation, direct instruction, or one-to-one tutoring necessary to learn and master the basic skills. When children don't learn, they become anxious, depressed, angry, frustrated, and demoralized. Later, these children may be labeled with "emotional problems" when the child is actually reacting normally to chronic stress, frustration and failure.

➡ **CHILD'S INVOLVEMENT AND PROGRESS IN GENERAL CURRICULUM**
One goal of special education is that the child will "be involved in and progress in the general curriculum." What will happen to a child who is placed in the general curriculum, but doesn't know how to read, write, spell, or do arithmetic? This child will not be able to "participate in the general curriculum." It is unlikely that the child will receive individualized instruction or remediation in the regular classroom.

➡ **ACCOUNTABILITY AND MEASURABLE OUTCOMES**
IDEA emphasizes accountability and improved, measurable outcomes. When an IEP goal says "CHILD will have 80% success" with success "measured" by subjective teacher observations and teacher-made tests, this IEP goal is meaningless.

➡ **SHANNON CARTER'S IEP**
In Shannon Carter's case, the Supreme Court found that the IEP proposed by Shannon's school district was not appropriate. This IEP proposed that after one year of special education, 16 year old Shannon would make four months of progress on standardized educational achievement tests. Her reading skills would improve from the 5.4 to 5.8 grade equivalent level, as measured by the Woodcock Johnson Reading Mastery Test. In the aftermath of *Carter*, many school districts stopped using standardized tests to measure educational progress objectively and began to use subjective teacher observations and teacher made tests. Educational progress should be measured with objective, measurable grade equivalents, standard scores, or percentile ranks.

(B) Individualized education program team. The term 'individualized education program team' or 'IEP Team' means a group of individuals composed of-
   (i) the **parents** of a child with a disability;
   (ii) at least one **regular education teacher** of such child (if the child is, or may be, participating in the regular education environment);
   (iii) at least **one special education teacher**, or where appropriate, at least one special education provider of such child;
   (iv) a **representative** of the local educational agency who -
      (I) is qualified **to provide, or supervise the provision of, specially designed instruction** to meet the unique needs of children with disabilities;
      (II) is **knowledgeable** about the general curriculum; and
      (III) **is knowledgeable about the availability of resources** of the local educational agency;
   (v) an individual who can **interpret the instructional implications of evaluation results**, who may be a member of the team described in clauses (ii) through (vi);
   (vi) at the **discretion of the parent** or the agency, other individuals who have knowledge or special expertise regarding the child, including related services personnel as appropriate; and
   (vii) whenever appropriate, the **child** with a disability.

➡ **IEP TEAM MEMBERS**
IEP teams **must** include the individuals listed above. If the IEP team does not include these individuals, this may be a procedural breach that triggers other remedies and sanctions. Parents can ask that the IEP meeting be rescheduled and that IEP document reflect that the required individuals did not attend the meeting. In making requests to the school, be polite.
If litigation, school board counsel will assert that the absence of one or more of the required IEP team members is a "harmless error" that did not adversely affect the outcome of the IEP meeting. If the child did not suffer "a loss of educational opportunity" due to a procedural violation of law, a court may agree that the breach was "harmless."

(2) Requirement that program be in effect.

(A) In general. At the **beginning of each school year**, each local educational agency, State educational agency, or other State agency, as the case may be, **shall have in effect, for each child with a disability in its jurisdiction, an individualized education program**, as defined in paragraph (1)(A).

➡ ALL STUDENTS, PUBLIC AND PRIVATE, SHALL HAVE AN IEP AT THE BEGINNING OF EACH YEAR
An IEP must be in effect at the beginning of each school year for all children in the school's jurisdiction, including children with disabilities who are enrolled in private programs. In many cases, parents who are unable to secure acceptable special education services for their child in a public school program have placed their child in a private program. School districts will claim that the child is no longer their responsibility. Under IDEA, it appears that public schools are responsible for offering an IEP to students at private schools.

(B) Program for child aged 3 through 5. In the case of a child with a disability aged 3 through 5 (or, at the discretion of the State educational agency, a 2 year-old child with a disability who will turn age 3 during the school year), an individualized family service plan that contains the material described in section 1436, and that is developed in accordance with this section, may serve as the IEP of the child if using that plan as the IEP is-
(i) consistent with State policy; and
(ii) agreed to by the agency and the child's parents.

(3) Development of IEP.

(A) In general. In developing each child's IEP, the IEP Team, subject to subparagraph (C), **shall** consider-
(i) the **strengths** of the child and the **concerns of the parents for enhancing the education of their child**; and
(ii) the **results** of the initial evaluation or **most recent evaluation** of the child.

➡ PARENT CONCERNS AND EVALUATIONS
The IEP team must consider the parents' concerns about the child's education, including concerns about inadequate progress. Sometimes, IEP teams refuse to accept or use any information from private sector evaluations on the child. The statute is clear that schools must consider the results from the most recent evaluation on the child.

(B) Consideration of special factors. The IEP Team shall -
(i) in the case of a child **whose behavior impedes his or her learning or that of others**, consider, when appropriate, strategies, including **positive behavioral interventions**, strategies, and supports to address that behavior;
(ii) in the case of a child with limited English proficiency, consider the language needs of the child as such needs relate to the child's IEP;
(iii) in the case of a child who is blind or visually impaired, provide for instruction in Braille and the use of Braille unless the IEP Team determines, after an evaluation of the child's reading and writing skills, needs, and appropriate reading and writing media (including an evaluation of the child's future needs for instruction in Braille or the use of Braille), that instruction in Braille or the use of Braille is not appropriate for the child;
(iv) consider the **communication needs of the child**, and in the case of a child who is deaf or hard of hearing, consider the child's language and communication needs, **opportunities for direct communications** with peers and professional personnel in the child's language and communication mode, academic level, and full range of needs, including opportunities **for direct instruction** in the child's language and communication mode; and
(v) consider whether the child requires assistive technology devices and services.

➡ SPECIAL FACTORS: CHILDREN WITH HEARING IMPAIRMENTS AND COMMUNICATION PROBLEMS
Advances in medicine have caused significant changes in the treatment of children with hearing impairments. With cochlear implants and/or hearing aids, many hearing impaired children can hear and speak. Parents and health care professionals are asking schools to provide auditory-verbal therapy which teaches the child to listen and speak. Problems arise when school districts have one service delivery model for all hearing-impaired children. Many districts offer a "Total Communication" model that teaches lip-reading and sign language, not how to listen or speak.

➡ SPECIAL FACTORS: YOUNG CHILDREN WITH AUTISM
Historically, autistic children were often placed in institutions or group homes. With ABA/Discrete Trial or Lovaas therapy, many autistic children "lose their labels" and are mainstreamed in regular education

classes. ABA/discrete trial/Lovaas therapy is expensive. Typically, young children receive at least 40 hours a week of one-on-one therapy (6 hours a day, 7 days a week) for two to three years. In 1997, the National Institutes of Health began to fund research projects about effective educational approaches to use for children with autism. As information from these research projects becomes available, we should see improvements in this area.

(C) Requirement with respect to regular education teacher. The regular education teacher of the child, as a member of the IEP Team, shall, to the extent appropriate, participate in the development of the IEP of the child, including the determination of appropriate **positive behavioral interventions and strategies** and the determination of supplementary aids and services, program modifications, and support for school personnel consistent with paragraph (1)(A)(iii).

➡ **ROLE OF CHILD'S REGULAR EDUCATION TEACHER**
Many children with disabilities receive most of their education in regular classes. Regular education teachers need accurate information about the child's intellectual and educational strengths and weaknesses. The regular education teacher is a member of the IEP team. This teacher must be consulted about special education decisions and should help the IEP team develop positive behavioral interventions.
When regular education teachers participate in IEP meetings, they will learn how the child's disability affects educational performance. When regular education teachers contribute to the IEP, they will have a stake in the child's success. Regular education teachers may provide fresh insights and new ideas that are based on observations of the child, not on the child's disability category. The regular education teacher will want to read the definition of supplementary aids and services in Section 1401 (Part A).

(4) Review and revision of IEP.
  (A) In general. The local educational agency **shall** ensure that, subject to subparagraph (B), the IEP Team—
    (i) **reviews** the child's IEP periodically, **but not less than annually** to determine whether the annual goals for the child are being achieved; and
    (ii) **revises** the IEP as appropriate to address -
      (I) any **lack of expected progress toward the annual goals and in the general curriculum**, where appropriate;
      (II) the results of **any reevaluation** conducted under this section;
      (III) **information about the child provided to, or by, the parents**, as described in subsection (c)(1)(B);
      (IV) the child's **anticipated needs**; or
      (V) other matters.

➡ **TIP: KEEP A CONTACT LOG**
You should keep a running log of your contacts with school personnel. If your child has behavior problems, document these problems and the strategies and/or interventions that the school is proposing to use to deal with these problems.

➡ **TIP: THE PARENT IEP ATTACHMENT**
If you have run into a wall of resistance from the IEP team, develop a "Parent Attachment" to your child's IEP. Parents are full members of the child's IEP team. Distribute the IEP attachment to the other team members and ask that your "Parent Attachment" be included as part of your child's IEP.

➡ **TIP: WRITE THANK YOU LETTERS**
Write courteous "thank you" letters after IEP meetings. Your letter should sum up discussions that took place during the IEP meeting, your understanding of the services your child will receive, and any concerns you have about your child's special education services.

(B) Requirement with respect to regular education teacher. The regular education teacher of the child, as a member of the IEP Team, shall, to the extent appropriate, participate in the review and revision of the IEP of the child.

(5) Failure to meet transition objectives. If a participating agency, other than the local educational agency, fails to provide the transition services described in the IEP in accordance with paragraph (1)(A)(vii), the local educational agency shall reconvene the IEP Team to identify alternative strategies to meet the transition objectives for the child set out in that program.

(6) Children with disabilities in adult prisons.

    (A) In general. The following requirements do not apply to children with disabilities who are convicted as adults under State law and incarcerated in adult prisons:

        (i) The requirements contained in section 1412(a)(17) and paragraph (1)(A)(v) of this subsection (relating to participation of children with disabilities in general assessments).

        (ii) The requirements of subclauses (I) and (II) of paragraph (1)(A)(vii) of this subsection (relating to transition planning and transition services), do not apply with respect to such children whose eligibility under this part will end, because of their age, before they will be released from prison.

    (B) Additional requirement. If a child with a disability is convicted as an adult under State law and incarcerated in an adult prison, the child's IEP team may modify the child's IEP or placement notwithstanding the requirements of sections 1412(a)(5)(A) and 1414(d)(1)(A) if the State has demonstrated a bona fide security or compelling penological interest that cannot otherwise be accommodated.

➡ ISSUES IN DISCIPLINE & IEPs

Some school districts still rely on suspensions and expulsions to deal with discipline and behavior problems. If the child's behavior interferes with learning, the IEP team should meet to develop positive behavioral interventions that address the child's behavior. If the IEP team fails to document efforts to develop positive behavioral plans, the district may have significant legal problems.

Suspensions and expulsions are negative interventions. These actions do not attempt to resolve the child's problems, nor do they teach the child new ways to behave. Suspensions and expulsions may be easier and more convenient for school authorities but there is no objective evidence that suspending or expelling children improves their educational performance.

➡ POSITIVE BEHAVIORAL INTERVENTION PLANS

IEP teams should devise positive behavioral intervention plans to deal with problem behavior. Removing the child from school by suspensions or expulsion is not a "positive behavioral intervention." If the child's situation worsens, a contact log is evidence of strategies and interventions that have been attempted. The IEP team should document their discussions and information about the positive behavioral intervention plans, making notes about works and what doesn't work.

(e) CONSTRUCTION. Nothing in this section shall be construed to require the IEP team to include information under one component of a child's IEP that is already contained under another component of such IEP.

(f) EDUCATIONAL PLACEMENTS. Each local educational agency or State educational agency shall ensure that **the parents** of each child with a disability **are members of any group that makes decisions on the educational placement** of their child.

➡ THE PARENT'S ROLE IN PLACEMENT MEETINGS

Decisions about placement cannot be made until after the IEP team, which includes the child's parent(s), has met and reached a consensus about the IEP goals and objectives.

Although the law is clear on this issue, school members of IEP teams often decide the child's placement before the IEP meeting. These unilateral actions prevent parents from "meaningful participation" in the educational decision-making process. By adding this provision to the statute, Congress has sent a message that unilateral decisions by school officials will not be tolerated.

20 U.S.C. §1415 - Procedural Safeguards

➡ SECTION OVERVIEW

Section 1415 includes the rules of procedure that attempt to level the playing field between schools and parents. These safeguards include the opportunity to examine the child's records, to have advance notice before any significant actions are taken, the right to pursue mediation and litigation, the right to view exhibits and to know the names of witnesses in advance of a hearing, the right to confront and cross-examine witnesses, the right to a fair hearing and, for parents, the right to possible reimbursement of reasonable attorney's fees. The statute provides for a proceeding before an impartial hearing officer in matters involving discipline. The losing party has the right to appeal an adverse decision and may have the matter heard in state or federal court.

(a) ESTABLISHMENT OF PROCEDURES. Any State educational agency, State agency, or local educational agency that receives assistance under this part **shall** establish and maintain procedures in accordance with this section **to ensure that children with disabilities and their parents are guaranteed procedural safeguards** with respect to the provision of free appropriate public education by such agencies.

(b) TYPES OF PROCEDURES. The procedures required by this section **shall** include-

(1) an opportunity for the parents of a child with a disability to **examine all records** relating to such child and to participate in meetings with respect to the **identification, evaluation, and educational placement** of the child, and the provision of a free appropriate public education to such child, **and to obtain an independent educational evaluation** of the child;

➡ PARENTS CAN EXAMINE ALL RECORDS

In some jurisdictions, school districts refuse to allow parents to examine their child's educational records. IDEA clarifies that parents have the right to examine all records. This right may include personal notes, if the notes have been shared with other staff. Parents are entitled to test data, and should ask for the raw scores, standard scores, percentile ranks, age equivalent scores, and grade equivalent scores. (For more information about educational records, see Section Four about FERPA in this book.)

(2) procedures to protect the rights of the child whenever te parents of the child are not known, the agency cannot, after reasonable efforts, locate the parents, or the child is a ward of the State, including the assignment of an individual (who shall not be an employee of the State educational agency, the local educational agency, or any other agency that is involved in the education or care of the child) to act as a surrogate for the parents;

(3) **written prior notice to the parents of the child whenever such agency-**
   (A) **proposes to initiate or change**; or
   (B) **refuses to initiate or change**; the **identification, evaluation, or educational placement** of the child, in accordance with subsection (c), or the provision of a free appropriate public education to the child;

➡ FAILURE TO PROVIDE NOTICE

It is often easier to prove that a parent did not receive notice than to prove that the school district's IEP is inappropriate or that the program secured by the parents is appropriate. Read 1415(c) to learn what should be included in notice to parents. Schools often fail to comply with section 1415(c).

When the school district refuses to change the identification or educational placement of a child after receiving a request to do so, and fails to provide the parents with written notice about their refusal, some courts, hearing officers, and Administrative Law Judges have viewed this as a serious procedural breach.

(4) procedures designed to ensure that the notice required by paragraph (3) is in the native language of the parents, unless it clearly is not feasible to do so;
(5) **an opportunity for mediation** in accordance with subsection (e);
(6) an opportunity to present **complaints** with respect **to any matter** relating to the **identification, evaluation, or educational placement** of the child, or the provision of a free appropriate public education to such child;

(7) procedures that **require the parent of a child with a disability, or the attorney representing the child**, to provide **notice** (which shall remain confidential)-

(A) to the State educational agency or local educational agency, as the case may be, in the complaint filed under paragraph (6); and

(B) **that shall include** -

(i) the name of the child, the address of the residence of the child, and the name of the school the child is attending;

(ii) a **description of the nature of the problem** of the child relating to such proposed initiation or change, including **facts** relating to such problem; and

(iii) **a proposed resolution** of the problem to the extent known and available to the parents at the time; and

➡ PARENTS MUST PROVIDE NOTICE

Written notice must include the name of the child, the address of the child (residence), the name of the school the child attends, a description of the problem that includes the factual history of the problem, and a proposal to resolve the problem. Failure to comply with this requirement may be ftal to the parent's claim.

(8) procedures that **require the State educational agency to develop a model form to assist parents in filing a complaint** in accordance with paragraph (7).

(c) **CONTENT OF PRIOR WRITTEN NOTICE.** The notice required by subsection (b)(3) **shall** include-

(1) a description of the action **proposed or refused** by the agency;

(2) an **explanation of why** the agency proposes or refuses to take the action;

(3) a description **of any other options** that the agency considered **and** the **reasons why** those options were rejected;

(4) a description of **each evaluation procedure, test, record, or report the agency used as a basis** for the proposed or refused action;

(5) a description of **any other factors** that are relevant to the agency's proposal or refusal;

(6) a statement that the parents of a child with a disability have protection under the procedural safeguards of this part and, if this notice is not an initial referral for evaluation, the means by which a copy of a description of the procedural safeguards can be obtained; and

(7) **sources** for parents to contact to obtain assistance in **understanding** the provisions of this part.

➡ SCHOOL MUST EXPLAIN BASIS OF DECISION

See the Note above in 1415(b)(3). The school district's failure to comply with this section can have serious consequences. Instead of saying that a number of options were considered and rejected, the document must explain the reasons and offer explanations. This cannot be a simple checklist.

(d) **PROCEDURAL SAFEGUARDS NOTICE.**

(1) **In General**. A copy of the procedural safeguards available to the parents of a child with a disability **shall be given to the parents, at a minimum**-

(A) upon initial referral for evaluation;

(B) upon each notification of an individualized education program meeting and upon reevaluation of the child; and

(C) upon registration of a complaint under subsection (b)(6).

➡ **MANDATORY REQUIREMENTS ABOUT NOTICE**

When a complaint is made in regard about any matter under 1415(b)(6), the school district must, at a minimum, provide the parents with a copy of the parental procedural safeguards. The components of the procedural safeguards notice are listed below.

(2) Contents. The procedural safeguards notice shall include a full explanation of the procedural safeguards, written in the native language of the parents, unless it clearly is not feasible to do so, and **written in an easily understandable manner**, available under this section and under regulations promulgated by the Secretary relating to-

(A) independent educational evaluation;

(B) prior written notice;

(C) parental consent;

(D) access to educational records;

(E) opportunity to present complaints;

(F) the child's placement during pendency of due process proceedings;

(G) procedures for students who are subject to placement in an interim alternative educational setting;

(H) requirements for unilateral placement by parents of children in private schools at public expense;

(I) mediation;

(J) due process hearings, including requirements for disclosure of evaluation results and recommendations;

(K) State-level appeals (if applicable in that State);

(L) civil actions; and

(M) attorneys' fees.

➡ **PROCEDURAL SAFEGUARDS**

Procedural safeguards should be "easily understandable," i.e., easy to read. We used a word processing program to analyze one state's procedural safeguard notice. To be "easily understandable," reading clarity should be higher than 70% and the reading level should be no higher than 6th grade. In this safeguards notice, reading clarity was at the 33% level and the reading grade level was higher than 12th grade. This notice was not "easily understandable."

State departments of education and school districts should expect this to become an issue. There is increasing emphasis on the rights of families where English is the Second Language (ESL) and parents who have disabilities. Perhaps the Office for Civil Rights will examine the readability of Notices developed by school districts and states.

(e) MEDIATION.

(1) In General. Any State educational agency or local educational agency that receives assistance under this part **shall** ensure that procedures are established and implemented to allow parties to **disputes involving any matter described in subsection (b)(6)** to resolve such disputes through a mediation process which, at a minimum, shall be available whenever a hearing is requested under subsection (f) or (k).

(2) Requirements. Such procedures shall meet the following requirements:

(A) The procedures shall ensure that the mediation process -

(i) is **voluntary** on the part of the parties;

(ii) **is not used to deny or delay a parent's right to a due process hearing** under subsection (f), or to deny any other rights afforded under this part; and

(iii) is conducted by a **qualified and impartial mediator who is trained in effective mediation techniques**.

➡ **MEDIATION MAY ALLOW PARTIES TO RESOLVE A DISPUTE WITHOUT LITIGATION**

Mediation is a process that allows parties to resolve their dispute without litigation. The mediator's role is to help the parties express their views and positions, and to help the parties hear and understand these views and positions. Before entering mediation, both parties should understand their rights and the law.

(B) A **local educational agency or a State agency may establish procedures to require parents** who choose not to use the mediation process to meet, at a time and location convenient to the parents, with a **disinterested party** who is under **contract** with-

   (i) a **parent training and information center** or community parent resource center in the State established under section 1482 or 1483; **or**

   (ii) an appropriate **alternative dispute resolution entity**; to encourage the use, and explain the benefits, of the mediation process to the parents.

➡️ **MEETING AT PARENT TRAINING CENTER**

As a parent, you can be required to meet with a parent training center staff member or an ADR staff person to discuss mediation. If parents fail to comply, they will be viewed as "uncooperative" and may lose their rights.

(C) The **State shall maintain a list** of individuals who are **qualified mediators** and **knowledgeable** in laws and regulations relating to the provision of special education and related services.

➡️ **THE MEDIATOR'S ROLE**

The mediator's role is to facilitate the communication process. Mediators should not take positions or take sides. Some mediators believe that their role is to force a settlement, even if this means the mediator must take sides. If mediators are poorly trained and supervised, their personal and professional biases and opinions will influence the mediation process. This will destroy trust and cause cases to be litigated that could have been resolved.

(D) The State shall bear the cost of the mediation process, including the costs of meetings described in subparagraph (B).

(E) Each session in the mediation process shall be scheduled in a timely manner and shall be held in a location that is convenient to the parties to the dispute.

(F) An **agreement** reached by the parties to the dispute in the mediation process shall be set forth in **a written mediation agreement.**

(G) Discussions that occur during the **mediation process shall be confidential** and **may not** be used as **evidence** in any subsequent due process hearings or civil proceedings and the parties to the mediation process may be required to sign a confidentiality pledge prior to the commencement of such process.

➡️ **CONFIDENTIALITY IN SETTLEMENT AND MEDIATION DISCUSSIONS**

Confidentiality is vital to the success of mediation. Discussions and admissions by the parties are confidential. Without confidentiality, the purpose of mediation would be to gain a tactical advantage in subsequent litigation.

In law, settlement discussions are usually confidential. Information from settlement discussions may not be used or disclosed in a subsequent trial, if the case is not settled. Any attempt to use confidential information from mediation or settlement discussion could lead to dismissal or an adverse ruling if the case ends up in state or federal court.

➡️ **MEDIATION IS A TWO-WAY STREET**

I am a trained mediator. I have mediated divorce and child custody cases. I support mediation, if the mediator is and remains neutral through the process.

Mediation is a two-way street. Each side must be prepared to walk down the street together and discuss their differences frankly, without lawyers being present. Good mediators do not need to be knowledgeable about special education law and practice but they must know how to facilitate communication between parties. Mediators are not arbitrators. Arbitrators issue rulings in favor of one party or the other. If you have a dispute with the school, read *Getting to Yes* by Roger Fisher. In *Getting to Yes*, you will learn how to develop "win-win" solutions.

(f) IMPARTIAL DUE PROCESS HEARING.

(1) In General. Whenever a complaint has been received under subsection (b)(6) or (k) of this section, the parents involved in such complaint shall have an opportunity for an impartial due process hearing, which shall be conducted by the State educational agency or by the local educational agency, as determined by State law or by the State educational agency.

(2) Disclosure of evaluations and recommendations.

(A) In general. At least 5 business days prior to a hearing conducted pursuant to paragraph (1), **each party shall disclose to all other parties all evaluations completed by that date and recommendations based on the offering party's evaluations that the party intends to use at the hearing.**

(B) Failure to disclose. A hearing officer may **bar** any party that fails to comply with subparagraph (A) from introducing the relevant evaluation or recommendation at the hearing without the consent of the other party.

➡️ **IF CONFLICT, ASSUME LITIGATION**

If parents have conflict with the school and want to avoid a due process hearing, they should prepare for a due process hearing.

Preparation involves several critical concepts. Because parents are biased in favor of their child, they must assume that the decision-maker will not hear or believe their testimony. Assume that all school staff will testify against them. Assume that the Hearing Officer is biased against parents. Assume that they will initiate the hearing.

How can parents prevail? Write thank you letters that document areas of disagreement and restate what the school staff told you and your responses. Get evaluations by private sector experts. Do not rely on the school's testing or the school employees. If you develop a paper trail and have competent, qualified private experts who can testify about what your child needs, you will be in a good position if a due process hearing is necessary. And, if you take these steps, you will increase the odds that you will not have to request a hearing.

➡️ **EXCHANGE DOCUMENTS AND WITNESS LISTS**

If you are involved in a hearing, most state regulations require each party to disclose and provide a copy of all documents and the names of all witnesses to the other party at least one week before the hearing. Failure to comply will often result in dismissal of the case. An exhibit list should include all research reports, learned treatises, journal articles, pertinent book chapters, and other documents that may be relevant to the case.

(3) Limitation on conduct of hearing. A hearing conducted pursuant to paragraph (1) may not be conducted by an employee of the State educational agency or the local educational agency involved in the education or care of the child.

➡️ **HEARING OFFICERS SHOULD BE IMPARTIAL**

The quality of Hearing Officers varies. Some states use school district employees as Hearing Officers. Some people believe that Hearing Officers should be attorneys. Others believe that attorney Hearing Officers are rigid and cause hearings to be run as legal proceedings with the burden of proof on parents. There are no easy answers to these problems.

(g) APPEAL.

If the hearing required by subsection (f) is conducted by a local educational agency, any party aggrieved by the findings and decision rendered in such a hearing may appeal such findings and decision to the State educational agency. Such agency shall conduct an impartial review of such decision. **The officer conducting such review shall make an independent decision upon completion of such review.**

➡️ **APPEAL TO STATE REVIEW OR TO COURT**

If a due process hearing is conducted at the local level, the losing party may appeal to the State Educational Agency. The SEA appoints an independent Reviewing Officer who issues a decision. The losing party may appeal to state or federal Court. In "two tiered systems," there must be a due process hearing and a review hearing before going to court. In states that use a "one-tier system," the due process decision can be appealed to Court.

(h) SAFEGUARDS. Any party to a hearing conducted pursuant to subsection (f) or (k), or an appeal conducted pursuant to subsection (g), shall be accorded-

(1) the right to be accompanied and advised by counsel and by individuals with special knowledge or training with respect to the problems of children with disabilities;

(2) **the right to present evidence and confront, cross-examine, and compel the attendance of witnesses;**

(3) **the right to a written**, or, at the option of the parents, electronic **verbatim record of such hearing**; and

(4) the right to written, or, at the option of the parents, electronic findings of fact and decisions (which findings and **decisions shall be made available to the public** consistent with the requirements of section 1417(c) (relating to the confidentiality of data, information, and records) and shall also be transmitted to the advisory panel established pursuant to section 1412(a)(21)).

➡ **COURTROOM PROCEDURE**

A special education due process hearing is similar to a trial. Both parties are usually represented by counsel. In some jurisdictions, parents are well represented by advocates who prevail over school board counsel. The statute clarifies that parents are entitled to a written verbatim record, i.e., a transcript of the hearing, not a tape recording of the hearing, as was the practice in some states.

For many witnesses, going through cross-examination is a brutal experience. Ultimately, success depends on the law, the facts, the preparedness of the attorneys, and the life experiences of the hearing officer, judge, or other individual who decides the outcome.

➡ **USE SIMPLE THEMES**

In a due process hearing, it is essential to simplify the case to a short story that can be expressed in one minute - or less. Focus on the story, the theme, one minute, simplify.

(i) ADMINISTRATIVE PROCEDURES.

(1) In general.
(A) Decision made in hearing. A decision made in a hearing conducted pursuant to subsection (f) or (k) shall be final, except that any party involved in such hearing may appeal such decision under the provisions of subsection (g) and paragraph (2) of this subsection.
(B) Decision made at appeal. A decision made under subsection (g) shall be final, except that any party may bring an action under paragraph (2) of this subsection.

(2) Right to bring civil action.
(A) In general. Any party aggrieved by the findings and decision made under subsection (f) or (k) who does not have the right to an appeal under subsection (g), and any party aggrieved by the findings and decision under this subsection, **shall have the right to bring a civil action** with respect to the complaint presented pursuant to this section, which action may be brought **in any State court** of competent jurisdiction **or in a district court of the United States** without regard to the amount in controversy.
(B) Additional requirements. In any action brought under this paragraph, the court-
(i) **shall** receive the records of the administrative proceedings;
(ii) **shall** hear additional evidence at the request of a party; and
(iii) basing its decision on the preponderance of the evidence, shall grant such relief as the court determines is appropriate.

➡ **ADDITIONAL EVIDENCE USUALLY NOT PERMITTED**

Many Courts will not hear evidence that could have been furnished at the due process hearing. Courts may hear new evidence or "after discovered" evidence. This means that the parties at the due process hearing should put all of their evidence into the record at that time.

(3) Jurisdiction of district courts; attorneys' fees.

(A) In general. The district courts of the United States shall have jurisdiction of actions brought under this section without regard to the amount in controversy.

(B) Award of attorneys' fees. In any action or proceeding brought under this section, the court, in its discretion, may award **reasonable attorneys' fees** as part of the costs to the parents of a child with a disability who is the prevailing party.

(C) Determination of amount of attorneys' fees. Fees awarded under this paragraph shall be based on rates prevailing in the community in which the action or proceeding arose for the kind and quality of services furnished. No bonus or multiplier may be used in calculating the fees awarded under this subsection.

(D) Prohibition of attorneys' fees and related costs for certain services.

(i) **Attorneys' fees may not be awarded** and **related costs may not be reimbursed** in any action or proceeding under this section for services performed subsequent to the time of a written offer of settlement to a parent if-

(I) the offer is made within the time prescribed by Rule 68 of the Federal Rules of Civil Procedure or, in the case of an administrative proceeding, at any **time more than ten days before the proceeding begins**;

(II) the offer is not accepted within 10 days; and

(III) the court or administrative hearing officer **finds** that the relief finally obtained by the parents **is not more favorable to the parents than the offer of settlement**.

(ii) **Attorneys' fees may not be awarded** relating to any meeting of the IEP Team **unless such meeting is convened as a result of an administrative proceeding** or judicial action, or, at the discretion of the State, for a mediation described in subsection (e) that is conducted prior to the filing of a complaint under subsection (b)(6) or (k) of this section.

➡ **LIMITATIONS ON ATTORNEYS' FEES**

If the district makes a written settlement offer ten days before the due process hearing that is the same or similar to the relief received through litigation, the parents lose all entitlement to attorneys' fees.

Attorneys' fees will not be awarded for an IEP meeting unless the IEP meeting is convened as the result of a due process hearing. School board counsel will assert that the IEP meeting was not caused by the pending litigation. Some courts have ruled that only federal courts can award attorney's fees. Other courts have held that a state court or federal court can award attorneys' fees.

(E) Exception to prohibition on attorneys' fees and related costs. Notwithstanding subparagraph (D), an award of **attorneys' fees and related costs may be made to a parent who is the prevailing party** and who was substantially justified in rejecting the settlement offer.

(F) Reduction in amount of attorneys' fees. Except as provided in subparagraph (G), whenever the court finds that-

(i) the **parent**, during the course of the action or proceeding, **unreasonably protracted** the final resolution of the controversy;

(ii) the amount of the attorneys' fees otherwise authorized to be **awarded unreasonably exceeds the hourly rate prevailing** in the community for similar services by attorneys of reasonably comparable skill, reputation, and experience;

(iii) the time spent and legal services furnished were **excessive** considering the nature of the action or proceeding; or

(iv) the attorney representing the parent **did not provide to the school district the appropriate information** in the due process complaint in accordance with subsection (b)(7); the court shall reduce, accordingly, the amount of the attorneys' fees awarded under this section.

➡ **COMPLAINTS ABOUT EXCESSIVE ATTORNEYS' FEES**

During "off the record" committee meetings before Congress enacted IDEA-97, school districts complained that attorneys' fees for special education due process hearings were excessive. The school districts did not disclose the fees they paid to their counsel.

When parents seek attorneys' fees, they should request information about all fees charged, incurred, paid, and time expended by school district attorneys in their case under the Freedom of Information Act. In most cases, the fees that school boards pay their attorneys are much higher than the fees incurred by parents.

(G) Exception to reduction in amount of attorneys' fees. The provisions of subparagraph (F) shall not apply in any action or proceeding if the court finds that the State or **local educational agency unreasonably protracted the final resolution** of the action or proceeding or there was a violation of this section.

(j) MAINTENANCE OF CURRENT EDUCATIONAL PLACEMENT. Except as provided in subsection (k)(7), during the pendency of any proceedings conducted pursuant to this section, unless the State or local educational agency and the parents otherwise agree, the child shall remain in the then-current educational placement of such child, or, if applying for initial admission to a public school, shall, with the consent of the parents, be placed in the public school program until all such proceedings have been completed.

➡ **PARENTS ARE NOT BOUND BY CURRENT PLACEMENT PROVISION**

Pursuant to the U. S. Supreme Court decisions in *Burlington* and *Carter*, parents may remove their child from a damaging public school placement and seek reimbursement for a private placement, subject to the restrictions in 20 U.S.C. §1412. The *Burlington* First Circuit case, the Ninth Circuit's *Clovis* case and the Third Circuit's *Raelee S*. case assert that when a State Review Officer awards private placement, this is the state's agreement that the placement is proper. The private placement becomes the "current educational placement." If the school appeals, they must pay for the child's private placement during the pendency of the appeal. The regulations made this provision mandatory. (see 300.514)

(k) PLACEMENT IN ALTERNATIVE EDUCATIONAL SETTING.

➡ **PLACEMENT IN ALTERNATIVE EDUCATIONAL SETTING BY SCHOOL AND BY HEARING OFFICER**

A change in placement can be initiated by school district personnel, without the authority of a Hearing Officer under (k)(1). For a longer change in placement, the school must obtain an order from a Hearing Officer, pursuant to (k)(2). There are several steps that the school must take about convening IEP meetings, functional behavioral assessments, and behavioral implementation plans. The school may not deny educational services to a child with a disability.

(1) Authority of school personnel.

(A) School personnel under this section may order a **change in the placement of a child** with a disability-

(i) **to an appropriate interim alternative educational setting, another setting, or suspension**, for **not more than 10 school days** (to the extent such alternatives would be applied to children without disabilities); **and**

(ii) to an appropriate **interim alternative educational setting** for the same amount of time that a child without a disability would be subject to discipline, but **for not more than 45 days if-**

(I) the **child carries or possesses a weapon to or at school**, on school premises, or to or at a school function under the jurisdiction of a State or a local educational agency; **or**

(II) the child knowingly **possesses** or uses illegal **drugs** or sells or solicits the sale of a controlled substance while at school or a school function under the jurisdiction of a State or local educational agency.

➡ **ALTERNATIVE EDUCATIONAL SETTING: NO WEAPON, NO DRUGS**

If the child did not carry a weapon or illegal drugs to school, the child may be suspended for up to 10 days and/or sent to an alternative setting for 10 days. Before the school can place the child in an interim alternative setting for up to 45 days, the school must obtain an ORDER from an independent Hearing Officer (See subsection (2)). If the child carried a weapon or illegal drugs to school, the child can be suspended for 10 days and placed in an alternative setting for 45 days, without an Order from a Hearing Officer.

(B) Either before or not later than **10 days after taking a disciplinary action** described in subparagraph (A)-

(i) **if** the local educational agency **did not conduct a functional behavioral assessment and implement a be-**

havioral intervention plan for such child before the behavior that resulted in the suspension described in subparagraph (A), the agency **shall convene an IEP meeting** to develop an **assessment plan** to address that behavior; **or**

(ii) if the child already has a behavioral intervention plan, **the IEP Team shall review the plan** and modify it, as necessary, to address the behavior.

➡ **FUNCTIONAL BEHAVIORAL ASSESSMENTS & BEHAVIORAL INTERVENTION PLANS**

If the school did not develop a functional behavioral assessment or implement a behavioral intervention plan before the incident, the school must convene an IEP meeting to develop a behavioral intervention plan. If the IEP team has a behavioral intervention plan in place, the school must convene an IEP meeting so the IEP team can review and modify the plan to address the child's behavior problems.

(2) Authority of hearing officer. A **hearing officer** under this section **may order a change in the placement** of a child with a disability to an appropriate **interim alternative educational setting** for **not more than 45** days **if** the hearing officer-

(A) determines that the public agency has demonstrated by **substantial evidence** that maintaining the current placement of such child is **substantially likely to result in injury to the child or to others**;

(B) considers the appropriateness of the child's current placement;

(C) considers whether the public agency has made **reasonable efforts to minimize the risk of harm** in the child's current placement, **including** the use of **supplementary** aids and services; **and**

(D) determines that the interim alternative educational setting meets the requirements of paragraph (3)(B).

➡ **CHANGE OF PLACEMENT BY HEARING OFFICER: ELEMENTS THAT MUST BE SATISFIED**

Each of these clauses (above) is followed by a semicolon with (C) ending with the word "and." This means that each element must be satisfied before a Hearing Officer can order a 45-day placement. The setting must comply with (3)(B). Note the use of the phrase "supplementary aids and services." Did the school district provide the child with individualized tutoring as a supplementary aid and service to the regular education program?

(3) Determination of setting.

(A) In general. The alternative educational **setting** described in paragraph (1)(A)(ii) shall be determined by the IEP Team.

(B) Additional requirements - Any **interim alternative educational setting** in which a child is placed under paragraph (1) or (2) **shall**-

(i) be selected so as to enable the child to continue to **participate in the general curriculum**, although in another setting, and to **continue to receive those services** and modifications, including those described in the child's current IEP, **that will enable the child to meet the goals set out in that IEP**; and

(ii) include services and modifications designed to address the behavior described in paragraph (1) or paragraph (2) so that it does not recur.

(4) Manifestation Determination Review.

(A) In general. If a **disciplinary** action is contemplated as described in paragraph (1) or paragraph (2) for a behavior of a child with a disability described in either of those paragraphs, or if a disciplinary action involving a **change of placement for more than 10 days** is contemplated for a child with a disability who has engaged in other behavior that violated any rule or code of conduct of the local educational agency that applies to all children-

(i) not later than the date on which the decision to take that action is made, **the parents shall be notified of that decision** and of all procedural safeguards accorded under this section; and

(ii) immediately, if possible, but in no case later than 10 school days after the date on which the decision to take that action is made, **a review shall be conducted of the relationship between the child's disability and the behavior subject to the disciplinary action.**

(B) Individuals to carry out review. A review described in subparagraph (A) shall be conducted by the **IEP Team** and **other** qualified personnel.

(C) Conduct of review. In carrying out a review described in subparagraph (A), **the IEP Team may determine that the behavior** of the child **was not a manifestation of such child's disability only if the IEP Team-**

　(i) first **considers**, in terms of the behavior subject to disciplinary action, **all relevant information, including -**
　　(I) **evaluation** and diagnostic results, including such results or other relevant **information supplied by the parents** of the child;
　　(II) **observations** of the child; and
　　(III) the child's **IEP** and placement; **and**
　(ii) **then determines that -**
　　(I) in relationship to the behavior subject to disciplinary action, the child's **IEP and placement were appropriate** and the special education services, supplementary aids and services, **and** behavior intervention **strategies were provided** consistent with the child's IEP and placement;
　　(II) the child's **disability did not impair** the ability of the child to understand the **impact** and **consequences** of the behavior subject to disciplinary action; **and**
　　(III) **the child's disability did not impair the ability of the child to control the behavior subject to disciplinary action.**

➡ **REQUIREMENTS FOR MANIFESTATION DETERMINATION REVIEW**
Several questions must be answered in a manifestation determination review hearing. Is the child's IEP appropriate? Is the placement appropriate? Were behavior intervention strategies provided that were consistent with the IEP and placement? Did the child's disability impair the child's ability to understand the impact and consequences of the behavior? The IEP Team must determine that the child's disability did not affect the child's understanding of the impact and consequences of the behavior or the child's ability to control the behavior.

(5) Determination that behavior was not manifestation of disability.
　(A) In general. If the result of the review described in paragraph (4) **is a determination**, consistent with paragraph (4)(C), **that the behavior** of the child with a disability **was not a manifestation** of the child's disability, the relevant **disciplinary procedures applicable to children without disabilities** may be applied to the child in the same manner in which they would be applied to children without disabilities, **except as provided in section 1412(a)(1).**

➡ **CHILD WITH DISABILITY IS ENTITLED TO AN APPROPRIATE EDUCATION**
If the IEP team decides that the behavior is not a manifestation of the disability, the child with a disability may be treated as a non-disabled child, subject to 20 U.S.C. §1412(a)(1). However, 1412(a)(1) requires that a "free appropriate public education is available to all children with disabilities residing in the State between the ages of 3 and 21, inclusive, including children with disabilities who have been suspended or expelled from school."
If a child with a disability is suspended or expelled for behaviors that are not related to the disability, the school must provide the child with a free, appropriate public education. This requirement has led to the proliferation of "alternative educational settings."

　(B) Additional requirement. If the public agency initiates disciplinary procedures applicable to all children, the agency shall ensure that the special education and disciplinary records of the child with a disability are transmitted for **consideration** by the person or persons making the final determination regarding the disciplinary action.

(6) Parent appeal.
　(A) In general.
　　(i) If the child's **parent disagrees with a determination** that the child's behavior was not a manifestation of the child's disability or with any decision regarding placement, **the parent may request a hearing.**
　　(ii) The State or local educational agency **shall** arrange for an **expedited hearing** in any case described in this subsection when requested by a parent

(B) Review of decision.

(i) **In reviewing a decision** with respect to the manifestation determination, **the hearing officer shall determine whether the** public agency has demonstrated that the child's **behavior** was not a manifestation of such child's disability consistent with the requirements of paragraph (4)(C).

(ii) In reviewing a decision under paragraph (1)(A)(ii) to place the child in an **interim alternative educational setting**, the hearing officer shall apply the standards set out in paragraph (2).

(7) Placement during appeals.

(A) In general. When a parent requests a hearing regarding a **disciplinary action** described in paragraph (1)(A)(ii) or paragraph (2) to challenge the interim alternative educational setting **or the manifestation determination,** the child **shall remain in the interim alternative educational setting pending the decision** of the hearing officer or until the expiration of the time period provided for in paragraph (1)(A)(ii) or paragraph (2), whichever occurs first, unless the parent and the State or local educational agency agree otherwise.

➡ **INTERIM ALTERNATIVE EDUCATION SETTINGS: 45 DAY LIMIT**
During an appeal, the child will remain in the interim alternative educational setting but this placement may not continue beyond 10 or 45 days, depending on whether drugs or guns are involved. Note the words "interim" and "educational." This educational setting is to be an interim placement, not a permanent placement. Some school board attorneys advocate sidestepping this provision and seeking a court injunction that permits exclusion for a longer period of time.

(B) Current placement. If a child is placed in an interim alternative educational setting pursuant to paragraph (1)(A)(ii) or paragraph (2) and school personnel propose to change the child's placement after expiration of the interim alternative placement, during the pendency of any proceeding to challenge the proposed change in placement, the child shall remain in the current placement (the child's placement prior to the interim alternative educational setting), except as provided in subparagraph (C).

➡ **RETURN TO PRIOR PLACEMENT**
If the school district proposes to keep the child in the interim alternative educational setting after the 10 day or 45 day period, the child must be returned to the "placement prior to the interim alternative educational setting" except under the circumstances listed below. Remember that paragraph 1(at the beginning) refers to the authority of school personnel, i.e., 10 days if no drugs or guns, 45 days if guns or drugs. Paragraph 2 refers to the authority of the Hearing Officer.

(C) Expedited hearing.

(i) If school personnel maintain that it is dangerous for the child to be in the current placement (placement prior to removal to the interim alternative education setting) during the pendency of the due process proceedings, the local educational agency may request an expedited hearing.

(ii) In determining whether the child may be placed in the alternative educational setting or in another appropriate placement ordered by the hearing officer, the hearing officer shall apply the standards set out in paragraph (2).

(8) Protections for children not yet eligible for special education and related services.

(A) In general. A child who has **not** been determined to be eligible for special education and related services under this part and **who has engaged in behavior** that violated any rule or code of conduct of the local educational agency, including any behavior described in paragraph (1), **may assert any of the protections provided for in this part if the local educational agency had knowledge** (as determined in accordance with this paragraph) that the child was a child with a disability **before** the behavior that precipitated the disciplinary action occurred.

(B) Basis of knowledge. A local educational agency **shall be deemed to have knowledge** that a child is a child with a disability if-

(i) the **parent** of the child **has expressed concern in writing** (unless the parent is illiterate or has a disability that prevents compliance with the requirements contained in this clause) to personnel of the appropriate educational agency that the child is in need of special education and related services;

(ii) the **behavior** or **performance** of the child **demonstrates the need for such services**;

(iii) the **parent** of the child **has requested an evaluation** of the child pursuant to section 1414; or

(iv) the **teacher** of the child, or other personnel of the local educational agency, **has expressed concern about the behavior** or performance of the child to the director of special education of such agency or to other personnel of the agency.

➡ KNOWLEDGE ABOUT POSSIBLE DISABILITY

Parents who are concerned that their child may have a disability should report their concerns in writing. For purposes of law and litigation, verbal statements were never made. If it is not in writing, it did not happen. You should follow up important conversations, meetings, and telephone calls with letters that restate what transpired and your concerns. To do less is naive.

Courts have little sympathy for people who know they have rights, fail to safeguard their rights, then complain that their rights were violated. If you fail to take reasonable steps to protect your rights, do you think the Courts will protect you? Courts believe that the party who complains that their rights were violated must prove that they took all reasonable steps to protect themselves, yet their rights were still violated.

(C) Conditions that apply if no basis of knowledge.

(i) **In general**. If a local educational agency does **not** have knowledge that a child is a child with a disability (in accordance with subparagraph (B)) **prior** to taking disciplinary measures against the child, **the child may be subjected to the same disciplinary measures as measures applied to children without disabilities** who engaged in comparable behaviors consistent with clause (ii).

(ii) **Limitations**. If a **request is made for an evaluation** of a child during the time period in which the child is subjected to disciplinary measures under paragraph (1) or (2), **the evaluation shall be conducted in an expedited manner. If the child is determined to be a child with a disability**, taking into consideration information from the evaluation conducted by the agency and information provided by the parents, **the agency shall provide special education** and related services in accordance with the provisions of this part, **except that**, pending the results of the evaluation, the child shall remain in the educational placement determined by school authorities.

(9) Referral to and action by law enforcement and judicial authorities.

(A) Nothing in this part shall be construed to prohibit an agency from reporting a crime committed by a child with a disability to appropriate authorities or to prevent State law enforcement and judicial authorities from exercising their responsibilities with regard to the application of Federal and State law to crimes committed by a child with a disability.

(B) An agency reporting a crime committed by a child with a disability shall ensure that copies of the special education and disciplinary records of the child are transmitted for consideration by the appropriate authorities to whom it reports the crime.

(10) Definitions. For purposes of this subsection, the following definitions apply:

(A) Controlled substance. The term 'controlled substance' means a **drug** or other substance identified under schedules I, II, III, IV, or V in section 202(c) of the Controlled Substances Act (21 U.S.C. 812(c)).

➡ OVER-THE-COUNTER MEDICATIONS ARE NOT ILLEGAL DRUGS

According to this definition, over-the-counter medications (i.e., aspirin, ibuprofen, Pepto-Bismol, and Tums) are not controlled substances. Many school districts have labeled over-the-counter-medicines as "drugs" and are suspending and expelling children for possessing these medicines. A child with a disability who receives services under IDEA is protected from abuses of power by school officials. A child who receives Section 504 accommodations and modifications does not have the same protections.

(B) Illegal drug. The term 'illegal drug' -

(i) means a controlled substance; but

(ii) **does not include** such a **substance that is legally possessed** or used under the supervision of a licensed health-care professional or that is legally possessed or used under any other authority under that Act or under any other provision of Federal law.

➡ **PRESCRIPTION REQUIRED FOR CONTROLLED SUBSTANCE**

If your child takes Ritalin that is prescribed by a doctor, the school may not expel or suspend the child. However, if the child tries to sell or distribute this drug, the child faces sanctions that are described in the beginning of this section under (k)(1) and (k)(2).)

(C) Substantial evidence. The term 'substantial evidence' means **beyond a preponderance** of the evidence.

➡ **SUBSTANTIAL EVIDENCE IS A NEW, UNDEFINED LEVEL OF PROOF**

"Beyond a preponderance of the evidence" is a new standard of evidence. Normally, there are three levels of evidence that must be considered before a judge or jury makes a finding of fact:

     Preponderance of the evidence,

     Clear and convincing evidence, and

     Proof beyond a reasonable doubt.

This new standard means more than a preponderance of the evidence, but less than clear and convincing evidence. As courts issue rulings on this issue, the levels of proof may differ from one jurisdiction to another.

(D) Weapon. The term 'weapon' has the meaning given the term 'dangerous weapon' under paragraph (2) of the first subsection (g) of section 930 of title 18, United States Code.

➡ **ZERO TOLERANCE POLICIES: WHEN THE PUNISHMENT DOES NOT FIT THE CRIME**

Under "zero tolerance" policies where punishments do not fit the crime, many schools routinely suspend and expel non-disabled children for bringing toy knives and guns to school. IDEA clarifies that a weapon is a weapon, not a toy.

(l) RULE OF CONSTRUCTION. Nothing in this part shall be construed to restrict or limit the rights, procedures, and remedies available under the Constitution, the Americans with Disabilities Act of 1990, title V of the Rehabilitation Act of 1973, or other Federal laws protecting the rights of children with disabilities, except that before the filing of a civil action under such laws seeking relief that is also available under this part, the procedures under subsections (f) and (g) shall be exhausted to the same extent as would be required had the action been brought under this part.

➡ **SUITS UNDER SECTION 504 AND ADA**

If a parent or child with a disability has a case against a school district or employee for reasons, facts, and events other than IDEA, they may file suit under that legal theory, but must usually initiate their case through a due process hearing. The law is still developing in this area.

(m) TRANSFER OF PARENTAL RIGHTS AT AGE OF MAJORITY.

(1) In general. A State that receives amounts from a grant under this part **may** provide that, when a child with a disability **reaches** the age of majority under State law (except for a child with a disability who has been determined to be incompetent under State law)-

     (A) the public agency **shall** provide any **notice** required by this section to **both** the individual and the parents;

     (B) **all other rights** accorded to parents under this part **transfer** to the child; and

     (C) the agency shall notify the individual and the parents of the transfer of rights; and

     (D) all rights accorded to parents under this part transfer to children who are incarcerated in an adult or juvenile Federal, State, or local correctional institution.

(2) Special rule. If, under State law, a child with a disability who has reached the age of majority under State law, who has not been determined to be incompetent, but who is determined not to have the ability to provide **informed consent** with respect to the educational program of the child, **the State shall establish procedures for appointing the parent** of the child, or if the parent is not available, another appropriate individual, **to represent the educational interests of the child** throughout the period of eligibility of the child under this part.

➡ **WHEN CHILDREN BECOME ADULTS**

Notice must be provided to the parent and child that the parents' rights will transfer to child when the child reaches the "age of majority" which is usually at age eighteen. States must establish procedures so that parents can continue to represent the educational interests of their children.

If possible, have your child write a statement that says, "I [child name], pursuant to 20 U.S.C. Section 1415(m)(2) hereby appoint my parent, [your name], to represent my educational interests." If the child is able, have the statement written out longhand, signed and dated. After your state adopts regulations, use the regulatory language verbatim. Don't add or subtract from it, or rephrase it. Suggested wording, "I [child name], pursuant to 20 U.S.C. Section 1415(m)(2) and [your state special education regulation section], hereby appoint my parent [your name] to represent my educational interests.

20 U.S.C. §1416 - Withholding and Judicial Review

➡ **SECTION OVERVIEW**

This section describes the steps that the U. S. Department of Education must take to withhold funds from a state that is in violation of IDEA.

(a) WITHHOLDING OF PAYMENTS -

(1) In General - Whenever the Secretary, after reasonable notice and opportunity for hearing to the State educational agency involved (and to any local educational agency or State agency affected by any failure described in subparagraph (B)), finds - -

(A) that there has been a failure by the State to comply substantially with any provision of this part; or

(B) that there is a failure to comply with any condition of a local educational agency's or State agency's eligibility under this part, including the terms of any agreement to achieve compliance with this part within the timelines specified in the agreement; the Secretary shall, after notifying the State educational agency, withhold, in whole or in part, any further payments to the State under this part, or refer the matter for appropriate enforcement action, which may include referral to the Department of Justice.

(2) Nature of Withholding - If the Secretary withholds further payments under paragraph (1), the Secretary may determine that such withholding will be limited to programs or projects, or portions thereof, affected by the failure, or that the State educational agency shall not make further payments under this part to specified local educational agencies or State agencies affected by the failure. Until the Secretary is satisfied that there is no longer any failure to comply with the provisions of this part, as specified in subparagraph (A) or (B) of paragraph (1), payments to the State under this part shall be withheld in whole or in part, or payments by the State educational agency under this part shall be limited to local educational agencies and State agencies whose actions did not cause or were not involved in the failure, as the case may be. Any State educational agency, State agency, or local educational agency that has received notice under paragraph (1) shall, by means of a public notice, take such measures as may be necessary to bring the pendency of an action pursuant to this subsection to the attention of the public within the jurisdiction of such agency.

(b) JUDICIAL REVIEW

(1) In General - If any State is dissatisfied with the Secretary's final action with respect to the eligibility of the State under section 612, such State may, not later than 60 days after notice of such action, file with the United States court of appeals for the circuit in which such State is located a petition for review of that action. A copy of the petition shall be forthwith transmitted by the clerk of the court to the Secretary. The Secretary thereupon shall file in the court the record of the proceedings upon which the Secretary's action was based, as provided in section 2112 of title 28, United States Code.

➡ **VIRGINIA EXPELS STUDENTS, THEN SUES THE U. S. DEPARTMENT OF EDUCATION**

The U. S. Department of Education threatened to withhold funds from the Commonwealth of Virginia because of the state's expulsion and suspension policies for children with disabilities. Virginia filed suit against the U. S. Department of Education. The style of the case is *(Virginia) Department of Education v. Richard Riley, U. S. Secretary of Education.* In February, 1997, the Fourth Circuit ruled in favor of Virginia. In June, 1997, IDEA was amended and the effect of the Fourth Circuit's ruling was overturned.

(2) Jurisdiction - Review by United States Supreme Court - Upon the filing of such petition, the court shall have jurisdiction to affirm the action of the Secretary or to set it aside, in whole or in part. The judgment of the court shall be subject to review by the Supreme Court of the United States upon certiorari or certification as provided in section 1254 of title 28, United States Code.

(3) Standard of Review - The findings of fact by the Secretary, if supported by substantial evidence, shall be conclusive, but the court, for good cause shown, may remand the case to the Secretary to take further evidence, and the Secretary may thereupon make new or modified findings of fact and may modify the Secretary's previous action, and shall file in the court the record of the further proceedings. Such new or modified findings of fact shall likewise be conclusive if supported by substantial evidence.

(c) Divided State Agency Responsibility - For purposes of this section, where responsibility for ensuring that the requirements of this part are met with respect to children with disabilities who are convicted as adults under State law and incarcerated in adult prisons is assigned to a public agency other than the State educational agency pursuant to section 612(a)(11)(C), the Secretary, in instances where the Secretary finds that the failure to comply substantially with the provisions of this part are related to a failure by the public agency, shall take appropriate corrective action to ensure compliance with this part, except - -

(1) any reduction or withholding of payments to the State is proportionate to the total funds allotted under section 1411 to the State as the number of eligible children with disabilities in adult prisons under the supervision of the other public agency is proportionate to the number of eligible individuals with disabilities in the State under the supervision of the State educational agency; and

(2) any withholding of funds under paragraph (1) shall be limited to the specific agency responsible for the failure to comply

with this part.

20 U.S.C. §1417 - Administration

➡ **SECTION OVERVIEW**
This section discusses the responsibilities of the U. S. Department of Education.

(a) Responsibilities of Secretary - In carrying out this part, the Secretary shall

(1) cooperate with, and (directly or by grant or contract) furnish technical assistance necessary to, the State in matters relating to

(A) the education of children with disabilities; and

(B) carrying out this part; and

(2) provide short-term training programs and institutes.

(b) Rules and Regulations - In carrying out the provisions of this part, the Secretary shall issue regulations under this Act only to the extent that such regulations are necessary to ensure that there is compliance with the specific requirements of this Act.

(c) Confidentiality - The Secretary shall take appropriate action, in accordance with the provisions of section 444 of the General Education Provisions Act (20 U.S.C. 1232g), to assure the protection of the confidentiality of any personally identifiable data, information, and records collected or maintained by the Secretary and by State and local educational agencies pursuant to the provisions of this part.

(d) Personnel - The Secretary is authorized to hire qualified personnel necessary to carry out the Secretary's duties under subsection (a) and under sections 1418, 1461, and 1473 (or their predecessor authorities through October 1, 1997) without regard to the provisions of title 5, United States Code, relating to appointments in the competitive service and without regard to chapter 51 and subchapter III of chapter 53 of such title relating to classification and general schedule pay rates, except that no more than twenty such personnel shall be employed at any time.

20 U.S.C. §1418 - Program Information

➡ **SECTION OVERVIEW**

This section discusses the data that must be furnished to the U. S. Department of Education.

(a) IN GENERAL - Each State that receives assistance under this part, and the Secretary of the Interior, shall provide data each year to the Secretary - -

(1)(A) on -

(i) the number of children with disabilities, by race, ethnicity, and disability category, who are receiving a free appropriate public education;

(ii) the number of children with disabilities, by race and ethnicity, who are receiving early intervention services;

(iii) the number of children with disabilities, by race, ethnicity, and disability category, who are participating in regular education;

(iv) the number of children with disabilities, by race, ethnicity, and disability category, who are in separate classes, separate schools or facilities, or public or private residential facilities;

(v) the number of children with disabilities, by race, ethnicity, and disability category, who, for each year of age from age 14 to 21, stopped receiving special education and related services because of program completion or other reasons and the reasons why those children stopped receiving special education and related services;

(vi) the number of children with disabilities, by race and ethnicity, who, from birth through age 2, stopped receiving early intervention services because of program completion or for other reasons; and

(vii)

(I) the number of children with disabilities, by race, ethnicity, and disability category, who under subparagraphs (A)(ii) and (B) of section 615(k)(1), are removed to an interim alternative educational setting;

(II) the acts or items precipitating those removals; and

(III) the number of children with disabilities who are subject to long-term suspensions or expulsions; and

(B) on the number of infants and toddlers, by race and ethnicity, who are at risk of having substantial developmental delays (as described in section 1432), and who are receiving early intervention services under part C; and

(2) on any other information that may be required by the Secretary.

(b) SAMPLING - The Secretary may permit States and the Secretary of the Interior to obtain the data described in subsection (a) through sampling.

(c) DISPROPORTIONALITY -

(1) In General - Each State that receives assistance under this part, and the Secretary of the Interior, shall provide for the collection and examination of data to determine if significant disproportionality based on race is occurring in the State with respect to - -

(A) the identification of children as children with disabilities, including the identification of children as children with disabilities in accordance with a particular impairment described in section 1402(3); and

(B) the placement in particular educational settings of such children.

(2) Review and Revision of Policies, Practices, and Procedures - In the case of a determination of significant disproportionality with respect to the identification of children as children with disabilities, or the placement in particular educational settings of such children, in accordance with paragraph (1), the State or the Secretary of the Interior, as the case may be, shall provide for the review and, if appropriate, revision of the policies, procedures, and practices used in such identification or placement to ensure that such policies, procedures, and practices comply with the requirements of this Act.

20 U.S.C. §1419 - Preschool Grants

➡ **SECTION OVERVIEW**

This section discusses grants for children between two and five years of age.

(a) IN GENERAL - The Secretary shall provide grants under this section to assist States to provide special education and related services, in accordance with this part - -

(1) to children with disabilities aged 3 through 5, inclusive; and

(2) at the State's discretion, to 2-year-old children with disabilities who will turn 3 during the school year.

(b) ELIGIBILITY - A State shall be eligible for a grant under this section if such State -

(1) is eligible under section 1412 to receive a grant under this part; and

(2) makes a free appropriate public education available to all children with disabilities, aged 3 through 5, residing in the State.

(c) ALLOCATIONS TO STATES -

(1) In General - After reserving funds for studies and evaluations under section 1474(e), the Secretary shall allocate the remaining amount among the States in accordance with paragraph (2) or (3), as the case may be.

(2) Increase in Funds - If the amount available for allocations to States under paragraph (1) is equal to or greater than the amount allocated to the States under this section for the preceding fiscal year, those allocations shall be calculated as follows:

(A)

(i) Except as provided in subparagraph (B), the Secretary shall - -

(I) allocate to each State the amount it received for fiscal year 1997;

(II) allocate 85 percent of any remaining funds to States on the basis of their relative populations of children aged 3 through 5; and

(III) allocate 15 percent of those remaining funds to States on the basis of their relative populations of all children aged 3 through 5 who are living in poverty.

(ii) For the purpose of making grants under this paragraph, the Secretary shall use the most recent population data, including data on children living in poverty, that are available and satisfactory to the Secretary.

(B) Notwithstanding subparagraph (A), allocations under this paragraph shall be subject to the following:

(i) No State's allocation shall be less than its allocation for the preceding fiscal year.

(ii) No State's allocation shall be less than the greatest of - -

(I) the sum of -

(aa) the amount it received for fiscal year 1997; and

(bb) one third of one percent of the amount by which the amount appropriated under subsection (j) exceeds the amount appropriated under this section for fiscal year 1997;

(II) the sum of - -

(aa) the amount it received for the preceding fiscal year; and

(bb) that amount multiplied by the percentage by which the increase in the funds appropriated from the preceding fiscal year exceeds 1.5 percent; or

(III) the sum of - -

(aa) the amount it received for the preceding fiscal year; and

(bb) that amount multiplied by 90 percent of the percentage increase in the amount appropriated from the preceding fiscal year.

(iii) Notwithstanding clause (ii), no State's allocation under this paragraph shall exceed the sum of - -

(I) the amount it received for the preceding fiscal year; and

(II) that amount multiplied by the sum of 1.5 percent and the percentage increase in the amount appropriated.

(C) If the amount available for allocations under this paragraph is insufficient to pay those allocations in full, those allocations shall be ratably reduced, subject to subparagraph (B)(i).

(3) Decrease in Funds - If the amount available for allocations to States under paragraph (1) is less than the amount allocated to the States under this section for the preceding fiscal year, those allocations shall be calculated as follows:

(A) If the amount available for allocations is greater than the amount allocated to the States for fiscal year 1997, each State shall be allocated the sum of - -

(i) the amount it received for fiscal year 1997; and

(ii) an amount that bears the same relation to any remaining funds as the increase the State received for the preceding fiscal year over fiscal year 1997 bears to the total of all such increases for all States.

(B) If the amount available for allocations is equal to or less than the amount allocated to the States for fiscal year 1997, each State shall be allocated the amount it received for that year, ratably reduced, if necessary.

(4) Outlying Areas - The Secretary shall increase the fiscal year 1998 allotment of each outlying area under section 611 by at least the amount that that area received under this section for fiscal year 1997.

(d) RESERVATION FOR STATE ACTIVITIES -

(1) In General - Each State may retain not more than the amount described in paragraph (2) for administration and other State-level activities in accordance with subsections (e) and (f).

(2) Amount Described - For each fiscal year, the Secretary shall determine and report to the State educational agency an amount that is 25 percent of the amount the State received under this section for fiscal year 1997, cumulatively adjusted by the Secretary for each succeeding fiscal year by the lesser of - -

(A) the percentage increase, if any, from the preceding fiscal year in the State's allocation under this section; or

(B) the percentage increase, if any, from the preceding fiscal year in the Consumer Price Index For All Urban Consumers published by the Bureau of Labor Statistics of the Department of Labor.

(e) STATE ADMINISTRATION -

(1) In General - For the purpose of administering this section (including the coordination of activities under this part with, and providing technical assistance to, other programs that provide services to children with disabilities) a State may use not more than 20 percent of the maximum amount it may retain under subsection (d) for any fiscal year.

(2) Administration of Part C - Funds described in paragraph (1) may also be used for the administration of Part C of this Act, if the State educational agency is the lead agency for the State under that part.

(f) OTHER STATE LEVEL ACTIVITIES - Each State shall use any funds it retains under subsection (d) and does not use for administration under subsection (e) - -

(1) for support services (including establishing and implementing the mediation process required by section 615(e)), which may benefit children with disabilities younger than 3 or older than 5 as long as those services also benefit children with disabilities aged 3 through 5;

(2) for direct services for children eligible for services under this section;

(3) to develop a State improvement plan under subpart 1 of part D;

(4) for activities at the State and local levels to meet the performance goals established by the State under section 612(a)(16) and to support implementation of the State improvement plan under subpart 1 of part D if the State receives funds under that subpart; or

(5) to supplement other funds used to develop and implement a Statewide coordinated services system designed to improve results for children and families, including children with disabilities and their families, but not to exceed one percent of the amount received by the State under this section for a fiscal year.

(g) SUBGRANTS TO LOCAL EDUCATIONAL AGENCIES

(1) Subgrants Required - Each State that receives a grant under this section for any fiscal year shall distribute any of the grant funds that it does not reserve under subsection (d) to local educational agencies in the State that have established their eligibility under section 613, as follows:

(A) Base Payments - The State shall first award each agency described in paragraph (1) the amount that agency would have received under this section for fiscal year 1997 if the State had distributed 75 percent of its grant for that year under section 619(c)(3), as then in effect.

(B) Allocation of Remaining Funds - After making allocations under subparagraph (A), the State shall - -

(i) allocate 85 percent of any remaining funds to those agencies on the basis of the relative numbers of children enrolled in public and private elementary and secondary schools within the agency's jurisdiction; and

(ii) allocate 15 percent of those remaining funds to those agencies in accordance with their relative numbers of children living in poverty, as determined by the State educational agency.

(2) Reallocation of Funds - If a State educational agency determines that a local educational agency is adequately providing a free appropriate public education to all children with disabilities aged 3 through 5 residing in the area served by that agency with State and local funds, the State educational agency may reallocate any portion of the funds under this section that are not needed by that local agency to provide a free appropriate public education to other local educational agencies in the State that are not adequately providing special education and related services to all children with disabilities aged 3 through 5 residing in the areas they serve.

(h) **PART C INAPPLICABLE** - Part C of this Act does not apply to any child with a disability receiving a free appropriate public education, in accordance with this part, with funds received under this section.

(i) **DEFINITION** - For the purpose of this section, the term 'State' means each of the 50 States, the District of Columbia, and the Commonwealth of Puerto Rico.

(j) **AUTHORIZATION OF APPROPRIATIONS** - For the purpose of carrying out this section, there are authorized to be appropriated to the Secretary $500,000,000 for fiscal year 1998 and such sums as may be necessary for each subsequent fiscal year.

END OF PART B

Part C - Infants and Toddlers with Disabilities

➡ **OVERVIEW OF PART C**

Part C discusses special education services to infants and toddlers with disabilities.

20 U.S.C. §1431 - Findings and policy
20 U.S.C. §1432 - Definitions
20 U.S.C. §1433 - General authority
20 U.S.C. §1434 - Eligibility
20 U.S.C. §1435 - Requirements for statewide system
20 U.S.C. §1436 - Individualized family service plan
20 U.S.C. §1437 - State application and assurances
20 U.S.C. §1438 - Uses of funds
20 U.S.C. §1439 - Procedural safeguards
20 U.S.C. §1440 - Payor of last resort
20 U.S.C. §1441 - State Interagency Coordinating Council
20 U.S.C. §1442 - Federal administration
20 U.S.C. §1443 - Allocation of funds
20 U.S.C. §1444 - Federal Interagency Coordinating Council
20 U.S.C. §1445 - Authorization of appropriations

20 U.S.C. §1431 – Findings and Policy

➡ **SECTION OVERVIEW**

Section 1431 focuses on the need to provide early intervention services. When very young children receive appropriate early intervention services, many problems can be reduced or minimized. The law encourages states to provide early intervention services to children who are under age three.

(a) FINDINGS - The Congress finds that there is **an urgent and substantial need** -

(1) to **enhance the development** of infants and toddlers with disabilities and to **minimize** their potential for **developmental delay**;

(2) to reduce the educational costs to our society, including our Nation's schools, by **minimizing the need for special education** and related services **after infants and toddlers with disabilities reach school age**;

(3) to **minimize the likelihood of institutionalization** of individuals with disabilities and maximize the potential for their independently living in society;

(4) to enhance the capacity of families to meet the special needs of their infants and toddlers with disabilities; and

(5) to enhance the capacity of State and local agencies and service providers to identify, evaluate, and meet the needs of historically underrepresented populations, particularly minority, low-income, inner-city, and rural populations.

(b) POLICY - It is therefore the policy of the United States to provide financial assistance to States -

(1) to develop and implement a statewide, comprehensive, coordinated, multidisciplinary, interagency system that provides early intervention services for infants and toddlers with disabilities and their families;

(2) to facilitate the coordination of payment for early intervention services from Federal, State, local, and private sources (including public and private insurance coverage);

(3) to enhance their capacity to **provide quality early intervention services** and **expand and improve existing early intervention services** being provided to infants and toddlers with disabilities and their families; and

(4) to encourage States to expand opportunities for children under 3 years of age who would be at risk of having substantial developmental delay if they did not receive early intervention services.

20 U.S.C. §1432 - Definitions

➡ **SECTION OVERVIEW**

This section, much like 20 U.S.C. § 1401 in Part A, provides the critical definitions that are used in Part C of the statute.

As used in this part:

(1) AT-RISK INFANT OR TODDLER - The term 'at-risk infant or toddler' means an individual under 3 years of age who would be at risk of experiencing a substantial developmental delay if early intervention services were not provided to the individual.

(2) COUNCIL - The term 'council' means a State interagency coordinating council established under section 1441.

(3) DEVELOPMENTAL DELAY - The term 'developmental delay', when used with respect to an individual residing in a State, has the meaning given such term by the State under section 1435(a)(1).

(4) EARLY INTERVENTION SERVICES - The term 'early intervention services' means developmental services that -

(A) are provided under public supervision;

(B) are provided at no cost except where Federal or State law provides for a system of payments by families, including a schedule of sliding fees;

(C) are designed to meet the developmental needs of an infant or toddler with a disability in any one or more of the following areas -
    (i) physical development;
    (ii) cognitive development;
    (iii) communication development;
    (iv) social or emotional development; or
    (v) adaptive development;

➡ **SERVICES SHOULD ADDRESS CHILD'S NEEDS IN SEVERAL AREAS**

Early intervention services must be designed to meet the child's developmental needs in physical, cognitive, communication, social and emotional, and adaptive areas. Many school districts offer only school-based programs which are not "designed to meet the developmental needs of an infant or toddler with a disability." Early intervention services must be provided at no charge to the child's parents.

(D) meet the standards of the State in which they are provided, including the requirements of this part;

(E) include -
    (i) family training, counseling, and home visits;
    (ii) special instruction;
    (iii) speech-language pathology and audiology services;
    (iv) occupational therapy;
    (v) physical therapy;
    (vi) psychological services;
    (vii) service coordination services;
    (viii) medical services only for diagnostic or evaluation purposes;
    (ix) early identification, screening, and assessment services;

(x) health services necessary to enable the infant or toddler to benefit from the other early intervention services;

(xi) social work services;

(xii) vision services;

(xiii) assistive technology devices and assistive technology services; and

(xiv) transportation and related costs that are necessary to enable an infant or toddler and the infant's or toddler's family to receive another service described in this paragraph;

➡ RANGE OF SERVICES INCLUDED
Early intervention services include home visits, medical services when necessary for diagnostic or evaluation purposes, several types of therapy, and assistive technology services and devices.

(F) are provided by **qualified personnel**, including -

(i) special educators;

(ii) speech-language pathologists and audiologists;

(iii) occupational therapists;

(iv) physical therapists;

(v) psychologists;

(vi) social workers;

(vii) nurses;

(viii) nutritionists;

(ix) family therapists;

(x) orientation and mobility specialists; and

(xi) pediatricians and other physicians;

➡ SERVICES FROM QUALIFIED PERSONNEL, INCLUDING PHYSICIANS
The statute authorizes services from professional providers. One issue will be whether service providers are "qualified" or whether services are being provided by inadequately trained aides. The statute allows children to receive services from physicians if necessary for diagnostic and evaluation purposes.

(G) to the maximum extent appropriate, are provided in natural environments, including the home, and community settings in which children without disabilities participate; and

(H) are provided in conformity with an individualized family service plan adopted in accordance with Section 1436.

➡ INDIVIDUALIZED FAMILY SERVICE PLAN
The Individualized Family Service Plan (or IFSP) for the very young child is similar to the IEP discussed in 20 U.S.C. §1414.

(5) **INFANT OR TODDLER WITH A DISABILITY** - The term 'infant or toddler with a disability' -

(A) means an individual **under 3 years of age who needs early intervention services** because the individual -

(i) is experiencing developmental delays, as measured by appropriate diagnostic instruments and procedures in one or more of the areas of cognitive development, physical development, communication development, social or emotional development, and adaptive development; or

(ii) has a diagnosed physical or mental condition which has a high probability of resulting in developmental delay; and

(B) may also include, at a State's discretion, at-risk infants and toddlers.

➡ INFANT OR TODDLER WITH A DISABILITY V. "AT RISK INFANT OR TODDLER"
There is a legal distinction between these two terms. An "at-risk infant or toddler" is a child under 3 years of age who is at risk for a developmental delay without early intervention services. An "infant/toddler with a disability" is a child under 3 years of age who needs early intervention services because of developmental delays in one or more areas (cognitive development, physical development, communication development, social or emotional development, and adaptive development). If the child benefits from early intervention services, this

does not mean that the child becomes ineligible for these services. The child can continue to receive services as an "at risk infant or toddler."

20 U.S.C. §1433 – General Authority

➡ **SECTION OVERVIEW**
This section discusses authority of U. S. Department of Education.

The Secretary shall, in accordance with this part, make grants to States (from their allotments under section 1443) to assist each State to maintain and implement a statewide, comprehensive, coordinated, multidisciplinary, interagency system to provide early intervention services for infants and toddlers with disabilities and their families.

20 U.S.C. §1434 - Eligibility

➡ **SECTION OVERVIEW**
This Section discusses state eligibility for grants.

In order to be eligible for a grant under section 1433, a State shall demonstrate to the Secretary that the State -

(1) has adopted a policy that appropriate early intervention services are available to all infants and toddlers with disabilities in the State and their families, including Indian infants and toddlers with disabilities and their families residing on a reservation geographically located in the State; and

(2) has in effect a statewide system that meets the requirements of section 1435.

20 U.S.C. §1435 – Requirements for Statewide System

➡ **SECTION OVERVIEW**
This section describes the minimum requirements for early intervention programs and individualized family service plans.

(a) IN GENERAL - A statewide system described in section 1433 shall include, at a minimum, the following components:

(1) A definition of the term 'developmental delay' that will be used by the State in carrying out programs under this part.

(2) A State policy that is in effect and that **ensures that appropriate early intervention services are available to all infants and toddlers with disabilities and their families**, including Indian infants and toddlers and their families residing on a reservation geographically located in the State.

(3) A **timely, comprehensive, multidisciplinary evaluation** of the functioning of each infant or toddler with a disability in the State, and a family-directed identification of the needs of each family of such an infant or toddler, to appropriately assist in the development of the infant or toddler.

(4) For each infant or toddler with a disability in the State, an individualized family service plan in accordance with section 1436, including service coordination services in accordance with such service plan.

(5) A **comprehensive child find system**, consistent with part B, including a system for making referrals to service providers that includes timelines and provides for participation by primary referral sources.

➡ **CHILD FIND AND TIMELINES**
States must have a comprehensive Child Find system with clear timelines. If there is delay before a child receives services, the neurological "window of opportunity" to learn skills may begin to close. Later litigation and caselaw may rely on precedent interpreting 20 U.S.C. §1412(a)(3).

(6) A **public awareness program focusing on early identification** of infants and toddlers with disabilities, including the preparation and dissemination by the lead agency designated or established under paragraph (10) to all primary referral sources, especially hospitals and physicians, of information for parents on the availability of early intervention services, and procedures for determining the extent to which such sources disseminate such information to parents of infants and toddlers.

(7) A **central directory** which includes information on **early intervention services, resources, and experts** available in the State and **research and demonstration projects** being conducted in the State.

➡ **STATES MUST MAINTAIN A CENTRAL RESOURCE DIRECTORY**

Does your state have a central directory of early intervention services, resources, experts, and research and demonstration projects in your state? If you don't know, place a call to your state department of education and request a copy of the central resource directory. If your state does not publish a directory, request a copy when it is available.

If your state does not provide a directory, send a confirmation letter to the individual you spoke to, reiterating your understanding that the state does not provide a directory of early intervention services, resources, experts, and research and demonstration projects. Send a copy of your letter to the U.S. Department of Education for their files and subsequent monitoring of this issue.

(8) A **comprehensive system of personnel development**, including the training of paraprofessionals and the training of primary referral sources respecting the basic components of early intervention services available in the State, that is consistent with the comprehensive system of personnel development described in section 1412(a)(14) and **may** include -

(A) implementing innovative strategies and activities for the recruitment and retention of early education service providers;

(B) promoting the preparation of early intervention providers who are fully and appropriately qualified to provide early intervention services under this part;

(C) training personnel to work in rural and inner-city areas; and

(D) training personnel to coordinate transition services for infants and toddlers served under this part from an early intervention program under this part to preschool or other appropriate services.

(9) Subject to subsection (b), policies and procedures relating to the establishment and maintenance of standards to ensure that personnel necessary to carry out this part are appropriately and adequately prepared and trained, including -

(A) the establishment and maintenance of standards which are consistent with any State-approved or recognized certification, licensing, registration, or other comparable requirements which apply to the area in which such personnel are providing early intervention services; and

(B) to the extent such standards are not based on the highest requirements in the State applicable to a specific profession or discipline, the steps the State is taking to require the retraining or hiring of personnel that meet appropriate professional requirements in the State; except that nothing in this part, including this paragraph, prohibits the use of paraprofessionals and assistants who are appropriately trained and supervised, in accordance with State law, regulations, or written policy, to assist in the provision of early intervention services to infants and toddlers with disabilities under this part.

(10) A single line of responsibility in a lead agency designated or established by the Governor for carrying out-

(A) the general administration and supervision of programs and activities receiving assistance under section 1433, and the monitoring of programs and activities used by the State to carry out this part, whether or not such programs or activities are receiving assistance made available under section 1433, to ensure that the State complies with this part;

(B) the identification and coordination of all available resources within the State from Federal, State, local, and private sources;

(C) the assignment of financial responsibility in accordance with section 1437(a)(2) to the appropriate agencies; (D) the development of procedures to ensure that services are provided to infants and toddlers with disabilities and their families under this part in a timely manner pending the resolution of any disputes among public agencies or service providers;

(D) the development of procedures to ensure that services are provided to infants and toddlers with disabilities and their families under this part in a timely manner pending the resolution of any disputes among public agencies or service providers;

(E) the resolution of intra- and interagency disputes; and

(F) the entry into formal interagency agreements

➡ **PROCEDURES TO ENSURE SERVICES IN A TIMELY MANNER**
The preamble to this section says "the statewide system described in section 1433 shall include, at a minimum, the following components" and includes the "development of procedures."

(11) A policy pertaining to the contracting or making other arrangements with service providers to provide early intervention services in the State, consistent with the provisions of this part, including the contents of the application used and the conditions of the contract or other arrangements.

(12) A procedure for securing timely reimbursements of funds used under this part in accordance with section 1440(a).

(13) Procedural safeguards with respect to programs under this part, as required by section 1439.

➡ **PROCEDURAL SAFEGUARDS**
The statute has many procedural and legal similarities to 20 U.S.C. §1415 (Part B) about due process hearings.

(14) A system for compiling data requested by the Secretary under section 1418 that relates to this part.

(15) A State interagency coordinating council that meets the requirements of section 1441.

(16) Policies and procedures to ensure that, consistent with section 1436(d)(5) -

(A) to the maximum extent appropriate, early intervention services are provided in natural environments; and

(B) the provision of early intervention services for any infant or toddler occurs in a setting other than a natural environment only when early intervention cannot be achieved satisfactorily for the infant or toddler in a natural environment.

(b) Policy - In implementing subsection (a)(9), a State may adopt a policy that includes making ongoing good-faith efforts to recruit and hire appropriately and adequately trained personnel to provide early intervention services to infants and toddlers with disabilities, including, in a geographic area of the State where there is a shortage of such personnel, the most qualified individuals available who are making satisfactory progress toward completing applicable course work necessary to meet the standards described in subsection (a)(9), consistent with State law within 3 years.

20 U.S.C. §1436 – Individualized Family Service Plan

➡ **SECTION OVERVIEW**
There are clear legal requirements about Individualized Family Service Plans (IFSPs). The due process procedures are similar to the requirements about due process hearings in Sections 1414 and 1415 of Part B.

(a) Assessment and Program Development - A statewide system described in section 1433 shall provide, at a minimum, for each infant or toddler with a disability, and the infant's or toddler's family, to receive -

(1) a multidisciplinary assessment of the unique strengths and needs of the infant or toddler and the identification of services appropriate to meet such needs;

(2) a family-directed assessment of the resources, priorities, and concerns of the family and the identification of the supports and services necessary to enhance the family's capacity to meet the developmental needs of the infant or toddler; and

(3) a written individualized family service plan developed by a multidisciplinary team, including the parents, as required by subsection (e).

(b) PERIODIC REVIEW - The individualized family service plan shall be evaluated once a year and the family shall be provided a review of the plan at 6-month intervals (or more often where appropriate based on infant or toddler and family needs).

(c) PROMPTNESS AFTER ASSESSMENT - The individualized family service plan shall be developed within a reasonable time after the assessment required by subsection (a)(1) is completed. With the parents' consent, early intervention services may commence prior to the completion of the assessment.

(d) CONTENT OF PLAN - The individualized family service plan shall be in writing and contain -

(1) a statement of the infant's or toddler's **present levels** of physical development, cognitive development, communication development, social or emotional development, and adaptive **development, based on objective criteria**;

(2) a statement of the **family's resources, priorities, and concerns** relating to enhancing the development of the family's infant or toddler with a disability;

(3) a statement of the major **outcomes expected to be achieved** for the infant or toddler and the family, and the **criteria, procedures, and timelines** used to determine the **degree to which progress toward achieving the outcomes is being made** and whether modifications or revisions of the outcomes or services are necessary;

(4) a statement of specific early intervention **services necessary to meet the unique needs** of the infant or toddler and the family, including the **frequency, intensity, and method** of delivering services;

(5) a **statement of the natural environments** in which early intervention services shall appropriately be provided, including a **justification** of the extent, if any, to **which the services will not be provided in a natural environment**;

(6) the projected dates for initiation of services and the anticipated duration of the services;

(7) the identification of the service coordinator from the profession most immediately relevant to the infant's or toddler's or family's needs (or who is otherwise qualified to carry out all applicable responsibilities under this part) A statewide system described in section 1433 shall include, at a minimum, the following components for the implementation of the plan and coordination with other agencies and persons; and

(8) the steps to be taken to support the transition of the toddler with a disability to preschool or other appropriate services.

(e) PARENTAL CONSENT - The contents of the individualized family service plan shall be fully explained to the parents and informed written consent from the parents shall be obtained prior to the provision of early intervention services described in such plan. If the parents do not provide consent with respect to a particular early intervention service, then the early intervention services to which consent is obtained shall be provided.

20 U.S.C. §1437 – State Applications and Assurances

➡ **SECTION OVERVIEW**

State grant applications must provide specific information about early intervention services for infants and toddlers and their families.

(a) APPLICATION - A State desiring to receive a grant under section 1433 shall submit an application to the Secretary at such time and in such manner as the Secretary may reasonably require. The application shall contain -

(1) a designation of the lead agency in the State that will be responsible for the administration of funds provided under section 1433;

(2) a designation of an individual or entity responsible for assigning financial responsibility among appropriate agencies;

(3) information demonstrating eligibility of the State under section 1434, including -
(A) information demonstrating to the Secretary's satisfaction that the State has in effect the statewide system required by section 1433; and
(B) a description of services to be provided to infants and toddlers with disabilities and their families through the system;

(4) if the State provides services to at-risk infants and toddlers through the system, a description of such services;

(5) a description of the uses for which funds will be expended in accordance with this part;

(6) a description of the procedure used to ensure that resources are made available under this part for all geographic areas within the State;

(7) a description of State policies and procedures that ensure that, prior to the adoption by the State of any other policy or procedure necessary to meet the requirements of this part, there are public hearings, adequate notice of the hearings, and an opportunity for comment available to the general public, including individuals with disabilities and parents of infants and toddlers with disabilities;

(8) a description of the policies and procedures to be used -
(A) to **ensure a smooth transition for toddlers receiving early intervention services under this part to preschool or other appropriate services**, including a description of how -
(i) the families of such toddlers will be included in the transition plans required by subparagraph (C); and
(ii) the lead agency designated or established under section 1435(a)(10) will -
(I) notify the local educational agency for the area in which such a child resides that the child will shortly reach the age of eligibility for preschool services under part B, as determined in accordance with State law;
(II) in the case of a child who may be eligible for such preschool services, with the approval of the family of the child, convene a conference among the lead agency, the family, and the local educational agency **at least 90 days** (and at the discretion of all such parties, up to 6 months) **before the child is eligible for the preschool services**, to discuss any such services that the child may receive; and

➡ **CONFERENCE REQUIRED AT LEAST 90 DAYS BEFORE PRESCHOOL ELIGIBILITY**
At least 90 days before a child is eligible for preschool services, a conference must be convened to discuss services that the child may (not shall) receive. This is very precise language that may be overlooked by the lead agency. Procedural defaults by agencies may open doors to other services and reimbursement, if the child is damaged, or at risk for being damaged by the delay. If the parent has rights and sits on them, the parent cannot later expect a court to grant relief.

(III) in the case of a child who may not be eligible for such preschool services, with the approval of the family, make reasonable efforts to convene a conference among the lead agency, the family, and providers of other appropriate services for children who are not eligible for preschool services under part B, to discuss the appropriate services that the child may receive;
(B) to review the child's program options for the period from the child's third birthday through the remainder of the school year; and
(C) to establish a transition plan; and

(9) such other information and assurances as the Secretary may reasonably require.

(b) ASSURANCES - The application described in subsection (a) -

(1) shall provide satisfactory assurance that Federal funds made available under section 1443 to the State will be expended in accordance with this part;

(2) shall contain an assurance that the State will comply with the requirements of section 1440;

(3) shall provide satisfactory assurance that the control of funds provided under section 1443, and title to property derived from those funds, will be in a public agency for the uses and purposes provided in this part and that a public agency will administer such funds and property;

(4) shall provide for -
(A) making such reports in such form and containing such information as the Secretary may require to carry out the Secretary's functions under this part; and
(B) keeping such records and affording such access to them as the Secretary may find necessary to ensure the correctness and verification of those reports and proper disbursement of Federal funds under this part;

(5) provide satisfactory assurance that Federal funds made available under section 1443 to the State -
(A) will not be commingled with State funds; and
(B) will be used so as **to supplement the level** of State and local funds expended for infants and toddlers with disabilities and their families **and in no case to supplant** those State and local funds;

(6) shall provide satisfactory assurance that such fiscal control and fund accounting procedures will be adopted as may be necessary to ensure proper disbursement of, and accounting for, Federal funds paid under section 1443 to the State;

(7) shall provide satisfactory assurance that policies and procedures have been adopted to ensure meaningful involvement of underserved groups, including minority, low-income, and rural families, in the planning and implementation of all the requirements of this part; and

(8) shall contain such other information and assurances as the Secretary may reasonably require by regulation.

(c) STANDARD FOR DISAPPROVAL OF APPLICATION - The Secretary may not disapprove such an application unless the Secretary determines, after notice and opportunity for a hearing, that the application fails to comply with the requirements of this section.

➡ **WHEN STATES BALK**
See the discussion in 20 U.S.C. § 1416 and reference to the Virginia case, *Department of Education v. Richard Riley, U. S. Secretary of Education,* and ruling by the U. S. Court of Appeals for the Fourth Circuit.

(d) SUBSEQUENT STATE APPLICATION - If a State has on file with the Secretary a policy, procedure, or assurance that demonstrates that the State meets a requirement of this section, including any policy or procedure filed under part H (as in effect before July 1, 1998), the Secretary shall consider the State to have met the requirement for purposes of receiving a grant under this part.

(e) MODIFICATION OF APPLICATION - An application submitted by a State in accordance with this section shall remain in effect until the State submits to the Secretary such modifications as the State determines necessary. This section shall apply to a modification of an application to the same extent and in the same manner as this section applies to the original application.

(f) MODIFICATIONS REQUIRED BY THE SECRETARY - The Secretary may require a State to modify its application under this section, but only to the extent necessary to ensure the State's compliance with this part, if -

(1) an amendment is made to this Act, or a Federal regulation issued under this Act;

(2) a new interpretation of this Act is made by a Federal court or the State's highest court; or

(3) an official finding of noncompliance with Federal law or regulations is made with respect to the State.

20 U.S.C. §1438 – Uses of Funds

➡ **SECTION OVERVIEW**

This section explains the use of funds by the states which may include direct services to children with disabilities.

In addition to using funds provided under section 1433 to maintain and implement the statewide system required by such section, **a State may use such funds** -

(1) **for direct early intervention services** for infants and toddlers with disabilities, and their families, under this part that are not otherwise funded through other public or private sources;

(2) to **expand and improve on** services for infants and toddlers and their families under this part that are otherwise available;

(3) to provide a free appropriate public education, in accordance with part B, to children with disabilities from their third birthday to the beginning of the following school year; and

(4) in any State that does not provide services for at-risk infants and toddlers under section 1437(a)(4), to strengthen the statewide system by initiating, expanding, or improving collaborative efforts related to at-risk infants and toddlers, including establishing linkages with appropriate public or private community-based organizations, services, and personnel for the purposes of -

(A) Identifying and evaluating at-risk infants and toddlers;

(B) making referrals of the infants and toddlers identified and evaluated under subparagraph (A); and

(C) conducting periodic follow-up on each such referral to determine if the status of the infant or toddler involved has changed with respect to the eligibility of the infant or toddler for services under this part.

20 U.S.C. §1439 – Procedural Safeguards

➡ **SECTION OVERVIEW**

The wording, protections and rights in this section are similar to the Section 1415. Caselaw that has developed under Section 1415 will be used in these disputes. Parents should assume that they must exhaust administrative remedies before initiating any court action, despite silence in this Section in that regard. Assume that the usual five-day rule relating to Section 1415 applies.

If you arrive at a traffic intersection and the light displays both red and green, do you ignore the red light and drive though the intersection? Do you stop, then proceed cautiously? In all areas of law, statutes often appear to conflict with each other. You should obey both and proceed with caution.

(a) MINIMUM PROCEDURES - The procedural safeguards required to be included in a statewide system under section 1435(a)(13) shall provide, at a minimum, the following:

(1) The timely administrative resolution of complaints by parents. Any party aggrieved by the findings and decision regarding an administrative complaint shall have the right to bring a civil action with respect to the complaint in any State court of competent jurisdiction or in a district court of the United States without regard to the amount in controversy. In any action brought under this paragraph, the court shall receive the records of the administrative proceedings, shall hear additional

evidence at the request of a party, and, basing its decision on the preponderance of the evidence, shall grant such relief as the court determines is appropriate.

(2) The right to confidentiality of personally identifiable information, including the right of parents to written notice of and written consent to the exchange of such information among agencies consistent with Federal and State law.

(3) The **right of the parents** to determine whether they, their infant or toddler, or other family members **will accept or decline any early intervention service** under this part in accordance with State law **without jeopardizing other early intervention services** under this part.

(4) The opportunity for **parents to examine records relating to assessment, screening, eligibility determinations, and** the **development and implementation of the individualized family service plan.**

(5) Procedures to **protect the rights of the infant or toddler whenever the parents** of the infant or toddler **are not known or cannot be found** or the infant or toddler is a ward of the State, including the assignment of an individual (who shall not be an employee of the State lead agency, or other State agency, and who shall not be any person, or any employee of a person, providing early intervention services to the infant or toddler or any family member of the infant or toddler) to act as a surrogate for the parents.

(6) **Written prior notice to the parents** of the infant or toddler with a disability whenever the State agency or service provider **proposes to initiate or change or refuses to initiate or change the identification, evaluation, or placement** of the infant or toddler with a disability, or the provision of appropriate early intervention services to the infant or toddler.

(7) Procedures designed to ensure that the notice required by paragraph (6) fully informs the parents, in the parents' native language, unless it clearly is not feasible to do so, of all procedures available pursuant to this section.

(8) The **right of parents to use mediation** in accordance with section 1415(e), except that -
   (A) any reference in the section to **a State educational agency shall be considered to be a reference to a State's lead agency established or designated under section 1435(a)(10);**
   (B) any reference in the section to a local educational agency shall be considered to be a reference to a local service provider or the State's lead agency under this part, as the case may be; and
   (C) any reference in the section to the provision of free appropriate public education to children with disabilities shall be considered to be a reference to the provision of appropriate early intervention services to infants and toddlers with disabilities.

(b) SERVICES DURING PENDENCY OF PROCEEDINGS - During the pendency of any proceeding or action involving a complaint by the parents of an infant or toddler with a disability, unless the State agency and the parents otherwise agree, the **infant or toddler shall continue to receive the appropriate early intervention services currently being provided** or, if applying for initial services, shall receive the services not in dispute.

20 U.S.C. §1440 – Payor of Last Resort

> ➡ **SECTION OVERVIEW**
> Parents cannot be required to use the child's health insurance benefits to pay for a free appropriate public education.

(a) NONSUBSTITUTION - Funds provided under section 1443 may not be used to satisfy a financial commitment for services that would have been paid for from another public or private source, including any medical program administered by the Secretary of Defense, but for the enactment of this part, except that whenever considered necessary to prevent a delay in the receipt of appropriate early intervention services by an infant, toddler, or family in a timely fashion, funds provided under section 1443 may be used to pay the provider of services pending reimbursement from the agency that has ultimate responsibility for the payment.

(b) REDUCTION OF OTHER BENEFITS - Nothing in this part shall be construed to permit the State to reduce medical or other assistance available or to alter eligibility under title V of the Social Security Act (relating to maternal and child health) or title XIX of the Social Security Act (relating to Medicaid for infants or toddlers with disabilities) within the State.

20 U.S.C. §1441 – State Interagency Coordinating Council

➡ **SECTION OVERVIEW**
This section is similar to 20 U.S.C. §1412(21) and requires an interagency coordinating council to coordinate early intervention efforts.

(a) ESTABLISHMENT -

(1) In General - A State that desires to receive financial assistance under this part shall establish a State interagency coordinating council.

(2) Appointment - The council shall be appointed by the Governor. In making appointments to the council, the Governor shall ensure that the membership of the council reasonably represents the population of the State.

(3) Chairperson - The Governor shall designate a member of the council to serve as the chairperson of the council, or shall require the council to so designate such a member. Any member of the council who is a representative of the lead agency designated under section 1435(a)(10) may not serve as the chairperson of the council.

(b) COMPOSITION -

(1) In General - The council shall be composed as follows:
(A) Parents - At least 20 percent of the members shall be parents of infants or toddlers with disabilities or children with disabilities aged 12 or younger, with knowledge of, or experience with, programs for infants and toddlers with disabilities. At least one such member shall be a parent of an infant or toddler with a disability or a child with a disability aged 6 or younger.
(B) Service Providers - At least 20 percent of the members shall be public or private providers of early intervention services.
(C) State Legislature - At least one member shall be from the State legislature.
(D) Personnel Preparation - At least one member shall be involved in personnel preparation.
(E) Agency for Early Intervention Services - At least one member shall be from each of the State agencies involved in the provision of, or payment for, early intervention services to infants and toddlers with disabilities and their families and shall have sufficient authority to engage in policy planning and implementation on behalf of such agencies.
(F) Agency for Preschool Services - At least one member shall be from the State educational agency responsible for preschool services to children with disabilities and shall have sufficient authority to engage in policy planning and implementation on behalf of such agency.
(G) Agency for Health Insurance - At least one member shall be from the agency responsible for the State governance of health insurance.
(H) Head Start Agency - At least one representative from a Head Start agency or program in the State.
(I) Child Care Agency - At least one representative from a State agency responsible for child care.

(2) Other Members - The council may include other members selected by the Governor, including a representative from the Bureau of Indian Affairs, or where there is no BIA-operated or BIA-funded school, from the Indian Health Service or the tribe or tribal council.

(c) MEETINGS - The council shall meet at least quarterly and in such places as it deems necessary. The meetings shall be publicly announced, and, to the extent appropriate, open and accessible to the general public.

(d) MANAGEMENT AUTHORITY - Subject to the approval of the Governor, the council may prepare and approve a budget using funds under this part to conduct hearings and forums, to reimburse members of the council for reasonable and necessary expenses for attending council meetings and performing council duties (including child care for parent representatives), to pay compensation to a member of the council if the member is not employed or must forfeit wages from other employment when performing official council business, to hire staff, and to obtain the services of such professional, technical, and clerical personnel as may be necessary to carry out its functions under this part.

(e) FUNCTIONS OF COUNCIL -

   (1) Duties - The council shall -
   (A) advise and assist the lead agency designated or established under section 1435(a)(10) in the performance of the responsibilities set forth in such section, particularly the identification of the sources of fiscal and other support for services for early intervention programs, assignment of financial responsibility to the appropriate agency, and the promotion of the interagency agreements;
   (B) advise and assist the lead agency in the preparation of applications and amendments thereto;
   (C) advise and assist the State educational agency regarding the transition of toddlers with disabilities to preschool and other appropriate services; and
   (D) prepare and submit an annual report to the Governor and to the Secretary on the status of early intervention programs for infants and toddlers with disabilities and their families operated within the State.

   (2) Authorized Activity - The council may advise and assist the lead agency and the State educational agency regarding the provision of appropriate services for children from birth through age 5. The council may advise appropriate agencies in the State with respect to the integration of services for infants and toddlers with disabilities and at-risk infants and toddlers and their families, regardless of whether at-risk infants and toddlers are eligible for early intervention services in the State.

(f) CONFLICT OF INTEREST - No member of the council shall cast a vote on any matter that would provide direct financial benefit to that member or otherwise give the appearance of a conflict of interest under State law.

20 U.S.C. §1442 – Federal Administration
   ➡ **SECTION OVERVIEW**
      Much of the language in Part B applies to this section. If the "lead agency" in your state is not the State Education Agency (SEA), as in Part B, then the requirements shall apply to the State and local mental health, social service, early intervention, health department, or other such agency appointed as the "lead agency."

Sections 1416, 1417, and 1418 shall, to the extent not inconsistent with this part, apply to the program authorized by this part, except that -

(1) any reference in such sections to a State educational agency shall be considered to be a reference to a State's lead agency established or designated under section 1435(a)(10);

(2) any reference in such sections to a local educational agency, educational service agency, or a State agency shall be considered to be a reference to an early intervention service provider under this part; and

(3) any reference to the education of children with disabilities or the education of all children with disabilities shall be considered to be a reference to the provision of appropriate early intervention services to infants and toddlers with disabilities.

20 U.S.C. §1443 – Allocation of Funds

➡ **SECTION OVERVIEW**

This section provides the formulas and percentages related to the allocation and distribution of funds.

(a) RESERVATION OF FUNDS FOR OUTLYING AREAS -

(1) In General - From the sums appropriated to carry out this part for any fiscal year, the Secretary may reserve up to one percent for payments to Guam, American Samoa, the Virgin Islands, and the Commonwealth of the Northern Mariana Islands in accordance with their respective needs.

(2) Consolidation of Funds - The provisions of Public Law 95-134, permitting the consolidation of grants to the outlying areas, shall not apply to funds those areas receive under this part.

(b) PAYMENTS TO INDIANS -

(1) In General - The Secretary shall, subject to this subsection, make payments to the Secretary of the Interior to be distributed to tribes, tribal organizations (as defined under section 4 of the Indian Self-Determination and Education Assistance Act), or consortia of the above entities for the coordination of assistance in the provision of early intervention services by the States to infants and toddlers with disabilities and their families on reservations served by elementary and secondary schools for Indian children operated or funded by the Department of the Interior. The amount of such payment for any fiscal year shall be 1.25 percent of the aggregate of the amount available to all States under this part for such fiscal year.

(2) Allocation - For each fiscal year, the Secretary of the Interior shall distribute the entire payment received under paragraph (1) by providing to each tribe, tribal organization, or consortium an amount based on the number of infants and toddlers residing on the reservation, as determined annually, divided by the total of such children served by all tribes, tribal organizations, or consortia.

(3) Information - To receive a payment under this subsection, the tribe, tribal organization, or consortium shall submit such information to the Secretary of the Interior as is needed to determine the amounts to be distributed under paragraph (2).

(4) Use of Funds - The funds received by a tribe, tribal organization, or consortium shall be used to assist States in child find, screening, and other procedures for the early identification of Indian children under 3 years of age and for parent training. Such funds may also be used to provide early intervention services in accordance with this part. Such activities may be carried out directly or through contracts or cooperative agreements with the BIA, local educational agencies, and other public or private nonprofit organizations. The tribe, tribal organization, or consortium is encouraged to involve Indian parents in the development and implementation of these activities. The above entities shall, as appropriate, make referrals to local, State, or Federal entities for the provision of services or further diagnosis.

(5) Reports - To be eligible to receive a grant under paragraph (2), a tribe, tribal organization, or consortium shall make a biennial report to the Secretary of the Interior of activities undertaken under this subsection, including the number of contracts and cooperative agreements entered into, the number of children contacted and receiving services for each year, and the estimated number of children needing services during the 2 years following the year in which the report is made. The Secretary of the Interior shall include a summary of this information on a biennial basis to the Secretary of Education along with such other information as required under section 1411(i)(3)(E). The Secretary of Education may require any additional information from the Secretary of the Interior.

(6) Prohibited Uses of Funds - None of the funds under this subsection may be used by the Secretary of the Interior for administrative purposes, including child count, and the provision of technical assistance.

(c) STATE ALLOTMENTS -

(1) In General - Except as provided in paragraphs (2), (3), and (4), from the funds remaining for each fiscal year after the reservation and payments under subsections (a) and (b), the Secretary shall first allot to each State an amount that bears the same ratio to the amount of such remainder as the number of infants and toddlers in the State bears to the number of infants and toddlers in all States.

(2) Minimum Allotments - Except as provided in paragraphs (3) and (4), no State shall receive an amount under this section for any fiscal year that is less than the greatest of -
  (A) one-half of one percent of the remaining amount described in paragraph (1); or
  (B) $500,000.

(3) Special Rule for 1998 and 1999-
  (A) In General - Except as provided in paragraph (4), no State may receive an amount under this section for either fiscal year 1998 or 1999 that is less than the sum of the amounts such State received for fiscal year 1994 under (i) part H (as in effect for such fiscal year); and (ii) subpart 2 of part D of chapter 1 of title I of the Elementary and Secondary Education Act of 1965 (as in effect on the day before the date of the enactment of the Improving America's Schools Act of 1994) for children with disabilities under 3 years of age.
  (B) Exception - If, for fiscal year 1998 or 1999, the number of infants and toddlers in a State, as determined under paragraph (1), is less than the number of infants and toddlers so determined for fiscal year 1994, the amount determined under subparagraph (A) for the State shall be reduced by the same percentage by which the number of such infants and toddlers so declined.

(4) Ratable Reduction -
  (A) In General - If the sums made available under this part for any fiscal year are insufficient to pay the full amounts that all States are eligible to receive under this subsection for such year, the Secretary shall ratably reduce the allotments to such States for such year.
  (B) Additional Funds - If additional funds become available for making payments under this subsection for a fiscal year, allotments that were reduced under subparagraph (A) shall be increased on the same basis they were reduced.

(5) Definitions - For the purpose of this subsection -
  (A) the terms 'infants' and 'toddlers' mean children under 3 years of age; and
  (B) the term 'State' means each of the 50 States, the District of Columbia, and the Commonwealth of Puerto Rico.

(d) REALLOTMENT OF FUNDS - If a State elects not to receive its allotment under subsection (c), the Secretary shall reallot, among the remaining States, amounts from such State in accordance with such subsection.

20 U.S.C. §1444 – Federal Interagency Coordinating Council
➡ **SECTION OVERVIEW**
This section discusses the Federal Interagency Coordinating Council which should minimize duplication of programs and ensure that programs and policies are coordinated.

(a) ESTABLISHMENT AND PURPOSE -

(1) In General - The Secretary shall establish a Federal Interagency Coordinating Council in order to -
  (A) minimize duplication of programs and activities across Federal, State, and local agencies, relating to -
    (i) early intervention services for infants and toddlers with disabilities (including at-risk infants and toddlers) and their families; and
    (ii) preschool or other appropriate services for children with disabilities;
  (B) ensure the effective coordination of Federal early intervention and preschool programs and policies across Federal agencies;

(C) coordinate the provision of Federal technical assistance and support activities to States;

(D) identify gaps in Federal agency programs and services; and

(E) identify barriers to Federal interagency cooperation.

(2) Appointments - The council established under paragraph (1) (hereafter in this section referred to as the Council') and the chairperson of the Council shall be appointed by the Secretary in consultation with other appropriate Federal agencies. In making the appointments, the Secretary shall ensure that each member has sufficient authority to engage in policy planning and implementation on behalf of the department, agency, or program that the member represents.

(b) COMPOSITION - The Council shall be composed of -

(1) a representative of the Office of Special Education Programs;

(2) a representative of the National Institute on Disability and Rehabilitation Research and a representative of the Office of Educational Research and Improvement;

(3) a representative of the Maternal and Child Health Services Block Grant Program;

(4) a representative of programs administered under the Developmental Disabilities Assistance and Bill of Rights Act;

(5) a representative of the Health Care Financing Administration;

(6) a representative of the Division of Birth Defects and Developmental Disabilities of the Centers for Disease Control;

(7) a representative of the Social Security Administration;

(8) a representative of the special supplemental nutrition program for women, infants, and children of the Department of Agriculture;

(9) a representative of the National Institute of Mental Health;

(10) a representative of the National Institute of Child Health and Human Development;

(11) a representative of the Bureau of Indian Affairs of the Department of the Interior;

(12) a representative of the Indian Health Service;

(13) a representative of the Surgeon General;

(14) a representative of the Department of Defense;

(15) a representative of the Children's Bureau, and a representative of the Head Start Bureau, of the Administration for Children and Families;

(16) a representative of the Substance Abuse and Mental Health Services Administration;

(17) a representative of the Pediatric AIDS Health Care Demonstration Program in the Public Health Service;

(18) parents of children with disabilities age 12 or under (who shall constitute at least 20 percent of the members of the Council), of whom at least one must have a child with a disability under the age of 6;

(19) at least two representatives of State lead agencies for early intervention services to infants and toddlers, one of whom must be a representative of a State educational agency and the other a representative of a non-educational agency;

(20) other members representing appropriate agencies involved in the provision of, or payment for, early intervention services and special education and related services to infants and toddlers with disabilities and their families and preschool children with disabilities; and

(21) other persons appointed by the Secretary.

(c) MEETINGS - The Council shall meet at least quarterly and in such places as the Council deems necessary. The meetings shall be publicly announced, and, to the extent appropriate, open and accessible to the general public.

(d) FUNCTIONS OF THE COUNCIL - The Council shall -

(1) advise and assist the Secretary of Education, the Secretary of Health and Human Services, the Secretary of Defense, the Secretary of the Interior, the Secretary of Agriculture, and the Commissioner of Social Security in the performance of their responsibilities related to serving children from birth through age 5 who are eligible for services under this part or under part B;

(2) conduct policy analyses of Federal programs related to the provision of early intervention services and special educational and related services to infants and toddlers with disabilities and their families, and preschool children with disabilities, in order to determine areas of conflict, overlap, duplication, or inappropriate omission;

(3) identify strategies to address issues described in paragraph (2);

(4) develop and recommend joint policy memoranda concerning effective interagency collaboration, including modifications to regulations, and the elimination of barriers to interagency programs and activities;

(5) coordinate technical assistance and disseminate information on best practices, effective program coordination strategies, and recommendations for improved early intervention programming for infants and toddlers with disabilities and their families and preschool children with disabilities; and

(6) facilitate activities in support of States' interagency coordination efforts.

(e) CONFLICT OF INTEREST - No member of the Council shall cast a vote on any matter that would provide direct financial benefit to that member or otherwise give the appearance of a conflict of interest under Federal law.

(f) FEDERAL ADVISORY COMMITTEE ACT - The Federal Advisory Committee Act (5 U.S.C. App.) shall not apply to the establishment or operation of the Council.

20 U.S.C. §1445 – Authorization of Appropriations

For the purpose of carrying out this part, there are authorized to be appropriated $400,000,000 for fiscal year 1998 and such sums as may be necessary for each of the fiscal years 1999 through 2002.

END OF PART C

Part D - National Activities to Improve Education of Children with Disabilities

➡ **OVERVIEW OF PART D**

Part D organizes and funds activities to improve the education of children with disabilities. Part D includes two subparts, with two chapters under subpart two. **Subpart 1** includes Congressional findings and purpose, eligibility and collaboration, funds, grants, and appropriations. **Subpart 2** includes Section 1461 about administration of a plan to enhance education, related services, transition, and early intervention services to children with disabilities. **Chapter One of Subpart 2** (Sections 1471 to 1474) discusses the need to improve results by using research and personnel preparation. **Chapter Two of Subpart 2** (Sections 1481 - 1487) is about improving results by technical assistance, support, and dissemination of information.

Subpart 1 – State Program Improvement Grants for Children with Disabilities

20 U.S.C. §1451 - Congressional Findings and Purpose

20 U.S.C. §1452 - Eligibility and Collaborative Process

20 U.S.C. §1453 - Applications

20 U.S.C. §1454 - Use of Funds

20 U.S.C. §1455 - Minimum State Grant Amounts

20 U.S.C. §1456 - Authorization of Appropriations

Subpart 2 – Coordinated Research, Personnel Preparation, Technical Assistance, Support, and Dissemination of Information

20 U.S.C. §1461 – Administrative Provisions

Chapter One – Improving Early Intervention, Educational, and Transitional Services and Results for Children through Coordinated Research and Personnel Preparation

20 U.S.C. §1471 - Findings and Purpose

20 U.S.C. §1472 - Research and Innovation to Improve Services & Results for Children with Disabilities

20 U.S.C. §1473 - Personnel Preparation to Improve Services & Results for Children with Disabilities

20 U.S.C. §1474 - Studies and Evaluations

Chapter Two - Improving Early Intervention, Educational, and Transitional Services and Results for Children with Disabilities through Coordinated Technical Assistance, Support, and Dissemination of Information

20 U.S.C. §1481 - Congressional Findings and Purposes

20 U.S.C. §1482 - Parent Training and Information Centers

20 U.S.C. §1483 - Community Parent Resource Centers

20 U.S.C. §1484 - Technical Assistance for Parent Training and Information Centers

20 U.S.C. §1485 - Coordinated Technical Assistance and Dissemination

20 U.S.C. §1486 - Authorization of Appropriations

20 U.S.C. §1487 - Technology Development, Demonstration, and Utilization, and Media Services

Subpart 1 - State Program Improvement Grants for Children with Disabilities

20 U.S.C. §1451 – Findings and Purpose

➡ **SECTION OVERVIEW**

This section mirrors and tracks Findings and Purposes in Section 1400. Research-based practices have not been used, should be used, and special education outcomes must improve.

(a) **FINDINGS** - The Congress finds the following:

(1) States are responding with some success to multiple pressures to improve educational and transitional services and results for children with disabilities in response to growing demands imposed by ever-changing factors, such as demographics, social policies, and labor and economic markets.

(2) In order for States to address such demands and to facilitate lasting systemic change that is of benefit to all students, including children with disabilities, States must involve local educational agencies, parents, individuals with disabilities and

their families, teachers and other service providers, and other interested individuals and organizations in carrying out comprehensive strategies to improve educational results for children with disabilities.

(3) Targeted Federal financial resources are needed to assist States, working in partnership with others, to identify and make needed changes to address the needs of children with disabilities into the next century.

(4) State educational agencies, in partnership with local educational agencies and other individuals and organizations, are in the best position to identify and design ways to meet emerging and expanding demands to improve education for children with disabilities and to address their special needs.

(5) Research, demonstration, and practice over the past 20 years in special education and related disciplines have built a foundation of knowledge on which State and local systemic-change activities can now be based.

➡ SPECIAL EDUCATION SHOULD BE BASED ON RESEARCH

In many school districts, the methods used to teach children with disabilities are not based on research. For 20 years, The National Institutes of Health sponsored research at several universities. This research shows how children learn to read, why many children don't learn to read, and how children with language learning problems need to be taught. (See extensive comments in Section 1400.) The issues and concerns raised by Congress in this section are directly related to the concerns in Section 1400. Early intervention is one key to successfully educating children with disabilities.

(6) Such research, demonstration, and practice in special education and related disciplines have demonstrated that an effective educational system now and in the future must -

(A) maintain high academic standards and clear performance goals for children with disabilities, consistent with the standards and expectations for all students in the educational system, and provide for appropriate and effective strategies and methods to ensure that students who are children with disabilities have maximum opportunities to achieve those standards and goals;

(B) create a system that fully addresses the needs of all students, including children with disabilities, by addressing the needs of children with disabilities in carrying out educational reform activities;

(C) clearly define, in measurable terms, the school and post-school results that children with disabilities are expected to achieve;

(D) promote service integration, and the coordination of State and local education, social, health, mental health, and other services, in addressing the full range of student needs, particularly the needs of children with disabilities who require significant levels of support to maximize their participation and learning in school and the community;

➡ AGENCIES MUST COOPERATE AND COORDINATE

Turf battles and lack of communication between agencies often result in children not receiving services. Another obstacle to providing effective educational services is the failure to coordinate services between individuals and agencies in the public and private sectors.

(E) ensure that children with disabilities are provided assistance and support in making transitions as described in section 1474(b)(3)(C);

(F) promote comprehensive programs of professional development to ensure that the persons responsible for the education or a transition of children with disabilities possess the skills and knowledge necessary to address the educational and related needs of those children;

(G) disseminate to teachers and other personnel serving children with disabilities research-based knowledge about successful teaching practices and models and provide technical assistance to local educational agencies and schools on how to improve results for children with disabilities;

➡ TEACHERS NEED ACCURATE INFORMATION ABOUT EFFECTIVE PRACTICES

Although information about "effective practices" is available, many school districts do not use researched-based teaching practices. States are not providing local districts with the information they need to make informed decisions about effective educational programs.

(H) create school-based disciplinary strategies that will be used to reduce or eliminate the need to use suspension and expulsion as disciplinary options for children with disabilities;

> ➡ **EXPEL CHILDREN NOW, PAY LATER**
> Removing children from school by suspensions and expulsions is convenient for school administrators but there is no evidence that suspending and/or expelling children is an effective way to discipline children. Removing children from school encourages unwanted children to leave school early by dropping out and/or getting into trouble with the law.

(I) establish placement-neutral funding formulas and cost-effective strategies for meeting the needs of children with disabilities; and

(J) involve individuals with disabilities and parents of children with disabilities in planning, implementing, and evaluating systemic-change activities and educational reforms.

(b) PURPOSE - The purpose of this subpart is to assist State educational agencies, and their partners referred to in section 1452(b), in reforming and improving their systems for providing educational, early intervention, and transitional services, including their systems for professional development, technical assistance, and dissemination of knowledge about best practices, to improve results for children with disabilities.

20 U.S.C. §1452 – Eligibility and Collaborative Process

> ➡ **SECTION OVERVIEW**
> This section requires state educational agencies (SEAs) to develop partnerships with lead agencies for early intervention services (in some states, this may be the SEA but may also be a Health Department, etc.) and with the private sector in order to be eligible for grants.

(a) ELIGIBLE APPLICANTS - A State educational agency may apply for a grant under this subpart for a grant period of not less than 1 year and not more than 5 years.

(b) PARTNERS -

(1) Required Partners -
(A) Contractual Partners - In order to be considered for a grant under this subpart, a State educational agency shall establish a partnership with local educational agencies and other State agencies involved in, or concerned with, the education of children with disabilities.
(B) Other Partners - In order to be considered for a grant under this subpart, a State educational agency shall work in partnership with other persons and organizations involved in, and concerned with, the education of children with disabilities, including -
(i) the Governor;
(ii) parents of children with disabilities;
(iii) parents of non-disabled children;
(iv) individuals with disabilities;
(v) organizations representing individuals with disabilities and their parents, such as parent training and information centers;
(vi) community-based and other nonprofit organizations involved in the education and employment of individuals with disabilities;
(vii) the lead State agency for part C;
(viii) general and special education teachers, and early intervention personnel;
(ix) the State advisory panel established under part C;
(x) the State interagency coordinating council established under part C; and
(xi) institutions of higher education within the State.

(2) Optional Partners - A partnership under subparagraph (A) or (B) of paragraph (1) may also include -
   (A) individuals knowledgeable about vocational education;
   (B) the State agency for higher education;
   (C) the State vocational rehabilitation agency;
   (D) public agencies with jurisdiction in the areas of health, mental health, social services, and juvenile justice; and
   (E) other individuals.

20 U.S.C. §1453 - Applications

➡ **SECTION OVERVIEW**

A panel of experts will analyze grant applications, on a competitive and need basis. Applications must address uniform statewide assessments and benefit from special education.

(a) IN GENERAL -

(1) Submission - A State educational agency that desires to receive a grant under this subpart shall submit to the Secretary an application at such time, in such manner, and including such information as the Secretary may require.

(2) State Improvement Plan - The application shall include a State improvement plan that -
   (A) is integrated, to the maximum extent possible, with State plans under the Elementary and Secondary Education Act of 1965 and the Rehabilitation Act of 1973, as appropriate; and
   (B) meets the requirements of this section.

(b) DETERMINING CHILD AND PROGRAM NEEDS -

(1) In General - Each State improvement plan shall identify those critical aspects of early intervention, general education, and special education programs (including professional development, based on an assessment of State and local needs) that must be improved to enable children with disabilities to meet the goals established by the State under section 1412(a)(16).

➡ **GOALS AND PERFORMANCE INDICATORS TO ASSESS PROGRESS**

20 U.S.C. § 1412(A)(16) requires states to establish goals to promote the Act (see section 1401(d)). Performance indicators assess how children with disabilities perform on assessments, drop-out rates, and graduation rates.

(2) Required Analysis - To meet the requirement of paragraph (1), the State improvement plan shall include at least -
   (A) an analysis of all information, reasonably available to the State educational agency, on the performance of children with disabilities in the State, including -
      (i) their performance on State assessments and other performance indicators established for all children, including drop-out rates and graduation rates;
      (ii) their participation in post-secondary education and employment; and
      (iii) how their performance on the assessments and indicators described in clause (i) compares to that of non-disabled children;

➡ **ASSESSMENTS MAY TRIGGER LITIGATION**

Standardized assessments will provide parents with information about their child's progress. If parents receive this information earlier, they may know if their child is benefiting from special education.
This new emphasis on how children perform on statewide assessments and how many children drop out of school relates to the purpose of special education which is to increase independence and self-sufficiency.

   (B) an analysis of State and local needs for professional development for personnel to serve children with disabilities that includes, at a minimum -

(i) the number of personnel providing special education and related services; and

(ii) relevant information on current and anticipated personnel vacancies and shortages (including the number of individuals described in clause (i) with temporary certification), and on the extent of certification or retraining necessary to eliminate such shortages, that is based, to the maximum extent possible, on existing assessments of personnel needs;

(C) an analysis of the major findings of the Secretary's most recent reviews of State compliance, as they relate to improving results for children with disabilities; and

(D) an analysis of other information, reasonably available to the State, on the effectiveness of the State's systems of early intervention, special education, and general education in meeting the needs of children with disabilities.

(c) IMPROVEMENT STRATEGIES - Each State improvement plan shall -

(1) describe a partnership agreement that -

(A) specifies -

(i) the nature and extent of the partnership among the State educational agency, local educational agencies, and other State agencies involved in, or concerned with, the education of children with disabilities, and the respective roles of each member of the partnership; and

(ii) how such agencies will work in partnership with other persons and organizations involved in, and concerned with, the education of children with disabilities, including the respective roles of each of these persons and organizations; and

(B) is in effect for the period of the grant;

(2) describe how grant funds will be used in undertaking the systemic-change activities, and the amount and nature of funds from any other sources, including part B funds retained for use at the State level under sections 1411(f) and 1419(d), that will be committed to the systemic-change activities;

(3) describe the strategies the State will use to address the needs identified under subsection (b), including -

(A) how the State will change State policies and procedures to address systemic barriers to improving results for children with disabilities;

(B) how the State will hold local educational agencies and schools accountable for educational progress of children with disabilities;

(C) how the State will provide technical assistance to local educational agencies and schools to improve results for children with disabilities;

(D) how the State will address the identified needs for in-service and pre-service preparation to ensure that all personnel who work with children with disabilities (including both professional and paraprofessional personnel who provide special education, general education, related services, or early intervention services) have the skills and knowledge necessary to meet the needs of children with disabilities, including a description of how -

(i) the State will prepare general and special education personnel with the content knowledge and collaborative skills needed to meet the needs of children with disabilities, including how the State will work with other States on common certification criteria;

(ii) the State will prepare professionals and paraprofessionals in the area of early intervention with the content knowledge and collaborative skills needed to meet the needs of infants and toddlers with disabilities;

(iii) the State will work with institutions of higher education and other entities that (on both a pre-service and an in-service basis) prepare personnel who work with children with disabilities to ensure that those institutions and entities develop the capacity to support quality professional development programs that meet State and local needs;

(iv) the State will work to develop collaborative agreements with other States for the joint support and development of programs to prepare personnel for which there is not sufficient demand within a single State to justify support or development of such a program of preparation;

(v) the State will work in collaboration with other States, particularly neighboring States, to address the lack of uniformity and reciprocity in the credentialing of teachers and other personnel;

(vi) the State will enhance the ability of teachers and others to use strategies, such as behavioral interventions, to address the conduct of children with disabilities that impedes the learning of children with disabilities and others;

(vii) the State will acquire and disseminate, to teachers, administrators, school board members, and related services personnel, significant knowledge derived from educational research and other sources, and how the State will, when appropriate, adopt promising practices, materials, and technology;

(viii) the State will recruit, prepare, and retain qualified personnel, including personnel with disabilities and personnel from groups that are underrepresented in the fields of regular education, special education, and related services;

(ix) the plan is integrated, to the maximum extent possible, with other professional development plans and activities, including plans and activities developed and carried out under other Federal and State laws that address personnel recruitment and training; and

(x) the State will provide for the joint training of parents and special education, related services, and general education personnel;

(E) strategies that will address systemic problems identified in Federal compliance reviews, including shortages of qualified personnel;

(F) how the State will disseminate results of the local capacity-building and improvement projects funded under section 1411(f)(4);

(G) how the State will address improving results for children with disabilities in the geographic areas of greatest need; and

(H) how the State will assess, on a regular basis, the extent to which the strategies implemented under this subpart have been effective; and

(4) describe how the improvement strategies described in paragraph (3) will be coordinated with public and private sector resources.

(d) COMPETITIVE AWARDS -

(1) In General - The Secretary shall make grants under this subpart on a competitive basis.

(2) Priority - The Secretary may give priority to applications on the basis of need, as indicated by such information as the findings of Federal compliance reviews.

(e) PEER REVIEW -

(1) In General - The Secretary shall use a panel of experts who are competent, by virtue of their training, expertise, or experience, to evaluate applications under this subpart.

(2) Composition of Panel - A majority of a panel described in paragraph (1) shall be composed of individuals who are not employees of the Federal Government.

(3) Payment of Fees and Expenses of Certain Members - The Secretary may use available funds appropriated to carry out this subpart to pay the expenses and fees of panel members who are not employees of the Federal Government.

(f) REPORTING PROCEDURES - Each State educational agency that receives a grant under this subpart shall submit performance reports to the Secretary pursuant to a schedule to be determined by the Secretary, but not more frequently than annually. The reports shall describe the progress of the State in meeting the performance goals established under section 1412(a)(16), analyze the effectiveness of the State's strategies in meeting those goals, and identify any changes in the strategies needed to improve its performance.

20 U.S.C. §1454 – Use of Funds

➡ **SECTION OVERVIEW**
This section describes how states may use funds.

(a) IN GENERAL -

(1) Activities - A State educational agency that receives a grant under this subpart may use the grant to carry out any activities that are described in the State's application and that are consistent with the purpose of this subpart.

(2) Contracts and Subgrants - Each such State educational agency -
(A) shall, consistent with its partnership agreement under section 1452(b), award contracts or subgrants to local educational agencies, institutions of higher education, and parent training and information centers, as appropriate, to carry out its State improvement plan under this subpart; and
(B) may award contracts and subgrants to other public and private entities, including the lead agency under part C, to carry out such plan.

(b) USE OF FUNDS FOR PROFESSIONAL DEVELOPMENT - A State educational agency that receives a grant under this subpart -

(1) shall use not less than 75 percent of the funds it receives under the grant for any fiscal year -
(A) to ensure that there are sufficient regular education, special education, and related services personnel who have the skills and knowledge necessary to meet the needs of children with disabilities and developmental goals of young children; or
(B) to work with other States on common certification criteria; or

(2) shall use not less than 50 percent of such funds for such purposes, if the State demonstrates to the Secretary's satisfaction that it has the personnel described in paragraph (1)(A).

(c) GRANTS TO OUTLYING AREAS - Public Law 95-134, permitting the consolidation of grants to the outlying areas, shall not apply to funds received under this subpart.

20 U.S.C. §1455 – Minimum State Grant Amounts

(a) IN GENERAL - The Secretary shall make a grant to **each** State educational agency whose application the Secretary has selected for funding under this subpart in an amount for each fiscal year that is -
(1) not less than **$500,000**, nor more than **$2,000,000**, in the case of the 50 States, the District of Columbia, and the Commonwealth of Puerto Rico; and
(2) not less than $80,000, in the case of an outlying area.

(b) INFLATION ADJUSTMENT - Beginning with fiscal year 1999, the Secretary may increase the maximum amount described in subsection (a)(1) to account for inflation.

(c) FACTORS - The Secretary shall set the amount of each grant under subsection (a) after considering -
(1) the amount of funds available for making the grants;
(2) the relative population of the State or outlying area; and
(3) the types of activities proposed by the State or outlying area.

20 U.S.C. §1456 – Authorization of Appropriations

There are authorized to be appropriated to carry out this subpart such sums as may be necessary for each of the fiscal years 1998 through 2002.

SUBPART 2 - COORDINATED RESEARCH, PERSONNEL PREPARATION, TECHNICAL ASSISTANCE, SUPPORT, AND DISSEMINATION OF INFORMATION

20 U.S.C. §1461 – Administrative Provisions
➡ **SECTION OVERVIEW**
> The U. S. Department of Education shall develop and implement a comprehensive plan to enhance services to children with disabilities. Funds may be used for research, personnel preparation, parent training, technical assistance and development of media services. A panel of experts will plan, implement and evaluate projects. These panels shall include individuals with disabilities and parents of children with disabilities. A standing panel of experts will evaluate applications.

(a) COMPREHENSIVE PLAN -

(1) In General - The Secretary shall develop and implement a comprehensive plan for activities carried out under this subpart in order to enhance the provision of educational, related, transitional, and early intervention services to children with disabilities under parts B and C. The plan shall include mechanisms to address educational, related services, transitional, and early intervention needs identified by State educational agencies in applications submitted for State program improvement grants under subpart 1.

(2) Participants in Plan Development - In developing the plan described in paragraph (1), the Secretary shall consult with -
   (A) **individuals with disabilities**;
   (B) **parents of children with disabilities**;
   (C) appropriate **professionals**; and
   (D) representatives of State and local educational agencies, private schools, institutions of higher education, other Federal agencies, the National Council on Disability, and national organizations with an interest in, and **expertise in, providing services to children with disabilities and their families**.

(3) Public Comment - The Secretary shall take public comment on the plan.

(4) Distribution of Funds - In implementing the plan, the Secretary shall, to the extent appropriate, ensure that funds are awarded to recipients under this subpart to carry out activities that benefit, directly or indirectly, children with disabilities of all ages.

(5) Reports to Congress - The Secretary shall periodically report to the Congress on the Secretary's activities under this subsection, including an initial report not later than the date that is 18 months after the date of the enactment of the Individuals with Disabilities Education Act Amendments of 1997.

(b) ELIGIBLE APPLICANTS -

(1) In General - Except as otherwise provided in this subpart, the following entities are eligible to apply for a grant, contract, or cooperative agreement under this subpart:
   (A) A State educational agency.
   (B) A local educational agency.
   (C) An institution of higher education.
   (D) Any other public agency.

(E) A private nonprofit organization.

(F) An outlying area.

(G) An Indian tribe or a tribal organization (as defined under section 4 of the Indian Self-Determination and Education Assistance Act).

(H) A for-profit organization, if the Secretary finds it appropriate in light of the purposes of a particular competition for a grant, contract, or cooperative agreement under this subpart.

(2) Special Rule - The Secretary may limit the entities eligible for an award of a grant, contract, or cooperative agreement to one or more categories of eligible entities described in paragraph (1).

(c) USE OF FUNDS BY SECRETARY - Notwithstanding any other provision of law, and in addition to any authority granted the Secretary under chapter 1 or chapter 2, the Secretary may use up to 20 percent of the funds available under either chapter 1 or chapter 2 for any fiscal year to carry out any activity, or combination of activities, subject to such conditions as the Secretary determines are appropriate effectively to carry out the purposes of such chapters, that -

(1) is consistent with the purposes of chapter 1, chapter 2, or both; and

(2) involves -

(A) research;

(B) personnel preparation;

(C) parent training and information;

(D) technical assistance and dissemination;

(E) technology development, demonstration, and utilization; or

(F) media services.

(d) SPECIAL POPULATIONS -

(1) Application Requirement - In making an award of a grant, contract, or cooperative agreement under this subpart, the Secretary shall, as appropriate, require an applicant to demonstrate how the applicant will address the needs of children with disabilities from minority backgrounds.

(2) Outreach and Technical Assistance -

(A) Requirement - Notwithstanding any other provision of this Act, the Secretary shall ensure that **at least one percent** of the total amount of funds appropriated to carry out this subpart is used for either or both of the following activities:

(i) To provide outreach and technical assistance to **Historically Black Colleges and Universities**, and to institutions of higher education with minority enrollments of at least 25 percent, to promote the participation of such colleges, universities, and institutions in activities under this subpart.

(ii) To enable Historically Black Colleges and Universities, and the institutions described in clause (i), to assist other colleges, universities, institutions, and agencies in improving educational and transitional results for children with disabilities.

(B) Reservation of Funds - The Secretary may reserve funds appropriated under this subpart to satisfy the requirement of subparagraph (A).

(e) PRIORITIES -

(1) In General - Except as otherwise explicitly authorized in this subpart, the Secretary shall ensure that a grant, contract, or cooperative agreement under chapter 1 or 2 is awarded only -

(A) for activities that are designed to benefit children with disabilities, their families, or the personnel employed to work with such children or their families; or

(B) to benefit other individuals with disabilities that such chapter is intended to benefit.

(2) Priority for Particular Activities - Subject to paragraph (1), the Secretary, in making an award of a grant, contract, or cooperative agreement under this subpart, may, without regard to the rule making procedures under section 553 of title 5, United States Code, **limit competitions to, or otherwise give priority to** -

    (A) projects that address one or more -

        (i) age ranges;

        (ii) disabilities;

        (iii) school grades;

        (iv) types of educational placements or early intervention environments;

        (v) types of services;

        (vi) content areas, such as reading; or

        (vii) effective strategies for helping children with disabilities learn appropriate behavior in the school and other community-based educational settings;

    (B) projects that address the needs of children based on the severity of their disability;

    (C) projects that address the needs of -

        (i) low-achieving students;

        (ii) under-served populations;

        (iii) children from low-income families;

        (iv) children with limited English proficiency;

        (v) un-served and under-served areas;

        (vi) particular types of geographic areas; or

        (vii) children whose behavior interferes with their learning and socialization;

    (D) projects to reduce inappropriate identification of children as children with disabilities, particularly among minority children;

    (E) projects that are carried out in particular areas of the country, to ensure broad geographic coverage; and

    (F) any activity that is expressly authorized in chapter 1 or 2.

(f) APPLICANT AND RECIPIENT RESPONSIBILITIES -

(1) Development and Assessment of Projects - The Secretary shall require that an applicant for, and a recipient of, a grant, contract, or cooperative agreement for a project under this subpart -

    (A) involve individuals with disabilities or parents of individuals with disabilities in planning, implementing, and evaluating the project; and

    (B) where appropriate, determine whether the project has any potential for replication and adoption by other entities.

(2) Additional Responsibilities - The Secretary may require a recipient of a grant, contract, or cooperative agreement for a project under this subpart -

    (A) to share in the cost of the project;

    (B) to prepare the research and evaluation findings and products from the project in formats that are useful for specific audiences, including parents, administrators, teachers, early intervention personnel, related services personnel, and individuals with disabilities;

    (C) to disseminate such findings and products; and

    (D) to collaborate with other such recipients in carrying out subparagraphs (B) and (C).

(g) APPLICATION MANAGEMENT -

(1) Standing Panel -

    (A) In General - The Secretary shall establish and use a **standing panel of experts** who are competent, by virtue of their training, expertise, or experience, to evaluate applications under this subpart that, individually, request more than $75,000 per year in Federal financial assistance.

    (B) Membership - The standing panel shall include, at a minimum -

(i) individuals who are representatives of institutions of higher education that plan, develop, and carry out programs of personnel preparation;

(ii) individuals who design and carry out programs of research targeted to the improvement of special education programs and services;

(iii) individuals who have recognized experience and knowledge necessary to integrate and apply research findings to improve educational and transitional results for children with disabilities;

(iv) individuals who administer programs at the State or local level in which children with disabilities participate;

(v) individuals who prepare parents of children with disabilities to participate in making decisions about the education of their children;

(vi) individuals who establish policies that affect the delivery of services to children with disabilities;

(vii) individuals who are parents of children with disabilities who are benefiting, or have benefited, from coordinated research, personnel preparation, and technical assistance; and

(viii) individuals with disabilities.

(C) Training - The Secretary shall provide training to the individuals who are selected as members of the standing panel under this paragraph.

(D) Term - No individual shall serve on the standing panel for more than 3 consecutive years, unless the Secretary determines that the individual's continued participation is necessary for the sound administration of this subpart.

(2) Peer-Review Panels for Particular Competitions -

(A) Composition - The Secretary shall ensure that each sub-panel selected from the standing panel that reviews applications under this subpart includes -

(i) individuals with knowledge and expertise on the issues addressed by the activities authorized by the subpart; and

(ii) to the extent practicable, parents of children with disabilities, individuals with disabilities, and persons from diverse backgrounds.

(B) Federal Employment Limitation - A majority of the individuals on each sub-panel that reviews an application under this subpart shall be individuals who are not employees of the Federal Government.

(3) Use of Discretionary Funds for Administrative Purposes -

(A) Expenses and Fees of Non-Federal Panel Members - The Secretary may use funds available under this subpart to pay the expenses and fees of the panel members who are not officers or employees of the Federal Government.

(B) Administrative Support - The Secretary may use not more than 1 percent of the funds appropriated to carry out this subpart to pay non-Federal entities for administrative support related to management of applications submitted under this subpart.

(C) Monitoring - The Secretary may use funds available under this subpart to pay the expenses of Federal employees to conduct on-site monitoring of projects receiving $500,000 or more for any fiscal year under this subpart.

(h) PROGRAM EVALUATION - The Secretary may use funds appropriated to carry out this subpart to evaluate activities carried out under the subpart.

(i) MINIMUM FUNDING REQUIRED -

(1) In General - Subject to paragraph (2), the Secretary shall ensure that, for every fiscal year, at least the following amounts are provided under this subpart to address the following needs:

(A) $12,832,000 to address the educational, related services, transitional, and early intervention needs of children with deaf-blindness.

(B) $4,000,000 to address the post-secondary, vocational, technical, continuing, and adult education needs of individuals with deafness.

(C) $4,000,000 to address the educational, related services, and transitional needs of children with an emotional disturbance and those who are at risk of developing an emotional disturbance.

(2) Ratable Reduction - If the total amount appropriated to carry out sections 1472, 1473, and 1485 for any fiscal year is less than $130,000,000, the amounts listed in paragraph (1) shall be ratably reduced.

(j) ELIGIBILITY FOR FINANCIAL ASSISTANCE - Effective for fiscal years for which the Secretary may make grants under section 1419(b), no State or local educational agency or educational service agency or other public institution or agency may receive a grant under this subpart which relates exclusively to programs, projects, and activities pertaining to children aged 3 through 5, inclusive, unless the State is eligible to receive a grant under section 1419(b).

CHAPTER 1 - IMPROVING EARLY INTERVENTION, EDUCATIONAL, AND TRANSITIONAL SERVICES AND RESULTS FOR CHILDREN WITH DISABILITIES THROUGH COORDINATED RESEARCH AND PERSONNEL PREPARATION.

20 U.S.C. §1471 – Findings and Purpose

➡ **SECTION OVERVIEW**

The Federal government has an obligation to fund programs. Twenty years of research has provided a comprehensive base of knowledge that should be used to benefit and teach children with disabilities. The purpose of Chapter One is to provide funding for research, projects and other activities that might create systemic change.

(a) FINDINGS - The Congress finds the following:

(1) The Federal Government has an ongoing obligation to support programs, projects, and activities that contribute to positive results for children with disabilities, enabling them -

(A) to meet their early intervention, educational, and transitional goals and, to the maximum extent possible, educational standards that have been established for all children; and

(B) to **acquire the skills that will empower them to lead productive and independent adult lives**.

➡ **PURPOSE OF SPECIAL EDUCATION**

These statements describe what special education is supposed to accomplish:
(1) to provide special education so disabled children can meet educational goals and standards established for non-disabled children, and (2) to teach disabled children the skills they need to lead productive and independent lives after they leave school.

(2)

(A) As a result of **more than 20 years** of Federal support for research, demonstration projects, and personnel preparation, there is **an important knowledge base for improving results** for children with disabilities.

(B) Such knowledge should be used by States and local educational agencies to **design and implement state-of-the-art educational systems** that consider the needs of, and include, children with disabilities, especially in environments in which they can learn along with their peers and **achieve results measured by the same standards** as the results of their peers.

(3)

(A) Continued Federal support is essential for the development and maintenance of a coordinated and high-quality program of research, demonstration projects, dissemination of information, and personnel preparation.

(B) Such support -

(i) enables State educational agencies and local educational agencies to improve their educational systems and results for children with disabilities;

(ii) enables State and local agencies to improve early intervention services and results for infants and toddlers with disabilities and their families; and

(iii) enhances the opportunities for general and special education personnel, related services personnel, parents, and paraprofessionals to participate in pre-service and in-service training, to collaborate, and to improve results for children with disabilities and their families.

(4) The Federal Government plays a critical role in facilitating the availability of an adequate number of qualified personnel -

    (A) to serve effectively the **over 5,000,000 children with disabilities**;

    (B) to assume leadership positions in administrative and direct-service capacities related to teacher training and research concerning the provision of early intervention services, special education, and related services; and

    (C) to work with children with low-incidence disabilities and their families.

(5) The Federal Government performs the role described in paragraph (4) -

    (A) by supporting models of personnel development that reflect successful practice, including strategies for recruiting, preparing, and retaining personnel;

    (B) by promoting the coordination and integration of -

        (i) personnel-development activities for teachers of children with disabilities; and

        (ii) other personnel-development activities supported under Federal law, including this chapter;

    (C) by supporting the development and dissemination of information about teaching standards; and

    (D) by promoting the coordination and integration of personnel-development activities through linkage with systemic-change activities within States and nationally.

(b) PURPOSE - The purpose of this chapter is to provide Federal funding for coordinated research, demonstration projects, outreach, and personnel-preparation activities that -

(1) are described in sections 1472 through 1474;

(2) are linked with, and promote, **systemic change**; and

(3) **improve early intervention, educational, and transitional results** for children with disabilities.

20 U.S.C. §1472 – Research and Innovation to Improve Services and Results for Children with Disabilities

➡️ **SECTION OVERVIEW**

    Grants shall be awarded to improve services and educational results. Research shall focus on early identification, under and over identification of children with disabilities, behavioral issues, and transition services, and will require significant levels of support. Research shall be integrated with practice and staff training.

(a) IN GENERAL - The Secretary shall make competitive grants to, or enter into contracts or cooperative agreements with, eligible entities to produce, and advance the use of, knowledge

(1) **to improve -**

    (A) **services provided under this Act, including the practices of professionals and others involved in providing such services to children with disabilities**; and

    (B) **educational results for children with disabilities**;

(2) to address the special needs of preschool-aged children and infants and toddlers with disabilities, including **infants and toddlers** who would be **at risk of having substantial developmental delays if early intervention services were not provided to them**;

(3) to address the **specific problems of over-identification and under-identification of children with disabilities**;

(4) to develop and implement **effective strategies for addressing inappropriate behavior** of students with disabilities in schools, including strategies **to prevent children with emotional and behavioral problems from developing emotional disturbances** that require the provision of special education and related services;

(5) to improve secondary and post-secondary education and transitional services for children with disabilities; and

(6) to address the range of special education, related services, and early intervention needs of children with disabilities who need **significant levels of support to maximize their participation and learning in school and in the community**.

(b) NEW KNOWLEDGE PRODUCTION; AUTHORIZED ACTIVITIES -

(1) In General - In carrying out this section, the Secretary shall support activities, consistent with the objectives described in subsection (a), that lead to the production of new knowledge.

(2) Authorized Activities - Activities that may be carried out under this subsection include activities such as the following:

(A) Expanding understanding of the relationships between learning characteristics of children with disabilities and the diverse ethnic, cultural, linguistic, social, and economic backgrounds of children with disabilities and their families.

(B) Developing or identifying innovative, effective, and efficient curricula designs, instructional approaches, and strategies, and developing or identifying positive academic and social learning opportunities, that -

(i) enable children with disabilities to make effective transitions described in section 674(b)(3)(C) or transitions between educational settings; and

(ii) improve educational and transitional results for children with disabilities at all levels of the educational system in which the activities are carried out and, in particular, that improve the progress of the children, as measured by assessments within the general education curriculum involved.

(C) Advancing the design of **assessment tools and procedures** that will accurately and efficiently determine the special instructional, learning, and behavioral needs of children with disabilities, especially within the context of general education.

(D) Studying and promoting improved alignment and compatibility of general and special education reforms concerned with curricular and instructional reform, evaluation and accountability of such reforms, and administrative procedures.

(E) **Advancing the design, development, and integration of technology**, assistive technology devices, media, and materials, to improve early intervention, educational, and transitional services and results for children with disabilities.

(F) Improving designs, processes, and results of personnel preparation for personnel who provide services to children with disabilities through the acquisition of information on, and implementation of, research-based practices.

(G) Advancing knowledge about the coordination of education with health and social services.

(H) Producing information on the **long-term impact of early intervention and education on results** for individuals with disabilities through large-scale longitudinal studies.

(c) INTEGRATION OF RESEARCH AND PRACTICE; AUTHORIZED ACTIVITIES -

(1) In General - In carrying out this section, the Secretary shall support activities, consistent with the objectives described in subsection (a), that integrate research and practice, including activities that support State systemic-change and local capacity-building and improvement efforts.

(2) Authorized Activities - Activities that may be carried out under this subsection include activities such as the following:

(A) Model demonstration projects to apply and test research findings in typical service settings to determine the usability, effectiveness, and general applicability of such research findings in such areas as improving instructional methods, curricula, and tools, such as textbooks and media.

(B) Demonstrating and applying research-based findings to facilitate systemic changes, related to the provision of services to children with disabilities, in policy, procedure, practice, and the training and use of personnel.

(C) Promoting and demonstrating the coordination of early intervention and educational services for children with disabilities with services provided by health, rehabilitation, and social service agencies.

(D) Identifying and disseminating solutions that overcome systemic barriers to the effective and efficient delivery of early intervention, educational, and transitional services to children with disabilities.

(d) IMPROVING THE USE OF PROFESSIONAL KNOWLEDGE; AUTHORIZED ACTIVITIES -

(1) In General - In carrying out this section, the Secretary shall support activities, consistent with the objectives described in subsection (a), that improve the use of professional knowledge, including activities that support State systemic-change and local capacity-building and improvement efforts.

(2) Authorized Activities - Activities that may be carried out under this subsection include activities such as the following:

(A) Synthesizing useful research and other information relating to the provision of services to children with disabilities, including effective practices.

(B) Analyzing professional knowledge bases to advance an understanding of the relationships, and the effectiveness of practices, relating to the provision of services to children with disabilities.

(C) Ensuring that research and related products are in appropriate formats for distribution to teachers, parents, and individuals with disabilities.

(D) Enabling professionals, parents of children with disabilities, and other persons, to learn about, and implement, the findings of research, and successful practices developed in model demonstration projects, relating to the provision of services to children with disabilities.

(E) Conducting outreach, and disseminating information relating to successful approaches to overcoming systemic barriers to the effective and efficient delivery of early intervention, educational, and transitional services, to personnel who provide services to children with disabilities.

(e) BALANCE AMONG ACTIVITIES AND AGE RANGES - In carrying out this section, the Secretary shall ensure that there is an appropriate balance -

(1) among knowledge production, integration of research and practice, and use of professional knowledge; and

(2) across all age ranges of children with disabilities.

(f) APPLICATIONS - An eligible entity that wishes to receive a grant, or enter into a contract or cooperative agreement, under this section shall submit an application to the Secretary at such time, in such manner, and containing such information as the Secretary may require.

(g) AUTHORIZATION OF APPROPRIATIONS - There are authorized to be appropriated to carry out this section such sums as may be necessary for each of the fiscal years 1998 through 2002.

20 U.S.C. §1473 – Personnel Preparation to Improve Services and Results for Children with Disabilities

➡ SECTION OVERVIEW

Scholarships and grants shall address the needs for qualified personnel who have research based skills and knowledge. Grants will target low-incidence and high-incidence disabilities. Administrators and general education staff may be eligible to receive one year of financial assistance for two years of service.

(a) IN GENERAL - The Secretary shall, on a competitive basis, make grants to, or enter into contracts or cooperative agreements with, eligible entities -

(1) to help address State-identified needs for qualified personnel in special education, related services, early intervention, and regular education, to work with children with disabilities; and

(2) to ensure that those **personnel have the skills and knowledge, derived from practices that have been determined, through research and experience, to be successful,** that are needed to serve those children.

(b) LOW-INCIDENCE DISABILITIES; AUTHORIZED ACTIVITIES -

(1) In General - In carrying out this section, the Secretary shall support activities, consistent with the objectives described in subsection (a), that benefit children with low-incidence disabilities.

(2) Authorized Activities - Activities that may be carried out under this subsection include activities such as the following:
(A) Preparing persons who -
(i) have prior training in educational and other related service fields; and
(ii) are studying to obtain degrees, certificates, or licensure that will enable them to assist children with disabilities to achieve the objectives set out in their individualized education programs described in section 1414(d), or to assist infants and toddlers with disabilities to achieve the outcomes described in their individualized family service plans described in section 1436.
(B) Providing personnel from various disciplines with interdisciplinary training that will contribute to improvement in early intervention, educational, and transitional results for children with disabilities.
(C) Preparing personnel in the innovative uses and application of technology to enhance learning by children with disabilities through early intervention, educational, and transitional services.
(D) Preparing personnel who provide services to visually impaired or blind children to teach and use Braille in the provision of services to such children.
(E) Preparing personnel to be qualified educational interpreters, to assist children with disabilities, particularly deaf and hard-of-hearing children in school and school-related activities and deaf and hard-of-hearing infants and toddlers and preschool children in early intervention and preschool programs.
(F) Preparing personnel who provide services to **children with significant cognitive disabilities** and **children with multiple disabilities**.

(3) Definition - As used in this section, the term '**low-incidence disability**' means -
(A) a visual or hearing impairment, or simultaneous visual and hearing impairments;
(B) a significant cognitive impairment; or
(C) any impairment for which a small number of personnel with highly specialized skills and knowledge are needed in order for children with that impairment to receive early intervention services or a free appropriate public education.

(4) Selection of Recipients - In selecting recipients under this subsection, the Secretary may give preference to applications that propose to prepare personnel in more than one low-incidence disability, such as deafness and blindness.

(5) Preparation in Use of Braille - The Secretary shall ensure that all recipients of assistance under this subsection who will use that assistance to prepare personnel to provide services to visually impaired or blind children that can appropriately be provided in Braille will prepare those individuals to provide those services in Braille.

(c) LEADERSHIP PREPARATION; AUTHORIZED ACTIVITIES -

(1) In General - In carrying out this section, the Secretary shall support leadership preparation activities that are consistent with the objectives described in subsection (a).

(2) Authorized Activities - Activities that may be carried out under this subsection include activities such as the following:

(A) Preparing personnel at the advanced graduate, doctoral, and postdoctoral levels of training to administer, enhance, or provide services for children with disabilities.

(B) Providing interdisciplinary training for various types of leadership personnel, including teacher preparation faculty, administrators, researchers, supervisors, principals, and other persons whose work affects early intervention, educational, and transitional services for children with disabilities.

(d) PROJECTS OF NATIONAL SIGNIFICANCE; AUTHORIZED ACTIVITIES -

(1) In General - In carrying out this section, the Secretary shall support activities, consistent with the objectives described in subsection (a), that are of national significance and have broad applicability.

(2) Authorized Activities - Activities that may be carried out under this subsection include activities such as the following:

(A) Developing and demonstrating effective and efficient practices for preparing personnel to provide services to children with disabilities, including practices that address any needs identified in the State's improvement plan under part C;

(B) Demonstrating the **application of significant knowledge derived from research** and other sources in the development of programs to prepare personnel to provide services to children with disabilities.

(C) Demonstrating models for the preparation of, and interdisciplinary training of, early intervention, special education, and general education personnel, to enable the personnel -

(i) to acquire the collaboration skills necessary to work within teams to assist children with disabilities; and

(ii) to achieve results that meet challenging standards, particularly within the general education curriculum.

(D) Demonstrating **models that reduce shortages of teachers**, **and personnel from other relevant disciplines**, who serve children with disabilities, through reciprocity arrangements between States that are related to licensure and certification.

(E) Developing, evaluating, and disseminating model teaching standards for persons working with children with disabilities.

(F) Promoting the transferability, across State and local jurisdictions, of licensure and certification of teachers and administrators working with such children.

(G) Developing and disseminating models that prepare teachers with strategies, including **behavioral interventions, for addressing the conduct of children with disabilities that impedes** their **learning** and that of others in the classroom.

(H) Institutes that provide professional development that addresses the needs of children with disabilities to teachers or teams of teachers, and where appropriate, to school board members, administrators, principals, pupil-service personnel, and other staff from individual schools.

(I) Projects to **improve the ability of general education teachers, principals, and other administrators** to meet the needs of children with disabilities.

(J) Developing, evaluating, and disseminating innovative models for the recruitment, induction, retention, and assessment of new, qualified teachers, especially from groups that are underrepresented in the teaching profession, including individuals with disabilities.

(K) Supporting institutions of higher education with minority enrollments of at least 25 percent for the purpose of preparing personnel to work with children with disabilities.

(e) HIGH-INCIDENCE DISABILITIES; AUTHORIZED ACTIVITIES -

(1) In General - In carrying out this section, the Secretary shall support activities, consistent with the objectives described in subsection (a), to benefit children with high-incidence disabilities, such as children with specific learning disabilities, speech or language impairment, or mental retardation.

➡ **HIGH INCIDENCE DISABILITIES**
Children who are identified with "specific learning disabilities" make up more than 50% of the special education population.

(2) Authorized Activities - Activities that may be carried out under this subsection include the following:
(A) Activities undertaken by institutions of higher education, local educational agencies, and other local entities -
(i) to improve and reform their existing programs to prepare teachers and related services personnel -
(I) to meet the diverse needs of children with disabilities for early intervention, educational, and transitional services; and
(II) to work collaboratively in regular classroom settings; and
(ii) to incorporate best practices and research-based knowledge about preparing personnel so they will have the knowledge and skills to improve educational results for children with disabilities.
(B) Activities incorporating innovative strategies to recruit and prepare teachers and other personnel to meet the needs of areas in which there are acute and persistent shortages of personnel.
(C) Developing career opportunities for paraprofessionals to receive training as special education teachers, related services personnel, and early intervention personnel, including interdisciplinary training to enable them to improve early intervention, educational, and transitional results for children with disabilities.

(f) APPLICATIONS -

(1) In General - **Any eligible entity** that wishes to receive a grant, or enter into a contract or cooperative agreement, under this section shall submit an application to the Secretary at such time, in such manner, and containing such information as the Secretary may require.

(2) Identified State Needs -
(A) Requirement to Address Identified Needs - Any application under subsection (b), (c), or (e) shall include information demonstrating to the satisfaction of the Secretary that the activities described in the application will address needs identified by the State or States the applicant proposes to serve.
(B) Cooperation with State Educational Agencies - Any applicant that is not a local educational agency or a State educational agency shall include information demonstrating to the satisfaction of the Secretary that **the applicant and one or more State educational agencies have engaged in a cooperative effort** to plan the project to which the application pertains, and will cooperate in carrying out and monitoring the project.

(3) Acceptance by States of Personnel Preparation Requirements - The Secretary may require applicants to provide letters from one or more States stating that the States -
(A) intend to accept successful completion of the proposed personnel preparation program as meeting State personnel standards for serving children with disabilities or serving infants and toddlers with disabilities; and
(B) need personnel in the area or areas in which the applicant proposes to provide preparation, as identified in the States' comprehensive systems of personnel development under parts B and C.

(g) SELECTION OF RECIPIENTS -

(1) Impact of Project - In selecting recipients under this section, the Secretary may consider the impact of the project proposed in the application in meeting the need for personnel identified by the States.

(2) Requirement on Applicants to Meet State and Professional Standards -The Secretary shall make grants under this section only to eligible applicants that meet State and professionally-recognized standards for the preparation of special education and related services personnel, if the purpose of the project is to assist personnel in obtaining degrees.

(3) Preferences - In selecting recipients under this section, the Secretary may -

(A) **give preference to institutions of higher education that are educating regular education personnel to meet the needs of children with disabilities** in integrated settings and **educating special education personnel to work in collaboration with regular educators** in integrated settings; and

(B) **give preference to institutions of higher education** that are successfully recruiting and preparing individuals with disabilities and **individuals from groups that are underrepresented** in the profession for which they are preparing individuals.

(h) SERVICE OBLIGATION -

(1) **In General** - Each application for funds under subsections (b) and (e), and to the extent appropriate subsection (d), shall include an assurance that the applicant will ensure that individuals who receive a scholarship under the proposed project will subsequently provide **special education and related services to children with disabilities for a period of 2 years for every year for which assistance was received** or repay all or part of the cost of that assistance, in accordance with regulations issued by the Secretary.

(2) **Leadership Preparation** - Each application for funds under subsection (c) shall include an assurance that the applicant will ensure that individuals who receive a scholarship under the proposed project will subsequently perform work related to their preparation for a period of 2 years for every year for which assistance was received or repay all or part of such costs, in accordance with regulations issued by the Secretary.

(i) **SCHOLARSHIPS** - The Secretary may include funds for **scholarships**, with necessary stipends and allowances, in awards under subsections (b), (c), (d), and (e).

(j) **AUTHORIZATION OF APPROPRIATIONS** - There are authorized to be appropriated to carry out this section such sums as may be necessary for each of the fiscal years 1998 through 2002.

20 U.S.C. §1474 – Studies and Evaluations

➡ **SECTION OVERVIEW**

This section authorizes assessments, longitudinal studies, and a national assessment to determine if children are benefiting from special education. The purpose of the national assessment is to determine whether LEAs and SEAs are improving results, placing children in the least restrictive environments, reducing dropout rates, and addressing behavior problems of children with disabilites.

(a) STUDIES AND EVALUATIONS -

(1) **In General** - The Secretary shall, directly or through grants, contracts, or cooperative agreements, assess the progress in the implementation of this Act, including the effectiveness of State and local efforts to provide -

(A) a free appropriate public education to children with disabilities; and

(B) early intervention services to infants and toddlers with disabilities and infants and toddlers who would be at risk of having substantial developmental delays if early intervention services were not provided to them.

(2) **Authorized Activities** - In carrying out this subsection, the Secretary may support studies, evaluations, and assessments, including studies that -

(A) **analyze measurable impact, outcomes, and results** achieved by State educational agencies and local educational agencies through their activities to reform policies, procedures, and practices designed to improve educational and transitional services and results for children with disabilities;

(B) analyze State and local needs for professional development, parent training, and other appropriate activities that can reduce the need for disciplinary actions involving children with disabilities;

(C) assess educational and transitional services and results for children with disabilities from minority backgrounds, including

(i) data on -
    (I) the number of minority children who are referred for special education evaluation;
    (II) the number of minority children who are receiving special education and related services and their educational or other service placement; and
    (III) the number of minority children who graduated from secondary and post-secondary education programs; and
(ii) the performance of children with disabilities from minority backgrounds on State assessments and other performance indicators established for all students;
(D) measure educational and transitional services and results of children with disabilities under this Act, including **longitudinal studies** that -
    (i) examine educational and transitional services and results for children with disabilities who are 3 through 17 years of age and are receiving special education and related services under this Act, using a national, representative sample of distinct age cohorts and disability categories; and
    (ii) examine educational results, postsecondary placement, and employment status of individuals with disabilities, 18 through 21 years of age, who are receiving or have received special education and related services under this Act; and
(E) identify and report on the placement of children with disabilities by disability category.

(b) NATIONAL ASSESSMENT -

(1) In General - The Secretay shall carry out a national assessment of activities carried out with Federal funds under this Act in order -
    (A) to determine the effectiveness of this Act in achieving its purposes;
    (B) to provide information to the President, the Congress, the States, local educational agencies, and the public on how to implement the Act more effectively; and
    (C) to provide the President and the Congress with information that will be useful in developing legislation to achieve the purposes of this Act more effectively.

(2) Consultation - The Secretary shall plan, review, and conduct the national assessment under this subsection in consultation with researchers, State practitioners, local practitioners, parents of children with disabilities, individuals with disabilities, and other appropriate individuals.

(3) Scope of Assessment - The national assessment shall examine how well schools, local educational agencies, States, other recipients of assistance under this Act, and the Secretary are achieving the purposes of this Act, including -
    (A) **improving the performance of children with disabilities in general scholastic activities and assessments as compared to nondisabled children;**
    (B) providing for the **participation** of children with disabilities **in the general curriculum;**
    (C) helping children with disabilities make **successful transitions** from -
        (i) early intervention services to preschool education;
        (ii) preschool education to elementary school; and
        (iii) secondary school to adult life;
    (D) placing and serving children with disabilities, including minority children, in the **least restrictive environment** appropriate;
    (E) preventing children with disabilities, especially children with emotional disturbances and specific learning disabilities, from **dropping out of school;**
    (F) addressing behavioral problems of children with disabilities as compared to non-disabled children;
    (G) coordinating services provided under this Act with each other, with other educational and pupil services (including preschool services), and with health and social services funded from other sources;
    (H) providing for the participation of parents of children with disabilities in the education of their children; and
    (I) resolving disagreements between education personnel and parents through activities such as mediation.

(4) Interim and Final Reports - The Secretary shall submit to the President and the Congress -

(A) an interim report that summarizes the preliminary findings of the assessment not later than October 1, 1999; and

(B) a final report of the findings of the assessment not later than October 1, 2001.

(c) ANNUAL REPORT - The Secretary shall report annually to the Congress on -

(1) an analysis and summary of the data reported by the States and the Secretary of the Interior under section 1418;

(2) the results of activities conducted under subsection (a);

(3) the findings and determinations resulting from reviews of State implementation of this Act.

(d) TECHNICAL ASSISTANCE TO LEAS - The Secretary shall provide directly, or through grants, contracts, or cooperative agreements, technical assistance to local educational agencies to assist them in carrying out local capacity-building and improvement projects under section 1411(f)(4) and other LEA systemic improvement activities under this Act.

(e) RESERVATION FOR STUDIES AND TECHNICAL ASSISTANCE -

(1) In General - Except as provided in paragraph (2) and notwithstanding any other provision of this Act, the Secretary may reserve up to one-half of one percent of the amount appropriated under parts B and C for each fiscal year to carry out this section.

(2) Maximum Amount - For the first fiscal year in which the amount described in paragraph (1) is at least $20,000,000, the maximum amount the Secretary may reserve under paragraph (1) is $20,000,000. For each subsequent fiscal year, the maximum amount the Secretary may reserve under paragraph (1) is $20,000,000, increased by the cumulative rate of inflation since the fiscal year described in the previous sentence.

(3) Use of Maximum Amount - In any fiscal year described in paragraph (2) for which the Secretary reserves the maximum amount described in that paragraph, the Secretary shall use at least half of the reserved amount for activities under subsection (d).

CHAPTER 2 - IMPROVING EARLY INTERVENTION, EDUCATIONAL, AND TRANSITIONAL SERVICES AND RESULTS FOR CHILDREN WITH DISABILITIES THROUGH COORDINATED TECHNICAL ASSISTANCE, SUPPORT, AND DISSEMINATION OF INFORMATION

20 U.S.C. §1481 – Findings and Purposes

➡ **SECTION OVERVIEW**

Parents need information and education about their rights under Part B. With appropriate training, parents should be able to participate actively in special education decisions. Parents and teachers need technical assistance.

(a) IN GENERAL - The Congress finds as follows:

(1) National technical assistance, support, and dissemination activities are necessary to ensure that parts B and C are fully implemented and achieve quality early intervention, ducational, and transitional results for children with disabilities and their families.

(2) Parents, teachers, administrators, and related services personnel need technical assistance and information in a timely, coordinated, and accessible manner in order to improve early intervention, educational, and transitional services and results at the State and local levels for children with disabilities and their families.

(3) **Parent training and information** activities have taken on increased importance in efforts **to assist parents of a child with a disability in dealing with the multiple pressures of rearing such a child** and are of particular importance in -

(A) ensuring the **involvement of such parents** in **planning and decision-making** with respect to early intervention, educational, and transitional services;

(B) achieving **quality early intervention, educational, and transitional results** for children with disabilities;

(C) providing such parents **information on their rights and protections** under this Act to ensure improved early intervention, educational, and transitional results for children with disabilities;

(D) assisting such paents in the development of **skills to participate effectively** in the education and development of their children and in the transitions described in section 1474(b)(3)(C); and

(E) **supporting** the roles of such **parents as participants** within partnerships seeking to improve early intervention, educational, and transitional services and results for children with disabilities and their families.

(4) Providers of parent training and information activities need to ensure that such parents who have limited access to services and supports, due to economic, cultural, or linguistic barriers, are provided with access to appropriate parent training and information activities.

(5) **Parents** of children with disabilities **need information** that **helps the parents to understand the rights and responsibilities of their children under part B.**

(6) The provision of coordinated technical assistance and dissemination of information to State and local agencies, institutions of higher education, and other providers of services to children with disabilities is essential in -

(A) supporting the process of achieving **systemic change**;

(B) supporting actions in areas of priority specific to the improvement of early intervention, educational, and transitional results for children with disabilities;

(C) conveying information and assistance that are -

(i) **based on current research** (as of the date the information and assistance are conveyed);

(ii) accessible and meaningful for use in supporting systemic-change activities of State and local partnerships; and

(iii) linked directly to improving early intervention, educational, and transitional services and results for children with disabilities and their families; and

(D) organizing systems and information networks for such information, based on modern technology related to -

(i) storing and gaining access to information; and

(ii) distributing information in a systematic manner to parents, students, professionals, and policymakers.

(7) Federal support for carrying out technology research, technology development, and educational media services and activities has resulted in major innovations that have significantly improved early intervention, educational, and transitional services and results for children with disabilities and their families.

(8) Such Federal support is needed -

(A) to stimulate the development of software, interactive learning tools, and devices to address early intervention, educational, and transitional needs of children with disabilities who have certain disabilities;

(B) to make information available on technology research, technology development, and educational media services and activities to individuals involved in the provision of early intervention, educational, and transitional services to children with disabilities;

(C) to promote the integration of technology into curricula to improve early intervention, educational, and transitional results for children with disabilities;

(D) to provide incentives for the development of technology and media devices and tools that are not readily found or available because of the small size of potential markets;

(E) to make resources available to pay for such devices and tools and educational media services and activities;

(F) to promote the training of personnel -

(i) to provide such devices, tools, services, and activities in a competent manner; and

(ii) to assist children with disabilities and their families in using such devices, tools, services, and activities; and

(G) to coordinate the provision of such devices, tools, services, and activities -

(i) among State human services programs; and

(ii) between such programs and private agencies.

(b) **PURPOSES** - The purposes of this chapter are to ensure that -

(1) **children with disabilities, and their parents, receive training and information on their rights and protections under this Act**, in order to develop the skills necessary to **effectively participate in planning and decision-making** relating to **early intervention, educational, and transitional services** and in **systemic-change** activities;

(2) parents, teachers, administrators, early intervention personnel, related services personnel, and transition personnel receive coordinated and **accessible technical assistance and information** to assist such persons, through systemic-change activities and other efforts, **to improve early intervention, educational, and transitional services and results** for children with disabilities and their families;

(3) appropriate **technology and media** are researched, developed, demonstrated, and made **available in timely and accessible formats to parents, teachers**, and all types of personnel providing services to children with disabilities to support their roles as partners in the improvement and implementation of early intervention, educational, and transitional services and results for children with disabilities and their families;

(4) on reaching the age of majority under State law, children with disabilities understand their rights and responsibilities under part B, if the State provides for the transfer of parental rights under section 1415(m); and

(5) the general welfare of deaf and hard-of-hearing individuals is promoted by -
   (A) bringing to such individuals understanding and appreciation of the films and television programs that play an important part in the general and cultural advancement of hearing individuals;
   (B) providing, through those films and television programs, enriched educational and cultural experiences through which deaf and hard-of-hearing individuals can better understand the realities of their environment; and
   (C) providing wholesome and rewarding experiences that deaf and hard-of-hearing individuals may share.

20 U.S.C. §1482 - Parent Training and Information Centers
   ➡ **SECTION OVERVIEW**
      Grants shall be awarded to at least one parent organization in each state to support parent training and information centers. These centers are required to assist parents in understanding their rights and how to use their rights effectively. The centers will help parents learn about their children's disabilities and educational needs, how to communicate effectively with school personnel, and how to participate as members of educational decision-making teams.

(a) PROGRAM AUTHORIZED - The Secretary may make grants to, and enter into contracts and cooperative agreements with, parent organizations to support parent training and informaton centers to carry out activities under this section.

(b) REQUIRED ACTIVITIES - Each parent training and information center that receives assistance under this section shall -

(1) provide training and information that meets the training and information needs of parents of children with disabilities living in the area served by the center, particularly under-served parents and parents of children who may be inappropriately identified;

(2) **assist parents to understand** the availability of, and **how to effectively use, procedural safeguards** under this Act, including encouraging the use, and explaining the benefits, of alternative methods of dispute resolution, such as the mediation process described in section 1415(e);

(3) serve the parents of infants, toddlers, and children with the full range of disabilities;

(4) **assist parents to -**
   (A) better **understand the nature of their children's disabilities and their educational and developmental needs;**
   (B) **communicate effectively with personnel** responsible for providing special education, early intervention, and related services;
   (C) **participate in decision-making** processes and the **development of individualized education programs** under part B and **individualized family service plans** under part C;

(D) obtain appropriate information about the **range of options, programs, services, and resources** available to assist children with disabilities and their families;

(E) understand the provisions of this Act for the education of, and the provision of early intervention services to, children with disabilities; and

(F) participate in **school reform** activities;

(5) in States where the State elects to contract with the parent training and information center, contract with State educational agencies to provide, consistent with subparagraphs (B) and (D) of section 1415(e)(2), individuals who meet with parents to explain the mediation process to them;

(6) network with appropriate clearinghouses, including organizations conducting national dissemination activities under section 1485(d), and with other national, State, and local organizations and agencies, such as protection and advocacy agencies, that serve parents and families of children with the full range of disabilities; and

(7) annually report to the Secretary on -
(A) the number of parents to whom it provided information and training in the most recently concluded fiscal year; and
(B) the effectiveness of strategies used to reach and serve parents, including under-served parents of children with disabilities.

(c) OPTIONAL ACTIVITIES - A parent training and information center that receives assistance under this section may -
(1) provide information to teachers and other professionals who provide special education and related services to children with disabilities;

(2) assist students with disabilities to understand their rights and responsibilities under section 1415(m) on reaching the age of majority; and

(3) assist parents of children with disabilities to be informed participants in the development and implementation of the State's State improvement plan under subpart 1.

(d) APPLICATION REQUIREMENTS - Each application for assistance under this section shall identify with specificity the special efforts that the applicant will undertake -

(1) to ensure that the needs for training and information of under-served parents of children with disabilities in the area to be served are effectively met; and

(2) to work with community-based organizations.

(e) DISTRIBUTION OF FUNDS -

(1) In General - The Secretary shall make **at least 1 award to a parent organization in each State**, unless the Secretary does not receive an application from such an organization in each State of sufficient quality to warrant approval.
(2) Selection Requirement - The Secretary shall select among applications submitted by parent organizations in a State in a manner that ensures the most effective assistance to parents, including parents in urban and rural areas, in the State.

(f) QUARTERLY REVIEW -

(1) Requirements-
(A) Meetings - The board of directors or special governing committee of each organization that receives an award under this section shall meet at least once in each calendar quarter to review the activities for which the award was made.
(B) Advising Board - Each special governing committee shall directly advise the organization's governing board of its views and recommendations.

(2) Continuation Award - When an organization requests a continuation award under this section, the board of directors or special governing committee shall submit to the Secretary a written review of the parent training and information program conducted by the organization during the preceding fiscal year.

(g) DEFINITION OF PARENT ORGANIZATION - As used in this section, the term 'parent organization' means a private nonprofit organization (other than an institution of higher education) that -

(1) has a board of directors -
  (A) the **majority of whom are parents of children with disabilities**;
  (B) that includes -
    (i) individuals working in the fields of special education, related services, and early intervention; and
    (ii) individuals with disabilities; and
  (C) the parent and professional members of which are broadly representative of the population to be served; or

(2) has -
  (A) a membership that **represents the interests of individuals with disabilities** and has established a special governing committee that meets the requirements of paragraph (1); and
  (B) a memorandum of understanding between the special governing committee and the board of directors of the organization that clearly outlines the relationship between the board and the committee and the decision-making responsibilities and authority of each.

20 U.S.C. §1483 – Community Parent Resource Centers

➡ **SECTION OVERVIEW**
> Grants may be awarded to parent organizations that do not meet the criteria in the preceding section but focus on helping Limited English Proficient parents, low-income parents, and parents with disabilities.

(a) IN GENERAL - The Secretary may make grants to, and enter into contracts and cooperative agreements with, local parent organizations to support parent training and information centers that will help ensure that **under-served parents** of children with disabilities, including **low-income parents**, parents of **children with limited English proficiency**, and **parents with disabilities**, have the training and information they need to enable them to participate effectively in helping their children with disabilities -

(1) to meet developmental goals and, to the maximum extent possible, those challenging standards that have been established for all children; and

(2) to be prepared to lead productive independent adult lives, to the maximum extent possible.

(b) REQUIRED ACTIVITIES - Each parent training and information center assisted under this section shall -
(1) provide training and information that meets the training and information needs of parents of children with disabilities proposed to be served by the grant, contract, or cooperative agreement;

(2) carry out the activities required of parent training and information centers under paragraphs (2) through (7) of section 1482(b);

(3) establish cooperative partnerships with the parent training and information centers funded under section 1482; and

(4) be designed to meet the specific needs of families who experience significant isolation from available sources of information and support.

(c) D<small>EFINITION</small> - As used is this section, the term 'local parent organization' means a parent organization, as defined in section 1482(g), that either -

(1) has a board of directors the majority of whom are from the community to be served; or

(2) has -
(A) as a part of its **mission, serving the interests of individuals with disabilities** from such community; and
(B) a special governing committee to administer the grant, contract, or cooperative agreement, a majority of the members of which are individuals from such community.

20 U.S.C. §1484 – Technical Assistance for Parent Training and Information Centers
➡ **SECTION OVERVIEW**
Technical assistance may be provided to those groups discussed in the previous sections.

(a) I<small>N</small> G<small>ENERAL</small> - The Secretary may, directly or through awards to eligible entities, provide technical assistance for developing, assisting, and coordinating parent training and information programs carried out by parent training and information centers receiving assistance under sections 1482 and 1483.

(b) A<small>UTHORIZED</small> A<small>CTIVITIES</small> - The Secretary may provide technical assistance to a parent training and information center under this section in areas such as -

(1) effective coordination of parent training efforts;

(2) dissemination of information;

(3) evaluation by the center of itself;

(4) promotion of the use of technology, including assistive technology devices and assistive technology services;

(5) reaching under-served populations;

(6) including children with disabilities in general education programs;

(7) facilitation of transitions from -
(A) early intervention services to preschool;
(B) preschool to school; and
(C) secondary school to post-secondary environments; and
(8) promotion of alternative methods of dispute resolution.

20 U.S.C. §1485 – Coordinated Technical Assistance and Dissemination
➡ **SECTION OVERVIEW**
The U. S. Department of Education may support or provide direct technical assistance and information of national or regional scope that can include links to libraries and electronic materials. Technical assistance may include information to promote system change.

(a) I<small>N</small> G<small>ENERAL</small> - The Secretary shall, by competitively making grants or entering into contracts and cooperative agreements with eligible entities, provide technical assistance and information, through such mechanisms as institutes, Regional Resource Centers, clearinghouses, and programs that support States and local entities in building capacity, to improve early intervention, educational, and transitional services and results for children with disabilities and their families, and address systemic-change goals and priorities.

(b) SYSTEMIC TECHNICAL ASSISTANCE; AUTHORIZED ACTIVITIES -

(1) In General - In carrying out this section, the Secretary shall carry out or support technical assistance activities, consistent with the objectives described in subsection (a), relating to systemic change.

(2) Authorized Activities - Activities that may be carried out under this subsection include activities such as the following:

(A) Assisting States, local educational agencies, and other participants in partnerships established under subpart 1 with the process of planning systemic changes that will promote improved early intervention, educational, and transitional results for children with disabilities.

(B) Promoting change through a multi-state or regional framework that benefits States, local educational agencies, and other participants in partnerships that are in the process of achieving systemic-change outcomes.

(C) Increasing the depth and utility of information in ongoing and emerging areas of priority need identified by States, local educational agencies, and other participants in partnerships that are in the process of achieving systemic-change outcomes.

(D) Promoting communication and information exchange among States, local educational agencies, and other participants in partnerships, based on the needs and concerns identified by the participants in the partnerships, rather than on externally imposed criteria or topics, regarding -

(i) the practices, procedures, and policies of the States, local educational agencies, and other participants in partnerships; and

(ii) accountability of the States, local educational agencies, and other participants in partnerships for improved early intervention, educational, and transitional results for children with disabilities.

(c) SPECIALIZED TECHNICAL ASSISTANCE; AUTHORIZED ACTIVITIES -

(1) In General - In carrying out this section, the Secretary shall carry out or support activities, consistent with the objectives described in subsection (a), relating to areas of priority or specific populations.

(2) Authorized Activities - Examples of activities that may be carried out under this subsection include activities that -

(A) focus on specific areas of high-priority need that -

(i) are identified by States, local educational agencies, and other participants in partnerships;

(ii) require the development of new knowledge, or the analysis and synthesis of substantial bodies of information not readily available to the States, agencies, and other participants in partnerships; and

(iii) will contribute significantly to the improvement of early intervention, educational, and transitional services and results for children with disabilities and their families;

(B) focus on needs and issues that are specific to a population of children with disabilities, such as the provision of single-State and multi-State technical assistance and in-service training -

(i) to schools and agencies serving deaf-blind children and their families; and

(ii) to programs and agencies serving other groups of children with low-incidence disabilities and their families; or

(C) address the post-secondary education needs of individuals who are deaf or hard-of-hearing.

(d) NATIONAL INFORMATION DISSEMINATION; AUTHORIZED ACTIVITIES -

(1) In General - In carrying out this section, the Secretary shall carry out or support information dissemination activities that are consistent with the objectives described in subsection (a), including **activities that address national needs for the preparation and dissemination of information** relating to **eliminating barriers to systemic-change** and **improving early intervention, educational, and transitional results** for children with disabilities.

(2) Authorized Activities - Examples of activities that may be carried out under this subsection include activities relating to

(A) infants and toddlers with disabilities and their families, and children with disabilities and their families;

(B) services for populations of children with low-incidence disabilities, including deaf-blind children, and targeted age groupings;

(C) the provision of post-secondary services to individuals with disabilities;

(D) the need for and use of personnel to provide services to children with disabilities, and personnel recruitment, retention, and preparation;

(E) issues that are of critical interest to State educational agencies and local educational agencies, other agency personnel, parents of children with disabilities, and individuals with disabilities;

(F) educational reform and systemic change within States; and

(G) promoting schools that are safe and conducive to learning.

(3) Linking States to Information Sources - In carrying out this subsection, the Secretary may support projects that link States to technical assistance resources, including special education and general education resources, and may make research and related products available through libraries, electronic networks, parent training projects, and other information sources.

(e) APPLICATIONS - An eligible entity that wishes to receive a grant, or enter into a contract or cooperative agreement, under this section shall submit an application to the Secretary at such time, in such manner, and containing such information as the Secretary may require.

20 U.S.C. §1486 - Authorization of Appropriations

There are authorized to be appropriated to carry out sections 1481 through 1485 such sums as may be necessary for each of the fiscal years 1998 through 2002.

20 U.S.C. §1487 – Technology Development, Demonstration, and Utilization; and Media Services

➡ **SECTION OVERVIEW**
Grants are available to promote the development of technology and educational media services.

(a) IN GENERAL - The Secretary shall competitively make grants to, and enter into contracts and cooperative agreements with, eligible entities to support activities described in subsections (b) and (c).

(b) TECHNOLOGY DEVELOPMENT, DEMONSTRATION, AND UTILIZATION; AUTHORIZED ACTIVITIES -

(1) In General - In carrying out tis section, the Secretary shall support activities to promote the **development, demonstration, and utilization of technology**.

(2) Authorized Activities - Activities that may be carried out under this subsection include activities such as the following:

(A) Conducting **research and development** activities on the **use of innovative and emerging technologies** for children with disabilities.

(B) Promoting the demonstration and use of innovative and emerging technologies for children with disabilities by improving and expanding the transfer of technology from **research and development to practice**.

(C) Providing technical assistance to recipients of other assistance under this section, concerning the development of accessible, effective, and usable products.

(D) Communicating information on available technology and the uses of such technology to assist children with disabilities.

(E) Supporting the implementation of research programs on captioning or video description.

(F) Supporting research, development, and dissemination of technology with universal-design features, so that the technology is accessible to individuals with disabilities without further modification or adaptation.

(G) Demonstrating the use of publicly-funded telecommunications systems to provide parents and teachers with information and training concerning early diagnosis of, intervention for, and effective teaching strategies for, young children with reading disabilities.

(c) EDUCATIONAL MEDIA SERVICES; AUTHORIZED ACTIVITIES - In carrying out this section, the Secretary shall support -

(1) educational media activities that are designed to be of educational value to children with disabilities;

(2) providing video description, open captioning, or closed captioning of television programs, videos, or educational materials through September 30, 2001; and after fiscal year 2001, providing video description, open captioning, or closed captioning of educational, news, and informational television, videos, or materials;

(3) distributing captioned and described videos or educational materials through such mechanisms as a loan service;

(4) providing free educational materials, including textbooks, in accessible media for visually impaired and print-disabled students in elementary, secondary, post-secondary, and graduate schools;

(5) providing cultural experiences through appropriate nonprofit organizations, such as the National Theater of the Deaf, that
    (A) enrich the lives of deaf and hard-of-hearing children and adults;
    (B) increase public awareness and understanding of deafness and of the artistic and intellectual achievements of deaf and hard-of-hearing persons; or
    (C) promote the integration of hearing, deaf, and hard-of-hearing persons through shared cultural, educational, and social experiences; and

(6) compiling and analyzing appropriate data relating to the activities described in paragraphs (1) through (5).

(d) APPLICATIONS - Any eligible entity that wishes to receive a grant, or enter into a contract or cooperative agreement, under this section shall submit an application to the Secretary at such time, in such manner, and containing such information as the Secretary may require.

(e) AUTHORIZATION OF APPROPRIATIONS - There are authorized to be appropriated to carry out this section such sums as may be necessary for each of the fiscal years 1998 through 2002.

END OF PART D

Title II - Miscellaneous Provisions

(a) PARTS A AND B -

(1) In General - Except as provided in paragraph (2), parts A and B of the Individuals with Disabilities Education Act, as amended by title I, shall take effect upon the enactment of this Act.

(2) Exceptions -
    (A) In General - Sections 1412(a)(4), 1412(a)(14), 1412(a)(16), 1414(d) (except for paragraph (6)), and 1418 of the Individuals with Disabilities Education Act, as amended by title I, shall take effect on July 1, 1998.
    (B) Section 1417 - Section 1417 of the Individuals with Disabilities Education Act, as amended by title I, shall take effect on October 1, 1997.
    (C) Individualized Education Programs and Comprehensive System of Personnel Development - Section 1418 of the Individuals with Disabilities Education Act, as in effect on the day before the date of the enactment of this Act,

and the provisions of parts A and B of the Individuals with Disabilities Education Act relating to individualized education programs and the State's comprehensive system of personnel development, as so in effect, shall remain in effect until July 1, 1998.

(D) Sections 1411 and 1419 - Sections 1411 and 1419, as amended by title I, shall take effect beginning with funds appropriated for fiscal year 1998.

(b) PART C - Part C of the Individuals with Disabilities Education Act, as amended by title I, shall take effect on July 1, 1998.

(c) PART D -

(1) In General - Except as provided in paragraph (2), part D of the Individuals with Disabilities Education Act, as amended by title I, shall take effect on October 1, 1997.

(2) Exception - Paragraphs (1) and (2) of section 1461(g) of the Individuals with Disabilities Education Act, as amended by title I, shall take effect on January 1, 1998.

END OF INDIVIDUALS WITH DISABILITIES EDUCATION ACT

CHAPTER 6

TABLE OF IDEA REGULATIONS
34 C.F.R. Part 300

Confidentiality of Information

Department Procedures

SUBPART F—STATE ADMINISTRATION
General

Use of Funds

State Advisory Panel

State Complaint Procedures

SUBPART G—ALLOCATION OF FUNDS; REPORTS
Allocations

Reports

Appendix A to Part 300—Notice of Interpretation
Authority: Part B of the Individuals with Disabilities Education Act (20 U.S.C. 1401, et seq.), unless otherwise noted.

Individualized Education Programs (IEPs) and Other Selected Implementation Issues

I. Involvement and Progress of Each Child With a Disability in the General Curriculum

1. What are the major Part B IEP requirements that govern the involvement and progress of children with disabilities in the general curriculum?

2. Must a child's IEP address his or her involvement in the general curriculum, regardless of the nature and severity of the child's disability and the setting in which the child is educated?

3. What must public agencies do to meet the requirements at Secs. 300.344(a)(2) and 300.346(d) regarding the participation of a "regular education teacher" in the development, review, and revision of IEPs, for children aged 3 through 5 who are receiving preschool special education services?

4. Must the measurable annual goals in a child's IEP address all areas of the general curriculum, or only those areas in which the child's involvement and progress are affected by the child's disability?

II. Involvement of Parents and Students

5. What is the role of the parents, including surrogate parents, in decisions regarding the educational program of their children?

6. What are the Part B requirements regarding the participation of a student (child) with a disability in an IEP meeting?

7. Must the public agency inform the parents of who will be at the IEP meeting?

8. Do parents have the right to a copy of their child's IEP?

9. What is a public agency's responsibility if it is not possible to reach consensus on what services should be included in a child's IEP?

10. Does Part B require that public agencies inform parents regarding the educational progress of their children with disabilities?

III. Preparing Students With Disabilities for Employment and Other Post-School Experiences

11. What must the IEP team do to meet the requirements that the IEP include "a statement of * * * transition service needs" beginning at age 14 (Sec. 300.347(b)(1)(i))," and a statement of needed transition services" no later than age 16 (Sec. 300.347(b)(2)?

12. Must the IEP for each student with a disability, beginning no later than age 16, include all "needed transition services," as identified by the IEP team and consistent with the definition at Sec. 300.29, even if an agency other than the public agency will provide those services? What is the public agency's responsibility if another agency fails to provide agreed-upon transition services?

13. Under what circumstances must a public agency invite representatives from other agencies to an IEP meeting at which a child's need for transition services will be considered?

IV. Other Questions Regarding the Development and Content of IEPS

14. For a child with a disability receiving special education for the first time, when must an IEP be developed—before or after the child begins to receive special education and related services?

15. Who is responsible for ensuring the development of IEPs for children with disabilities served by a public agency other than an LEA?

16. For a child placed out of State by an educational or non- educational State or local agency, is the placing or receiving State responsible for the child's IEP?

17. If a disabled child has been receiving special education from one public agency and transfers to another public agency in the same State, must the new public agency develop an IEP before the child can be placed in a special education program?

18. What timelines apply to the development and implementation of an initial IEP for a child with a disability?

19. Must a public agency hold separate meetings to determine a child's eligibility for special education and related services, develop the child's IEP, and determine the child's placement, or may the agency meet all of these requirements in a single meeting?

20. How frequently must a public agency conduct meetings to review, and, if appropriate, revise the IEP for each child with a disability?

21. May IEP meetings be audio- or video-tape-recorded?

22. Who can serve as the representative of the public agency at an IEP meeting?

23. For a child with a disability being considered for initial provision of special education and related services, which teacher or teachers should attend the IEP meeting?

24. What is the role of a regular education teacher in the development, review and revision of the IEP for a child who is, or may be, participating in the regular education environment?

25. If a child with a disability attends several regular classes, must all of the child's regular education teachers be members of the child's IEP team?

26. How should a public agency determine which regular education teacher and special education teacher will be members of the IEP team for a particular child with a disability?

27. For a child whose primary disability is a speech impairment, may a public agency meet its responsibility under Sec. 300.344(a)(3) to ensure that the IEP team includes "at least one special education teacher, or, if appropriate, at least one special education provider of the child" by including a speech-language pathologist on the IEP team?

28. Do parents and public agencies have the option of inviting any individual of their choice be participants on their child's IEP team?

29. Can parents or public agencies bring their attorneys to IEP meetings, and, if so under what circumstances? Are attorney's fees available for parents' attorneys if the parents are prevailing parties in actions or proceedings brought under Part B?

30. Must related services personnel attend IEP meetings?

31. Must the public agency ensure that all services specified in a child's IEP are provided?

32. Is it permissible for an agency to have the IEP completed before the IEP meeting begins?

33. Must a public agency include transportation in a child's IEP as a related service?

34. Must a public agency provide related services that are required to assist a child with a disability to benefit from special education, whether or not those services are included in the list of related services in Sec. 300.24?

35. Must the IEP specify the amount of services or may it simply list the services to be provided?

36. Under what circumstances is a public agency required to permit a child with a disability to use a school-purchased assistive technology device in the child's home or in another setting?

37. Can the IEP team also function as the group making the placement decision for a child with a disability?

38. If a child's IEP includes behavioral strategies to address a particular behavior, can a child ever be suspended for engaging in that behavior?

39. If a child's behavior in the regular classroom, even with appropriate interventions, would significantly impair the learning of others, can the group that makes the placement decision determine that placement in the regular classroom is inappropriate for that child?

40. May school personnel during a school year implement more than one short-term removal of a child with disabilities from his or her classroom or school for misconduct?

ASSISTANCE TO STATES FOR THE EDUCATION OF CHILDREN WITH DISABILITIES
34 C.F.R. Part 300

SUBPART A—GENERAL

PURPOSES, APPLICABILITY, AND REGULATIONS THAT APPLY TO THIS PROGRAM

Sec. 300.1 Purposes.

The purposes of this part are—

(a) To ensure that all children with disabilities have available to them a free appropriate public education that emphasizes special education and related services designed to meet their unique needs and prepare them for employment and independent living;

(b) To ensure that the rights of children with disabilities and their parents are protected;

(c) To assist States, localities, educational service agencies, and Federal agencies to provide for the education of all children with disabilities; and

(d) To assess and ensure the effectiveness of efforts to educate children with disabilities. (Authority: 20 U.S.C. 1400 note)

Sec. 300.2 Applicability of this part to State, local, and private agencies.

(a) States. This part applies to each State that receives payments under Part B of the Act.

(b) Public agencies within the State. The provisions of this part—

(1) Apply to all political subdivisions of the State that are involved in the education of children with disabilities, including—

(i) The State educational agency (SEA);

(ii) Local educational agencies (LEAs), educational service agencies (ESAs), and public charter schools that are not otherwise included as LEAs or ESAs and are not a school of an LEA or ESA;

(iii) Other State agencies and schools (such as Departments of Mental Health and Welfare and State schools for children with deafness or children with blindness); and

(iv) State and local juvenile and adult correctional facilities; and

(2) Are binding on each public agency in the State that provides special education and related services to children with disabilities, regardless of whether that agency is receiving funds under Part B.

(c) Private schools and facilities. Each public agency in the State is responsible for ensuring that the rights and protections under Part B of the Act are given to children with disabilities—

(1) Referred to or placed in private schools and facilities by that public agency; or

(2) Placed in private schools by their parents under the provisions of Sec. 300.403(c). (Authority: 20 U.S.C. 1412)

Sec. 300.3 Regulations that apply.

The following regulations apply to this program:

(a) 34 CFR part 76 (State-Administered Programs) except for Secs. 76.125-76.137 and 76.650-76.662.

(b) 34 CFR part 77 (Definitions).

(c) 34 CFR part 79 (Intergovernmental Review of Department of Education Programs and Activities).

(d) 34 CFR part 80 (Uniform Administrative Requirements for Grants and Cooperative Agreements to State and Local Governments).

(e) 34 CFR part 81 (General Education Provisions Act—Enforcement).

(f) 34 CFR part 82 (New Restrictions on Lobbying).

(g) 34 CFR part 85 (Government-wide Debarment and Suspension (Nonprocurement) and Government-wide Requirements for Drug-Free Workplace (Grants)).

(h) The regulations in this part—34 CFR part 300 (Assistance for Education of Children with Disabilities). (Authority: 20 U.S.C. 1221e-3(a)(1))

DEFINITIONS USED IN THIS PART

Sec. 300.4 Act.

As used in this part, Act means the Individuals with Disabilities Education Act (IDEA), as amended. (Authority: 20 U.S.C. 1400(a))

Sec. 300.5 Assistive technology device.

As used in this part, Assistive technology device means any item, piece of equipment, or product system, whether acquired commercially off the shelf, modified, or customized, that is used to increase, maintain, or improve the functional capabilities of a child with a disability. (Authority: 20 U.S.C. 1401(1))

Sec. 300.6 Assistive technology service.

As used in this part, Assistive technology service means any service that directly assists a child with a disability in the selection, acquisition, or use of an assistive technology device. The term includes—

(a) The evaluation of the needs of a child with a disability, including a functional evaluation of the child in the child's customary environment;

(b) Purchasing, leasing, or otherwise providing for the acquisition of assistive technology devices by children with disabilities;

(c) Selecting, designing, fitting, customizing, adapting, applying, maintaining, repairing, or replacing assistive technology devices;

(d) Coordinating and using other therapies, interventions, or services with assistive technology devices, such as those associated with existing education and rehabilitation plans and programs;

(e) Training or technical assistance for a child with a disability or, if appropriate, that child's family; and

(f) Training or technical assistance for professionals (including individuals providing education or rehabilitation services), employers, or other individuals who provide services to, employ, or are otherwise substantially involved in the major life functions of that child. (Authority: 20 U.S.C. 1401(2))

Sec. 300.7 Child with a disability.

(a) General.

(1) As used in this part, the term child with a disability means a child evaluated in accordance with Secs. 300.530- 300.536 as having mental retardation, a hearing impairment including deafness, a speech or language impairment, a visual impairment including blindness, serious emotional disturbance (hereafter referred to as emotional disturbance), an orthopedic impairment, autism, traumatic brain injury, an other health impairment, a specific learning disability, deaf-blindness, or multiple disabilities, and who, by reason thereof, needs special education and related services.

(2)

(i) Subject to paragraph (a)(2)(ii) of this section, if it is determined, through an appropriate evaluation under Secs. 300.530- 300.536, that a child has one of the disabilities identified in paragraph (a)(1) of this section, but only needs a related service and not special education, the child is not a child with a disability under this part.

(ii) If, consistent with Sec. 300.26(a)(2), the related service required by the child is considered special education rather than a related service under State standards, the child would be determined to be a child with a disability under paragraph (a)(1) of this section.

(b) Children aged 3 through 9 experiencing developmental delays. The term child with a disability for children aged 3 through 9 may, at the discretion of the State and LEA and in accordance with Sec. 300.313, include a child—

(1) Who is experiencing developmental delays, as defined by the State and as measured by appropriate diagnostic instruments and procedures, in one or more of the following areas: physical development, cognitive development, communication development, social or emotional development, or adaptive development; and

(2) Who, by reason thereof, needs special education and related services.

(c) Definitions of disability terms. The terms used in this definition are defined as follows:

(1)

(i) Autism means a developmental disability significantly affecting verbal and nonverbal communication and social interaction, generally evident before age 3, that adversely affects a child's educational performance. Other characteristics often associated with autism are engagement in repetitive activities and stereotyped movements, resistance to environmental change or change in daily routines, and unusual responses to sensory experiences. The term does not apply if a child's educational performance is adversely affected primarily because the child has an emotional disturbance, as defined in paragraph (b)(4) of this section.

(ii) A child who manifests the characteristics of "autism" after age 3 could be diagnosed as having "autism" if the criteria in paragraph (c)(1)(i) of this section are satisfied.

(2) Deaf-blindness means concomitant hearing and visual impairments, the combination of which causes such severe communication and other developmental and educational needs that they cannot be accommodated in special education programs solely for children with deafness or children with blindness.

(3) Deafness means a hearing impairment that is so severe that the child is impaired in processing linguistic information through hearing, with or without amplification, that adversely affects a child's educational performance.

(4) Emotional disturbance is defined as follows:

(i) The term means a condition exhibiting one or more of the following characteristics over a long period of time and to a marked degree that adversely affects a child's educational performance:

(A) An inability to learn that cannot be explained by intellectual, sensory, or health factors.

(B) An inability to build or maintain satisfactory interpersonal relationships with peers and teachers.

(C) Inappropriate types of behavior or feelings under normal circumstances.

(D) A general pervasive mood of unhappiness or depression.

(E) A tendency to develop physical symptoms or fears associated with personal or school problems.

(ii) The term includes schizophrenia. The term does not apply to children who are socially maladjusted, unless it is determined that they have an emotional disturbance.

(5) Hearing impairment means an impairment in hearing, whether permanent or fluctuating, that adversely affects a child's educational performance but that is not included under the definition of deafness in this section.

(6) Mental retardation means significantly subaverage general intellectual functioning, existing concurrently with deficits in adaptive behavior and manifested during the developmental period, that adversely affects a child's educational performance.

(7) Multiple disabilities means concomitant impairments (such as mental retardation-blindness, mental retardation-orthopedic impairment, etc.), the combination of which causes such severe educational needs that they cannot be accommodated in special education programs solely for one of the impairments. The term does not include deaf-blindness.

(8) Orthopedic impairment means a severe orthopedic impairment that adversely affects a child's educational performance. The term includes impairments caused by congenital anomaly (e.g., clubfoot, absence of some member, etc.), impairments caused by disease (e.g., poliomyelitis, bone tuberculosis, etc.), and impairments from other causes (e.g., cerebral palsy, amputations, and fractures or burns that cause contractures).

(9) Other health impairment means having limited strength, vitality or alertness, including a heightened alertness to environmental stimuli, that results in limited alertness with respect to the educational environment, that—

(i) Is due to chronic or acute health problems such as asthma, attention deficit disorder or attention deficit hyperactivity disorder, diabetes, epilepsy, a heart condition, hemophilia, lead poisoning, leukemia, nephritis, rheumatic fever, and sickle cell anemia; and

(ii) Adversely affects a child's educational performance.

(10) Specific learning disability is defined as follows:

(i) **General.** The term means a disorder in one or more of the basic psychological processes involved in understanding or in using language, spoken or written, that may manifest itself in an imperfect ability to listen, think, speak, read, write, spell, or to do mathematical calculations, including conditions such as perceptual disabilities, brain injury, minimal brain dysfunction, dyslexia, and developmental aphasia.

(ii) **Disorders not included.** The term does not include learning problems that are primarily the result of visual, hearing, or motor disabilities, of mental retardation, of emotional disturbance, or of environmental, cultural, or economic disadvantage.

(11) Speech or language impairment means a communication disorder, such as stuttering, impaired articulation, a language impairment, or a voice impairment, that adversely affects a child's educational performance.

(12) Traumatic brain injury means an acquired injury to the brain caused by an external physical force, resulting in total or partial functional disability or psychosocial impairment, or both, that adversely affects a child's educational performance. The term applies to open or closed head injuries resulting in impairments in one or more areas, such as cognition; language; memory; attention; reasoning; abstract thinking; judgment; problem-solving; sensory, perceptual, and motor abilities; psychosocial behavior; physical functions; information processing; and speech. The term does not apply to brain injuries that are congenital or degenerative, or to brain injuries induced by birth trauma.

(13) Visual impairment including blindness means an impairment in vision that, even with correction, adversely affects a child's educational performance. The term includes both partial sight and blindness. (Authority: 20 U.S.C. 1401(3)(A) and (B); 1401(26))

Sec. 300.8 Consent.

As used in this part, consent has the meaning given that term in Sec. 300.500(b)(1). (Authority: 20 U.S.C. 1415(a))

Sec. 300.9 Day; business day; school day.

As used in this part, the term—

(a) **Day** means calendar day unless otherwise indicated as business day or school day;

(b) **Business day** means Monday through Friday, except for Federal and State holidays (unless holidays are specifically included in the designation of business day, as in Sec. 300.403(d)(1)(ii)); and

(c)

(1) **School day** means any day, including a partial day, that children are in attendance at school for instructional purposes.

(2) The term school day has the same meaning for all children in school, including children with and without disabilities. (Authority: 20 U.S.C. 1221e-3)

Sec. 300.10 Educational service agency.

As used in this part, the term **educational service agency**—

(a) Means a regional public multiservice agency—

(1) Authorized by State law to develop, manage, and provide services or programs to LEAs; and

(2) Recognized as an administrative agency for purposes of the provision of special education and related services provided within public elementary and secondary schools of the State;

(b) Includes any other public institution or agency having administrative control and direction over a public elementary or secondary school; and

(c) Includes entities that meet the definition of intermediate educational unit in section 602(23) of IDEA as in effect prior to June 4, 1997. (Authority: 20 U.S.C. 1401(4))

Sec. 300.11 Equipment.

As used in this part, the term **equipment** means—

(a) Machinery, utilities, and built-in equipment and any necessary enclosures or structures to house the machinery, utilities, or equipment; and

(b) All other items necessary for the functioning of a particular facility as a facility for the provision of educational services, including items such as instructional equipment and necessary furniture; printed, published and audio-visual instructional materials; telecommunications, sensory, and other technological aids and devices; and books, periodicals, documents, and other related materials. (Authority: 20 U.S.C. 1401(6))

Sec. 300.12 Evaluation.

As used in this part, the term evaluation has the meaning given that term in Sec. 300.500(b)(2). (Authority: 20 U.S.C. 1415(a))

Sec. 300.13 Free appropriate public education.

As used in this part, the term free appropriate public education or FAPE means special education and related services that—

(a) Are provided at public expense, under public supervision and direction, and without charge;

(b) Meet the standards of the SEA, including the requirements of this part;

(c) Include preschool, elementary school, or secondary school education in the State; and

(d) Are provided in conformity with an individualized education program (IEP) that meets the requirements of Secs. 300.340-300.350. (Authority: 20 U.S.C. 1401(8))

Sec. 300.14 Include.

As used in this part, the term include means that the items named are not all of the possible items that are covered, whether like or unlike the ones named. (Authority: 20 U.S.C. 1221e-3)

Sec. 300.15 Individualized education program.

As used in this part, the term individualized education program or IEP has the meaning given the term in Sec. 300.340(a). (Authority: 20 U.S.C. 1401(11))

Sec. 300.16 Individualized education program team.

As used in this part, the term individualized education program team or IEP team means a group of individuals described in Sec. 300.344 that is responsible for developing, reviewing, or revising an IEP for a child with a disability. (Authority: 20 U.S.C. 1221e-3)

Sec. 300.17 Individualized family service plan.

As used in this part, the term individualized family service plan or IFSP has the meaning given the term in 34 CFR 303.340(b). (Authority: 20 U.S.C. 1401(12))

Sec. 300.18 Local educational agency.

(a) As used in this part, the term local educational agency means a public board of education or other public authority legally constituted within a State for either administrative control or direction of, or to perform a service function for, public elementary or secondary schools in a city, county, township, school district, or other political subdivision of a State, or for a combination of school districts or counties as are recognized in a State as an administrative agency for its public elementary or secondary schools.

(b) The term includes—

(1) An educational service agency, as defined in Sec. 300.10;

(2) Any other public institution or agency having administrative control and direction of a public elementary or secondary school, including a public charter school that is established as an LEA under State law; and

(3) An elementary or secondary school funded by the Bureau of Indian Affairs, and not subject to the jurisdiction of any SEA other than the Bureau of Indian Affairs, but only to the extent that the inclusion makes the school eligible for programs for which specific eligibility is not provided to the school in another provision of law and the school does not have a student population that is smaller than the student population of the LEA receiving assistance under this Act with the smallest student population. (Authority: 20 U.S.C. 1401(15))

Sec. 300.19 Native language.

(a) As used in this part, the term native language, if used with reference to an individual of limited English proficiency, means the following:

(1) The language normally used by that individual, or, in the case of a child, the language normally used by the parents of the child, except as provided in paragraph (a)(2) of this section.

(2) In all direct contact with a child (including evaluation of the child), the language normally used by the child in the home or learning environment.

(b) For an individual with deafness or blindness, or for an individual with no written language, the mode of communication is that normally used by the individual (such as sign language, braille, or oral communication). (Authority: 20 U.S.C. 1401(16))

Sec. 300.20 Parent.

(a) **General**. As used in this part, the term parent means—

(1) A natural or adoptive parent of a child;

(2) A guardian but not the State if the child is a ward of the State;

(3) A person acting in the place of a parent (such as a grandparent or stepparent with whom the child lives, or a person who is legally responsible for the child's welfare); or

(4) A surrogate parent who has been appointed in accordance with Sec. 300.515.

(b) **Foster parent**. Unless State law prohibits a foster parent from acting as a parent, a State may allow a foster parent to act as a parent under Part B of the Act if—

(1) The natural parents' authority to make educational decisions on the child's behalf has been extinguished under State law; and

(2) The foster parent—

(i) Has an ongoing, long-term parental relationship with the child;

(ii) Is willing to make the educational decisions required of parents under the Act; and

(iii) Has no interest that would conflict with the interests of the child. (Authority: 20 U.S.C. 1401(19))

Sec. 300.21 Personally identifiable

As used in this part, the term personally identifiable has the meaning given that term in Sec. 300.500(b)(3). (Authority: 20 U.S.C. 1415(a))

Sec. 300.22 Public agency.

As used in this part, the term public agency includes the SEA, LEAs, ESAs, public charter schools that are not otherwise included as LEAs or ESAs and are not a school of an LEA or ESA, and any other political subdivisions of the State that are responsible for providing education to children with disabilities. (Authority: 20 U.S.C. 1412(a)(1)(A), (a)(11))

Sec. 300.23 Qualified personnel.

As used in this part, the term qualified personnel means personnel who have met SEA-approved or SEA-recognized certification, licensing, registration, or other comparable requirements that apply to the area in which the individuals are providing special education or related services. (Authority: 20 U.S.C. 1221e-3)

Sec. 300.24 Related services.

(a) **General**. As used in this part, the term related services means transportation and such developmental, corrective, and other supportive services as are required to assist a child with a disability to benefit from special education, and includes speech- language pathology and audiology services, psychological services, physical and occupational therapy, recreation, including therapeutic recreation, early identification and assessment of disabilities in children, counseling services, including rehabilitation counseling, orientation and mobility services, and medical services for diagnostic or evaluation purposes. The term also includes school health services, social work services in schools, and parent counseling and training.

(b) **Individual terms defined**. The terms used in this definition are defined as follows:

(1) **Audiology** includes—

(i) Identification of children with hearing loss;

(ii) Determination of the range, nature, and degree of hearing loss, including referral for medical or other professional attention for the habilitation of hearing;

(iii) Provision of habilitative activities, such as language habilitation, auditory training, speech reading (lip-reading), hearing evaluation, and speech conservation;

(iv) Creation and administration of programs for prevention of hearing loss;

(v) Counseling and guidance of children, parents, and teachers regarding hearing loss; and

(vi) Determination of children's needs for group and individual amplification, selecting and fitting an appropriate aid, and evaluating the effectiveness of amplification.

(2) **Counseling services** means services provided by qualified social workers, psychologists, guidance counselors, or other qualified personnel.

(3) **Early identification and assessment of disabilities in children** means the implementation of a formal plan for identifying a disability as early as possible in a child's life.

(4) **Medical services** means services provided by a licensed physician to determine a child's medically related disability that results in the child's need for special education and related services.

(5) **Occupational therapy**—

(i) Means services provided by a qualified occupational therapist; and

(ii) Includes—

    (A) Improving, developing or restoring functions impaired or lost through illness, injury, or deprivation;

    (B) Improving ability to perform tasks for independent functioning if functions are impaired or lost; and

    (C) Preventing, through early intervention, initial or further impairment or loss of function.

(6) Orientation and mobility services—

    (i) Means services provided to blind or visually impaired students by qualified personnel to enable those students to attain systematic orientation to and safe movement within their environments in school, home, and community; and

    (ii) Includes teaching students the following, as appropriate:

        (A) Spatial and environmental concepts and use of information received by the senses (such as sound, temperature and vibrations) to establish, maintain, or regain orientation and line of travel (e.g., using sound at a traffic light to cross the street);

        (B) To use the long cane to supplement visual travel skills or as a tool for safely negotiating the environment for students with no available travel vision;

        (C) To understand and use remaining vision and distance low vision aids; and

        (D) Other concepts, techniques, and tools.

(7) Parent counseling and training means—

    (i) Assisting parents in understanding the special needs of their child;

    (ii) Providing parents with information about child development; and

    (iii) Helping parents to acquire the necessary skills that will allow them to support the implementation of their child's IEP or IFSP.

(8) Physical therapy means services provided by a qualified physical therapist.

(9) Psychological services includes—

    (i) Administering psychological and educational tests, and other assessment procedures;

    (ii) Interpreting assessment results;

    (iii) Obtaining, integrating, and interpreting information about child behavior and conditions relating to learning;

    (iv) Consulting with other staff members in planning school programs to meet the special needs of children as indicated by psychological tests, interviews, and behavioral evaluations;

    (v) Planning and managing a program of psychological services, including psychological counseling for children and parents; and

    (vi) Assisting in developing positive behavioral intervention strategies.

(10) Recreation includes—

    (i) Assessment of leisure function;

    (ii) Therapeutic recreation services;

    (iii) Recreation programs in schools and community agencies; and

    (iv) Leisure education.

(11) Rehabilitation counseling services means services provided by qualified personnel in individual or group sessions that focus specifically on career development, employment preparation, achieving independence, and integration in the workplace and community of a student with a disability. The term also includes vocational rehabilitation services provided to a student with disabilities by vocational rehabilitation programs funded under the Rehabilitation Act of 1973, as amended.

(12) School health services means services provided by a qualified school nurse or other qualified person.

(13) Social work services in schools includes—

    (i) Preparing a social or developmental history on a child with a disability;

    (ii) Group and individual counseling with the child and family;

    (iii) Working in partnership with parents and others on those problems in a child's living situation (home, school, and community) that affect the child's adjustment in school;

    (iv) Mobilizing school and community resources to enable the child to learn as effectively as possible in his or her educational program; and

    (v) Assisting in developing positive behavioral intervention strategies.

(14) Speech-language pathology services includes—

    (i) Identification of children with speech or language impairments;

    (ii) Diagnosis and appraisal of specific speech or language impairments;

    (iii) Referral for medical or other professional attention necessary for the habilitation of speech or language impairments;

    (iv) Provision of speech and language services for the habilitation or prevention of communicative impairments; and

    (v) Counseling and guidance of parents, children, and teachers regarding speech and language impairments.

(15) Transportation includes—

    (i) Travel to and from school and between schools;

    (ii) Travel in and around school buildings; and

    (iii) Specialized equipment (such as special or adapted buses, lifts, and ramps), if required to provide special transportation for a child with a disability. (Authority: 20 U.S.C. 1401(22))

Sec. 300.25 Secondary school.

As used in this part, the term secondary school means a nonprofit institutional day or residential school that provides secondary education, as determined under State law, except that it does not include any education beyond grade 12. (Authority: 20 U.S.C. 1401(23))

Sec. 300.26 Special education.

(a) General.

(1) As used in this part, the term special education means specially designed instruction, at no cost to the parents, to meet the unique needs of a child with a disability, including—

(i) Instruction conducted in the classroom, in the home, in hospitals and institutions, and in other settings; and

(ii) Instruction in physical education.

(2) The term includes each of the following, if it meets the requirements of paragraph (a)(1) of this section:

(i) Speech-language pathology services, or any other related service, if the service is considered special education rather than a related service under State standards;

(ii) Travel training; and

(iii) Vocational education.

(b) Individual terms defined. The terms in this definition are defined as follows:

(1) At no cost means that all specially-designed instruction is provided without charge, but does not preclude incidental fees that are normally charged to nondisabled students or their parents as a part of the regular education program.

(2) Physical education—

(i) Means the development of—

(A) Physical and motor fitness;

(B) Fundamental motor skills and patterns; and

(C) Skills in aquatics, dance, and individual and group games and sports (including intramural and lifetime sports); and

(ii) Includes special physical education, adapted physical education, movement education, and motor development.

(3) Specially-designed instruction means adapting, as appropriate to the needs of an eligible child under this part, the content, methodology, or delivery of instruction—

(i) To address the **unique needs of the child that result from the child's disability**; and

(ii) To ensure **access of the child to the general curriculum**, so that he or she can **meet the educational standards** within the jurisdiction of the public agency **that apply to all children**.

(4) Travel training means providing instruction, as appropriate, to children with significant cognitive disabilities, and any other children with disabilities who require this instruction, to enable them to—

(i) Develop an awareness of the environment in which they live; and

(ii) Learn the skills necessary to move effectively and safely from place to place within that environment (e.g., in school, in the home, at work, and in the community).

(5) Vocational education means organized educational programs that are directly related to the preparation of individuals for paid or unpaid employment, or for additional preparation for a career requiring other than a baccalaureate or advanced degree. (Authority: 20 U.S.C. 1401(25))

Sec. 300.27 State.

As used in this part, the term State means each of the 50 States, the District of Columbia, the Commonwealth of Puerto Rico, and each of the outlying areas. (Authority: 20 U.S.C. 1401(27))

Sec. 300.28 Supplementary aids and services.

As used in this part, the term supplementary aids and services means, aids, services, and other supports that are provided in regular education classes or other education-related settings to enable children with disabilities to be educated with nondisabled children to the maximum extent appropriate in accordance with Secs. 300.550- 300.556. (Authority: 20 U.S.C. 1401(29))

Sec. 300.29 Transition services.

(a) As used in this part, transition services means a coordinated set of activities for a student with a disability that—

(1) Is designed within an outcome-oriented process, that promotes movement from school to post-school activities, including postsecondary education, vocational training, integrated employment (including supported employment), continuing and adult education, adult services, independent living, or community participation;

(2) Is based on the individual student's needs, taking into account the student's preferences and interests; and

(3) Includes—

(i) Instruction;

(ii) Related services;

(iii) Community experiences;

(iv) The development of employment and other post-school adult living objectives; and

(v) If appropriate, acquisition of daily living skills and functional vocational evaluation.

(b) Transition services for students with disabilities may be special education, if provided as specially designed instruction, or related services, if required to assist a student with a disability to benefit from special education. (Authority: 20 U.S.C. 1401(30))

Sec. 300.30 Definitions in EDGAR.

The following terms used in this part are defined in 34 CFR 77.1:

Application Award Contract Department EDGAR Elementary school Fiscal year Grant Nonprofit Project Secretary Subgrant State educational agency (Authority: 20 U.S.C. 1221e-3(a)(1))

SUBPART B—STATE AND LOCAL ELIGIBILITY

STATE ELIGIBILITY—GENERAL

Sec. 300.110 Condition of assistance.

(a) A State is eligible for assistance under Part B of the Act for a fiscal year if the State demonstrates to the satisfaction of the Secretary that the State has in effect policies and procedures to ensure that it meets the conditions in Secs. 300.121-300.156.

(b) To meet the requirement of paragraph (a) of this section, the State must have on file with the Secretary—

(1) The information specified in Secs. 300.121-300.156 that the State uses to implement the requirements of this part; and

(2) Copies of all applicable State statutes, regulations, and other State documents that show the basis of that information. (Authority: 20 U.S.C. 1412(a))

Sec. 300.111 Exception for prior State policies and procedures on file with the Secretary.

If a State has on file with the Secretary policies and procedures approved by the Secretary that demonstrate that the State meets any requirement of Sec. 300.110, including any policies and procedures filed under Part B of the Act as in effect before June 4, 1997, the Secretary considers the State to have met the requirement for purposes of receiving a grant under Part B of the Act. (Authority: 20 U.S.C. 1412(c)(1))

Sec. 300.112 Amendments to State policies and procedures.

(a) Modifications made by a State.

(1) Subject to paragraph (b) of this section, policies and procedures submitted by a State in accordance with this subpart remain in effect until the State submits to the Secretary the modifications that the State decides are necessary.

(2) The provisions of this subpart apply to a modification to a State's policies and procedures in the same manner and to the same extent that they apply to the State's original policies and procedures.

(b) Modifications required by the Secretary. The Secretary may require a State to modify its policies and procedures, but only to the extent necessary to ensure the State's compliance with this part, if—

(1) After June 4, 1997, the provisions of the Act or the regulations in this part are amended;

(2) There is a new interpretation of this Act or regulations by a Federal court or a State's highest court; or

(3) There is an official finding of noncompliance with Federal law or regulations. (Authority: 20 U.S.C. 1412(c)(2) and (3))

Sec. 300.113 Approval by the Secretary.

(a) General. If the Secretary determines that a State is eligible to receive a grant under Part B of the Act, the Secretary notifies the State of that determination.

(b) Notice and hearing before determining a State is not eligible. The Secretary does not make a final determination that a State is not eligible to receive a grant under Part B of the Act until after providing the State reasonable notice and an opportunity for a hearing in accordance with the procedures in Secs. 300.581-300.586. (Authority: 20 U.S.C. 1412(d))

Secs. 300.114—300.120 [Reserved]

STATE ELIGIBILITY—SPECIFIC CONDITIONS

Sec. 300.121 Free appropriate public education (FAPE).

(a) General. Each State must have on file with the Secretary information that shows that, subject to Sec. 300.122, the State has in effect a policy that ensures that all children with disabilities aged 3 through 21 residing in the State have the right to FAPE, including children with disabilities who have been suspended or expelled from school.

(b) Required information. The information described in paragraph (a) of this section must—

(1) Include a copy of each State statute, court order, State Attorney General opinion, and other State documents that show the source of the State's policy relating to FAPE; and

(2) Show that the policy—

(i) (A) Applies to all public agencies in the State; and

(B) Is consistent with the requirements of Secs. 300.300-300.313; and

(ii) Applies to all children with disabilities, including children who have been suspended or expelled from school.

(c) FAPE for children beginning at age 3.

(1) Each State shall ensure that—

(i) The obligation to make FAPE available to each eligible child residing in the State begins no later than the child's third birthday; and

(ii) An IEP or an IFSP is in effect for the child by that date, in accordance with Sec. 300.342(c).

(2) If a child's third birthday occurs during the summer, the child's IEP team shall determine the date when services under the IEP or IFSP will begin.

(d) FAPE for children suspended or expelled from school.

(1) A public agency need not provide services during periods of removal under Sec. 300.520(a)(1) to a child with a disability who has been removed from his or her current placement for 10 school days or less in that school year, if services are not provided to a child without disabilities who has been similarly removed.

(2) In the case of a child with a disability who has been removed from his or her current placement for more than 10 school days in that school year, the public agency, for the remainder of the removals, must—

(i) Provide services to the extent necessary to enable the child to appropriately progress in the general curriculum and appropriately advance toward achieving the goals set out in the child's IEP, if the removal is—

(A) Under the school personnel's authority to remove for not more than 10 consecutive school days as long as that removal does not constitute a change of placement under Sec. 300.519(b) (Sec. 300.520((a)(1)); or

(B) For behavior that is not a manifestation of the child's disability, consistent with Sec. 300.524; and

(ii) Provide services consistent with Sec. 300.522, regarding determination of the appropriate interim alternative educational setting, if the removal is—

(A) For drug or weapons offenses under Sec. 300.520(a)(2); or

(B) Based on a hearing officer determination that maintaining the current placement of the child is substantially likely to result in injury to the child or to others if he or she remains in the current placement, consistent with Sec. 300.521.

(3)

(i) School personnel, in consultation with the child's special education teacher, determine the extent to which services are necessary to enable the child to appropriately progress in the general curriculum and appropriately advance toward achieving the goals set out in the child's IEP if the child is removed under the authority of school personnel to remove for not more than 10 consecutive school days as long as that removal does not constitute a change of placement under Sec. 300.519 (Sec. 300.520(a)(1)).

(ii) The child's IEP team determines the extent to which services are necessary to enable the child to appropriately progress in the general curriculum and appropriately advance toward achieving the goals set out in the child's IEP if the child is removed because of behavior that has been determined not to be a manifestation of the child's disability, consistent with Sec. 300.524.

(e) Children advancing from grade to grade.

(1) Each State shall ensure that FAPE is available to any individual child with a disability who needs special education and related services, even though the child is advancing from grade to grade.

(2) The determination that a child described in paragraph (a)(1) of this section is eligible under this part, must be made on an individual basis by the group responsible within the child's LEA for making those determinations. (Authority: 20 U.S.C. 1412(a)(1))

Sec. 300.122 Exception to FAPE for certain ages.

(a) General. The obligation to make FAPE available to all children with disabilities does not apply with respect to the following:

(1) Children aged 3, 4, 5, 18, 19, 20, or 21 in a State to the extent that its application to those children would be inconsistent with State law or practice, or the order of any court, respecting the provision of public education to children in one or more of those age groups.

(2)

(i) Students aged 18 through 21 to the extent that State law does not require that special education and related services under Part B of the Act be provided to students with disabilities who, in the last educational placement prior to their incarceration in an adult correctional facility—

(A) Were not actually identified as being a child with a disability under Sec. 300.7; and

(B) Did not have an IEP under Part B of the Act.

(ii) The exception in paragraph (a)(2)(i) of this section does not apply to students with disabilities, aged 18 through 21, who—

(A) Had been identified as a child with disability and had received services in accordance with an IEP, but who left school prior to their incarceration; or

        (B) Did not have an IEP in their last educational setting, but who had actually been identified as a "child with a disability" under Sec. 300.7.

    (3)

        (i) Students with disabilities who have graduated from high school with a regular high school diploma.

        (ii) The exception in paragraph (a)(3)(i) of this section does not apply to students who have graduated but have not been awarded a regular high school diploma.

        (iii) Graduation from high school with a regular diploma constitutes a change in placement, requiring written prior notice in accordance with Sec. 300.503.

(b) Documents relating to exceptions. The State must have on file with the Secretary—

    (1)

        (i) Information that describes in detail the extent to which the exception in paragraph (a)(1) of this section applies to the State; and

        (ii) A copy of each State law, court order, and other documents that provide a basis for the exception; and

    (2) With respect to paragraph (a)(2) of this section, a copy of the State law that excludes from services under Part B of the Act certain students who are incarcerated in an adult correctional facility. (Authority: 20 U.S.C. 1412(a)(1)(B))

Sec. 300.123 Full educational opportunity goal (FEOG).

The State must have on file with the Secretary detailed policies and procedures through which the State has established a goal of providing full educational opportunity to all children with disabilities aged birth through 21. (Authority: 20 U.S.C. 1412(a)(2))

Sec. 300.124 FEOG—timetable.

The State must have on file with the Secretary a detailed timetable for accomplishing the goal of providing full educational opportunity for all children with disabilities. (Authority: 20 U.S.C. 1412(a)(2))

Sec. 300.125 Child find.

(a) General requirement.

    (1) The State must have in effect policies and procedures to ensure that—

        (i) All children with disabilities residing in the State, including children with disabilities attending private schools, regardless of the severity of their disability, and who are in need of special education and related services, are identified, located, and evaluated; and

        (ii) A practical method is developed and implemented to determine which children are currently receiving needed special education and related services.

    (2) The requirements of paragraph (a)(1) of this section apply to—

        (i) Highly mobile children with disabilities (such as migrant and homeless children); and

        (ii) Children who are suspected of being a child with a disability under Sec. 300.7 and in need of special education, even though they are advancing from grade to grade.

(b) Documents relating to child find. The State must have on file with the Secretary the policies and procedures described in paragraph (a) of this section, including—

    (1) The name of the State agency (if other than the SEA) responsible for coordinating the planning and implementation of the policies and procedures under paragraph (a) of this section;

    (2) The name of each agency that participates in the planning and implementation of the child find activities and a description of the nature and extent of its participation;

    (3) A description of how the policies and procedures under paragraph (a) of this section will be monitored to ensure that the SEA obtains—

        (i) The number of children with disabilities within each disability category that have been identified, located, and evaluated; and

        (ii) Information adequate to evaluate the effectiveness of those policies and procedures; and

    (4) A description of the method the State uses to determine which children are currently receiving special education and related services.

(c) Child find for children from birth through age 2 when the SEA and lead agency for the Part C program are different.

    (1) In States where the SEA and the State's lead agency for the Part C program are different and the Part C lead agency will be participating in the child find activities described in paragraph (a) of this section, a description of the nature and extent of the Part C lead agency's participation must be included under paragraph (b)(2) of this section.

    (2) With the SEA's agreement, the Part C lead agency's participation may include the actual implementation of child find activities for infants and toddlers with disabilities.

    (3) The use of an interagency agreement or other mechanism for providing for the Part C lead agency's participation does not alter or diminish the responsibility of the SEA to ensure compliance with the requirements of this section.

(d) Construction. Nothing in the Act requires that children be classified by their disability so long as each child who has a disability listed in Sec. 300.7 and who, by reason of that disability, needs special education and related services is regarded as a child with a disability under Part B of the Act.

(e) Confidentiality of child find data. The collection and use of data to meet the requirements of this section are subject to the confidentiality requirements of Secs. 300.560-300.577. (Authority: 20 U.S.C. 1412 (a)(3)(A) and (B))

Sec. 300.126 Procedures for evaluation and determination of eligibility.

The State must have on file with the Secretary policies and procedures that ensure that the requirements of Secs. 300.530-300.536 are met. (Authority: 20 U.S.C. 1412(a)(6)(B), (7))

Sec. 300.127 Confidentiality of personally identifiable information.

(a) The State must have on file in detail the policies and procedures that the State has undertaken to ensure protection of the confidentiality of any personally identifiable information, collected, used, or maintained under Part B of the Act.

(b) The Secretary uses the criteria in Secs. 300.560-300.576 to evaluate the policies and procedures of the State under paragraph (a) of this section. (Authority: 20 U.S.C. 1412(a)(8))

Sec. 300.128 Individualized education programs.

(a) General. The State must have on file with the Secretary information that shows that an IEP, or an IFSP that meets the requirements of section 636(d) of the Act, is developed, reviewed, and revised for each child with a disability in accordance with Secs. 300.340-300.350.

(b) Required information. The information described in paragraph (a) of this section must include—

(1) A copy of each State statute, policy, and standard that regulates the manner in which IEPs are developed, implemented, reviewed, and revised; and

(2) The procedures that the SEA follows in monitoring and evaluating those IEPs or IFSPs. (Authority: 20 U.S.C. 1412(a)(4))

Sec. 300.129 Procedural safeguards.

(a) The State must have on file with the Secretary procedural safeguards that ensure that the requirements of Secs. 300.500-300.529 are met.

(b) Children with disabilities and their parents must be afforded the procedural safeguards identified in paragraph (a) of this section. (Authority: 20 U.S.C. 1412(a)(6)(A))

Sec. 300.130 Least restrictive environment.

(a) General. The State must have on file with the Secretary procedures that ensure that the requirements of Secs. 300.550-300.556 are met, including the provision in Sec. 300.551 requiring a continuum of alternative placements to meet the unique needs of each child with a disability.

(b) Additional requirement.

(1) If the State uses a funding mechanism by which the State distributes State funds on the basis of the type of setting where a child is served, the funding mechanism may not result in placements that violate the requirements of paragraph (a) of this section.

(2) If the State does not have policies and procedures to ensure compliance with paragraph (b)(1) of this section, the State must provide the Secretary an assurance that the State will revise the funding mechanism as soon as feasible to ensure that the mechanism does not result in placements that violate that paragraph. (Authority: 20 U.S.C. 1412(a)(5))

Sec. 300.131 [Reserved]

Sec. 300.132 Transition of children from Part C to preschool programs.

The State must have on file with the Secretary policies and procedures to ensure that—

(a) Children participating in early-intervention programs assisted under Part C of the Act, and who will participate in preschool programs assisted under Part B of the Act, experience a smooth and effective transition to those preschool programs in a manner consistent with section 637(a)(8) of the Act;

(b) By the third birthday of a child described in paragraph (a) of this section, an IEP or, if consistent with Sec. 300.342(c) and section 636(d) of the Act, an IFSP, has been developed and is being implemented for the child consistent with Sec. 300.121(c); and

(c) Each LEA will participate in transition planning conferences arranged by the designated lead agency under section 637(a)(8) of the Act. (Authority: 20 U.S.C. 1412(a)(9))

Sec. 300.133 Children in private schools.

The State must have on file with the Secretary policies and procedures that ensure that the requirements of Secs. 300.400-300.403 and Secs. 300.450-300.462 are met. (Authority: 20 U.S.C. 1413(a)(4))

Sec. 300.134 [Reserved]

Sec. 300.135 Comprehensive system of personnel development.

  (a) General. The State must have in effect, consistent with the purposes of this part and with section 635(a)(8) of the Act, a comprehensive system of personnel development that—

    (1) Is designed to ensure an adequate supply of qualified special education, regular education, and related services personnel; and

    (2) Meets the requirements for a State improvement plan relating to personnel development in section 653(b)(2)(B) and (c)(3)(D) of the Act.

  (b) Information. The State must have on file with the Secretary information that shows that the requirements of paragraph (a) of this section are met. (Authority: 20 U.S.C. 1412(a)(14))

Sec. 300.136 Personnel standards.

  (a) Definitions. As used in this part—

    (1) Appropriate professional requirements in the State means entry level requirements that—

      (i) Are based on the highest requirements in the State applicable to the profession or discipline in which a person is providing special education or related services; and

      (ii) Establish suitable qualifications for personnel providing special education and related services under Part B of the Act to children with disabilities who are served by State, local, and private agencies (see Sec. 300.2);

    (2) Highest requirements in the State applicable to a specific profession or discipline means the highest entry-level academic degree needed for any State-approved or -recognized certification, licensing, registration, or other comparable requirements that apply to that profession or discipline;

    (3) Profession or discipline means a specific occupational category that—

      (i) Provides special education and related services to children with disabilities under Part B of the Act;

      (ii) Has been established or designated by the State;

      (iii) Has a required scope of responsibility and degree of supervision; and

      (iv) Is not limited to traditional occupational categories; and

    (4) State-approved or -recognized certification, licensing, registration, or other comparable requirements means the requirements that a State legislature either has enacted or has authorized a State agency to promulgate through rules to establish the entry-level standards for employment in a specific profession or discipline in that State.

  (b) Policies and procedures.

    (1)

      (i) The State must have on file with the Secretary policies and procedures relating to the establishment and maintenance of standards to ensure that personnel necessary to carry out the purposes of this part are appropriately and adequately prepared and trained.

      (ii) The policies and procedures required in paragraph (b)(1)(i) of this section must provide for the establishment and maintenance of standards that are consistent with any State-approved or -recognized certification, licensing, registration, or other comparable requirements that apply to the profession or discipline in which a person is providing special education or related services.

    (2) Each State may—

      (i) Determine the specific occupational categories required to provide special education and related services within the State; and

      (ii) Revise or expand those categories as needed.

    (3) Nothing in this part requires a State to establish a specified training standard (e.g., a masters degree) for personnel who provide special education and related services under Part B of the Act.

    (4) A State with only one entry-level academic degree for employment of personnel in a specific profession or discipline may modify that standard as necessary to ensure the provision of FAPE to all children with disabilities in the State without violating the requirements of this section.

  (c) Steps for retraining or hiring personnel. To the extent that a State's standards for a profession or discipline, including standards for temporary or emergency certification, are not based on the highest requirements in the State applicable to a specific profession or discipline, the State must provide the steps the State is taking and the procedures for notifying public agencies and personnel of those steps and the timelines it has established for the retraining or hiring of personnel to meet appropriate professional requirements in the State.

  (d) Status of personnel standards in the State.

    (1) In meeting the requirements in paragraphs (b) and (c) of this section, a determination must be made about the status of personnel standards in the State. That determination must be based on current information that accurately describes, for each profession or discipline in which personnel are providing special education or related services, whether the applicable standards are consistent with the highest requirements in the State for that profession or discipline.

    (2) The information required in paragraph (d)(1) of this section must be on file in the SEA and available to the public.

  (e) Applicability of State statutes and agency rules. In identifying the highest requirements in the State for purposes of this section, the requirements of all State statutes and the rules of all State agencies applicable to serving children with disabilities must be considered.

  (f) Use of paraprofessionals and assistants. A State may allow paraprofessionals and assistants who are appropriately trained and supervised, in accordance with State law, regulations, or written policy, in meeting the requirements of this part to be used to assist in the provision of special education and related services to children with disabilities under Part B of the Act.

(g) Policy to address shortage of personnel.

(1) In implementing this section, a State may adopt a policy that includes a requirement that LEAs in the State make an ongoing good faith effort to recruit and hire appropriately and adequately trained personnel to provide special education and related services to children with disabilities, including, in a geographic area of the State where there is a shortage of personnel that meet these qualifications, the most qualified individuals available who are making satisfactory progress toward completing applicable course work necessary to meet the standards described in paragraph (b)(2) of this section, consistent with State law and the steps described in paragraph (c) of this section, within three years.

(2) If a State has reached its established date under paragraph (c) of this section, the State may still exercise the option under paragraph (g)(1) of this section for training or hiring all personnel in a specific profession or discipline to meet appropriate professional requirements in the State.

(3)(i) Each State must have a mechanism for serving children with disabilities if instructional needs exceed available personnel who meet appropriate professional requirements in the State for a specific profession or discipline.

(ii) A State that continues to experience shortages of qualified personnel must address those shortages in its comprehensive system of personnel development under Sec. 300.135. (Authority: 20 U.S.C. 1412(a)(15))

Sec. 300.137 Performance goals and indicators.

The State must have on file with the Secretary information to demonstrate that the State—

(a) Has established goals for the performance of children with disabilities in the State that—

(1) Will promote the purposes of this part, as stated in Sec. 300.1; and

(2) Are consistent, to the maximum extent appropriate, with other goals and standards for all children established by the State;

(b) Has established performance indicators that the State will use to assess progress toward achieving those goals that, at a minimum, address the performance of children with disabilities on assessments, drop-out rates, and graduation rates;

(c) Every two years, will report to the Secretary and the public on the progress of the State, and of children with disabilities in the State, toward meeting the goals established under paragraph (a) of this section; and

(d) Based on its assessment of that progress, will revise its State improvement plan under subpart 1 of Part D of the Act as may be needed to improve its performance, if the State receives assistance under that subpart. (Authority: 20 U.S.C. 1412(a)(16))

Sec. 300.138 Participation in assessments.

The State must have on file with the Secretary information to demonstrate that—

(a) Children with disabilities are included in general State and district-wide assessment programs, with appropriate accommodations and modifications in administration, if necessary;

(b) As appropriate, the State or LEA—

(1) Develops guidelines for the participation of children with disabilities in alternate assessments for those children who cannot participate in State and district-wide assessment programs;

(2) Develops alternate assessments in accordance with paragraph (b)(1) of this section; and

(3) Beginning not later than, July 1, 2000, conducts the alternate assessments described in paragraph (b)(2) of this section. (Authority: 20 U.S.C. 1412(a)(17)(A))

Sec. 300.139 Reports relating to assessments.

(a) General. In implementing the requirements of Sec. 300.138, the SEA shall make available to the public, and report to the public with the same frequency and in the same detail as it reports on the assessment of nondisabled children, the following information:

(1) The number of children with disabilities participating—

(i) In regular assessments; and

(ii) In alternate assessments.

(2) The performance results of the children described in paragraph (a)(1) of this section if doing so would be statistically sound and would not result in the disclosure of performance results identifiable to individual children—

(i) On regular assessments (beginning not later than July 1, 1998); and

(ii) On alternate assessments (not later than July 1, 2000).

(b) Combined reports. Reports to the public under paragraph (a) of this section must include—

(1) Aggregated data that include the performance of children with disabilities together with all other children; and

(2) Disaggregated data on the performance of children with disabilities.

(c) Timeline for disaggregation of data. Data relating to the performance of children described under paragraph (a)(2) of this section must be disaggregated—

(1) For assessments conducted after July 1, 1998; and

(2) For assessments conducted before July 1, 1998, if the State is required to disaggregate the data prior to July 1, 1998. (Authority: 20 U.S.C. 612(a)(17)(B))

Sec. 300.140 [Reserved]

Sec. 300.141 SEA responsibility for general supervision.
(a) The State must have on file with the Secretary information that shows that the requirements of Sec. 300.600 are met.

(b) The information described under paragraph (a) of this section must include a copy of each State statute, State regulation, signed agreement between respective agency officials, and any other documents that show compliance with that paragraph. (Authority: 20 U.S.C. 1412(a)(11))

Sec. 300.142 Methods of ensuring services.
(a) Establishing responsibility for services. The Chief Executive Officer or designee of that officer shall ensure that an interagency agreement or other mechanism for interagency coordination is in effect between each noneducational public agency described in paragraph (b) of this section and the SEA, in order to ensure that all services described in paragraph (b)(1) of this section that are needed to ensure FAPE are provided, including the provision of these services during the pendency of any dispute under paragraph (a)(3) of this section. The agreement or mechanism must include the following:

(1) Agency financial responsibility. An identification of, or a method for defining, the financial responsibility of each agency for providing services described in paragraph (b)(1) of this section to ensure FAPE to children with disabilities. The financial responsibility of each noneducational public agency described in paragraph (b) of this section, including the State Medicaid agency and other public insurers of children with disabilities, must precede the financial responsibility of the LEA (or the State agency responsible for developing the child's IEP).

(2) Conditions and terms of reimbursement. The conditions, terms, and procedures under which an LEA must be reimbursed by other agencies.

(3) Interagency disputes. Procedures for resolving interagency disputes (including procedures under which LEAs may initiate proceedings) under the agreement or other mechanism to secure reimbursement from other agencies or otherwise implement the provisions of the agreement or mechanism.

(4) Coordination of services procedures. Policies and procedures for agencies to determine and identify the interagency coordination responsibilities of each agency to promote the coordination and timely and appropriate delivery of services described in paragraph (b)(1) of this section.

(b) Obligation of noneducational public agencies.
(1) General.
(i) If any public agency other than an educational agency is otherwise obligated under Federal or State law, or assigned responsibility under State policy or pursuant to paragraph (a) of this section, to provide or pay for any services that are also considered special education or related services (such as, but not limited to, services described in Sec. 300.5 relating to assistive technology devices, Sec. 300.6 relating to assistive technology services, Sec. 300.24 relating to related services, Sec. 300.28 relating to supplementary aids and services, and Sec. 300.29 relating to transition services) that are necessary for ensuring FAPE to children with disabilities within the State, the public agency shall fulfill that obligation or responsibility, either directly or through contract or other arrangement.

(ii) A noneducational public agency described in paragraph (b)(1)(i) of this section may not disqualify an eligible service for Medicaid reimbursement because that service is provided in a school context.

(2) Reimbursement for services by noneducational public agency. If a public agency other than an educational agency fails to provide or pay for the special education and related services described in paragraph (b)(1) of this section, the LEA (or State agency responsible for developing the child's IEP) shall provide or pay for these services to the child in a timely manner. The LEA or State agency may then claim reimbursement for the services from the noneducational public agency that failed to provide or pay for these services and that agency shall reimburse the LEA or State agency in accordance with the terms of the interagency agreement or other mechanism described in paragraph (a)(1) of this section, and the agreement described in paragraph (a)(2) of this section.

(c) Special rule. The requirements of paragraph (a) of this section may be met through—
(1) State statute or regulation;
(2) Signed agreements between respective agency officials that clearly identify the responsibilities of each agency relating to the provision of services; or
(3) Other appropriate written methods as determined by the Chief Executive Officer of the State or designee of that officer.

(d) Information. The State must have on file with the Secretary information to demonstrate that the requirements of paragraphs (a) through (c) of this section are met.

(e) Children with disabilities who are covered by public insurance.
(1) A public agency may use the Medicaid or other public insurance benefits programs in which a child participates to provide or pay for services required under this part, as permitted under the public insurance program, except as provided in paragraph (e)(2) of this section.
(2) With regard to services required to provide FAPE to an eligible child under this part, the public agency—
(i) May not require parents to sign up for or enroll in public insurance programs in order for their child to receive FAPE under Part B of the Act;

(ii) May not require parents to incur an out-of-pocket expense such as the payment of a deductible or co-pay amount incurred in filing a claim for services provided pursuant to this part, but pursuant to paragraph (g)(2) of this section, may pay the cost that the parent otherwise would be required to pay; and

(iii) May not use a child's benefits under a public insurance program if that use would—

(A) Decrease available lifetime coverage or any other insured benefit;

(B) Result in the family paying for services that would otherwise be covered by the public insurance program and that are required for the child outside of the time the child is in school;

(C) Increase premiums or lead to the discontinuation of insurance; or

(D) Risk loss of eligibility for home and community-based waivers, based on aggregate health-related expenditures.

(f) Children with disabilities who are covered by private insurance.

(1) With regard to services required to provide FAPE to an eligible child under this part, a public agency may access a parent's private insurance proceeds only if the parent provides informed consent consistent with Sec. 300.500(b)(1).

(2) Each time the public agency proposes to acess the parent's private insurance proceeds, it must—

(i) Obtain parent consent in accordance with paragraph (f)(1) of this section; and

(ii) Inform the parents that their refusal to permit the public agency to access their private insurance does not relieve the public agency of its responsibility to ensure that all required services are provided at no cost to the parents.

(g) Use of Part B funds.

(1) If a public agency is unable to obtain parental consent to use the parent's private insurance, or public insurance when the parent would incur a cost for a specified service required under this part, to ensure FAPE the public agency may use its Part B funds to pay for the service.

(2) To avoid financial cost to parents who otherwise would consent to use private insurance, or public inurance if the parent would incur a cost, the public agency may use its Part B funds to pay the cost the parents otherwise would have to pay to use the parent's insurance (e.g., the deductible or co-pay amounts).

(h) Proceeds from public or private insurance.

(1) Proceeds from public or private insurance will not be treated as program income for purposes of 34 CFR 80.25.

(2) If a public agency spends reimbursements from Federal funds (e.g., Medicaid) for services under this part, those funds will not be considered "State or local" funds for purposes of the maintenance of effort provisions in Secs. 300.154 and 300.231.

(i) Construction. Nothing in this part should be construed to alter the requirements imposed on a State Medicaid agency, or any other agency administering a public insurance program by Federal statute, regulations or policy under title XIX, or title XXI of the Social Security Act, or any other public insurance program. (Authority: 20 U.S.C. 1412(a)(12)(A), (B), and (C); 1401(8))

Sec. 300.143 SEA implementation of procedural safeguards.

The State must have on file with the Secretary the procedures that the SEA (and any agency assigned responsibility pursuant to Sec. 300.600(d)) follows to inform each public agency of its responsibility for ensuring effective implementation of procedural safeguards for the children with disabilities served by that public agency. (Authority: 20 U.S.C. 1412(a)(11); 1415(a))

Sec. 300.144 Hearings relating to LEA eligibility.

The State must have on file with the Secretary procedures to ensure that the SEA does not make any final determination that an LEA is not eligible for assistance under Part B of the Act without first giving the LEA reasonable notice and an opportunity for a hearing under 34 CFR 76.401(d). (Authority: 20 U.S.C. 1412(a)(13))

ec. 300.145 Recovery of funds for misclassified children.

The State must have on file with the Secretary policies and procedures that ensure that the State seeks to recover any funds provided under Part B of the Act for services to a child who is determined to be erroneously classified as eligible to be counted under section 611(a) or (d) of the Act. (Authority: 20 U.S.C. 1221e-3(a)(1))

Sec. 300.146 Suspension and expulsion rates.

The State must have on file with the Secretary information to demonstrate that the following requirements are met:

(a) General. The SEA examines data to determine if significant discrepancies are occurring in the rate of long-term suspensions and expulsions of children with disabilities—

(1) Among LEAs in the State; or

(2) Compared to the rates for nondisabled children within the agencies.

(b) Review and revision of policies. If the discrepancies described in paragraph (a) of this section are occurring, the SEA reviews and, if appropriate, revises (or requires the affected State agency or LEA to revise) its policies, procedures, and practices relating to the development and implementation of IEPs, the use of behavioral interventions, and procedural safeguards, to ensure that these policies, procedures, and practices comply with the Act. (Authority: 20 U.S.C. 612(a)(22))

Sec. 300.147 Additional information if SEA provides direct services.

(a) If the SEA provides FAPE to children with disabilities, or provides direct services to these children, the agency—

(1) Shall comply with any additional requirements of Secs. 300.220- 300.230(a) and 300.234-300.250 as if the agency were an LEA; and

(2) May use amounts that are otherwise available to the agency under Part B of the Act to serve those children without regard to Sec. 300.184 (relating to excess costs).

(b) The SEA must have on file with the Secretary information to demonstrate that it meets the requirements of paragraph (a)(1) of this section. (Authority: 20 U.S.C. 1412(b))

Sec. 300.148 Public participation.

(a) General; exception.

(1) Subject to paragraph (a)(2) of this section, each State must ensure that, prior to the adoption of any policies and procedures needed to comply with this part, there are public hearings, adequate notice of the hearings, and an opportunity for comment available to the general public, including individuals with disabilities and parents of children with disabilities consistent with Secs. 300.280-300.284.

(2) A State will be considered to have met paragraph (a)(1) of this section with regard to a policy or procedure needed to comply with this part if it can demonstrate that prior to the adoption of that policy or procedure, the policy or procedure was subjected to a public review and comment process that is required by the State for other purposes and is comparable to and consistent with the requirements of Secs. 300.280-300.284.

(b) Documentation. The State must have on file with the Secretary information to demonstrate that the requirements of paragraph (a) of this section are met. (Authority: 20 U.S.C. 1412(a)(20))

Sec. 300.149 [Reserved]

Sec. 300.150 State advisory panel.

The State must have on file with the Secretary information to demonstrate that the State has established and maintains an advisory panel for the purpose of providing policy guidance with respect to special education and related services for children with disabilities in the State in accordance with the requirements of Secs. 300.650- 300.653. (Authority: 20 U.S.C. 1412(a)(21)(A))

Sec. 300.151 [Reserved]

Sec. 300.152 Prohibition against commingling.

(a) The State must have on file with the Secretary an assurance satisfactory to the Secretary that the funds under Part B of the Act are not commingled with State funds.

(b) The assurance in paragraph (a) of this section is satisfied by the use of a separate accounting system that includes an audit trail of the expenditure of the Part B funds. Separate bank accounts are not required. (See 34 CFR 76.702 (Fiscal control and fund accounting procedures).) (Authority: 20 U.S.C. 1412(a)(18)(B))

Sec. 300.153 State-level nonsupplanting.

(a) General.

(1) Except as provided in Sec. 300.230, funds paid to a State under Part B of the Act must be used to supplement the level of Federal, State, and local funds (including funds that are not under the direct control of the SEA or LEAs) expended for special education and related services provided to children with disabilities under Part B of the Act and in no case to supplant these Federal, State, and local funds.

(2) The State must have on file with the Secretary information to demonstrate to the satisfaction of the Secretary that the requirements of paragraph (a)(1) of this section are met.

(b) Waiver. If the State provides clear and convincing evidence that all children with disabilities have available to them FAPE, the Secretary may waive, in whole or in part, the requirements of paragraph (a) of this section if the Secretary concurs with the evidence provided by the State under Sec. 300.589. (Authority: 20 U.S.C. 1412(a)(18)(c))

Sec. 300.154 Maintenance of State financial support.

(a) General. The State must have on file with the Secretary information to demonstrate, on either a total or per-capita basis, that the State will not reduce the amount of State financial support for special education and related services for children with disabilities, or otherwise made available because of the excess costs of educating those children, below the amount of that support for the preceding fiscal year.

(b) Reduction of funds for failure to maintain support. The Secretary reduces the allocation of funds under section 611 of the Act for any fiscal year following the fiscal year in which the State fails to comply with the requirement of paragraph (a) of this section by the same amount by which the State fails to meet the requirement.

(c) Waivers for exceptional or uncontrollable circumstances. The Secretary may waive the requirement of paragraph (a) of this section for a State, for one fiscal year at a time, if the Secretary determines that—

(1) Granting a waiver would be equitable due to exceptional or uncontrollable circumstances such as a natural disaster or a precipitous and unforeseen decline in the financial resources of the State; or

(2) The State meets the standard in Sec. 300.589 for a waiver of the requirement to supplement, and not to supplant, funds received under Part B of the Act.

(d) Subsequent years. If, for any fiscal year, a State fails to meet the requirement of paragraph (a) of this section, including any year for which the State is granted a waiver under paragraph (c) of this section, the financial support required of the State in future years under paragraph (a) of this section must be the amount that would have been required in the absence of that failure and not the reduced level of the State's support. (Authority: 20 U.S.C. 1412(a)(19))

Sec. 300.155 Policies and procedures for use of Part B funds.

The State must have on file with the Secretary policies and procedures designed to ensure that funds paid to the State under Part B of the Act are spent in accordance with the provisions of Part B. (Authority: 20 U.S.C. 1412(a)(18)(A))

Sec. 300.156 Annual description of use of Part B funds.

(a) In order to receive a grant in any fiscal year a State must annually describe—

(1) How amounts retained for State-level activities under Sec. 300.602 will be used to meet the requirements of this part;

(2) How those amounts will be allocated among the activities described in Secs. 300.621 and 300.370 to meet State priorities based on input from LEAs; and

(3) The percentage of those amounts, if any, that will be distributed to LEAs by formula.

(b) If a State's plans for use of its funds under Secs. 300.370 and 300.620 for the forthcoming year do not change from the prior year, the State may submit a letter to that effect to meet the requirement in paragraph (a) of this section. (Authority: 20 U.S.C. 1411(f)(5))

LEA AND STATE AGENCY ELIGIBILITY—GENERAL

Sec. 300.180 Condition of assistance.

An LEA or State agency is eligible for assistance under Part B of the Act for a fiscal year if the agency demonstrates to the satisfaction of the SEA that it meets the conditions in Secs. 300.220- 300.250. (Authority: 20 U.S.C. 1413(a))

Sec. 300.181 Exception for prior LEA or State agency policies and procedures on file with the SEA.

If an LEA or a State agency described in Sec. 300.194 has on file with the SEA policies and procedures that demonstrate that the LEA or State agency meets any requirement of Sec. 300.180, including any policies and procedures filed under Part B of the Act as in effect before June 4, 1997, the SEA shall consider the LEA or State agency to have met the requirement for purposes of receiving assistance under Part B of the Act. (Authority: 20 U.S.C. 1413(b)(1))

Sec. 300.182 Amendments to LEA policies and procedures.

(a) Modification made by an LEA or a State agency.

(1) Subject to paragraph (b) of this section, policies and procedures submitted by an LEA or a State agency in accordance with this subpart remain in effect until it submits to the SEA the modifications that the LEA or State agency decides are necessary.

(2) The provisions of this subpart apply to a modification to an LEA's or State agency's policies and procedures in the same manner and to the same extent that they apply to the LEA's or State agency's original policies and procedures.

(b) Modifications required by the SEA. The SEA may require an LEA or a State agency to modify its policies and procedures, but only to the extent necessary to ensure the LEA's or State agency's compliance with this part, if—

(1) After June 4, 1997, the provisions of the Act or the regulations in this part are amended;

(2) There is a new interpretation of the Act by Federal or State courts; or

(3) There is an official finding of noncompliance with Federal or State law or regulations. (Authority: 20 U.S.C. 1413(b))

Sec. 300.183 [Reserved]

Sec. 300.184 Excess cost requirement.

(a) General. Amounts provided to an LEA under Part B of the Act may be used only to pay the excess costs of providing special education and related services to children with disabilities.

(b) Definition. As used in this part, the term excess costs means those costs that are in excess of the average annual per-student expenditure in an LEA during the preceding school year for an elementary or secondary school student, as may be appropriate. Excess costs must be computed after deducting—

(1) Amounts received—

   (i) Under Part B of the Act;

   (ii) Under Part A of title I of the Elementary and Secondary Education Act of 1965; or

   (iii) Under Part A of title VII of that Act; and

(2) Any State or local funds expended for programs that would qualify for assistance under any of those parts.

(c) Limitation on use of Part B funds.

(1) The excess cost requirement prevents an LEA from using funds provided under Part B of the Act to pay for all of the costs directly attributable to the education of a child with a disability, subject to paragraph (c)(2) of this section.

(2) The excess cost requirement does not prevent an LEA from using Part B funds to pay for all of the costs directly attributable to the education of a child with a disability in any of the ages 3, 4, 5, 18, 19, 20, or 21, if no local or State funds are available for nondisabled children in that age range. However, the LEA must comply with the nonsupplanting and other requirements of this part in providing the education and services for these children. (Authority: 20 U.S.C. 1401(7), 1413(a)(2)(A))

Sec. 300.185 Meeting the excess cost requirement.

(a)(1) General. An LEA meets the excess cost requirement if it has spent at least a minimum average amount for the education of its children with disabilities before funds under Part B of the Act are used.

(2) The amount described in paragraph (a)(1) of this section is determined using the formula in Sec. 300.184(b). This amount may not include capital outlay or debt service.

(b) Joint establishment of eligibility. If two or more LEAs jointly establish eligibility in accordance with Sec. 300.190, the minimum average amount is the average of the combined minimum average amounts determined under Sec. 300.184 in those agencies for elementary or secondary school students, as the case may be. (Authority: 20 U.S.C. 1413(a)(2)(A))

Secs. 300.186-300.189 [Reserved]

Sec. 300.190 Joint establishment of eligibility.

(a) General. An SEA may require an LEA to establish its eligibility jointly with another LEA if the SEA determines that the LEA would be ineligible under this section because the agency would not be able to establish and maintain programs of sufficient size and scope to effectively meet the needs of children with disabilities.

(b) Charter school exception. An SEA may not require a charter school that is an LEA to jointly establish its eligibility under paragraph (a) of this section unless it is explicitly permitted to do so under the State's charter school statute.

(c) Amount of payments. If an SEA requires the joint establishment of eligibility under paragraph (a) of this section, the total amount of funds made available to the affected LEAs must be equal to the sum of the payments that each LEA would have received under Secs. 300.711- 300.714 if the agencies were eligible for these payments. (Authority: 20 U.S.C. 1413(e)(1), and (2))

Sec. 300.191 [Reserved]

Sec. 300.192 Requirements for establishing eligibility.

(a) Requirements for LEAs in general. LEAs that establish joint eligibility under this section must—

   (1) Adopt policies and procedures that are consistent with the State's policies and procedures under Secs. 300.121-300.156; and

   (2) Be jointly responsible for implementing programs that receive assistance under Part B of the Act.

(b) Requirements for educational service agencies in general. If an educational service agency is required by State law to carry out programs under Part B of the Act, the joint responsibilities given to LEAs under Part B of the Act—

   (1) Do not apply to the administration and disbursement of any payments received by that educational service agency; and

   (2) Must be carried out only by that educational service agency.

(c) Additional requirement. Notwithstanding any other provision of Secs. 300.190-300.192, an educational service agency shall provide for the education of children with disabilities in the least restrictive environment, as required by Sec. 300.130. (Authority: 20 U.S.C. 1413(e)(3), and (4))

Sec. 300.193 [Reserved]

Sec. 300.194 State agency eligibility.

Any State agency that desires to receive a subgrant for any fiscal year under Secs. 300.711-300.714 must demonstrate to the satisfaction of the SEA that—

(a) All children with disabilities who are participating in programs and projects funded under Part B of the Act receive FAPE, and that those children and their parents are provided all the rights and procedural safeguards described in this part; and

(b) The agency meets the other conditions of this subpart that apply to LEAs. (Authority: 20 U.S.C. 1413(i))

Sec. 300.195 [Reserved]

Sec. 300.196 Notification of LEA or State agency in case of ineligibility.

If the SEA determines that an LEA or State agency is not eligible under Part B of the Act, the SEA shall—

(a) Notify the LEA or State agency of that determination; and

(b) Provide the LEA or State agency with reasonable notice and an opportunity for a hearing. (Authority: 20 U.S.C. 1413(c))

Sec. 300.197 LEA and State agency compliance.

(a) **General**. If the SEA, after reasonable notice and an opportunity for a hearing, finds that an LEA or State agency that has been determined to be eligible under this section is failing to comply with any requirement described in Secs. 300.220-300.250, the SEA shall reduce or may not provide any further payments to the LEA or State agency until the SEA is satisfied that the LEA or State agency is complying with that requirement.

(b) **Notice requirement**. Any State agency or LEA in receipt of a notice described in paragraph (a) of this section shall, by means of public notice, take the measures necessary to bring the pendency of an action pursuant to this section to the attention of the public within the jurisdiction of the agency.

(c) In carrying out its functions under this section, each SEA shall consider any decision resulting from a hearing under Secs. 300.507-300.528 that is adverse to the LEA or State agency involved in the decision. (Authority: 20 U.S.C. 1413(d))

LEA AND STATE AGENCY ELIGIBILITY—SPECIFIC CONDITIONS

Sec. 300.220 Consistency with State policies.

(a) **General**. The LEA, in providing for the education of children with disabilities within its jurisdiction, must have in effect policies, procedures, and programs that are consistent with the State policies and procedures established under Secs. 300.121-300.156.

(b) **Policies on file with SEA**. The LEA must have on file with the SEA the policies and procedures described in paragraph (a) of this section. (Authority: 20 U.S.C. 1413(a)(1))

Sec. 300.221 Implementation of CSPD.

The LEA must have on file with the SEA information to demonstrate that—

(a) All personnel necessary to carry out Part B of the Act within the jurisdiction of the agency are appropriately and adequately prepared, consistent with the requirements of Secs. 300.380-300.382; and

(b) To the extent the LEA determines appropriate, it shall contribute to and use the comprehensive system of personnel development of the State established under Sec. 300.135. (Authority: 20 U.S.C. 1413(a)(3))

Secs. 300.222-300.229 [Reserved]

Sec. 300.230 Use of amounts.

The LEA must have on file with the SEA information to demonstrate that amounts provided to the LEA under Part B of the Act—

(a) Will be expended in accordance with the applicable provisions of this part;

(b) Will be used only to pay the excess costs of providing special education and related services to children with disabilities, consistent with Secs. 300.184-300.185; and

(c) Will be used to supplement State, local, and other Federal funds and not to supplant those funds. (Authority: 20 U.S.C. 1413(a)(2)(A))

Sec. 300.231 Maintenance of effort.

(a) **General**. Except as provided in Secs. 300.232 and 300.233, funds provided to an LEA under Part B of the Act may not be used to reduce the level of expenditures for the education of children with disabilities made by the LEA from local funds below the level of those expenditures for the preceding fiscal year.

(b) **Information**. The LEA must have on file with the SEA information to demonstrate that the requirements of paragraph (a) of this section are met.

(c) **Standard**.

(1) Except as provided in paragraph (c)(2) of this section, the SEA determines that an LEA complies with paragraph (a) of this section for purposes of establishing the LEA's eligibility for an award for a fiscal year if the LEA budgets, for the education of children with disabilities, at least the same total or per-capita amount from either of the following sources as the LEA spent for that purpose from the same source for the most recent prior year for which information is available:

(i) Local funds only.

(ii) The combination of State and local funds.

(2) An LEA that relies on paragraph (c)(1)(i) of this section for any fiscal year must ensure that the amount of local funds it budgets for the education of children with disabilities in that year is at least the same, either in total or per capita, as the amount it spent for that purpose in—

(i) The most recent fiscal year for which information is available, if that year is, or is before, the first fiscal year beginning on or after July 1, 1997; or

(ii) If later, the most recent fiscal year for which information is available and the standard in paragraph (c)(1)(i) of this section was used to establish its compliance with this section.

(3) The SEA may not consider any expenditures made from funds provided by the Federal Government for which the SEA is required to account to the Federal Government or for which the LEA is required to account to the Federal Government directly or through the SEA in determining an LEA's compliance with the requirement in paragraph (a) of this section. (Authority: 20 U.S.C. 1413(a)(2)(A))

Sec. 300.232 Exception to maintenance of effort.

An LEA may reduce the level of expenditures by the LEA under Part B of the Act below the level of those expenditures for the preceding fiscal year if the reduction is attributable to the following:

(a)

(1) The voluntary departure, by retirement or otherwise, or departure for just cause, of special education or related services personnel, who are replaced by qualified, lower-salaried staff.

(2) In order for an LEA to invoke the exception in paragraph (a)(1) of this section, the LEA must ensure that those voluntary retirements or resignations and replacements are in full conformity with:

(i) Existing school board policies in the agency;

(ii) The applicable collective bargaining agreement in effect at that time; and

(iii) Applicable State statutes.

(b) A decrease in the enrollment of children with disabilities.

(c) The termination of the obligation of the agency, consistent with this part, to provide a program of special education to a particular child with a disability that is an exceptionally costly program, as determined by the SEA, because the child—

(1) Has left the jurisdiction of the agency;

(2) Has reached the age at which the obligation of the agency to provide FAPE to the child has terminated; or

(3) No longer needs the program of special education.

(d) The termination of costly expenditures for long-term purchases, such as the acquisition of equipment or the construction of school facilities. (Authority: 20 U.S.C. 1413(a)(2)(B))

Sec. 300.233 Treatment of Federal funds in certain fiscal years.

(a)

(1) Subject to paragraphs (a)(2) and (b) of this section, for any fiscal year for which amounts appropriated to carry out section 611 of the Act exceeds $4,100,000,000, an LEA may treat as local funds up to 20 percent of the amount of funds it receives under Part B of the Act that exceeds the amount it received under Part B of the Act for the previous fiscal year.

(2) The requirements of Secs. 300.230(c) and 300.231 do not apply with respect to the amount that may be treated as local funds under paragraph (a)(1) of this section.

(b) If an SEA determines that an LEA is not meeting the requirements of this part, the SEA may prohibit the LEA from treating funds received under Part B of the Act as local funds under paragraph (a)(1) of this section for any fiscal year, but only if it is authorized to do so by the State constitution or a State statute. (Authority: 20 U.S.C. 1413(a)(2)(C))

Sec. 300.234 Schoolwide programs under title I of the ESEA.

(a) General; limitation on amount of Part B funds used. An LEA may use funds received under Part B of the Act for any fiscal year to carry out a schoolwide program under section 1114 of the Elementary and Secondary Education Act of 1965, except that the amount used in any schoolwide program may not exceed—

(1)

(i) The amount received by the LEA under Part B for that fiscal year; divided by

(ii) The number of children with disabilities in the jurisdiction of the LEA; and multiplied by

(2) The number of children with disabilities participating in the schoolwide program.

(b) Funding conditions. The funds described in paragraph (a) of this section are subject to the following conditions:

(1) The funds must be considered as Federal Part B funds for purposes of the calculations required by Secs. 300.230(b) and (c).

(2) The funds may be used without regard to the requirements of Sec. 300.230(a).

(c) Meeting other Part B requirements. Except as provided in paragraph (b) of this section, all other requirements of Part B must be met by an LEA using Part B funds in accordance with paragraph (a) of this section, including ensuring that children with disabilities in schoolwide program schools—

(1) Receive services in accordance with a properly developed IEP; and

(2) Are afforded all of the rights and services guaranteed to children with disabilities under the IDEA. (Authority: 20 U.S.C. 1413(a)(2)(D))

Sec. 300.235 Permissive use of funds.

(a) **General**. Subject to paragraph (b) of this section, funds provided to an LEA under Part B of the Act may be used for the following activities:

(1) **Services and aids that also benefit nondisabled children**. For the costs of special education and related services and supplementary aids and services provided in a regular class or other education- related setting to a child with a disability in accordance with the IEP of the child, even if one or more nondisabled children benefit from these services.

(2) **Integrated and coordinated services system**. To develop and implement a fully integrated and coordinated services system in accordance with Sec. 300.244.

(b) **Non-applicability of certain provisions**. An LEA does not violate Secs. 300.152, 300.230, and 300.231 based on its use of funds provided under Part B of the Act in accordance with paragraphs (a)(1) and (a)(2) of this section. (Authority: 20 U.S.C. 1413(a)(4))

Secs. 300.236-300.239 [Reserved]

Sec. 300.240 Information for SEA.

(a) The LEA shall provide the SEA with information necessary to enable the SEA to carry out its duties under Part B of the Act, including, with respect to Secs. 300.137 and 300.138, information relating to the performance of children with disabilities participating in programs carried out under Part B of the Act.

(b) The LEA must have on file with the SEA an assurance satisfactory to the SEA that the LEA will comply with the requirements of paragraph (a) of this section. (Authority: 20 U.S.C. 1413(a)(6))

Sec. 300.241 Treatment of charter schools and their students.

The LEA must have on file with the SEA information to demonstrate that in carrying out this part with respect to charter schools that are public schools of the LEA, the LEA will—

(a) Serve children with disabilities attending those schools in the same manner as it serves children with disabilities in its other schools; and

(b) Provide funds under Part B of the Act to those schools in the same manner as it provides those funds to its other schools. (Authority: 20 U.S.C. 1413(a)(5))

Sec. 300.242 Public information.

The LEA must have on file with the SEA information to demonstrate to the satisfaction of the SEA that it will make available to parents of children with disabilities and to the general public all documents relating to the eligibility of the agency under Part B of the Act. (Authority: 20 U.S.C. 1413(a)(7))

Sec. 300.243 [Reserved]

Sec. 300.244 Coordinated services system.

(a) **General**. An LEA may not use more than 5 percent of the amount the agency receives under Part B of the Act for any fiscal year, in combination with other amounts (which must include amounts other than education funds), to develop and implement a coordinated services system designed to improve results for children and families, including children with disabilities and their families.

(b) **Activities**. In implementing a coordinated services system under this section, an LEA may carry out activities that include—

(1) Improving the effectiveness and efficiency of service delivery, including developing strategies that promote accountability for results;

(2) Service coordination and case management that facilitate the linkage of IEPs under Part B of the Act and IFSPs under Part C of the Act with individualized service plans under multiple Federal and State programs, such as title I of the Rehabilitation Act of 1973 (vocational rehabilitation), title XIX of the Social Security Act (Medicaid), and title XVI of the Social Security Act (supplemental security income);

(3) Developing and implementing interagency financing strategies for the provision of education, health, mental health, and social services, including transition services and related services under the Act; and

(4) Interagency personnel development for individuals working on coordinated services.

(c) **Coordination with certain projects under Elementary and Secondary Education Act of 1965**. If an LEA is carrying out a coordinated services project under title XI of the Elementary and Secondary Education Act of 1965 and a coordinated services project under Part B of the Act in the same schools, the agency shall use the amounts under Sec. 300.244 in accordance with the requirements of that title. (Authority: 20 U.S.C. 1413(f))

SCHOOL-BASED IMPROVEMENT PLAN

Sec. 300.245 School-based improvement plan.

(a) **General**. Each LEA may, in accordance with paragraph (b) of this section, use funds made available under Part B of the Act to permit a public school within the jurisdiction of the LEA to design, implement, and evaluate a school-based improvement plan that—

(1) Is consistent with the purposes described in section 651(b) of the Act; and

(2) Is designed to improve educational and transitional results for all children with disabilities and, as appropriate, for other children consistent with Sec. 300.235(a) and (b) in that public school.

(b) Authority.

(1) General. An SEA may grant authority to an LEA to permit a public school described in Sec. 300.245 (through a school-based standing panel established under Sec. 300.247(b)) to design, implement, and evaluate a school-based improvement plan described in Sec. 300.245 for a period not to exceed 3 years.

(2) Responsibility of LEA. If an SEA grants the authority described in paragraph (b)(1) of this section, an LEA that is granted this authority must have the sole responsibility of oversight of all activities relating to the design, implementation, and evaluation of any school-based improvement plan that a public school is permitted to design under this section. (Authority: 20 U.S.C. 1413(g)(1) and (g)(2)).

Sec. 300.246 Plan requirements.

A school-based improvement plan described in Sec. 300.245 must—

(a) Be designed to be consistent with the purposes described in section 651(b) of the Act and to improve educational and transitional results for all children with disabilities and, as appropriate, for other children consistent with Sec. 300.235(a) and (b), who attend the school for which the plan is designed and implemented;

(b) Be designed, evaluated, and, as appropriate, implemented by a school-based standing panel established in accordance with Sec. 300.247(b);

(c) Include goals and measurable indicators to assess the progress of the public school in meeting these goals; and

(d) Ensure that all children with disabilities receive the services described in their IEPs. (Authority: 20 U.S.C. 1413(g)(3))

Sec. 300.247 Responsibilities of the LEA.

An LEA that is granted authority under Sec. 300.245(b) to permit a public school to design, implement, and evaluate a school-based improvement plan shall—

(a) Select each school under the jurisdiction of the agency that is eligible to design, implement, and evaluate the plan;

(b) Require each school selected under paragraph (a) of this section, in accordance with criteria established by the LEA under paragraph (c) of this section, to establish a school-based standing panel to carry out the duties described in Sec. 300.246(b);

(c) Establish—

(1) Criteria that must be used by the LEA in the selection of an eligible school under paragraph (a) of this section;

(2) Criteria that must be used by a public school selected under paragraph (a) of this section in the establishment of a school-based standing panel to carry out the duties described in Sec. 300.246(b) and that ensure that the membership of the panel reflects the diversity of the community in which the public school is located and includes, at a minimum—

(i) Parents of children with disabilities who attend a public school, including parents of children with disabilities from unserved and underserved populations, as appropriate;

(ii) Special education and general education teachers of public schools;

(iii) Special education and general education administrators, or the designee of those administrators, of those public schools; and

(iv) Related services providers who are responsible for providing services to the children with disabilities who attend those public schools; and

(3) Criteria that must be used by the LEA with respect to the distribution of funds under Part B of the Act to carry out this section;

(d) Disseminate the criteria established under paragraph (c) of this section to local school district personnel and local parent organizations within the jurisdiction of the LEA;

(e) Require a public school that desires to design, implement, and evaluate a school-based improvement plan to submit an application at the time, in the manner and accompanied by the information, that the LEA shall reasonably require; and

(f) Establish procedures for approval by the LEA of a school-based improvement plan designed under Part B of the Act. • (Authority:1413(g)(4))

Sec. 300.248 Limitation.

A school-based improvement plan described in Sec. 300.245(a) may be submitted to an LEA for approval only if a consensus with respect to any matter relating to the design, implementation, or evaluation of the goals of the plan is reached by the school-based standing panel that designed the plan. (Authority: 20 U.S.C. 1413(g)(5))

Sec. 300.249 Additional requirements.

(a) Parental involvement. In carrying out the requirements of Secs. 300.245-300.250, an LEA shall ensure that the parents of children with disabilities are involved in the design, evaluation, and, if appropriate, implementation of school-based improvement plans in accordance with this section.

(b) Plan approval. An LEA may approve a school-based improvement plan of a public school within the jurisdiction of the agency for a period of 3 years, if—

(1) The approval is consistent with the policies, procedures, and practices established by the LEA and in accordance with Secs. 300.245-300.250; and

(2) A majority of parents of children who are members of the school-based standing panel, and a majority of other members of the school-based standing panel that designed the plan, agree in writing to the plan. (Authority: 20 U.S.C. 1413(g)(6))

Sec. 300.250 Extension of plan.

If a public school within the jurisdiction of an LEA meets the applicable requirements and criteria described in Secs. 300.246 and 300.247 at the expiration of the 3-year approval period described Sec. 300.249(b), the agency may approve a school-based improvement plan of the school for an additional 3-year period. (Authority: 20 U.S.C. 1413(g)(7))

SECRETARY OF THE INTERIOR—ELIGIBILITY

Sec. 300.260 Submission of information.

The Secretary may provide the Secretary of the Interior amounts under Sec. 300.715(b) and (c) for a fiscal year only if the Secretary of the Interior submits to the Secretary information that—

(a) Meets the requirements of section 612(a)(1), (3)—(9), (10)(B), (C), (11)—(12), (14)—(17), (20), (21) and (22) of the Act (including monitoring and evaluation activities);

(b) Meets the requirements of section 612(b) and (e) of the Act;

(c) Meets the requirements of section 613(a)(1), (2)(A)(i), (6), and (7) of the Act;

(d) Meets the requirements of this part that implement the sections of the Act listed in paragraphs (a)-(c) of this section;

(e) Includes a description of how the Secretary of the Interior will coordinate the provision of services under Part B of the Act with LEAs, tribes and tribal organizations, and other private and Federal service providers;

(f) Includes an assurance that there are public hearings, adequate notice of the hearings, and an opportunity for comment afforded to members of tribes, tribal governing bodies, and affected local school boards before the adoption of the policies, programs, and procedures described in paragraph (a) of this section;

(g) Includes an assurance that the Secretary of the Interior will provide the information that the Secretary may require to comply with section 618 of the Act, including data on the number of children with disabilities served and the types and amounts of services provided and needed;

(h)

(1) Includes an assurance that the Secretary of the Interior and the Secretary of Health and Human Services have entered into a memorandum of agreement, to be provided to the Secretary, for the coordination of services, resources, and personnel between their respective Federal, State, and local offices and with the SEAs and LEAs and other entities to facilitate the provision of services to Indian children with disabilities residing on or near reservations.

(2) The agreement must provide for the apportionment of responsibilities and costs, including child find, evaluation, diagnosis, remediation or therapeutic measures, and (if appropriate) equipment and medical or personal supplies, as needed for a child with a disability to remain in a school or program; and

(i) Includes an assurance that the Department of the Interior will cooperate with the Department in its exercise of monitoring and oversight of the requirements in this section and Secs. 300.261- 300.267, and any agreements entered into between the Secretary of the Interior and other entities under Part B of the Act, and will fulfill its duties under Part B of the Act. Section 616(a) of the Act applies to the information described in this section. (Authority: 20 U.S.C. 1411(i)(2))

Sec. 300.261 Public participation.

In fulfilling the requirements of Sec. 300.260 the Secretary of the Interior shall provide for public participation consistent with Secs. 300.280-300.284. (Authority: 20 U.S.C. 1411(i))

Sec. 300.262 Use of Part B funds.

(a) The Department of the Interior may use five percent of its payment under Sec. 300.715(b) and (c) in any fiscal year, or $500,000, whichever is greater, for administrative costs in carrying out the provisions of this part.

(b) Payments to the Secretary of the Interior under Sec. 300.716 must be used in accordance with that section. (Authority: 20 U.S.C. 1411(i))

Sec. 300.263 Plan for coordination of services.

(a) The Secretary of the Interior shall develop and implement a plan for the coordination of services for all Indian children with disabilities residing on reservations covered under Part B of the Act.

(b) The plan must provide for the coordination of services benefiting these children from whatever source, including tribes, the Indian Health Service, other BIA divisions, and other Federal agencies.

(c) In developing the plan, the Secretary of the Interior shall consult with all interested and involved parties.

(d) The plan must be based on the needs of the children and the system best suited for meeting those needs, and may involve the establishment of cooperative agreements between the BIA, other Federal agencies, and other entities.

(e) The plan also must be distributed upon request to States, SEAs and LEAs, and other agencies providing services to infants, toddlers, and children with disabilities, to tribes, and to other interested parties. (Authority: 20 U.S.C. 1411(i)(4))

Sec. 300.264 Definitions.

(a) **Indian**. As used in this part, the term Indian means an individual who is a member of an Indian tribe.

(b) **Indian tribe**. As used in this part, the term Indian tribe means any Federal or State Indian tribe, band, rancheria, pueblo, colony, or community, including any Alaska Native village or regional village corporation (as defined in or established under the Alaska Native Claims Settlement Act). (Authority: 20 U.S.C. 1401(9) and (10))

Sec. 300.265 Establishment of advisory board.

(a) To meet the requirements of section 612(a)(21) of the Act, the Secretary of the Interior shall establish, not later than December 4, 1997 under the BIA, an advisory board composed of individuals involved in or concerned with the education and provision of services to Indian infants, toddlers, and children with disabilities, including Indians with disabilities, Indian parents of the children, teachers, service providers, State and local educational officials, representatives of tribes or tribal organizations, representatives from State Interagency Coordinating Councils under section 641 of the Act in States having reservations, and other members representing the various divisions and entities of the BIA. The chairperson must be selected by the Secretary of the Interior.

(b) The advisory board shall—

(1) Assist in the coordination of services within the BIA and with other local, State, and Federal agencies in the provision of education for infants, toddlers, and children with disabilities;

(2) Advise and assist the Secretary of the Interior in the performance of the Secretary's responsibilities described in section 611(i) of the Act;

(3) Develop and recommend policies concerning effective inter- and intra-agency collaboration, including modifications to regulations, and the elimination of barriers to inter- and intra-agency programs and activities;

(4) Provide assistance and disseminate information on best practices, effective program coordination strategies, and recommendations for improved educational programming for Indian infants, toddlers, and children with disabilities; and

(5) Provide assistance in the preparation of information required under Sec. 300.260(g). (Authority: 20 U.S.C. 1411(i)(5))

Sec. 300.266 Annual report by advisory board.

(a) **General**. The advisory board established under Sec. 300.265 shall prepare and submit to the Secretary of the Interior and to the Congress an annual report containing a description of the activities of the advisory board for the preceding year.

(b) **Report to the Secretary.** The Secretary of the Interior shall make available to the Secretary the report described in paragraph (a) of this section. (Authority: 20 U.S.C. 1411(i)(6)(A))

Sec. 300.267 Applicable regulations.

The Secretary of the Interior shall comply with the requirements of Secs. 300.301-300.303, 300.305-300.309, 300.340-300.348, 300.351, 300.360-300.382, 300.400-300.402, 300.500-300.586, 300.600-300.621, and 300.660-300.662. (Authority: 20 U.S.C. 1411(i)(2)(A))

PUBLIC PARTICIPATION

Sec. 300.280 Public hearings before adopting State policies and procedures.

Prior to its adoption of State policies and procedures related to this part, the SEA shall—

(a) Make the policies and procedures available to the general public;

(b) Hold public hearings; and

(c) Provide an opportunity for comment by the general public on the policies and procedures. (Authority: 20 U.S.C. 1412(a)(20))

Sec. 300.281 Notice.

(a) The SEA shall provide adequate notice to the general public of the public hearings.

(b) The notice must be in sufficient detail to inform the general public about—

(1) The purpose and scope of the State policies and procedures and their relation to Part B of the Act;

(2) The availability of the State policies and procedures;

(3) The date, time, and location of each public hearing;

(4) The procedures for submitting written comments about the policies and procedures; and

(5) The timetable for submitting the policies and procedures to the Secretary for approval.

(c) The notice must be published or announced—

(1) In newspapers or other media, or both, with circulation adequate to notify the general public about the hearings; and

(2) Enough in advance of the date of the hearings to afford interested parties throughout the State a reasonable opportunity to participate. (Authority: 20 U.S.C. 1412(a)(20))

Sec. 300.282 Opportunity to participate; comment period.

(a) The SEA shall conduct the public hearings at times and places that afford interested parties throughout the State a reasonable opportunity to participate.

(b) The policies and procedures must be available for comment for a period of at least 30 days following the date of the notice under Sec. 300.281. (Authority: 20 U.S.C. 1412(a)(20))

Sec. 300.283 Review of public comments before adopting policies and procedures.

Before adopting the policies and procedures, the SEA shall—

(a) Review and consider all public comments; and

(b) Make any necessary modifications in those policies and procedures. (Authority: 20 U.S.C. 1412(a)(20))

Sec. 300.284 Publication and availability of approved policies and procedures.

After the Secretary approves a State's policies and procedures, the SEA shall give notice in newspapers or other media, or both, that the policies and procedures are approved. The notice must name places throughout the State where the policies and procedures are available for access by any interested person. (Authority: 20 U.S.C. 1412(a)(20))

Subpart C—Services

FREE APPROPRIATE PUBLIC EDUCATION

Sec. 300.300 Provision of FAPE.

(a) **General**.

(1) Subject to paragraphs (b) and (c) of this section and Sec. 300.311, each State receiving assistance under this part shall ensure that FAPE is available to all children with disabilities, aged 3 through 21, residing in the State, including children with disabilities who have been suspended or expelled from school.

(2) As a part of its obligation under paragraph (a)(1) of this section, each State must ensure that the requirements of Sec. 300.125 (to identify, locate, and evaluate all children with disabilities) are implemented by public agencies throughout the State.

(3)

    (i) The services provided to the child under this part address all of the child's identified special education and related services needs described in paragraph (a) of this section.

    (ii) The services and placement needed by each child with a disability to receive FAPE must be based on the child's unique needs and not on the child's disability.

(b) **Exception for age ranges 3-5 and 18-21**. This paragraph provides the rules for applying the requirements in paragraph (a) of this section to children with disabilities aged 3, 4, 5, 18, 19, 20, and 21 within the State:

(1) If State law or a court order requires the State to provide education for children with disabilities in any disability category in any of these age groups, the State must make FAPE available to all children with disabilities of the same age who have that disability.

(2) If a public agency provides education to nondisabled children in any of these age groups, it must make FAPE available to at least a proportionate number of children with disabilities of the same age.

(3) If a public agency provides education to 50 percent or more of its children with disabilities in any disability category in any of these age groups, it must make FAPE available to all its children with disabilities of the same age who have that disability. This provision does not apply to children aged 3 through 5 for any fiscal year for which the State receives a grant under section 619(a)(1) of the Act.

(4) If a public agency provides education to a child with a disability in any of these age groups, it must make FAPE available to that child and provide that child and his or her parents all of the rights under Part B of the Act and this part.

(5) A State is not required to make FAPE available to a child with a disability in one of these age groups if—

    (i) State law expressly prohibits, or does not authorize, the expenditure of public funds to provide education to nondisabled children in that age group; or

    (ii) The requirement is inconsistent with a court order that governs the provision of free public education to children with disabilities in that State.

(c) **Children aged 3 through 21 on Indian reservations**. With the exception of children identified in Sec. 300.715(b) and (c), the SEA shall ensure that all of the requirements of Part B of the Act are implemented for all children with disabilities aged 3 through 21 on reservations. (Authority: 20 U.S.C. 1412(a)(1), 1411(i)(1)(C), S. Rep. No. 94— 168, p. 19 (1975))

Sec. 300.301 FAPE—methods and payments.

(a) Each State may use whatever State, local, Federal, and private sources of support are available in the State to meet the requirements of this part. For example, if it is necessary to place a child with a disability in a residential facility, a State could use joint agreements between the agencies involved for sharing the cost of that placement.

(b) Nothing in this part relieves an insurer or similar third party from an otherwise valid obligation to provide or to pay for services provided to a child with a disability.

(c) Consistent with Secs. 300.342(b)(2) and 300.343(b), the State must ensure that there is no delay in implementing a child's IEP, including any case in which the payment source for providing or paying for special education and related services to the child is being determined. (Authority: 20 U.S.C. 1401(8), 1412(a)(1))

Sec. 300.302 Residential placement.

If placement in a public or private residential program is necessary to provide special education and related services to a child with a disability, the program, including non-medical care and room and board, must be at no cost to the parents of the child. (Authority: 20 U.S.C. 1412(a)(1), 1412(a)(10)(B))

Sec. 300.303 Proper functioning of hearing aids.

Each public agency shall ensure that the hearing aids worn in school by children with hearing impairments, including deafness, are functioning properly. (Authority: 20 U.S.C. 1412(a)(1))

Sec. 300.304 Full educational opportunity goal.

Each SEA shall ensure that each public agency establishes and implements a goal of providing full educational opportunity to all children with disabilities in the area served by the public agency. (Authority: 20 U.S.C. 1412(a)(2))

Sec. 300.305 Program options.

Each public agency shall take steps to ensure that its children with disabilities have available to them the variety of educational programs and services available to nondisabled children in the area served by the agency, including art, music, industrial arts, consumer and homemaking education, and vocational education. (Authority: 20 U.S.C. 1412(a)(2), 1413(a)(1))

Sec. 300.306 Nonacademic services.

(a) Each public agency shall take steps to provide nonacademic and extracurricular services and activities in the manner necessary to afford children with disabilities an equal opportunity for participation in those services and activities.

(b) Nonacademic and extracurricular services and activities may include counseling services, athletics, transportation, health services, recreational activities, special interest groups or clubs sponsored by the public agency, referrals to agencies that provide assistance to individuals with disabilities, and employment of students, including both employment by the public agency and assistance in making outside employment available. (Authority: 20 U.S.C. 1412(a)(1))

Sec. 300.307 Physical education.

(a) General. Physical education services, specially designed if necessary, must be made available to every child with a disability receiving FAPE.

(b) Regular physical education. Each child with a disability must be afforded the opportunity to participate in the regular physical education program available to nondisabled children unless—

    (1) The child is enrolled full time in a separate facility; or

    (2) The child needs specially designed physical education, as prescribed in the child's IEP.

(c) Special physical education. If specially designed physical education is prescribed in a child's IEP, the public agency responsible for the education of that child shall provide the services directly or make arrangements for those services to be provided through other public or private programs.

(d) Education in separate facilities. The public agency responsible for the education of a child with a disability who is enrolled in a separate facility shall ensure that the child receives appropriate physical education services in compliance with paragraphs (a) and (c) of this section. (Authority: 20 U.S.C. 1412(a)(25), 1412(a)(5)(A))

Sec. 300.308 Assistive technology.

(a) Each public agency shall ensure that assistive technology devices or assistive technology services, or both, as those terms are defined in Secs. 300.5-300.6, are made available to a child with a disability if required as a part of the child's—

    (1) Special education under Sec. 300.26;

    (2) Related services under Sec. 300.24; or

    (3) Supplementary aids and services under Secs. 300.28 and 300.550(b)(2).

(b) On a case-by-case basis, the use of school-purchased assistive technology devices in a child's home or in other settings is required if the child's IEP team determines that the child needs access to those devices in order to receive FAPE. (Authority: 20 U.S.C. 1412(a)(12)(B)(i))

Sec. 300.309 Extended school year services.

(a) **General.**

(1) Each public agency shall ensure that extended school year services are available as necessary to provide FAPE, consistent with paragraph (a)(2) of this section.

(2) Extended school year services must be provided only if a child's IEP team determines, on an individual basis, in accordance with Secs. 300.340-300.350, that the services are necessary for the provision of FAPE to the child.

(3) In implementing the requirements of this section, a public agency may not—

(i) Limit extended school year services to particular categories of disability; or

(ii) Unilaterally limit the type, amount, or duration of those services.

(b) Definition. As used in this section, the term extended school year services means special education and related services that—

(1) Are provided to a child with a disability—

(i) Beyond the normal school year of the public agency;

(ii) In accordance with the child's IEP; and

(iii) At no cost to the parents of the child; and

(2) Meet the standards of the SEA. (Authority: 20 U.S.C. 1412(a)(1))

Sec. 300.310 [Reserved]

Sec. 300.311 FAPE requirements for students with disabilities in adult prisons.

(a) **Exception to FAPE for certain students.** Except as provided in Sec. 300.122(a)(2)(ii), the obligation to make FAPE available to all children with disabilities does not apply with respect to students aged 18 through 21 to the extent that State law does not require that special education and related services under Part B of the Act be provided to students with disabilities who, in the last educational placement prior to their incarceration in an adult correctional facility—

(1) Were not actually identified as being a child with a disability under Sec. 300.7; and

(2) Did not have an IEP under Part B of the Act.

(b) **Requirements that do not apply.** The following requirements do not apply to students with disabilities who are convicted as adults under State law and incarcerated in adult prisons:

(1) The requirements contained in Sec. 300.138 and Sec. 300.347(a)(5)(i) (relating to participation of children with disabilities in general assessments).

(2) The requirements in Sec. 300.347(b) (relating to transition planning and transition services), with respect to the students whose eligibility under Part B of the Act will end, because of their age, before they will be eligible to be released from prison based on consideration of their sentence and eligibility for early release.

(c) **Modifications of IEP or placement.**

(1) Subject to paragraph (c)(2) of this section, the IEP team of a student with a disability, who is convicted as an adult under State law and incarcerated in an adult prison, may modify the student's IEP or placement if the State has demonstrated a bona fide security or compelling penological interest that cannot otherwise be accommodated.

(2) The requirements of Secs. 300.340(a) and 300.347(a) relating to IEPs, and 300.550(b) relating to LRE, do not apply with respect to the modifications described in paragraph (c)(1) of this section. (Authority: 20 U.S.C. 1412(a)(1), 1414(d)(6))

Sec. 300.312 Children with disabilities in public charter schools.

(a) Children with disabilities who attend public charter schools and their parents retain all rights under this part.

(b) If the public charter school is an LEA, consistent with Sec. 300.17, that receives funding under Secs. 300.711-300.714, that charter school is responsible for ensuring that the requirements of this part are met, unless State law assigns that responsibility to some other entity.

(c) If the public charter school is a school of an LEA that receives funding under Secs. 300.711-300.714 and includes other public schools—

(1) The LEA is responsible for ensuring that the requirements of this part are met, unless State law assigns that responsibility to some other entity; and

(2) The LEA must meet the requirements of Sec. 300.241.

(d)

(1) If the public charter school is not an LEA receiving funding under Secs. 300.711-300.714, or a school that is part of an LEA receiving funding under Secs. 300.711-300.714, the SEA is responsible for ensuring that the requirements of this part are met.

(2) Paragraph (d)(1) of this section does not preclude a State from assigning initial responsibility for ensuring the requirements of this part are met to another entity; however, the SEA must maintain the ultimate responsibility for ensuring compliance with this part, consistent with Sec. 300.600. (Authority: 20 U.S.C. 1413(a)(5))

Sec. 300.313 Children experiencing developmental delays.

(a) Use of term developmental delay.

(1) A State that adopts the term developmental delay under Sec. 300.7(b) determines whether it applies to children aged 3 through 9, or to a subset of that age range (e.g., ages 3 through 5).

(2) A State may not require an LEA to adopt and use the term developmental delay for any children within its jurisdiction.

(3) If an LEA uses the term developmental delay for children described in Sec. 300.7(b), the LEA must conform to both the State's definition of that term and to the age range that has been adopted by the State.

(4) If a State does not adopt the term developmental delay, an LEA may not independently use that term as a basis for establishing a child's eligibility under this part.

(b) Use of individual disability categories.

(1) Any State or LEA that elects to use the term developmental delay for children aged 3 through 9 may also use one or more of the disability categories described in Sec. 300.7 for any child within that age range if it is determined, through the evaluation conducted under Secs. 300.530- 300.536, that the child has an impairment described in Sec. 300.7, and because of that impairment needs special education and related services.

(2) The State or LEA shall ensure that all of the child's special education and related services needs that have been identified through the evaluation described in paragraph (b)(1) of this section are appropriately addressed.

(c) Common definition of developmental delay. A State may adopt a common definition of developmental delay for use in programs under Parts B and C of the Act. (Authority: 20 U.S.C. 1401(3)(A) and (B))

EVALUATIONS AND REEVALUATIONS

Sec. 300.320 Initial evaluations.

(a) Each public agency shall ensure that a full and individual evaluation is conducted for each child being considered for special education and related services under Part B of the Act—

(1) To determine if the child is a "child with a disability" under Sec. 300.7; and

(2) To determine the educational needs of the child.

(b) In implementing the requirements of paragraph (a) of this section, the public agency shall ensure that—

(1) The evaluation is conducted in accordance with the procedures described in Secs. 300.530-300.535; and

(2) The results of the evaluation are used by the child's IEP team in meeting the requirements of Secs. 300.340-300.350. (Authority: 20 U.S.C. 1414(a), (b), and (c))

Sec. 300.321 Reevaluations.

Each public agency shall ensure that—

(a) A reevaluation of each child with a disability is conducted in accordance with Sec. 300.536; and

(b) The results of any reevaluations are addressed by the child's IEP team under Secs. 300.340-300.349 in reviewing and, as appropriate, revising the child's IEP. (Authority: 20 U.S.C. 1414(a)(2))

Secs. 300.322-300.324 [Reserved]

INDIVIDUALIZED EDUCATION PROGRAMS

Sec. 300.340 Definitions related to IEPs.

(a) Individualized education program. As used in this part, the term individualized education program or IEP means a written statement for a child with a disability that is developed, reviewed, and revised in a meeting in accordance with Secs. 300.341-300.350.

(b) Participating agency. As used in Sec. 300.348, participating agency means a State or local agency, other than the public agency responsible for a student's education, that is financially and legally responsible for providing transition services to the student. (Authority: 20 U.S.C. 1401(11), 1412(a)(10)(B))

Sec. 300.341 Responsibility of SEA and other public agencies for IEPs.

(a) The SEA shall ensure that each public agency—

(1) Except as provided in Secs. 300.450-300.462, develops and implements an IEP for each child with a disability served by that agency; and

(2) Ensures that an IEP is developed and implemented for each eligible child placed in or referred to a private school or facility by the public agency.

(b) Paragraph (a) of this section applies to—

(1) The SEA, if it is involved in providing direct services to children with disabilities, in accordance with Sec. 300.370(a) and (b)(1); and

(2) Except as provided in Sec. 300.600(d), the other public agencies described in Sec. 300.2, including LEAs and other State agencies that provide special education and related services either directly, by contract, or through other arrangements. (Authority: 20 U.S.C. 1412(a)(4), (a)(10)(B))

Sec. 300.342 When IEPs must be in effect.

(a) General. At the beginning of each school year, each public agency shall have an IEP in effect for each child with a disability within its jurisdiction.

(b) Implementation of IEPs. Each public agency shall ensure that—

(1) An IEP—

(i) Is in effect before special education and related services are provided to an eligible child under this part; and

(ii) Is implemented as soon as possible following the meetings described under Sec. 300.343;

(2) The child's IEP is accessible to each regular education teacher, special education teacher, related service provider, and other service provider who is responsible for its implementation; and

(3) Each teacher and provider described in paragraph (b)(2) of this section is informed of—

(i) His or her specific responsibilities related to implementing the child's IEP; and

(ii) The specific accommodations, modifications, and supports that must be provided for the child in accordance with the IEP.

(c) IEP or IFSP for children aged 3 through 5.

(1) In the case of a child ith a disability aged 3 through 5 (or, at the discretion of the SEA a 2-year-old child with a disability who will turn age 3 during the school year), an IFSP that contains the material described in section 636 of the Act, and that is developed in accordance with Secs. 300.341- 300.346 and Secs. 300.349-300.350, may serve as the IEP of the child if using that plan as the IEP is—

(i) Consistent with State policy; and

(ii) Agreed to by the agency and the child's parents.

(2) In implementing the requirements of paragraph (c)(1) of this section, the public agency shall—

(i) Provide to the child's parents a detailed explanation of the differences between an IFSP and an IEP; and

(ii) If the parents choose an IFSP, obtain written informed consent from the parents.

(d) Effective date for new requirements. All IEPs developed, reviewed, or revised on or after July 1, 1998 must meet the requirements of Secs. 300.340-300.350. (Authority: 20 U.S.C. 1414(d)(2)(A) and (B), Pub. L. 105-17, sec. 201(a)(2)(A), (C)

Sec. 300.343 IEP meetings.

(a) General. Each public agency is responsible for initiating and conducting meetings for the purpose of developing, reviewing, and revising the IEP of a child with a disability (or, if consistent with Sec. 300.342(c), an IFSP).

(b) Initial IEPs; provision of services.

(1) Each public agency shall ensue that within a reasonable period of time following the agency's receipt of parent consent to an initial evaluation of a child—

(i) The child is evaluated; and

(ii) If determined eligible under this part, special education and related services are made available to the child in accordance with an IEP.

(2) In meeting the requirement in paragraph (b)(1) of this section, a meeting to develop an IEP for the child must be conducted within 30-days of a determination that the child needs special education and related services.

(c) Review and revision of IEPs. Each public agency shall ensure that the IEP team—

(1) Reviews the child's IEP periodically, but not less than annually, to determine whether the annual goals for the child are being achieved; and

(2) Revises the IEP as appropriate to address—

(i) Any lack of expected progress toward the annual goals described in Sec. 300.347(a), and in the general curriculum, if appropriate;

(ii) The results of any reevaluation conducted under Sec. 300.536;

(iii) Information about the child provided to, or by, the parents, as described in Sec. 300.533(a)(1);

(iv) The child's anticipated needs; or

(v) Other matters. (Authority: 20 U.S.C. 1413(a)(1), 1414(d)(4)(A))

Sec. 300.344 IEP team.

(a) General. The public agency shall ensure that the IEP team for each child with a disability includes—

(1) The **parents** of the child;

(2) **At least one regular education teacher of the child** (if the child is, or may be, paricipating in the regular education environment);

(3) **At least one special education teacher of the child, or** if appropriate, at least one**special education provider of the child**;

(4) A **representative of the public agency** who—

(i) Is qualified to provide, o supervise the provision of, specially designed instruction to meet the unique needs of children with disabilities;

(ii) Is knowledgeable about the general curriculum; and

(iii) Is knowledgeable about the availability of resources of the public agency;

(5) An **individual who can interpret the instructional implications of evaluation results**, who may be a member of the team described in paragraphs (a)(2) through (6) of this section;

(6) At the discretion of the parent or the agency, **other individuals who have knowledge or special expertise regarding the child,** including related services personnel as appropriate; and

(7) **If appropriate, the child.**

(b) Transition services participants.

(1) Under paragraph (a) () of this sction, the public agency shall invite a student with a disability of any age to attend his or her IEP meeting if a purpose of the meeting will be the consideration of—

(i) The student's transition services needs under Sec. 300.347(b)(1);

(ii) The needed transition services for the student under Sec. 300.347(b)(2); or

(iii) Both.

(2) If the student does not attend the IEP meeting, the public agency shall take other steps to ensure that the student's preferences and interests are considered.

(3)

(i) In implementing the requirements of Sec. 300.347(b)(2), the public agency also shall invite a representative of any other agency that is likely to be responsible for providing or paying for transition services.

(ii) If an agency invited to send a representative to a meeting does not do so, the public agency shall take other steps to obtain participation of the other agency in the planning of any transition services.

(c) Determination of knowledge and special expertise. The determination of the knowledge or pecial expertise of any individual described in paragraph (a)(6) of this section shall be made by the party (parents or public agency) who invited the individual to be a member of the IEP.

(d) Designating a public agency representative. A public agency may designate another public agency member of the IEP team to also serve as the agency representative, if the criteria in paragraph (a)(4) of this section are satisfied. (Authority: 20 U.S.C. 1401(30), 1414(d)(1)(A)(7), (B))

Sec. 300.345 Parent participation.

(a) Public agency responsibility—general. Each public agency shall take steps to ensure that one or both of the parents of a child with a disability are present at each IEP meeting or are afforded the opportunity to participate, including—

(1) Notifying parents of the meeting early enough to ensure that they will have an opportunity to attend; and

(2) Scheduling the meeting at a mutually agreed on time and place.

(b) Information provided to parents.

(1) The notice required under paragraph (a)(1) of this section must—

(i) Indicate the purpose, time, and location of the meeting and who will be in attendance; and

(ii) Inform the parents of the provisions in Sec. 300.344(a)(6) and (c) (relating to the participation of other individuals on the IEP team who have knowledge or special expertise about the child).

(2) For a student with a disability beginning at age 14, or younger, if appropriate, the notice must also—

(i) Indicate that a purpose of the meeting will be the development of a statement of the transition services needs of the student required in Sec. 300.347(b)(1); and

(ii) Indicate that the agency will invite the student.

(3) For a student with a disability beginning at age 16, or younger, if appropriate, the notice must—

(i) Indicate that a purpose of the meeting is the consideration of needed transition services for the student required in Sec. 300.347(b)(2);

(ii) Indicate that the agency will invite the student; and

(iii) Identify any other agency that will be invited to send a representative.

(c) Other methods to ensure parent participation. If neither parent can attend, the public agency shall use other methods to ensure parent participation, including individual or conference telephone calls.

(d) Conducting an IEP meeting without a parent in attendance. A meeting may be conducted without a parent in attendance if the public agency is unable to convince the parents that they should attend. In this case the public agency must have a record of its attempts to arrange a mutually agreed on time and place, such as—

(1) Detailed records of telephone calls made or attempted and the results of those calls;

(2) Copies of correspondence sent to the parents and any responses received; and

(3) Detailed records of visits made to the parent's home or place of employment and the results of those visits.

(e) Use of interpreters or other action, as appropriate. The public agency hall take whatever action is necessary to ensure that the parent understands the proceedings at the IEP meeting, including arranging for an interpreter for parents with deafness or whose native language is other than English.

(f) Parent copy of child's IEP. The public agency shall give the parent a copy of the child's IEP at no cost to the parent. (Authority: 20 U.S.C. 1414(d)(1)(B)(i))

Sec. 300.346 Development, review, and revision of IEP.

  (a) Development of IEP.

    (1) General. In developing each child's IEP, the IP team, shall consider—

      (i) The strengths of the child and the concerns of the parents for enhancing the education of their child;

      (ii) The results of the initial or most recent evaluation of the child; and

      (iii) As appropriate, the results of the child's performance on any general State or district-wide assessment programs.

    (2) Consideration of special factors. The IEP team also shall—

      (i) In the case of a child whose **behavior impedes his or her learning or that of others**, consider, if appropriate, strategies, including positive behavioral interventions, strategies, and supports to address that behavior;

      (ii) In the case of a child with **limited English proficiency,** consider the language needs of the child as those needs relate to the child's IEP;

      (iii) In the case of a child who is **blind or visually impaired**, provide for instruction in Braille and theuse of Braille unless the IEP team determines, after an evaluation of the child's reading and writing skills, needs, and appropriate reading and writing media (including an evaluation of the child's future needs for instruction in Braille or the use of Braille), that instruction in Braille or the use of Braille is not appropriate for the child;

      (iv) Consider the **communication needs of the child**, and in the case of a child who is **deaf or hard of hearing**, consider the child's language an communication needs, opportunities for direct communications with peers and professional personnel in the child's language and communication mode, academic level, and full range of needs, including opportunities for direct instruction in the child's language and communication mode; and

      (v) Consider whether the child requires **assistive technology devices and services**.

  (b) Review and Revision of IEP. In conducting a meeting to review, and, if ppropriate, revise a child's IEP, the IEP team shall consider the factors described in paragraph (a) of this section.

  (c) Statement in IEP. If, in considering the special factors described in paragraphs (a)(1) and (2) of this section, the IEP team determines that a child needs a particular device or service (including an intervention, accommodation, or other program modification) in order for the child to receive FAPE, the IEP team must include a statement to that effect in the child's IEP.

  (d) Requirement with respect to regular education teacher. The regular education teacher of a child with a disability, as a member of the IEP team, must, to the extent appropriate, participate in the development, review, and revision of the child's IEP, including assisting in the determination of—

    (1) Appropriate positive behavioral interventions and strategies for the child; and

    (2) Supplementary aids and services, program modifications or supports for school personnel that will be provided for the child, consistent with Sec. 300.347(a)(3).

  (e) Construction. Nothing in this section shall be construed to require the IEP team to include information under one component of a child's IEP that is already contained under another component of the child's IEP. (Authority: 20 U.S.C. 1414(d)(3) and (4)(B) and (e))

Sec. 300.347 Content of IEP.

  (a) General. The IEP for each child with a disability must include—

    (1) A statement of the child's present levels of educational performance, including—

      (i) How the child's disability affects the child's involvement and progress in the general curriculum (i.e., the same curriculum as for nondisabled children); or

      (ii) For preschool children, as appropriate, how the disability affects the child's participation in appropriate activities;

    (2) A statement of measurable annual goals, including benchmarks or short-term objectives, related to—

      (i) Meeting the child's needs that result from the child's disability to enable the child to be involved in and progress in the general curriculum (i.e., the same curriculum as for nondisabled children), or for preschool children, as appropriate, to participate in appropriate activities; and

      (ii) Meeting each of the child's other educational needs that result from the child's disability;

    (3) A statement of the special education and related services and supplementary aids and services to be provided to the child, or on behalf of the child, **and a statement of the program modifications or supports for school personnel that will be provided for the child**—

      (i) To advance appropriately toward attaining the annual goals;

      (ii) To be involved and progress in the general curriculum in accordance with paragraph (a)(1) of this section and to participate in extra-curricular and other nonacademic activities; and

      (iii) To be educated and participate with other children with disabilities and nondisabled children in the activities described in this section;

    (4) An explanation of the extent, if any, to which the child will not participate with nondisabled children in the regular class and in the activities described in paragraph (a)(3) of this section;

(5)

(i) A statement of any **individual modifications** in the administration of **State or district-wide assessments** of student achievement that are needed in order for the child to participate in the assessment; and

(ii) If the IEP team determines that the child will not participate in a particular State or district-wide assessment of student achievement (or part of an assessment), a statement of—

(A) Why that assessment is not appropriate for the child; and

(B) How the child will be assessed;

(6) The **projected date for the beginning of the services** and modifications described in paragraph (a)(3) of this section, and the **anticipated frequency, location, and duration of those services** and modifications; and

(7) A statement of—

(i) **How the child's progress toward the annual goals described in paragraph (a)(2) of this section will be measured**; and

(ii) **How the child's parents will be regularly informed** (through such means as periodic report cards), at least as often as parents are informed of their nondisabled children's progress, of—

(A) Their **child's progress toward the annual goals**; and

(B) **The extent to which that progress is sufficient to enable the child to achieve the goals by the end of the year**.

(b) Transition services. The IEP must include—

(1) For each student with a disability beginning at age 14 (or younger, if determined appropriate by the IEP team), and updated annually, a statement of the transition service needs of the student under the applicable components of the student's IEP that focuses on the student's courses of study (such as participation in advanced- placement courses or a vocational education program); and

(2) For each student beginning at age 16 (or younger, if determined appropriate by the IEP team), a statement of needed transition services for the student, including, if appropriate, a statement of the interagency responsibilities or any needed linkages.

(c) Transfer of rights. In a State that transfers rights at the age majority, beginning at least one year before a student reaches the age of majority under State law, the student's IEP must include a statement that the student has been informed of his or her rights under Part B of the Act, if any, that will transfer to the student on reaching the age of majority, consistent with Sec. 300.517.

(d) Students with disabilities convicted as adults and incarcerated in adult prisons. Special rules concerning the content of IEPs for students with disabilities convicted as adults and incarcerated in adult prisons are contained in Sec. 300.311(b) and (c). (Authority: 20 U.S.C. 1414(d)(1)(A) and (d)(6)(A)(ii))

Sec. 300.348 Agency responsibilities for transition services.

(a) If a participating agency, other than the public agency, fails to provide the transition services described in the IEP in accordance with Sec. 300.347(b)(1), the public agency shall reconvene the IEP team to identify alternative strategies to meet the transition objectives for the student set out in the IEP.

(b) Nothing in this part relieves any participating agency, including a State vocational rehabilitation agency, of the responsibility to provide or pay for any transition service that the agency would otherwise provide to students with disabilities who meet the eligibility criteria of that agency. (Authority: 20 U.S.C. 1414(d)(5); 1414(d)(1)(A)(vii))

Sec. 300.349 Private school placements by public agencies.

(a) Developing IEPs.

(1) Before a public agency places a child with a disability in, or refers a child to, a private school or facility, the agency shall initiate and conduct a meeting to develop an IEP for the child in accordance with Secs. 300.346 and 300.347.

(2) The agency shall ensure that a representative of the private school or facility attends the meeting. If the representative cannot attend, the agency shall use other methods to ensure participation by the private school or facility, including individual or conference telephone calls.

(b) Reviewing and revising IEPs.

(1) After a child with a disability enters a private school or facility, any meetings to review and revise the child's IEP may be initiated and conducted by the private school or facility at the discretion of the public agency.

(2) If the private school or facility initiates and conducts these meetings, the public agency shall ensure that the parents and an agency representative—

(i) Are involved in any decision about the child's IEP; and

(ii) Agree to any proposed changes in the IEP before those changes are implemented.

(c) Responsibility. Even if a private school or facility implements a child's IEP, responsibility for compliance with this part remains with the public agency and the SEA. (Authority: 20 U.S.C. 1412(a)(10)(B))

Sec. 300.350 IEP—accountability.

(a) Provision of services. Subject to paragraph (b) of this section, each public agency must—

(1) Provide special education and related services to a child with a disability in accordance with the child's IEP; and

(2) Make a good faith effort to assist the child to achieve the goals and objectives or benchmarks listed in the IEP.

(b) Accountability. Part B of the Act does not require that any agency, teacher, or other person be held accountable if a child does not achieve the growth projected in the annual goals and benchmarks or objectives. However, the Act does not prohibit a State or public agency from establishing its own accountability systems regarding teacher, school, or agency performance.

(c) Construction—parent rights. Nothing in this section limits a parent's right to ask for revisions of the child's IEP or to invoke due process procedures if the parent feels that the efforts required in paragraph (a) of this section are not being made. (Authority: 20 U.S.C. 1414(d)); Cong. Rec. at H7152 (daily ed., July 21, 1975))

DIRECT SERVICES BY THE SEA

Sec. 300.360 Use of LEA allocation for direct services.

(a) General. An SEA shall use the payments that would otherwise have been available to an LEA or to a State agency to provide special education and related services directly to children with disabilities residing in the area served by that local agency, or for whom that State agency is responsible, if the SEA determines that the LEA or State agency—

(1) Has not provided the information needed to establish the eligibility of the agency under Part B of the Act;

(2) Is unable to establish and maintain programs of FAPE that meet the requirements of this part;

(3) Is unable or unwilling to be consolidated with one or more LEAs in order to establish and maintain the programs; or

(4) Has one or more children with disabilities who can best be served by a regional or State program or service-delivery system designed to meet the needs of these children.

(b) SEA responsibility if an LEA does not apply for Part B funds.

(1) If an LEA elects not to apply for its Part B allotment, the SEA must use those funds to ensure that FAPE is available to all eligible children residing in the jurisdiction of the LEA.

(2)

(i) If the local allotment is not sufficient to meet the purpose described in paragraph (b)(1) of this section, the SEA must ensure compliance with Secs. 300.121(a) and 300.300(a).

(ii) Consistent with Sec. 300.301(a), the [State; SEA] may use whatever funding sources are available in the State to implement paragraph (b)(2)(i) of this section.

(c) SEA administrative procedures.

(1) In meeting the requirements in paragraph (a) of this section, the SEA may provide special education and related services directly, by contract, or through other arrangements.

(2) The excess cost requirements of Secs. 300.184 and 300.185 do not apply to the SEA. (Authority: 20 U.S.C. 1413(h)(1))

Sec. 300.361 Nature and location of services.

The SEA may provide special education and related services under Sec. 300.360(a) in the manner and at the location it considers appropriate (including regional and State centers). However, the manner in which the education and services are provided must be consistent with the requirements of this part (including the LRE provisions of Secs. 300.550-300.556). (Authority: 20 U.S.C. 1413(h)(2))

Secs. 300.362-300.369 [Reserved]

Sec. 300.370 Use of SEA allocations.

(a) Each State shall use any funds it retains under Sec. 300.602 and does not use for administration under Sec. 300.620 for any of the following:

(1) Support and direct services, including technical assistance and personnel development and training.

(2) Administrative costs of monitoring and complaint investigation, but only to the extent that those costs exceed the costs incurred for those activities during fiscal year 1985.

(3) To establish and implement the mediation process required by Sec. 300.506, including providing for the costs of mediators and support personnel.

(4) To assist LEAs in meeting personnel shortages.

(5) To develop a State Improvement Plan under subpart 1 of Part D of the Act.

(6) Activities at the State and local levels to meet the performance goals established by the State under Sec. 300.137 and to support implementation of the State Improvement Plan under subpart 1 of Part D of the Act if the State receives funds under that subpart.

(7) To supplement other amounts used to develop and implement a Statewide coordinated services system designed to improve results for children and families, including children with disabilities and their families, but not to exceed one percent of the amount received by the State under section 611 of the Act. This system must be coordinated with and, to the extent appropriate, build on the system of coordinated services developed by the State under Part C of the Act.

(8) For subgrants to LEAs for the purposes described in Sec. 300.622 (local capacity building).

(b) For the purposes of paragraph (a) of this section—

(1) Direct services means services provided to a child with a disability by the State directly, by contract, or through other arrangements; and

(2) Support services includes implementing the comprehensive system of personnel development under Secs. 300.380-300.382, recruitment and training of mediators, hearing officers, and surrogate parents, and public information and parent training activities relating to FAPE for children with disabilities.

(c) Of the funds an SEA retains under paragraph (a) of this section, the SEA may use the funds directly, or distribute them to LEAs on a competitive, targeted, or formula basis. (Authority: 20 U.S.C. 1411(f)(3))

Sec. 300.371 [Reserved]

Sec. 300.372 Nonapplicability of requirements that prohibit commingling and supplanting of funds.

A State may use funds it retains under Sec. 300.602 without regard to—

(a) The prohibition on commingling of funds in Sec. 300.152; and

(b) The prohibition on supplanting other funds in Sec. 300.153. (Authority: 20 U.S.C. 1411(f)(1)(C))

COMPREHENSIVE SYSTEM OF PERSONNEL DEVELOPMENT (CSPD)

Sec. 300.380 General CSPD requirements.

(a) Each State shall develop and implement a comprehensive system of personnel development that—

(1) Is consistent with the purposes of this part and with section 635(a)(8) of the Act;

(2) Is designed to ensure an adequate supply of qualified special education, regular education, and related services personnel;

(3) Meets the requirements of Secs. 300.381 and 300.382; and

(4) Is updated at least every five years.

(b) A State that has a State improvement grant has met the requirements of paragraph (a) of this section. (Authority: 20 U.S.C. 1412(a)(14))

Sec. 300.381 Adequate supply of qualified personnel.

Each State must include, at least, an analysis of State and local needs for professional development for personnel to serve children with disabilities that includes, at a minimum—

(a) The number of personnel providing special education and related services; and

(b) Relevant information on current and anticipated personnel vacancies and shortages (including the number of individuals described in paragraph (a) of this section with temporary certification), and on the extent of certification or retraining necessary to eliminate these shortages, that is based, to the maximum extent possible, on existing assessments of personnel needs. (Authority: 20 U.S.C. 1453(b)(2)(B))

Sec. 300.382 Improvement strategies.

Each State must describe the strategies the State will use to address the needs identified under Sec. 300.381. These strategies must include how the State will address the identified needs for in-service and pre-service preparation to ensure that all personnel who work with children with disabilities (including both professional and paraprofessional personnel who provide special education, general education, related services, or early intervention services) have the skills and knowledge necessary to meet the needs of children with disabilities. The plan must include a description of how the State will—

(a) Prepare general and special education personnel with the content knowledge and collaborative skills needed to meet the needs of children with disabilities including how the State will work with other States on common certification criteria;

(b) Prepare professionals and paraprofessionals in the area of early intervention with the content knowledge and collaborative skills needed to meet the needs of infants and toddlers with disabilities;

(c) Work with institutions of higher education and other entities that (on both a pre-service and an in-service basis) prepare personnel who work with children with disabilities to ensure that those institutions and entities develop the capacity to support quality professional development programs that meet State and local needs;

(d) Work to develop collaborative agreements with other States for the joint support and development of programs to prepare personnel for which there is not sufficient demand within a single State to justify support or development of a program of preparation;

(e) Work in collaboration with other States, particularly neighboring States, to address the lack of uniformity and reciprocity in credentialing of teachers and other personnel;

(f) Enhance the ability of teachers and others to use strategies, such as behavioral interventions, to address the conduct of children with disabilities that impedes the learning of children with disabilities and others;

(g) Acquire and disseminate, to teachers, administrators, school board members, and related services personnel, significant knowledge derived from educational research and other sources, and how the State will, if appropriate, adopt promising practices, materials, and technology;

(h) Recruit, prepare, and retain qualified personnel, including personnel with disabilities and personnel from groups that are under- represented in the fields of regular education, special education, and related services;

(i) Insure that the plan is integrated, to the maximum extent possible, with other professional development plans and activities, including plans and activities developed and carried out under other Federal and State laws that address personnel recruitment and training; and

(j) Provide for the joint training of parents and special education, related services, and general education personnel. (Authority: 20 U.S.C. 1453 (c)(3)(D))

Secs. 300.383-300.387 [Reserved]

SUBPART D—CHILDREN IN PRIVATE SCHOOLS

CHILDREN WITH DISABILITIES IN PRIVATE SCHOOLS PLACED OR REFERRED BY PUBLIC AGENCIES

Sec. 300.400 Applicability of Secs. 300.400-300.402.

Sections 300.401-300.402 apply only to children with disabilities who are or have been placed in or referred to a private school or facility by a public agency as a means of providing special education and related services. (Authority: 20 U.S.C. 1412(a)(10)(B))

Sec. 300.401 Responsibility of State educational agency.

Each SEA shall ensure that a child with a disability who is placed in or referred to a private school or facility by a public agency—

(a) Is provided special education and related services—

    (1) In conformance with an IEP that meets the requirements of Secs. 300.340-300.350; and

    (2) At no cost to the parents;

(b) Is provided an education that meets the standards that apply to education provided by the SEA and LEAs (including the requirements of this part); and

(c) Has all of the rights of a child with a disability who is served by a public agency. (Authority: 20 U.S.C. 1412(a)(10)(B))

Sec. 300.402 Implementation by State educational agency.

In implementing Sec. 300.401, the SEA shall—

(a) Monitor compliance through procedures such as written reports, on-site visits, and parent questionnaires;

(b) Disseminate copies of applicable standards to each private school and facility to which a public agency has referred or placed a child with a disability; and

(c) Provide an opportunity for those private schools and facilities to participate in the development and revision of State standards that apply to them. (Authority: 20 U.S.C. 1412(a)(10)(B))

CHILDREN WITH DISABILITIES ENROLLED BY THEIR PARENTS IN PRIVATE SCHOOLS WHEN FAPE IS AT ISSUE

Sec. 300.403 Placement of children by parents if FAPE is at issue.

(a) **General**. This part does not require an LEA to pay for the cost of education, including special education and related services, of a child with a disability at a private school or facility if that agency made FAPE available to the child and the parents elected to place the child in a private school or facility. However, the public agency shall include that child in the population whose needs are addressed consistent with Secs. 300.450-300.462.

(b) **Disagreements about FAPE**. Disagreements between a parent and a public agency regarding the availability of a program appropriate for the child, and the question of financial responsibility, are subject to the due process procedures of Secs. 300.500-300.517.

(c) **Reimbursement for private school placement**. If the parents of a child with a disability, who previously received special education and related services under the authority of a public agency, enroll the child in a private preschool, elementary, or secondary school without the consent of or referral by the public agency, a court or a hearing officer may require the agency to reimburse the parents for the cost of that enrollment if the court or hearing officer finds that the agency had not made FAPE available to the child in a timely manner prior to that enrollment and that the private placement is appropriate. A parental placement may be found to be appropriate by a hearing officer or a court even if it does not meet the State standards that apply to education provided by the SEA and LEAs.

(d) **Limitation on reimbursement**. The cost of reimbursement described in paragraph (c) of this section may be reduced or denied—

    (1) If—

        (i) **At the most recent IEP meeting** that the parents attended prior to removal of the child from the public school, the parents did not inform the IEP team that they were rejecting the placement proposed by the public agency to provide FAPE to their child, including stating their concerns and their intent to enroll their child in a private school at public expense; or

        (ii) **At least ten (10) business days** (including any holidays that occur on a business day) prior to the removal of the child from the public school, the parents did not give written notice to the public agency of the information described in paragraph (d)(1)(i) of this section;

    (2) If, prior to the parents' removal of the child from the public school, the public agency informed the parents, through the notice requirements described in Sec. 300.503(a)(1), of its intent to evaluate the child (including a statement of the purpose of the evaluation that was appropriate and reasonable), but the parents did not make the child available for the evaluation; or

    (3) Upon a judicial finding of unreasonableness with respect to actions taken by the parents.

(e) Exception. Notwithstanding the notice requirement in paragraph (d)(1) of this section, the cost of reimbursement may not be reduced or denied for failure to provide the notice if—

(1) The parent is illiterate and cannot write in English;

(2) Compliance with paragraph (d)(1) of this section would likely result in physical or serious emotional harm to the child;

(3) The school prevented the parent from providing the notice; or

(4) The parents had not received notice, pursuant to section 615 of the Act, of the notice requirement in paragraph (d)(1) of this section. (Authority: 20 U.S.C. 1412(a)(10)(C))

CHILDREN WITH DISABILITIES ENROLLED BY THEIR PARENTS IN PRIVATE SCHOOLS

Sec. 300.450 Definition of "private school children with disabilities."

As used in this part, private school children with disabilities means children with disabilities enrolled by their parents in private schools or facilities other than children with disabilities covered under Secs. 300.400-300.402. (Authority: 20 U.S.C. 1412(a)(10)(A))

Sec. 300.451 Child find for private school children with disabilities.

(a) Each LEA shall locate, identify, and evaluate all private school children with disabilities, including religious-school children residing in the jurisdiction of the LEA, in accordance with Secs. 300.125 and 300.220. The activities undertaken to carry out this responsibility for private school children with disabilities must be comparable to activities undertaken for children with disabilities in public schools.

(b) Each LEA shall consult with appropriate representatives of private school children with disabilities on how to carry out the activities described in paragraph (a) of this section. (Authority: 20 U.S.C. 1412(a)(10)(A)(ii))

Sec. 300.452 Provision of services—basic requirement.

(a) General. To the extent consistent with their number and location in the State, provision must be made for the participation of private school children with disabilities in the program assisted or carried out under Part B of the Act by providing them with special education and related services in accordance with Secs. 300.453- 300.462.

(b) SEA Responsibility—services plan. Each SEA shall ensure that, in accordance with paragraph (a) of this section and Secs. 300.454-300.456, a services plan is developed and implemented for each private school child with a disability who has been designated to receive special education and related services under this part. (Authority: 20 U.S.C. 1412(a)(10)(A)(i))

Sec. 300.453 Expenditures.

(a) Formula. To meet the requirement of Sec. 300.452(a), each LEA must spend on providing special education and related services to private school children with disabilities—

(1) For children aged 3 through 21, an amount that is the same proportion of the LEA's total subgrant under section 611(g) of the Act as the number of private school children with disabilities aged 3 through 21 residing in its jurisdiction is to the total number of children with disabilities in its jurisdiction aged 3 through 21; and

(2) For children aged 3 through 5, an amount that is the same proportion of the LEA's total subgrant under section 619(g) of the Act as the number of private school children with disabilities aged 3 through 5 residing in its jurisdiction is to the total number of children with disabilities in its jurisdiction aged 3 through 5.

(b) Child count.

(1) Each LEA shall—

(i) Consult with representatives of private school children in deciding how to conduct the annual count of the number of private school children with disabilities; and

(ii) Ensure that the count is conducted on December 1 or the last Friday of October of each year.

(2) The child count must be used to determine the amount that the LEA must spend on providing special education and related services to private school children with disabilities in the next subsequent fiscal year.

(c) Expenditures for child find may not be considered. Expenditures for child find activities described in Sec. 300.451 may not be considered in determining whether the LEA has met the requirements of paragraph (a) of this section.

(d) Additional services permissible. State and local educational agencies are not prohibited from providing services to private school children with disabilities in excess of those required by this part, consistent with State law or local policy. (Authority: 20 U.S.C. 1412(a)(10)(A))

Sec. 300.454 Services determined.

(a) No individual right to special education and related services.

(1) No private school child with a disability has an individual right to receive some or all of the special education and related services that the child would receive if enrolled in a public school.

(2) Decisions about the services that will be provided to private school children with disabilities under Secs. 300.452-300.462, must be made in accordance with paragraphs (b), and (c) of this section.

(b) Consultation with representatives of private school children with disabilities.

(1) General. Each LEA shall consult, in a timely and meaningful way, with appropriate representatives of private school children with disabilities in light of the funding under Sec. 300.453, the number of private school children with disabilities, the needs of private school children with disabilities, and their location to decide—

(i) Which children will receive services under Sec. 300.452;

(ii) What services will be provided;

(iii) How and where the services will be provided; and

(iv) How the services provided will be evaluated.

(2) Genuine opportunity. Each LEA shall give appropriate representatives of private school children with disabilities a genuine opportunity to express their views regarding each matter that is subject to the consultation requirements in this section.

(3) Timing. The consultation required by paragraph (b)(1) of this section must occur before the LEA makes any decision that affects the opportunities of private school children with disabilities to participate in services under Secs. 300.452-300.462.

(4) Decisions. The LEA shall make the final decisions with respect to the services to be provided to eligible private school children.

(c) Services plan for each child served under Secs. 300.450- 300.462. If a child with a disability is enrolled in a religious or other private school and will receive special education or related services from an LEA, the LEA shall—

(1) Initiate and conduct meetings to develop, review, and revise a services plan for the child, in accordance with Sec. 300.455(b); and

(2) Ensure that a representative of the religious or other private school attends each meeting. If the representative cannot attend, the LEA shall use other methods to ensure participation by the private school, including individual or conference telephone calls. (Authority: 1412(a)(10)(A))

Sec. 300.455 Services provided.

(a) General.

(1) The services provided to private school children with disabilities must be provided by personnel meeting the same standards as personnel providing services in the public schools.

(2) Private school children with disabilities may receive a different amount of services than children with disabilities in public schools.

(3) No private school child with a disability is entitled to any service or to any amount of a service the child would receive if enrolled in a public school.

(b) Services provided in accordance with a services plan.

(1) Each private school child with a disability who has been designated to receive services under Sec. 300.452 must have a services plan that describes the specific special education and related services that the LEA will provide to the child in light of the services that the LEA has determined, through the process described in Secs. 300.453-300.454, it will make available to private school children with disabilities.

(2) The services plan must, to the extent appropriate—

(i) Meet the requirements of Sec. 300.347, with respect to the services provided; and

(ii) Be developed, reviewed, and revised consistent with Secs. 300.342-300.346. (Authority: 20 U.S.C. 1412(a)(10)(A))

Sec. 300.456 Location of services; transportation.

(a) On-site. Services provided to private school children with disabilities may be provided on-site at a child's private school, including a religious school, to the extent consistent with law.

(b) Transportation.

(1) General.

(i) If necessary for the child to benefit from or participate in the services provided under this part, a private school child with a disability must be provided transportation—

(A) From the child's school or the child's home to a site other than the private school; and

(B) From the service site to the private school, or to the child's home, depending on the timing of the services.

(ii) LEAs are not required to provide transportation from the child's home to the private school.

(2) Cost of transportation. The cost of the transportation described in paragraph (b)(1)(i) of this section may be included in calculating whether the LEA has met the requirement of Sec. 300.453. (Authority: 20 U.S.C. 1412(a)(10)(A))

Sec. 300.457 Complaints.

(a) Due process inapplicable. The procedures in Secs. 300.504- 300.515 do not apply to complaints that an LEA has failed to meet the requirements of Secs. 300.452-300.462, including the provision of services indicated on the child's services plan.

(b) Due process applicable. The procedures in Secs. 300.504-300.515 do apply to complaints that an LEA has failed to meet the requirements of Sec. 300.451, including the requirements of Secs. 300.530-300.543.

(c) State complaints. Complaints that an SEA or LEA has failed to meet the requirements of Secs. 300.451-300.462 may be filed under the procedures in Secs. 300.660-300.662. (Authority: 20 U.S.C. 1412(a)(10)(A))

Sec. 300.458 Separate classes prohibited.

An LEA may not use funds available under section 611 or 619 of the Act for classes that are organized separately on the basis of school enrollment or religion of the students if—

(a) The classes are at the same site; and

(b) The classes include students enrolled in public schools and students enrolled in private schools. (Authority: 20 U.S.C. 1412(a)(10)(A))

Sec. 300.459 Requirement that funds not benefit a private school.

(a) An LEA may not use funds provided under section 611 or 619 of the Act to finance the existing level of instruction in a private school or to otherwise benefit the private school.

(b) The LEA shall use funds provided under Part B of the Act to meet the special education and related services needs of students enrolled in private schools, but not for—

(1) The needs of a private school; or

(2) The general needs of the students enrolled in the private school. (Authority: 20 U.S.C. 1412(a)(10)(A))

Sec. 300.460 Use of public school personnel.

An LEA may use funds available under sections 611 and 619 of the Act to make public school personnel available in other than public facilities—

(a) To the extent necessary to provide services under Secs. 300.450-300.462 for private school children with disabilities; and

(b) If those services are not normally provided by the private school. (Authority: 20 U.S.C. 1412(a)(10)(A))

Sec. 300.461 Use of private school personnel.

An LEA may use funds available under section 611 or 619 of the Act to pay for the services of an employee of a private school to provide services under Secs. 300.450-300.462 if—

(a) The employee performs the services outside of his or her regular hours of duty; and

(b) The employee performs the services under public supervision and control. (Authority: 20 U.S.C. 1412(a)(10)(A))

Sec. 300.462 Requirements concerning property, equipment, and supplies for the benefit of private school children with disabilities.

(a) A public agency must keep title to and exercise continuing administrative control of all property, equipment, and supplies that the public agency acquires with funds under section 611 or 619 of the Act for the benefit of private school children with disabilities.

(b) The public agency may place equipment and supplies in a private school for the period of time needed for the program.

(c) The public agency shall ensure that the equipment and supplies placed in a private school—

(1) Are used only for Part B purposes; and

(2) Can be removed from the private school without remodeling the private school facility.

(d) The public agency shall remove equipment and supplies from a private school if—

(1) The equipment and supplies are no longer needed for Part B purposes; or

(2) Removal is necessary to avoid unauthorized use of the equipment and supplies for other than Part B purposes.

(e) No funds under Part B of the Act may be used for repairs, minor remodeling, or construction of private school facilities. (Authority: 20 U.S.C. 1412(a)(10)(A))

PROCEDURES FOR BY-PASS

Sec. 300.480 By-pass—general.

(a) The Secretary implements a by-pass if an SEA is, and was on December 2, 1983, prohibited by law from providing for the participation of private school children with disabilities in the program assisted or carried out under Part B of the Act, as required by section 612(a)(10)(A) of the Act and by Secs. 300.452-300.462.

(b) The Secretary waives the requirement of section 612(a)(10)(A) of the Act and of Secs. 300.452-300.462 if the Secretary implements a by-pass. (Authority: 20 U.S.C. 1412(f)(1))

Sec. 300.481 Provisions for services under a by-pass.

(a) Before implementing a by-pass, the Secretary consults with appropriate public and private school officials, including SEA officials, in the affected State to consider matters such as—

(1) The prohibition imposed by State law that results in the need for a by-pass;

(2) The scope and nature of the services required by private school children with disabilities in the State, and the number of children to be served under the by-pass; and

(3) The establishment of policies and procedures to ensure that private school children with disabilities receive services consistent with the requirements of section 612(a)(10)(A) of the Act and Secs. 300.452-300.462.

(b) After determining that a by-pass is required, the Secretary arranges for the provision of services to private school children with disabilities in the State in a manner consistent with the requirements of section 612(a)(10)(A) of the Act and Secs. 300.452-300.462 by providing services through one or more agreements with appropriate parties.

(c) For any fiscal year that a by-pass is implemented, the Secretary determines the maximum amount to be paid to the providers of services by multiplying—

(1) A per child amount that may not exceed the amount per child provided by the Secretary under Part B of the Act for all children with disabilities in the State for the preceding fiscal year; by

(2) The number of private school children with disabilities (as defined by Secs. 300.7(a) and 300.450) in the State, as determined by the Secretary on the basis of the most recent satisfactory data available, which may include an estimate of the number of those children with disabilities.

(d) The Secretary deducts from the State's allocation under Part B of the Act the amount the Secretary determines is necessary to implement a by-pass and pays that amount to the provider of services. The Secretary may withhold this amount from the State's allocation pending final resolution of any investigation or complaint that could result in a determination that a by-pass must be implemented. (Authority: 20 U.S.C. 1412(f)(2))

Sec. 300.482 Notice of intent to implement a by-pass.

(a) Before taking any final action to implement a by-pass, the Secretary provides the affected SEA with written notice.

(b) In the written notice, the Secretary—

(1) States the reasons for the proposed by-pass in sufficient detail to allow the SEA to respond; and

(2) Advises the SEA that it has a specific period of time (at least 45 days) from receipt of the written notice to submit written objections to the proposed by-pass and that it may request in writing the opportunity for a hearing to show cause why a by-pass should not be implemented.

(c) The Secretary sends the notice to the SEA by certified mail with return receipt requested. (Authority: 20 U.S.C. 1412(f)(3)(A))

Sec. 300.483 Request to show cause.

An SEA seeking an opportunity to show cause why a by-pass should not be implemented shall submit a written request for a show cause hearing to the Secretary. (Authority: 20 U.S.C. 1412(f)(3))

Sec. 300.484 Show cause hearing.

(a) If a show cause hearing is requested, the Secretary—

(1) Notifies the SEA and other appropriate public and private school officials of the time and place for the hearing; and

(2) Designates a person to conduct the show cause hearing. The designee must not have had any responsibility for the matter brought for a hearing.

(b) At the show cause hearing, the designee considers matters such as—

(1) The necessity for implementing a by-pass;

(2) Possible factual errors in the written notice of intent to implement a by-pass; and

(3) The objections raised by public and private school representatives.

(c) The designee may regulate the course of the proceedings and the conduct of parties during the pendency of the proceedings. The designee takes all steps necessary to conduct a fair and impartial proceeding, to avoid delay, and to maintain order.

(d) The designee may interpret applicable statutes and regulations, but may not waive them or rule on their validity.

(e) The designee arranges for the preparation, retention, and, if appropriate, dissemination of the record of the hearing. (Authority: 20 U.S.C. 1412(f)(3))

Sec. 300.485 Decision.

(a) The designee who conducts the show cause hearing—

(1) Issues a written decision that includes a statement of findings; and

(2) Submits a copy of the decision to the Secretary and sends a copy to each party by certified mail with return receipt requested.

(b) Each party may submit comments and recommendations on the designee's decision to the Secretary within 15 days of the date the party receives the designee's decision.

(c) The Secretary adopts, reverses, or modifies the designee's decision and notifies the SEA of the Secretary's final action. That notice is sent by certified mail with return receipt requested. (Authority: 20 U.S.C. 1412(f)(3))

Sec. 300.486 Filing requirements.

(a) Any written submission under Secs. 300.482-300.485 must be filed by hand-delivery, by mail, or by facsimile transmission. The Secretary discourages the use of facsimile transmission for documents longer than five pages.

(b) The filing date under paragraph (a) of this section is the date the document is—

(1) Hand-delivered;

(2) Mailed; or

(3) Sent by facsimile transmission.

(c) A party filing by facsimile transmission is responsible for confirming that a complete and legible copy of the document was received by the Department.

(d) If a document is filed by facsimile transmission, the Secretary or the hearing officer, as applicable, may require the filing of a follow-up hard copy by hand-delivery or by mail within a reasonable period of time.

(e) If agreed upon by the parties, service of a document may be made upon the other party by facsimile transmission. (Authority: 20 U.S.C. 1412(f)(3))

Sec. 300.487 Judicial review.

If dissatisfied with the Secretary's final action, the SEA may, within 60 days after notice of that action, file a petition for review with the United States Court of Appeals for the circuit in which the State is located. The procedures for judicial review are described in section 612(f)(3)(B)-(D) of the Act. (Authority: 20 U.S.C. 1412(f)(3)(B)-(D))

SUBPART E—PROCEDURAL SAFEGUARDS

DUE PROCESS PROCEDURES FOR PARENTS AND CHILDREN

Sec. 300.500 General responsibility of public agencies; definitions.

(a) **Responsibility of SEA and other public agencies**. Each SEA shall ensure that each public agency establishes, maintains, and implements procedural safeguards that meet the requirements of Secs. 300.500- 300.529.

(b) **Definitions of "consent," "evaluation," and "personally identifiable."** As used in this part —

(1) **Consent** means that —

(i) The parent has been fully informed of all information relevant to the activity for which consent is sought, in his or her native language, or other mode of communication;

(ii) The parent understands and agrees in writing to the carrying out of the activity for which his or her consent is sought, and the consent describes that activity and lists the records (if any) that will be released and to whom; and

(iii)

(A) The parent understands that the granting of consent is voluntary on the part of the parent and may be revoked at anytime.

(B) If a parent revokes consent, that revocation is not retroactive (i.e., it does not negate an action that has occurred after the consent was given and before the consent was revoked).

(2) **Evaluation** means procedures used in accordance with Secs. 300.530-300.536 to determine whether a child has a disability and the nature and extent of the special education and related services that the child needs; and

(3) **Personally identifiable** means that information includes—

(i) The name of the child, the child's parent, or other family member;

(ii) The address of the child;

(iii) A personal identifier, such as the child's social security number or student number; or

(iv) A list of personal characteristics or other information that would make it possible to identify the child with reasonable certainty. (Authority: 20 U.S.C. 1415(a))

Sec. 300.501 Opportunity to examine records; parent participation in meetings.

(a) **General**. The parents of a child with a disability must be afforded, in accordance with the procedures of Secs. 300.562-300.569, an opportunity to—

(1) Inspect and review all education records with respect to—

(i) The identification, evaluation, and educational placement of the child; and

(ii) The provision of FAPE to the child; and

(2) Participate in meetings with respect to —

(i) The identification, evaluation, and educational placement of the child; and

(ii) The provision of FAPE to the child.

(b) **Parent participation in meetings**.

(1) Each public agency shall provide notice consistent with Sec. 300.345(a)(1) and (b)(1) to ensure that parents of children with disabilities have the opportunity to participate in meetings described in paragraph (a)(2) of this section.

(2) A meeting does not include informal or unscheduled conversations involving public agency personnel and conversations on issues such as teaching methodology, lesson plans, or coordination of service provision if those issues are not addressed in the child's IEP. A meeting also does not include preparatory activities that public agency personnel engage in to develop a proposal or response to a parent proposal that will be discussed at a later meeting.

(c) **Parent involvement in placement decisions**.

(1) Each public agency shall ensure that the parents of each child with a disability are members of any group that makes decisions on the educational placement of their child.

(2) In implementing the requirements of paragraph (c)(1) of this section, the public agency shall use procedures consistent with the procedures described in Sec. 300.345(a) through (b)(1).

(3) If neither parent can participate in a meeting in which a decision is to be made relating to the educational placement of their child, the public agency shall use other methods to ensure their participation, including individual or conference telephone calls, or video conferencing.

(4) A placement decision may be made by a group without the involvement of the parents, if the public agency is unable to obtain the parents' participation in the decision. In this case, the public agency must have a record of its attempt to ensure their involvement, including information that is consistent with the requirements of Sec. 300.345(d).

(5) The public agency shall make reasonable efforts to ensure that the parents understand, and are able to participate in, any group discussions relating to the educational placement of their child, including arranging for an interpreter for parents with deafness, or whose native language is other than English. (Authority: 20 U.S.C. 1414(f), 1415(b)(1))

Sec. 300.502 Independent educational evaluation.

(a) General.

(1) The parents of a child with a disability have the right under this part to obtain an independent educational evaluation of the child, subject to paragraphs (b) through (e) of this section.

(2) Each public agency shall provide to parents, upon request for an independent educational evaluation, information about where an independent educational evaluation may be obtained, and the agency criteria applicable for independent educational evaluations as set forth in paragraph (e) of this section.

(3) For the purposes of this part—

(i) **Independent educational evaluation** means an evaluation conducted by a qualified examiner who is not employed by the public agency responsible for the education of the child in question; and

(ii) **Public expense** means that the public agency either pays for the full cost of the evaluation or ensures that the evaluation is otherwise provided at no cost to the parent, consistent with Sec. 300.301.

(b) Parent right to evaluation at public expense.

(1) A parent has the right to an independent educational evaluation at public expense if the parent disagrees with an evaluation obtained by the public agency.

(2) If a parent requests an independent educational evaluation at public expense, the public agency must, without unnecessary delay, either—

(i) Initiate a hearing under Sec. 300.507 to show that its evaluation is appropriate; or

(ii) Ensure that an independent educational evaluation is provided at public expense, unless the agency demonstrates in a hearing under Sec. 300.507 that the evaluation obtained by the parent did not meet agency criteria.

(3) If the public agency initiates a hearing and the final decision is that the agency's evaluation is appropriate, the parent still has the right to an independent educational evaluation, but not at public expense.

(4) If a parent requests an independent educational evaluation, the public agency may ask for the parent's reason why he or she objects to the public evaluation. However, the explanation by the parent may not be required and the public agency may not unreasonably delay either providing the independent educational evaluation at public expense or initiating a due process hearing to defend the public evaluation.

(c) Parent-initiated evaluations. If the parent obtains an independent educational evaluation at private expense, the results of the evaluation—

(1) Must be considered by the public agency, if it meets agency criteria, in any decision made with respect to the provision of FAPE to the child; and

(2) May be presented as evidence at a hearing under this subpart regarding that child.

(d) Requests for evaluations by hearing officers. If a hearing officer requests an independent educational evaluation as part of a hearing, the cost of the evaluation must be at public expense.

(e) Agency criteria.

(1) If an independent educational evaluation is at public expense, the criteria under which the evaluation is obtained, including the location of the evaluation and the qualifications of the examiner, must be the same as the criteria that the public agency uses when it initiates an evaluation, to the extent those criteria are consistent with the parent's right to an independent educational evaluation.

(2) Except for the criteria described in paragraph (e)(1) of this section, a public agency may not impose conditions or timelines related to obtaining an independent educational evaluation at public expense. (Authority: 20 U.S.C. 1415(b)(1))

Sec. 300.503 Prior notice by the public agency; content of notice.

(a) Notice.

(1) Written notice that meets the requirements of paragraph (b) of this section must be given to the parents of a child with a disability a reasonable time before the public agency—

(i) **Proposes to initiate or change the identification, evaluation, or educational placement of the child or the provision of FAPE** to the child; or

(ii) **Refuses to initiate or change the identification, evaluation, or educational placement of the child or the provision of FAPE** to the child.

(2) If the notice described under paragraph (a)(1) of this section relates to an action proposed by the public agency that also requires parental consent under Sec. 300.505, the agency may give notice at the same time it requests parent consent.

(b) Content of notice. The notice required under paragraph (a) of this section must include—

(1) A description of the action proposed or refused by the agency;

(2) An explanation of why the agency proposes or refuses to take the action;

(3) A description of any other options that the agency considered and the reasons why those options were rejected;

(4) A description of each evaluation procedure, test, record, or report the agency used as a basis for the proposed or refused action;

(5) A description of any other factors that are relevant to the agency's proposal or refusal;

(6) A statement that the parents of a child with a disability have protection under the procedural safeguards of this part and, if this notice is not an initial referral for evaluation, the means by which a copy of a description of the procedural safeguards can be obtained; and

(7) Sources for parents to contact to obtain assistance in understanding the provisions of this part.

(c) Notice in understandable language.

(1) The notice required under paragraph (a) of this section must be—

(i) Written in language understandable to the general public; and

(ii) Provided in the native language of the parent or other mode of communication used by the parent, unless it is clearly not feasible to do so.

(2) If the native language or other mode of communication of the parent is not a written language, the public agency shall take steps to ensure—

(i) That the notice is translated orally or by other means to the parent in his or her native language or other mode of communication;

(ii) That the parent understands the content of the notice; and

(iii) That there is written evidence that the requirements in paragraphs (c)(2)(i) and (ii) of this section have been met. (Authority: 20 U.S.C. 1415(b)(3), (4) and (c), 1414(b)(1))

Sec. 300.504 Procedural safeguards notice.

(a) General. A copy of the procedural safeguards available to the parents of a child with a disability must be given to the parents, at a minimum—

(1) Upon initial referral for evaluation;

(2) Upon each notification of an IEP meeting;

(3) Upon reevaluation of the child; and

(4) Upon receipt of a request for due process under Sec. 300.507.

(b) Contents. The procedural safeguards notice must include a full explanation of all of the procedural safeguards available under Secs. 300.403, 300.500-300.529, and 300.560-300.577, and the State complaint procedures available under Secs. 300.660-300.662 relating to—

(1) Independent educational evaluation;

(2) Prior written notice;

(3) Parental consent;

(4) Access to educational records;

(5) Opportunity to present complaints to initiate due process hearings;

(6) The child's placement during pendency of due process proceedings;

(7) Procedures for students who are subject to placement in an interim alternative educational setting;

(8) Requirements for unilateral placement by parents of children in private schools at public expense;(9) Mediation;

(10) Due process hearings, including requirements for disclosure of evaluation results and recommendations;

(11) State-level appeals (if applicable in that State);

(12) Civil actions;

(13) Attorneys' fees; and

(14) The State complaint procedures under Secs. 300.660-300.662, including a description of how to file a complaint and the timelines under those procedures.

(c) Notice in understandable language. The notice required under paragraph (a) of this section must meet the requirements of Sec. 300.503(c). (Authority: 20 U.S.C. 1415(d))

Sec. 300.505 Parental consent.

(a) General.

(1) Subject to paragraphs (a)(3), (b) and (c) of this section, informed parent consent must be obtained before—

(i) Conducting an initial evaluation or reevaluation; and

(ii) Initial provision of special education and related services to a child with a disability.

(2) Consent for initial evaluation may not be construed as consent for initial placement described in paragraph (a)(1)(ii) of this section.

(3) Parental consent is not required before—

(i) Reviewing existing data as part of an evaluation or a reevaluation; or

(ii) Administering a test or other evaluation that is administered to all children unless, before administration of that test or evaluation, consent is required of parents of all children.

(b) Refusal. If the parents of a child with a disability refuse consentfor initial evaluation or a reevaluation, the agency may continue to pursue those evaluations by using the due process procedures under Secs. 300.507-300.509, or the mediation procedures under Sec. 300.506 if appropriate, except to the extent inconsistent with State law relating to parental consent.

(c) Failure to respond to request for reevaluation.

(1) Informed parental consent need not be obtained for reevaluation if the public agency can demonstrate that it has taken reasonable measures to obtain that consent, and the child's parent has failed to respond.

(2) To meet the reasonable measures requirement in paragraph (c)(1) of this section, the public agency must use procedures consistent with those in Sec. 300.345(d).

(d) Additional State consent requirements. In addition to the parental consent requirements described in paragraph (a) of this section, a State may require parental consent for other services and activities under this part if it ensures that each public agency in the State establishes and implements effective procedures to ensure that a parent's refusal to consent does not result in a failure to provide the child with FAPE.

(e) Limitation. A public agency may not use a parent's refusal to consent to one service or activity under paragraphs (a) and (d) of this section to deny the parent or child any other service, benefit, or activity of the public agency, except as required by this part. (Authority: 20 U.S.C. 1415(b)(3); 1414(a)(1)(C) and (c)(3))

Sec. 300.506 Mediation.

(a) General. Each public agency shall ensure that procedures are established and implemented to allow parties to disputes involving any matter described in Sec. 300.503(a)(1) to resolve the disputes through a mediation process that, at a minimum, must be available whenever a hearing is requested under Secs. 300.507 or 300.520-300.528.

(b) Requirements. The procedures must meet the following requirements:

(1) The procedures must ensure that the mediation process—

(i) Is voluntary on the part of the parties;

(ii) Is not used to deny or delay a parent's right to a due process hearing under Sec. 300.507, or to deny any other rights afforded under Part B of the Act; and

(iii) Is conducted by a qualified and impartial mediator who is trained in effective mediation techniques.

(2)

(i) The State shall maintain a list of individuals who are qualified mediators and knowledgeable in laws and regulations relating to the provision of special education and related services.

(ii) If a mediator is not selected on a random (e.g., a rotation) basis from the list described in paragraph (b)(2)(i) of this section, both parties must be involved in selecting the mediator andagree with the selection of the individual who will mediate.

(3) The State shall bear the cost of the mediation process, including the costs of meetings described in paragraph (d) of this section.

(4) Each session in the mediation process must be scheduled in a timely manner and must be held in a location that is convenient to the parties to the dispute.

(5) An ageement reached by the parties to the dispute in the mediation process must be set forth in a written mediation agreement.

(6) Discussions that occur during the mediation process must be confidential and may not be used as evidence in any subsequent due process hearings or civil proceedings, and the parties to the mediation process may be required to sign a confidentiality pledge prior to the commencement of the process.

(c) Impartiality of mediator.

(1) An individual who serves as a mediator under this part—

(i) May not be an employee of—

(A) Any LEA or any State agency described under Sec. 300.194; or

(B) An SEA that is providing direct services to a child who is the subject of the mediation process; and

(ii) Must not have a personal or professional conflict of interest.

(2) A person who otherwise qualifies as a mediator is not an employee of an LEA or State agency desribed under Sec. 300.194 solely because he or she is paid by the agency to serve as a mediator.

(d) Meeting to encourage mediation.

(1) A public agency may establish procedures to require parents who elect not to use the mediation process to meet, at a time and locatio convenient to the parents, with a disinterested party—

(i) Who is under contract with a parent training and information center or community parent resource center in the State established under section 682 or 683 of the Act, or an appropriate alternative dispute resolution entity; and

(ii) Who would explain the benefits of the mediation process, and encourage the parents to use the process.

(2) A public agency may not deny or delay a parent's right to a due process hearing under Sec. 300.507 if the parent fails to participate in the meeting described in paragraph (d)(1) of this section. (Authority: 20 U.S.C. 1415(e))

Sec. 300.507 Impartial due process hearing; parent notice.

   (a) General.

      (1) A parent or a public agency may initiate a hearing on any of the matters described in Sec. 300.503(a)(1) and (2) (relating to the identification, evaluation or educational placement of a child with a disability, or the provision of FAPE to the child).

      (2) When a hearing is initiated under paragraph (a)(1) of this section, the public agency shall inform the parents of the availability of mediation described in Sec. 300.506.

      (3) The public agency shall inform the parent of any free or low- cost legal and other relevant services available in the area if—

         (i) The parent requests the information; or

         (ii) The parent or the agency initiates a hearing under this section.

   (b) Agency responsible for conducting hearing. The hearing described in paragraph (a) of this section must be conducted by the SEA or the public agency directly responsible for the education of the child, as determined under State statute, State regulation, or a written policy of the SEA.

   (c) Parent notice to the public agency.

      (1) General. The public agency must have procedures that require the parent of a child with a disability or the attorney representing the child, to provide notice (which must remain confidential) to the public agency in a request for a hearing under paragraph (a)(1) of this section.

      (2) Content of parent notice. The notice required in paragraph (c)(1) of this section must include—

         (i) The name of the child;

         (ii) The address of the residence of the child;

         (iii) The name of the school the child is attending;

         (iv) A description of the nature of the problem of the child relating to the proposed or refused initiation or change, including facts relating to the problem; and

         (v) A proposed resolution of the problem to the extent known and available to the parents at the time.

      (3) Model form to assist parents. Each SEA shall develop a model form to assist parents in filing a request for due process that includes the information required in paragraphs (c)(1) and (2) of this section.

      (4) Right to due process hearing. A public agency may not deny or delay a parent's right to a due process hearing for failure to provide the notice required in paragraphs (c)(1) and (2) of this section. (Authority: 20 U.S.C. 1415(b)(5), (b)(6), (b)(7), (b)(8), (e)(1) and (f)(1))

Sec. 300.508 Impartial hearing officer.

   (a) A hearing may not be conducted—

      (1) By a person who is an employee of the State agency or the LEA that is involved in the education or care of the child; or

      (2) By any person having a personal or professional interest that would conflict with his or her objectivity in the hearing.

   (b) A person who otherwise qualifies to conduct a hearing under paragraph (a) of this section is not an employee of the agency solely because he or she is paid by the agency to serve as a hearing officer.

   (c) Each public agency shall keep a list of the persons who serve as hearing officers. The list must include a statement of the qualifications of each of those persons. (Authority: 20 U.S.C. 1415(f)(3))

Sec. 300.509 Hearing rights.

   (a) General. Any party to a hearing conducted pursuant to Secs. 300.507 or 300.520-300.528, or an appeal conducted pursuant to Sec. 300.510, has the right to—

      (1) Be accompanied and advised by counsel and by individuals with special knowledge or training with respect to the problems of children with disabilities;

      (2) Present evidence and confront, cross-examine, and compel the attendance of witnesses;

      (3) Prohibit the introduction of any evidence at the hearing that has not been disclosed to that party at least 5 business days before the hearing;

      (4) Obtain a written, or, at the option of the parents, electronic, verbatim record of the hearing; and

      (5) Obtain written, or, at the option of the parents, electronic findings of fact and decisions.

   (b) Additional disclosure of information.

      (1) At least 5 business days prior to a hearing conducted pursuant to Sec. 300.507(a), each party shall disclose to all other parties all evaluations completed by that date and recommendations based on the offering party's evaluations that the party intends to use at the hearing.

      (2) A hearing officer may bar any party that fails to comply with paragraph (b)(1) of this section from introducing the relevant evaluation or recommendation at the hearing without the consent of the other party.

   (c) Parental rights at hearings.

      (1) Parents involved in hearings must be given the right to—

         (i) Have the child who is the subject of the hearing present; and

         (ii) Open the hearing to the public.

      (2) The record of the hearing and the findings of fact and decisions described in paragraphs (a)(4) and (a)(5) of this section must be provided at no cost to parents.

(d) Findings and decision to advisory panel and general public. The public agency, after deleting any personally identifiable information, shall —

(1) Transmit the findings and decisions referred to in paragraph (a)(5) of this section to the State advisory panel established under Sec. 300.650; and

(2) Make those findings and decisions available to the public. (Authority: 20 U.S.C. 1415(f)(2) and (h))

Sec. 300.510 Finality of decision; appeal; impartial review.

(a) Finality of decision. A decision made in a hearing conducted pursuant to Secs. 300.507 or 300.520-300.528 is final, except that any party involved in the hearing may appeal the decision under the provisions of paragraph (b) of this section and Sec. 300.512. (Authority: 20 U.S.C. 1415(i)(1)(A))

(b) Appeal of decisions; impartial review.

(1) General. If the hearing required by Sec. 300.507 is conducted by a public agency other than the SEA, any party aggrieved by the findings and decision in the hearing may appeal to the SEA.

(2) SEA responsibility for review. If there is an appeal, the SEA shall conduct an impartial review of the hearing. The official conducting the review shall—

(i) Examine the entire hearing record;

(ii) Ensure that the procedures at the hearing were consistent with the requirements of due process;

(iii) Seek additional evidence if necessary. If a hearing is held to receive additional evidence, the rights in Sec. 300.509 apply;

(iv) Afford the parties an opportunity for oral or written argument, or both, at the discretion of the reviewing official;

(v) Make an independent decision on completion of the review; and

(vi) Give a copy of the written, or, at the option of the parents, electronic findings of fact and decisions to the parties.

(c) Findings and decision to advisory panel and general public. The SEA, after deleting any personally identifiable information, shall—

(1) Transmit the findings and decisions referred to in paragraph (b)(2)(vi) of this section to the State advisory panel established under Sec. 300.650; and

(2) Make those findings and decisions available to the public.

(d) Finality of review decision. The decision made by the reviewing official is final unless a party brings a civil action under Sec. 300.512. (Authority: 20 U.S.C. 1415(g); H. R. Rep. No. 94-664, at p. 49 (1975))

Sec. 300.511 Timelines and convenience of hearings and reviews.

(a) The public agency shall ensure that not later than 45 days after the receipt of a request for a hearing—

(1) A final decision is reached in the hearing; and

(2) A copy of the decision is mailed to each of the parties.

(b) The SEA shall ensure that not later than 30 days after the receipt of a request for a review—

(1) A final decision is reached in the review; and

(2) A copy of the decision is mailed to each of the parties.

(c) A hearing or reviewing officer may grant specific extensions of time beyond the periods set out in paragraphs (a) and (b) of this section at the request of either party.

(d) Each hearing and each review involving oral arguments must be conducted at a time and place that is reasonably convenient to the parents and child involved. (Authority: 20 U.S.C. 1415)

Sec. 300.512 Civil action.

(a) General. Any party aggrieved by the findings and decision made under Secs. 300.507 or 300.520-300.528 who does not have the right to an appeal under Sec. 300.510(b), and any party aggrieved by the findings and decision under Sec. 300.510(b), has the right to bring a civil action with respect to the complaint presented pursuant to Sec. 300.507. The action may be brought in any State court of competent jurisdiction or in a district court of the United States without regard to the amount in controversy.

(b) Additional requirements. In any action brought under paragraph (a) of this section, the court—

(1) Shall receive the records of the administrative proceedings;

(2) Shall hear additional evidence at the request of a party; and

(3) Basing its decision on the preponderance of the evidence, shall grant the relief that the court determines to be appropriate.

(c) Jurisdiction of district courts. The district courts of the United States have jurisdiction of actions brought under section 615 of the Act without regard to the amount in controversy.

(d) Rule of construction. Nothing in this part restricts or limits the rights, procedures, and remedies available under the Constitution, the Americans with Disabilities Act of 1990, title V of the Rehabilitation Act of 1973, or other Federal laws protecting the rights of children with disabilities, except that before the filing of a civil action under these laws seeking relief that is also available under section 615 of the Act, the procedures under Secs. 300.507 and 300.510 must be exhausted to the same extent as would be required had the action been brought under section 615 of the Act. (Authority: 20 U.S.C. 1415(i)(2), (i)(3)(A), and 1415(l))

Sec. 300.513 Attorneys' fees.

(a) In any action or proceeding brought under section 615 of the Act, the court, in its discretion, may award reasonable attorneys' fees as part of the costs to the parents of a child with a disability who is the prevailing party.

(b)

(1) Funds under Part B of the Act may not be used to pay attorneys' fees or costs of a party related to an action or proceeding under section 615 of the Act and subpart E of this part.

(2) Paragraph (b)(1) of this section does not preclude a public agency from using funds under Part B of the Act for conducting an action or proceeding under section 615 of the Act.

(c) A court awards reasonable attorney's fees under section 615(i)(3) of the Act consistent with the following:

(1) Determination of amount of attorneys' fees. Fees awarded under section 615(i)(3) of the Act must be based on rates prevailing in the community in which the action or proceeding arose for the kind and quality of services furnished. No bonus or multiplier may be used in calculating the fees awarded under this subsection.

(2) Prohibition of attorneys' fees and related costs for certain services.

(i) Attorneys' fees may not be awarded and related costs may not be reimbursed in any action or proceeding under section 615 of the Act for services performed subsequent to the time of a written offer of settlement to a parent if—

(A) The offer is made within the time prescribed by Rule 68 of the Federal Rules of Civil Procedure or, in the case of an administrative proceeding, at any time more than 10 days before the proceeding begins;

(B) The offer is not accepted within 10 days; and

(C) The court or administrative hearing officer finds that the relief finally obtained by the parents is not more favorable to the parents than the offer of settlement.

(ii) Attorneys' fees may not be awarded relating to any meeting of the IEP team unless the meeting is convened as a result of an administrative proceeding or judicial action, or at the discretion of the State, for a mediation described in Sec. 300.506 that is conducted prior to the filing of a request for due process under Secs. 300.507 or 300.520-300.528.

(3) Exception to prohibition on attorneys' fees and related costs. Notwithstanding paragraph (c)(2) of this section, an award of attorneys' fees and related costs may be made to a parent who is the prevailing party and who was substantially justified in rejecting the settlement offer.

(4) Reduction of amount of attorneys' fees. Except as provided in paragraph (c)(5) of this section, the court reduces, accordingly, the amount of the attorneys' fees awarded under section 615 of the Act, if the court finds that—

(i) The parent, during the course of the action or proceeding, unreasonably protracted the final resolution of the controversy;

(ii) The amount of the attorneys' fees otherwise authorized to be awarded unreasonably exceeds the hourly rate prevailing in the community for similar services by attorneys of reasonably comparable skill, reputation, and experience;

(iii) The time spent and legal services furnished were excessive considering the nature of the action or proceeding; or

(iv) The attorney representing the parent did not provide to the school district the appropriate information in the due process complaint in accordance with Sec. 300.507(c).

(5) Exception to reduction in amount of attorneys' fees. The provisions of paragraph (c)(4) of this section do not apply in any action or proceeding if the court finds that the State or local agency unreasonably protracted the final resolution of the action or proceeding or there was a violation of section 615 of the Act. (Authority: 20 U.S.C. 1415(i)(3)(B)-(G))

Sec. 300.514 Child's status during proceedings.

(a) Except as provided in Sec. 300.526, during the pendency of any administrative or judicial proceeding regarding a complaint under Sec. 300.507, unless the State or local agency and the parents of the child agree otherwise, the child involved in the complaint must remain in his or her current educational placement.

(b) If the complaint involves an application for initial admission to public school, the child, with the consent of the parents, must be placed in the public school until the completion of all the proceedings.

(c) If the decision of a hearing officer in a due process hearing conducted by the SEA or a State review official in an administrative appeal agrees with the child's parents that a change of placement is appropriate, that placement must be treated as an agreement between the State or local agency and the parents for purposes of paragraph (a) of this section. (Authority: 20 U.S.C. 1415(j))

Sec. 300.515 Surrogate parents.

(a) General. Each public agency shall ensure that the rights of a child are protected if—

(1) No parent (as defined in Sec. 300.20) can be identified;

(2) The public agency, after reasonable efforts, cannot discover the whereabouts of a parent; or

(3) The child is a ward of the State under the laws of that State.

(b) Duty of public agency. The duty of a public agency under paragraph (a) of this section includes the assignment of an individual to act as a surrogate for the parents. This must include a method—

(1) For determining whether a child needs a surrogate parent; and

(2) For assigning a surrogate parent to the child.

(c) Criteria for selection of surrogates.

(1) The public agency may select a surrogate parent in any way permitted under State law.

(2) Except as provided in paragraph (c)(3) of this section, public agencies shall ensure that a person selected as a surrogate—

(i) Is not an employee of the SEA, the LEA, or any other agency that is involved in the education or care of the child;

(ii) Has no interest that conflicts with the interest of the child he or she represents; and

(iii) Has knowledge and skills that ensure adequate representation of the child.

(3) A public agency may select as a surrogate a person who is an employee of a nonpublic agency that only provides non-educational care for the child and who meets the standards in paragraphs (c)(2)(ii) and (iii) of this section.

(d) Non-employee requirement; compensation. A person who otherwise qualifies to be a surrogate parent under paragraph (c) of this section is not an employee of the agency solely because he or she is paid by the agency to serve as a surrogate parent.

(e) Responsibilities. The surrogate parent may represent the child in all matters relating to—

(1) The identification, evaluation, and educational placement of the child; and

(2) The provision of FAPE to the child. (Authority: 20 U.S.C. 1415(b)(2))

Sec. 300.516 [Reserved].

Sec. 300.517 Transfer of parental rights at age of majority.

(a) General. A State may provide that, when a student with a disability reaches the age of majority under State law that applies to all students (except for a student with a disability who has been determined to be incompetent under State law)—

(1)

(i) The public agency shall provide any notice required by this part to both the individual and the parents; and

(ii) All other rights accorded to parents under Part B of the Act transfer to the student; and

(2) All rights accorded to parents under Part B of the Act transfer to students who are incarcerated in an adult or juvenile, State or local correctional institution.

(3) Whenever a State transfers rights under this part pursuant to paragraph (a)(1) or (a)(2) of this section, the agency shall notify the individual and the parents of the transfer of rights.

(b) Special rule. If, under State law, a State has a mechanism to determine that a student with a disability, who has reached the age of majority under State law that applies to all children and has not been determined incompetent under State law, does not have the ability to provide informed consent with respect to his or her educational program, the State shall establish procedures for appointing the parent, or, if the parent is not available another appropriate individual, to represent the educational interests of the student throughout the student's eligibility under Part B of the Act. (Authority: 20 U.S.C. 1415(m))

DISCIPLINE PROCEDURES

Sec. 300.519 Change of placement for disciplinary removals.

For purposes of removals of a child with a disability from the child's current educational placement under Secs. 300.520-300.529, a change of placement occurs if—

(a) The removal is for more than 10 consecutive school days; or

(b) The child is subjected to a series of removals that constitute a pattern because they cumulate to more than 10 school days in a school year, and because of factors such as the length of each removal, the total amount of time the child is removed, and the proximity of the removals to one another. (Authority: 20 U.S.C. 1415(k))

Sec. 300.520 Authority of school personnel.

(a) School personnel may order—

(1)

(i) To the extent removal would be applied to children without disabilities, the removal of a child with a disability from the child's current placement for not more than 10 consecutive school days for any violation of school rules, and additional removals of not more than 10 consecutive school days in that same school year for separate incidents of misconduct (as long as those removals do not constitute a change of placement under Sec. 300.519(b));

(ii) After a child with a disability has been removed from his or her current placement for more than 10 school days in the same school year, during any subsequent days of removal the public agency must provide services to the extent required under Sec. 300.121(d); and

(2) A change in placement of a child with a disability to an appropriate interim alternative educational setting for the same amount of time that a child without a disability would be subject to discipline, but for not more than 45 days, if—

(i) The child carries a weapon to school or to a school function under the jurisdiction of a State or a local educational agency; or

(ii) The child knowingly possesses or uses illegal drugs or sells or solicits the sale of a controlled substance while at school or a school function under the jurisdiction of a State or local educational agency.

(b)

(1) Either before or not later than 10 business days after either first removing the child for more than 10 school days in a school year or commencing a removal that constitutes a change of placement under Sec. 300.519, including the action described in paragraph (a)(2) of this section—

(i) If the LEA did not conduct a functional behavioral assessment and implement a behavioral intervention plan for the child before the behavior that resulted in the removal described in paragraph (a) of this section, the agency shall convene an IEP meeting to develop an assessment plan.

(ii) If the child already has a behavioral intervention plan, the IEP team shall meet to review the plan and its implementation, and, modify the plan and its implementation as necessary, to address the behavior.

(2) As soon as practicable after developing the plan described in paragraph (b)(1)(i) of this section, and completing the assessments required by the plan, the LEA shall convene an IEP meeting to develop appropriate behavioral interventions to address that behavior and shall implement those interventions.

(c)

(1) If subsequently, a child with a disability who has a behavioral intervention plan and who has been removed from the child's current educational placement for more than 10 school days in a school year is subjected to a removal that does not constitute a change of placement under Sec. 300.519, the IEP team members shall review the behavioral intervention plan and its implementation to determine if modifications are necessary.

(2) If one or more of the team members believe that modifications are needed, the team shall meet to modify the plan and its implementation, to the extent the team determines necessary.

(d) For purposes of this section, the following definitions apply:

(1) **Controlled substance means a drug or other substance identified under schedules I, II, III, IV, or V in section 202(c) of the Controlled Substances Act** (21 U.S.C. 812(c)).

(2) **Illegal drug—**

(i) Means a controlled substance; but

(ii) Does not include a substance that is legally possessed or used under the supervision of a licensed health-care professional or that is legally possessed or used under any other authority under that Act or under any other provision of Federal law.

(3) **Weapon has the meaning given the term "dangerous weapon"** under paragraph (2) of the first subsection (g) of section 930 of title 18, United States Code. (Authority: 20 U.S.C. 1415(k)(1), (10))

Sec. 300.521 Authority of hearing officer.

A hearing officer under section 615 of the Act may order a change in the placement of a child with a disability to an appropriate interim alternative educational setting for not more than 45 days if the hearing officer, in an expedited due process hearing—

(a) Determines that the public agency has demonstrated by substantial evidence that maintaining the current placement of the child is substantially likely to result in injury to the child or to others;

(b) Considers the appropriateness of the child's current placement;

(c) Considers whether the public agency has made reasonable efforts to minimize the risk of harm in the child's current placement, including the use of supplementary aids and services; and

(d) Determines that the interim alternative educational setting that is proposed by school personnel who have consulted with the child's special education teacher, meets the requirements of Sec. 300.522(b).

(e) As used in this section, the term substantial evidence means beyond a preponderance of the evidence. (Authority: 20 U.S.C. 1415(k)(2), (10))

Sec. 300.522 Determination of setting.

(a) **General**. The interim alternative educational setting referred to in Sec. 300.520(a)(2) must be determined by the IEP team.

(b) **Additional requirements**. Any interim alternative educational setting in which a child is placed under Secs. 300.520(a)(2) or 300.521 must—

(1) Be selected so as to enable the child to continue to progress in the general curriculum, although in another setting, and to continue to receive those services and modifications, including those described in the child's current IEP, that will enable the child to meet the goals set out in that IEP; and

(2) Include services and modifications to address the behavior described in Secs. 300.520(a)(2) or 300.521, that are designed to prevent the behavior from recurring. (Authority: 20 U.S.C. 1415(k)(3))

Sec. 300.523 Manifestation determination review.

(a) **General**. If an action is contemplated regarding behavior described in Secs. 300.520(a)(2) or 300.521, or involving a removal that constitutes a change of placement under Sec. 300.519 for a child with a disability who has engaged in other behavior that violated any rule or code of conduct of the LEA that applies to all children—

(1) Not later than the date on which the decision to take that action is made, the parents must be notified of that decision and provided the procedural safeguards notice described in Sec. 300.504; and

(2) Immediately, if possible, but in no case later than 10 school days after the date on which the decision to take that action is made, a review must be conducted of the relationship between the child's disability and the behavior subject to the disciplinary action.

(b) Individuals to carry out review. A review described in paragraph (a) of this section must be conducted by the IEP team and other qualified personnel in a meeting.

(c) Conduct of review. In carrying out a review described in paragraph (a) of this section, the IEP team and other qualified personnel may determine that the behavior of the child was not a manifestation of the child's disability only if the IEP team and other qualified personnel—

(1) First consider, in terms of the behavior subject to disciplinary action, all relevant information, including —

(i) Evaluation and diagnostic results, including the results or other relevant information supplied by the parents of the child;

(ii) Observations of the child; and

(iii) The child's IEP and placement; and

(2) Then determine that—

(i) In relationship to the behavior subject to disciplinary action, the child's IEP and placement were appropriate and the special education services, supplementary aids and services, and behavior intervention strategies were provided consistent with the child's IEP and placement;

(ii) The child's disability did not impair the ability of the child to understand the impact and consequences of the behavior subject to disciplinary action; and

(iii) The child's disability did not impair the ability of the child to control the behavior subject to disciplinary action.

(d) Decision. If the IEP team and other qualified personnel determine that any of the standards in paragraph (c)(2) of this section were not met, the behavior must be considered a manifestation of the child's disability.

(e) Meeting. The review described in paragraph (a) of this section may be conducted at the same IEP meeting that is convened under Sec. 300.520(b).

(f) Deficiencies in IEP or placement. If, in the review in paragraphs (b) and (c) of this section, a public agency identifies deficiencies in the child's IEP or placement or in their implementation, it must take immediate steps to remedy those deficiencies. (Authority: 20 U.S.C. 1415(k)(4))

Sec. 300.524 Determination that behavior was not manifestation of disability.

(a) General. If the result of the review described in Sec. 300.523 is a determination, consistent with Sec. 300.523(d), that the behavior of the child with a disability was not a manifestation of the child's disability, the relevant disciplinary procedures applicable to children without disabilities may be applied to the child in the same manner in which they would be applied to children without disabilities, except as provided in Sec. 300.121(d).

(b) Additional requirement. If the public agency initiates disciplinary procedures applicable to all children, the agency shall ensure that the special education and disciplinary records of the child with a disability are transmitted for consideration by the person or persons making the final determination regarding the disciplinary action.

(c) Child's status during due process proceedings. Except as provided in Sec. 300.526, Sec. 300.514 applies if a parent requests a hearing to challenge a determination, made through the review described in Sec. 300.523, that the behavior of the child was not a manifestation of the child's disability. (Authority: 20 U.S.C. 1415(k)(5))

Sec. 300.525 Parent appeal.

(a) General.

(1) If the child's parent disagrees with a determination that the child's behavior was not a manifestation of the child's disability or with any decision regarding placement under Secs. 300.520-300.528, the parent may request a hearing.

(2) The State or local educational agency shall arrange for an expedited hearing in any case described in paragraph (a)(1) of this section if a hearing is requested by a parent.

(b) Review of decision.

(1) In reviewing a decision with respect to the manifestation determination, the hearing officer shall determine whether the public agency has demonstrated that the child's behavior was not a manifestation of the child's disability consistent with the requirements of Sec. 300.523(d).

(2) In reviewing a decision under Sec. 300.520(a)(2) to place the child in an interim alternative educational setting, the hearing officer shall apply the standards in Sec. 300.521. (Authority: 20 U.S.C. 1415(k)(6))

Sec. 300.526 Placement during appeals.

(a) General. If a parent requests a hearing or an appeal regarding a disciplinary action described in Sec. 300.520(a)(2) or 300.521 to challenge the interim alternative educational setting or the manifestation determination, the child must remain in the interim alternative educational setting pending the decision of the hearing officer or until the expiration of the time period provided for in Sec. 300.520(a)(2) or 300.521, whichever occurs first, unless the parent and the State agency or local educational agency agree otherwise.

(b) Current placement. If a child is placed in an interim alternative educational setting pursuant to Sec. 300.520(a)(2) or 300.521 and school personnel propose to change the child's placement after expiration of the interim alternative placement, during the pendency of any proceeding to challenge the proposed change in placement the child must remain in the current placement (the child's placement prior to the interim alternative educational setting), except as provided in paragraph (c) of this section.

(c) Expedited hearing.

(1) If school personnel maintain that it is dangerous for the child to be in the current placement (placement prior to removal to the interim alternative education setting) during the pendency of the due process proceedings, the LEA may request an expedited due process hearing.

(2) In determining whether the child may be placed in the alternative educational setting or in another appropriate placement ordered by the hearing officer, the hearing officer shall apply the standards in Sec. 300.521.

(3) A placement ordered pursuant to paragraph (c)(2) of this section may not be longer than 45 days.

(4) The procedure in paragraph (c) of this section may be repeated, as necessary. (Authority: 20 U.S.C. 1415(k)(7))

Sec. 300.527 Protections for children not yet eligible for special education and related services.

(a) General. A child who has not been determined to be eligible for special education and related services under this part and who has engaged in behavior that violated any rule or code of conduct of the local educational agency, including any behavior described in Secs. 300.520 or 300.521, may assert any of the protections provided for in this part if the LEA had knowledge (as determined in accordance with paragraph (b) of this section) that the child was a child with a disability before the behavior that precipitated the disciplinary action occurred.

(b) Basis of knowledge. An LEA must be deemed to have knowledge that a child is a child with a disability if—

(1) The parent of the child has expressed concern in writing (or orally if the parent does not know how to write or has a disability that prevents a written statement) to personnel of the appropriate educational agency that the child is in need of special education and related services;

(2) The behavior or performance of the child demonstrates the need for these services, in accordance with Sec. 300.7;

(3) The parent of the child has requested an evaluation of the child pursuant to Secs. 300.530-300.536; or

(4) The teacher of the child, or other personnel of the local educational agency, has expressed concern about the behavior or performance of the child to the director of special education of the agency or to other personnel in accordance with the agency's established child find or special education referral system.

(c) Exception. A public agency would not be deemed to have knowledge under paragraph (b) of this section if, as a result of receiving the information specified in that paragraph, the agency—

(1) Either—

(i) Conducted an evaluation under Secs. 300.530-300.536, and determined that the child was not a child with a disability under this part; or

(ii) Determined that an evaluation was not necessary; and

(2) Provided notice to the child's parents of its determination under paragraph (c)(1) of this section, consistent with Sec. 300.503.

(d) Conditions that apply if no basis of knowledge.

(1) General. If an LEA does not have knowledge that a child is a child with a disability (in accordance with paragraphs (b) and (c) of this section) prior to taking disciplinary measures against the child, the child may be subjected to the same disciplinary measures as measures applied to children without disabilities who engaged in comparable behaviors consistent with paragraph (d)(2) of this section.

(2) Limitations.

(i) If a request is made for an evaluation of a child during the time period in which the child is subjected to disciplinary measures under Sec. 300.520 or 300.521, the evaluation must be conducted in an expedited manner.

(ii) Until the evaluation is completed, the child remains in the educational placement determined by school authorities, which can include suspension or expulsion without educational services.

(iii) If the child is determined to be a child with a disability, taking into consideration information from the evaluation conducted by the agency and information provided by the parents, the agency shall provide special education and related services in accordance with the provisions of this part, including the requirements of Secs. 300.520- 300.529 and section 612(a)(1)(A) of the Act. (Authority: 20 U.S.C. 1415(k)(8))

Sec. 300.528 Expedited due process hearings.

(a) Expedited due process hearings under Secs. 300.521-300.526 must—

(1) Meet the requirements of Sec. 300.509, except that a State may provide that the time periods identified in Secs. 300.509(a)(3) and Sec. 300.509(b) for purposes of expedited due process hearings under Secs. 300.521-300.526 are not less than two business days; and

(2) Be conducted by a due process hearing officer who satisfies the requirements of Sec. 300.508.

(b)

(1) Each State shall establish a timeline for expedited due process hearings that results in a written decision being mailed to the parties within 45 days of the public agency's receipt of the request for the hearing, without exceptions or extensions.

(2) The timeline established under paragraph (b)(1) of this section must be the same for hearings requested by parents or public agencies.

(c) A State may establish different procedural rules for expedited hearings under Secs. 300.521-300.526 than it has established for due process hearings under Sec. 300.507.

(d) The decisions on expedited due process hearings are appealable consistent with Sec. 300.510. (Authority: 20 U.S.C. 1415(k)(2), (6), (7))

Sec. 300.529 Referral to and action by law enforcement and judicial authorities.

(a) Nothing in this part prohibits an agency from reporting a crime committed by a child with a disability to appropriate authorities or to prevent State law enforcement and judicial authorities from exercising their responsibilities with regard to the application of Federal and State law to crimes committed by a child with a disability.

(b)

(1) An agency reporting a crime committed by a child with a disability shall ensure that copies of the special education and disciplinary records of the child are transmitted for consideration by the appropriate authorities to whom it reports the crime.

(2) An agency reporting a crime under this section may transmit copies of the child's special education and disciplinary records only to the extent that the transmission is permitted by the Family Educational Rights and Privacy Act. (Authority: 20 U.S.C. 1415(k)(9))

PROCEDURES FOR EVALUATION AND DETERMINATION OF ELIGIBILITY

Sec. 300.530 General.

Each SEA shall ensure that each public agency establishes and implements procedures that meet the requirements of Secs. 300.531- 300.536. (Authority: 20 U.S.C. 1414(b)(3); 1412(a)(7))

Sec. 300.531 Initial evaluation.

Each public agency shall conduct a full and individual initial evaluation, in accordance with Secs. 300.532 and 300.533, before the initial provision of special education and related services to a child with a disability under Part B of the Act. (Authority: 20 U.S.C. 1414(a)(1))

Sec. 300.532 Evaluation procedures.

Each public agency shall ensure, at a minimum, that the following requirements are met:

(a)

(1) Tests and other evaluation materials used to assess a child under Part B of the Act—

(i) Are selected and administered so as not to be discriminatory on a racial or cultural basis; and

(ii) Are provided and administered in the child's native language or other mode of communication, unless it is clearly not feasible to do so; and

(2) Materials and procedures used to assess a child with limited English proficiency are selected and administered to ensure that they measure the extent to which the child has a disability and needs special education, rather than measuring the child's English language skills.

(b) A variety of assessment tools and strategies are used to gather relevant functional and developmental information about the child, including information provided by the parent, and information related to enabling the child to be involved in and progress in the general curriculum (or for a preschool child, to participate in appropriate activities), that may assist in determining—

(1) Whether the child is a child with a disability under Sec. 300.7; and

(2) The content of the child's IEP.

(c)

(1) Any standardized tests that are given to a child—

(i) Have been validated for the specific purpose for which they are used; and

(ii) Are administered by trained and knowledgeable personnel in accordance with any instructions provided by the producer of the tests.

(2) If an assessment is not conducted under standard conditions, a description of the extent to which it varied from standard conditions (e.g., the qualifications of the person administering the test, or the method of test administration) must be included in the evaluation report.

(d) Tests and other evaluation materials include those tailored to assess specific areas of educational need and not merely those that are designed to provide a single general intelligence quotient.

(e) Tests are selected and administered so as best to ensure that if a test is administered to a child with impaired sensory, manual, or speaking skills, the test results accurately reflect the child's aptitude or achievement level or whatever other factors the test purports to measure, rather than reflecting the child's impaired sensory, manual, or speaking skills (unless those skills are the factors that the test purports to measure).

(f) No single procedure is used as the sole criterion for determining whether a child is a child with a disability and for determining an appropriate educational program for the child.

(g) The child is assessed in all areas related to the suspected disability, including, if appropriate, health, vision, hearing, social and emotional status, general intelligence, academic performance, communicative status, and motor abilities.

(h) In evaluating each child with a disability under Secs. 300.531- 300.536, the evaluation is sufficiently comprehensive to identify all of the child's special education and related services needs, whether or not commonly linked to the disability category in which the child has been classified.

(i) The public agency uses technically sound instruments that may assess the relative contribution of cognitive and behavioral factors, in addition to physical or developmental factors.

(j) The public agency uses assessment tools and strategies that provide relevant information that directly assists persons in determining the educational needs of the child. (Authority: 20 U.S.C. 1412(a)(6)(B), 1414(b)(2) and (3))

Sec. 300.533 Determination of needed evaluation data.

  (a) Review of existing evaluation data. As part of an initial evaluation (if appropriate) and as part of any reevaluation under Part B of the Act, a group that includes the individuals described in Sec. 300.344, and other qualified professionals, as appropriate, shall—

    (1) Review existing evaluation data on the child, including—

      (i) Evaluations and information provided by the parents of the child;

      (ii) Current classroom-based assessments and observations; and

      (iii) Observations by teachers and related services providers; and

    (2) On the basis of that review, and input from the child's parents, identify what additional data, if any, are needed to determine—

      (i) Whether the child has a particular category of disability, as described in Sec. 300.7, or, in case of a reevaluation of a child, whether the child continues to have such a disability;

      (ii) The present levels of performance and educational needs of the child;

      (iii) Whether the child needs special education and related services, or in the case of a reevaluation of a child, whether the child continues to need special education and related services; and

      (iv) Whether any additions or modifications to the special education and related services are needed to enable the child to meet the measurable annual goals set out in the IEP of the child and to participate, as appropriate, in the general curriculum.

  (b) Conduct of review. The group described in paragraph (a) of this section may conduct its review without a meeting.

  (c) Need for additional data. The public agency shall administer tests and other evaluation materials as may be needed to produce the data identified under paragraph (a) of this section.

  (d) Requirements if additional data are not needed.

    (1) If the determination under paragraph (a) of this section is that no additional data are needed to determine whether the child continues to be a child with a disability, the public agency shall notify the child's parents—

      (i) Of that determination and the reasons for it; and

      (ii) Of the right of the parents to request an assessment to determine whether, for purposes of services under this part, the child continues to be a child with a disability.

    (2) The public agency is not required to conduct the assessment described in paragraph (d)(1)(ii) of this section unless requested to do so by the child's parents. (Authority: 20 U.S.C. 1414(c)(1), (2) and (4))

Sec. 300.534 Determination of eligibility

  (a) Upon completing the administration of tests and other evaluation materials—

    (1) A group of qualified professionals and the parent of the child must determine whether the child is a child with a disability, as defined in Sec. 300.7; and

    (2) The public agency must provide a copy of the evaluation report and the documentation of determination of eligibility to the parent.

  (b) A child may not be determined to be eligible under this part if—

    (1) The determinant factor for that eligibility determination is—

      (i) Lack of instruction in reading or math; or

      (ii) Limited English proficiency; and

    (2) The child does not otherwise meet the eligibility criteria under Sec. 300.7(a).

  (c)

    (1) A public agency must evaluate a child with a disability in accordance with Secs. 300.532 and 300.533 before determining that the child is no longer a child with a disability.

    (2) The evaluation described in paragraph (c)(1) of this section is not required before the termination of a student's eligibility under Part B of the Act due to graduation with a regular high school diploma, or exceeding the age eligibility for FAPE under State law. (Authority: 20 U.S.C. 1414(b)(4) and (5), (c)(5))

Sec. 300.535 Procedures for determining eligibility and placement.

  (a) In interpreting evaluation data for the purpose of determining if a child is a child with a disability under Sec. 300.7, and the educational needs of the child, each public agency shall—

    (1) Draw upon information from a variety of sources, including aptitude and achievement tests, parent input, teacher recommendations, physical condition, social or cultural background, and adaptive behavior; and

    (2) Ensure that information obtained from all of these sources is documented and carefully considered.

  (b) If a determination is made that a child has a disability and needs special education and related services, an IEP must be developed for the child in accordance with Secs. 300.340-300.350. (Authority: 20 U.S.C. 1412(a)(6), 1414(b)(4))

Sec. 300.536 Reevaluation.

Each public agency shall ensure—

(a) That the IEP of each child with a disability is reviewed in accordance with Secs. 300.340-300.350; and

(b) That a reevaluation of each child, in accordance with Secs. 300.532-300.535, is conducted if conditions warrant a reevaluation, or if the child's parent or teacher requests a reevaluation, but at least once every three years. (Authority: 20 U.S.C. 1414(a)(2))

ADDITIONAL PROCEDURES FOR EVALUATING CHILDREN WITH SPECIFIC LEARNING DISABILITIES

Sec. 300.540 Additional team members.

The determination of whether a child suspected of having a specific learning disability is a child with a disability as defined in Sec. 300.7, must be made by the child's parents and a team of qualified professionals which must include—

(a)

(1) The child's regular teacher; or

(2) If the child does not have a regular teacher, a regular classroom teacher qualified to teach a child of his or her age; or

(3) For a child of less than school age, an individual qualified by the SEA to teach a child of his or her age; and

(b) At least one person qualified to conduct individual diagnostic examinations of children, such as a school psychologist, speech- language pathologist, or remedial reading teacher. (Authority: Sec. 5(b), Pub. L. 94-142)

Sec. 300.541 Criteria for determining the existence of a specific learning disability.

(a) A team may determine that a child has a specific learning disability if—

(1) The child does not achieve commensurate with his or her age and ability levels in one or more of the areas listed in paragraph (a)(2) of this section, if provided with learning experiences appropriate for the child's age and ability levels; and

(2) The team finds that a child has a severe discrepancy between achievement and intellectual ability in one or more of the following areas:

(i) Oral expression.

(ii) Listening comprehension.

(iii) Written expression.

(iv) Basic reading skill.

(v) Reading comprehension.

(vi) Mathematics calculation.

(vii) Mathematics reasoning.

(b) The team may not identify a child as having a specific learning disability if the severe discrepancy between ability and achievement is primarily the result of—

(1) A visual, hearing, or motor impairment;

(2) Mental retardation;

(3) Emotional disturbance; or

(4) Environmental, cultural or economic disadvantage. (Authority: Sec. 5(b), Pub. L. 94-142)

Sec. 300.542 Observation.

(a) At least one team member other than the child's regular teacher shall observe the child's academic performance in the regular classroom setting.

(b) In the case of a child of less than school age or out of school, a team member shall observe the child in an environment appropriate for a child of that age. (Authority: Sec. 5(b), Pub. L. 94-142)

Sec. 300.543 Written report.

(a) For a child suspected of having a specific learning disability, the documentation of the team's determination of eligibility, as required by Sec. 300.534(a)(2), must include a statement of—

(1) Whether the child has a specific learning disability;

(2) The basis for making the determination;

(3) The relevant behavior noted during the observation of the child;

(4) The relationship of that behavior to the child's academic functioning;

(5) The educationally relevant medical findings, if any;

(6) Whether there is a severe discrepancy between achievement and ability that is not correctable without special education and related services; and

(7) The determination of the team concerning the effects of environmental, cultural, or economic disadvantage.

(b) Each team member shall certify in writing whether the report reflects his or her conclusion. If it does not reflect his or her conclusion, the team member must submit a separate statement presenting his or her conclusions. (Authority: Sec. 5(b), Pub. L. 94-142)

LEAST RESTRICTIVE ENVIRONMENT (LRE)

Sec. 300.550 General LRE requirements.

(a) Except as provided in Sec. 300.311(b) and (c), a State shall demonstrate to the satisfaction of the Secretary that the State has in effect policies and procedures to ensure that it meets the requirements of Secs. 300.550-300.556.

(b) Each public agency shall ensure—

(1) That to the maximum extent appropriate, children with disabilities, including children in public or private institutions or other care facilities, are educated with children who are nondisabled; and

(2) That special classes, separate schooling or other removal of children with disabilities from the regular educational environment occurs only if the nature or severity of the disability is such that education in regular classes with the use of supplementary aids and services cannot be achieved satisfactorily. (Authority: 20 U.S.C. 1412(a)(5))

Sec. 300.551 Continuum of alternative placements.

(a) Each public agency shall ensure that a continuum of alternative placements is available to meet the needs of children with disabilities for special education and related services.

(b) The continuum required in paragraph (a) of this section must—

(1) Include the alternative placements listed in the definition of special education under Sec. 300.26 (instruction in regular classes, special classes, special schools, home instruction, and instruction in hospitals and institutions); and

(2) Make provision for supplementary services (such as resource room or itinerant instruction) to be provided in conjunction with regular class placement. (Authority: 20 U.S.C. 1412(a)(5))

Sec. 300.552 Placements.

In determining the educational placement of a child with a disability, including a preschool child with a disability, each public agency shall ensure that—

(a) The placement decision—

(1) Is made by a group of persons, including the parents, and other persons knowledgeable about the child, the meaning of the evaluation data, and the placement options; and

(2) Is made in conformity with the LRE provisions of this subpart, including Secs. 300.550-300.554;

(b) The child's placement—

(1) Is determined at least annually;

(2) Is based on the child's IEP; and

(3) Is as close as possible to the child's home;

(c) Unless the IEP of a child with a disability requires some other arrangement, the **child is educated in the school that he or she would attend if nondisabled**;

(d) In selecting the LRE, consideration is given to **any potential harmful effect on the child or on the quality of services** that he or she needs; and

(e) A child with a disability is not removed from education in age-appropriate regular classrooms solely because of needed modifications in the general curriculum. (Authority: 20 U.S.C. 1412(a)(5))

Sec. 300.553 Nonacademic settings.

In providing or arranging for the provision of nonacademic and extracurricular services and activities, including meals, recess periods, and the services and activities set forth in Sec. 300.306, each public agency shall ensure that each child with a disability participates with nondisabled children in those services and activities to the maximum extent appropriate to the needs of that child. (Authority: 20 U.S.C. 1412(a)(5))

Sec. 300.554 Children in public or private institutions.

Except as provided in Sec. 300.600(d), an SEA must ensure that Sec. 300.550 is effectively implemented, including, if necessary, making arrangements with public and private institutions (such as a memorandum of agreement or special implementation procedures). (Authority: 20 U.S.C. 1412(a)(5))

Sec. 300.555 Technical assistance and training activities.

Each SEA shall carry out activities to ensure that teachers and administrators in all public agencies—

(a) Are fully informed about their responsibilities for implementing Sec. 300.550; and

(b) Are provided with technical assistance and training necessary to assist them in this effort. (Authority: 20 U.S.C. 1412(a)(5))

Sec. 300.556 Monitoring activities.

(a) The SEA shall carry out activities to ensure that Sec. 300.550 is implemented by each public agency.

(b) If there is evidence that a public agency makes placements that are inconsistent with Sec. 300.550, the SEA shall—

(1) Review the public agency's justification for its actions; and

(2) Assist in planning and implementing any necessary corrective action. (Authority: 20 U.S.C. 1412(a)(5))

CONFIDENTIALITY OF INFORMATION

Sec. 300.560 Definitions.

As used in Secs. 300.560-300.577—

(a) Destruction means physical destruction or removal of personal identifiers from information so that the information is no longer personally identifiable.

(b) Education records means the type of records covered under the definition of "education records" in 34 CFR part 99 (the regulations implementing the Family Educational Rights and Privacy Act of 1974).

(c) Participating agency means any agency or institution that collects, maintains, or uses personally identifiable information, or from which information is obtained, under Part B of the Act. (Authority: 20 U.S.C. 1221e-3, 1412(a)(8), 1417(c))

Sec. 300.561 Notice to parents.

(a) The SEA shall give notice that is adequate to fully inform parents about the requirements of Sec. 300.127, including—

(1) A description of the extent that the notice is given in the native languages of the various population groups in the State;

(2) A description of the children on whom personally identifiable information is maintained, the types of information sought, the methods the State intends to use in gathering the information (including the sources from whom information is gathered), and the uses to be made of the information;

(3) A summary of the policies and procedures that participating agencies must follow regarding storage, disclosure to third parties, retention, and destruction of personally identifiable information; and

(4) A description of all of the rights of parents and children regarding this information, including the rights under the Family Educational Rights and Privacy Act of 1974 and implementing regulations in 34 CFR part 99.

(b) Before any major identification, location, or evaluation activity, the notice must be published or announced in newspapers or other media, or both, with circulation adequate to notify parents throughout the State of the activity. (Authority: 20 U.S.C. 1412(a)(8), 1417(c))

Sec. 300.562 Access rights.

(a) Each participating agency shall permit parents to inspect and review any education records relating to their children that are collected, maintained, or used by the agency under this part. The agency shall comply with a request without unnecessary delay and before any meeting regarding an IEP, or any hearing pursuant to Secs. 300.507 and 300.521-300.528, and in no case more than 45 days after the request has been made.

(b) The right to inspect and review education records under this section includes—

(1) The right to a response from the participating agency to reasonable requests for explanations and interpretations of the records;

(2) The right to request that the agency provide copies of the records containing the information if failure to provide those copies would effectively prevent the parent from exercising the right to inspect and review the records; and

(3) The right to have a representative of the parent inspect and review the records.

(c) An agency may presume that the parent has authority to inspect and review records relating to his or her child unless the agency has been advised that the parent does not have the authority under applicable State law governing such matters as guardianship, separation, and divorce. (Authority: 20 U.S.C. 1412(a)(8), 1417(c))

Sec. 300.563 Record of access.

Each participating agency shall keep a record of parties obtaining access to education records collected, maintained, or used under Part B of the Act (except access by parents and authorized employees of the participating agency), including the name of the party, the date access was given, and the purpose for which the party is authorized to use the records. (Authority: 20 U.S.C. 1412(a)(8), 1417(c))

Sec. 300.564 Records on more than one child.

If any education record includes information on more than one child, the parents of those children have the right to inspect and review only the information relating to their child or to be informed of that specific information. (Authority: 20 U.S.C. 1412(a)(8), 1417(c))

Sec. 300.565 List of types and locations of information.

Each participating agency shall provide parents on request a list of the types and locations of education records collected, maintained, or used by the agency. (Authority: 20 U.S.C. 1412(a)(8), 1417(c))

Sec. 300.566 Fees.

(a) Each participating agency may charge a fee for copies of records that are made for parents under this part if the fee does not effectively prevent the parents from exercising their right to inspect and review those records.

(b) A participating agency may not charge a fee to search for or to retrieve information under this part. (Authority: 20 U.S.C. 1412(a)(8), 1417(c))

Sec. 300.567 Amendment of records at parent's request.

(a) A parent who believes that information in the education records collected, maintained, or used under this part is inaccurate or misleading or violates the privacy or other rights of the child may request the participating agency that maintains the information to amend the information.

(b) The agency shall decide whether to amend the information in accordance with the request within a reasonable period of time of receipt of the request.

(c) If the agency decides to refuse to amend the information in accordance with the request, it shall inform the parent of the refusal and advise the parent of the right to a hearing under Sec. 300.568. (Authority: 20 U.S.C. 1412(a)(8); 1417(c))

Sec. 300.568 Opportunity for a hearing.

The agency shall, on request, provide an opportunity for a hearing to challenge information in education records to ensure that it is not inaccurate, misleading, or otherwise in violation of the privacy or other rights of the child. (Authority: 20 U.S.C. 1412(a)(8), 1417(c))

Sec. 300.569 Result of hearing.

(a) If, as a result of the hearing, the agency decides that the information is inaccurate, misleading or otherwise in violation of the privacy or other rights of the child, it shall amend the information accordingly and so inform the parent in writing.

(b) If, as a result of the hearing, the agency decides that the information is not inaccurate, misleading, or otherwise in violation of the privacy or other rights of the child, it shall inform the parent of the right to place in the records it maintains on the child a statement commenting on the information or setting forth any reasons for disagreeing with the decision of the agency.

(c) Any explanation placed in the records of the child under this section must—

(1) Be maintained by the agency as part of the records of the child as long as the record or contested portion is maintained by the agency; and

(2) If the records of the child or the contested portion is disclosed by the agency to any party, the explanation must also be disclosed to the party. (Authority: 20 U.S.C. 1412(a)(8), 1417(c))

Sec. 300.570 Hearing procedures.

A hearing held under Sec. 300.568 must be conducted according to the procedures under 34 CFR 99.22. (Authority: 20 U.S.C. 1412(a)(8), 1417(c))

Sec. 300.571 Consent.

(a) Except as to disclosures addressed in Sec. 300.529(b) for which parental consent is not required by Part 99, parental consent must be obtained before personally identifiable information is—

(1) Disclosed to anyone other than officials of participating agencies collecting or using the information under this part, subject to paragraph (b) of this section; or

(2) Used for any purpose other than meeting a requirement of this part.

(b) An educational agency or institution subject to 34 CFR part 99 may not release information from education records to participating agencies without parental consent unless authorized to do so under part 99.

(c) The SEA shall provide policies and procedures that are used in the event that a parent refuses to provide consent under this section. (Authority: 20 U.S.C. 1412(a)(8), 1417(c))

Sec. 300.572 Safeguards.

(a) Each participating agency shall protect the confidentiality of personally identifiable information at collection, storage, disclosure, and destruction stages.

(b) One official at each participating agency shall assume responsibility for ensuring the confidentiality of any personally identifiable information.

(c) All persons collecting or using personally identifiable information must receive training or instruction regarding the State's policies and procedures under Sec. 300.127 and 34 CFR part 99.

(d) Each participating agency shall maintain, for public inspection, a current listing of the names and positions of those employees within the agency who may have access to personally identifiable information. (Authority: 20 U.S.C. 1412(a)(8), 1417(c))

Sec. 300.573 Destruction of information.

(a) The public agency shall inform parents when personally identifiable information collected, maintained, or used under this part is no longer needed to provide educational services to the child.

(b) The information must be destroyed at the request of the parents. However, a permanent record of a student's name, address, and phone number, his or her grades, attendance record, classes attended, grade level completed, and year completed may be maintained without time limitation. (Authority: 20 U.S.C. 1412(a)(8), 1417(c))

Sec. 300.574 Children's rights.

(a) The SEA shall provide policies and procedures regarding the extent to which children are afforded rights of privacy similar to those afforded to parents, taking into consideration the age of the child and type or severity of disability.

(b) Under the regulations for the Family Educational Rights and Privacy Act of 1974 (34 CFR 99.5(a)), the rights of parents regarding education records are transferred to the student at age 18.

(c) If the rights accorded to parents under Part B of the Act are transferred to a student who reaches the age of majority, consistent with Sec. 300.517, the rights regarding educational records in Secs. 300.562-300.573 must also be transferred to the student. However, the public agency must provide any notice required under section 615 of the Act to the student and the parents. (Authority: 20 U.S.C. 1412(a)(8), 1417(c))

Sec. 300.575 Enforcement.

The SEA shall provide the policies and procedures, including sanctions, that the State uses to ensure that its policies and procedures are followed and that the requirements of the Act and the regulations in this part are met. (Authority: 20 U.S.C. 1412(a)(8), 1417(c))

Sec. 300.576 Disciplinary information.

(a) The State may require that a public agency include in the records of a child with a disability a statement of any current or previous disciplinary action that has been taken against the child and transmit the statement to the same extent that the disciplinary information is included in, and transmitted with, the student records of nondisabled children.

(b) The statement may include a description of any behavior engaged in by the child that required disciplinary action, a description of the disciplinary action taken, and any other information that is relevant to the safety of the child and other individuals involved with the child.

(c) If the State adopts such a policy, and the child transfers from one school to another, the transmission of any of the child's records must include both the child's current individualized education program and any statement of current or previous disciplinary action that has been taken against the child. (Authority: 20 U.S.C. 1413(j))

Sec. 300.577 Department use of personally identifiable information.

If the Department or its authorized representatives collect any personally identifiable information regarding children with disabilities that is not subject to 5 U.S.C. 552a (the Privacy Act of 1974), the Secretary applies the requirements of 5 U.S.C. 552a (b)(1)- (2), (4)-(11); (c); (d); (e)(1), (2), (3)(A), (B), and (D), (5)-(10); (h); (m); and (n); and the regulations implementing those provisions in 34 CFR part 5b. (Authority: 20 U.S.C. 1412(a)(8), 1417(c))

DEPARTMENT PROCEDURES

Sec. 300.580 Determination by the Secretary that a State is eligible.

If the Secretary determines that a State is eligible to receive a grant under Part B of the Act, the Secretary notifies the State of that determination. (Authority: 20 U.S.C. 1412(d))

Sec. 300.581 Notice and hearing before determining that a State is not eligible.

(a) General.

(1) The Secretary does not make a final determination that a State is not eligible to receive a grant under Part B of the Act until providing the State—

    (i) With reasonable notice; and

    (ii) With an opportunity for a hearing.

(2) In implementing paragraph (a)(1)(i) of this section, the Secretary sends a written notice to the SEA by certified mail with return receipt requested.

(b) Content of notice. In the written notice described in paragraph (a)(2) of this section, the Secretary—

(1) States the basis on which the Secretary proposes to make a final determination that the State is not eligible;

(2) May describe possible options for resolving the issues;

(3) Advises the SEA that it may request a hearing and that the request for a hearing must be made not later than 30 days after it receives the notice of the proposed final determination that the State is not eligible; and

(4) Provides information about the procedures followed for a hearing. (Authority: 20 U.S.C. (1412(d)(2))

Sec. 300.582 Hearing official or panel.

(a) If the SEA requests a hearing, the Secretary designates one or more individuals, either from the Department or elsewhere, not responsible for or connected with the administration of this program, to conduct a hearing.

(b) If more than one individual is designated, the Secretary designates one of those individuals as the Chief Hearing Official of the Hearing Panel. If one individual is designated, that individual is the Hearing Official. (Authority: 20 U.S.C. (1412(d)(2))

Sec. 300.583 Hearing procedures.

(a) As used in Secs. 300.581-300.586 the term party or parties means the following:

(1) An SEA that requests a hearing regarding the proposed disapproval of the State's eligibility under this part.

(2) The Department official who administers the program of financial assistance under this part.

(3) A person, group or agency with an interest in and having relevant information about the case that has applied for and been granted leave to intervene by the Hearing Official or Panel.

(b) Within 15 days after receiving a request for a hearing, the Secretary designates a Hearing Official or Panel and notifies the parties.

(c) The Hearing Official or Panel may regulate the course of proceedings and the conduct of the parties during the proceedings. The Hearing Official or Panel takes all steps necessary to conduct a fair and impartial proceeding, to avoid delay, and to maintain order, including the following:

(1) The Hearing Official or Panel may hold conferences or other types of appropriate proceedings to clarify, simplify, or define the issues or to consider other matters that may aid in the disposition of the case.

(2) The Hearing Official or Panel may schedule a prehearing conference of the Hearing Official or Panel and parties.

(3) Any party may request the Hearing Official or Panel to schedule a prehearing or other conference. The Hearing Official or Panel decides whether a conference is necessary and notifies all parties.

(4) At a prehearing or other conference, the Hearing Official or Panel and the parties may consider subjects such as—

(i) Narrowing and clarifying issues;

(ii) Assisting the parties in reaching agreements and stipulations;

(iii) Clarifying the positions of the parties;

(iv) Determining whether an evidentiary hearing or oral argument should be held; and

(v) Setting dates for—

(A) The exchange of written documents;

(B) The receipt of comments from the parties on the need for oral argument or evidentiary hearing;

(C) Further proceedings before the Hearing Official or Panel (including an evidentiary hearing or oral argument, if either is scheduled);

(D) Requesting the names of witnesses each party wishes to present at an evidentiary hearing and estimation of time for each presentation; or

(E) Completion of the review and the initial decision of the Hearing Official or Panel.

(5) A prehearing or other conference held under paragraph (b)(4) of this section may be conducted by telephone conference call.

(6) At a prehearing or other conference, the parties shall be prepared to discuss the subjects listed in paragraph (b)(4) of this section.

(7) Following a prehearing or other conference the Hearing Official or Panel may issue a written statement describing the issues raised, the action taken, and the stipulations and agreements reached by the parties.

(d) The Hearing Official or Panel may require parties to state their positions and to provide all or part of the evidence in writing.

(e) The Hearing Official or Panel may require parties to present testimony through affidavits and to conduct cross-examination through interrogatories.

(f) The Hearing Official or Panel may direct the parties to exchange relevant documents or information and lists of witnesses, and to send copies to the Hearing Official or Panel.

(g) The Hearing Official or Panel may receive, rule on, exclude, or limit evidence at any stage of the proceedings.

(h) The Hearing Official or Panel may rule on motions and other issues at any stage of the proceedings.

(i) The Hearing Official or Panel may examine witnesses.

(j) The Hearing Official or Panel may set reasonable time limits for submission of written documents.

(k) The Hearing Official or Panel may refuse to consider documents or other submissions if they are not submitted in a timely manner unless good cause is shown.

(l) The Hearing Official or Panel may interpret applicable statutes and regulations but may not waive them or rule on their validity.

(m)

(1) The parties shall present their positions through briefs and the submission of other documents and may request an oral argument or evidentiary hearing. The Hearing Official or Panel shall determine whether an oral argument or an evidentiary hearing is needed to clarify the positions of the parties.

(2) The Hearing Official or Panel gives each party an opportunity to be represented by counsel.

(n) If the Hearing Official or Panel determines that an evidentiary hearing would materially assist the resolution of the matter, the Hearing Official or Panel gives each party, in addition to the opportunity to be represented by counsel—

(1) An opportunity to present witnesses on the party's behalf; and

(2) An opportunity to cross-examine witnesses either orally or with written questions.

(o) The Hearing Official or Panel accepts any evidence that it finds is relevant and material to the proceedings and is not unduly repetitious.

(p)

(1) The Hearing Official or Panel—

(i) Arranges for the preparation of a transcript of each hearing;

(ii) Retains the original transcript as part of the record of the hearing; and

(iii) Provides one copy of the transcript to each party.

(2) Additional copies of the transcript are available on request and with payment of the reproduction fee.

(q) Each party shall file with the Hearing Official or Panel all written motions, briefs, and other documents and shall at the same time provide a copy to the other parties to the proceedings. (Authority: 20 U.S.C. (1412(d)(2))

Sec. 300.584 Initial decision; final decision.

(a) The Hearing Official or Panel prepares an initial written decision that addresses each of the points in the notice sent by the Secretary to the SEA under Sec. 300.581.

(b) The initial decision of a Panel is made by a majority of Panel members.

(c) The Hearing Official or Panel mails by certified mail with return receipt requested a copy of the initial decision to each party (or to the party's counsel) and to the Secretary, with a notice stating that each party has an opportunity to submit written comments regarding the decision to the Secretary.

(d) Each party may file comments and recommendations on the initial decision with the Hearing Official or Panel within 15 days of the date the party receives the Panel's decision.

(e) The Hearing Official or Panel sends a copy of a party's initial comments and recommendations to the other parties by certified mail with return receipt requested. Each party may file responsive comments and recommendations with the Hearing Official or Panel within seven days of the date the party receives the initial comments and recommendations.

(f) The Hearing Official or Panel forwards the parties' initial and responsive comments on the initial decision to the Secretary who reviews the initial decision and issues a final decision.

(g) The initial decision of the Hearing Official or Panel becomes the final decision of the Secretary unless, within 25 days after the end of the time for receipt of written comments, the Secretary informs the Hearing Official or Panel and the parties to a hearing in writing that the decision is being further reviewed for possible modification.

(h) The Secretary may reject or modify the initial decision of the Hearing Official or Panel if the Secretary finds that it is clearly erroneous.

(i) The Secretary conducts the review based on the initial decision, the written record, the Hearing Official's or Panel's proceedings, and written comments. The Secretary may remand the matter for further proceedings.

(j) The Secretary issues the final decision within 30 days after notifying the Hearing Official or Panel that the initial decision is being further reviewed. (Authority: 20 U.S.C. (1412(d)(2))

Sec. 300.585 Filing requirements.

(a) Any written submission under Secs. 300.581-300.585 must be filed by hand-delivery, by mail, or by facsimile transmission. The Secretary discourages the use of facsimile transmission for documents longer than five pages.

(b) The filing date under paragraph (a) of this section is the date the document is—

(1) Hand-delivered;

(2) Mailed; or

(3) Sent by facsimile transmission.

(c) A party filing by facsimile transmission is responsible for confirming that a complete and legible copy of the document was received by the Department.

(d) If a document is filed by facsimile transmission, the Secretary, the Hearing Official, or the Panel, as applicable, may require the filing of a follow-up hard copy by hand-delivery or by mail within a reasonable period of time.

(e) If agreed upon by the parties, service of a document may be made upon the other party by facsimile transmission. (Authority: 20 U.S.C. 1413(c))

Sec. 300.586 Judicial review.

If a State is dissatisfied with the Secretary's final action with respect to the eligibility of the State under section 612 of the Act, the State may, not later than 60 days after notice of that action, file with the United States Court of Appeals for the circuit in which that State is located a petition for review of that action. A copy of the petition must be forthwith transmitted by the clerk of the court to the Secretary. The Secretary then files in the court the record of the proceedings upon which the Secretary's action was based, as provided in section 2112 of title 28, United States Code. (Authority: 20 U.S.C. 1416(b))

Sec. 300.587 Enforcement.

  (a) **General**. The Secretary initiates an action described in paragraph (b) of this section if the Secretary finds—

    (1) That there has been a failure by the State to comply substantially with any provision of Part B of the Act, this part, or 34 CFR part 301; or

    (2) That there is a failure to comply with any condition of an LEA's or SEA's eligibility under Part B of the Act, this part or 34 CFR part 301, including the terms of any agreement to achieve compliance with Part B of the Act, this part, or Part 301 within the timelines specified in the agreement.

  (b) **Types of action**. The Secretary, after notifying the SEA (and any LEA or State agency affected by a failure described in paragraph (a)(2) of this section)—

    (1) Withholds in whole or in part any further payments to the State under Part B of the Act;

    (2) Refers the matter to the Department of Justice for enforcement; or

    (3) Takes any other enforcement action authorized by law.

  (c) **Nature of withholding**.

    (1) If the Secretary determines that it is appropriate to withhold further payments under paragraph (b)(1) of this section, the Secretary may determine that the withholding will be limited to programs or projects, or portions thereof, affected by the failure, or that the SEA shall not make further payments under Part B of the Act to specified LEA or State agencies affected by the failure.

    (2) Until the Secretary is satisfied that there is no longer any failure to comply with the provisions of Part B of the Act, this part, or 34 CFR part 301, as specified in paragraph (a) of this section, payments to the State under Part B of the Act are withheld in whole or in part, or payments by the SEA under Part B of the Act are limited to local educational agencies and State agencies whose actions did not cause or were not involved in the failure, as the case may be.

    (3) Any SEA, LEA, or other State agency that has received notice under paragraph (a) of this section shall, by means of a public notice, take such measures as may be necessary to bring the pendency of an action pursuant to this subsection to the attention of the public within the jurisdiction of that agency.

    (4) Before withholding under paragraph (b)(1) of this section, the Secretary provides notice and a hearing pursuant to the procedures in Secs. 300.581-300.586.

  (d) **Referral for appropriate enforcement**.

    (1) Before the Secretary makes a referral under paragraph (b)(2) of this section for enforcement, or takes any other enforcement action authorized by law under paragraph (b)(3), the Secretary provides the State—

      (i) With reasonable notice; and

      (ii) With an opportunity for a hearing.

    (2) The hearing described in paragraph (d)(1)(ii) of this section consists of an opportunity to meet with the Assistant Secretary for the Office of Special Education and Rehabilitative Services to demonstrate why the Department should not make a referral for enforcement.

  (e) **Divided State agency responsibility**. For purposes of this part, if responsibility for ensuring that the requirements of this part are met with respect to children with disabilities who are convicted as adults under State law and incarcerated in adult prisons is assigned to a public agency other than the SEA pursuant to Sec. 300.600(d), and if the Secretary finds that the failure to comply substantially with the provisions of Part B of the Act or this part are related to a failure by the public agency, the Secretary takes one of the enforcement actions described in paragraph (b) of this section to ensure compliance with Part B of the Act and this part, except—

    (1) Any reduction or withholding of payments to the State under paragraph (b)(1) of this section is proportionate to the total funds allotted under section 611 of the Act to the State as the number of eligible children with disabilities in adult prisons under the supervision of the other public agency is proportionate to the number of eligible individuals with disabilities in the State under the supervision of the State educational agency; and

    (2) Any withholding of funds under paragraph (e)(1) of this section is limited to the specific agency responsible for the failure to comply with Part B of the Act or this part. (Authority: 20 U.S.C. 1416)

Secs. 300.588 [Reserved]

Sec. 300.589 Waiver of requirement regarding supplementing and not supplanting with Part B funds.

  (a) Except as provided under Secs. 300.232-300.235, funds paid to a State under Part B of the Act must be used to supplement and increase the level of Federal, State, and local funds (including funds that are not under the direct control of SEAs or LEAs) expended for special education and related services provided to children with disabilities under Part B of the Act and in no case to supplant those Federal, State, and local funds. A State may use funds it retains under Sec. 300.602 without regard to the prohibition on supplanting other funds (see Sec. 300.372).

  (b) If a State provides clear and convincing evidence that all eligible children with disabilities throughout the State have FAPE available to them, the Secretary may waive for a period of one year in whole or in part the requirement under Sec. 300.153 (regarding State- level nonsupplanting) if the Secretary concurs with the evidence provided by the State.

  (c) If a State wishes to request a waiver under this section, it must submit to the Secretary a written request that includes—

(1) An assurance that FAPE is currently available, and will remain available throughout the period that a waiver would be in effect, to all eligible children with disabilities throughout the State, regardless of the public agency that is responsible for providing FAPE to them. The assurance must be signed by an official who has the authority to provide that assurance as it applies to all eligible children with disabilities in the State;

(2) All evidence that the State wishes the Secretary to consider in determining whether all eligible children with disabilities have FAPE available to them, setting forth in detail—

(i) The basis on which the State has concluded that FAPE is available to all eligible children in the State; and

(ii) The procedures that the State will implement to ensure that FAPE remains available to all eligible children in the State, which must include—

(A) The State's procedures under Sec. 300.125 for ensuring that all eligible children are identified, located and evaluated;

(B) The State's procedures for monitoring public agencies to ensure that they comply with all requirements of this part;

(C) The State's complaint procedures under Secs. 300.660-300.662; and

(D) The State's hearing procedures under Secs. 300.507-300.511 and 300.520-300.528;

(3) A summary of all State and Federal monitoring reports, and State complaint decisions (see Secs. 300.660-300.662) and hearing decisions (see Secs. 300.507-300.511 and 300.520-300.528), issued within three years prior to the date of the State's request for a waiver under this section, that includes any finding that FAPE has not been available to one or more eligible children, and evidence that FAPE is now available to all children addressed in those reports or decisions; and

(4) Evidence that the State, in determining that FAPE is currently available to all eligible children with disabilities in the State, has consulted with the State advisory panel under Sec. 300.650, the State's parent training and information center or centers, the State's protection and advocacy organization, and other organizations representing the interests of children with disabilities and their parents, and a summary of the input of these organizations.

(d) If the Secretary determines that the request and supporting evidence submitted by the State makes a prima facie showing that FAPE is, and will remain, available to all eligible children with disabilities in the State, the Secretary, after notice to the public throughout the State, conducts a public hearing at which all interested persons and organizations may present evidence regarding the following issues:

(1) Whether FAPE is currently available to all eligible children with disabilities in the State.

(2) Whether the State will be able to ensure that FAPE remains available to all eligible children with disabilities in the State if the Secretary provides the requested waiver.

(e) Following the hearing, the Secretary, based on all submitted evidence, will provide a waiver, in whole or in part, for a period of one year if the Secretary finds that the State has provided clear and convincing evidence that FAPE is currently available to all eligible children with disabilities in the State, and the State will be able to ensure that FAPE remains available to all eligible children with disabilities in the State if the Secretary provides the requested waiver.

(f) A State may receive a waiver of the requirement of section 612(a)(19)(A) and Sec. 300.154(a) if it satisfies the requirements of paragraphs (b) through (e) of this section.

(g) The Secretary may grant subsequent waivers for a period of one year each, if the Secretary determines that the State has provided clear and convincing evidence that all eligible children with disabilities throughout the State have, and will continue to have throughout the one-year period of the waiver, FAPE available to them. (Authority: 20 U.S.C. 1412(a)(18)(C), (19)(C)(ii) and (E))

SUBPART F—STATE ADMINISTRATION

GENERAL

Sec. 300.600 Responsibility for all educational programs.

(a) The SEA is responsible for ensuring—

(1) That the requirements of this part are carried out; and

(2) That each educational program for children with disabilities administered within the State, including each program administered by any other State or local agency—

(i) Is under the general supervision of the persons responsible for educational programs for children with disabilities in the SEA; and

(ii) Meets the education standards of the SEA (including the requirements of this part).

(b) The State must comply with paragraph (a) of this section through State statute, State regulation, signed agreement between respective agency officials, or other documents.

(c) Part B of the Act does not limit the responsibility of agencies other than educational agencies for providing or paying some or all of the costs of FAPE to children with disabilities in the State.

(d) Notwithstanding paragraph (a) of this section, the Governor (or another individual pursuant to State law) may assign to any public agency in the State the responsibility of ensuring that the requirements of Part B of the Act are met with respect to students with disabilities who are convicted as adults under State law and incarcerated in adult prisons. (Authority: 20 U.S.C. 1412(a)(11))

Sec. 300.601 Relation of Part B to other Federal programs.

Part B of the Act may not be construed to permit a State to reduce medical and other assistance available to children with disabilities, or to alter the eligibility of a child with a disability, under title V (Maternal and Child Health) or title XIX (Medicaid) of the Social Security Act, to receive services that are also part of FAPE. (Authority: 20 U.S.C. 1412(e))

Sec. 300.602 State-level activities.

(a) Each State may retain not more than the amount described in paragraph (b) of this section for administration in accordance with Secs. 300.620 and 300.621 and other State-level activities in accordance with Sec. 300.370.

(b) For each fiscal year, the Secretary determines and reports to the SEA an amount that is 25 percent of the amount the State received under this section for fiscal year 1997, cumulatively adjusted by the Secretary for each succeeding fiscal year by the lesser of—

(1) The percentage increase, if any, from the preceding fiscal year in the State's allocation under section 611 of the Act; or

(2) The rate of inflation, as measured by the percentage increase, if any, from the preceding fiscal year in the Consumer Price Index For All Urban Consumers, published by the Bureau of Labor Statistics of the Department of Labor. (Authority: 20 U.S.C. 1411(f)(1)(A) and (B))

USE OF FUNDS

Sec. 300.620 Use of funds for State administration.

(a) For the purpose of administering Part B of the Act, including section 619 of the Act (including the coordination of activities under Part B of the Act with, and providing technical assistance to, other programs that provide services to children with disabilities)—

(1) Each State may use not more than twenty percent of the maximum amount it may retain under Sec. 300.602(a) for any fiscal year or $500,000 (adjusted by the cumulative rate of inflation since fiscal year 1998, as measured by the percentage increase, if any, in the Consumer Price Index For All Urban Consumers, published by the Bureau of Labor Statistics of the Department of Labor), whichever is greater; and

(2) Each outlying area may use up to five percent of the amount it receives under this section for any fiscal year or $35,000, whichever is greater.

(b) Funds described in paragraph (a) of this section may also be used for the administration of Part C of the Act, if the SEA is the lead agency for the State under that part. (Authority: 20 U.S.C. 1411(f)(2))

Sec. 300.621 Allowable costs.

(a) The SEA may use funds under Sec. 300.620 for—

(1) Administration of State activities under Part B of the Act and for planning at the State level, including planning, or assisting in the planning, of programs or projects for the education of children with disabilities;

(2) Approval, supervision, monitoring, and evaluation of the effectiveness of local programs and projects for the education of children with disabilities;

(3) Technical assistance to LEAs with respect to the requirements of Part B of the Act;

(4) Leadership services for the program supervision and management of special education activities for children with disabilities; and

(5) Other State leadership activities and consultative services.

(b) The SEA shall use the remainder of its funds under Sec. 300.620 in accordance with Sec. 300.370. (Authority: 20 U.S.C. 1411(f)(2))

Sec. 300.622 Subgrants to LEAs for capacity-building and improvement.

In any fiscal year in which the percentage increase in the State's allocation under 611 of the Act exceeds the rate of inflation (as measured by the percentage increase, if any, from the preceding fiscal year in the Consumer Price Index For All Urban Consumers, published by the Bureau of Labor Statistics of the Department of Labor), each State shall reserve, from its allocation under 611 of the Act, the amount described in Sec. 300.623 to make subgrants to LEAs, unless that amount is less than $100,000, to assist them in providing direct services and in making systemic change to improve results for children with disabilities through one or more of the following:

(a) Direct services, including alternative programming for children who have been expelled from school, and services for children in correctional facilities, children enrolled in State-operated or State- supported schools, and children in charter schools.

(b) Addressing needs or carrying out improvement strategies identified in the State's Improvement Plan under subpart 1 of Part D of the Act.

(c) Adopting promising practices, materials, and technology, based on knowledge derived from education research and other sources.

(d) Establishing, expanding, or implementing interagency agreements and arrangements between LEAs and other agencies or organizations concerning the provision of services to children with disabilities and their families.

(e) Increasing cooperative problem-solving between parents and school personnel and promoting the use of alternative dispute resolution. (Authority: 20 U.S.C. 1411(f)(4)(A))

Sec. 300.623 Amount required for subgrants to LEAs.

For each fiscal year, the amount referred to in Sec. 300.622 is—

(a) The maximum amount the State was allowed to retain under Sec. 300.602(a) for the prior fiscal year, or, for fiscal year 1998, 25 percent of the State's allocation for fiscal year 1997 under section 611; multiplied by

(b) The difference between the percentage increase in the State's allocation under this section and the rate of inflation, as measured by the percentage increase, if any, from the preceding fiscal year in the Consumer Price Index For All Urban Consumers, published by the Bureau of Labor Statistics of the Department of Labor. (Authority: 20 U.S.C. 1411(f)(4)(B))

Sec. 300.624 State discretion in awarding subgrants.

The State may establish priorities in awarding subgrants under Sec. 300.622 to LEAs competitively or on a targeted basis. (Authority: 20 U.S.C. 1411(f)(4)(A))

STATE ADVISORY PANEL

Sec. 300.650 Establishment of advisory panels.

(a) Each State shall establish and maintain, in accordance with Secs. 300.650-300.653, a State advisory panel on the education of children with disabilities.

(b) The advisory panel must be appointed by the Governor or any other official authorized under State law to make those appointments.

(c) If a State has an existing advisory panel that can perform the functions in Sec. 300.652, the State may modify the existing panel so that it fulfills all of the requirements of Secs. 300.650-300.653, instead of establishing a new advisory panel. (Authority: 20 U.S.C. 1412(a)(21)(A))

Sec. 300.651 Membership.

(a) **General**. The membership of the State advisory panel must consist of members appointed by the Governor, or any other official authorized under State law to make these appointments, that is representative of the State population and that is composed of individuals involved in, or concerned with the education of children with disabilities, including—

(1) Parents of children with disabilities;

(2) Individuals with disabilities;

(3) Teachers;

(4) Representatives of institutions of higher education that prepare special education and related services personnel;

(5) State and local education officials;

(6) Administrators of programs for children with disabilities;

(7) Representatives of other State agencies involved in the financing or delivery of related services to children with disabilities;

(8) Representatives of private schools and public charter schools;

(9) At least one representative of a vocational, community, or business organization concerned with the provision of transition services to children with disabilities; and

(10) Representatives from the State juvenile and adult corrections agencies.

(b) **Special rule**. A majority of the members of the panel must be individuals with disabilities or parents of children with disabilities. (Authority: 20 U.S.C. 1412(a)(21)(B) and (C))

Sec. 300.652 Advisory panel functions.

(a) **General**. The State advisory panel shall—

(1) Advise the SEA of unmet needs within the State in the education of children with disabilities;

(2) Comment publicly on any rules or regulations proposed by the State regarding the education of children with disabilities;

(3) Advise the SEA in developing evaluations and reporting on data to the Secretary under section 618 of the Act;

(4) Advise the SEA in developing corrective action plans to address findings identified in Federal monitoring reports under Part B of the Act; and

(5) Advise the SEA in developing and implementing policies relating to the coordination of services for children with disabilities.

(b) **Advising on eligible students with disabilities in adult prisons**. The advisory panel also shall advise on the education of eligible students with disabilities who have been convicted as adults and incarcerated in adult prisons, even if, consistent with Sec. 300.600(d), a State assigns general supervision responsibility for those students to a public agency other than an SEA. (Authority: 20 U.S.C. 1412(a)(21)(D))

Sec. 300.653 Advisory panel procedures.

(a) The advisory panel shall meet as often as necessary to conduct its business.

(b) By July 1 of each year, the advisory panel shall submit an annual report of panel activities and suggestions to the SEA. This report must be made available to the public in a manner consistent with other public reporting requirements of Part B of the Act.

(c) Official minutes must be kept on all panel meetings and must be made available to the public on request.

(d) All advisory panel meetings and agenda items must be announced enough in advance of the meeting to afford interested parties a reasonable opportunity to attend. Meetings must be open to the public.

(e) Interpreters and other necessary services must be provided at panel meetings for panel members or participants. The State may pay for these services from funds under Sec. 300.620.

(f) The advisory panel shall serve without compensation but the State must reimburse the panel for reasonable and necessary expenses for attending meetings and performing duties. The State may use funds under Sec. 300.620 for this purpose. (Authority: 20 U.S.C. 1412(a)(21))

STATE COMPLAINT PROCEDURES

Sec. 300.660 Adoption of State complaint procedures.

(a) **General**. Each SEA shall adopt written procedures for—

(1) Resolving any complaint, including a complaint filed by an organization or individual from another State, that meets the requirements of Sec. 300.662 by—

(i) Providing for the filing of a complaint with the SEA; and

(ii) At the SEA's discretion, providing for the filing of a complaint with a public agency and the right to have the SEA review the public agency's decision on the complaint; and

(2) Widely disseminating to parents and other interested individuals, including parent training and information centers, protection and advocacy agencies, independent living centers, and other appropriate entities, the State's procedures under Secs. 300.660- 300.662.

(b) **Remedies for denial of appropriate services**. In resolving a complaint in which it has found a failure to provide appropriate services, an SEA, pursuant to its general supervisory authority under Part B of the Act, must address:

(1) How to remediate the denial of those services, including, as appropriate, the awarding of monetary reimbursement or other corrective action appropriate to the needs of the child; and

(2) Appropriate future provision of services for all children with disabilities. (Authority: 20 U.S.C. 1221e-3)

Sec. 300.661 Minimum State complaint procedures.

(a) **Time limit; minimum procedures**. Each SEA shall include in its complaint procedures a time limit of 60 days after a complaint is filed under Sec. 300.660(a) to—

(1) Carry out an independent on-site investigation, if the SEA determines that an investigation is necessary;

(2) Give the complainant the opportunity to submit additional information, either orally or in writing, about the allegations in the complaint;

(3) Review all relevant information and make an independent determination as to whether the public agency is violating a requirement of Part B of the Act or of this part; and

(4) Issue a written decision to the complainant that addresses each allegation in the complaint and contains—

(i) Findings of fact and conclusions; and

(ii) The reasons for the SEA's final decision.

(b) **Time extension; final decision; implementation**. The SEA's procedures described in paragraph (a) of this section also must—

(1) Permit an extension of the time limit under paragraph (a) of this section only if exceptional circumstances exist with respect to a particular complaint; and

(2) Include procedures for effective implementation of the SEA's final decision, if needed, including—

(i) Technical assistance activities;

(ii) Negotiations; and

(iii) Corrective actions to achieve compliance.

(c) **Complaints filed under this section, and due process hearings under Secs. 300.507 and 300.520-300.528**.

(1) If a written complaint is received that is also the subject of a due process hearing under Sec. 300.507 or Secs. 300.520-300.528, or contains multiple issues, of which one or more are part of that hearing, the State must set aside any part of the complaint that is being addressed in the due process hearing, until the conclusion of the hearing. However, any issue in the complaint that is not a part of the due process action must be resolved using the time limit and procedures described in paragraphs (a) and (b) of this section.

(2) If an issue is raised in a complaint filed under this section that has previously been decided in a due process hearing involving the same parties—

(i) The hearing decision is binding; and

(ii) The SEA must inform the complainant to that effect.

(3) A complaint alleging a public agency's failure to implement a due process decision must be resolved by the SEA. (Authority: 20 U.S.C. 1221e-3)

Sec. 300.662 Filing a complaint.

(a) An organization or individual may file a signed written complaint under the procedures described in Secs. 300.660-300.661.

(b) The complaint must include—

(1) A statement that a public agency has violated a requirement of Part B of the Act or of this part; and

(2) The facts on which the statement is based.

(c) The complaint must allege a violation that occurred not more than one year prior to the date that the complaint is received in accordance with Sec. 300.660(a) unless a longer period is reasonable because the violation is continuing, or the complainant is requesting compensatory services for a violation that occurred not more than three years prior to the date the complaint is received under Sec. 300.660(a). (Authority: 20 U.S.C. 1221e-3)

Subpart G—Allocation of Funds; Reports

ALLOCATIONS

Sec. 300.700 Special definition of the term "State".

For the purposes of Secs. 300.701, and 300.703-300.714, the term State means each of the 50 States, the District of Columbia, and the Commonwealth of Puerto Rico. (Authority: 20 U.S.C. 1411(h)(2))

Sec. 300.701 Grants to States.

(a) **Purpose of grants.** The Secretary makes grants to States and the outlying areas and provides funds to the Secretary of the Interior, to assist them to provide special education and related services to children with disabilities in accordance with Part B of the Act.

(b) **Maximum amounts.** The maximum amount of the grant a State may receive under section 611 of the Act for any fiscal year is—

(1) The number of children with disabilities in the State who are receiving special education and related services—

(i) Aged 3 through 5 if the State is eligible for a grant under section 619 of the Act; and

(ii) Aged 6 through 21; multiplied by—

(2) Forty (40) percent of the average per-pupil expenditure in public elementary and secondary schools in the United States. (Authority: 20 U.S.C. 1411(a))

Sec. 300.702 Definition.

For the purposes of this section the term average per-pupil expenditure in public elementary and secondary schools in the United States means—

(a) Without regard to the source of funds—

(1) The aggregate current expenditures, during the second fiscal year preceding the fiscal year for which the determination is made (or, if satisfactory data for that year are not available, during the most recent preceding fiscal year for which satisfactory data are available) of all LEAs in the 50 States and the District of Columbia); plus

(2) Any direct expenditures by the State for the operation of those agencies; divided by

(b) The aggregate number of children in average daily attendance to whom those agencies provided free public education during that preceding year. (Authority: 20 U.S.C. 1411(h)(1))

Sec. 300.703 Allocations to States.

(a) **General.** After reserving funds for studies and evaluations under section 674(e) of the Act, and for payments to the outlying areas, the freely associated States, and the Secretary of the Interior under Secs. 300.715 and 300.717-300.719, the Secretary allocates the remaining amount among the States in accordance with paragraph (b) of this section and Secs. 300.706-300.709.

(b) **Interim formula.** Except as provided in Secs. 300.706-300.709, the Secretary allocates the amount described in paragraph (a) of this section among the States in accordance with section 611(a)(3), (4), (5) and (b)(1), (2) and (3) of the Act, as in effect prior to June 4, 1997, except that the determination of the number of children with disabilities receiving special education and related services under section 611(a)(3) of the Act (as then in effect) may be calculated as of December 1, or, at the State's discretion, the last Friday in October, of the fiscal year for which the funds were appropriated. (Authority: 20 U.S.C. 1411(d))

Secs. 300.704-300.705 [Reserved]

Sec. 300.706 Permanent formula.

(a) **Establishment of base year.** The Secretary allocates the amount described in Sec. 300.703(a) among the States in accordance with Secs. 300.706-300.709 for each fiscal year beginning with the first fiscal year for which the amount appropriated under 611(j) of the Act is more than $4,924,672,200.

(b) **Use of base year.**

(1) **Definition.** As used in this section, the term base year means the fiscal year preceding the first fiscal year in which this section applies.

(2) **Special rule for use of base year amount.** If a State received any funds under section 611 of the Act for the base year on the basis of children aged 3 through 5, but does not make FAPE available to all children with disabilities aged 3 through 5 in the State in any subsequent fiscal year, the Secretary computes the State's base year amount, solely for the purpose of calculating the State's allocation in that subsequent year under Secs. 300.707-300.709, by subtracting the amount allocated to the State for the base year on the basis of those children. (Authority: 20 U.S.C. 1411(e)(1) and (2))

Sec. 300.707 Increase in funds.

If the amount available for allocations to States under Sec. 300.706 is equal to or greater than the amount allocated to the States under section 611 of the Act for the preceding fiscal year, those allocations are calculated as follows:

(a) Except as provided in Sec. 300.708, the Secretary—

    (1) Allocates to each State the amount it received for the base year;

    (2) Allocates 85 percent of any remaining funds to States on the basis of their relative populations of children aged 3 through 21 who are of the same age as children with disabilities for whom the State ensures the availability of FAPE under Part B of the Act; and

    (3) Allocates 15 percent of those remaining funds to States on the basis of their relative populations of children described in paragraph (a)(2) of this section who are living in poverty.

(b) For the purpose of making grants under this section, the Secretary uses the most recent population data, including data on children living in poverty, that are available and satisfactory to the Secretary. (Authority: 20 U.S.C. 1411(e)(3))

Sec. 300.708 Limitation.

(a) Allocations under Sec. 300.707 are subject to the following:

    (1) No State's allocation may be less than its allocation for the preceding fiscal year.

    (2) No State's allocation may be less than the greatest of—

        (i) The sum of—

            (A) The amount it received for the base year; and

            (B) One-third of one percent of the amount by which the amount appropriated under section 611(j) of the Act exceeds the amount appropriated under section 611 of the Act for the base year; or

        (ii) The sum of—

        (A) The amount it received for the preceding fiscal year; and

            (B) That amount multiplied by the percentage by which the increase in the funds appropriated from the preceding fiscal year exceeds 1.5 percent; or

        (iii) The sum of—

        (A) The amount it received for the preceding fiscal year; and

            (B) That amount multiplied by 90 percent of the percentage increase in the amount appropriated from the preceding fiscal year.

(b) Notwithstanding paragraph (a)(2) of this section, no State's allocation under Sec. 300.707 may exceed the sum of—

    (1) The amount it received for the preceding fiscal year; and

    (2) That amount multiplied by the sum of 1.5 percent and the percentage increase in the amount appropriated.

(c) If the amount available for allocations to States under Sec. 300.703 and paragraphs (a) and (b) of this section is insufficient to pay those allocations in full those allocations are ratably reduced, subject to paragraph (a)(1) of this section. (Authority: 20 U.S.C. 1411(e)(3)(B) and (C))

Sec. 300.709 Decrease in funds.

If the amount available for allocations to States under Sec. 300.706 is less than the amount allocated to the States under section 611 of the Act for the preceding fiscal year, those allocations are calculated as follows:

(a) If the amount available for allocations is greater than the amount allocated to the States for the base year, each State is allocated the sum of—

    (1) The amount it received for the base year; and

    (2) An amount that bears the same relation to any remaining funds as the increase the State received for the preceding fiscal year over the base year bears to the total of those increases for all States.

(b)

    (1) If the amount available for allocations is equal to or less than the amount allocated to the States for the base year, each State is allocated the amount it received for the base year.

    (2) If the amount available is insufficient to make the allocations described in paragraph (b)(1) of this section, those allocations are ratably reduced. (Authority: 20 U.S.C. 1411(e)(4))

Sec. 300.710 Allocation for State in which by-pass is implemented for private school children with disabilities.

In determining the allocation under Secs. 300.700-300.709 of a State in which the Secretary will implement a by-pass for private school children with disabilities under Secs. 300.451-300.487, the Secretary includes in the State's child count—

(a) For the first year of a by-pass, the actual or estimated number of private school children with disabilities (as defined in Secs. 300.7(a) and 300.450) in the State, as of the preceding December 1; and

(b) For succeeding years of a by-pass, the number of private school children with disabilities who received special education and related services under the by-pass in the preceding year. (Authority: 20 U.S.C. 1412(f)(2))

Sec. 300.711 Subgrants to LEAs.

Each State that receives a grant under section 611 of the Act for any fiscal year shall distribute in accordance with Sec. 300.712 any funds it does not retain under Sec. 300.602 and is not required to distribute under Secs. 300.622 and 300.623 to LEAs in the State that have established their eligibility under section 613 of the Act, and to State agencies that received funds under section 614A(a) of the Act for fiscal year 1997, as then in effect, and have established their eligibility under section 613 of the Act, for use in accordance with Part B of the Act. (Authority: 20 U.S.C. 1411(g)(1))

Sec. 300.712 Allocations to LEAs.

(a) **Interim procedure**. For each fiscal year for which funds are allocated to States under Sec. 300.703(b) each State shall allocate funds under Sec. 300.711 in accordance with section 611(d) of the Act, as in effect prior to June 4, 1997.

(b) **Permanent procedure**. For each fiscal year for which funds are allocated to States under Secs. 300.706-300.709, each State shall allocate funds under Sec. 300.711 as follows:

(1) **Base payments**. The State first shall award each agency described in Sec. 300.711 the amount that agency would have received under this section for the base year, as defined in Sec. 300.706(b)(1), if the State had distributed 75 percent of its grant for that year under section Sec. 300.703(b).

(2) **Base payment adjustments**. For any fiscal year after the base year fiscal year—

(i) If a new LEA is created, the State shall divide the base allocation determined under paragraph (b)(1) of this section for the LEAs that would have been responsible for serving children with disabilities now being served by the new LEA, among the new LEA and affected LEAs based on the relative numbers of children with disabilities ages 3 through 21, or ages 6 through 21 if a State has had its payment reduced under Sec. 300.706(b)(2), currently provided special education by each of the LEAs;

(ii) If one or more LEAs are combined into a single new LEA, the State shall combine the base allocations of the merged LEAs; and

(iii) If, for two or more LEAs, geographic boundaries or administrative responsibility for providing services to children with disabilities ages 3 through 21 change, the base allocations of affected LEAs shall be redistributed among affected LEAs based on the relative numbers of children with disabilities ages 3 through 21, or ages 6 through 21 if a State has had its payment reduced under Sec. 300.706(b)(2), currently provided special education by each affected LEA.

(3) **Allocation of remaining funds**. The State then shall—

(i) Allocate 85 percent of any remaining funds to those agencies on the basis of the relative numbers of children enrolled in public and private elementary and secondary schools within each agency's jurisdiction; and

(ii) Allocate 15 percent of those remaining funds to those agencies in accordance with their relative numbers of children living in poverty, as determined by the SEA.

(iii) For the purposes of making grants under this section, States must apply on a uniform basis across all LEAs the best data that are available to them on the numbers of children enrolled in public and private elementary and secondary schools and the numbers of children living in poverty. (Authority: 20 U.S.C. 1411(g)(2))

Sec. 300.713 Former Chapter 1 State agencies.

(a) To the extent necessary, the State—

(1) Shall use funds that are available under Sec. 300.602(a) to ensure that each State agency that received fiscal year 1994 funds under subpart 2 of Part D of chapter 1 of title I of the Elementary and Secondary Education Act of 1965 (as in effect in fiscal year 1994) receives, from the combination of funds under Sec. 300.602(a) and funds provided under Sec. 300.711, an amount no less than—

(i) The number of children with disabilities, aged 6 through 21, to whom the agency was providing special education and related services on December 1, or, at the State's discretion, the last Friday in October, of the fiscal year for which the funds were appropriated, subject to the limitation in paragraph (b) of this section; multiplied by

(ii) The per-child amount provided under that subpart for fiscal year 1994; and

(2) May use funds under Sec. 300.602(a) to ensure that each LEA that received fiscal year 1994 funds under that subpart for children who had transferred from a State-operated or State-supported school or program assisted under that subpart receives, from the combination of funds available under Sec. 300.602(a) and funds provided under Sec. 300.711, an amount for each child, aged 3 through 21 to whom the agency was providing special education and related services on December 1, or, at the State's discretion, the last Friday in October, of the fiscal year for which the funds were appropriated, equal to the per-child amount the agency received under that subpart for fiscal year 1994.

(b) The number of children counted under paragraph (a)(1)(i) of this section may not exceed the number of children aged 3 through 21 for whom the agency received fiscal year 1994 funds under subpart 2 of Part D of chapter 1 of title I of the Elementary and Secondary Education Act of 1965 (as in effect in fiscal year 1994). (Authority: 20 U.S.C. 1411(g)(3))

Sec. 300.714 Reallocation of LEA funds.

If an SEA determines that an LEA is adequately providing FAPE to all children with disabilities residing in the area served by that agency with State and local funds, the SEA may reallocate any portion of the funds under Part B of the Act that are not needed by that local agency to provide FAPE to other LEAs in the State that are not adequately providing special education and related services to all children with disabilities residing in the areas they serve. (Authority: 20 U.S.C. 1411(g)(4))

Sec. 300.715 Payments to the Secretary of the Interior for the education of Indian children.

(a) Reserved amounts for Secretary of Interior. From the amount appropriated for any fiscal year under 611(j) of the Act, the Secretary reserves 1.226 percent to provide assistance to the Secretary of the Interior in accordance with this section and Sec. 300.716.

(b) Provision of amounts for assistance. The Secretary provides amounts to the Secretary of the Interior to meet the need for assistance for the education of children with disabilities on reservations aged 5 to 21, inclusive, enrolled in elementary and secondary schools for Indian children operated or funded by the Secretary of the Interior. The amount of the payment for any fiscal year is equal to 80 percent of the amount allotted under paragraph (a) of this section for that fiscal year.

(c) Calculation of number of children. In the case of Indian students aged 3 to 5, inclusive, who are enrolled in programs affiliated with the Bureau of Indian Affairs (BIA) schools and that are required by the States in which these schools are located to attain or maintain State accreditation, and which schools have this accreditation prior to the date of enactment of the Individuals with Disabilities Education Act Amendments of 1991, the school may count those children for the purpose of distribution of the funds provided under this section to the Secretary of the Interior.

(d) Responsibility for meeting the requirements of Part B. The Secretary of the Interior shall meet all of the requirements of Part B of the Act for the children described in paragraphs (b) and (c) of this section, in accordance with Sec. 300.260. (Authority: 20 U.S.C. 1411(c); 1411(i)(1)(A) and (B))

Sec. 300.716 Payments for education and services for Indian children with disabilities aged 3 through 5.

(a) General. With funds appropriated under 611(j) of the Act, the Secretary makes payments to the Secretary of the Interior to be distributed to tribes or tribal organizations (as defined under section 4 of the Indian Self-Determination and Education Assistance Act) or consortia of those tribes or tribal organizations to provide for the coordination of assistance for special education and related services for children with disabilities aged 3 through 5 on reservations served by elementary and secondary schools for Indian children operated or funded by the Department of the Interior. The amount of the payments under paragraph (b) of this section for any fiscal year is equal to 20 percent of the amount allotted under Sec. 300.715(a).

(b) Distribution of funds. The Secretary of the Interior shall distribute the total amount of the payment under paragraph (a) of this section by allocating to each tribe or tribal organization an amount based on the number of children with disabilities ages 3 through 5 residing on reservations as reported annually, divided by the total of those children served by all tribes or tribal organizations.

(c) Submission of information. To receive a payment under this section, the tribe or tribal organization shall submit the figures to the Secretary of the Interior as required to determine the amounts to be allocated under paragraph (b) of this section. This information must be compiled and submitted to the Secretary.

(d) Use of funds.

(1) The funds received by a tribe or tribal organization must be used to assist in child find, screening, and other procedures for the early identification of children aged 3 through 5, parent training, and the provision of direct services. These activities may be carried out directly or through contracts or cooperative agreements with the BIA, LEAs, and other public or private nonprofit organizations. The tribe or tribal organization is encouraged to involve Indian parents in the development and implementation of these activities.

(2) The entities shall, as appropriate, make referrals to local, State, or Federal entities for the provision of services or further diagnosis.

(e) Biennial report. To be eligible to receive a grant pursuant to paragraph (a) of this section, the tribe or tribal organization shall provide to the Secretary of the Interior a biennial report of activities undertaken under this paragraph, including the number of contracts and cooperative agreements entered into, the number of children contacted and receiving services for each year, and the estimated number of children needing services during the two years following the one in which the report is made. The Secretary of the Interior shall include a summary of this information on a biennial basis in the report to the Secretary required under section 611(i) of the Act. The Secretary may require any additional information from the Secretary of the Interior.

(f) Prohibitions. None of the funds allocated under this section may be used by the Secretary of the Interior for administrative purposes, including child count and the provision of technical assistance. (Authority: 20 U.S.C. 1411(i)(3))

Sec. 300.717 Outlying areas and freely associated States.

From the amount appropriated for any fiscal year under section 611(j) of the Act, the Secretary reserves not more than one percent, which must be used—

(a) To provide assistance to the outlying areas in accordance with their respective populations of individuals aged 3 through 21; and

(b) For fiscal years 1998 through 2001, to carry out the competition described in Sec. 300.719, except that the amount reserved to carry out that competition may not exceed the amount reserved for fiscal year 1996 for the competition under Part B of the Act described under the heading "SPECIAL EDUCATION" in Public Law 104-134. (Authority: 20 U.S.C. 1411(b)(1))

Sec. 300.718 Outlying area—definition.

As used in this part, the term outlying area means the United States Virgin Islands, Guam, American Samoa, and the Commonwealth of the Northern Mariana Islands. (Authority: 20 U.S.C. 1402(18))

Sec. 300.719 Limitation for freely associated States.

(a) **Competitive grants.** The Secretary uses funds described in Sec. 300.717(b) to award grants, on a competitive basis, to Guam, American Samoa, the Commonwealth of the Northern Mariana Islands, and the freely associated States to carry out the purposes of this part.

(b) **Award basis.** The Secretary awards grants under paragraph (a) of this section on a competitive basis, pursuant to the recommendations of the Pacific Region Educational Laboratory in Honolulu, Hawaii. Those recommendations must be made by experts in the field of special education and related services.

(c) **Assistance requirements.** Any freely associated State that wishes to receive funds under Part B of the Act shall include, in its application for assistance—

(1) Information demonstrating that it will meet all conditions that apply to States under Part B of the Act;

(2) An assurance that, notwithstanding any other provision of Part B of the Act, it will use those funds only for the direct provision of special education and related services to children with disabilities and to enhance its capacity to make FAPE available to all children with disabilities;

(3) The identity of the source and amount of funds, in addition to funds under Part B of the Act, that it will make available to ensure that FAPE is available to all children with disabilities within its jurisdiction; and

(4) Such other information and assurances as the Secretary may require.

(d) **Termination of eligibility.** Notwithstanding any other provision of law, the freely associated States may not receive any funds under Part B of the Act for any program year that begins after September 30, 2001.

(e) **Administrative costs.** The Secretary may provide not more than five percent of the amount reserved for grants under this section to pay the administrative costs of the Pacific Region Educational Laboratory under paragraph (b) of this section.

(f) **Eligibility for award.** An outlying area is not eligible for a competitive award under Sec. 300.719 unless it receives assistance under Sec. 300.717(a). (Authority: 20 U.S.C. 1411(b)(2) and (3))

Sec. 300.720 Special rule.

The provisions of Public Law 95-134, permitting the consolidation of grants by the outlying areas, do not apply to funds provided to those areas or to the freely associated States under Part B of the Act. (Authority: 20 U.S.C. 1411(b)(4))

Sec. 300.721 [Reserved]

Sec. 300.722 Definition.

As used in this part, the term freely associated States means the Republic of the Marshall Islands, the Federated States of Micronesia, and the Republic of Palau. (Authority: 20 U.S.C. 1411(b)(6))

REPORTS

Sec. 300.750 Annual report of children served—report requirement.

(a) The SEA shall report to the Secretary no later than February 1 of each year the number of children with disabilities aged 3 through 21 residing in the State who are receiving special education and related services.

(b) The SEA shall submit the report on forms provided by the Secretary. (Authority: 20 U.S.C. 1411(d)(2); 1418(a))

Sec. 300.751 Annual report of children served—information required in the report.

(a) For any year the SEA shall include in its report a table that shows the number of children with disabilities receiving special education and related services on December 1, or at the State's discretion on the last Friday in October, of that school year—

(1) Aged 3 through 5;

(2) Aged 6 through 17; and

(3) Aged 18 through 21.

(b) For the purpose of this part, a child's age is the child's actual age on the date of the child count: December 1, or, at the State's discretion, the last Friday in October.

(c) Reports must also include the number of those children with disabilities aged 3 through 21 for each year of age (3, 4, 5, etc.) within each disability category, as defined in the definition of "children with disabilities" in Sec. 300.7; and

(d) The Secretary may permit the collection of the data in paragraph (c) of this section through sampling.

(e) The SEA may not report a child under paragraph (c) of this section under more than one disability category.

(f) If a child with a disability has more than one disability, the SEA shall report that child under paragraph (c) of this section in accordance with the following procedure:

(1) If a child has only two disabilities and those disabilities are deafness and blindness, and the child is not reported as having a developmental delay, that child must be reported under the category "deaf-blindness".

(2) A child who has more than one disability and is not reported as having deaf-blindness or as having a developmental delay must be reported under the category "multiple disabilities". (Authority: 20 U.S.C. 1411(d)(2); 1418(a) and (b))

Sec. 300.752 Annual report of children served—certification.

The SEA shall include in its report a certification signed by an authorized official of the agency that the information provided under Sec. 300.751(a) is an accurate and unduplicated count of children with disabilities receiving special education and related services on the dates in question. (Authority: 20 U.S.C. 1411(d)(2); 1417(b))

Sec. 300.753 Annual report of children served—criteria for counting children.

(a) The SEA may include in its report children with disabilities who are enrolled in a school or program that is operated or supported by a public agency, and that—

(1) Provides them with both special education and related services that meet State standards;

(2) Provides them only with special education, if a related service is not required, that meets State standards; or

(3) In the case of children with disabilities enrolled by their parents in private schools, provides them with special education or related services under Secs. 300.452-300.462 that meet State standards.

(b) The SEA may not include children with disabilities in its report who are receiving special education funded solely by the Federal Government, including children served by the Department of Interior, the Department of Defense, or the Department of Education. However, the State may count children covered under Sec. 300.184(c)(2). (Authority: 20 U.S.C. 1411(d)(2); 1417(b))

Sec. 300.754 Annual report of children served—other responsibilities of the SEA.

In addition to meeting the other requirements of Secs. 300.750- 300.753, the SEA shall—

(a) Establish procedures to be used by LEAs and other educational institutions in counting the number of children with disabilities receiving special education and related services;

(b) Set dates by which those agencies and institutions must report to the SEA to ensure that the State complies with Sec. 300.750(a);

(c) Obtain certification from each agency and institution that an unduplicated and accurate count has been made;

(d) Aggregate the data from the count obtained from each agency and institution, and prepare the reports required under Secs. 300.750- 300.753; and

(e) Ensure that documentation is maintained that enables the State and the Secretary to audit the accuracy of the count. (Authority: 20 U.S.C. 1411(d)(2); 1417(b))

Sec. 300.755 Disproportionality.

(a) General. Each State that receives assistance under Part B of the Act, and the Secretary of the Interior, shall provide for the collection and examination of data to determine if significant disproportionality based on race is occurring in the State or in the schools operated by the Secretary of the Interior with respect to—

(1) The identification of children as children with disabilities, including the identification of children as children with disabilities in accordance with a particular impairment described in section 602(3) of the Act; and

(2) The placement in particular educational settings of these children.

(b) Review and revision of policies, practices, and procedures. In the case of a determination of significant disproportionality with respect to the identification of children as children with disabilities, or the placement in particular educational settings of these children, in accordance with paragraph (a) of this section, the State or the Secretary of the Interior shall provide for the review and, if appropriate revision of the policies, procedures, and practices used in the identification or placement to ensure that the policies, procedures, and practices comply with the requirements of Part B of the Act. (Authority: 20 U.S.C. 1418(c))

Sec. 300.756 Acquisition of equipment; construction or alteration of facilities.

(a) General. If the Secretary determines that a program authorized under Part B of the Act would be improved by permitting program funds to be used to acquire appropriate equipment, or to construct new facilities or alter existing facilities, the Secretary may allow the use of those funds for those purposes.

(b) Compliance with certain regulations. Any construction of new facilities or alteration of existing facilities under paragraph (a) of this section must comply with the requirements of—

(1) Appendix A of part 36 of title 28, Code of Federal Regulations (commonly known as the "Americans with Disabilities Accessibility Guidelines for Buildings and Facilities"); or

(2) Appendix A of part 101-19.6 of title 41, Code of Federal Regulations (commonly known as the "Uniform Federal Accessibility Standards"). (Authority: 20 U.S.C. 1405)

APPENDIX A TO PART 300—NOTICE OF INTERPRETATION

AUTHORITY: PART B OF THE INDIVIDUALS WITH DISABILITIES EDUCATION ACT (20 U.S.C. 1401, ET SEQ.),
UNLESS OTHERWISE NOTED.

INDIVIDUALIZED EDUCATION PROGRAMS (IEPS) AND OTHER SELECTED IMPLEMENTATION ISSUES

INTRODUCTION

The IEP requirements under Part B off the IDEA emphasize the importance of three core concepts:

(1) the **involvement and progress of each child with a disability in the general curriculum** including addressing the unique needs that arise out of the child's disability;

(2) the **involvement of parents and students**, together with regular and special education personnel, **in making individual decisions** to support each student's (child's) educational success, and

(3) the **preparation** of students with disabilities **for employment and other post-school activities**.

The first three sections of this Appendix (I-III) provide guidance regarding the IEP requirements as they relate to the three core concepts described above. Section IV addresses other questions regarding the development and content of IEPs, including questions about the timelines and responsibility for developing and implementing IEPs, participation in IEP meetings, and IEP content. Section IV also addresses questions on other selected requirements under IDEA.

I. INVOLVEMENT AND PROGRESS OF EACH CHILD WITH A DISABILITY IN THE GENERAL CURRICULUM

In enacting the IDEA Amendments of 1997, the Congress found that research, demonstration, and practice over the past 20 years in special education and related disciplines have demonstrated that an effective educational system now and in the future must maintain high academic standards and clear performance goals for children with disabilities, consistent with the standards and expectations for all students in the educational system, and provide for appropriate and effective strategies and methods to ensure that students who are children with disabilities have maximum opportunities to achieve those standards and goals. [Section 651(a)(6)(A) of the Act.]

Accordingly, the evaluation and IEP provisions of Part B place great emphasis on the involvement and progress of children with disabilities in the general curriculum. (The term "general curriculum," as used in these regulations, including this Appendix, refers to the curriculum that is used with nondisabled children.)

While the Act and regulations recognize that IEP teams must make individualized decisions about the special education and related services, and supplementary aids and services provided to each child with a disability, they are driven by IDEA's strong preference that, to the maximum extent appropriate, children with disabilities be educated in regular classes with their nondisabled peers with appropriate supplementary aids and services.

In many cases, children with disabilities will need appropriate supports in order to successfully progress in the general curriculum, participate in State and district-wide assessment programs, achieve the measurable goals in their IEPs, and be educated together with their nondisabled peers. Accordingly, the Act requires the IEP team to determine, and the public agency to provide, the accommodations, modifications, supports, and supplementary aids and services, needed by each child with a disability to successfully be involved in and progress in the general curriculum achieve the goals of the IEP, and successfully demonstrate his or her competencies in State and district-wide assessments.

1. What are the major Part B IEP requirements that govern the involvement and progress of children with disabilities in the general curriculum?

PRESENT LEVELS OF EDUCATIONAL PERFORMANCE

Section 300.347(a)(1) requires that the IEP for each child with a disability include "* * * a statement of the child's present levels of educational performance, including—(i) how the child's disability affects the child's involvement and progress in the general curriculum; or (ii) for preschool children, as appropriate, how the child's disability affects the child's participation in appropriate activities * * *" ("Appropriate activities" in this context refers to age-relevant developmental abilities or milestones that typically developing children of the same age would be performing or would have achieved.)

The IEP team's determination of how each child's disability affects the child's involvement and progress in the general curriculum is a primary consideration in the development of the child's IEP. In assessing children with disabilities, school districts may use a variety of assessment techniques to determine the extent to which these children can be involved and progress in the general curriculum, such as criterion-referenced tests, standard achievement tests, diagnostic tests, other tests, or any combination of the above. The purpose of using these assessments is to determine the child's present levels of educational performance and areas of need arising from the child's disability so that approaches for ensuring the child's involvement and progress in the general curriculum and any needed adaptations or modifications to that curriculum can be identified.

MEASURABLE ANNUAL GOALS, INCLUDING BENCHMARKS OR SHORT-TERM OBJECTIVES

Measurable annual goals, including benchmarks or short-term objectives, are critical to the strategic planning process used to develop and implement the IEP for each child with a disability. Once the IEP team has developed measurable annual goals for a child, the team

(1) can develop strategies that will be most effective in realizing those goals and

(2) must develop either measurable, intermediate steps (short-term objectives) or major milestones (benchmarks) that will enable parents, students, and educators to monitor progress during the year, and, if appropriate, to revise the IEP consistent with the student's instructional needs.

The strong emphasis in Part B on linking the educational program of children with disabilities to the general curriculum is reflected in Sec. 300.347(a)(2), which requires that the IEP include:

a statement of measurable annual goals, including benchmarks or short-term objectives, related to—(i) meeting the child's needs that result from the child's disability to enable the child to be involved in and progress in the general curriculum; and (ii) meeting each of the child's other educational needs that result from the child's disability.

As noted above, each annual goal must include either short-term objectives or benchmarks. The purpose of both is to enable a child's teacher(s), parents, and others involved in developing and implementing the child's IEP, to gauge, at intermediate times during the year, how well the child is progressing toward achievement of the annual goal. IEP teams may continue to develop short-term instructional objectives that generally break the skills described in the annual goal down into discrete components. The revised statute and regulations also provide that, as an alternative, IEP teams may develop benchmarks, which can be thought of as describing the amount of progress the child is expected to make within specified segments of the year. Generally, benchmarks establish expected performance levels that allow for regular checks of progress that coincide with the reporting periods for informing parents of their child's progress toward achieving the annual goals. An IEP team may use either short term objectives or benchmarks or a combination of the two depending on the nature of the annual goals and the needs of the child.

SPECIAL EDUCATION AND RELATED SERVICES AND SUPPLEMENTARY AIDS AND SERVICES

The requirements regarding services provided to address a child's present levels of educational performance and to make progress toward the identified goals reinforce the emphasis on progress in the general curriculum, as well as maximizing the extent to which children with disabilities are educated with nondisabled children. Section 300.347(a)(3) requires that the IEP include:

a statement of the special education and related services and supplementary aids and services to be provided to the child, or on behalf of the child, and a statement of the program modifications or supports for school personnel that will be provided for the child— (i) to advance appropriately toward attaining the annual goals; (ii) to be involved and progress in the general curriculum * * * and to participate in extracurricular and other nonacademic activities; and (iii) to be educated and participate with other children with disabilities and nondisabled children in [extracurricular and other nonacademic activities] * * * [Italics added.]

EXTENT TO WHICH CHILD WILL PARTICIPATE WITH NONDISABLED CHILDREN

Section 300.347(a)(4) requires that each child's IEP include "An explanation of the extent, if any, to which the child will not participate with nondisabled children in the regular class and in [extracurricular and other nonacademic] activities * * *" This is consistent with the least restrictive environment (LRE) provisions at Secs. 300.550-300.553, which include requirements that:

(1) each child with a disability be educated with nondisabled children to the maximum extent appropriate (Sec. 300.550(b)(1));

(2) each child with a disability be removed from the regular educational environment only when the nature or severity of the child's disability is such that education in regular classes with the use of supplementary aids and services cannot be achieved satisfactorily (Sec. 300.550(b)(1)); and

(3) to the maximum extent appropriate to the child's needs, each child with a disability participates with nondisabled children in nonacademic and extracurricular services and activities (Sec. 300.553).

All services and educational placements under Part B must be individually determined in light of each child's unique abilities and needs, to reasonably promote the child's educational success. Placing children with disabilities in this manner should enable each disabled child to meet high expectations in the future.

Although Part B requires that a child with a disability not be removed from the regular educational environment if the child's education can be achieved satisfactorily in regular classes with the use of supplementary aids and services, Part B's LRE principle is intended to ensure that a child with a disability is served in a setting where the child can be educated successfully. Even though IDEA does not mandate regular class placement for every disabled student, IDEA presumes that the first placement option considered for each disabled student by the student's placement team, which must include the parent, is the school the child would attend if not disabled, with appropriate supplementary aids and services to facilitate such placement.

Thus, before a disabled child can be placed outside of the regular educational environment, the full range of supplementary aids and services that if provided would facilitate the student's placement in the regular classroom setting must be considered. Following that consideration, if a determination is made that particular disabled student cannot be educated satisfactorily in the regular educational environment, even with the provision of appropriate supplementary aids and services, that student then could be placed in a setting other than the regular classroom.

Later, if it becomes apparent that the child's IEP can be carried out in a less restrictive setting, with the provision of appropriate supplementary aids and services, if needed, Part B would require that the child's placement be changed from the more restrictive setting to a less restrictive setting. In all cases, placement decisions must be individually determined on the basis of each child's abilities and needs, and not solely on factors such as category of disability, significance of disability, availability of special education and related services, configuration of the service delivery system, availability of space, or administrative convenience. Rather, each student's IEP forms the basis for the placement decision.

Further, a student need not fail in the regular classroom before another placement can be considered. Conversely, IDEA does not require that a student demonstrate achievement of a specific performance level as a prerequisite for placement into a regular classroom.

PARTICIPATION IN STATE OR DISTRICT-WIDE ASSESSMENTS OF STUDENT ACHIEVEMENT

Consistent with Sec. 300.138(a), which sets forth a presumption that children with disabilities will be included in general State and district-wide assessment programs, and provided with appropriate accommodations if necessary, Sec. 300.347(a)(5) requires that the IEP for each student with a disability include: "(i) a statement of any individual modifications in the administration of State or district-wide assessments of student achievement that are needed in order for the child to participate in the assessment; and (ii) if the IEP team determines that the child will not participate in a particular State or district-wide assessment of student achievement (or part of an assessment of student achievement), a statement of— (A) Why that assessment is not appropriate for the child; and (B) How the child will be assessed."

REGULAR EDUCATION TEACHER PARTICIPATION IN THE DEVELOPMENT, REVIEW, AND REVISION OF IEPS

Very often, regular education teachers play a central role in the education of children with disabilities (H. Rep. No. 105-95, p. 103 (1997); S. Rep. No. 105-17, p. 23 (1997)) and have important expertise regarding the general curriculum and the general education environment. Further, with the emphasis on involvement and progress in the general curriculum added by the IDEA Amendments of 1997, regular education teachers have an increasingly critical role (together with special education and related services personnel) in implementing the program of FAPE for most children with disabilities, as described in their IEPs.

Accordingly, the IDEA Amendments of 1997 added a requirement that each child's IEP team must include at least one regular education teacher of the child, if the child is, or may be, participating in the regular education environment (see Sec. 300.344(a)(2)). (See also Secs. 300.346(d) on the role of a regular education teacher in the development, review and revision of IEPs.)

2. Must a child's IEP address his or her involvement in the general curriculum, regardless of the nature and severity of the child's disability and the setting in which the child is educated?

Yes. The IEP for each child with a disability (including children who are educated in separate classrooms or schools) must address how the child will be involved and progress in the general curriculum. However, the Part B regulations recognize that some children have other educational needs resulting from their disability that also must be met, even though those needs are not directly linked to participation in the general curriculum. Accordingly, Sec. 300.347(a)(1)(2) requires that each child's IEP include:

A statement of measurable annual goals, including benchmarks or short-term objectives related to—

(i) Meeting the child's needs that result from the child's disability to enable the child to be involved in and progress in the general curriculum; and

(ii) meeting each of the child's other educational needs that result from the child's disability. [Italics added.]

Thus, the IEP team for each child with a disability must make an individualized determination regarding

(1) how the child will be involved and progress in the general curriculum and what needs that result from the child's disability must be met to facilitate that participation;

(2) whether the child has any other educational needs resulting from his or her disability that also must be met; and

(3) what special education and other services and supports must be described in the child's IEP to address both sets of needs (consistent with Sec. 300.347(a)).

For example, if the IEP team determines that in order for a child who is deaf to participate in the general curriculum he or she needs sign language and materials which reflect his or her language development, those needs (relating to the child's participation in the general curriculum) must be addressed in the child's IEP. In addition, if the team determines that the child also needs to expand his or her vocabulary in sign language that service must also be addressed in the applicable components of the child's IEP. The IEP team may also wish to consider whether there is a need for members of the child's family to receive training in sign language in order for the child to receive FAPE.

3. What must public agencies do to meet the requirements at Secs. 300.344(a)(2) and 300.346(d) regarding the participation of a "regular education teacher" in the development, review, and revision of IEPs, for children aged 3 through 5 who are receiving preschool special education services?

If a public agency provides "regular education" preschool services to non-disabled children, then the requirements of Secs. 300.344(a)(2) and 300.346(d) apply as they do in the case of older children with disabilities. If a public agency makes kindergarten available to nondisabled children, then a regular education kindergarten teacher could appropriately be the regular education teacher who would be a member of the IEP team, and, as appropriate, participate in IEP meetings, for a kindergarten-aged child who is, or may be, participating in the regular education environment.

If a public agency does not provide regular preschool education services to nondisabled children, the agency could designate an individual who, under State standards, is qualified to serve nondisabled children of the same age.

4. Must the measurable annual goals in a child's IEP address all areas of the general curriculum, or only those areas in which the child's involvement and progress are affected by the child's disability?

Section 300.347(a)(2) requires that each child's IEP include "A statement of measurable annual goals, including benchmarks or short-term objectives, related to—(i) meeting the child's needs that result from the child's disability to enable the child to be involved in and progress in the general curriculum * * *; and (ii) meeting each of the child's other educational needs that result from the child's disability. . . ." (Italics added).

Thus, a public agency is not required to include in an IEP annual goals that relate to areas of the general curriculum in which the child's disability does not affect the child's ability to be involved in and progress in the general curriculum. If a child with a disability needs only modifications or accommodations in order to progress in an area of the general curriculum, the IEP does not need to include a goal for that area; however, the IEP would need to specify those modifications or accommodations.

Public agencies often require all children, including children with disabilities, to demonstrate mastery in a given area of the general curriculum before allowing them to progress to the next level or grade in that area. Thus, in order to ensure that each child with a disability can effectively demonstrate competencies in an applicable area of the general curriculum, it is important for the IEP team to consider the accommodations and modifications that the child needs to assist him or her in demonstrating progress in that area.

II. INVOLVEMENT OF PARENTS AND STUDENTS

The Congressional Committee Reports on the IDEA Amendments of 1997 express the view that the Amendments provide an opportunity for strengthening the role of parents, and emphasize that one of the purposes of the Amendments is to expand opportunities for parents and key public agency staff (e.g., special education, related services, regular education, and early intervention service providers, and other personnel) to work in new partnerships at both the State and local levels (H. Rep. 105-95, p. 82 (1997); S. Rep. No. 105-17, p. 4 and 5 (1997)). Accordingly, the IDEA Amendments of 1997 require that parents have an opportunity to participate in meetings with respect to the identification, evaluation, and educational placement of the child, and the provision of FAPE to the child. (Sec. 300.501(a)(2)). Thus, parents must now be part of: (1) the group that determines what additional data are needed as part of an evaluation of their child (Sec. 300.533(a)(1)); (2) the team that determines their child's eligibility (Sec. 300.534(a)(1)); and (3) the group that makes decisions on the educational placement of their child (Sec. 300.501(c)).

In addition, the concerns of parents and the information that they provide regarding their children must be considered in developing and reviewing their children's IEPs (Secs. 300.343(c)(iii) and 300.346(a)(1)(i) and (b)); and the requirements for keeping parents informed about the educational progress of their children, particularly as it relates to their progress in the general curriculum, have been strengthened (Sec. 300.347(a)(7)).

The IDEA Amendments of 1997 also contain provisions that greatly strengthen the involvement of students with disabilities in decisions regarding their own futures, to facilitate movement from school to post-school activities. For example, those amendments (1) retained, essentially verbatim, the "transition services" requirements from the IDEA Amendments of 1990 (which provide that a statement of needed transition services must be in the IEP of each student with a disability, beginning no later than age 16); and (2) significantly expanded those provisions by adding a new annual requirement for the IEP to include "transition planning" activities for students beginning at age 14. (See section IV of this appendix for a description of the transition services requirements and definition.)

With respect to student involvement in decisions regarding transition services, Sec. 300.344(b) provides that (1) "the public agency shall invite a student with a disability of any age to attend his or her IEP meeting if a purpose of the meeting will be the consideration of—(i) The student's transition services needs under Sec. 300.347(b)(1); or (ii) The needed transition services for the student under Sec. 300.347(b)(2); or (iii) Both;" and (2) "If the student does not attend the IEP meeting, the public agency shall take other steps to ensure that the student's preferences and interests are considered." (Sec. 300.344(b)(2)).

The IDEA Amendments of 1997 also give States the authority to elect to transfer the rights accorded to parents under Part B to each student with a disability upon reaching the age of majority under State law (if the student has not been determined incompetent under State law) (Sec. 300.517). (Part B requires that if the rights transfer to the student, the public agency must provide any notice required under Part B to both the student and the parents.) If the State elects to provide for the transfer of rights from the parents to the student at the age of majority, the IEP must, beginning at least one year before a student reaches the age of majority under State law, include a statement that the student has been informed of any rights that will transfer to him or her upon reaching the age of majority. (Sec. 300.347(c)).

The IDEA Amendments of 1997 also permit, but do not require, States to establish a procedure for appointing the parent, or another appropriate individual if the parent is not available, to represent the educational interests of a student with a disability who has reached the age of majority under State law and has not been determined to be incompetent, but who is determined not to have the ability to provide informed consent with respect to his or her educational program.

5. What is the role of the parents, including surrogate parents, in decisions regarding the educational program of their children?

The parents of a child with a disability are expected to be equal participants along with school personnel, in developing, reviewing, and revising the IEP for their child. This is an active role in which the parents

(1) provide critical information regarding the strengths of their child and express their concerns for enhancing the education of their child;

(2) participate in discussions about the child's need for special education and related services and supplementary aids and services; and

(3) join with the other participants in deciding how the child will be involved and progress in the general curriculum and participate in State and district-wide assessments, and what services the agency will provide to the child and in what setting.

As previously noted in the introduction to section II of this Appendix, Part B specifically provides that parents of children with disabilities—

Have an opportunity to participate in meetings with respect to the identification, evaluation, and educational placement of their child, and the provision of FAPE to the child (including IEP meetings) (Secs. 300.501(b), 300.344(a)(1), and 300.517;

Be part of the groups that determine what additional data are needed as part of an evaluation of their child (Sec. 300.533(a)(1)), and determine their child's eligibility (Sec. 300.534(a)(1)) and educational placement (Sec. 300.501(c));

Have their concerns and the information that they provide regarding their child considered in developing and reviewing their child's IEPs (Secs. 300.343(c)(iii) and 300.346(a)(1)(i) and (b)); and

Be regularly informed (by such means as periodic report cards), as specified in their child's IEP, at least as often as parents are informed of their nondisabled children's progress, of their child's progress toward the annual goals in the IEP and the extent to which that progress is sufficient to enable the child to achieve the goals by the end of the year (Sec. 300.347(a)(7)).

A surrogate parent is a person appointed to represent the interests of a child with a disability in the educational decision- making process when no parent (as defined at Sec. 300.20) is known, the agency, after reasonable efforts, cannot locate the child's parents, or the child is a ward of the State under the laws of the State. A surrogate parent has all of the rights and responsibilities of a parent under Part B (Sec. 300.515.)

6. What are the Part B requirements regarding the participation of a student (child) with a disability in an IEP meeting?

If a purpose of an IEP meeting for a student with a disability will be the consideration of the student's transition services needs or needed transition services under Sec. 300.347(b)(1) or (2), or both, the public agency **must invite the student** and, as part of the notification to the parents of the IEP meeting, inform the parents that the agency will invite the student to the IEP meeting. If the student does not attend, the public agency must take other steps to ensure that the student's preferences and interests are considered. (See Sec. 300.344(b)).

Section Sec. 300.517 permits, but does not require, States to transfer procedural rights under Part B from the parents to students with disabilities who reach the age of majority under State law, if they have not been determined to be incompetent under State law. If those rights are to be transferred from the parents to the student, the public agency would be required to ensure that the student has the right to participate in IEP meetings set forth for parents in Sec. 300.345. However, at the discretion of the student or the public agency, the parents also could attend IEP meetings as "* * * individuals who have knowledge or special expertise regarding the child * * *" (see Sec. 300.344(a)(6)).

In other circumstances, a child with a disability may attend "if appropriate." (Sec. 300.344(a)(7)). Generally, a child with a disability should attend the IEP meeting if the parent decides that it is appropriate for the child to do so. If possible, the agency and parents should discuss the appropriateness of the child's participation before a decision is made, in order to help the parents determine whether or not the child's attendance would be (1) helpful in developing the IEP or (2) directly beneficial to the child or both. The agency should inform the parents before each IEP meeting—as part of notification under Sec. 300.345(a)(1)—that they may invite their child to participate.

7. Must the public agency inform the parents of who will be at the IEP meeting?

Yes. In notifying parents about the meeting, the agency "must indicate the purpose, time, and location of the meeting, and who will be in attendance." (Sec. 300.345(b), italics added.) In addition, if a purpose of the IEP meeting will be the consideration of a student's transition services needs or needed transition services under Sec. 300.347(b)(1) or (2) or both, the notice must also inform the parents that the agency is inviting the student, and identify any other agency that will be invited to send a representative.

The public agency also must inform the parents of the right of the parents and the agency to invite other individuals who have knowledge or special expertise regarding the child, including related services personnel as appropriate to be members of the IEP team. (Sec. 300.345(b)(1)(ii).) It also may be appropriate for the agency to ask the parents to inform the agency of any individuals the parents will be bringing to the meeting. Parents are encouraged to let the agency know whom they intend to bring. Such cooperation can facilitate arrangements for the meeting, and help ensure a productive, child-centered meeting.

8. Do parents have the right to a copy of their child's IEP?

Yes. Section 300.345(f) states that the public agency shall give the parent a copy of the IEP at no cost to the parent.

9. What is a public agency's responsibility if it is not possible to reach consensus on what services should be included in a child's IEP?

The IEP meeting serves as a communication vehicle between parents and school personnel, and enables them, as equal participants, to make joint, informed decisions regarding the

(1) child's needs and appropriate goals;

(2) extent to which the child will be involved in the general curriculum and participate in the regular education environment and State and district-wide assessments; and

(3) services needed to support that involvement and participation and to achieve agreed-upon goals.

Parents are considered equal partners with school personnel in making these decisions, and the IEP team must consider the parents' concerns and the information that they provide regarding their child in developing, reviewing, and revising IEPs (Secs. 300.343(c)(iii) and 300.346(a)(1) and (b)).

The IEP team should work toward consensus, but the public agency has ultimate responsibility to ensure that the IEP includes the services that the child needs in order to receive FAPE. It is not appropriate to make IEP decisions based upon a majority "vote." If the team cannot reach consensus, the public agency must provide the parents with prior written notice of the agency's proposals or refusals, or both, regarding the child's educational program, and the parents have the right to seek resolution of any disagreements by initiating an impartial due process hearing.

Every effort should be made to resolve differences between parents and school staff through voluntary mediation or some other informal step, without resort to a due process hearing. However, mediation or other informal procedures may not be used to deny or delay a parent's right to a due process hearing, or to deny any other rights afforded under Part B.

10. Does Part B require that public agencies inform parents regarding the educational progress of their children with disabilities?

Yes. The Part B statute and regulations include a number of provisions to help ensure that parents are involved in decisions regarding, and are informed about, their child's educational progress, including the child's progress in the general curriculum. First, the parents will be informed regarding their child's present levels of educational performance through the development of the IEP. Section 300.347(a)(1) requires that each IEP include:

* * * A statement of the child's present levels of educational performance, including—

(i) how the child's disability affects the child's involvement and progress in the general curriculum; or

(ii) for preschool children, as appropriate, how the disability affects the child's participation in appropriate activities * * *

Further, Sec. 300.347(a)(7) sets forth new requirements for regularly informing parents about their child's educational progress, as regularly as parents of nondisabled children are informed of their child's progress. That section requires that the IEP include:

A statement of—

(i) How the child's progress toward the annual goals * * * will be measured; and

(ii) how the child's parents will be regularly informed (by such means as periodic report cards), at least as often as parents are informed of their nondisabled children's progress, of—

(A) their child's progress toward the annual goals; and

(B) the extent to which that progress is sufficient to enable the child to achieve the goals by the end of the year.

One method that public agencies could use in meeting this requirement would be to provide periodic report cards to the parents of students with disabilities that include both (1) the grading information provided for all children in the agency at the same intervals; and (2) the specific information required by Sec. 300.347(a)(7)(ii)(A) and (B).

Finally, the parents, as part of the IEP team, will participate at least once every 12 months in a review of their child's educational progress. Section 300.343(c) requires that a public agency initiate and conduct a meeting, at which the IEP team:

(1) Reviews the child's IEP periodically, but not less than annually to determine whether the annual goals for the child are being achieved; and

(2) revises the IEP as appropriate to address—

(i) any lack of expected progress toward the annual goals * * * and in the general curriculum, if appropriate;

(ii) The results of any reevaluation * * *;

(iii) Information about the child provided to, or by, the parents * * *;

(iv) The child's anticipated needs; or

(v) Other matters.

III. Preparing Students With Disabilities for Employment and Other Post-School Experiences

One of the primary purposes of the IDEA is to "* * * ensure that all children with disabilities have available to them a free appropriate public education that emphasizes special education and related services designed to meet their unique needs and prepare them for employment and independent living * * *" (Sec. 300.1(a)). Section 701 of the Rehabilitation Act of 1973 describes the philosophy of independent living as including a philosophy of consumer control, peer support, self-help, self-determination, equal access, and individual and system advocacy, in order to maximize the leadership, empowerment, independence, and productivity of individuals with disabilities, and the integration and full inclusion of individuals with disabilities into the mainstream of American society. Because many students receiving services under IDEA will also receive services under the Rehabilitation Act, it is important, in planning for their future, to consider the impact of both statutes.

Similarly, one of the key purposes of the IDEA Amendments of 1997 was to "promote improved educational results for children with disabilities through early intervention, preschool, and educational experiences that prepare them for later educational challenges and employment." (H. Rep. No. 105-95, p. 82 (1997); S. Rep. No. 105-17, p. 4 (1997)).

Thus, throughout their preschool, elementary, and secondary education, the IEPs for children with disabilities must, to the extent appropriate for each individual child, focus on providing instruction and experiences that enable the child to prepare himself or herself for later educational experiences and for post-school activities, including formal education, if appropriate, employment, and independent living. Many students with disabilities will obtain services through State vocational rehabilitation programs to ensure that their educational goals are effectively implemented in post-school activities. Services available through rehabilitation programs are consistent with the underlying purpose of IDEA.

Although preparation for adult life is a key component of FAPE throughout the educational experiences of students with disabilities, Part B sets forth specific requirements related to transition planning and transition services that must be implemented no later than ages 14 and 16, respectively, and which require an intensified focus on that preparation as these students begin and prepare to complete their secondary education.

11. What must the IEP team do to meet the requirements that the IEP include "a statement of * * * transition service needs" beginning at age 14 (Sec. 300.347(b)(1)(i))," and a statement of needed transition services" no later than age 16 (Sec. 300.347(b)(2)?

Section 300.347(b)(1) requires that, beginning no later than age 14, each student's IEP include specific transition-related content, and, beginning no later than age 16, a statement of needed transition services:

Beginning at age 14 and younger if appropriate, and updated annually, each student's IEP must include:

"* * * a statement of the transition service needs of the student under the applicable components of the student's IEP that focuses on the student's courses of study (such as participation in advanced-placement courses or a vocational education program)" (Sec. 300.347(b)(1)(i)).

Beginning at age 16 (or younger, if determined appropriate by the IEP team), each student's IEP must include:

"* * * a statement of needed transition services for the student, including, if appropriate, a statement of the interagency responsibilities or any needed linkages." (Sec. 300.347(b)(2)).

The Committee Reports on the IDEA Amendments of 1997 make clear that the requirement added to the statute in 1997 that beginning at age 14, and updated annually, the IEP include "a statement of the transition service needs" is "* * * designed to augment, and not replace," the separate, preexisting requirement that the IEP include, "* * * beginning at age 16 (or younger, if determined appropriate by the IEP team), a statement of needed transition services * * *" (H. Rep. No. 105-95, p. 102 (1997); S. Rep. No. 105-17, p. 22 (1997)).

As clarified by the Reports,

The purpose of [the requirement in Sec. 300.347(b)(1)(i)] is to focus attention on how the child's educational program can be planned to help the child make a successful transition to his or her goals for life after secondary school." (H. Rep. No. 105-95, pp. 101-102 (1997); S. Rep. No. 105-17, p. 22 (1997)).

The Reports further explain that "For example, for a child whose transition goal is a job, a transition service could be teaching the child how to get to the job site on public transportation." (H. Rep. No. 105-95, p. 102 (1997); S. Rep. No. 105-17, p. 22 (1997)).

Thus, beginning at age 14, the IEP team, in determining appropriate measurable annual goals (including benchmarks or short- term objectives) and services for a student, must determine what instruction and educational experiences will assist the student to prepare for transition from secondary education to post-secondary life.

The statement of transition service needs should relate directly to the student's goals beyond secondary education, and show how planned studies are linked to these goals. For example, a student interested in exploring a career in computer science may have a statement of transition services needs connected to technology course work, while another student's statement of transition services needs could describe why public bus transportation training is important for future independence in the community.

Although the focus of the transition planning process may shift as the student approaches graduation, the IEP team must discuss specific areas beginning at least at the age of 14 years and review these areas annually. As noted in the Committee Reports, a disproportionate number of students with disabilities drop out of school before they complete their secondary education: "Too many students with disabilities are failing courses and dropping out of school. Almost twice as many students with disabilities drop out as compared to students without disabilities." (H. Rep. No. 105-95, p. 85 (1997), S. Rep. No. 105-17, p. 5 (1997).)

To help reduce the number of students with disabilities that drop out, it is important that the IEP team work with each student with a disability and the student's family to select courses of study that will be meaningful to the student's future and motivate the student to complete his or her education. This requirement is distinct from the requirement, at Sec. 300.347(b)(2), that the IEP include:

> * * * beginning at age 16 (or younger, if determined appropriate by the IEP team), a statement of needed transition services for the child, including, if appropriate, a statement of the interagency responsibilities or any needed linkages.

The **term "transition services"** is defined at Sec. 300.29 to mean:

> * * * a coordinated set of activities for a student with a disability that—
>
> (1) Is designed within **an outcome-oriented process, that promotes movement from school to post-school activities, including postsecondary education, vocational training, integrated employment** (including supported employment), continuing and adult education, adult services, independent living, or community participation;
>
> (2) Is **based on the individual student's needs**, taking into account the student's preferences and interests; and
>
> (3) Includes—
>
> > (i) Instruction;
> >
> > (ii) Related services;
> >
> > (iii) Community experiences;
> >
> > (iv) The development of employment and other post-school adult living objectives; and
> >
> > (v) If appropriate, acquisition of daily living skills and functional vocational evaluation.

Thus, while Sec. 300.347(b)(1) requires that the IEP team begin by age 14 to address the student's need for instruction that will assist the student to prepare for transition, the IEP must include by age 16 a statement of needed transition services under Sec. 300.347(b)(2) that includes a "coordinated set of activities * * *, designed within an outcome-oriented process, that promotes movement from school to post-school activities * * *." (Sec. 300.29)

Section 300.344(b)(3) further requires that, in implementing Sec. 300.347(b)(1), public agencies (in addition to required participants for all IEP meetings), must also invite a representative of any other agency that is likely to be responsible for providing or paying for transition services. Thus, Sec. 300.347(b)(2) requires a broader focus on coordination of services across, and linkages between, agencies beyond the SEA and LEA.

12. Must the IEP for each student with a disability, beginning no later than age 16, include all "needed transition services," as identified by the IEP team and consistent with the definition at Sec. 300.29, even if an agency other than the public agency will provide those services? What is the public agency's responsibility if another agency fails to provide agreed-upon transition services?

Section 300.347(b)(2) requires that the IEP for each child with a disability, beginning no later than age 16, or younger if determined appropriate by the IEP team, include all "needed transition services," as identified by the IEP team and consistent with the definition at Sec. 300.29, regardless of whether the public agency or some other agency will provide those services. Section 300.347(b)(2) specifically requires that the statement of needed transition services include, "* * * if appropriate, a statement of the interagency responsibilities or any needed linkages."

Further, the IDEA Amendments of 1997 also permit an LEA to use up to five percent of the Part B funds it receives in any fiscal year in combination with other amounts, which must include amounts other than education funds, to develop and implement a coordinated services system. These funds may be used for activities such as:

> (1) linking IEPs under Part B and Individualized Family Service Plans (IFSPs) under Part C, with Individualized Service Plans developed under multiple Federal and State programs, such as Title I of the Rehabilitation Act; and
>
> (2) developing and implementing interagency financing strategies for the provision of services, including transition services under

Part B.

The need to include, as part of a student's IEP, transition services to be provided by agencies other than the public agency is contemplated by Sec. 300.348(a), which specifies what the public agency must do if another agency participating in the development of the statement of needed transition services fails to provide a needed transition service that it had agreed to provide.

If an agreed-upon service by another agency is not provided, the public agency responsible for the student's education must implement alternative strategies to meet the student's needs. This requires that the public agency provide the services, or convene an IEP meeting as soon as possible to identify alternative strategies to meet the transition services objectives, and to revise the IEP accordingly. Alternative strategies might include the identification of another funding source, referral to another agency, the public agency's identification of other district-wide or community resources that it can use to meet the student's identified needs appropriately, or a combination of these strategies. As emphasized by Sec. 300.348(b), however:

Nothing in [Part B] relieves any participating agency, including a State vocational rehabilitation agency, of the responsibility to provide or pay for any transition service that the agency would otherwise provide to students with disabilities who meet the eligibility criteria of that agency.

However, the fact that an agency other than the public agency does not fulfill its responsibility does not relieve the public agency of its responsibility to ensure that FAPE is available to each student with a disability. (Section 300.142(b)(2) specifically requires that if an agency other than the LEA fails to provide or pay for a special education or related service (which could include a transition service), the LEA must, without delay, provide or pay for the service, and may then claim reimbursement from the agency that failed to provide or pay for the service.)

13. Under what circumstances must a public agency invite representatives from other agencies to an IEP meeting at which a child's need for transition services will be considered?

Section 300.344 requires that, "In implementing the requirements of [Sec. 300.347(b)(1)(ii) requiring a statement of needed transition services], the public agency shall also invite a representative of any other agency that is likely to be responsible for providing or paying for transition services." To meet this requirement, the public agency must identify all agencies that are "likely to be responsible for providing or paying for transition services" for each student addressed by Sec. 300.347(b)(1), and must invite each of those agencies to the IEP meeting; and if an agency invited to send a representative to a meeting does not do so, the public agency must take other steps to obtain the participation of that agency in the planning of any transition services.

If, during the course of an IEP meeting, the team identifies additional agencies that are "likely to be responsible for providing or paying for transition services" for the student, the public agency must determine how it will meet the requirements of Sec. 300.344.

IV. OTHER QUESTIONS REGARDING THE DEVELOPMENT AND CONTENT OF IEPS

14. For a child with a disability receiving special education for the first time, when must an IEP be developed—before or after the child begins to receive special education and related services?

Section 300.342(b)(1) requires that an IEP be "in effect before special education and related services are provided to an eligible child * * *" (Italics added.) The appropriate placement for a particular child with a disability cannot be determined until after decisions have been made about the child's needs and the services that the public agency will provide to meet those needs. These decisions must be made at the IEP meeting, and it would not be permissible first to place the child and then develop the IEP. Therefore, the IEP must be developed before placement. (Further, the child's placement must be based, among other factors, on the child's IEP.)

This requirement does not preclude temporarily placing an eligible child with a disability in a program as part of the evaluation process—before the IEP is finalized—to assist a public agency in determining the appropriate placement for the child. However, it is essential that the temporary placement not become the final placement before the IEP is finalized. In order to ensure that this does not happen, the State might consider requiring LEAs to take the following actions:

a. Develop an interim IEP for the child that sets out the specific conditions and timelines for the trial placement. (See paragraph c, following.)

b. Ensure that the parents agree to the interim placement before it is carried out, and that they are involved throughout the process of developing, reviewing, and revising the child's IEP.

c. Set a specific timeline (e.g., 30 days) for completing the evaluation, finalizing the IEP, and determining the appropriate placement for the child.

d. Conduct an IEP meeting at the end of the trial period in order to finalize the child's IEP.

15. Who is responsible for ensuring the development of IEPs for children with disabilities served by a public agency other than an LEA?

The answer as to which public agency has direct responsibility for ensuring the development of IEPs for children with disabilities served by a public agency other than an LEA will vary from State to State, depending upon State law, policy, or practice. The SEA is ultimately responsible for ensuring that all Part B requirements, including the IEP requirements, are met for eligible children within the State, including those children served by a public agency other than an LEA. Thus, the SEA must ensure that every eligible child with a disability in the State has FAPE available, regardless of which State or local agency is responsible for educating the child. (The only exception to this responsibility is that the SEA is not responsible for ensuring that FAPE is made available to children with disabilities who are convicted as adults under State law and incarcerated in adult prisons, if the State has assigned that responsibility to a public agency other than the SEA. (See Sec. 300.600(d)).

Although the SEA has flexibility in deciding the best means to meet this obligation (e.g., through interagency agreements), the SEA must ensure that no eligible child with a disability is denied FAPE due to jurisdictional disputes among agencies. When an LEA is responsible for the education of a child with a disability, the LEA remains responsible for developing the child's IEP, regardless of the public or private school setting into which it places the child.

16. For a child placed out of State by an educational or non- educational State or local agency, is the placing or receiving State responsible for the child's IEP?

Regardless of the reason for the placement, the "placing" State is responsible for ensuring that the child's IEP is developed and that it is implemented. The determination of the specific agency in the placing State that is responsible for the child's IEP would be based on State law, policy, or practice. However, the SEA in the placing State is ultimately responsible for ensuring that the child has FAPE available.

17. If a disabled child has been receiving special education from one public agency and transfers to another public agency in the same State, must the new public agency develop an IEP before the child can be placed in a special education program?

If a child with a disability moves from one public agency to another in the same State, the State and its public agencies have an ongoing responsibility to ensure that FAPE is made available to that child. This means that if a child moves to another public agency the new agency is responsible for ensuring that the child has available special education and related services in conformity with an IEP.

The new public agency must ensure that the child has an IEP in effect before the agency can provide special education and related services. The new public agency may meet this responsibility by either adopting the IEP the former public agency developed for the child or by developing a new IEP for the child. (The new public agency is strongly encouraged to continue implementing the IEP developed by the former public agency, if appropriate, especially if the parents believe their child was progressing appropriately under that IEP.)

Before the child's IEP is finalized, the new public agency may provide interim services agreed to by both the parents and the new public agency. If the parents and the new public agency are unable to agree on an interim IEP and placement, the new public agency must implement the old IEP to the extent possible until a new IEP is developed and implemented.

In general, while the new public agency must conduct an IEP meeting, it would not be necessary if: (1) A copy of the child's current IEP is available; (2) the parents indicate that they are satisfied with the current IEP; and (3) the new public agency determines that the current IEP is appropriate and can be implemented as written. If the child's current IEP is not available, or if either the new public agency or the parent believes that it is not appropriate, the new public agency must develop a new IEP through appropriate procedures within a short time after the child enrolls in the new public agency (normally, within one week).

18. What timelines apply to the development and implementation of an initial IEP for a child with a disability?

Section 300.343(b) requires each public agency to ensure that within a reasonable period of time following the agency's receipt of parent consent to an initial evaluation of a child, the child is evaluated and, if determined eligible, special education and related services are made available to the child in accordance with an IEP. The section further requires the agency to conduct a meeting to develop an IEP for the child within 30 days of determining that the child needs special education and related services. Section 300.342(b)(2) provides that an IEP must be implemented as soon as possible following the meeting in which the IEP is developed.

19. Must a public agency hold separate meetings to determine a child's eligibility for special education and related services, develop the child's IEP, and determine the child's placement, or may the agency meet all of these requirements in a single meeting?

A public agency may, after a child is determined by "a group of qualified professionals and the parent" (see Sec. 300.534(a)(1)) to be a child with a disability, continue in the same meeting to develop an IEP for the child and then to determine the child's placement. However, the public agency must ensure that it meets:

(1) the requirements of Sec. 300.535 regarding eligibility decisions;

(2) all of the Part B requirements regarding meetings to develop IEPs (including providing appropriate notification to the parents, consistent with the requirements of Secs. 300.345, 300.503, and 300.504, and ensuring that all the required team members participate in the development of the IEP, consistent with the requirements of Sec. 300.344;) and

(3) ensuring that the placement is made by the required individuals, including the parent, as required by Secs. 300.552 and 300.501(c).

20. How frequently must a public agency conduct meetings to review, and, if appropriate, revise the IEP for each child with a disability?

A public agency must initiate and conduct meetings periodically, but at least once every twelve months, to review each child's IEP, in order to determine whether the annual goals for the child are being achieved, and to revise the IEP, as appropriate, to address:

(a) Any lack of expected progress toward the annual goals and in the general curriculum, if appropriate;

(b) the results of any reevaluation;

(c) information about the child provided to, or by, the parents;

(d) the child's anticipated needs; or

(e) other matters (Sec. 300.343(c)).

A public agency also must ensure that an IEP is in effect for each child at the beginning of each school year (Sec. 300.342(a)). It may conduct IEP meetings at any time during the year. However, if the agency conducts the IEP meeting prior to the beginning of the next school year, it must ensure that the IEP contains the necessary special education and related services and supplementary aids and services to ensure that the student's IEP can be appropriately implemented during the next school year. Otherwise, it would be necessary for the public agency to conduct another IEP meeting.

Although the public agency is responsible for determining when it is necessary to conduct an IEP meeting, the parents of a child with a disability have the right to request an IEP meeting at any time. For example, if the parents believe that the child is not progressing satisfactorily or that there is a problem with the child's current IEP, it would be appropriate for the parents to request an IEP meeting.

If a child's teacher feels that the child's IEP or placement is not appropriate for the child, the teacher should follow agency procedures with respect to: (1) calling or meeting with the parents or (2) requesting the agency to hold another IEP meeting to review the child's IEP.

The legislative history of Public Law 94-142 makes it clear that there should be as many meetings a year as any one child may need (121 Cong. Rec. S20428-29 (Nov. 19, 1975) (remarks of Senator Stafford)). Public agencies should grant any reasonable parent request for an IEP meeting. For example, if the parents question the adequacy of services that are provided while their child is suspended for short periods of time, it would be appropriate to convene an IEP meeting.

In general, if either a parent or a public agency believes that a required component of the student's IEP should be changed, the public agency must conduct an IEP meeting if it believes that a change in the IEP may be necessary to ensure the provision of FAPE. If a parent requests an IEP meeting because the parent believes that a change is needed in the provision of FAPE to the child or the educational placement of the child, and the agency refuses to convene an IEP meeting to determine whether such a change is needed, the agency must provide written notice to the parents of the refusal, including an explanation of why the agency has determined that conducting the meeting is not necessary to ensure the provision of FAPE to the student.

Under Sec. 300.507(a), the parents or agency may initiate a due process hearing at any time regarding any proposal or refusal regarding the identification, evaluation, or educational placement of the child, or the provision of FAPE to the child, and the public agency must inform parents about the availability of mediation.

21. May IEP meetings be audio- or video-tape-recorded?

Part B does not address the use of audio or video recording devices at IEP meetings, and no other Federal statute either authorizes or prohibits the recording of an IEP meeting by either a parent or a school official. Therefore, an SEA or public agency has the option to require, prohibit, limit, or otherwise regulate the use of recording devices at IEP meetings.

If a public agency has a policy that prohibits or limits the use of recording devices at IEP meetings, that policy must provide for exceptions if they are necessary to ensure that the parent understands the IEP or the IEP process or to implement other parental rights guaranteed under Part B. An SEA or school district that adopts a rule regulating the tape recording of IEP meetings also should ensure that it is uniformly applied.

Any recording of an IEP meeting that is maintained by the public agency is an "education record," within the meaning of the Family Educational Rights and Privacy Act ("FERPA"; 20 U.S.C. 1232g), and would, therefore, be subject to the confidentiality requirements of the regulations under both FERPA (34 CFR part 99) and part B (Secs. 300.560-300.575). Parents wishing to use audio or video recording devices at IEP meetings should consult State or local policies for further guidance.

22. Who can serve as the representative of the public agency at an IEP meeting?

The IEP team must include a representative of the public agency who:

(a) Is qualified to provide, or supervise the provision of, specially designed instruction to meet the unique needs of children with disabilities;

(b) is knowledgeable about the general curriculum; and

(c) is knowledgeable about the availability of resources of the public agency (Sec. 300.344(a)(4)).

Each public agency may determine which specific staff member will serve as the agency representative in a particular IEP meeting, so long as the individual meets these requirements. It is important, however, that the agency representative have the authority to commit agency resources and be able to ensure that whatever services are set out in the IEP will actually be provided.

A public agency may designate another public agency member of the IEP team to also serve as the agency representative, so long as that individual meets the requirements of Sec. 300.344(a)(4).

23. For a child with a disability being considered for initial provision of special education and related services, which teacher or teachers should attend the IEP meeting?

A child's IEP team must include at least one of the child's regular education teachers (if the child is, or may be participating in the regular education environment) and at least one of the child's special education teachers, or, if appropriate, at least one of the child's special education providers (Sec. 300.344(a)(2) and (3)).

Each IEP must include a statement of the present levels of educational performance, including a statement of how the child's disability affects the child's involvement and progress in the general curriculum (Sec. 300.347(a)(1)). At least one regular education teacher is a required member of the IEP team of a child who is, or may be, participating in the regular educational environment, regardless of the extent of that participation. The requirements of Sec. 300.344(a)(3) can be met by either:

(1) a special education teacher of the child; or

(2) another special education provider of the child, such as a speech pathologist, physical or occupational therapist, etc., if the related service consists of specially designed instruction and is considered special education under applicable State standards.

Sometimes more than one meeting is necessary in order to finalize a child's IEP. In this process, if the special education teacher or special education provider who will be working with the child is identified, it would be useful to have that teacher or provider participate in the meeting with the parents and other members of the IEP team in finalizing the IEP. If this is not possible, the public agency must ensure that the teacher or provider has access to the child's IEP as soon as possible after it is finalized and before beginning to work with the child.

Further, (consistent with Sec. 300.342(b)), the public agency must ensure that each regular education teacher, special education teacher, related services provider and other service provider of an eligible child under this part

(1) has access to the child's IEP, and

(2) is informed of his or her specific responsibilities related to implementing the IEP, and of the specific accommodations, modifications, and supports that must be provided to the child in accordance with the IEP.

This requirement is crucial to ensuring that each child receives FAPE in accordance with his or her IEP, and that the IEP is appropriately and effectively implemented.

24. What is the role of a regular education teacher in the development, review and revision of the IEP for a child who is, or may be, participating in the regular education environment?

As required by Sec. 300.344(a)(2), the IEP team for a child with a disability must include at least one regular education teacher of the child if the child is, or may be, participating in the regular education environment. Section 300.346(d) further specifies that the regular education teacher of a child with a disability, as a member of the IEP team, must, to the extent appropriate, participate in the development, review, and revision of the child's IEP, including assisting in—

(1) the determination of appropriate positive behavioral interventions and strategies for the child; and

(2) the determination of supplementary aids and services, program modifications, and supports for school personnel that will be provided for the child, consistent with 300.347(a)(3) (Sec. 300.344(d)).

Thus, while a regular education teacher must be a member of the IEP team if the child is, or may be, participating in the regular education environment, the teacher need not (depending upon the child's needs and the purpose of the specific IEP team meeting) be required to participate in all decisions made as part of the meeting or to be present throughout the entire meeting or attend every meeting. For example, the regular education teacher who is a member of the IEP team must participate in discussions and decisions about how to modify the general curriculum in the regular classroom to ensure the child's involvement and progress in the general curriculum and participation in the regular education environment.

Depending upon the specific circumstances, however, it may not be necessary for the regular education teacher to participate in discussions and decisions regarding, for example, the physical therapy needs of the child, if the teacher is not responsible for implementing that portion of the child's IEP.

In determining the extent of the regular education teacher's participation at IEP meetings, public agencies and parents should discuss and try to reach agreement on whether the child's regular education teacher that is a member of the IEP team should be present at a particular IEP meeting and, if so, for what period of time. The extent to which it would be appropriate for the regular education teacher member of the IEP team to participate in IEP meetings must be decided on a case-by-case basis.

25. If a child with a disability attends several regular classes, must all of the child's regular education teachers be members of the child's IEP team?

No. The IEP team need not include more than one regular education teacher of the child. If the participation of more than one regular education teacher would be beneficial to the child's success in school (e.g., in terms of enhancing the child's participation in the general curriculum), it would be appropriate for them to attend the meeting.

26. How should a public agency determine which regular education teacher and special education teacher will be members of the IEP team for a particular child with a disability?

The regular education teacher who serves as a member of a child's IEP team should be a teacher who is, or may be, responsible for implementing a portion of the IEP, so that the teacher can participate in discussions about how best to teach the child.

If the child has more than one regular education teacher responsible for carrying out a portion of the IEP, the LEA may designate which teacher or teachers will serve as IEP team member(s), taking into account the best interest of the child.

In a situation in which not all of the child's regular education teachers are members of the child's IEP team, the LEA is strongly encouraged to seek input from the teachers who will not be attending. In addition, (consistent with Sec. 300.342(b)), the LEA must ensure that each regular education teacher (as well as each special education teacher, related services provider, and other service provider) of an eligible child under this part (1) has access to the child's IEP, and (2) is informed of his or her specific responsibilities related to implementing the IEP, and of the specific accommodations, modifications and supports that must be provided to the child in accordance with the IEP.

In the case of a child whose behavior impedes the learning of the child or others, the LEA is encouraged to have a regular education teacher or other person knowledgeable about positive behavior strategies at the IEP meeting. This is especially important if the regular education teacher is expected to carry out portions of the IEP. Similarly, the special education teacher or provider of the child who is a member of the child's IEP team should be the person who is, or will be, responsible for implementing the IEP. If, for example, the child's disability is a speech impairment, the special education teacher on the IEP team could be the speech-language pathologist.

27. For a child whose primary disability is a speech impairment, may a public agency meet its responsibility under Sec. 300.344(a)(3) to ensure that the IEP team includes "at least one special education teacher, or, if appropriate, at least one special education provider of the child" by including a speech-language pathologist on the IEP team?

Yes, if speech is considered special education under State standards. As with other children with disabilities, the IEP team must also include at least one of the child's regular education teachers if the child is, or may be, participating in the regular education environment.

28. Do parents and public agencies have the option of inviting any individual of their choice be participants on their child's IEP team?

The IEP team may, at the discretion of the parent or the agency, include "other individuals who have knowledge or special expertise regarding the child * * *" (Sec. 300.344(a)(6), italics added). Under Sec. 300.344(a)(6), these individuals are members of the IEP team. This is a change from prior law, which provided, without qualification, that parents or agencies could have other individuals as members of the IEP team at the discretion of the parents or agency.

Under Sec. 300.344(c), the determination as to whether an individual has knowledge or special expertise, within the meaning of Sec. 300.344(a)(6), shall be made by the parent or public agency who has invited the individual to be a member of the IEP team.

Part B does not provide for including individuals such as representatives of teacher organizations as part of an IEP team, unless they re included because of knowledge or special expertise regarding the child. (Because a representative of a teacher organization would generally be concerned with the interests of the teacher rather than the interests of the child, and generally would not possess knowledge or expertise regarding the child, it generally would be inappropriate for such an official to be a member of the IEP team or to otherwise participate in an IEP meeting.)

29. Can parents or public agencies bring their attorneys to IEP meetings, and, if so under what circumsances? Are attorney's fees available for parents' attorneys if the parents are prevailing parties in actions or proceedings brought under Part B?

Section 300.344(a)(6) authorizes the addition to the IEP team of other individuals at the discretion of the parent or the public agency only if those other individuals have knowledge or special expertise regarding the child. The determination of whether an attorney possesses knowledge or special expertise regarding the child would have to be made on a case-by-case basis by the parent or public agency inviting the attorney to be a member of the team.

The presence of the agency's attorney could contribute to a potentially adversarial atmosphere at the meeting. The same is true with regard to the presence of an attorney accompanying the parents at the IEP meeting. Even if the attorney possessed knowledge or special expertise regarding the child (Sec. 300.344(a)(6)), an attorney's presence would have the potential for creating an adversarial atmosphere that would not necessarily be in the best interests of the child. Therefore, **the attendance of attorneys at IEP meetings should be strongly discouraged**. Further, as specified in Section 615(i)(3)(D)(ii) of the Act and Sec. 300.513(c)(2)(ii), Attorneys' fees may not be awarded relating to any meeting of the IEP team unless the meeting is convened as a result of an administrative proceeding or judicial action, or, at the discretion of the State, for a mediation conducted prior to the request for a due process hearing.

30. Must related services personnel attend IEP meetings?

Although Part B does not expressly require that the IEP team include related services personnel as part of the IEP team (Sec. 300.344(a)), it is appropriate for those persons to be included if a particular related service is to be discussed as part of the IEP meeting. Section 300.344(a)(6) provides that the IEP team also includes "at the discretion of the parent or the agency, other individuals who have knowledge or special expertise regarding the child, including related services personnel as appropriate. * * *" (Italics added.)

Further, Sec. 300.344(a)(3) requires that the IEP team for each child with a disability include "at least one special education teacher, or, if appropriate, at least one special education provider of the child * * *" This requirement can be met by the participation of either (1) a special education teacher of the child, or (2) another special education provider such as a speech- language pathologist, physical or occupational therapist, etc., if the related service consists of specially designed instruction and is considered special education under the applicable State standard.

If a child with a disability has an identified need for related services, it would be appropriate for the related services personnel to attend the meeting or otherwise be involved in developing the IEP. As explained in the Committee Reports on the IDEA Amendments of 1997, "Related services personnel should be included on the team when a particular related service will be discussed at the request of the child's parents or the school." (H. Rep. No. 105-95, p. 103 (1997); S. Rep. No. 105-17, p. 23 (1997)).

For example, if the child's evaluation indicates the need for a specific related service (e.g., physical therapy, occupational therapy, special transportation services, school social work services, school health services, or counseling), the agency should ensure that a qualified provider of that service either (1) attends the IEP meeting, or (2) provides a written recommendation concerning the nature, frequency, and amount of service to be provided to the child. This written recommendation could be a part of the evaluation report.A public agency must ensure that all individuals who are necessary to develop an IEP that will meet the child's unique needs, and ensure the provision of FAPE to the child, participate in the child's IEP meeting.

31. Must the public agency ensure that all services specified in a child's IEP are provided?

Yes. The public agency must ensure that all services set forth in the child's IEP are provided, consistent with the child's needs as identified in the IEP. The agency may provide each of those services directly, through its own staff resources; indirectly, by contracting with another public or private agency; or through other arrangements. In providing the services, the agency may use whatever State, local, Federal, and private sources of support are available for those purposes (see Sec. 300.301(a)); but the services must be at no cost to the parents, and the public agency remains responsible for ensuring that the IEP services are provided in a manner that appropriately meets the student's needs as specified in the IEP. The SEA and responsible public agency may not allow the failure of another agency to provide service(s) described in the child's IEP to deny or delay the provision of FAPE to the child. (See Sec. 300.142, Methods of ensuring services.)

32. Is it permissible for an agency to have the IEP completed before the IEP meeting begins?

No. Agency staff may come to an IEP meeting prepared with evaluation findings and proposed recommendations regarding IEP content, but the agency must make it clear to the parents at the outset of the meeting that the services proposed by the agency are only recommendations for review and discussion with the parents. Parents have the right to bring questions, concerns, and recommendations to an IEP meeting as part of a full discussion of the child's needs and the services to be provided to meet those needs before the IEP is finalized.

Public agencies must ensure that, if agency personnel bring drafts of some or all of the IEP content to the IEP meeting, there is a full discussion with the child's parents, before the child's IEP is finalized, regarding drafted content and the child's needs and the services to be provided to meet those needs.

33. Must a public agency include transportation in a child's IEP as a related service?

As with other related services, a public agency must provide transportation as a related service if it is required to assist the disabled child to benefit from special education. (This includes transporting a preschool-aged child to the site at which the public agency provides special education and related services to the child, if that site is different from the site at which the child receives other preschool or day care services.)

In determining whether to include transportation in a child's IEP, and whether the child needs to receive transportation as a related service, it would be appropriate to have at the IEP meeting a person with expertise in that area. In making this determination, the IEP team must consider how the child's disability affects the child's need for transportation, including determining whether the child's disability prevents the child from using the same transportation provided to nondisabled children, or from getting to school in the same manner as nondisabled children. The public agency must ensure that any transportation service included in a child's IEP as a related service is provided at public expense and at no cost to the parents, and that the child's IEP describes the transportation arrangement.

Even if a child's IEP team determines that the child does not require transportation as a related service, Section 504 of the Rehabilitation Act of 1973, as amended, requires that the child receive the same transportation provided to nondisabled children. If a public agency transports nondisabled children, it must transport disabled children under the same terms and conditions. However, if a child's IEP team determines that the child does not need transportation as a related service, and the public agency transports only those children whose IEPs specify transportation as a related service, and does not transport nondisabled children, the public agency would not be required to provide transportation to a disabled child. It should be assumed that most children with disabilities receive the same transportation services as nondisabled children. For some children with disabilities, integrated transportation may be achieved by providing needed accommodations such as lifts and other equipment adaptations on regular school transportation vehicles.

34. Must a public agency provide related services that are required to assist a child with a disability to benefit from special education, whether or not those services are included in the list of related services in Sec. 300.24?

The list of related services is not exhaustive and may include other developmental, corrective, or supportive services if they are required to assist a child with a disability to benefit from special education. This could, depending upon the unique needs of a child, include such services as nutritional services or service coordination. These determinations must be made on an individual basis by each child's IEP team.

35. Must the IEP specify the amount of services or may it simply list the services to be provided?

The amount of services to be provided must be stated in the IEP, so that the level of the agency's commitment of resources will be clear to parents and other IEP team members (Sec. 300.347(a)(6)). The amount of time to be committed to each of the various services to be provided must be (1) appropriate to the specific service, and (2) stated in the IEP in a manner that is clear to all who are involved in both the development and implementation of the IEP.

The amount of a special education or related service to be provided to a child may be stated in the IEP as a range (e.g., speech therapy to be provided three times per week for 30-45 minutes per session) only if the IEP team determines that stating the amount of services as a range is necessary to meet the unique needs of the child. For example, it would be appropriate for the IEP to specify, based upon the IEP team's determination of the student's unique needs, that particular services are needed only under specific circumstances, such as the occurrence of a seizure or of a particular behavior. A range may not be used because of personnel shortages or uncertainty regarding the availability of staff.

36. Under what circumstances is a public agency required to permit a child with a disability to use a school-purchased assistive technology device in the child's home or in another setting?

Each child's IEP team must consider the child's need for assistive technology (AT) in the development of the child's IEP (Sec. 300.346(a)(2)(v)); and the nature and extent of the AT devices and services to be provided to the child must be reflected in the child's IEP (Sec. 300.346(c)).

A public agency **must permit a child to use school-purchased assistive technology devices at home or in other settings**, if the IEP team determines that the child needs access to those devices in nonschool settings in order to receive FAPE (to complete homework, for example). Any assistive technology devices that are necessary to ensure FAPE must be provided at no cost to the parents, and the parents cannot be charged for normal use, wear and tear. However, while ownership of the devices in these circumstances would remain with the public agency, State law, rather than Part B, generally would govern whether parents are liable for loss, theft, or damage due to negligence or misuse of publicly owned equipment used at home or in other settings in accordance with a child's IEP.

37. Can the IEP team also function as the group making the placement decision for a child with a disability?

Yes, a public agency may use the IEP team to make the placement decision for a child, so long as the group making the placement decision meets the requirements of Secs. 300.552 and 300.501(c), which requires that the placement decision be made by a group of persons, including the parents, and other persons knowledgeable about the child, the meaning of the evaluation data, and the placement options.

38. If a child's IEP includes behavioral strategies to address a particular behavior, can a child ever be suspended for engaging in that behavior?

If a child's behavior impedes his or her learning or that of others, the IEP team, in developing the child's IEP, must consider, if appropriate, development of strategies, including positive behavioral interventions, strategies and supports to address that behavior, consistent with Sec. 300.346(a)(2)(i). This means that in most cases in which a child's behavior that impedes his or her learning or that of others is, or can be readily anticipated to be, repetitive, proper development of the child's IEP will include the development of strategies, including positive behavioral interventions, strategies and supports to address that behavior. See Sec. 300.346(c). This includes behavior that could violate a school code of conduct.

A failure to, if appropriate, consider and address these behaviors in developing and implementing the child's IEP would constitute a denial of FAPE to the child.

Of course, in appropriate circumstances, the IEP team, which includes the child's parents, might determine that the child's behavioral intervention plan includes specific regular or alternative disciplinary measures, such as denial of certain privileges or short suspensions, that would result from particular infractions of school rules, along with positive behavior intervention strategies and supports, as a part of a comprehensive plan to address the child's behavior. Of course, if short suspensions that are included in a child's IEP are being implemented in a manner that denies the child access to the ability to progress in the educational program, the child would be denied FAPE.

Whether other disciplinary measures, including suspension, are ever appropriate for behavior that is addressed in a child's IEP will have to be determined on a case by case basis in light of the particular circumstances of that incident. However, **school personnel may not use their ability to suspend a child for 10 days or less at a time on multiple occasions in a school year as a means of avoiding appropriately considering and addressing the child's behavior as a part of providing FAPE to the child.**

39. If a child's behavior in the regular classroom, even with appropriate interventions, would significantly impair the learning of others, can the group that makes the placement decision determine that placement in the regular classroom is inappropriate for that child?

The IEP team, in developing the IEP, is required to consider, when appropriate, strategies, including positive behavioral interventions, strategies and supports to address the behavior of a child with a disability whose behavior impedes his or her learning or that of others. If the IEP team determines that such supports, strategies or interventions are necessary to address the behavior of the child, those services must be included in the child's IEP. These provisions are designed to foster increased participation of children with disabilities in regular education environments or other less restrictive environments, not to serve as a basis for placing children with disabilities in more restrictive settings.

The determination of appropriate placement for a child whose behavior is interfering with the education of others requires careful consideration of whether the child can appropriately function in the regular classroom if provided appropriate behavioral supports, strategies and interventions. If the child can appropriately function in the regular classroom with appropriate behavioral supports, strategies or interventions, placement in a more restrictive environment would be inconsistent with the least restrictive environment provisions of the IDEA. If the child's behavior in the regular classroom, even with the provision of appropriate behavioral supports, strategies or interventions, would significantly impair the learning of others, that placement would not meet his or her needs and would not be appropriate for that child.

40. May school personnel during a school year implement more than one short-term removal of a child with disabilities from his or her classroom or school for misconduct?

Yes. Under Sec. 300.520(a)(1), school personnel may order removal of a child with a disability from the child's current placement for not more than 10 consecutive school days for any violation of school rules, and additional removals of not more than 10 consecutive school days in that same school year for separate incidents of misconduct, as long as these removals do not constitute a change of placement under Sec. 300.519(b). However, these removals are permitted only to the extent they are consistent with discipline that is applied to children without disabilities. Also, school personnel should be aware of constitutional due process protections that apply to suspensions of all children. Goss v. Lopez, 419 U.S. 565 (1975). Section 300.121(d) addresses the extent of the obligation to provide services after a child with a disability has been removed from his or her current placement for more than 10 school days in the same school year.

END OF APPENDIX A TO THE REGULATIONS

TABLE OF EARLY INTERVENTION REGULATIONS
34 C.F.R. Part 303

EARLY INTERVENTION PROGRAM FOR INFANTS AND TODDLERS WITH DISABILITIES
34 C.F.R. Part 303

SUBPART A—GENERAL

PURPOSE, ELIGIBILITY, AND OTHER GENERAL PROVISIONS

Sec. 303.1 Purpose of the early intervention program for infants and toddlers with disabilities

The purpose of this part is to provide financial assistance to States to—

(a) Maintain and implement a statewide, comprehensive, coordinated, multidisciplinary, interagency program of early intervention services for infants and toddlers with disabilities and their families;

(b) Facilitate the coordination of payment for early intervention services from Federal, State, local, and private sources (including public and private insurance coverage);

(c) Enhance the States' capacity to provide quality early intervention services and expand and improve existing early intervention services being provided to infants and toddlers with disabilities and their families; and

(d) Enhance the capacity of State and local agencies and service providers to identify, evaluate, and meet the needs of historically underrepresented populations, particularly minority, low-income, inner-city, and rural populations. (Authority: 20 U.S.C. 1431-1445, unless otherwise noted.)

Sec. 303.2 Eligible recipients of an award

Eligible recipients include the 50 States, the Commonwealth of Puerto Rico, the District of Columbia, the Secretary of the Interior, and the following jurisdictions: Guam, American Samoa, the Virgin Islands, the Commonwealth of the Northern Mariana Islands. (Authority: 20 U.S.C. 1401(27), 1443)

Sec. 303.3 Activities that may be supported under this part

Funds under this part may be used for the following activities:

(a) To maintain and implement a statewide system of early intervention services for children eligible under this part and their families.

(b) For direct services for eligible children and their families that are not otherwise provided from other public or private sources.

(c) To expand and improve on services for eligible children and their families that are otherwise available, consistent with Sec. 303.527.

(d) To provide a free appropriate public education, in accordance with Part B of the Act, to children with disabilities from their third birthday to the beginning of the following school year.

(e) To strengthen the statewide system by initiating, expanding, or improving collaborative efforts related to at-risk infants and toddlers, including establishing linkages with appropriate public or private community-based organizations, services, and personnel for the purpose of—

(1) Identifying and evaluating at-risk infants and toddlers;

(2) Making referrals of the infants and toddlers identified and evaluated under paragraph (e)(1) of this section; and

(3) Conducting periodic follow-up on each referral under paragraph (e)(2) of this section to determine if the status of the infant or toddler involved has changed with respect to the eligibility of the infant or toddler for services under this part. (Authority: 20 U.S.C. 1433 and 1438)

Sec. 303.4 Limitation on eligible children

This part 303 does not apply to any child with disabilities receiving a free appropriate public education, in accordance with 34 CFR part 300, with funds received under 34 CFR part 301. (Authority: 20 U.S.C. 1419(h))

Sec. 303.5 Applicable regulations

(a) The following regulations apply to this part:

(1) The Education Department General Administrative Regulations (EDGAR), including—

(i) Part 76 (State Administered Programs), except for Sec. 76.103;

(ii) Part 77 (Definitions that Apply to Department Regulations);

(iii) Part 79 (Intergovernmental Review of Department of Education Programs and Activities);

(iv) Part 80 (Uniform Administrative Requirements for Grants and Cooperative Agreements to State and Local Governments);

(v) Part 81 (Grants and Cooperative Agreements under the General Education Provisions Act—Enforcement);

(vi) Part 82 (New Restrictions on Lobbying); and

(vii) Part 85 (Governmentwide Debarment and Suspension (Nonprocurement) and Governmentwide Requirements for Drug-Free Work Place (Grants)).

(2) The regulations in this part 303.

(3) The following regulations in 34 CFR part 300 (Assistance to States for Children with Disabilities Program): Secs. 300.560 through 300.577, and Secs. 300.580 through 300.585.

(b) In applying the regulations cited in paragraphs (a)(1) and (a)(3) of this section, any reference to—

(1) State educational agency means the lead agency under this part;

(2) Special education, related services, free appropriate public education, free public education, or education means "early intervention services" under this part;

(3) Participating agency, when used in reference to a local educational agency or an intermediate educational agency, means a local service provider under this part;

(4) Sec. 300.128 means Secs. 303.164 and 303.321; and

(5) Sec. 300.129 means Sec. 303.460. (Authority: 20 U.S.C. 1401, 1416, 1417)

Definitions

Note: Secs. 303.6-303.24 contain definitions, including a definition of "natural environments" in Sec. 303.18 that are used throughout these regulations. Other terms are defined in the specific subparts in which they are used. Below is a list of those terms and the specific sections in which they are defined:

Appropriate professional requirements in the State (Sec. 303.361(a)(1))

Assessment (Sec. 303.322(b)(2))

Consent (Sec. 303.401(a))

Evaluation (Sec. 303.322(b)(1))

Frequency and intensity (Sec. 303.344(d)(2)(i))

Highest requirements in the State applicable to a profession or discipline (Sec. 303.361)(a)(2))

Individualized family service plan and IFSP (Sec. 303.340(b))

Impartial (Sec. 303.421(b))

Location (Sec. 303.344(d)(3))

Method (Sec. 303.344(d)(2)(ii))

Native language (Sec. 303.401(b))

Personally identifiable (Sec. 303.401©)

Primary referral sources (Sec. 303.321(d)(3))

Profession or discipline (Sec. 303.361(a)(3))

Special definition of "aggregate amount" (Sec. 303.200(b)(1))

Special definition of "infants and toddlers" (Sec. 303.200(b)(2))

Special definition of "State" (Sec. 303.200(b)(3))

State approved or recognized certification, licensing, registration, or other comparable requirements (Sec. 303.361(a)(4))

Sec. 303.6 Act

As used in this part, "Act" means the Individuals with Disabilities Education Act. (Authority: 20 U.S.C. 1400)

Sec. 303.7 Children

As used in this part, "children" means "infants and toddlers with disabilities" as that term is defined in Sec. 303.16. (Authority: 20 U.S.C. 1432(5))

Sec. 303.8 Council

As used in this part, "Council" means the State Interagency Coordinating Council. (Authority: 20 U.S.C. 1432(2))

Sec. 303.9 Days

As used in this part, "days" means calendar days. (Authority: 20 U.S.C. 1431-1445)

Sec. 303.10 Developmental delay

As used in this part, "developmental delay," when used with respect to an individual residing in a State, has the meaning given to that term by a State under Sec. 303.300. (Authority: 20 U.S.C. 1432(3))

Sec. 303.11 Early intervention program

As used in this part, "early intervention program" means the total effort in a State that is directed at meeting the needs of children eligible under this part and their families. (Authority: 20 U.S.C. 1431-1445)

Sec. 303.12 Early intervention services

(a) General

As used in this part, early intervention services means services that—

(1) Are designed to meet the developmental needs of each child eligible under this part and the needs of the family related to enhancing the child's development;

(2) Are selected in collaboration with the parents;

(3) Are provided—

(i) Under public supervision;

(ii) By qualified personnel, as defined in Sec. 303.21, including the types of personnel listed in paragraph (e) of this section;

(iii) In conformity with an individualized family service plan; and

(iv) At no cost, unless, subject to Sec. 303.520(b)(3), Federal or State law provides for a system of payments by families, including a schedule of sliding fees; and

(4) Meet the standards of the State, including the requirements of this part.

(b) Natural environments

To the maximum extent appropriate to the needs of the child, early intervention services must be provided in natural environments, including the home and community settings in which children without disabilities participate.

(c) General role of service providers

To the extent appropriate, service providers in each area of early intervention services included in paragraph (d) of this section are responsible for—

(1) Consulting with parents, other service providers, and representatives of appropriate community agencies to ensure the effective provision of services in that area;

(2) Training parents and others regarding the provision of those services; and

(3) Participating in the multidisciplinary team's assessment of a child and the child's family, and in the development of integrated goals and outcomes for the individualized family service plan.

(d) Types of services; definitions

Following are types of services included under "early intervention services," and, if appropriate, definitions of those services:

(1) Assistive technology device means any item, piece of equipment, or product system, whether acquired commercially off the shelf, modified, or customized, that is used to increase, maintain, or improve the functional capabilities of children with disabilities. Assistive technology service means a service that directly assists a child with a disability in the selection, acquisition, or use of an assistive technology device.

Assistive technology services include—

(i) The evaluation of the needs of a child with a disability, including a functional evaluation of the child in the child's customary environment;

(ii) Purchasing, leasing, or otherwise providing for the acquisition of assistive technology devices by children with disabilities;

(iii) Selecting, designing, fitting, customizing, adapting, applying, maintaining, repairing, or replacing assistive technology devices;

(iv) Coordinating and using other therapies, interventions, or services with assistive technology devices, such as those associated with existing education and rehabilitation plans and programs;

(v) Training or technical assistance for a child with disabilities or, if appropriate, that child's family; and

(vi) Training or technical assistance for professionals (including individuals providing early intervention services) or other individuals who provide services to or are otherwise substantially involved in the major life functions of individuals with disabilities.

(2) Audiology includes—

(i) Identification of children with auditory impairment, using at risk criteria and appropriate audiologic screening techniques;

(ii) Determination of the range, nature, and degree of hearing loss and communication functions, by use of audiological evaluation procedures;

(iii) Referral for medical and other services necessary for the habilitation or rehabilitation of children with auditory impairment;

(iv) Provision of auditory training, aural rehabilitation, speech reading and listening device orientation and training, and other services;

(v) Provision of services for prevention of hearing loss; and

(vi) Determination of the child's need for individual amplification, including selecting, fitting, and dispensing appropriate listening and vibrotactile devices, and evaluating the effectiveness of those devices.

(3) Family training, counseling, and home visits means services provided, as appropriate, by social workers, psychologists, and other qualified personnel to assist the family of a child eligible under this part in understanding the special needs of the child and enhancing the child's development.

(4) Health services (See Sec. 303.13).

(5) Medical services only for diagnostic or evaluation purposes means services provided by a licensed physician to determine a child's developmental status and need for early intervention services.

(6) Nursing services includes—

(i) The assessment of health status for the purpose of providing nursing care, including the identification of patterns of human response to actual or potential health problems;

(ii) Provision of nursing care to prevent health problems, restore or improve functioning, and promote optimal health and development; and

(iii) Administration of medications, treatments, and regimens prescribed by a licensed physician.

(7) Nutrition services includes—

(i) Conducting individual assessments in—

(A) Nutritional history and dietary intake;

(B) Anthropometric, biochemical, and clinical variables;

(C) Feeding skills and feeding problems; and

(D) Food habits and food preferences;

(ii) Developing and monitoring appropriate plans to address the nutritional needs of children eligible under this part, based on the findings in paragraph (d)(7)(i) of this section; and

(iii) Making referrals to appropriate community resources to carry out nutrition goals.

(8) Occupational therapy includes services to address the functional needs of a child related to adaptive development, adaptive behavior and play, and sensory, motor, and postural development. These services are designed to improve the child's functional ability to perform tasks in home, school, and community settings, and include—

(i) Identification, assessment, and intervention;

(ii) Adaptation of the environment, and selection, design, and fabrication of assistive and orthotic devices to facilitate development and promote the acquisition of functional skills; and

(iii) Prevention or minimization of the impact of initial or future impairment, delay in development, or loss of functional ability.

(9) Physical therapy includes services to address the promotion of sensorimotor function through enhancement of musculoskeletal status, neurobehavioral organization, perceptual and motor development, cardiopulmonary status, and effective environmental adaptation. These services include—

(i) Screening, evaluation, and assessment of infants and toddlers to identify movement dysfunction;

(ii) Obtaining, interpreting, and integrating information appropriate to program planning to prevent, alleviate, or compensate for movement dysfunction and related functional problems; and

(iii) Providing individual and group services or treatment to prevent, alleviate, or compensate for movement dysfunction and related functional problems.

(10) Psychological services includes—

(i) Administering psychological and developmental tests and other assessment procedures;

(ii) Interpreting assessment results;

(iii) Obtaining, integrating, and interpreting information about child behavior, and child and family conditions related to learning, mental health, and development; and

(iv) Planning and managing a program of psychological services, including psychological counseling for children and parents, family counseling, consultation on child development, parent training, and education programs.

(11) Service coordination services means assistance and services provided by a service coordinator to a child eligible under this part and the child's family that are in addition to the functions and activities included under Sec. 303.23.

(12) Social work services includes—

(i) Making home visits to evaluate a child's living conditions and patterns of parent-child interaction;

(ii) Preparing a social or emotional developmental assessment of the child within the family context;

(iii) Providing individual and family-group counseling with parents and other family members, and appropriate social skill- building activities with the child and parents;

(iv) Working with those problems in a child's and family's living situation (home, community, and any center where early intervention services are provided) that affect the child's maximum utilization of early intervention services; and

(v) Identifying, mobilizing, and coordinating community resources and services to enable the child and family to receive maximum benefit from early intervention services.

(13) Special instruction includes—

    (i) The design of learning environments and activities that promote the child's acquisition of skills in a variety of developmental areas, including cognitive processes and social interaction;

    (ii) Curriculum planning, including the planned interaction of personnel, materials, and time and space, that leads to achieving the outcomes in the child's individualized family service plan;

    (iii) Providing families with information, skills, and support related to enhancing the skill development of the child; and

    (iv) Working with the child to enhance the child's development.

(14) Speech-language pathology includes—

    (i) Identification of children with communicative or oropharyngeal disorders and delays in development of communication skills, including the diagnosis and appraisal of specific disorders and delays in those skills;

    (ii) Referral for medical or other professional services necessary for the habilitation or rehabilitation of children with communicative or oropharyngeal disorders and delays in development of communication skills; and

    (iii) Provision of services for the habilitation, rehabilitation, or prevention of communicative or oropharyngeal disorders and delays in development of communication skills.

(15) Transportation and related costs includes the cost of travel (e.g., mileage, or travel by taxi, common carrier, or other means) and other costs (e.g., tolls and parking expenses) that are necessary to enable a child eligible under this part and the child's family to receive early intervention services.

(16) Vision services means—

    (i) Evaluation and assessment of visual functioning, including the diagnosis and appraisal of specific visual disorders, delays, and abilities;

    (ii) Referral for medical or other professional services necessary for the habilitation or rehabilitation of visual functioning disorders, or both; and

    (iii) Communication skills training, orientation and mobility training for all environments, visual training, independent living skills training, and additional training necessary to activate visual motor abilities.

(e) Qualified personnel

Early intervention services must be provided by qualified personnel, including—

    (1) Audiologists;

    (2) Family therapists;

    (3) Nurses;

    (4) Nutritionists;

    (5) Occupational therapists;

    (6) Orientation and mobility specialists;

    (7) Pediatricians and other physicians;

    (8) Physical therapists;

    (9) Psychologists;

    (10) Social workers;

    (11) Special educators; and

    (12) Speech and language pathologists. (Authority: 20 U.S.C. 1401(1) and (2); 1432(4))

Note: The lists of services in paragraph (d) and qualified personnel in paragraph (e) of this section are not exhaustive. Early intervention services may include such services as the provision of respite and other family support services. Qualified personnel may include such personnel as vision specialists, paraprofessionals, and parent-to-parent support personnel.

Sec. 303.13 Health services

    (a) As used in this part, health services means services necessary to enable a child to benefit from the other early intervention services under this part during the time that the child is receiving the other early intervention services.

    (b) The term includes—

        (1) Such services as clean intermittent catheterization, tracheostomy care, tube feeding, the changing of dressings or colostomy collection bags, and other health services; and

        (2) Consultation by physicians with other service providers concerning the special health care needs of eligible children that will need to be addressed in the course of providing other early intervention services.

    (c) The term does not include the following:

        (1) Services that are—

            (i) Surgical in nature (such as cleft palate surgery, surgery for club foot, or the shunting of hydrocephalus); or

            (ii) Purely medical in nature (such as hospitalization for management of congenital heart ailments, or the prescribing of medicine or drugs for any purpose).

(2) Devices necessary to control or treat a medical condition.

(3) Medical-health services (such as immunizations and regular "well-baby" care) that are routinely recommended for all children. (Authority: 20 U.S.C. 1432(4))

Note: The definition in this section distinguishes between the health services that are required under this part and the medical- health services that are not required. The IFSP requirements in subpart D of this part provide that, to the extent appropriate, these other medical-health services are to be included in the IFSP, along with the funding sources to be used in paying for the services or the steps that will be taken to secure the services through public or private sources. Identifying these services in the IFSP does not impose an obligation to provide the services if they are otherwise not required to be provided under this part. (See Sec. 303.344(e) and the note 3 following that section.)

Sec. 303.14 IFSP

As used in this part, IFSP means the individualized family service plan, as that term is defined in Sec. 303.340(b). (Authority: 20 U.S.C. 1436)

Sec. 303.15 Include; including

As used in this part, include or including means that the items named are not all of the possible items that are covered whether like or unlike the ones named. (Authority: 20 U.S.C. 1431-1445)

Sec. 303.16 Infants and toddlers with disabilities

(a) As used in this part, infants and toddlers with disabilities means individuals from birth through age two who need early intervention services because they—

(1) Are experiencing developmental delays, as measured by appropriate diagnostic instruments and procedures, in one or more of the following areas:

(i) Cognitive development.

(ii) Physical development, including vision and hearing.

(iii) Communication development.

(iv) Social or emotional development.

(v) Adaptive development; or

(2) Have a diagnosed physical or mental condition that has a high probability of resulting in developmental delay.

(b) The term may also include, at a State's discretion, children from birth through age two who are at risk of having substantial developmental delays if early intervention services are not provided. (Authority: 20 U.S.C. 1432(5))

Note 1: The phrase "a diagnosed physical or mental condition that has a high probability of resulting in developmental delay," as used in paragraph (a)(2) of this section, applies to a condition if it typically results in developmental delay. Examples of these conditions include chromosomal abnormalities; genetic or congenital disorders; severe sensory impairments, including hearing and vision; inborn errors of metabolism; disorders reflecting disturbance of the development of the nervous system; congenital infections; disorders secondary to exposure to toxic substances, including fetal alcohol syndrome; and severe attachment disorders.

Note 2: With respect to paragraph (b) of this section, children who are at risk may be eligible under this part if a State elects to extend services to that population, even though they have not been identified as disabled. Under this provision, States have the authority to define who would be "at risk of having substantial developmental delays if early intervention services are not provided." In defining the "at risk" population, States may include well-known biological and environmental factors that can be identified and that place infants and toddlers "at risk" for developmental delay. Commonly cited factors include low birth weight, respiratory distress as a newborn, lack of oxygen, brain hemorrhage, infection, nutritional deprivation, and a history of abuse or neglect. It should be noted that "at risk" factors do not predict the presence of a barrier to development, but they may indicate children who are at higher risk of developmental delay than children without these problems.

Sec. 303.17 Multidisciplinary

As used in this part, multidisciplinary means the involvement of two or more disciplines or professions in the provision of integrated and coordinated services, including evaluation and assessment activities in Sec. 303.322 and development of the IFSP in Sec. 303.342. (Authority: 20 U.S.C. 1435(a)(3), 1436(a))

Sec. 303.18 Natural environments

As used in this part, natural environments means settings that are natural or normal for the child's age peers who have no disabilities. (Authority: 20 U.S.C. 1435 and 1436)

Sec. 303.19 Parent

(a) General. As used in this part, "parent" means —

(1) A natural or adoptive parent of a child;

(2) A guardian;

(3) A person acting in the place of a parent (such as a grandparent or stepparent with whom a child lives, or a person who is legally responsible for the child's welfare); or

(4) A surrogate parent who has been assigned in accordance with Sec. 303.406.

(b) Foster parent. Unless State law prohibits a foster parent from acting as a parent, a State may allow a foster parent to act as a parent under Part C of the Act if -

(1) The natural parents' authority to make the decisions required of parents under the Act has been extinguished under State law; and

(2) The foster parent -

(i) Has an ongoing, long-term parental relationship with the child;

(ii) Is willing to make the decisions required of parents under the Act; and

(iii) Has no interest that would conflict with the interests of the child. (Authority: 20 U.S.C. 14301(19), 1431-1445)

Sec. 303.20 Policies

(a) As used in this part, policies means State statutes, regulations, Governor's orders, directives by the lead agency, or other written documents that represent the State's position concerning any matter covered under this part.

(b) State policies include—

(1) A State's commitment to maintain the statewide system (see Sec. 303.140);

(2) A State's eligibility criteria and procedures (see Sec. 303.300);

(3) A statement that, consistent with Sec. 303.520(b), provides that services under this part will be provided at no cost to parents, except where a system of payments is provided for under Federal or State law.

(4) A State's standards for personnel who provide services to children eligible under this part (see Sec. 303.361);

(5) A State's position and procedures related to contracting or making other arrangements with service providers under subpart F of this part; and

(6) Other positions that the State has adopted related to implementing any of the other requirements under this part. (Authority: 20 U.S.C. 1431-1445)

Sec. 303.21 Public agency

As used in this part, public agency includes the lead agency and any other political subdivision of the State that is responsible for providing early intervention services to children eligible under this part and their families. (Authority: 20 U.S.C. 1432(4))

Sec. 303.22 Qualified

As used in this part, qualified means that a person has met State approved or recognized certification, licensing, registration, or other comparable requirements that apply to the area in which the person is providing early intervention services. (Authority: 20 U.S.C. 1432(4))

Note: These regulations contain the following provisions relating to a State's responsibility to ensure that personnel are qualified to provide early intervention services:

1. Sec. 303.12(a)(4) provides that early intervention services must meet State standards. This provision implements a requirement that is similar to a longstanding provision under Part B of the Act (i.e., that the State educational agency establish standards and ensure that those standards are currently met for all programs providing special education and related services).

2. Sec. 303.12(a)(3)(ii) provides that early intervention services must be provided by qualified personnel.

3. Sec. 303.361(b) requires statewide systems to have policies and procedures relating to personnel standards.

Sec. 303.23 Service coordination (case management)

(a) General

(1) As used in this part, except in Sec. 303.12(d)(11), service coordination means the activities carried out by a service coordinator to assist and enable a child eligible under this part and the child's family to receive the rights, procedural safeguards, and services that are authorized to be provided under the State's early intervention program.

(2) Each child eligible under this part and the child's family must be provided with one service coordinator who is responsible for—

(i) Coordinating all services across agency lines; and

(ii) Serving as the single point of contact in helping parents to obtain the services and assistance they need.

(3) Service coordination is an active, ongoing process that involves—

(i) Assisting parents of eligible children in gaining access to the early intervention services and other services identified in the individualized family service plan;

(ii) Coordinating the provision of early intervention services and other services (such as medical services for other than diagnostic and evaluation purposes) that the child needs or is being provided;

(iii) Facilitating the timely delivery of available services; and

(iv) Continuously seeking the appropriate services and situations necessary to benefit the development of each child being served for the duration of the child's eligibility.

(b) Specific service coordination activities

Service coordination activities include—

(1) Coordinating the performance of evaluations and assessments;

(2) Facilitating and participating in the development, review, and evaluation of individualized family service plans;

(3) Assisting families in identifying available service providers;

(4) Coordinating and monitoring the delivery of available services;

(5) Informing families of the availability of advocacy services;

(6) Coordinating with medical and health providers; and

(7) Facilitating the development of a transition plan to preschool services, if appropriate.

(c) Employment and assignment of service coordinators

(1) Service coordinators may be employed or assigned in any way that is permitted under State law, so long as it is consistent with the requirements of this part.

(2) A State's policies and procedures for implementing the statewide system of early intervention services must be designed and implemented to ensure that service coordinators are able to effectively carry out on an interagency basis the functions and services listed under paragraphs (a) and (b) of this section.

(d) Qualifications of service coordinators

Service coordinators must be persons who, consistent with Sec. 303.344(g), have demonstrated knowledge and understanding about—

(1) Infants and toddlers who are eligible under this part;

(2) Part H of the Act and the regulations in this part; and

(3) The nature and scope of services available under the State's early intervention program, the system of payments for services in the State, and other pertinent information. (Authority: 20 U.S.C. 1401(27))

Note 1: If States have existing service coordination systems, the States may use or adapt those systems, so long as they are consistent with the requirements of this part.

Note 2: The legislative history of the 1991 amendments to the Act indicates that the use of the term "service coordination" was not intended to affect the authority to seek reimbursement for services provided under Medicaid or any other legislation that makes reference to "case management" services. See H.R. REP. NO. 198, 102d Cong., 1st Sess. 12 (1991); S. REP. NO. 84, 102d Cong., 1st Sess. 20 (1991).

Sec. 303.24 State

Except as provided in Sec. 303.200(b)(3), State means each of the 50 States, the Commonwealth of Puerto Rico, the District of Columbia, and the jurisdictions of Guam, American Samoa, the Virgin Islands, the Commonwealth of the Northern Mariana Islands. (Authority: 20 U.S.C. 1431-1445)

Sec. 303.25 EDGAR definitions that apply

The following terms used in this part are defined in 34 CFR 77.1:

Applicant

Award

Contract

Department

EDGAR

Fiscal year

Grant

Grantee

Grant period

Private

Public

Secretary

(Authority: 20 U.S.C. 1471-1485)

SUBPART B—STATE APPLICATION FOR A GRANT

GENERAL REQUIREMENTS

Sec. 303.100 Conditions of assistance

(a) In order to receive funds under this part for any fiscal year, a State must have—

(1) An approved application that contains the information required in this part, including—

(i) The information required in Secs. 303.140 through 303.148; and

(ii) The information required in Secs. 303.161 through 303.176; and

(2) The statement of assurances required under Secs. 303.120 through 303.128, on file with the Secretary.

(b) If a State has on file with the Secretary a policy, procedure, or assurance that demonstrates that the State meets an application requirement, including any policy or procedure filed under this part before July 1, 1998, that meets such a requirement, the Secretary considers the State to have met that requirement for purposes of receiving a grant under this part.

(c) An application that meets the requirements of this part remains in effect until the State submits to the Secretary modifications of that application.

(d) The Secretary may require a State to modify its application under this part to the extent necessary to ensure the State's compliance with this part if—

(1) An amendment is made to the Act, or to a regulation under this part;

(2) A new interpretation is made of the Act by a Federal court or the State's highest court; or

(3) An official finding of noncompliance with Federal law or regulations is made with respect to the State. (Authority: 20 U.S.C. 1434 and 1437)

Sec. 303.101 How the Secretary disapproves a State's application or statement of assurances

The Secretary follows the procedures in 34 CFR 300.581 through 300.586 before disapproving a State's application or statement of assurances submitted under this part. (Authority: 20 U.S.C. 1478)

PUBLIC PARTICIPATION

Sec. 303.110 General requirements and timelines for public participation

(a) Before submitting to the Secretary its application under this part, and before adopting a new or revised policy that is not in its current application, a State shall—

(1) Publish the application or policy in a manner that will ensure circulation throughout the State for at least a 60-day period, with an opportunity for comment on the application or policy for at least 30 days during that period;

(2) Hold public hearings on the application or policy during the 60-day period required in paragraph (a)(1) of this section; and

(3) Provide adequate notice of the hearings required in paragraph (a)(2) of this section at least 30 days before the dates that the hearings are conducted.

(b) A State may request the Secretary to waive compliance with the timelines in paragraph (a) of this section. The Secretary grants the request if the State demonstrates that—

(1) There are circumstances that would warrant such an exception; and

(2) The timelines that will be followed provide an adequate opportunity for public participation and comment. (Authority: 20 U.S.C. 1437(a)(3))

Sec. 303.111 Notice of public hearings and opportunity to comment

The notice required in Sec. 303.110(a)(3) must—

(a) Be published in newspapers or announced in other media, or both, with coverage adequate to notify the general public, including individuals with disabilities and parents of infants and toddlers with disabilities, throughout the State about the hearings and opportunity to comment on the application or policy; and

(b) Be in sufficient detail to inform the public about—

(1) The purpose and scope of the State application or policy, and its relationship to Part C of the Act;

(2) The length of the comment period and the date, time, and location of each hearing; and

(3) The procedures for providing oral comments or submitting written comments. (Authority: 20 U.S.C. 1437(a)(7))

Sec. 303.112 Public hearings

Each State shall hold public hearings in a sufficient number and at times and places that afford interested parties throughout the State a reasonable opportunity to participate. (Authority: 20 U.S.C. 1478(a)(4))

Sec. 303.113 Reviewing public comments received

(a) Review of comments

Before adopting its application, and before the adoption of a new or revised policy not in the application, the lead agency shall—

(1) Review and consider all public comments; and

(2) Make any modifications it deems necessary in the application or policy.

(b) Submission to the Secretary

In submitting the State's application or policy to the Secretary, the lead agency shall include copies of news releases, advertisements, and announcements used to provide notice to the general public, including individuals with disabilities and parents of infants and toddlers with disabilities. (Authority: 20 U.S.C. 1437(a)(7))

STATEMENT OF ASSURANCES

Sec. 303.120 General

(a) A State's statement of assurances must contain the information required in Secs. 303.121 through 303.128.

(b) Unless otherwise required by the Secretary, the statement is submitted only once, and remains in effect throughout the term of a State's participation under this part.

(c) A State may submit a revised statement of assurances if the statement is consistent with the requirements in Secs. 303.121 through 303.128. (Authority: 20 U.S.C. 1437(b))

Sec. 303.121 Reports and records

The statement must provide for—

(a) Making reports in such form and containing such information as the Secretary may require; and

(b) Keeping such records and affording such access to those records as the Secretary may find necessary to assure compliance with the requirements of this part, the correctness and verification of reports, and the proper disbursement of funds provided under this part. (Authority: 20 U.S.C. 1437(b)(4))

Sec. 303.122 Control of funds and property

The statement must provide assurance satisfactory to the Secretary that—

(a) The control of funds provided under this part, and title to property acquired with those funds, will be in a public agency for the uses and purposes provided in this part; and

(b) A public agency will administer the funds and property. (Authority: 20 U.S.C. 1437(b)(3))

Sec. 303.123 Prohibition against commingling

The statement must include an assurance satisfactory to the Secretary that funds made available under this part will not be commingled with State funds. (Authority: 20 U.S.C. 1437(b)(5)(A))

Note: As used in this part, commingle means depositing or recording funds in a general account without the ability to identify each specific source of funds for any expenditure. Under that general definition, it is clear that commingling is prohibited. However, to the extent that the funds from each of a series of Federal, State, local, and private funding sources can be identified-with a clear audit trail for each source-it is appropriate for those funds to be consolidated for carrying out a common purpose. In fact, a State may find it essential to set out a funding plan that incorporates, and accounts for, all sources of funds that can be targeted on a given activity or function related to the State's early intervention program. Thus, the assurance in this section is satisfied by the use of an accounting system that includes an "audit trail" of the expenditure of funds awarded under this part. Separate bank accounts are not required.

Sec. 303.124 Prohibition against supplanting

(a) The statement must include an assurance satisfactory to the Secretary that Federal funds made available under this part will be used to supplement the level of State and local funds expended for children eligible under this part and their families and in no case to supplant those State and local funds.

(b) To meet the requirement in paragraph (a) of this section, the total amount of State and local funds budgeted for expenditures in the current fiscal year for early intervention services for children eligible under this part and their families must be at least equal to the total amount of State and local funds actually expended for early intervention services for these children and their families in the most recent preceding fiscal year for which the information is available. Allowance may be made for—

(1) Decreases in the number of children who are eligible to receive early intervention services under this part; and

(2) Unusually large amounts of funds expended for such long- term purposes as the acquisition of equipment and the construction of facilities. (Authority: 20 U.S.C. 1437(b)(5)(B))

Sec. 303.125 Fiscal control

The statement must provide assurance satisfactory to the Secretary that such fiscal control and fund accounting procedures will be adopted as may be necessary to assure proper disbursement of, and accounting for, Federal funds paid under this part.
(Authority: 20 U.S.C. 1437(b)(6))

Sec. 303.126 Payor of last resort

The statement must include an assurance satisfactory to the Secretary that the State will comply with the provisions in Sec. 303.527, including the requirements on—
(a) Nonsubstitution of funds; and
(b) Non-reduction of other benefits. (Authority: 20 U.S.C. 1437(b)(2))

Sec. 303.127 Assurance regarding expenditure of funds

The statement must include an assurance satisfactory to the Secretary that the funds paid to the State under this part will be expended in accordance with the provisions of this part, including the requirements in Sec. 303.3.
(Authority: 20 U.S.C. 1437(b)(1))

Sec. 303.128 Traditionally underserved groups

The statement must include an assurance satisfactory to the Secretary that policies and practices have been adopted to ensure—
(a) That traditionally underserved groups, including minority, low-income, and rural families, are meaningfully involved in the planning and implementation of all the requirements of this part; and
(b) That these families have access to culturally competent services within their local geographical areas. (Authority: 20 U.S.C. 1437(b)(7))

GENERAL REQUIREMENTS FOR A STATE APPLICATION

Sec. 303.140 General

A State's application under this part must contain information and assurances demonstrating to the satisfaction of the Secretary that—
(a) The statewide system of early intervention services required in this part is in effect; and
(b) A State policy is in effect that ensures that appropriate early intervention services are available to all infants and toddlers with disabilities and their families, including Indian infants and toddlers with disabilities in the State. (Authority: 20 U.S.C. 1434 and 1435(a)(2))

Sec. 303.141 Information about the Council

Each application must include information demonstrating that the State has established a State Interagency Coordinating Council that meets the requirements of Subpart G of this part. (Authority: 20 U.S.C. 1437(a)(3))

Sec. 303.142 Designation of lead agency

Each application must include a designation of the lead agency in the State that will be responsible for the administration of funds provided under this part. (Authority: 20 U.S.C. 1437(a)(1))

Sec. 303.143 Designation regarding financial responsibility

Each application must include a designation by the State of an individual or entity responsible for assigning financial responsibility among appropriate agencies. (Authority: 20 U.S.C. 1437(a)(2))

Sec. 303.144 Assurance regarding use of funds

Each application must include an assurance that funds received under this part will be used to assist the State to maintain and implement the statewide system required under subparts D through F of this part. (Authority: 20 U.S.C. 1475, 1437(a)(3))

Sec. 303.145 Description of use of funds

(a) General

Each application must include a description of how a State proposes to use its funds under this part for the fiscal year or years covered by the application. The description must be presented separately for the lead agency and the Council, and include the information required in paragraphs (b) through (e) of this section.

(b) Administrative positions

Each application must include—

(1) A list of administrative positions, with salaries, and a description of the duties for each person whose salary is paid in whole or in part with funds awarded under this part; and

(2) For each position, the percentage of salary paid with those funds.

(c) Maintenance and implementation activities

Each application must include—

(1) A description of the nature and scope of each major activity to be carried out under this part in maintaining and implementing the statewide system of early intervention services; and

(2) The approximate amount of funds to be spent for each activity.

(d) Direct services

(1) Each application must include a description of any direct services that the State expects to provide to eligible children and their families with funds under this part, including a description of any services provided to at-risk infants and toddlers as defined in Sec. 303.16(b), and their families, consistent with Secs. 303.521 and 303.527.

(2) The description must include information about each type of service to be provided, including—

(i) A summary of the methods to be used to provide the service (e.g., contracts or other arrangements with specified public or private organizations); and

(ii) The approximate amount of funds under this part to be used for the service.

(e) At-risk infants and toddlers

For any State that does not provide direct services for at-risk infants and toddlers described in paragraph (d)(1) of this section, but chooses to use funds as described in Sec. 303.3(e), each application must include a description of how those funds will be used.

(f) Activities by other agencies

If other agencies are to receive funds under this part, the application must include—

(1) The name of each agency expected to receive funds;

(2) The approximate amount of funds each agency will receive; and

(3) A summary of the purposes for which the funds will be used. (Authority: 20 U.S.C. 1437(a)(3) and (a)(5))

Sec. 303.146 Information about public participation

Each application must include the information on public participation that is required in Sec. 303.113(b). (Authority: 20 U.S.C. 1437(a)(7))

Sec. 303.147 Services to all geographic areas

Each application must include a description of the procedure used to ensure that resources are made available under this part for all geographic areas within the State. (Authority: 20 U.S.C. 1437(a)(6))

Sec. 303.148 Transition to preschool programs

Each application must include a description of the policies and procedures to be used to ensure a smooth transition for children receiving early intervention services under this part to preschool or other appropriate services, including—

(a) A description of how the families will be included in the transition plans;

(b) A description of how the lead agency under this part will—

(1) Notify the local educational agency for the area in which the child resides that the child will shortly reach the age of eligibility for preschool services under Part B of the Act, as determined in accordance with State law;

(2)(i) In the case of a child who may be eligible for preschool services under Part B of the Act, with the approval of the family of the child, convene a conference among the lead agency, the family, and the local educational agency at least 90 days, and at the discretion of the parties, up to 6 months, before the child is eligible for the preschool services, to discuss any services that the child may receive; or

(ii) In the case of a child who may not be eligible for preschool services under Part B of the Act, with the approval of the family, make reasonable efforts to convene a conference among the lead agency, the family, and providers of other appropriate services for children who are not eligible for preschool services under Part B, to discuss the appropriate services that the child may receive;

(3) Review the child's program options for the period from the child's third birthday through the remainder of the school year; and

(4) Establish a transition plan; and

(c) If the State educational agency, which is responsible for administering preschool programs under Part B of the Act, is not the lead agency under this part, an interagency agreement between the two agencies to ensure coordination on transition matters. (Authority: 20 U.S.C. 1437(a)(8))

Note 1: Among the matters that should be considered in developing policies and procedures to ensure a smooth transition of children from one program to the other are the following:

The financial responsibilities of all appropriate agencies.

The responsibility for performing evaluations of children.

The development and implementation of an individualized education program ("IEP") or an individualized family service plan ("IFSP") for each child, consistent with the requirements of law (see Sec. 303.344(h) and Sec. 612(a)(9) of the Act).

The coordination of communication between agencies and the child's family.

The mechanisms to ensure the uninterrupted provision of appropriate services to the child.

Sec. 303.149-.155   [REMOVED]

COMPONENTS OF A STATEWIDE SYSTEM—APPLICATION REQUIREMENTS

Sec. 303.160 Minimum components of a statewide system

Each application must address the minimum components of a statewide system of coordinated, comprehensive, multidisciplinary, interagency programs providing appropriate early intervention services to all infants and toddlers with disabilities and their families, including Indian infants and toddlers with disabilities and their families residing on a reservation geographically located in the State. The minimum components of a statewide system are described in Secs. 303.161 through 303.176. (Authority: 20 U.S.C. 1435(a), 1437(a)(9))

Sec. 303.161 State definition of developmental delay

Each application must include the State's definition of "developmental delay," as described in Sec. 303.300. (Authority: 20 U.S.C. 1435(b)(1))

Sec. 303.162 Central directory

Each application must include information and assurances demonstrating to the satisfaction of the Secretary that the State has developed a central directory of information that meets the requirements in Sec. 303.301.(Authority: 20 U.S.C. 1435(b)(7))

Sec. 303.163 [RESERVED]

Sec. 303.164 Public awareness program

Each application must include information and assurances demonstrating to the satisfaction of the Secretary that the State has established a public awareness program that meets the requirements in Sec. 303.320. (Authority: 20 U.S.C. 1435(b)(6))

Sec. 303.165 Comprehensive child find system

Each application must include—

(a) The policies and procedures required in Sec. 303.321(b);

(b) Information demonstrating that the requirements on coordination in Sec. 303.321(c) are met;

(c) The referral procedures required in Sec. 303.321(d), and either—

(1) A description of how the referral sources are informed about the procedures; or

(2) A copy of any memorandum or other document used by the lead agency to transmit the procedures to the referral sources; and

(d) The timelines in Sec. 303.321(e). (Authority: 20 U.S.C. 1435(b)(5))

Sec. 303.166 Evaluation, assessment, and nondiscriminatory procedures

Each application must include information to demonstrate that the requirements in Secs. 303.322 and 303.323 are met. (Authority: 20 U.S.C. 1435(a)(3); 1436(a)(1), (d)(2), and (d)(3))

Sec. 303.167 Individualized family service plans

Each application must include—

(a) An assurance that a current IFSP is in effect and implemented for each eligible child and the child's family;

(b) Information demonstrating that—

(1) The State's procedures for developing, reviewing, and evaluating IFSPs are consistent with the requirements in Secs. 303.340, 303.342, 303.343 and 303.345; and

(2) The content of IFSPs used in the State is consistent with the requirements in Sec. 303.344; and

(c) Policies and procedures to ensure that—

(1) To the maximum extent appropriate, early intervention services are provided in natural environments; and

(2) The provision of early intervention services for any infant or toddler occurs in a setting other than a natural environment only if early intervention cannot be achieved satisfactorily for the infant or toddler in a natural environment. (Authority: 20 U.S.C. 1476(b)(4), 1477(d))

Sec. 303.168 Comprehensive system of personnel development (CSPD)

Each application must include information to show that the requirements in Sec. 303.360(b) are met. (Authority: 20 U.S.C. 1435(a)(8))

Sec. 303.169 Personnel standards

(a) Each application must include policies and procedures that are consistent with the requirements in Sec. 303.361. (Authority: 20 U.S.C. 1435(a)(9))

Sec. 303.170 Procedural safeguards

Each application must include procedural safeguards that—

(a) Are consistent with Secs. 303.400 through 303.406, 303.419 through 303.425 and 303.460; and

(b) Incorporate either—

(1) The due process procedures in 34 CFR 300.506 through 300.512; or

(2) The procedures that the State has developed to meet the requirements in Secs. 303.419, 303.420(b) and 303.421 through 303.425. (Authority: 20 U.S.C. 1476(6)(12))

Sec. 303.171 Supervision and monitoring of programs

Each application must include information to show that the requirements in Sec. 303.501 are met. (Authority: 20. U.S.C. 1435(a)(10)(A))

Sec. 303.172 Lead agency procedures for resolving complaints

Each application must include procedures that are consistent with the requirements in Secs. 303.510 through 303.512. (Authority: 20 U.S.C. 1435(a)(10))

Sec. 303.173 Policies and procedures related to financial matters

Each application must include—

(a) Funding policies that meet the requirements in Secs. 303.520 and 303.521;

(b) Information about funding sources, as required in Sec. 303.522;

(c) Procedures to ensure the timely delivery of services, in accordance with Sec. 303.525; and

(d) A procedure related to the timely reimbursement of funds under this part, in accordance with Secs. 303.527(b) and 303.528. (Authority: 20 U.S.C. 1435(a)(10)(D) and (E), 1435(a)(12), 1440)

Sec. 303.174 Interagency agreements; resolution of individual disputes

Each application must include—

(a) A copy of each interagency agreement that has been developed under Sec. 303.523; and

(b) Information to show that the requirements in Sec. 303.524 are met. (Authority: 20 U.S.C. 1435(a)(10)(E) and (F))

Sec. 303.175 Policy for contracting or otherwise arranging for services

Each application must include a policy that meets the requirements in Sec. 303.526. (Authority: 20 U.S.C. 1435(a)(11))

Sec. 303.176 Data collection

Each application must include procedures that meet the requirements in Sec. 303.540. (Authority: 20 U.S.C. 1435(a)(14))

PARTICIPATION BY THE SECRETARY OF THE INTERIOR

Sec. 303.180 Payments to the Secretary of the Interior for Indian tribes and tribal organizations

(a) The Secretary makes payments to the Secretary of the Interior for the coordination of assistance in the provision of early intervention services by the States to infants and toddlers with disabilities and their families on reservations served by elementary and secondary schools for Indian children operated or funded by the Department of the Interior.

(b)

(1) The Secretary of the Interior shall distribute payments under this part to tribes or tribal organizations (as defined under Sec. 4 of the Indian Self-Determination and Education Assistance Act), or combinations of those entities, in accordance with Sec. 684(b) of the Act.

(2) A tribe or tribal organization is eligible to receive a payment under this section if the tribe is on a reservation that is served by an elementary or secondary school operated or funded by the Bureau of Indian Affairs ("BIA").

(c) (1) Within 90 days after the end of each fiscal year the Secretary of the Interior shall provide the Secretary with a report on the payments distributed under this section.

(2) The report must include—

(i) The name of each tribe, tribal organization, or combination of those entities that received a payment for the fiscal year;

(ii) The amount of each payment; and

(iii) The date of each payment. (Authority: 20 U.S.C. 1443(b))

SUBPART C—PROCEDURES FOR MAKING GRANTS TO STATES

Sec. 303.200 Formula for State allocations

(a) For each fiscal year, from the aggregate amount of funds available under this part for distribution to the States, the Secretary allots to each State an amount that bears the same ratio to the aggregate amount as the number of infants and toddlers in the State bears to the number of infants and toddlers in all States.

(b) For the purpose of allotting funds to the States under paragraph (a) of this section—

(1) Aggregate amount means the amount available for distribution to the States after the Secretary determines the amount of payments to be made to the Secretary of the Interior under Sec. 303.203 and to the jurisdictions under Sec. 303.204;

(2) Infants and toddlers means children from birth through age two in the general population, based on the most recent satisfactory data as determined by the Secretary; and

(3) State means each of the 50 States, the District of Columbia, and the Commonwealth of Puerto Rico. (Authority: 20 U.S.C. 1443(C))

Sec. 303.201 Distribution of allotments from non-participating States

If a State elects not to receive its allotment, the Secretary reallots those funds among the remaining States, in accordance with Sec. 303.200(a). (Authority: 20 U.S.C. 1443(d))

Sec. 303.202 Minimum grant that a State may receive

No State receives less than 0.5 percent of the aggregate amount available under Sec. 303.200 or $500,000, whichever is greater. (Authority: 20 U.S.C. 1443(C)(2))

Sec. 303.203 Payments to the Secretary of the Interior

The amount of the payment to the Secretary of the Interior under Sec. 303.180 for any fiscal year is 1.25 percent of the aggregate amount available to States after the Secretary determines the amount of payments to be made to the jurisdictions under Sec. 303.204. (Authority: 20 U.S.C. 1443(b))

Sec. 303.204 Payments to the jurisdictions

(a) From the sums appropriated to carry out this part for any fiscal year, the Secretary may reserve up to 1 percent for payments to the jurisdictions listed in Sec. 303.2 in accordance with their respective needs.

(b) The provisions of Pub. L. 95-134, permitting the consolidation of grants to the outlying areas, do not apply to funds provided under paragraph (a) of this section. (Authority: 20 U.S.C. 1443(a))

Sec. 303.205 [REMOVED]

SUBPART D—PROGRAM AND SERVICE COMPONENTS OF A STATEWIDE SYSTEM OF EARLY INTERVENTION SERVICES

GENERAL

Sec. 303.300 State eligibility criteria and procedures

Each statewide system of early intervention services must include the eligibility criteria and procedures, consistent with Sec. 303.16, that will be used by the State in carrying out programs under this part.

(a) The State shall define developmental delay by—

(1) Describing, for each of the areas listed in Sec. 303.16(a)(1), the procedures, including the use of informed clinical opinion, that will be used to measure a child's development; and

(2) Stating the levels of functioning or other criteria that constitute a developmental delay in each of those areas.

(b) The State shall describe the criteria and procedures, including the use of informed clinical opinion, that will be used to determine the existence of a condition that has a high probability of resulting in developmental delay under Sec. 303.16(a)(2).

(c) If the State elects to include in its system children who are at risk under Sec. 303.16(b), the State shall describe the criteria and procedures, including the use of informed clinical opinion, that will be used to identify those children. (Authority: 20 U.S.C. 1432(5), 1435(a)(1))

Note: Under this section and Sec. 303.322(C)(2), States are required to ensure that informed clinical opinion is used in determining a child's eligibility under this part. Informed clinical opinion is especially important if there are no standardized measures, or if the standardized procedures are not appropriate for a given age or developmental area. If a given standardized procedure is considered to be appropriate, a State's criteria could include percentiles or percentages of levels of functioning on standardized measures.

Sec. 303.301 Central directory

(a) Each system must include a central directory of information about—

(1) Public and private early intervention services, resources, and experts available in the State;

(2) Research and demonstration projects being conducted in the State; and

(3) Professional and other groups that provide assistance to children eligible under this part and their families.

(b) The information required in paragraph (a) of this section must be in sufficient detail to—

(1) Ensure that the general public will be able to determine the nature and scope of the services and assistance available from each of the sources listed in the directory; and

(2) Enable the parent of a child eligible under this part to contact, by telephone or letter, any of the sources listed in the directory.

(c) The central directory must be—

(1) Updated at least annually; and

(2) Accessible to the general public.

(d) To meet the requirements in paragraph © (2) of this section, the lead agency shall arrange for copies of the directory to be available—

(1) In each geographic region of the State, including rural areas; and

(2) In places and a manner that ensure accessibility by persons with disabilities. (Authority: 20 U.S.C. 1435(a)(7))

Note: Examples of appropriate groups that provide assistance to eligible children and their families include parent support groups and advocate associations.

Sec. 303.302 [REMOVED]

IDENTIFICATION AND EVALUATION

Sec. 303.320 Public awareness program

Each system must include a public awareness program that focuses on the early identification of children who are eligible to receive early intervention services under this part and includes the preparation and dissemination by the lead agency to all primary referral sources, especially hospitals and physicians, of materials for parents on the availability of early intervention services. The public awareness program must provide for informing the public about—

(a) The State's early intervention program;

(b) The child find system, including—

(1) The purpose and scope of the system;

(2) How to make referrals; and

(3) How to gain access to a comprehensive, multidisciplinary evaluation and other early intervention services; and

(c) The central directory. (Authority: 20 U.S.C. 1435(a)(6))

Note 1: An effective public awareness program is one that does the following:

1. Provides a continuous, ongoing effort that is in effect throughout the State, including rural areas;

2. Provides for the involvement of, and communication with, major organizations throughout the State that have a direct interest in this part, including public agencies at the State and local level, private providers, professional associations, parent groups, advocate associations, and other organizations;

3. Has coverage broad enough to reach the general public, including those who have disabilities; and

4. Includes a variety of methods for informing the public about the provisions of this part.

Note 2: Examples of methods for informing the general public about the provisions of this part include: (1) Use of television, radio, and newspaper releases, (2) pamphlets and posters displayed in doctors' offices, hospitals, and other appropriate locations, and (3) the use of a toll-free telephone service.

Sec. 303.321 Comprehensive child find system

(a) General

(1) Each system must include a comprehensive child find system that is consistent with Part B of the Act (see 34 CFR 300.128), and meets the requirements of paragraphs (b) through (e) of this section.

(2) The lead agency, with the advice and assistance of the Council, shall be responsible for implementing the child find system.

(b) Procedures

The child find system must include the policies and procedures that the State will follow to ensure that—

(1) All infants and toddlers in the State who are eligible for services under this part are identified, located, and evaluated; and

(2) An effective method is developed and implemented to determine which children are receiving needed early intervention services.

(c) Coordination

(1) The lead agency, with the assistance of the Council, shall ensure that the child find system under this part is coordinated with all other major efforts to locate and identify children conducted by other State agencies responsible for administering the various education, health, and social service programs relevant to this part, tribes and tribal organizations that receive payments under this part, and other tribes and tribal organizations as appropriate, including efforts in the—

(i) Program authorized under Part B of the Act;

(ii) Maternal and Child Health program under Title V of the Social Security Act;

(iii) Early Periodic Screening, Diagnosis and Treatment (EPSDT) program under Title XIX of the Social Security Act;

(iv) Developmental Disabilities Assistance and Bill of Rights Act;

(v) Head Start Act; and

(vi) Supplemental Security Income program under Title XVI of the Social Security Act.

(2) The lead agency, with the advice and assistance of the Council, shall take steps to ensure that—

(i) There will not be unnecessary duplication of effort by the various agencies involved in the State's child find system under this part; and

(ii) The State will make use of the resources available through each public agency in the State to implement the child find system in an effective manner.

(d) Referral procedures

(1) The child find system must include procedures for use by primary referral sources for referring a child to the appropriate public agency within the system for—

(i) Evaluation and assessment, in accordance with Secs. 303.322 and 303.323; or

(ii) As appropriate, the provision of services, in accordance with Sec. 303.342(a) or Sec. 303.345.

(2) The procedures required in paragraph (b)(1) of this section must—

(i) Provide for an effective method of making referrals by primary referral sources;

(ii) Ensure that referrals are made no more than two working days after a child has been identified; and

(iii) Include procedures for determining the extent to which primary referral sources, especially hospitals and physicians, disseminate the information, as described in Sec. 303.320, prepared by the lead agency on the availability of early intervention services to parents of infants and toddlers with disabilities.

(3) As used in paragraph (d)(1) of this section, primary referral sources includes—

(i) Hospitals, including prenatal and postnatal care facilities;

(ii) Physicians;

(iii) Parents;

(iv) Day care programs;

(v) Local educational agencies;

(vi) Public health facilities;

(vii) Other social service agencies; and

(viii) Other health care providers.

(e) Timelines for public agencies to act on referrals

(1) Once the public agency receives a referral, it shall appoint a service coordinator as soon as possible.

(2) Within 45 days after it recives a referral, the public agency shall—

(i) Complete the evaluation and assessment activities in Sec. 303.322; and

(ii) Hold an IFSP meeting, in accordance with Sec. 303.342. (Authority: 20 U.S.C. 1432(4)(E)(vii), 1435(a)(5))

Note: In developing the child find system under this part, States should consider (1) tracking systems based on high-risk conditions at birth, and (2) other activities that are being conducted by various agencies or organizations in the State.

Sec. 303.322 Evaluation and Assessment

(a) General

(1) Each system must include the performance of a timely, comprehensive, multidisciplinary evaluation of each child, birth through age two, referred for evaluation, and a family-directed identification of the needs of each child's family to appropriately assist n the development of the child.

(2) The lead agency shall be responsible for ensuring that the requirements of this section are implemented by all affected public agencies and service providers in the State.

(b) Definitions of evaluation and assessment

As used in this part—

(1) **Evaluation** means the procedures used by appropriate qualified personnel to determine a child's initial and continuing eligibility under this part, consistent with the definition of "infants and toddlers with disabilities" in Sec. 303.16, including determining the status of the child in each of the developmental areas in paragraph ©(3)(ii) of this section.

(2) **Assessment** means the ongoing procedures used by appropriate qualified personnel throughout the period of a child's eligibility under this part to identify—

(i) The child's unique strengths and needs and the services appropriate to meet those needs; and

(ii) The resources, priorities, and concerns of the family and the supports and services necessary to enhance the family's capacity to meet the developmental needs of their infant or toddler with a disability.

(c) Evaluation and assessment of the child

The evaluation and assessment of each child must—

(1) Be conducted by personnel trained to utilize appropriate methods and procedures;

(2) Be based on informed clinical opinion; and

(3) Include the following:

(i) A review of pertinent records related to the child's current health status and medical history.

(ii) An evaluation of the child's level of functioning in each of the following developmental areas:

(A) Cognitive development.

(B) Physical development, including vision and hearing.

(C) Communication development.

(D) Social or emotional development.

(E) Adaptive development.

(iii) An assessment of the unique needs of the child in terms of each of the developmental areas in paragraph ©(3)(ii) of this section, including the identification of services appropriate to meet those needs.

(d) Family assessment

(1) Family assessments under this part must be family-directed and designed to determine the resources, priorities, and concerns of the family and the identification of the supports and services necessary to enhance the family's capacity to meet the developmental needs of the child.

(2) Any assessment that is conducted must be voluntary on the part of the family.

(3) If an assessment of the family is carried out, the assessment must—

(i) Be conducted by personnel trained to utilize appropriate methods and procedures;

(ii) Be based on information provided by the family through a personal interview; and

(iii) Incorporate the family's description of its resources, priorities, and concerns related to enhancing the child's development.

(e) Timelines

(1) Except as provided in paragraph (e)(2) of this section, the evaluation and initial assessment of each child (including the family assessment) must be completed within the 45-day time period required in Sec. 303.321(e).

(2) The lead agency shall develop procedures to ensure that in the event of exceptional circumstances that make it impossible to complete the evaluation and assessment within 45 days (e.g., if a child is ill), public agencies will—

(i) Document those circumstances; and

(ii) Develop and implement an interim IFSP, to the extent appropriate and consistent with Sec. 303.345 (b)(1) and (b)(2). (Authority: 20 U.S.C. 1435(a)(3); 1436(a)(1), (a)(2), (d)(1), and (d)(2))

Sec. 303.323 Nondiscriminatory procedures

Each lead agency shall adopt nondiscriminatory evaluation and assessment procedures. The procedures must provide that public agencies responsible for the evaluation and assessment of children and families under this part shall ensure, at a minimum, that—

(a) Tests and other evaluation materials and procedures are administered in the native language of the parents or other mode of communication, unless it is clearly not feasible to do so;

(b) Any assessment and evaluation procedures and materials that are used are selected and administered so as not to be racially or culturally discriminatory;

(c) No single procedure is used as the sole criterion for determining a child's eligibility under this part; and

(d) Evaluations and assessments are conducted by qualified personnel. (Authority: 20 U.S.C. 1435(a)(3); 1436(a)(1), (d)(2), and (d)(3))

INDIVIDUALIZED FAMILY SERVICE PLANS (IFSPs)

Sec. 303.340 General

(a) Each system must include **policies and procedures** regarding individualized family service plans (IFSPs) that meet the requirements of this section and Secs. 303.341 through 303.346.

(b) As used in this part, individualized family service plan and IFSP mean a written plan for providing early intervention services to a child eligible under this part and the child's family. The plan must—

(1) Be developed in accordance with Secs. 303.342 and 303.343;

(2) Be based on the evaluation and assessment described in Sec. 303.322; and

(3) Include the matters specified in Sec. 303.344.

(c) Lead agency responsibility

The lead agency shall ensure that an IFSP is developed and implemented for each eligible child, in accordance with the requirements of this part. If there is a dispute between agencies as to who has responsibility for developing or implementing an IFSP, the lead agency shall resolve the dispute or assign responsibility. (Authority: 20 U.S.C. 1436)

Note: In instances where an eligible child must have both an IFSP and an individualized service plan under another Federal program, it may be possible to develop a single consolidated document, provided that it (1) contains all of the required information in Sec. 303.344, and (2) is developed in accordance with the requirements of this part.

Sec. 303.341 [RESERVED]

Sec. 303.342 Procedures for IFSP development, review, and evaluation

(a) Meeting to develop initial IFSP-timelines

For a child who has been evaluated for the first time and determined to be eligible, a meeting to develop the initial IFSP must be conducted within the 45-day time period in Sec. 303.321(e).

(b) Periodic review

(1) A review of the IFSP for a child and the child's family must be conducted every six months, or more frequently if conditions warrant, or if the family requests such a review. The purpose of the periodic review is to determine—

(i) The degree to which progress toward achieving the outcomes is being made; and

(ii) Whether modification or revision of the outcomes or services is necessary.

(2) The review may be carried out by a meeting or by another means that is acceptable to the parents and other participants.

(c) Annual meeting to evaluate the IFSP

A meeting must be conducted on at least an annual basis to evaluate the IFSP for a child and the child's family, and, as appropriate, to revise its provisions. The results of any current evaluations conducted under Sec. 303.322©, and other information available from the ongoing assessment of the child and family, must be used in determining what services are needed and will be provided.

(d) Accessibility and convenience of meetings

(1) IFSP meetings must be conducted—

(i) In settings and at times that are convenient to families; and

(ii) In the native language of the family or other mode of communication used by the family, unless it is clearly not feasible to do so.

(2) Meeting arrangements must be made with, and written notice provided to, the family and other participants early enough before the meeting date to ensure that they will be able to attend.

(e) Parental consent

The contents of the IFSP must be fully explained to the parents and informed written consent from the parents must be obtained prior to the provision of early intervention services described in the plan. If the parents do not provide consent with respect to a particular early intervention service or withdraw consent after first providing it, that service may not be provided. The early intervention services to which parental consent is obtained must be provided. (Authority: 20 U.S.C. 1436)

Note: The requirement for the annual evaluation incorporates the periodic review process. Therefore, it is necessary to have only one separate periodic review each year (i.e., six months after the initial and subsequent annual IFSP meetings), unless conditions warrant otherwise. Because the needs of infants and toddlers change so rapidly during the course of a year, certain evaluation procedures may need to be repeated before conducting the periodic reviews and annual evaluation meetings in paragraphs (b) and (c) of this section.

Sec. 303.343 Participants in IFSP meetings and periodic reviews

(a) Initial and annual IFSP meetings

(1) Each initial meeting and each annual meeting to evaluate the IFSP must include the following participants:

(i) The parent or parents of the child.

(ii) Other family members, as requested by the parent, if feasible to do so;

(iii) An advocate or person outside of the family, if the parent requests that the person participate.

(iv) The service coordinator who has been working with the family since the initial referral of the child for evaluation, or who has been designated by the public agency to be responsible for implementation of the IFSP.

(v) A person or persons directly involved in conducting the evaluations and assessments in Sec. 303.322.

(vi) As appropriate, persons who will be providing services to the child or family.

(2) If a person listed in paragraph (a)(1)(v) of this section is unable to attend a meeting, arrangements must be made for the person's involvement through other means, including—

(i) Participating in a telephone conference call;

(ii) Having a knowledgeable authorized representative attend the meeting; or

(iii) Making pertinent records available at the meeting.

(b) Periodic review

Each periodic review must provide for the participation of persons in paragraphs (a)(1)(i) through (a)(1)(iv) of this section. If conditions warrant, provisions must be made for the participation of other representatives identified in paragraph (a) of this section. (Authority: 20 U.S.C. 1436(b))

Sec. 303.344 Content of an IFSP

(a) Information about the child's status

(1) The IFSP must include a statement of the child's present levels of physical development (including vision, hearing, and health status), cognitive development, communication development, social or emotional development, and adaptive development.

(2) The statement in paragraph (a)(1) of this section must be based on professionally acceptable objective criteria.

(b) Family information

With the concurrence of the family, the IFS must include a statement of the family's resources, priorities, and concerns related to enhancing the development of the child.

(c) Outcomes

The IFSP must include a statement of the major outcomes expected to be achieved for the child and family, and the criteria, procedures, and timeliness used to determine—

(1) The degree to which progress toward achieving the outcomes is being made; and

(2) Whether modifications or revisions of the outcomes or services are necessary.

(d) Early intervention services

(1) The IFSP must include a statement of the specific early intervention services necessary to meet the unique needs of the child and the family to achieve the outcomes identified in paragraph © of this section, including—

(i) The frequency, intensity, and method of delivering the services;

(ii) The natural environments, as described in Sec. 303.12(b) and Sec. 303.318, in which early intervention services will be provided, and a justification of the extent, if any, to which the services will not be provided in a natural environment;

(iii) The location of the services; and

(iv) The payment arrangements, if any.

(2) As used in paragraph (d)(1)(i) of this section—

(i) Frequency and intensity mean the number of days or sessions that a service will be provided, the length of time the service is provided during each session, and whether the service is provided on an individual or group basis; and

(ii) Method means how a service is provided.

(3) As used in paragraph (d)(1)(iii) of this section, location means the actual place or places where a service will be provided.

(e) Other services

(1) To the extent appropriate, the IFSP must include—

(i) Medical and other services that the child needs, but that are not required under this part; and

(ii) The funding sources to be used in paying for those services or the steps that will be taken to secure those services through public or private sources.

(2) The requirement in paragraph (e)(1) of this section does not apply to routine medical services (e.g., immunizations and "well-baby" care), unless a child needs those services and the services are not otherwise available or being provided.

(f) Dates; duration of services

The IFSP must include—

(1) The projected dates for initiation of the services in paragraph (d)(1) of this section as soon as possible after the IFSP meetings described in Sec. 303.342; and

(2) The anticipated duration of those services.

(g) Service coordinator

(1) The IFSP must include the name of the service coordinator from the profession most immediately relevant to the child's or family's needs (or who is otherwise qualified to carry out all applicable responsibilities under this part), who will be responsible for the implementation of the IFSP and coordination with other agencies and persons.

(2) In meeting the requirements in paragraph (g)(1) of this section, the public agency may—

(i) Assign the same service coordinator who was appointed at the time that the child was initially referred for evaluation to be responsible for implementing a child's and family's IFSP; or

(ii) Appoint a new service coordinator.

(3) As used in paragraph (g)(1) of this section, the term "profession" includes "service coordination."

(h) Transition from Part C services

(1) The IFSP must include the steps to be taken to support the transition of the child, in accordance with Sec. 303.148, to—

(i) Preschool services under Part B of th Act, to the extent that those services are appropriate; or

(ii) Other services that may be available, if appropriate.

(2) The steps required in paragraph (h)(1) of this section include—

(i) Discussions with, and training of, parents regarding future placements and other matters related to the child's transition;

(ii) Procedures to prepare the child for changes in service delivery, including steps to help the child adjust to, and function in, a new setting; and

(iii) With parental consent, the transmission of information about the child to the local educational agency, to ensure continuity of services, including evaluation and assessment information required in Sec. 303.322, and copies of IFSPs that have been developed and implemented in accordance with Secs. 303.340 through 303.346. (Authority: 20 U.S.C. 1436(d))

Note 1: With respect to the requirements in paragraph (d) of this section, the appropriate location of services for some infants and toddlers might be a hospital setting-during the period in which they require extensive medical intervention. However, for these and other eligible children, early intervention services must be provided in natural environments (e.g., the home, child care centers, or other community settings) to the maximum extent appropriate to the needs of the child.

Note 2: Throughout the process of developing and implementing IFSPs for an eligible child and the child's family, it is important for agencies to recognize the variety of roles that family members play in enhancing the child's development. It also is important that the degree to which the needs of the family are addressed in the IFSP process is determined in a collaborative manner with the full agreement and participation of the parents of the child. Parents retain the ultimate decision in determining whether they, their child, or other family members will accept or decline services under this part.

Note 3: The early intervention services in paragraph (d) of this section are those services that a State is required to provide to a child in accordance with Sec. 303.12. The "other services" in paragraph (e) of this section are services that a child or family needs, but that are neither required nor covered under this part. While listing the non- required services in the IFSP does not mean that those services must be provided, their identification can be helpful to both the child's family and the service coordinator, for the following reasons: First, the IFSP would provide a comprehensive picture of the child's total service needs (including the need for medical and health services, as well as early intervention services). Second, it is appropriate for the service coordinator to assist the family in securing the non-required services (e.g., by (1) determining if there is a public agency that could provide financial assistance, if needed, (2) assisting in the preparation of eligibility claims or insurance claims, if needed, and (3) assisting the family in seeking out and arranging for the child to receive the needed medical-health services). Thus, to the extent appropriate, it is important for a State's procedures under this part to provide for ensuring that other needs of the child, and of the family related to enhancing the development of the child, such as medical and health needs, are considered and addressed, including determining (1) who will provide each service, and when, where, and how it will be provided, and (2) how the service will be paid for (e.g., through private insurance, an existing Federal-State funding source, such as Medicaid or EPSDT, or some other funding arrangement).

Note 4: Although the IFSP must include information about each of the items in paragraphs (b) through (h) of this section, this does not mean that the IFSP must be a detailed, lengthy document. It might be a brief outline, with appropriate attachments that address each of the points in the paragraphs under this section. It is important for the IFSP itself to be clear about (a) what services are to be provided, (b) the actions that are to be taken by the service coordinator in initiating those services, and (c) what actions will be taken by the parents.

Sec. 303.345 Provision of services before evaluation and assessment are completed

Early intervention services for an eligible child and the child's family may commence before the completion of the evaluation and assessment in Sec. 303.322, if the following conditions are met:

(a) Parental consent is obtained.

(b) An interim IFSP is developed that includes—

(1) The name of the service coordinator who will be responsible, consistent with Sec. 303.344(g), for implementation of the interim IFSP and coordination with other agencies and persons; and

(2) The early intervention services that have been determined to be needed immediately by the child and the child's family.

(c) The evaluation and assessment are completed within the time period required in Sec. 303.322(e). (Authority: 20 U.S.C. 1436(c)

Note: This section is intended to accomplish two specific purposes: (1) To facilitate the provision of services in the event that a child has obvious immediate needs that are identified, even at the time of referral (e.g., a physician recommends that a child with cerebral palsy begin receiving physical therapy as soon as possible), and (2) to ensure that the requirements for the timely evaluation and assessment are not circumvented.

Sec. 303.346 Responsibility and accountability

Each agency or person who has a direct role in the provision of early intervention services is responsible for making a good faith effort to assist each eligible child in achieving the outcomes in the child's IFSP. However, Part H of the Act does not require that any agency or person be held accountable if an eligible child does not achieve the growth projected in the child's IFSP. (Authority: 20 U.S.C. 1436)

PERSONNEL TRAINING AND STANDARDS

Sec. 303.360 Comprehensive system of personnel development

(a) Each system must include a comprehensive system of personnel development.

(b) The personnel development system under this part must—

(1) Be consistent with the comprehensive system of personnel development required under Part B of the Act (34 CFR 300.380 through 300.387);

(2) Provide for preservice and inservice training to be conducted on an interdisciplinary basis, to the extent appropriate;

(3) Provide for the training of a variety of personnel needed to meet the requirements of this part, including public and private providers, primary referral sources, paraprofessionals, and persons who will serve as service coordinators; and

(4) Ensure that the training provided relates specifically to—

(i) Understanding the basic components of early intervention services available in the State;

(ii) Meeting the interrelated social or emotional, health, developmental, and educational needs of eligible children under this part; and

(iii) Assisting families in enhancing the development of their children, and in participating fully in the development and implementation of IFSPs.

(c) A personnel development system under this part may include—

(1) Implementing innovative strategies and activities for the recruitment and retention of early intervention service providers;

(2) Promoting the preparation of early intervention providers who are fully and appropriately qualified to provide early intervention services under this part;

(3) Training personnel to work in rural and inner-city areas; and

(4) Training personnel to coordinate transition services for infants and toddlers with disabilities from an early intervention program under this part to a preschool program under Part B of the Act or to other preschool or other appropriate services. (Authority: 20 U.S.C. 1435(a)(8))

Sec. 303.361 Personnel standards

(a) As used in this part—

(1) Appropriate professional requirements in the State means entry level requirements that—

(i) Are based on the highest requirements in the State applicable to the profession or discipline in which a person is providing early intervention services; and

(ii) Establish suitable qualifications for personnel providing early intervention services under this part to eligible children and their families who are served by State, local, and private agencies.

(2) **Highest requirements in the State** applicable to a specific profession or discipline means the highest entry-level academic degree needed for any State approved or recognized certification, licensing, registration, or other comparable requirements that apply to that profession or discipline.

(3) **Profession or discipline** means a specific occupational category that—

(i) Provides early intervention services to children eligible under this part and their families;

(ii) Has been established or designated by the State; and

(iii) Has a required scope of responsibility and degree of supervision.

(4) **State approved or recognized certification**, licensing, registration, or other comparable requirements means the requirements that a State legislature either has enacted or has authorized a State agency to promulgate through rules to establish the entry-level standards for employment in a specific profession or discipline in that State.

(b)(1) Each statewide system must have policies and procedures relating to the establishment and maintenance of standards to ensure that personnel necessary to carry out the purposes of this part are appropriately and adequately prepared and trained.

(2) The policies and procedures required in paragraph (b)(1) of this section must provide for the establishment and maintenance of standards that are consistent with any State-approved or State- recognized certification, licensing, registration, or other comparable requirements that apply to the profession or discipline in which a person is providing early intervention services.

(c) To the extent that a State's standards for a profession or discipline, including standards for temporary or emergency certification, are not based on the highest requirements in the State applicable to a specific profession or discipline, the State's application for assistance under this part must include the steps the State is taking, the procedures for notifying public agencies and personnel of those steps, and the timelines it has established for the retraining or hiring of personnel that meet appropriate professional requirements in the State.

(d)(1) In meeting the requirements in paragraphs (b) and (c) of this section, a determination must be made about the status of personnel standards in the State. That determination must be based on current information that accurately describes, for each profession or discipline in which personnel are providing early intervention services, whether the applicable standards are consistent with the highest requirements in the State for that profession or discipline.

(2) The information required in paragraph (d)(1) of this section must be on file in the lead agency, and available to the public.

(e) In identifying the "highest requirements in the State" for purposes of this section, the requirements of all State statutes and the rules of all State agencies applicable to serving children eligible under this part and their families must be considered.

(f) A State may allow paraprofessionals and assistants who are appropriately trained and supervised, in accordance with State law, regulations, or written policy, to assist in the provision of early intervention services to eligible children under this part.

(g) In implementing this section, a State may adopt a policy that includes making ongoing good-faith efforts to recruit and hire appropriately and adequately trained personnel to provide early intervention services to eligible children, including, in a geographic area of the State where there is a shortage of personnel that meet these qualifications, the most qualified individuals available who are making satisfactory progress toward completing applicable course work necessary to meet the standards described in paragraph (b)(2) of this section, consistent with State law, within three years. (Authority: 20 U.S.C. 1435(a)(9))

Note: This section requires that a State use its own existing highest requirements to determine the standards appropriate to personnel who provide early intervention services under this part. The regulations do not require States to set any specified training standard, such as a master's degree, for employment of personnel who provide services under this part.

The regulations permit each State to determine the specific occupational categories required to provide early intervention services to children eligible under this part and their families, and to revise or expand these categories as needed. The professions or disciplines need not be limited to traditional occupational categories.

SUBPART E—PROCEDURAL SAFEGUARDS

GENERAL

Sec. 303.400 General responsibility of lead agency for procedural safeguards

Each lead agency shall be responsible for—

(a) Establishing or adopting procedural safeguards that meet the requirements of this subpart; and

(b) Ensuring effective implementation of the safeguards by each public agency in the State that is involved in the provision of early intervention services under this part. (Authority: 20 U.S.C. 1439)

Sec. 303.401 Definitions of consent, native language, and personally identifiable information

As used in this subpart—

(a) **Consent** means that—

(1) The parent has been fully informed of all information relevant to the activity for which consent is sought, in the parent's native language or other mode of communication;

(2) The parent understands and agrees in writing to the carrying out of the activity for which consent is sought, and the consent describes that activity and lists the records (if any) that will be released and to whom; and

(3) The parent understands that the granting of consent is voluntary on the part of the parent and may be revoked at any time;

(b) **Native language**, where used with reference to persons of limited English proficiency, means the language or mode of communication normally used by the parent of a child eligible under this part;

(c) **Personally identifiable** means that information includes—

    (1) The name of the child, the child's parent, or other family member;

    (2) The address of the child;

    (3) A personal identifier, such as the child's or parent's social security number; or

    (4) A list of personal characteristics or other information that would make it possible to identify the child with reasonable certainty. (Authority: 20 U.S.C. 1439)

Sec. 303.402 Opportunity to examine records

In accordance with the confidentiality procedures in the regulations under Part B of the Act (34 CFR 300.560 through 300.576), the parents of a child eligible under this part must be afforded the opportunity to inspect and review records relating to evaluations and assessments, eligibility determinations, development and implementation of IFSPs, individual complaints dealing with the child, and any other area under this part involving records about the child and the child's family. (Authority: 20 U.S.C. 1439(a)(4))

Sec. 303.403 Prior notice; native language

(a) General

Written prior notice must be given to the parents of a child eligible under this part a reasonable time before a public agency or service provider proposes, or refuses, to initiate or change the identification, evaluation, or placement of the child, or the provision of appropriate early intervention services to the child and the child's family.

(b) Content of notice

The notice must be in sufficient detail to inform the parents about—

    (1) The action that is being proposed or refused;

    (2) The reasons for taking the action;

    (3) All procedural safeguards that are available under Sec. 303.401-303.460 of this part; and

    (4) The State complaint procedures under Sec. 303.510 - 303. 512, including a description of how to file a complaint and the timelines under those procedures.

(c) Native language

    (1) The notice must be—

        (i) Written in language understandable to the general public; and

        (ii) Provided in the native language of the parents, unless it is clearly not feasible to do so.

    (2) If the native language or other mode of communication of the parent is not a written language, the public agency, or designated service provider, shall take steps to ensure that—

        (i) The notice is translated orally or by other means to the parent in the parent's native language or other mode of communication;

        (ii) The parent understands the notice; and

        (iii) There is written evidence that the requirements of this paragraph have been met.

    (3) If a parent is deaf or blind, or has no written language, the mode of communication must be that normally used by the parent (such as sign language, braille, or oral communication). (Authority: 20 U.S.C. 1439(a)(6) and (7))

Sec. 303.404 Parent consent

(a) Written parental consent must be obtained before—

    (1) Conducting the initial evaluation and assessment of a child under Sec. 303.322; and

    (2) Initiating the provision of early intervention services (see Sec. 303.342(e)).

(b) If consent is not given, the public agency shall make reasonable efforts to ensure that the parent—

    (1) Is fully aware of the nature of the evaluation and assessment or the services that would be available; and

    (2) Understands that the child will not be able to receive the evaluation and assessment or services unless consent is given. (Authority: 20 U.S.C. 1439)

Note 1: In addition to the consent requirements in this section, other consent requirements are included in (1) Sec. 303.460(a), regarding the exchange of personally identifiable information among agencies, and (2) the confidentiality provisions in the regulations under Part B of the Act (34 CFR 300.571) and 34 CFR part 99 (Family Educational Rights and Privacy), both of which apply to this part.

Note 2: Under Sec. 300.504(b) of the Part B regulations, a public agency may initiate procedures to challenge a parent's refusal to consent to the initial evaluation of the parent's child and, if successful, obtain the evaluation. This provision applies to eligible children under this part, since the Part B evaluation requirement applies to all children with disabilities in a State, including infants and toddlers.

Sec. 303.405 Parent right to decline service

The parents of a child eligible under this part may determine whether they, their child, or other family members will accept or decline any early intervention service under this part in accordance with State law, and may decline such a service after first accepting it, without jeopardizing other early intervention services under this part. (Authority: 20 U.S.C. 1439(a)(3))

Sec. 303.406 Surrogate parents

(a) General

Each lead agency shall ensure that the rights of children eligible under this part are protected if—

(1) No parent (as defined in Sec. 303.18) can be identified;

(2) The public agency, after reasonable efforts, cannot discover the whereabouts of a parent; or

(3) The child is a ward of the State under the laws of that State.

(b) Duty of lead agency and other public agencies

The duty of the lead agency, or other public agency under paragraph (a) of this section, includes the assignment of an individual to act as a surrogate for the parent. This must include a method for—

(1) Determining whether a child needs a surrogate parent; and

(2) Assigning a surrogate parent to the child.

(c) Criteria for selecting surrogates

(1) The lead agency or other public agency may select a surrogate parent in any way permitted under State law.

(2) Public agencies shall ensure that a person selected as a surrogate parent—

(i) Has no interest that conflicts with the interests of the child he or she represents; and

(ii) Has knowledge and skills that ensure adequate representation of the child.

(d) Non-employee requirement; compensation

(1) A person assigned as a surrogate parent may not be—

(i) An employee of any State agency; or

(ii) A person or an employee of a person providing early intervention services to the child or to any family member of the child.

(2) A person who otherwise qualifies to be a surrogate parent under paragraph (d)(1) of this section is not an employee solely because he or she is paid by a public agency to serve as a surrogate parent.

(e) Responsibilities

A surrogate parent may represent a child in all matters related to—

(1) The evaluation and assessment of the child;

(2) Development and implementation of the child's IFSPs, including annual evaluations and periodic reviews;

(3) The ongoing provision of early intervention services to the child; and

(4) Any other rights established under this part. (Authority: 20 U.S.C. 1439(a)(5))

MEDIATION AND DUE PROCESS PROCEDURES FOR PARENTS AND CHILDREN

Sec. 303.419 Mediation

(a) General

Each State shall ensure that procedures are established and implemented to allow parties to disputes involving any matter described in Sec. 303.403(a) to resolve the disputes through a mediation process which, at a minimum, must be available whenever a hearing is requested under Sec. 303.420. The lead agency may either use the mediation system established under Part B of the Act or establish its own system.

(b) Requirements

The procedures must meet the following requirements:

(1) The procedures must ensure that the mediation process—

(i) Is voluntary on the part of the parties;

(ii) Is not used to deny or delay a parent's right to a due process hearing under Sec. 303.420, or to deny any other rights afforded under Part C of the Act; and

(iii) Is conducted by a qualified and impartial mediator who is trained in effective mediation techniques.

(2) The State shall maintain a list of individuals who are qualified mediators and knowledgeable in laws and regulations relating to the provision of special education and related services.

(3) The State shall bear the cost of the mediation process, including the costs of meetings described in paragraph © of this section.

(4) Each session in the mediation process must be scheduled in a timely manner and must be held in a location that is convenient to the parties to the dispute.

(5) An agreement reached by the parties to the dispute in the mediation process must be set forth in a written mediation agreement.

(6) Discussions that occur during the mediation process must be confidential and may not be used as evidence in any subsequent due process hearings or civil proceedings, and the parties to the mediation process may be required to sign a confidentiality pledge prior to the commencement of the process.

(c) Meeting to encourage mediation

A State may establish procedures to require parents who elect not to use the mediation process to meet, at a time and location convenient to the parents, with a disinterested party—

(1) Who is under contract with a parent training and information center or community parent resource center in the State established under Secs. 682 or 683 of the Act, or an appropriate alternative dispute resolution entity; and

(2) Who would explain the benefits of the mediation process and encourage the parents to use the process.   (Authority: 20 U.S.C. 1415(e) and 1439(a)(8))

Sec. 303.420 Due process procedures

Each system must include written procedures including procedures for mediation as described in Sec. 303.419, for the timely administrative resolution of individual child complaints by parents concerning any of the matters in Sec. 303.403(a). A State may meet this requirement by—

(a) Adopting the mediation and due process procedures in 34 CFR 300.506 through 300.512 and developing procedures that meet the requirements of Sec. 303.425; or

(b) Developing procedures that—

(1) Meet the requirements in Secs. 303.419, 303.421 through 303.425; and

(2) Provide parents a means of filing a complaint. (Authority: 20 U.S.C. 1439(a)(1))

Note 1: Secs. 303.420 through 303.425 are concerned with the adoption of impartial procedures for resolving individual child complaints (i.e., complaints that generally affect only a single child or the child's family). These procedures require the appointment of a decision-maker who is impartial, as defined in Sec. 303.421(b), to resolve a dispute concerning any of the matters in Sec. 303.403(a). The decision of the impartial decision-maker is binding unless it is reversed on appeal.

A different type of administrative procedure is included in Secs. 303.510 through 303.512 of subpart F of this part. Under those procedures, the lead agency is responsible for (1) investigating any complaint that it receives (including individual child complaints and those that are systemic in nature), and (2) resolving the complaint if the agency determines that a violation has occurred.

Note 2: It is important that the administrative procedures developed by a State be designed to result in speedy resolution of complaints. An infant's or toddler's development is so rapid that undue delay could be potentially harmful.

Sec. 303.421 Appointment of an impartial person

(a) Qualifications and duties

An impartial person must be appointed to implement the complaint resolution process in this subpart. The person must—

(1) Have knowledge about the provisions of this part and the needs of, and services available for, eligible children and their families; and

(2) Perform the following duties:

(i) Listen to the presentation of relevant viewpoints about the complaint, examine all information relevant to the issues, and seek to reach a timely resolution of the complaint.

(ii) Provide a record of the proceedings, including a written decision.

(b) Definition of impartial

(1) As used in this section, impartial means that the person appointed to implement the complaint resolution process—

(i) Is not an employee of any agency or other entity involved in the provision of early intervention services or care of the child; and

(ii) Does not have a personal or professional interest that would conflict with his or her objectivity in implementing the process.

(2) A person who otherwise qualifies under paragraph (b)(1) of this section is not an employee of an agency solely because the person is paid by the agency to implement the complaint resolution process. (Authority: 20 U.S.C. 1439(a)(1))

Sec. 303.422 Parent rights in administrative proceedings

(a) General

Each lead agency shall ensure that the parents of children eligible under this part are afforded the rights in paragraph (b) of this section in any administrative proceedings carried out under Sec. 303.420.

(b) Rights

Any parent involved in an administrative proceeding has the right to—

(1) Be accompanied and advised by counsel and by individuals with special knowledge or training with respect to early intervention services for children eligible under this part;

(2) Present evidence and confront, cross-examine, and compel the attendance of witnesses;

(3) Prohibit the introduction of any evidence at the proceeding that has not been disclosed to the parent at least five days before the proceeding;

(4) Obtain a written or electronic verbatim transcription of the proceeding; and

(5) Obtain written findings of fact and decisions. (Authority: 20 U.S.C. 1439)

Sec. 303.423 Convenience of proceedings; timelines

(a) Any proceeding for implementing the complaint resolution process in this subpart must be carried out at a time and place that is reasonably convenient to the parents.

(b) Each lead agency shall ensure that, not later than 30 days after the receipt of a parent's complaint, the impartial proceeding required under this subpart is completed and a written decision mailed to each of the parties. (Authority: 20 U.S.C. 1439(a)(1))

Note: Under Part B of the Act, States are allowed 45 days to conduct an impartial due process hearing (i.e., within 45 days after the receipt of a request for a hearing, a decision is reached and a copy of the decision is mailed to each of the parties). (See 34 CFR 300.512.) Thus, if a State, in meeting the requirements of Sec. 303.420, elects to adopt the due process procedures under Part B, that State would also have 45 days for hearings. However, any State in that situation is encouraged (but not required) to accelerate the timeline for the due process hearing for children who are eligible under this part-from 45 days to the 30-day timeline in this section. Because the needs of children in the birth-through-two-age range change so rapidly, quick resolution of complaints is important.

Sec. 303.424 Civil action

Any party aggrieved by the findings and decision regarding an administrative complaint has the right to bring a civil action in State or Federal court under Sec. 639(a)(1) of the Act. (Authority: 20 U.S.C. 1439(a)(1))

Sec. 303.425 Status of a child during proceedings

(a) During the pendency of any proceeding involving a complaint under this subpart, unless the public agency and parents of a child otherwise agree, the child must continue to receive the appropriate early intervention services currently being provided.

(b) If the complaint involves an application for initial services under this part, the child must receive those services that are not in dispute. (Authority: 20 U.S.C. 1439(a)(7))

CONFIDENTIALITY
Sec. 303.460 Confidentiality of information

(a) Each State shall adopt or develop policies and procedures that the State will follow in order to ensure the protection of any personally identifiable information collected, used, or maintained under this part, including the right of parents to written notice of and written consent to the exchange of this information among agencies consistent with Federal and State law.

(b) These policies and procedures must meet the requirements in 34 CFR 300.560 through 300.576, with the modifications specified in Sec. 303.5(b). (Authority: 20 U.S.C. 1439(a)(2), 1442)

Note: With the modifications referred to in paragraph (b) of this section, the confidentiality requirements in the regulations implementing Part B of the Act (34 CFR 300.560 through 300.576) are to be used by public agencies to meet the confidentiality requirements under Part H of the Act and this section (Sec. 303.460). The Part B provisions incorporate by reference the regulations in 34 CFR Part 99 (Family Educational Rights and Privacy); therefore, those regulations also apply to this part.

SUBPART F—STATE ADMINISTRATION

GENERAL
Sec. 303.500 Lead agency establishment or designation

Each system must include a single line of responsibility in a lead agency that—

(a) Is established or designated by the Governor; and

(b) Is responsible for the administration of the system, in accordance with the requirements of this part. (Authority: 20 U.S.C. 1435(a)(10))

Sec. 303.501 Supervision and monitoring of programs

(a) General

Each lead agency is responsible for—

(1) The general administration and supervision of programs and activities receiving assistance under this part; and

(2) The monitoring of programs and activities used by the State to carry out this part, whether or not these programs or activities are receiving assistance under this part, to ensure that the State complies with this part.

(b) Methods of administering programs

In meeting the requirement in paragraph (a) of this section, the lead agency shall adopt and use proper methods of administering each program, including—

(1) Monitoring agencies, institutions, and organizations used by the State to carry out this part;

(2) Enforcing any obligations imposed on those agencies under Part H of the Act and these regulations;

(3) Providing technical assistance, if necessary, to those agencies, institutions, and organizations; and

(4) Correcting deficiencies that are identified through monitoring. (Authority: 20 U.S.C. 1435(a)(10)(A))

LEAD AGENCY PROCEDURES FOR RESOLVING COMPLAINTS

Sec. 303.510 Adopting complaint procedures

Each lead agency shall adopt written procedures for—

(a) General. Each lead agency shall adopt written procedures for

(1) Resolving any complaint, including a complaint filed by an organization or individual from another State, that any public agency or private service provider is violating a requirement of Part C of the Act or this part by—

(i) Providing for the filing of a complaint with the lead agency; and

(ii) At the lead agency's discretion, providing for the filing of a complaint with a public agency and the right to have the lead agency review the public agency's decision on the complaint; and

(2) Widely disseminating to parents and other interested individuals, including parent training centers, protection and advocacy agencies, independent living centers, and other appropriate entities, the State's procedures under Secs. 303.510 - 303.512.

(b) Remedies for denial of appropriate services. In resolving a complaint in which it finds a failure to provide appropriate services, a lead agency, pursuant to its general supervisory authority under Part C of the Act , must address:

(1) How to remediate the denial of those services, including, as appropriate, the awarding of monetary reimbursement or other corrective action appropriate to the needs of the child and the child's family; and

(2) Appropriate future provision of services for all infants and toddlers with disabilities and their families. (Authority: 20 U.S.C. 1435(a)(10))

Note: Because of the interagency nature of Part H of the Act, complaints received under these regulations could concern violations by (1) any public agency in the State that receives funds under this part (e.g., the lead agency and the Council), (2) other public agencies that are involved in the State's early intervention program, or (3) private service providers that receive Part H funds on a contract basis from a public agency to carry out a given function or provide a given service required under this part. These complaint procedures are in addition to any other rights under State or Federal law. The lead agency must provide for the filing of a complaint with the lead agency and, at the lead agency's discretion, with a public agency subject to a right of appeal to the lead agency.

Sec. 303.511 An organization or individual may file a complaint

(a) General. An individual or organization may file a written signed complaint under Sec. 303.510. The complaint must include—

(1) A statement that the State has violated a requirement of part C of the Act or the regulations in this part; and

(2) The facts on which the complaint is based.

(b) Limitations. The alleged violation must have occurred not more than one year before the date that the complaint is received by the public agency unless a longer period is reasonable because -

(1) The alleged violation continues for that child or other children; or

(2) The complainant is requesting reimbursement or corrective action for a violation that occurred not more than three years before the date on which the complaint is received by the public agency. (Authority: 20 U.S.C. 1435(a)(10))

Sec. 303.512 Minimum State complaint procedures

(a) Time limit, minimum procedures. Each lead agency shall include in its complaint procedures a time limit of 60 calendar days after a complaint is filed under Sec. 303.510(a) to—

(1) Carry out an independent on-site investigation, if the lead agency determines that such an investigation is necessary;

(2) Give the complainant the opportunity to submit additional information, either orally or in writing, about the allegations in the complaint;

(3) Review all relevant information and make an independent determination as to whether the public agency is violating a requirement of Part C of the Act or of this Part; and

(4) Issue a written decision to the complainant that addresses each allegation in the complaint and contains—

(i) Findings of fact and conclusions; and

(ii) The reasons for the lead agency's final decision.

(b) Time extension; final decisions; implementation. The lead agency's procedures described in paragraph (a) of this section also must —

(1) Permit an extension of the time limit under paragraph (a) of this section only if exceptional circumstances exist with respect to a particular complaint; and

(2) Include procedures for effective implementation of the lead agency's final decision, if needed, including —

(i) Technical assistance activities;

(ii) Negotiations;

(iii) Corrective actions to achieve compliance.

(c) Complaints filed under this section, and due process hearings under Sec. 303.420.

(1) If a written complaint is received that is also the subject of a due process hearing under Sec. 303.420, or contains multiple issues, of which one or more are part of that hearing, the State must set aside any part of the complaint that is being addressed in the due process hearing until the conclusion of the hearing. However, any issue in the complaint that is not a part of the due process action must be resolved within the 60-calendar day timeline using the complaint procedures described in paragraphs (a) and (b) of this section.

(2) If an issue is raised in a complaint filed under this section that has previously been decided in a due process hearing involving the same parties -

    (i) The hearing decision is binding; and

    (ii) The lead agency must inform the complainant to that effect.

(3) A complaint alleging a public agency's or private service provider's failure to implement a due process decision must be resolved by the lead agency. (Authority: 20 U.S.C. 1435(a)(10))

POLICIES AND PROCEDURES RELATED TO FINANCIAL MATTERS

Sec. 303.520 Policies related to payment for services

(a) General

Each lead agency is responsible for establishing State policies related to how services to children eligible under this part and their families will be paid for under the State's early intervention program. The policies must—

    (1) Meet the requirements in paragraph (b) of this section; and

    (2) Be reflected in the interagency agreements required in Sec. 303.523.

(b) Specific funding policies

A State's policies must—

    (1) Specify which functions and services will be provided at no cost to all parents;

    (2) Specify which functions or services, if any, will be subject to a system of payments, and include—

        (i) Information about the payment system and schedule of sliding fees that will be used; and

        (ii) The basis and amount of payments; and

    (3) Include an assurance that—

        (i) Fees will not be charged for the services that a child is otherwise entitled to receive at no cost to parents; and

        (ii) The inability of the parents of an eligible child to pay for services will not result in the denial of services to the child or the child's family; and

    (4) Set out any fees that will be charged for early intervention services and the basis for those fees.

(c) Procedures to ensure the timely provision of services

No later than the beginning of the fifth year of a State's participation under this part, the State shall implement a mechanism to ensure that no services that a child is entitled to receive are delayed or denied because of disputes between agencies regarding financial or other responsibilities.

(d) Proceeds from public or private insurance.

    (1) Proceeds from public or private insurance not treated as program income for purposes of 34 CFR 80.25.

    (2) If a public agency spends reimbursements from Federal funds (e.g. Medicaid) for services under this part, those funds are not considered State or local funds for purposes of the provisions contained in Sec. 303.124. (Authority: 20 U.S.C. 1432(4)(B)), 1435(a)(10))

Sec. 303.521 Fees

(a) General

A State may establish, consistent with Sec. 303.12(a)(3)(iv), a system of payments for early intervention services, including a schedule of sliding fees.

(b) Functions not subject to fees

The following are required functions that must be carried out at public expense by a State, and for which no fees may be charged to parents:

    (1) Implementing the child find requirements in Sec. 303.321.

    (2) Evaluation and assessment, as included in Sec. 303.322, and including the functions related to evaluation and assessment in Sec. 303.12.

    (3) Service coordination, as included in Secs. 303.22 and 303.344(g).

    (4) Administrative and coordinative activities related to—

        (i) The development, review, and evaluation of IFSPs in Secs. 303.340 through 303.346; and

        (ii) Implementation of the procedural safeguards in subpart E of this part and the other components of the statewide system of early intervention services in subparts D and F of this part.

(c) States with mandates to serve children from birth

If a State has in effect a State law requiring the provision of a free appropriate public education to children with disabilities from birth, the State may not charge parents for any services (e.g., physical or occupational therapy) required under that law that are provided to children eligible under this part and their families. (Authority: 20 U.S.C. 1432(4))

Sec. 303.522 Identification and coordination of resources

(a) Each lead agency is responsible for—

(1) The identification and coordination of all available resources for early intervention services within the State, including those from Federal, State, local, and private sources; and

(2) Updating the information on the funding sources in paragraph (a)(1) of this section, if a legislative or policy change is made under any of those sources.

(b) The Federal funding sources in paragraph (a)(1) of this section include—

(1) Title V of the Social Security Act (relating to Maternal and Child Health);

(2) Title XIX of the Social Security Act (relating to the general Medicaid Program, and EPSDT);

(3) The Head Start Act;

(4) Parts B and H of the Act;

(5) The Developmental Disabilities Assistance and Bill of Rights Act (Pub. L. 94-103); and

(6) Other Federal programs. (Aut hority: 20 U.S.C. 1435(a)(10)(B))

Sec. 303.523 Interagency agreements

(a) General

Each lead agency is responsible for entering into formal interagency agreements with other State-level agencies involved in the State's early intervention program. Each agreement must meet the requirements in paragraphs (b) through (d) of this section.

(b) Financial responsibility

Each agreement must define the financial responsibility, in accordance with Sec. 303.143, of the agency for paying for early intervention services (consistent with State law and the requirements of this part).

(c) Procedures for resolving disputes

(1) Each agreement must include procedures for achieving a timely resolution of intra-agency and interagency disputes about payments for a given service, or disputes about other matters related to the State's early intervention program. Those procedures must include a mechanism for making a final determination that is binding upon the agencies involved.

(2) The agreement with each agency must—

(i) Permit the agency to resolve its own internal disputes (based on the agency's procedures that are included in the agreement), so long as the agency acts in a timely manner; and

(ii) Include the process that the lead agency will follow in achieving resolution of intra-agency disputes, if a given agency is unable to resolve its own internal disputes in a timely manner.

(d) Additional components

Each agreement must include any additional components necessary to ensure effective cooperation and coordination among all agencies involved in the State's early intervention program. (Authority: 20 U.S.C. 1435(a)(10)(C) and (a)(10)(F))

Note: A State may meet the requirement in paragraph ©(1) of this section in any way permitted under State law, including (1) providing for a third party (e.g., an administrative law judge) to review a dispute and render a decision, (2) assignment of the responsibility by the Governor to the lead agency or Council, or (3) having the final decision made directly by the Governor.

Sec. 303.524 Resolution of disputes

(a) Each lead agency is responsible for resolving individual disputes, in accordance with the procedures in Sec. 303.523(c)(2)(ii).

(b)(1) During a dispute, the individual or entity responsible for assigning financial responsibility among appropriate agencies under Sec. 303.143 ("financial designee") shall assign financial responsibility to—

(i) An agency, subject to the provisions in paragraph (b)(2) of this section; or

(ii) The lead agency, in accordance with the "payor of last resort" provisions in Sec. 303.527.

(2) If, during the lead agency's resolution of the dispute, the financial designee determines that the assignment of financial responsibility under paragraph (b)(1)(i) of this section was inappropriately made—

(i) The financial designee shall reassign the responsibility to the appropriate agency; and

(ii) The lead agency shall make arrangements for reimbursement of any expenditures incurred by the agency originally assigned responsibility.

(c) To the extent necessary to ensure compliance with its action in paragraph (b)(2) of this section, the lead agency shall—

    (1) Refer the dispute to the Council or the Governor; and

    (2) Implement the procedures to ensure the delivery of services in a timely manner in accordance with Sec. 303.525. (Authority: 20 U.S.C. 1435(a)(10)(C) and (a)(10)(E))

Sec. 303.525 Delivery of services in a timely manner

Each lead agency is responsible for the development of procedures to ensure that services are provided to eligible children and their families in a timely manner, pending the resolution of disputes among public agencies or service providers. (Authority: 20 U.S.C. 1435(a)(10)(D))

Sec. 303.526 Policy for contracting or otherwise arranging for services

Each system must include a policy pertaining to contracting or making other arrangements with public or private service providers to provide early intervention services. The policy must include—

(a) A requirement that all early intervention services must meet State standards and be consistent with the provisions of this part;

(b) The mechanisms that the lead agency will use in arranging for these services, including the process by which awards or other arrangements are made; and

(c) The basic requirements that must be met by any individual or organization seeking to provide these services for the lead agency. (Authority: 20 U.S.C. 1435(a)(11))

Note: In implementing the statewide system, States may elect to continue using agencies and individuals in both the public and private sectors that have previously been involved in providing early intervention services, so long as those agencies and individuals meet the requirements of this part.

Sec. 303.527 Payor of last resort

(a) Nonsubstitution of funds

Except as provided in paragraph (b)(1) of this section, funds under this part may not be used to satisfy a financial commitment for services that would otherwise have been paid for from another public or private source, including any medical program administered by the Secretary of Defense, but for the enactment of Part C of the Act. Therefore, funds under this part may be used only for early intervention services that an eligible child needs but is not currently entitled to under any other Federal, State, local, or private source.

(b) Interim payments—reimbursement

    (1) If necessary to prevent a delay in the timely provision of services to an eligible child or the child's family, funds under this part may be used to pay the provider of services, pending reimbursement from the agency or entity that has ultimate responsibility for the payment.

    (2) Payments under paragraph (b)(1) of this section may be made for—

        (i) Early intervention services, as described in Sec. 303.12;

        (ii) Eligible health services (see Sec. 303.13); and

        (iii) Other functions and services authorized under this part, including child find and evaluation and assessment.

    (3) The provisions of paragraph (b)(1) of this section do not apply to medical services or "well-baby" health care (see Sec. 303.13(c)(1)).

(c) Non-reduction of benefits

Nothing in this part may be construed to permit a State to reduce medical or other assistance available or to alter eligibility under Title V of the Social Security Act (SSA) (relating to maternal and child health) or Title XIX of the SSA (relating to Medicaid for children eligible under this part) within the State. (Authority: 20 U.S.C. 1440)

Note: The Congress intended that the enactment of Part H not be construed as a license to any agency (including the lead agency and other agencies in the State) to withdraw funding for services that currently are or would be made available to eligible children but for the existence of the program under this part. Thus, the Congress intended that other funding sources would continue, and that there would be greater coordination among agencies regarding the payment of costs.

The Congress further clarified its intent concerning payments under Medicaid by including in Sec. 411(k)(13) of the Medicare Catastrophic Coverage Act of 1988 (Pub. L. 100-360) an amendment to Title XIX of the Social Security Act. That amendment states, in effect, that nothing in this title shall be construed as prohibiting or restricting, or authorizing the Secretary of Health and Human Services to prohibit or restrict, payment under subsection (a) of Sec. 1903 of the Social Security Act for medical assistance for covered services furnished to an infant or toddler with a disability because those services are included in the child's IFSP adopted pursuant to Part H of the Act.

Sec. 303.528 Reimbursement procedure

Each system must include a procedure for securing the timely reimbursement of funds used under this part, in accordance with Sec. 303.527(b). (Authority: 20 U.S.C. 1435(a)(12))

REPORTING REQUIREMENTS

Sec. 303.540 Data collection

(a) Each system must include the procedures that the State uses to compile data on the statewide system. The procedures must—

    (1) Include a process for—

        (i) Collecting data from various agencies and service providers in the State;

        (ii) Making use of appropriate sampling methods, if sampling is permitted; and

        (iii) Describing the sampling methods used, if reporting to the Secretary; and

    (2) Provide for reporting data required under Sec. 618 of the Act that relates to this part.

(b) The information required in paragraph (a)(2) of this section must be provided at the time and in the manner specified by the Secretary. (Authority: 20 U.S.C. 1435(a)(14))

USE OF FUNDS FOR STATE ADMINISTRATION

Sec. 303.560 Use of funds by the lead agency

A lead agency may use funds under this part that are reasonable and necessary for administering the State's early intervention program for infants and toddlers with disabilities. (Authority: 20 U.S.C. 1433, 1435(a)(10))

SUBPART G—STATE INTERAGENCY COORDINATING COUNCIL

GENERAL

Sec. 303.600 Establishment of Council

(a) A State that desires to receive financial assistance under this part shall establish a State Interagency Coordinating Council.

(b) The Council must be appointed by the Governor. The Governor shall ensure that the membership of the Council reasonably represents the population of the State.

(c) The Governor shall designate a member of the Council to serve as the chairperson of the Council or require the Council to do so. Any member of the Council who is a representative of the lead agency designated under Sec. 303.500 may not serve as the chairperson of the Council. (Authority: 20 U.S.C. 1441(a))

Note: To avoid a potential conflict of interest, it is recommended that parent representatives who are selected to serve on the Council not be employees of any agency involved in providing early intervention services. It is suggested that consideration be given to maintaining an appropriate balance between the urban and rural communities of the State.

Sec. 303.601 Composition

(a) The Council must be composed as follows:

    (1)(i) At least 20 percent of the members must be parents, including minority parents, of infants or toddlers with disabilities or children with disabilities aged 12 or younger, with knowledge of, or experience with, programs for infants and toddlers with disabilities.

        (ii) At least one member must be a parent of an infant or toddler with a disability or a child with a disability aged six or younger.

    (2) At least 20 percent of the members must be public or private providers of early intervention services.

    (3) At least one member must be from the State legislature.

    (4) At least one member must be involved in personnel preparation.

    (5) At least one member must—

        (i) Be from each of the State agencies involved in the provisions of, or payment for, early intervention services to infants and toddlers with disabilities and their families; and

        (ii) Have sufficient authority to engage in policy planning and implementation on behalf of these agencies.

    (6) At least one member must—

        (i) Be from the State educational agency responsible for preschool services to children with disabilities; and

        (ii) Have sufficient authority to engage in policy planning and implementation on behalf of that agency.

    (7) At least one member must be from the agency responsible for the State governance of health insurance.

    (8) At least one member must be from a Head Start agency or program in the State.

    (9) At least one member must be from a State agency responsible for child care.

(b) The Council may include other members selected by the Governor, including a representative from the BIA or, where there is no school operated or funded by the BIA, from the Indian Health Service or the tribe or tribal council. (Authority: 20 U.S.C. 1441(b))

Sec. 303.602 Use of funds by the Council

(a) General

Subject to the approval of the Governor, the Council may use funds under this part—

(1) To conduct hearings and forums;

(2) To reimburse members of the Council for reasonable and necessary expenses for attending Council meetings and performing Council duties (including child care for parent representatives);

(3) To pay compensation to a member of the Council if the member is not employed or must forfeit wages from other employment when performing official Council business;

(4) To hire staff; and

(5) To obtain the services of professional, technical, and clerical personnel, as may be necessary to carry out the performance of its functions under this part.

(b) Compensation and expenses of Council members

Except as provided in paragraph (a) of this section, Council members shall serve without compensation from funds available under this part. (Authority: 20 U.S.C. 1438, 1441(C) and (d))

Sec. 303.603 Meetings

(a) The Council shall meet at least quarterly and in such places as it deems necessary.

(b) The meetings must—

(1) Be publicly announced sufficiently in advance of the dates they are to be held to ensure that all interested parties have an opportunity to attend; and

(2) To the extent appropriate, be open and accessible to the general public.

(c) Interpreters for persons who are deaf and other necessary services must be provided at Council meetings, both for Council members and participants. The Council may use funds under this part to pay for those services. (Authority: 20 U.S.C. 1441(C) and (d))

Sec. 303.604 Conflict of interest

No member of the Council may cast a vote on any matter that would provide direct financial benefit to that member or otherwise give the appearance of a conflict of interest. (Authority: 20 U.S.C. 1441(f))

FUNCTIONS OF THE COUNCIL

Sec. 303.650 General

(a) Each Council shall—

(1) Advise and assist the lead agency in the development and implementation of the policies that constitute the statewide system;

(2) Assist the lead agency in achieving the full participation, coordination, and cooperation of all appropriate public agencies in the State;

(3) Assist the lead agency in the effective implementation of the statewide system, by establishing a process that includes—

(i) Seeking information from service providers, service coordinators, parents, and others about any Federal, State, or local policies that impede timely service delivery; and

(ii) Taking steps to ensure that any policy problems identified under paragraph (a)(3)(i) of this section are resolved; and

(4) To the extent appropriate, assist the lead agency in the resolution of disputes.

(b) Each Council may advise and assist the lead agency and the State educational agency regarding the provision of appropriate services for children aged birth to five, inclusive.

(c) Each Council may advise appropriate agencies in the State with respect to the integration of services for infants and toddlers with disabilities and at-risk infants and toddlers and their families, regardless of whether at-risk infants and toddlers are eligible for early intervention services in the State. (Authority: 20 U.S.C. 1441(e)(1)(A) and (e)(2))

Sec. 303.651 Advising and assisting the lead agency in its administrative duties

Each Council shall advise and assist the lead agency in the—

(a) Identification of sources of fiscal and other support for services for early intervention programs under this part;

(b) Assignment of financial responsibility to the appropriate agency; and

(c) Promotion of the interagency agreements under Sec. 303.523. (Authority: 20 U.S.C. 1441(e)(1)(A))

Sec. 303.652 Applications

Each Council shall advise and assist the lead agency in the preparation of applications under this part and amendments to those applications. (Authority: 20 U.S.C. 1441(e)(1)(B))

Sec. 303.653 Transitional services

Each Council shall advise and assist the State educational agency regarding the transition of toddlers with disabilities to preschool and other appropriate services. (Authority: 20 U.S.C. 1441(e)(1)©)

Sec. 303.654 Annual report to the Secretary

(a) Each Council shall—

(1) Prepare an annual report to the Governor and to the Secretary on the status of early intervention programs operated within the State for children eligible under this part and their families; and

(2) Submit the report to the Secretary by a date that the Secretary establishes.

(b) Each annual report must contain the information required by the Secretary for the year for which the report is made. (Authority: 20 U.S.C. 1441(e)(1)(D))

Sec. 303.670 [REMOVED]

CHAPTER 7
OVERVIEW OF SECTION 504

Many parents want their children to be classified as Section 504 children, not as "special ed" children under IDEA. They believe that Section 504 of the Rehabilitation Act will provide the child with more benefits and rights. This is clearly wrong.

The child who receives protections under Section 504 of the Rehabilitation Act has fewer rights than the child who receives special education services under IDEA. The child who is eligible for special education under IDEA automatically receives protections under Section 504.

If the child has a disability that adversely affects educational performance, the child is covered under IDEA. If the child has a disability that does not adversely affect educational performance, the child is usually covered under Section 504 but does not receive services under IDEA.

Change the facts to illustrate the differences between these two laws. A handicapped child is in a wheelchair. Under Section 504, this child shall not be discriminated against because of the disability. The child shall be provided with access to an education, to and through the schoolhouse door. However, under Section 504 there is no guarantee that this wheelchair-bound child will receive an education from which the child benefits. The child simply has access to the same education that children without disabilities receive.

Now assume that the child in a wheelchair also has neurological problems that adversely affect the child's ability to learn. Under IDEA, the child with a disability that adversely affects educational performance is entitled to an education that is individually designed to meet the child's unique needs and from which the child receives educational benefit.

Many parents believe that if the child has a Section 504 plan, the child will remain in the regular classroom. Some parents and educators believe that under IDEA, children must be placed in special education classes. This is incorrect. For these reasons, parents often assume that IDEA is less desirable.

Who? Definition of Section 504 Child

Section 504 is a civil rights law. To be eligible for Section 504 protections, the child must have a physical or mental impairment that substantially limits one or more major life activities; have a record of such an impairment; or be regarded as having such an impairment.

The law offers protections to children who meet the criteria for "handicapped:" children who have a physical or mental impairment that substantially limits a major life activity or is regarded as handicapped by others.

"Major life activities" include walking, seeing, hearing, speaking, breathing, **learning**, reading, writing, performing math calculations, working, caring for oneself, and performing manual tasks. The handicapping condition must "substantially limit" at least one major life activity for the child to be eligible.

Section 504 at 29 U.S.C. § 706(7)(B) says "handicapped individual" means "any person who (i) has a physical or mental impairment which substantially limits one or more of such person's major life activities, (ii) has a record of such impairment, or (iii) is regarded as having such an impairment. For our purposes, the key is whether the child has an "impairment" that "substantially limits . . . one or more . . . major life activities . . ."

Litigation often focuses on the terms "substantially" and "major life activities." Learning is a "major life activity." Is learning "substantially limited"? Does the child's disability adversely affect educational performance?

Educational performance is often assessed by looking at the child's grades. Yet, according to the National Educational Longitudinal Study, the average grade in American schools is now a "B." ("What Do Student Grades Mean?" available from ERIC). In some school districts, children receive honor roll grades but cannot read, write, spell, or do arithmetic .

What? A Section 504 Education

The Code of Federal Regulations at 34 C. F.R. § 104.33(b)(1) defines a free appropriate public education as "the provision of regular or special education and related aids and services that . . . are designed to meet individual educational needs of persons with disabilities as adequately as the needs of persons without disabilities are met and . . . are based upon adherence to specified procedures."

Under Section 504, the handicapped child should receive an education that is comparable to the education provided to children who are not handicapped. To make education comparable, Section 504 plans often include classroom accommodations and modifications. Section 504 does not require that the child will benefit from the education. Section 504 does not require that an IEP be designed to meet the child's unique needs, from which the child will receive educational benefit.

Under IDEA, the term "free appropriate public education" means that the child will receive clear educational benefit. The IDEA child may receive educational remediation where the child is taught how to speak, read, write, spell, and do arithmetic. Older children must have transition plans to help them secure more education or enter the world of work. The concepts of "access" and "educational benefit" are important.

Eligible children under Section 504 include those with chronic health conditions, those identified as "at risk" or potential for dropping out of school, children with substance abuse problems, and children who return to school after a serious illness or injury. (Weber, "Section 504")

Under Section 504, there is a requirement for an evaluation that draws on information from a variety of sources in the area of concerns. No meeting is required for a change in placement.

Discipline: Section 504 v. IDEA

Before Public Law 94-142 was passed in 1975, children with disabilities were routinely excluded from school. School districts often used disciplinary measures to keep unwanted disabled children out of school. Some school districts refused to provide any education to children with disabilities and used expulsions to evade the law.

As a condition of receiving federal funding under IDEA, schools must now provide disabled students with access to and benefit from an education. Schools cannot evade their responsibility to provide disabled children with an appropriate education, even if they expel these children.

The IDEA child has the right to FAPE, even if expelled from school. The Section 504 child does not have this protection. If the Section 504 child misbehaves and the school decides that the child's behavior is not a manifestation of the disability, the child can be expelled from school permanently.

Accessibility

Section 504 includes regulations about accessibility of schools and educational programs. Section 504 requires that "reasonable accommodations" be made. Assume that the high school child in a wheelchair needs to take biology. The biology class is on the second floor of the school. Under Section 504, the child is entitled to "reasonable access" which usually means that the child must be provided with a way to get to the second floor.

Procedural Safeguards

Under Section 504, there is no written notice requirement. Notice is not required before a "significant change" in placement. In contrast, IDEA includes an elaborate system of procedural safeguards to protect the child and parents. Safeguards include written notice before any change of placement and the right to an independent educational evaluation at public expense. Section 504 contains no provision for an independent educational evaluation at public expense.

Section 504 and IDEA require school districts to have impartial hearings for parents who disagree with the identification, evaluation or placement of a child. Under Section 504, the parent has an opportunity to participate and be represented by counsel. Other details are left to the discretion of the school district.

References

Education Research Report. (1994) "What Do Student Grades Mean: Differences Across Schools" ERIC database.

Weber, Mark. (1992) *Special Education Law and Litigation Treatise* (Horsham, PA: LRP Publications, Inc.)

CHAPTER 8
THE REHABILITATION ACT OF 1973
29 U.S.C. CHAPTER 16

Sec. 701 Congressional findings; purpose; policy

(a) Findings

Congress finds that—

(1) millions of Americans have one or more physical or mental disabilities and the number of Americans with such disabilities is increasing;

(2) individuals with disabilities constitute one of the most disadvantaged groups in society;

(3) disability is a natural part of the human experience and in no way diminishes the right of individuals to—

    (A) live independently;

    (B) enjoy self-determination;

    (C) make choices;

    (D) contribute to society;

    (E) pursue meaningful careers; and

    (F) enjoy full inclusion and integration in the economic, political, social, cultural, and educational mainstream of American society;

(4) increased employment of individuals with disabilities can be achieved through the provision of individualized training, independent living services, educational and support services, and meaningful opportunities for employment in integrated work settings through the provision of reasonable accommodations;

(5) individuals with disabilities continually encounter various forms of discrimination in such critical areas as employment, housing, public accommodations, education, transportation, communication, recreation, institutionalization, health services, voting, and public services; and

(6) the goals of the Nation properly include the goal of providing individuals with disabilities with the tools necessary to—

    (A) make informed choices and decisions; and

    (B) achieve equality of opportunity, full inclusion and integration in society, employment, independent living, and economic and social self-sufficiency, for such individuals.

(b) Purpose

The purposes of this chapter are—

(1) to empower individuals with disabilities to maximize employment, economic self-sufficiency, independence, and inclusion and integration into society, through—

    (A) comprehensive and coordinated state-of-the-art programs of vocational rehabilitation;

    (B) independent living centers and services;

    (C) research;

    (D) training;

    (E) demonstration projects; and

    (F) the guarantee of equal opportunity; and

(2) to ensure that the Federal Government plays a leadership role in promoting the employment of individuals with disabilities, especially individuals with severe disabilities, and in assisting States and providers of services in fulfilling the aspirations of such individuals with disabilities for meaningful and gainful employment and independent living.

(c) Policy

It is the policy of the United States that all programs, projects, and activities receiving assistance under this chapter shall be carried out in a manner consistent with the principles of—

(1) respect for individual dignity, personal responsibility, self-determination, and pursuit of meaningful careers, based on informed choice, of individuals with disabilities;

(2) respect for the privacy, rights, and equal access (including the use of accessible formats), of the individuals;

(3) inclusion, integration, and full participation of the individuals;

(4) support for the involvement of a parent, a family member, a guardian, an advocate, or an authorized representative if an individual with a disability requests, desires, or needs such support; and

(5) support for individual and systemic advocacy and community involvement.

(Pub. L. 93-112, Sec. 2, Sept. 26, 1973, 87 Stat. 357; Pub. L. 95-602, title I, Sec. 122(a)(1), Nov. 6, 1978, 92 Stat. 2984; Pub. L. 99-506, title I, Sec. 101, Oct. 21, 1986, 100 Stat. 1808; Pub. L. 102-569, title I, Sec. 101, Oct. 29, 1992, 106 Stat. 4346.)

Sec. 705 Definitions

(20) Individual with a disability

(A) In general. Except as otherwise provided in subparagraph (B), the term 'individual with a disability' means any individual who—

(i) has a physical or mental impairment which for such individual constitutes or results in a substantial impediment to employment; and

(ii) can benefit in terms of an employment outcome from vocational rehabilitation services provided pursuant to title I, III, or VI.

(B) Certain programs; limitations on major life activities

Subject to subparagraphs (C), (D), (E), and (F), the term 'individual with a disability' means, for purposes of Secs. 701, 713, and 714, and titles II, IV, V, and VII of this Act, any person who—

(i) has a physical or mental impairment which substantially limits one or more of such person's major life activities;

(ii) has a record of such an impairment; or

(iii) is regarded as having such an impairment.

(C) Rights and advocacy provisions

(i) In general; exclusion of individuals engaging in drug use

For purposes of title V, the term 'individual with a disability' does not include an individual who is currently engaging in the illegal use of drugs, when a covered entity acts on the basis of such use.

(ii) Exception for individuals no longer engaging in drug use

Nothing in clause (i) shall be construed to exclude as an individual with a disability an individual who—

(I) has successfully completed a supervised drug rehabilitation program and is no longer engaging in the illegal use of drugs, or has otherwise been rehabilitated successfully and is no longer engaging in such use;

(II) is participating in a supervised rehabilitation program and is no longer engaging in such use; or

(III) is erroneously regarded as engaging in such use, but is not engaging in such use;

except that it shall not be a violation of this Act for a covered entity to adopt or administer reasonable policies or procedures, including but not limited to drug testing, designed to ensure that an individual described in subclause (I) or (II) is no longer engaging in the illegal use of drugs.

(iii) Exclusion for certain services

Notwithstanding clause (i), for purposes of programs and activities providing health services and services provided under titles I, II, and III, an individual shall not be excluded from the benefits of such programs or activities on the basis of his or her current illegal use of drugs if he or she is otherwise entitled to such services.

(iv) Disciplinary action

For purposes of programs and activities providing educational services, local educational agencies may take disciplinary action pertaining to the use or possession of illegal drugs or alcohol against any student who is an individual with a disability and who currently is engaging in the illegal use of drugs or in the use of alcohol to the same extent that such disciplinary action is taken against students who are not individuals with disabilities.

Furthermore, the due process procedures at Sec. 104.36 of title 34, Code of Federal Regulations (or any corresponding similar regulation or ruling) shall not apply to such disciplinary actions.

(v) Employment; exclusion of alcoholics

For purposes of Secs. 793 and 794 as such sections relate to employment, the term 'individual with a disability' does not include any individual who is an alcoholic whose current use of alcohol prevents such individual from performing the duties of the job in question or whose employment, by reason of such current alcohol abuse, would constitute a direct threat to property or the safety of others.

(D) Employment; exclusion of individuals with certain diseases or infections

For the purposes of Secs. 793 and 794, as such sections relate to employment, such term does not include an individual who has a currently contagious disease or infection and who, by reason of such disease or infection, would constitute a direct threat to the health or safety of other individuals or who, by reason of the currently contagious disease or infection, is unable to perform the duties of the job.

(E) Rights provisions; Exclusion of individuals on basis of homosexuality or bisexuality

For the purposes of Secs. 488, 791, 793, and 794—

(i) for purposes of the application of subparagraph (B) to such sections, the term 'impairment' does not include homosexuality or bisexuality; and

(ii) therefore the term 'individual with a disability' does not include an individual on the basis of homosexuality or bisexuality.

(F) Rights provisions; exclusion of individuals on basis of certain disorders

For the purposes of Secs. 791, 793, and 794, the term 'individual with a disability' does not include an individual on the basis of—

(i) transvestism, transsexualism, pedophilia, exhibitionism, voyeurism, gender identity disorders not resulting from physical impairments, or other sexual behavior disorders;

(ii) compulsive gambling, kleptomania, or pyromania; or

(iii) psychoactive substance use disorders resulting from current illegal use of drugs.

(G) Individuals with disabilities

The term 'individuals with disabilities' means more than one individual with a disability.

Section 794 Nondiscrimination under Federal grants and programs

(a) Promulgation of nondiscriminatory rules and regulations; copies to appropriate committees

No otherwise qualified individual with a disability in the United States, as defined in Sec. 705(20) of this title, shall, solely by reason of her or his disability, be excluded from the participation in, be denied the benefits of, or be subjected to discrimination under any program or activity receiving Federal financial assistance or under any program or activity conducted by any Executive agency or by the United States Postal Service. The head of each such agency shall promulgate such regulations as may be necessary to carry out the amendments to this section made by the Rehabilitation, Comprehensive Services, and Developmental Disabilities Act of 1978. Copies of any proposed regulation shall be submitted to appropriate authorizing committees of the Congress, and such regulation may take effect no earlier than the thirtieth day after the date on which such regulation is so submitted to such committees.

(b) "Program or activity" defined

For the purposes of this section, the term "program or activity" means all of the operations of—

(1) (A) a department, agency, special purpose district, or other instrumentality of a State or of a local government; or

(B) the entity of such State or local government that distributes such assistance and each such department or agency (and each other State or local government entity) to which the assistance is extended, in the case of assistance to a State or local government;

(2) (A) a college, university, or other postsecondary institution, or a public system of higher education; or

(B) a local educational agency (as defined in Sec. 8801 of title 20), system of vocational education, or other school system;

(3) (A) an entire corporation, partnership, or other private organization, or an entire sole proprietorship—

(i) if assistance is extended to such corporation, partnership, private organization, or sole proprietorship as a whole; or

(ii) which is principally engaged in the business of providing education, health care, housing, social services, or parks and recreation; or

(B) the entire plant or other comparable, geographically separate facility to which Federal financial assistance is extended, in the case of any other corporation, partnership, private organization, or sole proprietorship; or

(4) any other entity which is established by two or more of the entities described in paragraph (1), (2), or (3);

any part of which is extended Federal financial assistance.

(c) Significant structural alterations by small providers

Small providers are not required by subsection (a) of this section to make significant structural alterations to their existing facilities for the purpose of assuring program accessibility, if alternative means of providing the services are available. The terms used in this subsection shall be construed with reference to the regulations existing on March 22, 1988.

(d) Standards used in determining violation of section

The standards used to determine whether this section has been violated in a complaint alleging employment discrimination under this section shall be the standards applied under title I of the Americans with Disabilities Act of 1990 (42 U.S.C. 12111 et seq.) and the provisions of Secs. 501 through 504, and 510, of the Americans with Disabilities Act of 1990 (42 U.S.C. 122010912204 and 12210), as such sections relate to employment.

Sec. 794a Remedies and attorneys' fees

(a)

(1) The remedies, procedures, and rights set forth in Sec. 717 of the Civil Rights Act of 1964 (42 U.S.C. 2000e-16), including the application of Secs. 706(f) through 706(k) (42 U.S.C. 2000e-5(f) through (k)), shall be available, with respect to any complaint under Sec. 791 of this title, to any employee or applicant for employment aggrieved by the final disposition of such complaint, or by the failure to take final action on such complaint. In fashioning an equitable or affirmative action remedy under such section, a court may take into account the reasonableness of the cost of any necessary work place accommodation, and the availability of alternatives therefor or other appropriate relief in order to achieve an equitable and appropriate remedy.

(2) The remedies, procedures, and rights set forth in title VI of the Civil Rights Act of 1964 [42 U.S.C. 2000d et seq.] shall be available to any person aggrieved by any act or failure to act by any recipient of Federal assistance or Federal provider of such assistance under Sec. 794 of this title.

(b) In any action or proceeding to enforce or charge a violation of a provision of this subchapter, the court, in its discretion, may allow the prevailing party, other than the United States, a reasonable attorney's fee as part of the costs.
section.

END SECTION 504 STATUTE

CHAPTER 9

TABLE OF SECTION 504 REGULATIONS
34 C.F.R. Part 104

Nondiscrimination on the Basis of Handicap in Programs and Activities Receiving or Benefiting From Federal Financial Assistance

NONDISCRIMINATION ON THE BASIS ON HANDICAP IN PROGRAMS AND ACTIVITIES RECEIVING OR BENEFITING FROM FEDERAL FINANCIAL ASSISTANCE
34 C.F.R. PART 104

Subpart A—General Provisions
Subpart B—Employment Practices
Subpart C—Program Accessibility
Subpart D—Preschool, Elementary, and Secondary Education
Subpart E—Postsecondary Education
Subpart F—Health, Welfare, and Social Services
Subpart G—Procedures

SUBPART A—GENERAL PROVISIONS

Sec. 104.1 Purpose.

The purpose of this part is to effectuate Sec. 504 of the Rehabilitation Act of 1973, which is designed to eliminate discrimination on the basis of handicap in any program or activity receiving Federal financial assistance.

Sec. 104.2 Application.

This part applies to each recipient of Federal financial assistance from the Department of Education and to each program or activity that receives or benefits from such assistance.

Sec. 104.3 Definitions

As used in this part, the term:

(a) "**The Act**" means the Rehabilitation Act of 1973, Pub. L. 93-112, as amended by the Rehabilitation Act Amendments of 1974, Pub. L. 93-516, 29 U.S.C. 794.

(b) "**Sec. 504**" means Sec. 504 of the Act.

(c) "**Education of the Handicapped Act**" means that statute as amended by the Education for all Handicapped Children Act of 1975, Pub. L. 94-142, 20 U.S.C. 1401 et seq.

(d) "**Department**" means the Department of Education.

(e) "Assistant Secretary" means the Assistant Secretary for Civil Rights of the Department of Education.

(f) "**Recipient**" means any state or its political subdivision, any instrumentality of a state or its political subdivision, any public or private agency, institution, organization, or other entity, or any person to which Federal financial assistance is extended directly or through another recipient, including any successor, assignee, or transferee of a recipient, but excluding the ultimate beneficiary of the assistance.

(g) "**Applicant for assistance**" means one who submits an application, request, or plan required to be approved by a Department official or by a recipient as a condition to becoming a recipient.

(h) "**Federal financial assistance**" means any grant, loan, contract (other than a procurement contract or a contract of insurance or guaranty), or any other arrangement by which the Department provides or otherwise makes available assistance in the form of:

  (1) Funds;

  (2) Services of Federal personnel; or

  (3) Real and personal property or any interest in or use of such property, including:

    (i) Transfers or leases of such property for less than fair market value or for reduced consideration; and

    (ii) Proceeds from a subsequent transfer or lease of such property if the Federal share of its fair market value is not returned to the Federal Government.

(i) "**Facility**" means all or any portion of buildings, structures, equipment, roads, walks, parking lots, or other real or personal property or interest in such property.

(j) "**Handicapped person**."

  (1) "Handicapped persons" means any person who

    (i) has a physical or mental impairment which substantially limits one or more major life activities,

    (ii) has a record of such an impairment, or

    (iii) is regarded as having such an impairment.

(2) As used in paragraph (j)(1) of this section, the phrase:

(i) **"Physical or mental impairment"** means (A) any physiological disorder or condition, cosmetic disfigurement, or anatomical loss affecting one or more of the following body systems: neurological; musculoskeletal; special sense organs; respiratory, including speech organs; cardiovascular; reproductive, digestive, genito-urinary; hemic and lymphatic; skin; and endocrine; or (B) any mental or psychological disorder, such as mental retardation, organic brain syndrome, emotional or mental illness, and specific learning disabilities.

(ii) **"Major life activities"** means functions such as caring for one's self, performing manual tasks, walking, seeing, hearing, speaking, breathing, learning, and working.

(iii) **"Has a record of such an impairment"** means has a history of, or has been misclassified as having, a mental or physical impairment that substantially limits one or more major life activities.

(iv) **"Is regarded as having an impairment"** means (A) has a physical or mental impairment that does not substantially limit major life activities but that is treated by a recipient as constituting such a limitation; (B) has a physical or mental impairment that substantially limits major life activities only as a result of the attitudes of others toward such impairment; or (C) has none of the impairments defined in paragraph (j)(2)(i) of this section but is treated by a recipient as having such an impairment.

(k) **"Qualified handicapped person"** means:

(1) With respect to employment, a handicapped person who, with reasonable accommodation, can perform the essential functions of the job in question;

(2) With respect to public preschool elementary, secondary, or adult educational services, a handicapped person

(i) of an age during which nonhandicapped persons are provided such services,

(ii) of any age during which it is mandatory under state law to provide such services to handicapped persons, or

(iii) to whom a state is required to provide a free appropriate public education under Sec. 612 of the Education of the Handicapped Act; and

(3) With respect to postsecondary and vocational education services, a handicapped person who meets the academic and technical standards requisite to admission or participation in the recipient's education program or activity;

(4) With respect to other services, a handicapped person who meets the essential eligibility requirements for the receipt of such services.

(l) **"Handicap"** means any condition or characteristic that renders a person a handicapped person as defined in paragraph (j) of this section.

Sec. 104.4 Discrimination prohibited

(a) General

No qualified handicapped person shall, on the basis of handicap, be excluded from participation in, be denied the benefits of, or otherwise be subjected to discrimination under any program or activity which receives or benefits from Federal financial assistance.

(b) Discriminatory actions prohibited

(1) A recipient, in providing any aid, benefit, or service, may not, directly or through contractual, licensing, or other arrangements, on the basis of handicap:

(i) Deny a qualified handicapped person the opportunity to participate in or benefit from the aid, benefit, or service;

(ii) Afford a qualified handicapped person an opportunity to participate in or benefit from the aid, benefit, or service that is not equal to that afforded others;

(iii) Provide a qualified handicapped person with an aid, benefit, or service that is not as effective as that provided to others;

(iv) Provide different or separate aid, benefits, or services to handicapped persons or to any class of handicapped persons unless such action is necessary to provide qualified handicapped persons with aid, benefits, or services that are as effective as those provided to others;

(v) Aid or perpetuate discrimination against a qualified handicapped person by providing significant assistance to an agency, organization, or person that discriminates on the basis of handicap in providing any aid, benefit, or service to beneficiaries of the recipients program;

(vi) Deny a qualified handicapped person the opportunity to participate as a member of planning or advisory boards; or

(vii) Otherwise limit a qualified handicapped person in the enjoyment of any right, privilege, advantage, or opportunity enjoyed by others receiving an aid, benefit, or service.

(2) For purposes of this part, aids, benefits, and services, to be equally effective, are not required to produce the identical result or level of achievement for handicapped and nonhandicapped persons, but must afford handicapped persons equal opportunity to obtain the same result, to gain the same benefit, or to reach the same level of achievement, in the most integrated setting appropriate to the person's needs.

(3) Despite the existence of separate or different programs or activities provided in accordance with this part, a recipient may not deny a qualified handicapped person the opportunity to participate in such programs or activities that are not separate or different.

(4) A recipient may not, directly or through contractual or other arrangements, utilize criteria or methods of administration (i) that have

the effect of subjecting qualified handicapped persons to discrimination on the basis of handicap, (ii) that have the purpose or effect of defeating or substantially impairing accomplishment of the objectives of the recipient's program with respect to handicapped persons, or (iii) that perpetuate the discrimination of another recipient if both recipients are subject to common administrative control or are agencies of the same State.

(5) In determining the site or location of a facility, an applicant for assistance or a recipient may not make selections (i) that have the effect of excluding handicapped persons from, denying them the benefits of, or otherwise subjecting them to discrimination under any program or activity that receives or benefits from Federal financial assistance or (ii) that have the purpose or effect of defeating or substantially impairing the accomplishment of the objectives of the program or activity with respect to handicapped persons.

(6) As used in this section, the aid, benefit, or service provided under a program or activity receiving or benefiting from Federal financial assistance includes any aid, benefit, or service provided in or through a facility that has been constructed, expanded, altered, leased or rented, or otherwise acquired, in whole or in part, with Federal financial assistance.

(c) Programs limited by Federal law

The exclusion of nonhandicapped persons from the benefits of a program limited by Federal statute or executive order to handicapped persons or the exclusion of a specific class of handicapped persons from a program limited by Federal statute or executive order to a different class of handicapped persons is not prohibited by this part.

Sec. 104.5 Assurances required

(a) Assurances

An applicant for Federal financial assistance for a program or activity to which this part applies shall submit an assurance, on a form specified by the Assistant Secretary, that the program will be operated in compliance with this part. An applicant may incorporate these assurances by reference in subsequent applications to the Department.

(b) Duration of obligation

(1) In the case of Federal financial assistance extended in the form of real property or to provide real property or structures on the property, the assurance will obligate the recipient or, in the case of a subsequent transfer, the transferee, for the period during which the real property or structures are used for the purpose for which Federal financial assistance is extended or for another purpose involving the provision of similar services or benefits.

(2) In the case of Federal financial assistance extended to provide personal property, the assurance will obligate the recipient for the period during which it retains ownership or possession of the property.

(3) In all other cases the assurance will obligate the recipient for the period during which Federal financial assistance is extended.

(c) Covenants

(1) Where Federal financial assistance is provided in the form of real property or interest in the property from the Department, the instrument effecting or recording this transfer shall contain a covenant running with the land to assure nondiscrimination for the period during which the real property is used for a purpose for which the Federal financial assistance is extended or for another purpose involving the provision of similar services or benefits.

(2) Where no transfer of property is involved but property is purchased or improved with Federal financial assistance, the recipient shall agree to include the covenant described in paragraph (b)(2) of this section in the instrument effecting or recording any subsequent transfer of the property.

(3) Where Federal financial assistance is provided in the form of real property or interest in the property from the Department, the covenant shall also include a condition coupled with a right to be reserved by the Department to revert title to the property in the event of a breach of the covenant. If a transferee of real property proposes to mortgage or otherwise encumber the real property as security for financing construction of new, or improvement of existing, facilities on the property for the purposes for which the property was transferred, the Assistant Secretary may, upon request of the transferee and if necessary to accomplish such financing and upon such conditions as he or she deems appropriate, agree to forbear the exercise of such right to revert title for so long as the lien of such mortgage or other encumbrance remains effective.

Sec. 104.6 Remedial action, voluntary action, and self-evaluation

(a) Remedial action

(1) If the Assistant Secretary finds that a recipient has discriminated against persons on the basis of handicap in violation of Sec. 504 or this part, the recipient shall take such remedial action as the Assistant Secretary deems necessary to overcome the effects of the discrimination.

(2) Where a recipient is found to have discriminated against persons on the basis of handicap in violation of Sec. 504 or this part and where another recipient exercises control over the recipient that has discriminated, the Assistant Secretary, where appropriate, may require either or both recipients to take remedial action.

(3) The Assistant Secretary may, where necessary to overcome the effects of discrimination in violation of Sec. 504 or this part, require a recipient to take remedial action (i) with respect to handicapped persons who are no longer participants in the recipient's program but

who were participants in the program when such discrimination occurred or (ii) with respect to handicapped persons who would have been participants in the program had the discrimination not occurred.

(b) Voluntary action

A recipient may take steps, in addition to any action that is required by this part, to overcome the effects of conditions that resulted in limited participation in the recipient's program or activity by qualified handicapped persons.

(c) Self-evaluation

(1) A recipient shall, within one year of the effective date of this part:

(i) Evaluate, with the assistance of interested persons, including handicapped persons or organizations representing handicapped persons, its current policies and practices and the effects thereof that do not or may not meet the requirements of this part; (ii) Modify, after consultation with interested persons, including handicapped persons or organizations representing handicapped persons, any policies and practices that do not meet the requirements of this part; and

(iii) Take, after consultation with interested persons, including handicapped persons or organizations representing handicapped persons, appropriate remedial steps to eliminate the effects of any discrimination that resulted from adherence to these policies and practices.

(2) A recipient that employs fifteen or more persons shall, for at least three years following completion of the evaluation required under paragraph (c)(1) of this section, maintain on file, make available for public inspection, and provide to the Assistant Secretary upon request:

(i) A list of the interested persons consulted

(ii) a description of areas examined and any problems identified, and (iii) a description of any modifications made and of any remedial steps taken.

Sec. 104.7 Designation of responsible employee and adoption of grievance procedures

(a) Designation of responsible employee

A recipient that employs fifteen or more persons shall designate at least one person to coordinate its efforts to comply with this part.

(b) Adoption of grievance procedures

A recipient that employs fifteen or more persons shall adopt grievance procedures that incorporate appropriate due process standards and that provide for the prompt and equitable resolution of complaints alleging any action prohibited by this part. Such procedures need not be established with respect to complaints from applicants for employment or from applicants for admission to postsecondary educational institutions.

Sec. 104.8 Notice

(a) A recipient that employs fifteen or more persons shall take appropriate initial and continuing steps to notify participants, beneficiaries, applicants, and employees, including those with impaired vision or hearing, and unions or professional organizations holding collective bargaining or professional agreements with the recipient that it does not discriminate on the basis of handicap in violation of Sec. 504 and this part. The notification shall state, where appropriate, that the recipient does not discriminate in admission or access to, or treatment or employment in, its programs and activities. The notification shall also include an identification of the responsible employee designated pursuant to 104.7(a). A recipient shall make the initial notification required by this paragraph within 90 days of the effective date of this part. Methods of initial and continuing notification may include the posting of notices, publication in newspapers and magazines, placement of notices in recipients' publication, and distribution of memoranda or other written communications.

(b) If a recipient publishes or uses recruitment materials or publications containing general information that it makes available to participants, beneficiaries, applicants, or employees, it shall include in those materials or publications a statement of the policy described in paragraph (a) of this section. A recipient may meet the requirement of this paragraph either by including appropriate inserts in existing materials and publications or by revising and reprinting the materials and publications.

Sec. 104.9 Administrative requirements for small recipients

The Assistant Secretary may require any recipient with fewer than fifteen employees, or any class of such recipients, to comply with 104.7 and 104.8, in whole or in part, when the Assistant Secretary finds a violation of this part or finds that such compliance will not significantly impair the ability of the recipient or class of recipients to provide benefits or services.

Sec. 104.10 Effect of state or local law or other requirements and effect of employment opportunities

(a) The obligation to comply with this part is not obviated or alleviated by the existence of any state or local law or other requirement that, on the basis of handicap, imposes prohibitions or limits upon the eligibility of qualified handicapped persons to receive services or to practice any occupation or profession.

(b) The obligation to comply with this part is not obviated or alleviated because employment opportunities in any occupation or profession are or may be more limited for handicapped persons than for nonhandicapped persons.

SUBPART B—EMPLOYMENT PRACTICES

Sec. 104.11 Discrimination prohibited
(a) General

(1) No qualified handicapped person shall, on the basis of handicap, be subjected to discrimination in employment under any program or activity to which this part applies.

(2) A recipient that receives assistance under the Education of the Handicapped Act shall take positive steps to employ and advance in employment qualified handicapped persons in programs assisted under that Act.

(3) A recipient shall make all decisions concerning employment under any program or activity to which this part applies in a manner which ensures that discrimination on the basis of handicap does not occur and may not limit, segregate, or classify applicants or employees in any way that adversely affects their opportunities or status because of handicap.

(4) A recipient may not participate in a contractual or other relationship that has the effect of subjecting qualified handicapped applicants or employees to discrimination prohibited by this subpart. The relationships referred to in this paragraph include relationships with employment and referral agencies, with labor unions, with organizations providing or administering fringe benefits to employees of the recipient, and with organizations providing training and apprenticeship programs.

(b) Specific activities. The provisions of this subpart apply to:

(1) Recruitment, advertising, and the processing of applications for employment;

(2) Hiring, upgrading, promotion, award of tenure, demotion, transfer, layoff, termination, right of return from layoff and rehiring;

(3) Rates of pay or any other form of compensation and changes in compensation;

(4) Job assignments, job classifications, organizational structures, position descriptions, lines of progression, and seniority lists;

(5) Leaves of absence, sick leave, or any other leave;

(6) Fringe benefits available by virtue of employment, whether or not administered by the recipient;

(7) Selection and financial support for training, including apprenticeship, professional meetings, conferences, and other related activities, and selection for leaves of absence to pursue training;

(8) Employer sponsored activities, including social or recreational programs; and

(9) Any other term, condition, or privilege of employment.

(c) A recipient's obligation to comply with this subpart is not affected by any inconsistent term of any collective bargaining agreement to which it is a party.

Sec. 104.12 Reasonable accommodation

(a) A recipient shall make reasonable accommodation to the known physical or mental limitations of an otherwise qualified handicapped applicant or employee unless the recipient can demonstrate that the accommodation would impose an undue hardship on the operation of its program.

(b) Reasonable accommodation may include:

(1) Making facilities used by employees readily accessible to and usable by handicapped persons, and

(2) job restructuring, part-time or modified work schedules, acquisition or modification of equipment or devices, the provision of readers or interpreters, and other similar actions.

(c) In determining pursuant to paragraph (a) of this section whether an accommodation would impose an undue hardship on the operation of a recipient's program, factors to be considered include:

(1) The overall size of the recipient's program with respect to number of employees, number and type of facilities, and size of budget;

(2) The type of the recipient's operation, including the composition and structure of the recipient's workforce; and

(3) The nature and cost of the accommodation needed.

(d) A recipient may not deny any employment opportunity to a qualified handicapped employee or applicant if the basis for the denial is the need to make reasonable accommodation to the physical or mental limitations of the employee or applicant.

Sec. 104.13 Employment criteria

(a) A recipient may not make use of any employment test or other selection criterion that screens out or tends to screen out handicapped persons or any class of handicapped persons unless:

(1) The test score or other selection criterion, as used by the recipient, is shown to be job-related for the position in question, and

(2) alternative job-related tests or criteria that do not screen out or tend to screen out as many handicapped persons are not shown by the Director to be available.

(b) A recipient shall select and administer tests concerning employment so as best to ensure that, when administered to an applicant or employee who has a handicap that impairs sensory, manual, or speaking skills, the test results accurately reflect the applicant's or employee's job skills, aptitude, or whatever other factor the test purports to measure, rather than reflecting the applicant's or employee's impaired sensory, manual, or speaking skills (except where those skills are the factors that the test purports to measure).

Sec. 104.14 Preemployment inquiries

(a) Except as provided in paragraphs (b) and (c) of this section, a recipient may not conduct a preemployment medical examination or may not make preemployment inquiry of an applicant as to whether the applicant is a handicapped person or as to the nature or severity of a handicap. A recipient may, however, make preemployment inquiry into an applicant's ability to perform job-related functions.

(b) When a recipient is taking remedial action to correct the effects of past discrimination pursuant to 104.6(a), when a recipient is taking voluntary action to overcome the effects of conditions that resulted in limited participation in its federally assisted program or activity pursuant to 104.6(b), or when a recipient is taking affirmative action pursuant to Sec. 503 of the Act, the recipient may invite applicants for employment to indicate whether and to what extent they are handicapped, provided that:

(1) The recipient states clearly on any written questionnaire used for this purpose or makes clear orally if no written questionnaire is used that the information requested is intended for use solely in connection with its remedial action obligations or its voluntary or affirmative action efforts; and

(2) The recipient states clearly that the information is being requested on a voluntary basis, that it will be kept confidential as provided in paragraph (d) of this section, that refusal to provide it will not subject the applicant or employee to any adverse treatment, and that it will be used only in accordance with this part.

(c) Nothing in this section shall prohibit a recipient from conditioning an offer of employment on the results of a medical examination conducted prior to the employee's entrance on duty, provided that:

(1) All entering employees are subjected to such an examination regardless of handicap, and

(2) the results of such an examination are used only in accordance with the requirements of this part.

(d) Information obtained in accordance with this section as to the medical condition or history of the applicant shall be collected and maintained on separate forms that shall be accorded confidentiality as medical records, except that:

(1) Supervisors and managers may be informed regarding restrictions on the work or duties of handicapped persons and regarding necessary accommodations;

(2) First aid and safety personnel may be informed, where appropriate, if the condition might require emergency treatment; and

(3) Government officials investigating compliance with the Act shall be provided relevant information upon request.

SUBPART C—PROGRAM ACCESSIBILITY

Sec. 104.21 Discrimination prohibited

No qualified handicapped person shall, because a recipient's facilities are inaccessible to or unusable by handicapped persons, be denied the benefits of, be excluded from participation in, or otherwise be subjected to discrimination under any program or activity to which this part applies.

Sec. 104.22 Existing facilities

(a) Program accessibility

A recipient shall operate each program or activity to which this part applies so that the program or activity, when viewed in its entirety, is readily accessible to handicapped persons. This paragraph does not require a recipient to make each of its existing facilities or every part of a facility accessible to and usable by handicapped persons.

(b) Methods

A recipient may comply with the requirements of paragraph (a) of this section through such means as redesign of equipment, reassignment of classes or other services to accessible buildings, assignment of aides to beneficiaries, home visits, delivery of health, welfare, or other social services at alternate accessible sites, alteration of existing facilities and construction of new facilities in conformance with the requirements of 104.23, or any other methods that result in making its program or activity accessible to handicapped persons. A recipient is not required to make structural changes in existing facilities where other methods are effective in achieving compliance with paragraph (a) of this section. In choosing among available methods for meeting the requirement of paragraph (a) of this section, a recipient shall give priority to those methods that offer programs and activities to handicapped persons in the most integrated setting appropriate.

(c) Small health, welfare, or other social service providers

If a recipient with fewer than fifteen employees that provides health, welfare, or other social services finds, after consultation with a handicapped person seeking its services, that there is no method of complying with paragraph (a) of this section other than making a significant alteration in its existing facilities, the recipient may, as an alternative, refer the handicapped person to other providers of those services that are accessible.

(d) Time period

A recipient shall comply with the requirement of paragraph (a) of this section within sixty days of the effective date of this part except that where structural changes in facilities are necessary, such changes shall be made within three years of the effective date of this part, but in any event as expeditiously as possible.

(e) Transition plan

In the event that structural changes to facilities are necessary to meet the requirement of paragraph (a) of this section, a recipient shall develop, within six months of the effective date of this part, a transition plan setting forth the steps necessary to complete such changes. The plan shall be developed with the assistance of interested persons, including handicapped persons or organizations representing handicapped persons. A copy of the transition plan shall be made available for public inspection. The plan shall, at a minimum:

(1) Identify physical obstacles in the recipient's facilities that limit the accessibility of its program or activity to handicapped persons;

(2) Describe in detail the methods that will be used to make the facilities accessible;

(3) Specify the schedule for taking the steps necessary to achieve full program accessibility and, if the time period of the transition plan is longer than one year, identify the steps of that will be taken during each year of the transition period; and

(4) Indicate the person responsible for implementation of the plan.

(f) Notice

The recipient shall adopt and implement procedures to ensure that interested persons, including persons with impaired vision or hearing, can obtain information as to the existence and location of services, activities, and facilities that are accessible to and usable by handicapped persons.

Sec. 104.23 New construction

(a) Design and construction

Each facility or part of a facility constructed by, on behalf of, or for the use of a recipient shall be designed and constructed in such manner that the facility or part of the facility is readily accessible to and usable by handicapped persons, if the construction was commenced after the effective date of this part.

(b) Alteration

Each facility or part of a facility which is altered by, on behalf of, or for the use of a recipient after the effective date of this part in a manner that affects or could affect the usability of the facility or part of the facility shall, to the maximum extent feasible, be altered in such manner that the altered portion of the facility is readily accessible to and usable by handicapped persons.

(c) Conformance with Uniform Federal Accessibility Standards

(1) Effective as of January 18, 1991, design, construction, or alteration of buildings in conformance with Secs. 3-8 of the Uniform Accessibility Standards (UFAS) (Appendix A to 41 CFR Subpart 101-19.6) shall be deemed to comply with the requirements of this section with respect to those buildings. Departures from particular technical and scoping requirements of UFAS by the use of other methods are permitted where substantially equivalent or greater access to and usability of the building is provided.

(2) For purposes of this section, Sec. 4.1.6(1)(g) of UFAS shall be interpreted to exempt from the requirements of UFAS only mechanical rooms and other spaces that, because of their intended use, will not require accessibility to the public or beneficiaries or result in the employment or residence therein of persons with physical handicaps.

(3) This section does not require recipients to make building alterations that have little likelihood of being accomplished without removing or altering a load-bearing structural member. [45 FR 30936, May 9, 1980; 45 FR 37426, June 3, 1980]

SUBPART D—PRESCHOOL, ELEMENTARY, AND SECONDARY EDUCATION

Sec. 104.31 Application of this subpart

Subpart D applies to preschool, elementary, secondary, and adult education programs and activities that receive or benefit from Federal financial assistance and to recipients that operate, or that receive or benefit from Federal financial assistance for the operation of, such programs or activities.

Sec. 104.32 Location and notification

A recipient that operates a public elementary or secondary education program shall annually:

(a) Undertake to identify and locate every qualified handicapped person residing in the recipient's jurisdiction who is not receiving a public education; and

(b) Take appropriate steps to notify handicapped persons and their parents or guardians of the recipient's duty under this subpart.

Sec. 104.33 Free appropriate public education

(a) General

A recipient that operates a public elementary or secondary education program shall provide a free appropriate public education to each qualified handicapped person who is in the recipient's jurisdiction, regardless of the nature or severity of the person's handicap.

(b) Appropriate education

(1) For the purpose of this subpart, the provision of an appropriate education is the provision of regular or special education and related aids and services that (i) are designed to meet individual educational needs of handicapped persons as adequately as the needs of nonhandicapped persons are met and (ii) are based upon adherence to procedures that satisfy the requirements of 104.34, 104.35, and 104.36.

(2) Implementation of an individualized education program developed in accordance with the Education of the Handicapped Act is one means of meeting the standard established in paragraph (b)(1)(i) of this section.

(3) A recipient may place a handicapped person in or refer such person to a program other than the one that it operates as its means of carrying out the requirements of this subpart. If so, the recipient remains responsible for ensuring that the requirements of this subpart are met with respect to any handicapped person so placed or referred.

(c) Free education

(1) General

For the purpose of this section, the provision of a free education is the provision of educational and related services without cost to the handicapped person or to his or her parents or guardian, except for those fees that are imposed on non-handicapped persons or their parents or guardian. It may consist either of the provision of free services or, if a recipient places a handicapped person in or refers such person to a program not operated by the recipient as its means of carrying out the requirements of this subpart, of payment for the costs of the program. Funds available from any public or private agency may be used to meet the requirements of this subpart. Nothing in this section shall be construed to relieve an insurer or similar third party from an otherwise valid obligation to provide or pay for services provided to a handicapped person.

(2) Transportation

If a recipient places a handicapped person in or refers such person to a program not operated by the recipient as its means of carrying out the requirements of this subpart, the recipient shall ensure that adequate transportation to and from the program is provided at no greater cost than would be incurred by the person or his or her parents or guardian if the person were placed in the program operated by the recipient.

(3) Residential placement

If placement in a public or private residential program is necessary to provide a free appropriate public education to a handicapped person because of his or her handicap, the program, including non-medical care and room and board, shall be provided at no cost to the person or his or her parents or guardian.

(4) Placement of handicapped persons by parents

If a recipient has made available, in conformance with the requirements of this section and 104.34, a free appropriate public education to a handicapped person and the person's parents or guardian choose to place the person in a private school, the recipient is not required to pay for the person's education in the private school. Disagreements between a parent or guardian and a recipient regarding whether the recipient has made such a program available or otherwise regarding the question of financial responsibility are subject to the due process procedures of 104.36.

(d) Compliance

A recipient may not exclude any qualified handicapped person from a public elementary or secondary education after the effective date of this part. A recipient that is not, on the effective date of this regulation, in full compliance with the other requirements of the preceding paragraphs of this section shall meet such requirements at the earliest practicable time and in no event later than September 1, 1978.

Sec. 104.34 Educational setting

(a) Academic setting

A recipient to which this subpart applies shall educate, or shall provide for the education of, each qualified handicapped person in its jurisdiction with persons who are not handicapped to the maximum extent appropriate to the needs of the handicapped person. A recipient shall place a handicapped person in the regular educational environment operated by the recipient unless it is demonstrated by the recipient that the education of the person in the regular environment with the use of supplementary aids and services cannot be achieved satisfactorily. Whenever a recipient places a person in a setting other than the regular educational environment pursuant to this paragraph, it shall take into account the proximity of the alternate setting to the person's home.

(b) Nonacademic settings

In providing or arranging for the provision of nonacademic and extracurricular services and activities, including meals, recess periods, and the services and activities set forth in 104.37(a)(2), a recipient shall ensure that handicapped persons participate with nonhandicapped persons in such activities and services to the maximum extent appropriate to the needs of the handicapped person in question.

(c) Comparable facilities

If a recipient, in compliance with paragraph (a) of this section, operates a facility that is identifiable as being for handicapped persons, the recipient shall ensure that the facility and the services and activities provided therein are comparable to the other facilities, services, and activities of the recipient.

Sec. 104.35 Evaluation and placement

(a) Preplacement evaluation

A recipient that operates a public elementary or secondary education program shall conduct an evaluation in accordance with the requirements of paragraph (b) of this section of any person who, because of handicap, needs or is believed to need special education or related services before taking any action with respect to the initial placement of the person in a regular or special education program and any subsequent significant change in placement.

(b) Evaluation procedures

A recipient to which this subpart applies shall establish standards and procedures for the evaluation and placement of persons who, because of handicap, need or are believed to need special education or related services which ensure that:

(1) Tests and other evaluation materials have been validated for the specific purpose for which they are used and are administered by trained personnel in conformance with the instructions provided by their producer;

(2) Tests and other evaluation materials include those tailored to assess specific areas of educational need and not merely those which are designed to provide a single general intelligence quotient; and

(3) Tests are selected and administered so as best to ensure that, when a test is administered to a student with impaired sensory, manual, or speaking skills, the test results accurately reflect the student's aptitude or achievement level or whatever other factor the test purports to measure, rather than reflecting the student's impaired sensory, manual, or speaking skills (except where those skills are the factors that the test purports to measure).

(c) Placement procedures

In interpreting evaluation data and in making placement decisions, a recipient shall (1) draw upon information from a variety of sources, including aptitude and achievement tests, teacher recommendations, physical condition, social or cultural background, and adaptive behavior, (2) establish procedures to ensure that information obtained from all such sources is documented and carefully considered, (3) ensure that the placement decision is made by a group of persons, including persons knowledgeable about the child, the meaning of the evaluation data, and the placement options, and (4) ensure that the placement decision is made in conformity with 104.34.

(d) Reevaluation

A recipient to which this section applies shall establish procedures, in accordance with paragraph (b) of this section, for periodic reevaluation of students who have been provided special education and related services. A reevaluation procedure consistent with the Education for the Handicapped Act is one means of meeting this requirement.

Sec. 104.36 Procedural safeguards

A recipient that operates a public elementary or secondary education program shall establish and implement, with respect to actions regarding the identification, evaluation, or educational placement of persons who, because of handicap, need or are believed to need special instruction or related services, a system of procedural safeguards that includes notice, an opportunity for the parents or guardian of the person to examine relevant records, an impartial hearing with opportunity for participation by the person's parents or guardian and representation by counsel, and a review procedure. Compliance with the procedural safeguards of Sec. 615 of the Education of the Handicapped Act is one means of meeting this requirement.

Sec. 104.37 Nonacademic services

(a) General

(1) A recipient to which this subpart applies shall provide non-academic and extracurricular services and activities in such manner as is necessary to afford handicapped students an equal opportunity for participation in such services and activities.

(2) Nonacademic and extracurricular services and activities may include counseling services, physical recreational athletics, transportation, health services, recreational activities, special interest groups or clubs sponsored by the recipients, referrals to agencies which provide assistance to handicapped persons, and employment of students, including both employment by the recipient and assistance in making available outside employment.

(b) Counseling services

A recipient to which this subpart applies that provides personal, academic, or vocational counseling, guidance, or placement services to its students shall provide these services without discrimination on the basis of handicap. The recipient shall ensure that qualified handicapped students are not counseled toward more restrictive career objectives than are nonhandicapped students with similar interests and abilities.

(c) Physical education and athletics

(1) In providing physical education courses and athletics and similar programs and activities to any of its students, a recipient to which this subpart applies may not discriminate on the basis of handicap. A recipient that offers physical education courses or that operates or sponsors interscholastic, club, or intramural athletics shall provide to qualified handicapped students an equal opportunity for participation in these activities.

(2) A recipient may offer to handicapped students physical education and athletic activities that are separate or different from those offered to nonhandicapped students only if separation or differentiation is consistent with the requirements of 104.34 and only if no qualified handicapped student is denied the opportunity to compete for teams or to participate in courses that are not separate or different.

Sec. 104.38 Preschool and adult education programs

A recipient to which this subpart applies that operates a preschool education or day care program or activity or an adult education program or activity may not, on the basis of handicap, exclude qualified handicapped persons from the program or activity and shall take into account the needs of such persons in determining the aid, benefits, or services to be provided under the program or activity.

Sec. 104.39 Private education programs

(a) A recipient that operates a private elementary or secondary education program may not, on the basis of handicap, exclude a qualified handicapped person from such program if the person can, with minor adjustments, be provided an appropriate education, as defined in 104.33(b)(1), within the recipient's program.

(b) A recipient to which this section applies may not charge more for the provision of an appropriate education to handicapped persons than to nonhandicapped persons except to the extent that any additional charge is justified by a substantial increase in cost to the recipient.

(c) A recipient to which this section applies that operates special education programs shall operate such programs in accordance with the provisions of 104.35 and 104.36. Each recipient to which this section applies is subject to the provisions of 104.34, 104.37, and 104.38.

SUBPART E—POSTSECONDARY EDUCATION

Sec. 104.41 Application of this subpart

Subpart E applies to postsecondary education programs and activities, including postsecondary vocational education programs and activities, that receive or benefit from Federal financial assistance and to recipients that operate, or that receive or benefit from Federal financial assistance for the operation of, such programs or activities.

Sec. 104.42 Admissions and recruitment

(a) General

Qualified handicapped persons may not, on the basis of handicap, be denied admission or be subjected to discrimination in admission or recruitment by a recipient to which this subpart applies.

(b) Admissions

In administering its admission policies, a recipient to which this subpart applies:

(1) May not apply limitations upon the number or proportion of handicapped persons who may be admitted;

(2) May not make use of any test or criterion for admission that has a disproportionate, adverse effect on handicapped persons or any class of handicapped persons unless (i) the test or criterion, as used by the recipient, has been validated as a predictor of success in the education program or activity in question and (ii) alternate tests or criteria that have a less disproportionate, adverse effect are not shown by the Assistant Secretary to be available.

(3) Shall assure itself that (i) admissions tests are selected and administered so as best to ensure that, when a test is administered to an applicant who has a handicap that impairs sensory, manual, or speaking skills, the test results accurately reflect the applicant's aptitude or achievement level or whatever other factor the test purports to measure, rather than reflecting the applicant's impaired sensory, manual, or speaking skills (except where those skills are the factors that the test purports to measure); (ii) admissions tests that are designed for persons with impaired sensory, manual, or speaking skills are offered as often and in as timely a manner as are other admissions tests; and (iii) admissions tests are administered in facilities that, on the whole, are accessible to handicapped persons; and

(4) Except as provided in paragraph (c) of this section, may not make preadmission inquiry as to whether an applicant for admission is a handicapped person but, after admission, may make inquiries on a confidential basis as to handicaps that may require accommodation.

(c) Preadmission inquiry exception

When a recipient is taking remedial action to correct the effects of past discrimination pursuant to 104.6(a) or when a recipient is taking voluntary action to overcome the effects of conditions that resulted in limited participation in its federally assisted program or activity pursuant to 104.6(b), the recipient may invite applicants for admission to indicate whether and to what extent they are handicapped, Provided, That:

(1) The recipient states clearly on any written questionnaire used for this purpose or makes clear orally if no written questionnaire is used

that the information requested is intended for use solely in connection with its remedial action obligations or its voluntary action efforts; and

(2) The recipient states clearly that the information is being requested on a voluntary basis, that it will be kept confidential, that refusal to provide it will not subject the applicant to any adverse treatment, and that it will be used only in accordance with this part.

(d) Validity studies

For the purpose of paragraph (b)(2) of this section, a recipient may base prediction equations on first year grades, but shall conduct periodic validity studies against the criterion of overall success in the education program or activity in question in order to monitor the general validity of the test scores.

Sec. 104.43 Treatment of students; general

(a) No qualified handicapped student shall, on the basis of handicap, be excluded from participation in, be denied the benefits of, or otherwise be subjected to discrimination under any academic, research, occupational training, housing, health insurance, counseling, financial aid, physical education, athletics, recreation, transportation, other extracurricular, or other postsecondary education program or activity to which this subpart applies.

(b) A recipient to which this subpart applies that considers participation by students in education programs or activities not operated wholly by the recipient as part of, or equivalent to, and education program or activity operated by the recipient shall assure itself that the other education program or activity, as a whole, provides an equal opportunity for the participation of qualified handicapped persons.

(c) A recipient to which this subpart applies may not, on the basis of handicap, exclude any qualified handicapped student from any course, course of study, or other part of its education program or activity.

(d) A recipient to which this subpart applies shall operate its programs and activities in the most integrated setting appropriate.

Sec. 104.44 Academic adjustments

(a) Academic requirements

A recipient to which this subpart applies shall make such modifications to its academic requirements as are necessary to ensure that such requirements do not discriminate or have the effect of discriminating, on the basis of handicap, against a qualified handicapped applicant or student. Academic requirements that the recipient can demonstrate are essential to the program of instruction being pursued by such student or to any directly related licensing requirement will not be regarded as discriminatory within the meaning of this section. Modifications may include changes in the length of time permitted for the completion of degree requirements, substitution of specific courses required for the completion of degree requirements, and adaptation of the manner in which specific courses are conducted.

(b) Other rules

A recipient to which this subpart applies may not impose upon handicapped students other rules, such as the prohibition of tape recorders in classrooms or of dog guides in campus buildings, that have the effect of limiting the participation of handicapped students in the recipient's education program or activity.

(c) Course examinations

In its course examinations or other procedures for evaluating students' academic achievement in its program, a recipient to which this subpart applies shall provide such methods for evaluating the achievement of students who have a handicap that impairs sensory, manual, or speaking skills as will best ensure that the results of the evaluation represents the student's achievement in the course, rather than reflecting the student's impaired sensory, manual, or speaking skills (except where such skills are the factors that the test purports to measure).

(d) Auxiliary aids

(1) A recipient to which this subpart applies shall take such steps as are necessary to ensure that no handicapped student is denied the benefits of, excluded from participation in, or otherwise subjected to discrimination under the education program or activity operated by the recipient because of the absence of educational auxiliary aids for students with impaired sensory, manual, or speaking skills.

(2) Auxiliary aids may include taped texts, interpreters or other effective methods of making orally delivered materials available to students with hearing impairments, readers in libraries for students with visual impairments, classroom equipment adapted for use by students with manual impairments, and other similar services and actions. Recipients need not provide attendants, individually prescribed devices, readers for personal use or study, or other devices or services of a personal nature.

Sec. 104.45 Housing

(a) Housing provided by the recipient

A recipient that provides housing to its nonhandicapped students shall provide comparable, convenient, and accessible housing to handicapped students at the same cost as to others. At the end of the transition period provided for in Subpart C, such housing shall be available in sufficient quantity and variety so that the scope of handicapped students' choice of living accommodations is, as a whole, comparable to that of nonhandicapped students.

(b) Other housing

A recipient that assists any agency, organization, or person in making housing available to any of its students shall take such action as may be necessary to assure itself that such housing is, as a whole, made available in a manner that does not result in discrimination on the basis of handicap.

Sec. 104.46 Financial and employment assistance to students

(a) Provision of financial assistance

(1) In providing financial assistance to qualified handicapped persons, a recipient to which this subpart applies may not

(i), on the basis of handicap, provide less assistance than is provided to nonhandicapped persons, limit eligibility for assistance, or otherwise discriminate or

(ii) assist any entity or person that provides assistance to any of the recipient's students in a manner that discriminates against qualified handicapped persons on the basis of handicap.

(2) A recipient may administer or assist in the administration of scholarships, fellowships, or other forms of financial assistance established under wills, trusts, bequests, or similar legal instruments that require awards to be made on the basis of factors that discriminate or have the effect of discriminating on the basis of handicap only if the overall effect of the award of scholarships, fellowships, and other forms of financial assistance is not discriminatory on the basis of handicap.

(b) Assistance in making available outside employment

A recipient that assists any agency, organization, or person in providing employment opportunities to any of its students shall assure itself that such employment opportunities, as a whole, are made available in a manner that would not violate Subpart B if they were provided by the recipient.

(c) Employment of students by recipients

A recipient that employs any of its students may not do so in a manner that violates Subpart B.

Sec. 104.47 Nonacademic services

(a) Physical education and athletics

(1) In providing physical education courses and athletics and similar programs and activities to any of its students, a recipient to which this subpart applies may not discriminate on the basis of handicap. A recipient that offers physical education courses or that operates or sponsors intercollegiate, club, or intramural athletics shall provide to qualified handicapped students an equal opportunity for participation in these activities.

(2) A recipient may offer to handicapped students physical education and athletic activities that are separate or different only if separation or differentiation is consistent with the requirements of 104.43(d) and only if no qualified handicapped student is denied the opportunity to compete for teams or to participate in courses that are not separate or different.

(b) Counseling and placement services

A recipient to which this subpart applies that provides personal, academic, or vocational counseling, guidance, or placement services to its students shall provide these services without discrimination on the basis of handicap. The recipient shall ensure that qualified handicapped students are not counseled toward more restrictive career objectives than are nonhandicapped students with similar interests and abilities. This requirement does not preclude a recipient from providing factual information about licensing and certification requirements that may present obstacles to handicapped persons in their pursuit of particular careers.

(c) Social organizations

A recipient that provides significant assistance to fraternities, sororities, or similar organizations shall assure itself that the membership practices of such organizations do not permit discrimination otherwise prohibited by this subpart.

SUBPART F—HEALTH, WELFARE, AND SOCIAL SERVICES

Sec. 104.51 Application of this subpart

Subpart F applies to health, welfare, and other social service programs and activities that receive or benefit from Federal financial assistance and to recipients that operate, or that receive or benefit from Federal financial assistance for the operation of, such programs or activities.

Sec. 104.52 Health, welfare, and other social services

(a) General

In providing health, welfare, or other social services or benefits, a recipient may not, on the basis of handicap:

(1) Deny a qualified handicapped person these benefits or services;

(2) Afford a qualified handicapped person an opportunity to receive benefits or services that is not equal to that offered nonhandicapped persons;

(3) Provide a qualified handicapped person with benefits or services that are not as effective (as defined in 104.4(b)) as the benefits or services provided to others;

(4) Provide benefits or services in a manner that limits or has the effect of limiting the participation of qualified handicapped persons; or

(5) Provide different or separate benefits or services to handicapped persons except where necessary to provide qualified handicapped persons with benefits and services that are as effective as those provided to others.

(b) Notice

A recipient that provides notice concerning benefits or services or written material concerning waivers of rights or consent to treatment shall take such steps as are necessary to ensure that qualified handicapped persons, including those with impaired sensory or speaking skills, are not denied effective notice because of their handicap.

(c) Emergency treatment for the hearing impaired

A recipient hospital that provides health services or benefits shall establish a procedure for effective communication with persons with impaired hearing for the purpose of providing emergency health care.

(d) Auxiliary aids

(1) A recipient to which this subpart applies that employs fifteen or more persons shall provide appropriate auxiliary aids to persons with impaired sensory, manual, or speaking skills, where necessary to afford such persons an equal opportunity to benefit from the service in question.

(2) The Assistant Secretary may require recipients with fewer than fifteen employees to provide auxiliary aids where the provision of aids would not significantly impair the ability of the recipient to provide its benefits or services.

(3) For the purpose of this paragraph, auxiliary aids may include brailled and taped material, interpreters, and other aids for persons with impaired hearing or vision.

Sec. 104.53 Drug and alcohol addicts

A recipient to which this subpart applies that operates a general hospital or outpatient facility may not discriminate in admission or treatment against a drug or alcohol abuser or alcoholic who is suffering from a medical condition, because of the person's drug or alcohol abuse or alcoholism.

Sec. 104.54 Education of institutionalized persons

A recipient to which this subpart applies and that operates or supervises a program or activity for persons who are institutionalized because of handicap shall ensure that each qualified handicapped person, as defined in 104.3(k)(2), in its program or activity is provided an appropriate education, as defined in 104.33(b). Nothing in this section shall be interpreted as altering in any way the obligations of recipients under Subpart D.

SUBPART G—PROCEDURES

Sec. 104.61 Procedures

The procedural provisions applicable to title VI of the Civil Rights Act of 1964 apply to this part. These procedures are found in 100.6-100.10 and Part 101 of this title.

END SECTION 504 REGULATIONS

CHAPTER 10
OVERVIEW OF THE FAMILY EDUCATIONAL RIGHTS AND PRIVACY ACT

The Family Educational Rights and Privacy Act (FERPA) deals with privacy and confidentiality, parent access to educational records, parent amendment of records, and destruction of records.

The purpose of this statute is to protect the privacy of parents and students. The statute is in the United States Code at 20 U.S.C. 1232. The regulations are in the Code of Federal Regulations at 34 C.F.R Part 99.

FERPA applies to all agencies and institutions that receive federal funds, including elementary and secondary schools, colleges, and universities.

Educational Records

Educational records include "all instructional materials, including teacher's manuals, films, tapes, or other supplementary material which will be used in connection with any survey, analysis, or evaluation as part of any applicable program shall be available for inspection by the parents or guardians of the children."

Test materials, including test protocols and answer sheets are educational records and must be disclosed. The Office for Civil Rights has determined that the test protocols used by a psychologist to prepare a report are educational records and must be produced to the parents. Destruction of records violates the parents rights of access. (Weber, "Records")

Personal notes and memory aids that are used only by the person who made them are not educational records. However, if the notes are shared with or disclosed to another individual, they become educational records.

The Office for Civil Rights found that the transcript of a hearing is an educational record for purposes of Section 504. Due process decisions are educational records. Tapes of IEP meetings are educational records as are IEPs.

Right to Inspect and Review Educational Records

Parents have a right to inspect and review all educational records relating to their child. This right to "inspect and review" includes the right to have copies of records and to receive explanations and interpretations from school officials. Agencies must comply with requests to inspect and review records within forty-five days.

Copies of records must be provided to the parent if failure to do so would prevent the parent from exercising the right to view records. Schools may charge reasonable copying fees unless the fee would "effectively prevent" the parent or student from exercising the right to inspect and review the records. Fees may not be charged for searching and retrieving records.

According to the FERPA regulations "If circumstances effectively prevent the parent or eligible student from exercising the right to inspect and review the student's education records, the educational agency or institution, or SEA or its component, shall (1) Provide the parent or eligible student with a copy of the records requested; or (2) Make other arrangements for the parent or eligible student to inspect and review the requested records."

If the parent believes that the educational record contains inaccurate or misleading information, the parent may ask the agency to amend the record. The parent may also request a hearing to correct or challenge misleading or inaccurate information.

Confidentiality and Disclosure of Personally identifiable Information

Personally identifiable information may not be disclosed without written consent of the parent.

"Personally identifiable information" includes, but is not limited to:
(a) The student's name;
(b) The name of the student's parent or other family member;
(c) The address of the student or student's family;

(d) A personal identifier, such as the student's social security number or student number;

(e) A list of personal characteristics that would make the student's identity easily traceable; or

(f) Other information that would make the student's identity easily traceable.

Disclosures

Records may be released without consent to "other school officials, including teachers within the educational institution or local educational agency, who have been determined by such agency or institution to have legitimate educational interests."

Records may be released to "officials of other schools or school systems in which the student seeks or intends to enroll, upon condition that the student's parents be notified of the transfer, receive a copy of the record if desired, and have an opportunity for a hearing to challenge the content of the record . . ."

Disclosures may be made without consent in health and safety emergencies. Law enforcement agencies and monitoring agencies have access to confidential records.

The agency must maintain a log of all disclosures without parental consent. Consent for disclosure must be signed and dated and must include specific information about the recipients of information.

Destruction of Records

Pursuant to the General Educational Provisions Act, schools must retain records for at least five years. The school may not destroy any education records if there is an outstanding request to inspect and review the records under this section.

References

Weber, Mark. (1992) *Special Education Law and Litigation Treatise* (Horsham, PA: LRP Publications)

CHAPTER 11
FAMILY EDUCATIONAL RIGHTS AND PRIVACY ACT
20 U.S.C. 1232(g); 20 U.S.C. 1232(h)

Sec. 1232 (g).

(a) Conditions for availability of funds to educational agencies or institutions; inspection and review of education records; specific information to be made available; procedure for access to education records; reasonableness of time for such access; hearings; written explanations by parents; definitions.

   (1)

      (A) No funds shall be made available under any applicable program to any educational agency or institution which has a policy of denying, or which effectively prevents, the parents of students who are or have been in attendance at a school of such agency or at such institution, as the case may be, the right to inspect and review the education records of their children. If any material or document in the education record of a student includes information on more than one student, the parents of one of such students shall have the right to inspect and review only such part of such material or document as relates to such student or to be informed of the specific information contained in such part of such material. Each educational agency or institution shall establish appropriate procedures for the granting of a request by parents for access to the education records of their children within a reasonable period of time, but in no case more than forty-five days after the request has been made.

      (B) No funds under any applicable program shall be made available to any State educational agency (whether or not that agency is an educational agency or institution under this section) that has a policy of denying, or effectively prevents, the parents of students the right to inspect and review the education records maintained by the State educational agency on their children who are or have been in attendance at any school of an educational agency or institution that is subject to the provisions of this section.

      (C) The first sentence of subparagraph (A) shall not operate to make available to students in institutions of post-secondary education the following materials:

         (i) financial records of the parents of the student or any information contained therein;

         (ii) confidential letters and statements of recommendation, which were placed in the education records prior to January 1, 1975, if such letters or statements are not used for purposes other than those for which they were specifically intended;

         (iii) if the student has signed a waiver of the student's right of access under this subsection in accordance with subparagraph (D), confidential recommendations—

            (I) respecting admission to any educational agency or institution,

            (II) respecting an application for employment, and

            (III) respecting the receipt of an honor or honorary recognition.

      (D) A student or a person applying for admission may waive his right of access to confidential statements described in clause (iii) of subparagraph (c) except that such waiver shall apply to recommendations only if

         (i) the student is, upon request, notified of the names of all persons making confidential recommendations and

         (ii) such recommendations are used solely for the purpose for which they were specifically intended. Such waivers may not be required as a condition for admission to, receipt of financial aid from, or receipt of any other services or benefits from such agency or institution.

(2) No funds shall be made available under any applicable program to any educational agency or institution unless the parents of students who are or have been in attendance at a school of such agency or at such institution are provided an opportunity for a hearing by such agency or institution, in accordance with regulations of the Secretary, to challenge the content of such student's education records, in order to insure that the records are not inaccurate, misleading, or otherwise in violation of the privacy rights of students, and to provide an opportunity for the correction or deletion of any such inaccurate, misleading or otherwise inappropriate data contained therein and to insert into such records a written explanation of the parents respecting the content of such records.

(3) For the purposes of this section the term **"educational agency or institution"** means any public or private agency or institution which is the recipient of funds under any applicable program.

(4)

(A) For the purposes of this section, the term **"education records"** means, except as may be provided otherwise in subparagraph (B), those records, files, documents, and other materials which—

(i) contain information directly related to a student; and

(ii) are maintained by an educational agency or institution or by a person acting for such agency or institution.

(B) The term **"education records" does not include**—

(i) records of instructional, supervisory, and administrative personnel and educational personnel ancillary thereto which are in the sole possession of the maker thereof and which are not accessible or revealed to any other person except a substitute;

(ii) records maintained by a law enforcement unit of the educational agency or institution that were created by that law enforcement unit for the purpose of law enforcement;

(iii) in the case of persons who are employed by an educational agency or institution but who are not in attendance at such agency or institution, records made and maintained in the normal course of business which relate exclusively to such person in that person's capacity as an employee and are not available for use for any other purpose; or

(iv) records on a student who is eighteen years of age or older, or is attending an institution of post-secondary education, which are made or maintained by a physician, psychiatrist, psychologist or other recognized professional or paraprofessional acting in his professional or paraprofessional capacity, or assisting in that capacity, and which are made, maintained, or used only in connection with the provision of treatment to the student, and are not available to anyone other than persons providing such treatment, except that such records can be personally reviewed by a physician or other appropriate professional of the student's choice.

(5)

(A) For the purposes of this section the term **"directory information"** relating to a student includes the following: the student's name, address, telephone listing, date and place of birth, major field of study, participation in officially recognized activities and sports, weight and height of members of athletic teams, dates of attendance, degrees and awards received, and the most recent previous educational agency or institution attended by the student.

(B) Any educational agency or institution making public directory information shall give public notice of the categories of information which it has designated as such information with respect to each student attending the institution or agency and shall allow a reasonable period of time after such notice has been given for a parent to inform the institution or agency that any or all of the information designated should not be released without the parent's prior consent.

(6) For the purposes of this section, the term **"student"** includes any person with respect to whom an educational agency or institution maintains education records or personally identifiable information, but does not include a person who has not been in attendance at such agency or institution.

(b) Release of education records; parental consent requirement; exceptions; compliance with judicial orders and subpoenas; audit and evaluation of federally-supported education programs; recordkeeping.

(1) No funds shall be made available under any applicable program to any educational agency or institution which has a policy or practice of permitting the release of education records (or personally identifiable information contained therein other than directory information, as defined in paragraph (5) of subsection (a) of this section) of students without the written consent of their parents to any individual, agency, or organization, other than to the following—

(A) other school officials, including teachers within the educational institution or local educational agency, who have been determined by such agency or institution to have legitimate educational interests, including the educational interests of the child for whom consent would otherwise be required;

(B) officials of other schools or school systems in which the student seeks or intends to enroll, upon condition that the student's parents be notified of the transfer, receive a copy of the record if desired, and have an opportunity for a hearing to challenge the content of the record;

(C) authorized representatives of

(i) the Comptroller General of the United States,

(ii) the Secretary,

(iii) an administrative head of an education agency (as defined in section 1221e-3(c) of this title), or

(iv) State educational authorities under the conditions set forth in paragraph (3) of this subsection;

(D) in connection with a student's application for, or receipt of, financial aid;

(E) State and local officials or authorities to whom such information is specifically allowed to be reported or disclosed pursuant to State statute adopted—

(i) before November 19, 1974, if the allowed reporting or disclosure concerns the juvenile justice system and such system's ability to effectively serve the student whose records are released, or

(ii) after November 19, 1974, if—

(I) the allowed reporting or disclosure concerns the juvenile justice system and such system's ability to effectively serve, prior to adjudication, the student whose records are released; and

(II) the officials and authorities to whom such information is disclosed certify in writing to the educational agency or institution that the information will not be disclosed to any other party except as provided under State law without the prior written consent of the parent of the student.

(F) organizations conducting studies for, or on behalf of, educational agencies or institutions for the purpose of developing, validating, or administering predictive tests, administering student aid programs, and improving instruction, if such studies are conducted in such a manner as will not permit the personal identification of students and their parents by persons other than representatives of such organizations and such information will be destroyed when no longer needed for the purpose for which it is conducted;

(G) accrediting organizations in order to carry out their accrediting functions;

(H) parents of a dependent student of such parents, as defined in section 152 of Title 26;

(I) subject to regulations of the Secretary, in connection with an emergency, appropriate persons if the knowledge of such information is necessary to protect the health or safety of the student or other persons; and

(J)

(i) the entity or persons designated in a Federal grand jury subpoena, in which case the court shall order, for good cause shown, the educational agency or institution (and any officer, director, employee, agent, or attorney for such agency or institution) on which the subpoena is served, to not disclose to any person the existence or contents of the subpoena or any information furnished to the grand jury in response to the subpoena; and

(ii) the entity or persons designated in any other subpoena issued for a law enforcement purpose, in which case the court or other issuing agency may order, for good cause shown, the educational agency or institution (and any officer, director, employee, agent, or attorney for such agency or institution) on which the subpoena is served, to not disclose to any person the existence or contents of the subpoena or any information furnished in response to the subpoena. Nothing in clause (E) of this paragraph shall prevent a State from further limiting the number or type of State or local officials who will continue to have access thereunder.

(2) No funds shall be made available under any applicable program to any educational agency or institution which has a policy or practice of releasing, or providing access to, any personally identifiable information in education records other than directory information, or as is permitted under paragraph (1) of this subsection unless—

(A) there is written consent from the student's parents specifying records to be released, the reasons for such release, and to whom, and with a copy of the records to be released to the student's parents and the student if desired by the parents, or

(B) except as provided in paragraph (1)(J), such information is furnished in compliance with judicial order, or pursuant to any lawfully issued subpoena, upon condition that parents and the students are notified of all such orders or subpoenas in advance of the compliance therewith by the educational institution or agency.

(3) Nothing contained in this section shall preclude authorized representatives of
(A) the Comptroller General of the United States,

(B) the Secretary,

(C) State educational authorities from having access to student or other records which may be necessary in connection with the audit and evaluation of Federally-supported education programs, or in connection with the enforcement of the Federal legal requirements which relate to such programs: Provided, That except when collection of personally identifiable information is specifically authorized by Federal law, any data collected by such officials shall be protected in a manner which will not permit the personal identification of students and their parents by other than those officials, and such personally identifiable data shall be destroyed when no longer needed for such audit, evaluation, and enforcement of Federal legal requirements.

(4)

(A) Each educational agency or institution shall maintain a record, kept with the education records of each student, which will indicate all individuals (other than those specified in paragraph (1)(A) of this subsection), agencies, or organizations which have requested or obtained access to a student's education records maintained by such educational agency or institution, and which will indicate specifically the legitimate interest that each such person, agency, or organization has in obtaining this information. Such record of access shall be available only to parents, to the school official and his assistants who are responsible for the custody of such records, and to persons or organizations authorized in, and under the conditions of, clauses (A) and (C) of paragraph (1) as a means of auditing the operation of the system.

(B) With respect to this subsection, personal information shall only be transferred to a third party on the condition that such party will not permit any other party to have access to such information without the written consent of the parents of the student. If a third party outside the educational agency or institution permits access to information in violation of paragraph (2)(A), or fails to destroy information in violation of paragraph (1)(F), the educational agency or institution shall be prohibited from permitting access to information from education records to that third party for a period of not less than five years.

(5) Nothing in this section shall be construed to prohibit State and local educational officials from having access to student or other records which may be necessary in connection with the audit and evaluation of any federally or State supported education program or in connection with the enforcement of the Federal legal requirements which relate to any such program, subject to the conditions specified in the proviso in paragraph (3).

(6) Nothing in this section shall be construed to prohibit an institution of post-secondary education from disclosing, to an alleged victim of any crime of violence (as that term is defined in section 16 of Title 18), the results of any disciplinary proceeding conducted by such institution against the alleged perpetrator of such crime with respect to such crime.

(c) Surveys or data-gathering activities; regulations

Not later than 240 days after the date of enactment of the Improving America's Schools Act of 1994, the Secretary shall adopt appropriate regulations or procedures, or identify existing regulations or procedures, which protect the rights of privacy of students and their families in connection with any surveys or data-gathering activities conducted, assisted, or authorized by the Secretary or an administrative head of an education agency. Regulations established under this subsection shall include provisions controlling the use, dissemination, and protection of such data. No survey or data-gathering activities shall be conducted by the Secretary, or an administrative head of an education agency under an applicable program, unless such activities are authorized by law.

(d) Students' rather than parents' permission or consent

For the purposes of this section, whenever a student has attained eighteen years of age, or is attending an institution of post-secondary education the permission or consent required of and the rights accorded to the parents of the student shall thereafter only be required of and accorded to the student.

(e) Informing parents or students of rights under this section

No funds shall be made available under any applicable program to any educational agency or institution unless such agency or institution effectively informs the parents of students, or the students, if they are eighteen years of age or older, or are attending an institution of post-secondary education, of the rights accorded them by this section.

(f) Enforcement; termination of assistance

The Secretary, or an administrative head of an education agency, shall take appropriate actions to enforce provisions of this section and to deal with violations of this section, according to the provisions of this chapter, except that action to terminate assistance may be taken only if the Secretary finds there has been a failure to comply with the provisions of this section, and he has determined that compliance cannot be secured by voluntary means.

(g) Office and review board; creation; functions

The Secretary shall establish or designate an office and review board within the Department of Education for the purpose of investigating, processing, reviewing, and adjudicating violations of the provisions of this section and complaints which may be filed concerning alleged violations of this section. Except for the conduct of hearings, none of the functions of the Secretary under this section shall be carried out in any of the regional offices of such Department.

(h) Nothing in this section shall prohibit an educational agency or institution from—

(1) including appropriate information in the education record of any student concerning disciplinary action taken against such student for conduct that posed a significant risk to the safety or well-being of that student, other students, or other members of the school community; or

(2) disclosing such information to teachers and school officials, including teachers and school officials in other schools , who have legitimate educational interests in the behavior of the student.

Sec. 1232h Protection of pupil rights

(a) All instructional materials, including teacher's manuals, films, tapes, or other supplementary material which will be used in connection with any survey, analysis, or evaluation as part of any applicable program shall be available for inspection by the parents or guardians of the children.

(b) No student shall be required, as part of any applicable program, to submit to a survey, analysis, or evaluation that reveals information concerning—
   (1) political affiliations;
   (2) mental and psychological problems potentially embarrassing to the student or his family;
   (3) sex behavior and attitudes;
   (4) illegal, anti-social, self-incriminating and demeaning behavior;
   (5) critical appraisals of other individuals with whom respondents have close family relationships;
   (6) legally recognized privileged or analogous relationships, such as those of lawyers, physicians, and ministers; or
   (7) income (other than that required by law to determine eligibility for participation in a program or for receiving financial assistance under such program), without the prior consent of the student (if the student is an adult or emancipated minor), or in the case of an unemancipated minor, without the prior written consent of the parent.

(c) Educational agencies and institutions shall give parents and students effective notice of their rights under this section.

(d) Enforcement—

The Secretary shall take such action as the Secretary determines appropriate to enforce this section, except that action to terminate assistance provided under an applicable program shall be taken only if the Secretary determines that—
   (1) there has been a failure to comply with such section; and
   (2) compliance with such section cannot be secured by voluntary means.

(e) Office and review board

The Secretary shall establish or designate an office and review board within the Department of Education to investigate, process, review, and adjudicate violations of the rights established under this section.

(Pub. L. 90-247, title IV, Sec. 433, formerly Sec. 439, as added Pub. L. 93-380, title V, Sec. 514(a), Aug. 21, 1974, 88 Stat. 574, and amended Pub. L. 95-561, title XII, Sec. 1250, Nov. 1, 1978, 92 Stat. 2355; Pub. L. 103-227, title X, Sec. 1017, Mar. 31, 1994, 108 Stat. 268; renumbered Sec. 433, Pub. L. 103-382, title II, Sec. 212(b)(1), Oct. 20, 1994, 108 Stat. 3913.)

END OF FERPA STATUTE

THIS PAGE DELIBERATELY LEFT BLANK

CHAPTER 12
TABLE OF FERPA REGULATIONS
34 C.F.R. Part 99

Subpart A—General
Subpart B—What are the Rights of Inspection and Review of Education Records?
Subpart C—What are the Procedures for Amending Education Records?
Subpart D—May an Educational Agency or Institution Disclose Personally Identifiable Information from Education Records?
Subpart E—What are the Enforcement Procedures?

SUBPART A—GENERAL

Sec. 99.1 To which educational agencies or institutions do these regulations apply?
Sec. 99.2 What is the purpose of these regulations?
Sec. 99.3 What definitions apply to these regulations?
Sec. 99.4 What are the rights of parents?
Sec. 99.5 What are the rights of students?
Sec. 99.6 [Reserved]
Sec. 99.7 What must an educational agency or institution include in its annual notification?
Sec. 99.8 What provisions apply to records of a law enforcement unit?

SUBPART B—WHAT ARE RIGHTS OF INSPECTION AND REVIEW OF EDUCATION RECORDS?

Sec. 99.10 What rights exist for a parent or eligible student to inspect and review education records?
Sec. 99.11 May an educational agency or institution charge a fee for copies of education records?
Sec. 99.12 What limitations exist on the right to inspect and review records?

SUBPART C—WHAT ARE THE PROCEDURES FOR AMENDING EDUCATION RECORDS?

99.20 How can a parent or eligible student request amendment of the student's education records?
99.21 Under what conditions does a parent or eligible student have the right to a hearing?
99.22 What minimum requirements exist for the conduct of a hearing?

SUBPART D—MAY AN EDUCATIONAL AGENCY OR INSTITUTION DISCLOSE PERSONALLY IDENTIFIABLE INFORMATION FROM EDUCATION RECORDS?

Sec. 99.30 Under what conditions is prior consent required to disclose information?
Sec. 99.31 Under what conditions is prior consent not required to disclose information?
Sec. 99.32 What recordkeeping requirements exist concerning requests and disclosures?
Sec. 99.33 What limitations apply to the redisclosure of information?
Sec. 99.34 What conditions apply to disclosure of information to other educational agendes or institutions?
Sec. 99.35 What conditions apply to disclosure of information for Federal or State program purposes?
Sec. 99.36 What conditions apply to disclosure of information in health and safety emergencies?
Sec. 99.37 What conditions apply to disclosing directory information?
Sec. 99.38 What conditions apply to disclosure of information as permitted by State statute adopted after November 19, 1974 concerning the juvenile justice system?

SUBPART E – WHAT ARE ENFORCEMENT PROCEDURES?

Reg. 99.60 What functions has the Secretary delegated to the Office and to the Office of Administrative Law Judges?
Reg. 99.61 What responsibility does an educational agency or institution have concerning conflict with State or local laws?
Reg. 99.62 What information must an educational agency or institution submit to the Office?
Sec. 99.63 Where are complaints filed?
Sec. 99.64 What is the complaint procedure?
Sec. 99.65 What is the content of the notice of complaint issued by the Office?
Sec. 99.66 What are the responsibilities of the Office in the enforcement process?
Sec. 99.67 How does the Secretary enforce decisions?

FERPA REGULATIONS
34 C.F.R., Part 99

Subpart A—General
Subpart B—What are the Rights of Inspection and Review of Education Records?
Subpart C—What are the Procedures for Amending Education Records?
Subpart D—May an Educational Agency or Institution Disclose Personally Identifiable Information from Education Records?
Subpart E—What are the Enforcement Procedures?

SUBPART A—GENERAL

Sec. 99.1 To which educational agencies or institutions do these regulations apply?

(a) Except as otherwise noted in Sec. 99.10, this part applies to an educational agency or institution to which funds have been made available under any program administered by the Secretary of Education if -

(1) The educational institution provides educational services or instruction, or both, to student; or

(2) The educational agency provides administrative control or direction of, or performs service functions for, public elementary or secondary schools or postsecondary institutions.

(b) This part does not apply to an educational agency or institution solely because students attending that agency or institution receive non–monetary benefits under a program referenced in paragraph (a) of this section, if no funds under that program are made available to the agency or institution.

(c) The Secretary considers funds to be made available to an educational agency or institution if funds under one or more of the programs referenced in paragraph (a) of this section

(1) are provided to the agency or institution by grant, cooperative agreement, contract, subgrant , or subcontract; or

(2) are provided to students attending the agency or institution and the funds may be paid to the agency or institution by those students for educational purposes, such as under the Pell Grant Program and the Guaranteed Student Loan Program (Titles IV-A-1 and IV-B, respectively, of the Higher Education Act of 1965, as amended).

(d) If an educational agency or institution receives funds under one or more of the programs covered by this section, the regulations in this part apply to the recipient as a whole, including each of its components (such as a department within a university).

Sec. 99.2 What is the purpose of these regulations?

The purpose of this part is to set out requirements for the protection of privacy of parents and students under section 444 of the General Education Provisions Act, as amended. (Note: 34 C.F.R. 300.560-300.576 contain requirements regarding confidentiality of information relating to handicapped children who receive benefits under IDEA.)

Sec. 99.3 What definitions apply to these regulations?

The following definitions apply to this part:

"Act" means the Family Educational Rights and Privacy Act of 1974, as mended, enacted as Sec. 438 of the General Education Provisions Act.

"Attendance" includes, but is not limited to:

(a) Attendance in person or by correspondence; and

(b) The period during which a person is working under a work-study program.

"Directory information" means information contained in an education record of a student which would not generally be considered harmful or an invasion of privacy if disclosed. It includes, but is not limited to the student's name, address, telephone listing, date and place of birth, major field of study, participation in officially recognized activities and sports, weight and height of members of athletic teams, dates of attendance, degrees and awards received, and the most recent previous educational agency or institution attended.

"Disciplinary action or proceeding" means the investigation, adjudication, or imposition of sanctions by an educational agency or institution with respect to an infraction or violation of the internal rules of conduct applicable to students of the agency or institution.

"Disclosure" means to permit access to or the release, transfer, or other communication of education records, or the personally identifiable information contained in those records, to any party, by any means, including oral, written, or electronic means.

"Educational agency or institution" means any public or private agency or institution to which this part applies under Sec. 99. 1(a).

"Education records"

(a) The term means those records that are:

(1) Directly related to a student; and

(2) Maintained by an educational agency or institution or by a party acting for the agency or institution.

(b) The term does not include:

(1) Records of instructional, supervisory, and administrative personnel and educational personnel ancillary to those persons that axe kept in the sole possession of the maker of the record, and are not accessible or revealed to any other person except a temporary substitute for the maker of the record;

(2) Records of a law enforcement unit of an educational agency or institution, but only if education records maintained by the agency or institution are not disclosed to the unit, and the law enforcement records a~:

(i) Maintained separately from education records;

(ii) Maintained solely for law enforcement purposes; and

(iii) Disclosed only to law enforcement officials of the same jurisdiction;

(3)

(i) Records relating to an individual who is employed by an educational agency or institution, that:

(A) Are made and maintained in the normal course of business;

(B) Relate exclusively to the individual in that individual's capacity as an employee; and

(C) Are not available for use for any other purpose.

(ii) Records relating to an individual in attendance at the agency or institution who is employed as a result of his or her status as a student are education records and not excepted under paragraph (b)(3)(i) of this definition.

(4) Records on a student who is 18 years of age or older, or is attending an institution of postsecondary education, that are:

(i) Made or maintained by a physician, psychiatrist, psychologist, or other recognized professional or paraprofessional acting in his or her professional capacity or assisting in a paraprofessional capacity;

(ii) Made, maintained, or used only in connection with treatment of the student; and

(iii) Disclosed only to individuals providing the treatment. For the purpose of this definition, "treatment' does not include remedial educational activities or activities that are part of the program of instruction at the agency or institution; and

(5) Records that only contain information about an individual after he or she is no longer a student at that agency or institution.

"Eligible student" means a student who has reached 18 years of age or is attending an institution of postsecondary education.

"Institution of postsecondary education" means an institution that provides education to students beyond the secondary school level; "secondary school level" means the educational level (not beyond grade 12) at which secondary education is provided as determined under State law.

"Parent" means a parent of a student and includes a natural parent, a guardian, or an individual acting as a parent in the absence of a parent or a guardian.

"Party" means an individual, agency, institution, or organization.

"Personally identifiable information" includes, but is not limited to:

(a) The student's name;

(b) The name of the student's parent or other family member;

(c) The address of the student or student's family;

(d) A personal identifier, such as the student's social security number or student number;

(e) A list of personal characteristics that would make the student's identity easily traceable; or

(f) Other information that would make the student's identity easily traceable.

"Record" means any information recorded in any way, including, but not limited to, handwriting, print, tape, film, microfilm, and microfiche.

"Secretary" means the Secretary of the U.S. Department of Education or an official or employee of the Department of Education acting for the Secretary under a delegation of authority.

"Student," except as otherwise specifically provided in this part means any individual who is or has been in attendance at an educational agency or institution and regarding whom the agency or institution maintains education records.

Sec. 99.4 What are the rights of parents?

An educational agency or institution shall give full rights under the Act to either parent, unless the agency or institution has been provided with evidence that there is a court order, State statute, or legally binding document relating to such matters as divorce, separation, or custody that specifically revokes these rights.

Sec. 99.5 What are the rights of students?

(a) When a student becomes an eligible student, the rights accorded to, and consent required of, parents under this part transfer from the parents to the student.

(b) The Act and this part do not prevent educational agencies or institutions from giving students rights in addition to those given to parents.

(c) If an individual is or has been in attendance at one component of an educational agency or institution, that attendance does not give the individual rights as a student in other components of the agency or institution to which the individual has applied for admission, but has never been in attendance.

Sec. 99.6 [Reserved]

Sec. 99.7 What must an educational agency or institution include in its annual notification?

(a)

    (1) Each educational agency or institution shall annually notify parents of students currently in attendance, or eligible students currently in attendance, of their rights under the Act and this part.

    (2) The notice must inform parents or eligible students that they have the right to —

        (i) Inspect and review the student's education records;

        (ii) Seek amendment of the student's education records that the parent or eligible student believes to be inaccurate, misleading, or otherwise in violation of the student's privacy rights;

        (iii) Consent to disclosures of personally identifiable information contained in the student's education records, except to the extent that the Act and Reg. 99.31 authorize disclosure without consent; and

        (iv) File with the Department a complaint under Regs. 99.63 and 99.64 concerning alleged failures by the educational agency or institution to comply with the requirements of the Act and this part.

    (3) The notice must include all of the following:

        (i) The procedure for exercising the right to inspect and review education records.

        (ii) The procedure for requesting amendment of records under Reg. 99.20;

        (iii) If the educational agency or institution has a policy of disclosing education records under Reg. 99.31(a)(1), a specification of criteria for determining who constitutes a school official and what constitutes a legitimate educational interest.

(b) An educational agency or institution may provide this notice by any means that are reasonably likely to inform the parents or eligible students of their rights.

    (1) An educational agency or institution shall effectively notify parents or eligible students who are disabled.

    (2) An agency or institution of elementary or secondary education shall effectively notify parents who have a primary or home language other than English.

Reg. 99.8 What provisions apply to records of a law enforcement unit?

(a)

    (1) Law enforcement unit means any individual, office, department, division, or other component of an educational agency or institution, such as a unit of commissioned police officers or non-commissioned security guards, that is officially authorized or designated by that agency or institution to —

        (i) Enforce any local, State, or Federal law, or refer to appropriate authorities a matter for enforcement of any local, State, or Federal law against any individual or organization other than the agency or institution itself; or

        (ii) Maintain the physical security and safety of the agency or institution.

    (2) A component of an educational agency or institution does not lose its status as a law enforcement unit if it also performs other, non-law enforcement functions for the agency or institution, including investigation of incidents or conduct that constitutes or leads to a disciplinary action or proceedings against the student.

(b)

    (1) Records of a law enforcement unit means those records, files, documents, and other materials that are —

        (i) Created by a law enforcement unit;

        (ii) Created for a law enforcement purpose; and

        (iii) Maintained by the law enforcement unit.

    (2) Records of a law enforcement unit does not mean-

        (i) Records created by a law enforcement unit for a law enforcement purpose that are maintained by a component of the educational agency or institution other than the law enforcement unit; or

        (ii) Records created and maintained by a law enforcement unit exclusively for a non-law enforcement purpose, such as a disciplinary action or proceeding conducted by the educational agency or institution.

(c)

    (1) Nothing in the Act prohibits an educational agency or institution from contacting its law enforcement unit, orally or in writing, for the purpose of asking that unit to investigate a possible violation of, or to enforce, any local, State, or Federal law.

(2) Education records, and personally identifiable information contained in education records, do not lose their status as education records and remain subject to the Act, including the disclosure provisions of Sec. 99.30, while in the possession of the law enforcement unit.

(d) The Act neither requires nor prohibits the disclosure by an educational agency or institution of its law enforcement unit records.

SUBPART B—WHAT ARE RIGHTS OF INSPECTION AND REVIEW OF EDUCATION RECORDS?

Sec. 99.10 What rights exist for a parent or eligible student to inspect and review education records?

a) Except as limited under Reg. 99.12, a parent or eligible student must be given the opportunity to inspect and review the student's education records. This provision applies to —

(1) Any educational agency or institution; and

(2) Any State educational agency (SEA) and its components.

(i) For the purposes of subpart B of this part, an SEA and its components constitute an educational agency or institution.

(ii) An SEA and its components are subject to Subpart B of this part if the SEA maintains education records on students who are or have been in attendance at any school of an educational agency or institution subject to the Act and this part.

(b) The educational agency or institution, or SEA or its component, shall comply with a request for access to records within a reasonable period of time, but not more than 45 days after it has received the request.

(c) The educational agency or institution, or SEA or its component, shall respond to reasonable requests for explanations and interpretations of the records.

(d) If circumstances effectively prevent the parent or eligible student from exercising the right to inspect and review the student's education records, the educational agency or institution, or SEA or its component, shall —

(1) Provide the parent or eligible student with a copy of the records requested; or

(2) Make other arrangements for the parent or eligible student to inspect and review the requested records.

(e) The educational agency or institution, or SEA or its component, shall not destroy any education records if there is an outstanding request to inspect and review the records under this section.

(f) While an educational agency or institution is not required to give an eligible student access to treatment records under paragraph (b)(4) of the definition of "Education records" in Reg. 99.3, the student may have those records reviewed by a physician or other appropriate professional of the student's choice.

Sec. 99.11 May an educational agency or institution charge a fee for copies of education records?

(a) Unless the imposition of a fee effectively prevents a parent or eligible student from exercising the right to inspect and review the student's education records, an educational agency or institution may charge a fee for a copy of an education record which is made for the parent or eligible student.

(b) An educational agency or institution may not charge a fee to search for or to retrieve the education records of a student.

Sec. 99.12 What limitations exist on the right to inspect and review records?

(a) If the education records of a student contain information on more than one student, the parent or eligible student may inspect and review or be informed of only the specific information about that student.

(b) A postsecondary institution does not have to permit a student to inspect and review education records that are:

(1) Financial records, including any information those records contain, of his or her parents;

(2) Confidential letters and confidential statements of recommendation placed in the education records of the student before January 1, 1975, as long as the statements are used only for the purposes for which they were specifically intended; and

(3) Confidential letters and confidential statements of recommendation placed in the student's education records after January 1, 1975, if:

(i) The student has waived his or her right to inspect and review these letters and statements; and

(ii) Those letters and statements are related to the student's:

(A) Admission to an educational institution;

(B) Application for employment; or

(C) Receipt of an honor or honorary recognition.

(c)

(1) A waiver under paragraph (b)(3)(i) of this section is valid only if:

(i) The educational agency or institution does not require the waiver as a condition for admission to or receipt of a service or benefit from the agency or institution; and

(ii) The waiver is made in writing and signed by the student, regardless of age.

(2) If a student has waived his or her rights under paragraph (b)(3)(i) of this section, the educational institution shall:

(i) Give the student, on request, the names of the individuals who provided the letters and statements of recommendation; and

(ii) Use the letters and statements of recommendation only for the purpose for which they were intended.

(3)

(i) A waiver under paragraph (b)(3)(i) of this section may be revoked with respect to any actions occurring after the revocation.

(ii) A revocation under paragraph (c)(3)(i) of this section must be in writing.

SUBPART C—WHAT ARE THE PROCEDURES FOR AMENDING EDUCATION RECORDS?

99.20 How can a parent or eligible student request amendment of the student's education records?

(a) If a parent or eligible student believes the education records relating to the student contain information that is inaccurate, misleading, or in violation of the student's rights of privacy, he or she may ask the educational agency or institution to amend the record.

(b) The educational agency or institution shall decide whether to amend the record as requested within a reasonable time after the agency or institution receives the request.

(c) If the educational agency or institution decides not to amend the record as requested, it shall inform the parent or eligible student of its decision and of his or her right to a hearing under Reg. 99.21.

99.21 Under what conditions does a parent or eligible student have the right to a hearing?

(a) An educational agency or institution shall give a parent or eligible student, on request, an opportunity for a hearing to challenge the content of the student's education records on the grounds that the information contained in the education records is inaccurate, misleading, or otherwise in violation of the privacy rights of the student.

(b)

(1) If, as a result of the hearing, the educational agency or institution decides that the information is inaccurate, misleading, or otherwise in violation of the privacy rights of the student, it shall:

(i) Amend the record accordingly; and

(ii) Inform the parent or eligible student of the amendment in writing.

(2) If, as a result of the hearing, the educational agency or institution decides that the information in the education record is not inaccurate, misleading, or otherwise in violation of the privacy rights of the student, it shall inform the parent or eligible student of the right to place a statement in the record commenting on the contested information in the record or stating why he or she disagrees with the decision of the agency or institution, or both.

(c) If an educational agency or institution places a statement in the education records of a student under paragraph (b)(2) of this section, the agency or institution shall:

(1) Maintain the statement with the contested part of the record for as long as the record is maintained; and

(2) Disclose the statement whenever it discloses the portion of the record to which the statement relates.

99.22 What minimum requirements exist for the conduct of a hearing?

The hearing required by Reg. 99.21 must meet, at a minimum, the following requirements:

(a) The educational agency or institution shall hold the hearing within a reasonable time after it has received the request for the hearing from the parent or eligible student.

(b) The educational agency or institution shall give the parent or eligible student notice of the date, time, and place reasonably in advance of the hearing.

(c) The hearing may be conducted by any individual, including an official of the educational agency or institution, who does not have a direct interest in the outcome of the hearing.

(d) The educational agency or institution shall give the parent or eligible student a full and fair opportunity to present evidence relevant to the issues raised under Reg. 99.21. The parent or eligible student may, at their own expense, be assisted or represented by one or more individuals of his or her own choice, including an attorney.

(e) The educational agency or institution shall make its decision in writing within a reasonable period of time after the hearing.

(f) The decision must be based solely on the evidence presented at the hearing, and must include a summary of the evidence and the reasons for the decision.

SUBPART D—MAY AN EDUCATIONAL AGENCY OR INSTITUTION DISCLOSE PERSONALLY IDENTIFIABLE INFORMATION FROM EDUCATION RECORDS?

Sec. 99.30 Under what conditions is prior consent required to disclose information?

(a) The parent or eligible student shall provide a signed and dated written consent before an educational agency or institution discloses personally identifiable information from the student's education records, eExcept as provided in Reg. 99.31.

(b) The written consent must:

(1) Specify the records that may be disclosed;

(2) State the purpose of the disclosure; and

(3) Identify the party or class of parties to whom the disclosure may be made.

(c) When a disclosure is made under paragraph (a) of this section:

(1) If a parent or eligible student so requests, the educational agency or institution shall provide him or her with a copy of the records disclosed; and

(2) If the parent of a student who is not an eligible student so requests, the agency or institution shall provide the student with a copy of the records disclosed.

Sec. 99.31 Under what conditions is prior consent not required to disclose information?

(a) An educational agency or institution may disclose personally identifiable information from an education record of a student without the consent required by Reg. 99.30 if the disclosure meets one or more of the following conditions:

(1) The disclosure is to other school officials, including teachers, within the agency or institution whom the agency or nstitution has determined to have legitimate educational interests.

(2) The disclosure is, subject to the requirements of Reg. 99.34, to officials of another school, school system, or institution of postsecondary education where the student seeks or intends to enroll.

(3) The disclosure is, subject to the requirements of Reg. 99.35, to authorized representatives of:

(i) The Comptroller General of the United States;

(ii) The Secretary; or

(iii) State and local educational authorities.

(4)

(i) The disclosure is in connection with financial aid for which the student has applied or which the student has received, if the information is necessary for such purposes as to:

(A) Determine eligibility for the aid;

(B) Determine the amount of the aid;

(C) Determine the conditions for the aid; or

(D) Enforce the terms and conditions of the aid.

(ii) As used in paragraph (a)(4)(i) of this section, "financial aid" means a payment of funds provided to an individual (or a payment in kind of tangible or intangible property to the individual) that is conditioned on the individual's attendance at an educational agency or institution. (Authority: 20 U.S.C. 1232g(b)(1)(D))

(5)

(i) The disclosure is to State and local officials or authorities to whom this information is specifically —

(A) Allowed to be reported or disclosed pursuant to State statute adopted before November 19, 1974, if the allowed reporting or disclosure concerns the juvenile justice system and the system's ability to effectively serve the student whose records are released; or

(B) Allowed to be reported or disclosed pursuant to State statute adopted after November 19, 1974, subject to the requirements of Reg. 99.38.

(ii) Paragraph (a)(5)(i) of this section does not prevent a State from further limiting the number or type of State or local officials to whom disclosures may be made under that paragraph.

(6)

(i) The disclosure is to organizations conducting studies for, or on behalf of, educational agencies or institutions to:

(A) Develop, validate, or administer predictive tests;

(B) Administer student aid programs; or

(C) Improve instruction.

(ii) The agency or institution may disclose information under paragraph (a)(6)(i) of this section only if:

(A) The study is conducted in a manner that does not permit personal identification of parents and students by individuals other than representatives of the organization; and

(B) The information is destroyed when no longer needed for the purposes for which the study was conducted.

(iii) If this Office determines that a third party outside the educational agency or institution to whom information is disclosed under this paragraph (a)(6) violates paragraph (a)(6)(ii)(B) of this section, the educational agency or institution may not allow that third party access to personally identifiable information from education records for at least five years.

(iv) For the purposes of paragraph (a)(6) of this section, the term "organization" includes, but is not limited to, Federal, State and local agencies, and independent organizations.

(7) The disclosure is to accrediting organizations to carry out their accrediting functions.

(8) The disclosure is to parents of a dependent student, as defined in section 152 of the Internal Revenue Code of 1954.

(9)

(i) The disclosure is to comply with a judicial order or lawfully issued subpoena.

(ii) The educational agency or institution may disclose information under paragraph (a)(9)(i) of this section only if the agency or institution makes a reasonable effort to notify the parent or eligible student of the order or subpoena in advance of compliance, so that the parent or eligible student may seek protective action, unless the disclosure is in compliance with —

(A) A Federal grand jury subpoena and the court has ordered that the existence or the contents of the subpoena or the information furnished in response to the subpoena not be disclosed; or

(B) Any other subpoena issued for a law enforcement purpose and the court or other issuing agency has ordered that the existence or the contents of the subpoena or the information furnished in response to the subpoena not be disclosed.

(iii) If the educational agency or institution initiates legal action against a parent or student and has complied with paragraph (a)(9)(ii) of this section, it may disclose education records that are relevant to the action to the court without a court order or subpoena.

(10) The disclosure is in connection with a health or safety emergency, under the conditions described in Reg. 99.36.

(11) The disclosure is information the educational agency or institution has designated as "directory information," under the conditions described in Reg. 99.37.

(12) The disclosure is to the parent of a student who is not an eligible student or to the student.

(13) The disclosure is to an alleged victim of any crime of violence, as that term is defined in section 16 of title 18, U.S.C., of the results of any disciplinary proceeding conducted by an institution of postsecondary education against the alleged perpetrator of that crime with respect to that crime.

(b) This section does not forbid or require an educational agency or institution to disclose, nor does it require an educational agency or institution to disclose, personally identifiable information from the education records of a student to any parties under paragraph (a)(1) through (11) and (13) of this section.

Sec. 99.32 What recordkeeping requirements exist concerning requests and disclosures?

(a) (1) An educational agency or institution shall maintain a record of each request for access to and each disclosure of personally identifiable information from the education records of each student.

(2) The agency or institution shall maintain the record with the education records of the student as long as the records are maintained.

(3) For each request or disclosure the record must include:

(i) The parties who have requested or received personally identifiable information from the education records; and

(ii) The legitimate interests the parties had in requesting or obtaining the information.

(b) If an educational agency or institution discloses personally identifiable information from an education record with the understanding authorized under Reg. 99.33(b), the record of the disclosure required under this section must include:

(1) The names of the additional parties to which the receiving party may disclose the information on behalf of the educational agency or institution; and

(2) The legitimate interests under Reg. 99.31 which each of the additional parties has in requesting or obtaining the information.

(c) The following parties may inspect the record relating to each student:

(1) The parent or eligible student.

(2) The school official or his or her assistants who are responsible for the custody of the records.

(3) Those parties authorized in Reg. 99.31(a)(1) and (3) for the purposes of auditing the recordkeeping procedures of the educational agency or institution.

(d) Paragraph (a) of this section does not apply if the request was from, or the disclosure was to:

(1) The parent or eligible student;

(2) A school official under Reg. 99.31(a)(1);

(3) A party with written consent from the parent or eligible student;

(4) A party seeking directory information; or

(5) A party seeking or receiving the records as directed by a Federal grand jury or other law enforcement subpoena and the issuing court or other issuing agency has ordered that the existence or the contents of the subpoena or the information furnished in response to the subpoena not be disclosed.

Sec. 99.33 What limitations apply to the redisclosure of information?

(a) (1) An educational agency or institution may disclose personally identifiable information from an education record only on the condition that the party to whom the information is disclosed will not disclose the information to any other party without the prior consent of the parent or eligible student.

(2) The officers, employees, and agents of a party that receives information under paragraph (a)(1) of this section may use the information, but only for the purposes for which the disclosure was made.

(b) Paragraph (a) of this section does not prevent an educational agency or institution from disclosing personally identifiable information with the understanding that the party receiving the information may make further disclosures of the information on behalf of the educational agency or institution if:

(1) The disclosures meet the requirements of Reg. 99.31; and

(2) The educational agency or institution has complied with the requirements of Reg. 99.32(b).

(c) Paragraph (a) of this section does not apply to disclosures made pursuant to court orders or lawfully issued subpoenas under Sec. 99.31(a)(9), to disclosures of directory information under Sec. 99.31(a)(11) or to disclosures to a parent or student under Reg. 99.31(a)(12).

(d) Except for disclosures under Sec. 99.31(a)(9), (11) and (12), an educational agency or institution shall inform a party to whom disclosure is made of the requirements of this section.

(e) If this Office determines that a third party improperly rediscloses personally identifiable information from education records in violation of Reg. 99.33(a) of this section, the educational agency or institution may not allow that third party access to personally identifiable information from education records for at least five years.

Sec. 99.34 What conditions apply to disclosure of information to other educational agendes or institutions?

(a) An educational agency or institution that discloses an education record under Reg. 99.31(a)(2) shall:

(1) Make a reasonable attempt to notify the parent or eligible student at the last known address of the parent or eligible student, unless:

(i) The disclosure is initiated by the parent or eligible student; or

(ii) The annual notification of the agency or institution under Reg. 99.6 includes a notice that the agency or institution forwards education records to other agencies or institutions that have requested the records and in which the student seeks or intends to enroll;

(2) Give the parent or eligible student, upon request, a copy of the record that was disclosed; and

(3) Give the parent or eligible student, upon request, an opportunity for a hearing under Subpart C.

(b) An educational agency or institution may disclose an education record of a student in attendance to another educational agency or institution if:

(1) The student is enrolled in or receives services from the other agency or institution; and

(2) The disclosure meets the requirements of paragraph (a) of this section.

Sec. 99.35 What conditions apply to disclosure of information for Federal or State program purposes?

(a) The officials listed in Reg. 99.31(a)(3) may have access to education records in connection with an audit or evaluation of Federal or State supported education programs, or for the enforcement of or compliance with Federal legal requirements which relate to those programs.

(b) Information that is collected under paragraph (a) of this section must:

(1) Be protected in a manner that does not permit personal identification of individuals by anyone except the officials referred to in paragraph (a) of this section; and

(2) Be destroyed when no longer needed for the purposes listed in paragraph (a) of this section.

(c) Paragraph (b) of this section does not apply if:

(1) The parent or eligible student has given written consent for the disclosure under Reg. 99.30; or

(2) The collection of personally identifiable information is specifically authorized by Federal law.

Sec. 99.36 What conditions apply to disclosure of information in health and safety emergencies?

(a) An educational agency or institution may disclose personally identifiable information from an education record to appropriate parties in connection with an emergency if knowledge of the information is necessary to protect the health or safety of the student or other individuals.

(b) Nothing in this Act or this part shall prevent an educational agency or institution from —

(1) Including in the education records of a student appropriate information concerning disciplinary action taken against the student for conduct that posed a significant risk to the safety or well-being of that student, other students, or other members of the school community;

(2) Disclosing appropriate information maintained under paragraph (b)(1) of this section to teachers and school officials within the agency or institution who the agency or institution has determined have legitimate educational interests in the behavior of the student; or

(3) Disclosing appropriate information maintained under paragraph (b)(1) of this section to teachers and school officials in other schools who have been determined to have legitimate educational interests in the behavior of the student.

(c) Paragraphs (a) and (b) of this section shall be strictly construed.

Sec. 99.37 What conditions apply to disclosing directory information?

(a) An educational agency or institution may disclose directory information if it has given public notice to parents of students in attendance and eligible students in attendance at the agency or institution of:

(1) The types of personally identifiable information that the agency or institution has designated as directory information;

(2) A parent's or eligible student's right to refuse to let the agency or institution designate any or all of those types of information about the student as directory information; and

(3) The period of time within which a parent or eligible student has to notify the agency or institution in writing that he or she does not want any or all of those types of information about the student designated as directory information.

(b) An educational agency or institution may disclose directory information about former students without meeting the conditions in paragraph (a) of this section.

Sec. 99.38 What conditions apply to disclosure of information as permitted by State statute adopted after November 19, 1974 concerning the juvenile justice system?

(a) If reporting or disclosure allowed by State statute concerns the juvenile justice system and the system's ability to effectively serve, prior to adjudication, the student whose records are released, an educational agency or institution may disclose education records under Reg. 99.31(a)(5)(i)(B).

(b) The officials and authorities to whom the records are disclosed shall certify in writing to the educational agency or institution that the information will not be disclosed to any other party, except as provided under State law, without the prior written consent of the parent of the student.

SUBPART E – WHAT ARE ENFORCEMENT PROCEDURES?

Reg. 99.60 What functions has the Secretary delegated to the Office and to the Office of Administrative Law Judges?

(a) For the purposes of this subpart, "Office" means the Family Policy Compliance Office, U.S. Department of Education.

(b) The Secretary designates the Office to:

(1) Investigate, process, and review complaints and violations under the Act and this part; and

(2) Provide technical assistance to ensure compliance with the Act and this part.

(c) The Secretary designates the Office of Administrative Law Judges to act as the Review Board required under the Act to enforce the Act with respect to all applicable programs. The term "applicable program" is defined in section 400 of the General Education Provisions Act.

Reg. 99.61 What responsibility does an educational agency or institution have concerning conflict with State or local laws?

If an educational agency or institution determines that it cannot comply with the Act or this part due to a conflict with State or local law, it shall notify the Office within 45 days, giving the text and citation of the conflicting law.

Reg. 99.62 What information must an educational agency or institution submit to the Office?

The Office may require an educational agency or institution to submit reports containing information necessary to resolve complaints under the Act and the regulations in this part.

Sec. 99.63 Where are complaints filed?

A person may file a written complaint with the Office regarding an alleged violation under the Act and this part. The Office's address is: Family Policy Compliance Office, U. S. Department of Education, Washington, D.C. 20202-4605.

Sec. 99.64 What is the complaint procedure?

(a) A complaint filed under Sec. 99.63 must contain specific allegations of fact giving reasonable cause to believe that a violation of the Act or this part has occurred.

b) The Office investigates each timely complaint to determine whether the educational agency or institution has failed to comply with the provisions of the Act or this part.

(c) A timely complaint is defined as an allegation of a violation of the Act that is submitted to the Office within 180 days of the date of the alleged violation or of the date that the complainant knew or reasonably should have known of the alleged violation.

(d) The Office extends the time limit in this section if the complainant shows that he or she was prevented by circumstances beyond the complainant's control from submitting the matter within the time limit, or for other reasons considered sufficient by the Office.

Sec. 99.65 What is the content of the notice of complaint issued by the Office?

(a) The Office notifies the complainant and the educational agency or institution in writing if it initiates an investigation of a complaint under section 99.64(b). The notice to the educational agency or institution —

(1) Includes the substance of the alleged violation; and

(2) Asks the agency or institution to submit a written response to the complaint.

(b) The Office notifies the complainant if it does not initiate an investigation of a complaint because the complaint fails to meet the requirements of section 99.64.

Sec. 99.66 What are the responsibilities of the Office in the enforcement process?

(a) The Office reviews the complaint and response and may permit the parties to submit further written or oral arguments or information.

(b) Following its investigation, the Office provides to the complainant and the educational agency or institution written notice of its findings and the basis for its findings.

(c) If the Office finds that the educational agency or institution has not complied with the Act or this part, the notice under paragraph (b) of this section:

(1) Includes a statement of the specific steps that the agency or institution must take to comply; and

(2) Provides a reasonable period of time, given all of the circumstances of the case, during which the educational agency or institution may comply voluntarily.

Sec. 99.67 How does the Secretary enforce decisions?

(a) If the educational agency or institution does not comply during the period of time set under Reg. 99.66(c), the Secretary may, in accordance with part E of the General Education Provisions Act —

(1) Withhold further payments under any applicable program;

(2) Issue a complaint to compel compliance through a cease and desist order; or

(3) Terminate eligibility to receive funding under any applicable program.

(b) If, after an investigation under Reg. 99.66, the Secretary finds that an educational agency or institution has complied voluntarily with the Act or this part, the Secretary provides the complainant and the agency or institution written notice of the decision and the basis for the decision.

END FERPA REGULATIONS

THE PAGE INTENTIONALLY LEFT BLANK

CHAPTER 13
OVERVIEW OF SPECIAL EDUCATION CASELAW

The Individuals with Disabilities Act requires school districts to provide a free appropriate public education (FAPE) to children with disabilities. The child's special education must be at no cost to the child's parent.

After Congress passed Public Law 94-142, courts issued different rulings about the meaning of the term "appropriate." As cases were litigated, some courts decided that "appropriate" meant that handicapped children were entitled to an education that would help the child become **self-sufficient**. Other courts decided that school systems were required "to **maximize** the potential of each handicapped child commensurate with the opportunity provided non-handicapped children." (from *Rowley*)

Board of Education v. Rowley, 458 U.S. 176 (1982)

In 1982, the U. S. Supreme Court issued their first decision in a special education case. In *Board of Education v. Rowley*, the high court defined the terms "special education" and "appropriate" as follows:

> Special education . . . means specially designed instruction, at no cost to parents or guardians to meet the unique needs of a handicapped child . . . (At 189) [an appropriate education] provides personalized instruction with sufficient support services to permit the child to benefit educationally from that instruction . . . and if the child is being educated in the regular classrooms of the public education system, (it) should be reasonably calculated to enable the child to achieve passing marks and advance from grade to grade. *Board of Educ. v. Rowley*, 458 U.S. 176, 204, 205 (1982)

After the *Rowley* decision, terms like "maximizing," and "self-sufficiency" were stricken. Parents were not entitled to the "best" education nor were they entitled to an education that would "maximize" their child's potential. The use of these terms is fatal to the parent's case. Parents and school districts continued to disagree about the adequacy (and appropriateness) of special education services.

Tuition Reimbursement

Dissatisfied about their children's lack of progress in public school programs, parents removed their children from public programs and placed the children into private special education programs. Some parents requested that their school districts reimburse them for the costs of their child's special education in these private programs.

If the public school provides an appropriate educational program, parents are not entitled to be reimbursed for a private placement. If the school district defaults on their obligation to provide a child with an appropriate education and the parent places the child into a private special education program where the child does receive an appropriate education, should the parent be reimbursed?

Some Courts decided that reimbursement was retroactive to the date of placement or the date of denial of an appropriate education. Other courts held that parents could not be reimbursed until after the case was litigated and won by the parents, a process that often took several years to complete.

In 1980, the U. S. Court of Appeals for the Fourth Circuit held that parents who had withdrawn their children from public school placements could not receive reimbursement retroactively because the parents violated the "stay put" provisions of the Act. (*Stemple v. Board of Education*, 623 F.2d 893 (4th Cir. 1980)).

The U.S. Court of Appeals for the First Circuit disagreed. In the First Circuit, parents could be reimbursed from the date of placement. This created a split among Circuits on this issue.

Burlington School Committee v. Dept. of Education, 471 U.S. 359 (1985)

To resolve the split, the U.S. Supreme Court agreed to hear the case of Michael Panico in *Burlington School Committee v. Department of Education*, 471 U. S. 359, 105 S. Ct. 1996, 85 L. Ed. 2d 385 (1985).

In *Burlington*, the legal issue was whether Michael Panico's parents could be reimbursed for his education at a private special education school that was on the state's list of approved schools. The Panico family and the Massachusetts Department of Education brought the suit against the Town of Burlington, Massachusetts.

The decision in *Burlington* was written by Justice William Rehnquist. In this unanimous decision, Justice Rehnquist explained that the special education statutes were enacted for the benefit of handicapped children. He discussed the issues that parents face in deciding whether to remove their child from an inadequate public school program:

> . . . the parents who disagree with the proposed IEP are faced with a choice: go along with the IEP to the detriment of their child if it turns out to be inappropriate or pay for what they consider to be the appropriate placement. If they choose the latter course, which conscientious parents who have adequate means and who are reasonably confident of their assessment normally would, it would be an empty victory several years later that they were right but that these expenditures could not in a proper case be reimbursed by the school officials. (At 370)

> In a case where a court determines that a private placement desired by the parents was proper under the Act and that an IEP calling for placement in a public school was inappropriate, it seems clear beyond cavil that "appropriate" relief would include a prospective injunction directing the school officials to develop and implement at public expense an IEP placing the child in a private school. (At 370)

In closing, Justice Rehnquist wrote:

> We do think that the (lower) court was correct in concluding that 'such relief the court determines is appropriate,' within the meaning of 20 U.S.C. § 1415(e)(2), means that equitable considerations are relevant in fashioning relief. (At 374)

Honig v Doe, 484 U.S. 305 (1988)

In *Honig v. Doe*, 484 U.S. 305 108 S. Ct. 592, 98 L. Ed. 686 (1988), the Supreme Court issued their first and only decision in a school discipline case.

The Court found that John Doe had peer relationship problems since first grade. His social skills were poor and minor frustrations caused him to explode. Jack Smith was identified as emotionally disturbed in the second grade. Smith had academic and social problems, extreme hyperactivity, low self esteem, and frequent verbal and physical outbursts. The San Francisco school system sought to suspend and expel both boys for behaviors relating to their handicaps. Referring to the *Mills* case and congressional intent, the Supreme Court held that the special education law:

> . . . demonstrates a congressional intent to strip schools of the unilateral authority they had traditionally employed to exclude disabled students, particularly emotionally disturbed students, from school. This Court will not rewrite the statute to infer a "dangerousness" exception on the basis of obviousness or congressional inadvertence, since, in drafting the statute, Congress devoted close attention to *Mills* . . . thereby establishing that the omission of an emergency exception for dangerous students was intentional. (At 306)

Although the Supreme Court issued a strong decision in *Honig*, school authorities have continued to expel and suspend handicapped children for behaviors related to their handicaps.

Florence County School District IV v. Shannon Carter, 510 U.S. 7 (1993)

The U.S. Supreme Court agreed to review *Florence County School District Four v. Shannon Carter*, 950 F. 2d 156 (4th Cir. 1991) after a Second Circuit Court of Appeals ruling in a similar case created a split among circuits.

In *Tucker v. Bay Shore Union Free School District*, 873 F. 2d 563 (2d Cir. 1989), the Second Circuit followed a decision in an earlier Fourth Circuit case:

> . . . (T)he Tuckers might have sought to exploit the Education for the Handicapped Act (EHA) by selecting Eagle Hill (private special education school) without first fulfilling their obligation to work together with school officials to find a placement that was "appropriate" within the meaning of the EHA.

On the other hand, it may be that the Tuckers did everything in their power to find a school for Jonas that was on the state's "approved list," but were unable to do so. We find no indication in the record of any effort on the part of the School District to assist the Tuckers in any way in finding a mutually acceptable alternative to the proposed IEP. We find this troubling as the School District was no freer than were the Tuckers to leave to the other party the responsibility of searching for an acceptable placement. It may be that having made its recommendation, the School District meant to leave the Tuckers alone with a "take it or leave it" crisis ... Such an "unfortunate" situation ... would constitute a "less than complete" safeguarding of Jonas' rights under the EHA ... (At 567)

In *Tucker*, the Second Circuit held that the parents could not be reimbursed for their son's education although " ... the placement at the Eagle Hill School had been appropriate to meet Jonas' educational needs" because Eagle Hill was not on New York's list of approved special education placements (at 564).

The *Tucker* rule created inequities for children like Jack Straube who resided in the Second Circuit. Although Jack Straube had an average to above average abilities, at the end of ninth grade his reading skills were at the third grade level. Jack had dyslexia and an attention deficit disorder. He had received special education services in a public school program since third grade. *Straube v. Florida Union Free School Dist.*, 801 F. Supp. 1164 (S.D.N.Y. 1992)

By the end of ninth grade, Jack Straube's parents:

... decided that the school district had enough time to teach their son to read and challenged his IEP as inappropriate. Their goal was to place Jack in the Kildonan School in Amenia, New York, a residential school which purportedly has a high degree of success in teaching dyslexic children to read. The Kildonan School utilizes a teaching method known as Orton-Gillingham, which is a multi-sensory approach to learning.

(T)he school district agreed to place Jack at Kildonan. The Straubes began the enrollment process but were then told that the district could not authorize the Kildonan placement because the school was not "approved" by the New York State Education Department. The Straubes nevertheless enrolled Jack at Kildonan after allegedly investigating other alternatives drawn from the "approved" list. (At 1170)

In Jack's case, a Hearing Officer found that " ... no private school either within or without the state dealing with this Child's severe learning disability, at his chronological age, is registered as an approved school." (At 1170) Kildonan School was on the approved list of states other than New York. (At 1180) Pursuant to the *Tucker* rule, which was binding on Hearing Officers and Courts in the Second Circuit, the Hearing and Reviewing Officers were forced to rule against Jack Straube's parents.

The parents appealed to the U.S. District Court. Ultimately, New York was a party to the suit because the state failed to provide a "continuum of alternative placements," as is required by the Code of Federal Regulations. (At 1172, 1175)

"After nine months in Kildonan, Jack's reading scores had improved dramatically." (Reading comprehension at 9.0, word identification at 9.8, passage comprehension at 7.0 grade levels). The District Court wrote that "we have been returned to the question of whether in its private placement approvals, the State provided a continuum of alternative placements. This question invites us into investigating state educational policies and facilities which is far beyond the scope of review permitted." (At 1177)

The Court ruled that although Jack received an appropriate education at The Kildonan School, his education could not be free because of the *Tucker* rule.

In *Florence County School District IV v. Shannon Carter*, the U. S. District Court and the Fourth Circuit found that the IEP developed for Shannon was not appropriate. The courts ordered Florence County to reimburse Shannon's parents for her education at Trident Academy. Florence County argued that they should not have to pay for Shannon's education at a non-approved school because this would not be "proper under the Act." The district claimed that the Court did not have the legal authority to award reimbursement to a school that may not meet state standards.

Several states and powerful interest groups states filed amicus briefs on behalf of Florence County claiming that a ruling in Shannon's favor would bring financial ruin to school districts. The "financial ruin argument" was not raised by the Justices during Pete's oral argument before the Supreme Court, but was addressed in the written opinion.

Cedar Rapids v. Garret F. (1999)

On March 3, 1999, the U. S. Supreme Court issued a favorable decision for Garret in *Cedar Rapids v. Garret F.* In a 7-2 decision, the Supreme Court ruled that the Individuals with Disabilities Education Act (IDEA) requires school districts to provide nursing services if such services are necessary for the disabled child to receive an education.

The majority's decision was written by Justice John Paul Stevens who wrote:

> Respondent Garret F. is a friendly, creative, and intelligent young man. When Garret was four years old, his spinal column was severed in a motorcycle accident. Though paralyzed from the neck down, his mental capacities were unaffected. He is able to speak, to control his motorized wheelchair through use of a puff and suck straw, and to operate a computer with a device that responds to head movements.

> Garret is currently a student in the Cedar Rapids Community School District (District), he attends regular classes in a typical school program, and his academic performance has been a success. Garret is, however, ventilator dependent, and therefore requires a responsible individual nearby to attend to certain physical needs while he is in school.

> This case is about whether meaningful access to the public schools will be assured, not the level of education that a school must finance once access is attained. It is undisputed that the services at issue must be provided if Garret is to remain in school.

> Under the statute, our precedent and the purposes of the IDEA, the district must fund such related services to help guarantee that students like Garret are integrated into the public schools.

> Congress intended to open the door of public education to all qualified children and required participating states to educate handicapped children with non-handicapped children whenever possible.

Chief Justice William H. Rehnquist and Justices Sandra Day O'Connor, Antonin Scalia, David H. Souter, Ruth Bader Ginsburg and Stephen G. Breyer joined Justice Stevens in the decision for Garret. Two Justices, Clarence Thomas and Anthony M. Kennedy, dissented.

THE UNITED STATES SUPREME COURT

458 U.S. 176

**BOARD OF EDUCATION OF THE HENDRICK HUDSON CENTRAL
SCHOOL DISTRICT, WESTCHESTER COUNTY, et al.,
Petitioners**

v.

**AMY ROWLEY, by her parents, ROWLEY et. al.
Respondent**

No. 80-1002
On a Writ of Certiorari to the United States Court of Appeals for The Second Circuit. 632 F. 2d 945, reversed and remanded.
June 28, 1982
Before Burger, C.J., and Brennan, White, Marshall, Blackmun, Powell, Rehnquist, Stevens, O'Connor, JJ.
REHNQUIST, J., delivered the opinion of the Court, in which BURGER, C. J., and POWELL, STEVENS, and O'CONNOR, JJ., joined. BLACKMUN, J., filed an opinion, concurring in the judgment.
WHITE, J., filed a dissenting opinion, in which BRENNAN and MARSHALL, JJ., joined.
JUSTICE REHNQUIST delivered the opinion of the Court.

This case presents a question of statutory interpretation. Petitioners contend that the Court of Appeals and the District Court misconstrued the requirements imposed by the Congress upon States which receive federal funds under the Education for All Handicapped Children Act. We agree and reverse the judgment of the Court of Appeals.

I

The Education for All Handicapped Children Act of 1975 (Act), 20 U.S.C. 1401 et seq., provides federal money to assist state and local agencies in educating handicapped children, and conditions such funding upon a States compliance with extensive goals and procedures. The Act represents an ambitious federal effort to promote the education of handicapped children, and was passed in response to Congress' perception that a majority of handicapped in the United States "were either totally excluded from schools or [were] sitting idly in regular classrooms awaiting the time when they were old enough to 'drop out.'" H.R. Rep. No. 94-332. P.2 (1975). The Acts evolution and major provisions shed light on the question of statutory interpretation which is at he heart of this case.

Congress first addressed the problem of education the handicapped in 1966 when it amended the Elementary and Secondary Education Act of 1965 to establish a grant program "for the purpose of assisting the States in the initiation, expansion, and improvement of programs and projects . . . for the education of handicapped children." *Pub. L. No. 89-750*, 161, 80 Stat. 1204 (1966). That program was repealed in 1970 by the *Education for the Handicapped Act*, Pub. L. No. 91-230, 175, Part B of which established a grant program similar in purpose to the repealed legislation. Neither the 1966 nor 1970 legislation contained specific guidelines for state use of the grant money; both were aimed primarily at stimulating the States to develop educational resources and to train personnel for educating the handicapped.[1]

Dissatisfied with the progress being made under these earlier enactments, and spurred by two district court decisions holding that handicapped children should be given access to a public education, Congress in 1974 greatly increased federal funding for education of the handicapped and for the first time required recipient States to adopt "a goal of providing full educational opportunities to all handicapped children." *Pub. L. 93-380*, 88 Stat. 579, 583 (1974) (the 1974 statue). The 1974 statute was recognized as an interim measure only, adopted "in order to give the Congress an additional year in which to study what if any additional Federal assistance

[was] required to enable the States to meet the needs of handicapped children." H.R. Rep. No. 94-332, supra, p.4. The ensuing year of study produced the Education for All Handicapped Children Act of 1975.

In order to qualify for federal financial assistance under the Act, a State must demonstrate that it "has in effect a policy that assures all handicapped children the right to a free appropriate public education." 20 U.S.C. 1412(1). That policy must be reflected in a state plan submitted to and approved by the Commissioner of Education, 3 1413, which describes in detail the goals, programs, and time-tables under which the State intends to educate handicapped children within its borders. 1412. 1413. States receiving money under the Act must provide education to the handicapped by priority, first "to handicapped children who are not receiving an education" and second "to handicapped children . . . with the most severe handicaps who are receiving an inadequate education," 1413(3), and to the maximum extent appropriate" must educate handicapped children "with children who are not handicapped." 1412(5). [4] The Act broadly defines "handicapped children" to include "mentally retarded, hard of hearing, deaf, speech impaired, visually handicapped, seriously emotionally disturbed, orthopedically impaired, [and] other health impaired children, [and] children with specific learning disabilities." 1401(1).[5]

The "free appropriate public education" required by the Act is tailored to the unique needs of the handicapped child by means of an 'individualized educational program" (IEP). 1401(18). The IEP, which is prepared at a meeting between a qualified representative of the local educational agency, the child's teacher, the child parents or guardian, and, where appropriate, the child, consists of a written document containing

> (A) a student of the present levels of educational performance of the child,
> (B) a statement of annual goals, including short-term instructional objectives,
> (C) a statement of the specific educational services to be provided to such child, and the extent to which such child will be able to participate in regular educational programs,
> (D) the projected date for initiation and anticipated duration of such service, and
> (E) appropriate objective criteria and evaluation procedures and schedules for determining, on at least an annual basis, whether instructional objectives are being achieved. 1401(19).

Local or regional educational agencies must review, and where appropriate revise, each child's IEP at least annually. 1404(a)(5). See also 1413(a)(11), 1414(a)(5).

In addition to the state plan and the IEP already described, the Act imposes extensive procedural requirements upon State receiving federal funds under its provisions. Parents or guardians of handicapped children must be notified of any proposed change in "the identification, evaluation, or educational placement of the child or the provision of a free appropriate public education to the child," and must be permitted to being a complaint about "any matter relating to" such evaluation and education. 1415(b)(1)(D) and (E).[6] Complaints brought by parents or guardians must be resolved at "an impartial due process hearing," and appeal to the State educational agency must be provided if the initial hearing is held at the local or regional level. 1415(B)(2) and (c)[7] Thereafter, "any party aggrieved by the findings and decisions" of the state administrative hearing has "the right to bring a civil action with respect to the complaint . . . in any State court of competent jurisdiction or in a district court of the United Stated without regard to the amount in controversy." 1415(e)(2).

Thus, although the Act leaves to the States the primary responsibility for developing and executing educational programs for handicapped children, it imposes significant requirements to be followed in the discharge of that responsibility. Compliance is assured by provisions permitting the withholding of federal funds upon determination that a participating state or local agency has failed to satisfy the requirements of the Act, 1414(b)(A), 1416, and by the provision for judicial review. At present, all States except New Mexico receive federal funds under the portions of the Act at issue today. Brief for the United States as Amicus Curiae 2, n. 2.

II

This case arose in connection with the education of Amy Rowley, a deaf student at the Furnace Woods School in the Hendrick Hudson Central School District, Peekskill, New York. Amy has minimal residual hearing and is an excellent lip reader. During the year before she began attending furnace Woods, a meeting between her parents and school administrators resulted in a decision to place in a regular kindergarten class in order to determine what supplemental services would be necessary to her education. Several members of the school administration prepared for Amy's arrival by attending a course in sign-language interpretation, and a teletype machine was installed in the principal's office to facilitate communication with her parents who are also deaf. At the end of the trial period it was determined that Amy should remain in the kindergarten class, but that she should be provided with an FM hearing aid which would amplify words spoken into a wireless receiver by the teacher or fellow students during certain classroom activities. Amy successfully completed her kindergarten year.

As required by the Act, an IEP was prepared for Amy during the fall of her first-grade year. The IEP provided that Amy should be educated in a regular classroom at Furnace Woods, should continue to use the FM hearing aid, and should receive instruction from a tutor for the deaf for one hour each day and from a speech therapist for three hours each week. The Rowleys agreed with the IEP but insisted that Amy also be provided a qualified sign-language interpreter in all of her academic classes. Such an interpreter had been placed in Amy's kindergarten class for a two-week experimental period, but the interpreter had reported that Amy did not need his services at that time. The school administrators likewise concluded that Amy did not need such an interpreter in her first-grade classroom. They reached this conclusion after consulting the school district's Committee on the Handicapped, which had received expert evidence from Amy's parents on the importance of a sign-language interpreter, received testimony from Amy's teacher and other persons familiar with her academic and social progress, and visited a class for the deaf.

When their request for an interpreter was denied, the Rowleys demanded and received a hearing before an independent examiner. After receiving evidence from both sides, the examiner agreed with the administrators' determination that an interpreter was not necessary because "Amy was achieving educationally, academically, and socially" without such assistance. App. to Pet. for Cert. F-22. The examiner's decision was affirmed on appeal by the New York Commissioner of Education on the basis of substantial evidence in the record. *Id.*, at E-4. Pursuant to the Act's provision for judicial review, the Rowleys then brought an action in the United States District Court for the Southern District of New York, claiming that the administrators' denial of the sign-language interpreter constituted a denial of the "free appropriate public education" guaranteed by the Act.

The District Court found that Amy "is a remarkably well adjusted child" who interacts and communicates well with her classmates and has "developed an extraordinary rapport" with her teachers. 483 F. Supp, 528, 531. It also found that "she performs better than the average child in her class and is advancing easily from grade to grade," *id.*, at 534, but "that she understands considerably less of what goes on in class than she would if she were not deaf" and thus "is not learning as much, or performing as well academically, as she would without her handicap," *id.*, at 532. This disparity between Amy's achievement and her potential led the court to decide that she was not receiving a "free appropriate public education" which the court defined as "an opportunity to achieve [her] full potential commensurate with the opportunity provided to other children." *id.*, at 534. According to the District Court, such a standard "requires that the potential of the handicapped child be measured and compared to his or her performance, and that the remaining differential or 'shortfall' be compared to the shortfall experienced by nonhandicapped children.' *Ibid.* The District Court's definition arose from its assumption that the responsibility for "giving content to the requirement of an 'appropriate education'" had 'been left entirely to the federal courts and the hearing officers.' *Id.*, at 533.[8]

A divided panel of the United States Court of Appeals for the Second Circuit affirmed. The Court of Appeals "agree[d] with the [D]istrict [C]ourt's conclusions of law," and held that its 'findings of fact [were] not clearly erroneous." 632 F. 2d 945, 947 (1980).

We granted certiorari to review the lower courts' interpretation of the Act. Such review requires us to consider two questions: What is meant by the Act's requirement of a "free appropriate public education"? And what is the role of state and federal courts in exercising the review granted by 1415 of the Act? We consider these questions separately.[9]

III

A

This is the first case in which this Court has been called upon to interpret any provision of the Act. As noted previously, the District Court and Court of Appeals concluded that "the Act itself does nor define 'appropriate education,'" 483 F. Supp., at 533, but leaves "to the courts and the hearing officers" the responsibility of "giv[ing] content to the requirement of an appropriate education." *Ibid.* see also 632 F. 2d, at 947. Petitioners contend that the definition of the phrase "free appropriate public education" used by the courts below overlooks the definition of the phrase actually found in the Act. Respondents agree that the Act defines "free appropriate public education," but contend that the statutory definition is not "functional" and thus "offers judges no guidance in their consideration of controversies involving the 'identification, evaluation, or educational placement of the child or the provision of a free appropriate public education," Brief for Respondents 28. The United States, appearing as *amicus curiae* on behalf of respondents, states that '[a]though the Act includes definitions of 'free appropriate public education' and other related terms, the statutory definitions do not adequately explain what is meant by 'appropriate," Brief for United States as Amicus Curiae. [13]

We are loath to conclude that Congress failed to offer any assistance in defining the meaning of the principal substantive phrase used in the Act. It is beyond dispute that, contrary to the conclusions of the courts below, the Act does expressly define "free appropriate public education:"

> The term 'free appropriate public education' means **special education** and **related services** which (A) have been provided at public expenses, under public supervision and direction, and without charge, (B) meet the standards of the State educational agency, (C) include an appropriate preschool, elementary, or secondary school education in the State involved, and (D) are provided in conformity with the individualized education program required under section 1414(a)(5) of this title. 1401(18) (emphasis added).

"Special education," as referred to in this definition, means "specially designed instruction, at no cost to parents or guardians, to meet the unique needs of a handicapped child, including classroom instruction, instruction in physical education, home instruction, and instruction in hospitals and institutions." 1401(16). "Related services" are defined as "transportation, and such developmental, corrective, and other supportive services...as may be required to assist a handicapped child to benefit from special education." 1401(17). [10]

Like many statutory definitions, this one tends toward the cryptic rather than the comprehensive, but that is scarcely a reason for abandoning the quest for legislative intent. Whether or not the definition is a "functional" one, as respondents contend it is not, it is the principal tool which Congress has given us for parsing the critical phrase of the Act, we think more must be made of it than either respondents or the United States seems willing to admit.

According to the definitions contained in the Act, a "free appropriate public education" consists of educational instruction specially designed to meet the unique needs of the handicapped child, supported by such services as are necessary to permit the child "to benefit" from the instruction. Almost as a checklist for adequacy under the Act, the definition also requires that such instruction and services be provided at public expense and under public supervision, meet the State's educational standards, approximate the grade levels used in the State's regular education, and comport with the child's IEP. Thus, if personalized instruction is being provided with sufficient supportive services to permit the child to benefit from the instruction, and the other items on the definitional checklist are satisfied, the child is receiving a "free appropriate public education" as defined by the Act.

Other portions of the statute also shed light on congressional intent. Congress found that of the roughly eight million handicapped children in the United States at the time of enactment, one million were "excluded entirely form the public school system" and more than half were receiving an inappropriate education. Note to 1401. In addition, as mentioned in Part I, the Act requires States to extend educational services first to those children who are receiving no education and second to those children who are receiving an "inadequate education." 1412(3). When these express statutory findings and priorities are read together with the Act's extensive procedural requirements and its definition of "free appropriate public education," the face of the statute evinces a congressional intent to bring previously excluded handicapped children into public education systems of the States and to require the States to adopt procedures which would result in individualized consideration of and instruction for each child.

Noticeably absent from the language of the statue is any substantive standard prescribing the level of education to be accorded handicapped children. Certainly the language of the statute contains no requirement like the one imposed by the lower courts—that States maximize the potential of handicapped children "commensurate with the opportunity provided to other children." 483 F. Supp., at 534. That standard was expounded by the District court without reference to the statutory definitions or even to the legislative history of the Act. Although we find the statutory definition of "free appropriates public education" to be helpful in our interpretation of the Act, there remains the question of whether the legislative history indicates a congressional intent that such education meet some additional substantive standard. For an answer, we turn to that history.

B
(i)

As suggested in Part I, federal support for education of the handicapped is a fairly recent development. Before passage of the Act some States has passed laws to improve the educational services afford handicapped children [12] but many of these children were excluded completely form any form of public education or were left to fend for themselves in classrooms designed for the education of their nonhandicapped peers. The House Report begins by emphasizing this exclusion and misplacement, noting that millions of handicapped children "were either totally excluded form schools or [were] sitting idly in regular classrooms awaiting the time when they were old enough to 'drop out.'" *H.R. Rep, No. 94-332*, supra, at 2. See also *S. Rep. No. 94-168*, p. 8 (1975). One of the Act's two principal sponsors in the Senate urged its passage in similar terms:

> While much progress has been made in the last few years, we can take no solace in that progress until all handicapped children are, in fact, receiving an education. The most recent statistics provided by the Bureau of Education for the Handicapped estimate that . . . 1.75 million handicapped children do not receive any educational services, and 2.5 million handicapped children are not receiving an appropriate education. *121 Cong. Rec. 1946* (1975) (remarks of Sen. Williams).

This concern, stressed repeatedly throughout the legislative history [13], confirms the impression conveyed by the language of statute: By passing the Act, Congress sought primarily to make public education available to handicapped children. But in seeking to provide such access to public education, Congress did not impose upon the states any greater substantive educational standard than would be necessary to make such access meaningful. Indeed, Congress expressly "recognized that in many instances the process of providing special education and related services to handicapped children is not guaranteed to produce any particular outcome." *S. Rep. No. 94-168*, supra, at 11. Thus, the intent of the Act was more to open the door of public education to handicapped children on appropriate terms than to guarantee any particular level of education once inside.

Both the House and the Senate reports attribute the impetus for the Act and its predecessors to two federal court judgments rendered in 1971 and 1972. As the Senate Report states, passage of the act "followed a series of landmark court cases establishing in law the right to education for all handicapped children." *S. Rep. No. 94-168*, supra, at 6.14 The first case, *Pennsylvania Association for Retarded Children v. Commonwealth of Pennsylvania (PARC)*, 334 F. Supp. 1257 (1971) 343 F. Supp. 279(ED pa 1972), was a suit on behalf of retarded children challenging the constitutionality of a Pennsylvania statue which acted to exclude them from public education and training. The case ended in a consent decree which enjoined the State from "den[ying] to any mentally retarded child *access* to a free public program of education and training." 334 F. Supp. at 1258 (emphasis added).

PARC was followed by *Mills v. Board of Education of the District of Columbia*, 343 F. Supp. 866 (DC 1972), a case in which the plaintiff handicapped children had been excluded from the District of Columbia public schools. The court judgment, quoted at page 6 of the Senate Report on the Act, provided

> that no handicapped child eligible for publicly supported education in the District of Columbia public schools shall be *excluded* from a regular school assignment by a Rule, policy, or practice of the Board of Education of the District of Columbia or its agents unless such child is provided (a) *adequate* alternative educational services suited to the child's needs, which may include special education or tuition grants, and (b) a constitutionally adequate prior hearing and periodic review of the child's status, progress, and the *adequacy* of any educational alternative. 348 F. Supp., at 878 (emphasis added).

Mills and *PARC* both held that handicapped children must be given access to an adequate, publicly supported education. Neither case purports to require any particular substantive level of education.[15] Rather, like the language of the Act, the cases set forth extensive procedures to be followed in formulating personalized educational programs for handicapped children. See 348 F. Supp., at 878-883; 334 F. Supp., at 1258-1267.16. The fact that both *PARC* and *Mills* are discussed at length in the legislative reports suggest that the principles which they established are the principles which, to a significant extent, guided the drafters of the Act. Indeed, immediately after discussing these cases the Senate Report describes the 1974 statue as having "incorporated the major principles of the right to education cases." S. Rep. No 94-168, *supra*, at 8. Those principles in turn became the basis of the Act, which itself was designed to effectuate the purposes of the 1974 statue. H.R. Rep. No. 94-332, *supra*, at 5.18

That the Act imposes no clear obligation upon recipient States beyond the requirement that handicapped children receive some form of specialized education is perhaps best demonstrated by the fact that Congress, in explaining the need for the Act, equated an "appropriate education" to the receipt of some specialized educational services. The Senate report states: 'The most recent statistics provided by the Bureau of education for the Handicapped estimate that of the more than 8 million children...with handicapping conditions requiring special education and related services, only 3.9 million such children are receiving an appropriate education." S. Rep. No. 94-332, *supra*, at 8. 19 This statement, which reveals Congress' view that 3.9 million handicapped children were "receiving an appropriate education" in 1975, is followed immediately in the Senate Report by a table showing that 3.9 million handicapped children were "served " in 1975 and a slightly larger numbers were "unserved." A similar statement and table appear in the House report. H.R. Rep. No. 94-332, *supra*, at 11-12.

It is evident from the legislative history that the characterization of handicapped children as "served" referred to children who were receiving some form of specialized educational services from the States, and that the characterization of children as "unserved" referred to those who were receiving no specialized educational services. For example, a letter sent to the United States Commissioner of Education by the House Committee on Education and Labor, signed by two key sponsors of the Act in the House, asked the commissioner to identify the number of handicapped " children served" in each State. The letter asked for statistics on the number of children "being served" in various types of "special education programs" and the number of children who were not "receiving educational services." Hearing on S. 6 before the Subcommittee on the Handicapped of the Senate Committee on Labor and Public Welfare, 94th Cong. 1st Sess., 205-207 (1975). Similarly, Senator Randolph, one of the Act 's principal sponsors in the Senate, noted that roughly one-half of the handicapped children in the United States "are receiving special educational services." *Id.*, at 1.[20] By characterizing the 3.9 million handicapped children who were "served" as children who were receiving an appropriate education," the Senate and House reports unmistakably disclose Congress' perception of the type of education required by the Act: an "appropriate education" is provided when personalized educational services are provided.[21]

(ii)

Respondents contend that "the goal of the Act is to provide each handicapped child with an equal educational opportunity." Brief for Respondents 35. We think, however, that the requirement that a State provides specialized educational services to handicapped children generates no additional requirement that the services so provided be sufficient to maximize each child's potential "commensurate with the opportunity provided other children." Respondents and the United States correctly note that Congress sought "to provide assistance to the States carrying out their responsibilities under the Constitution of the United States to provide equal protection of the laws." *S. Rep. No. 94-168*, supra, at 13.22 But we do not think that such statements imply a congressional intent to achieve: strict equality of opportunity or services.

The educational opportunities provided by our public school systems undoubtedly differ from student to student, depending upon a myriad of factors that might affect a particular student's ability to assimilate information presented in the classroom. The requirement that States provide "equal" educational opportunities would thus seem to present an entirely unworkable standard requiring impossible measurements and comparisons. Similarly, furnishing handicapped children with only such services as are available to nonhandicapped children would in all probability fall short of the statutory requirement of "free appropriate public education." To require, on the other hand, the furnishing of every special service necessary to maximize each handicapped child's potential is, we think, further than Congress intended to go. Thus, to speak in terms of "equal" services in one instance gives less than what is required by the Act and in another instance more. The theme of the Act is "free appropriate public education," a phrase which is too complex to be captured by the word "equal" whether on is speaking of opportunities or services.

The legislative conception of the requirements of equal protection was undoubtedly informed by the two district court decisions referred to above. But cases such as *Mills* and *PARC* held simply that handicapped children may not be excluded from entirely public education. In *Mills*, the District Court said:

> If sufficient funds are not available to finance all of the services and programs that are needed and desirable in the system, then the available funds must be expended equitably in such a manner that no child is entirely excluded from a publicly supported education consistent with his needs and ability to benefit therefrom. 348 F Supp., at 876.

The *PARC* Court used similar language, saying "[i]t is the commonwealth's obligation to place each mentally retarded child in a free, public program of education and training appropriate to the child's capacity . . ." 334 F. Supp., at 1260. The right of access to free public education enunciated by these cases is significantly different from any notion of absolute equality of opportunity regardless of capacity. To the extent the Congress might have looked further than these cases which are mentioned in the legislative history at the time of enactment of the Act, this Court has held at least twice that the Equal Protection Clause of the Fourteenth Amendment does not require States to expend equal financial resources on the education of each child. *San Antonio School District v. Rodriguez*, 411 U.S. 1(1975); *Mcinnis v. Shapiro*, 238 F.Supp. 327 (ND Ill. 1968), aff'd sub nom, *Mcinnis v. Ogilvie*, 394 U.S. 322 (1969).

In explaining the need for federal legislation, the House Report noted that "no congressional legislation has required a precise guarantee for handicapped children, i.e., a basic floor of opportunity that would bring into compliance all school districts with the constitutional right of equal protection with respect to handicapped children." H.R. Rep. No. 94-332, *supra*, at 14. Assuming that the Act was designed to fill the need identified in the House Report—that is, to provide a "basic floor of opportunity' consistent with equal protection—neither the Act nor its history persuasively demonstrate that Congress thought that equal protection required anything more than equal access. Therefore, Congress' desire to provide specialized educational services, even in furtherance of "equality," cannot be read as imposing any particular substantive educational standard upon the States.

The District Court and the Court of Appeals thus erred when they held that the Act requires New York to maximize the potential of each handicapped child commensurate with the opportunity provided nonhandicapped children. Desirable though that goal might be, it is not the standard that Congress imposed upon States which receive funding under the Act. Rather, Congress sought primarily to identify and evaluate handicapped children, and to provide them with access to a free public education.

(iii)

Implicit in the congressional purpose of providing access to a "free appropriate public education" is the requirement that the education to which access is provided be sufficient to confer some educational benefit upon the handicapped child. It would do little good for Congress to spend millions of dollars in providing access to public education only to have the handicapped child receive no benefit from that education. The statutory definition of "free appropriate public education," in addition to requiring that States provide each child with "specially designed instruction," expressly requires the provision of "such . . . supportive services . . . as may be required to assist a handicapped child to benefit from special education." 1401(17) (emphasis added). We therefore conclude that the "basic floor of opportunity" provided by the Act consists of access to specialized instruction and related services which are individually designed to provide educational benefit to the handicapped child.[23]

The determination of when handicapped children are receiving sufficient educational benefits to satisfy the requirements of the Act presents a more difficult problem. The Act requires participating States to educate a wide spectrum of handicapped children, from the marginally hearing-impaired to the profoundly retarded palsied. It is clear that the benefits obtainable by children at one end of the spectrum will differ dramatically form those obtainable by children at the other end, with infinite variations in between. One child may have little difficulty competing successfully in an academic setting with nonhandicapped children while another child may encounter great difficulty in acquiring even the most basic of self-maintenance skills. We do not attempt today to establish any one test for determining the adequacy of educational benefits conferred upon all children covered by the Act. Because in this case we are presented with a handicapped child who is receiving substantial specialized instruction and related services, and who is performing above average in the regular classrooms of a public school system, we confine our analysis to the situation.

The Act requires participating States to educate handicapped children with nonhandicapped children whenever possible.[24] When the "mainstreaming" preference of the Act has been met and a child is being educated in the regular classrooms of a public school system, the system itself monitors the educational progress of the child. Regular examinations are administered, grades are awarded, and yearly advancement to higher grade levels is permitted for those children who attain an adequate knowledge of the course material. The grading and advancement system thus constitutes an important factor in determining educational benefit. Children who graduate from our public school systems are considered by our society to have been "educated" at least to the grade level they have completed, and access to an "education" for handicapped children is precisely what Congress sought to provide in the Act.[25]

C

When the language of the Act and its legislative history are considered together, the requirements imposed by Congress become tolerably clear. Insofar as a State is required to provide a handicapped child with a "free appropriate public education," we hold that it satisfies this requirements by providing personalized instruction with sufficient support services to permit the child to benefit educationally from that instruction. Such instruction and services must be provided at public expense, must meet the State's educational standards, must approximate the grade levels used in the State's regular education, and must comport with the child's IEP. In addition, the IEP, and therefore the personalized instruction, should be formulated in accordance with the requirements of the Act, and if the child is being educated in the regular classrooms of the public education system, should be reasonably calculated to enable the child to achieve passing marks and advance from grade to grade.[26]

IV

A

As mentioned in Part I, the Act permits "any party aggrieved by the findings and decision" of the state administrative hearings "to bring a civil action "in" any State Court of competent jurisdiction or in a district court of the United States without regard to the amount in controversy." 1415(e)(2). The complaint, and therefore the civil action, may concern "any matter relating to the identification, evaluation, or educational placement of the child, or the provision of a free appropriate public education to such child." 1415(b)(1)(E). In reviewing the complaint, the Act provides that a court "shall receive the record of the state administrative proceedings, shall hear additional evidence at the request of a party, and, basing its decision on the preponderance of the evidence, shall grant such relief as the court determines is appropriate." 1415(e)(2).

The parties disagree sharply over the meaning of these provisions, petitioners contending that courts are given only limited authority to review for state compliance with the Act's procedural requirements and no power to review the substance of the state program, and respondents contending that the Act requires courts to exercise de novo review over state educational decisions and policies. We find petitioners' contention unpersuasive, for Congress expressly rejected provisions that would have so severely restricted the role of reviewing courts. In substituting the current language of the statue for language that would have made state administrative findings conclusive if supported by substantial evidence, the Conference Committee explained that courts were to make "independent decisions based on a preponderance of the evidence." S. Conf. Rep.No. 94-455, *supra*, at 50. (See also 121 Cong. Rec. 37416 (1975), remarks of Senator Williams).

But although we find that this grant of authority is broader than claimed by petitioners, we think the fact that it is found in 1415 of the Act, which is entitled "Procedural Safeguards," is not without significance when the elaborate and highly specific procedural safeguards embodied in 1415 are contrasted with the general and somewhat imprecise substantive admonitions contained in the Act, we think that the importance Congress attached to these procedural safeguards cannot be gainsaid. It seems to us no exaggeration to say that Congress placed every bit as much emphasis upon compliance with procedures giving parents and guardians a large measure of participation at every stage of the administrative process, see, e.g. 1415(a)-(d), as it did upon the measurement of the resulting IEP against a substantive standard. We think that the congressional emphasis upon full participation of concerned parties throughout the development of the IEP, as well as the requirements that state and local plans be submitted to the Commissioner for approval, demonstrate the legislative conviction that adequate compliance with the procedures prescribed would in most cases assure much if not all of what Congress wished in the way of substantive content in an IEP.

Thus, the provision that a reviewing court base its decision on the "preponderance of the evidence" is by no means an invitation to the court to substitute their own notions of sound educational policy for those of the school authorities which they review. The very importance which Congress has attached to compliance with certain procedures in the preparation of an IEP would be frustrated if a court were permitted simply to set state decisions aside. The fact that 1415(e) requires that the reviewing court "receive the records of the [state] administrative proceedings" carries with it the implied requirement that due weight shall be given to these proceedings. And we find nothing in the Act to suggest that merely because Congress was rather sketchy in establishing substantive requirements, as opposed to procedural requirements for the preparation of an IEP, it intended that reviewing courts should have a free hand to impose substantive standards of review which cannot be derived from the Act itself. In short, the statutory authorization to grant "such relief as the court determines is appropriate' cannot be read without reference to the obligations, largely procedural in nature, which are imposed upon recipient States by Congress.

Therefore, a court's inquiry in suits brought under 1415(e)(2) is twofold. First, has the State complied with the procedures set forth in the Act?[27] And second, is the individualized educational program developed through the Act's procedures reasonably calculated to enable the child to receive educational benefits?[28] If these requirements are met, the State has complied with the obligations imposed by Congress and the courts can require no more.

B

In assuring that the requirements of the Act have been met, courts must be careful to avoid imposing their view of preferable educational methods upon the States.[29] The primary responsibility for formulating the education to be accorded a handicapped child, and for choosing the educational method most suitable to the child's needs, was left by the Act to state and local educational agencies in cooperation with the parents or guardian of the child. The Act expressly charges States with the responsibility of "acquiring and disseminating to teachers and administrators of programs for handicapped children significant information derived form educational research, demonstration, and similar projects, and of adopting, where appropriate, promising educational practices and materials." 1413(a)(3). In the face of such a clear statutory directive, it seems highly unlikely that congress intended courts to overturn a State's choice of appropriate educational theories in a proceeding conducted pursuant to 1415(e)(2).[30]

We previously have cautioned that courts lack the "specialized knowledge and experience" necessary to resolve "persistent and difficult questions of educational policy." *San Antonio School District v. Rodriguez*, 411 U.S. 1, 42 (1973). We think that Congress shared that view when it passed the Act. As already demonstrated, Congress' intention was not that the Act displace the primacy of States in the field of education, but that the states receive funds to assist them in extending their educational systems to handicapped. Therefore, once a court determines that the requirements of the Act have been met, questions of methodology are for resolution by the States.

V

Entrusting a child's education to state and local agencies does not leave the child without protection. Congress sought to protect individual children by providing for parental involvement in the development of State plans and policies, *supra*, at 4-5 and n. 6, and in the formulation of the child's individual educational program. As the Senate Report states:

> The Committee recognizes that in may instances the process of providing special education and related services to handicapped children is not guaranteed to produce any particular outcome. By changing the language of the provision relating to individualized educational programs to emphasize the process of parent and child involvement, and to provide a written record of reasonable expectations, the Committee intends to clarify that such individualized planning conferences are a way to provide parent involvement and protection to assure that appropriate services are provided to a handicapped child. S. Rep. No.94-168, *supra*, at 11-12. See also *S. Conf. Rep. No. 94-445*, p. 30 (1975); 45 CFR 121a.345 (1980).

As this very case demonstrates, parents and guardians will not lack ardor in seeking to ensure that handicapped children receive all the benefits to which they are entitled by the Act.[31]

IV

Applying these principles to the facts of this case, we conclude that the court of Appeals erred in affirming the decision of the District Court. Neither the District Court nor the Court of Appeals found that petitioners had failed to comply with the procedures of the Act, and the findings of neither court would support a conclusion that Amy's educational program failed to comply with the substantive requirements of the Act. On the contrary, the District Court found that the "evidence firmly establishes that Amy is receiving an 'adequate' education, since she performs better than the average child in her class and is advancing easily from grade to grade." 483 F Supp., at 534. In light of this finding, and of the fact that Amy was receiving personalized instruction and related services calculated by the Furnace Woods school administrators to meet her educational needs, the lower courts should not have concluded that the Act requires the provision of a sign-language interpreter. Accordingly, the decision of the Court of appeals is reversed and the case is remanded for further proceedings consistent with this opinion.[32]

SO ORDERED.

JUSTICE BLACKMUN, concurring in the judgment.

Although I reach the same result as the Court does today, I read the legislative history of the Education for All Handicapped Children Act differently. Congress unambiguously stated that it intended to "to take a more active role under its responsibility for equal protection of the laws to guarantee that handicapped children are provided ***equal educational opportunity***." *S. Rep. No. 94-168*, p. 9 (1975) (emphasis added). See also 20 U.S.C. 1412(2)(A)(i) (requiring States to establish plans with the 'goal of providing full educational opportunity to all handicapped children").

As I have observed before, "[i]t seems plain to me that Congress, in enacting [this statue], intended to do more than merely set out politically self-serving but essentially meaningless language about what the [handicapped] deserve at the hands of state . . . authorities." *Pennhurst State School v. Halderman*, 451 U.S. 1, 32 (1981) (opinion concurring in part and concurring in judgment). The clarity of the legislative intent convinces me that the relevant question here is not, as the court says, whether Amy Rowley's individualized education program was "reasonably calculated to enable [her] to receive educational benefits," measured in part by whether or not she "achieves passing marks and advances from grade to grade."[27] Rather, the question is whether Amy's program, viewed as a whole, offered her an opportunity to understand and participate in the classroom that was substantially equal to that given her nonhandicapped classmates. This is a standard predicated on equal educational opportunity and equal access to the educational process, rather than upon Amy's achievement of any particular educational outcome.

In answering this question, I believe that the District Court and the court of Appeals should have given greater deference than they did to the findings of the School District's impartial hearing officer and the State's Commissioner of Education, both of whom sustained petitioner's refusal to add sign-language interpreter to Amy's individualized education program. 20 U.S.C. 1415(e)(2) (requiring reviewing court to "receive the records of the administrative proceeding" before granting relief). I would suggest further that those courts focused too narrowly on the presence or absence of a particular service, a sign-language interpreter, rather than on the total package of services furnished to Amy by the School Board.

As the Court demonstrates, petitioner Board has provided Amy Rowley considerably more than "a teacher with a loud voice." See post, at 4 (dissenting opinion). By concentrating on whether Amy was "learning as much, or performing as well academically, as she would without her handicap," 483 F. Supp. 528, 532 (SDNY 1980), the District Court and the Court of Appeals paid too little attention to whether, on the entire record, respondent's individualized education program offered her an educational equal to that provided her nonhandicapped classmates. Because I believe that standard has been satisfied here, I agree that the judgment of the Court of Appeals should be reversed.

FOOTNOTES:

[1] See *S. Rep. No. 94-168*, p. 5 (1975; *H.R. Rep. No. 94-332*, pp. 2-3 (1975).

[2] Two cases, *Mills v. Board of Education of the District of Columbia*, 348 F. Supp. 866 (DC 1972), and *Pennsylvania Association for Retarded Children v. Commonwealth of Pennsylvania*, 334 F. Supp. 1257 (1971), 343 F. Supp. 279(ED Pa 1972), were later identified as the most prominent of the cases contributing to Congress' enactment of the Act and the statutes which preceded it. H.R. Rep. No. 94-332, supra , at 3-4. Both decisions are discussed in Part III of this opinion, infra.

[3] All functions of the Commissioner of Education, formerly an officer in the Department of Health, Education, and Welfare, were transferred to the Secretary of Education, in 1979 when congress passed the Department of Education Organization Act 20, U.S.C. 3401 et seq. See 20 U.S.C. 3441(a)(1).

[4] Despite this preference for "mainstreaming" handicapped children—educating them with nonhandicapped children—Congress organized that regular classrooms simply would not be a suitable setting for the education of many handicapped children. The Act expressly acknowledge that "the nature or severity of the handicap [may be] such that education in regular classes with the use of supplementary aids and services cannot be achieved satisfactorily." 1412(5). The Act thus provides for the education of some handicapped children in separate classes or institutional settings. See *ibid.*; 1413(a)(4).

[5] In addition to covering a wide variety of handicapped conditions, the Act requires special educational services for children "regardless of the severity of their handicap." 1412(2), 1414(a)(A).

[6] The requirements that parents be permitted to file complaints regarding their child's education, and present when the child's IEP is formulated, represent only two examples of Congress' effort to maximize parental involvement in the education of each handicapped child. In addition, the Act requires that parents be permitted "to examine all relevant records with respect to the identification, evaluation, and educational placement of the child, and . . . to obtain an independent educational evaluation of the child." 1415(b)(1)(A). See also 1412(4), 1414(a)(4). State educational policies and the state plan submitted to the Commissioner of Education must be formulated in "consultation with individuals involved in

or concerned with the education of handicapped children, including handicapped individuals and parents or guardians of handicapped children." 1412(7). See also 1412(2)(E). Local agencies, which receive funds under the act by applying to the state agency, must submit applications which assure that they have developed procedures for "participation and consultation of the parents or guardians[s] of [handicapped] children" in local educational programs, 1414(a)(1)(C)(iii), and the application itself, along with "all pertinent documents related to such application," must be made "available to parents, guardians, and other members of the general public." 1414(a)(4).

[7] "Any Party" to a state or local administrative hearing must "be accorded (1) the right to be accompanied and advised by counsel and by individuals with special knowledge or training with respect to the problems of handicapped children, (2) the right to present evidence and confront, cross examine, and compel the attendance of witnesses, (3) the right to a written or electronic verbatim record of such hearing, and (4) the right to written findings of fact and decisions." 1415(d).

[8] For reasons that are not revealed in the record, the District Court concluded that "the Act itself does not define 'appropriate education." 483 F. Supp. 533. In fact, the Act expressly defines the phrase "free appropriate public education." See 1401(18), to which the District Court was referring. See 483 F. Supp., at 533. After overlooking the statutory definition, the District Court sought guidance not from regulations interpreting the Act, but from regulations promulgated under Section 504 of the Rehabilitation Act. See 483 F. Supp., at 533, citing 45 CFR 84.33(b).

[9] The IEP which respondents challenged in the District Court was created for the 1978-1979 school year. Petitioners contend that the District Court erred in reviewing that IEP after the school year had ended and before the school administrators were able to develop another IEP for subsequent years. We disagree. Judicial review invariably takes more than nine months to complete, not to mention the time consumed during the preceding state administrative hearings. The District Court thus correctly ruled that it retained jurisdiction to grant relief because the alleged deficiencies in the IEP were capable of repetition as to the parties before it yet evading review. *Rowley v. The board of Education of the Hendrick Hudson Central School District*, 483 F. Supp. 536. 538 (1980). See *Murphy v. Hunt*, 455 U.S.—,—(1982); *Weinstein v. Bradford*, 423 U.S. 147, 149 (1975).

[10] Examples of "related services" identified in the Act are "speech pathology and audiology, psychological services, physical and occupational therapy, recreation, and medical and counseling services, except that such medical services shall be for diagnosis and evaluation purposes only." 1401(17).

[11] The dissent, finding that "the standard of the courts below seems to reflect the congressional purpose' of the Act, concludes that our answer to this question "is not a satisfactory one." *Id.*, at 5. Presumably, the dissent also agrees with the District Court's conclusion that "It has been left entirely to the courts and hearing officers to give content to the requirement of an 'appropriate education." 483 F. Supp., at 533. It thus seems that the dissent would give the courts carte blanche to impose upon the States whatever burden their various judgments indicate should be imposed. Indeed, the dissent clearly characterizes the requirement of an "appropriate education," as open-ended, noting that "if there are limits not evident from the face of the statute on what may be considered an ' appropriate education,' they must be found in the purpose of the statue or its legislative history." Not only are we unable to find any suggestion from the face of the statute that the requirement of an "appropriate education" was to be limitless, but we also view the dissent's approach as contrary to the fundamental proposition that Congress, when exercising its spending power, can impose no burden upon the States unless it does so unambiguously. See *infra*, at 27, n 26.

No one can doubt that this would have been an easier case if Congress had seen fit to provide a more comprehensive statutory definition of the phrase "free appropriate public education." But Congress did not do so, and our problem is to construe what Congress has written. After all, Congress expresses its purpose by words. It is for us to ascertain - neither to add nor to subtract - neither to delete nor to distort." 62 Cases of *Jam v. United States*, 340 U.S. 593. 596 (1951). We would be less than faithful to our obligation to construe what Congress has written if, in this case, we were to disregard the statutory language and legislative history of the Act by concluding that Congress had imposed upon the States a burden of unspecified proportions and weight, to be revealed only through case by case adjudication in this courts.

[12] See H.R. Rep. No. 94-332, *supra*, at 10; Note. *The Education of All Handicapped Children Act of 1975*, Mich. J.L Ref. 110, 119 (1976).

[13] See, e.g., 121 Cong. Rec. (1975)(remarks of Sen. Javits) ("all too often, our handicapped citizens have been denied opportunities to receive an adequate education"); 121 Cong Rec. (1975) (remarks of Sen. Cranston) (millions of handicapped "children are largely excluded from educational opportunities that we give to our other children"); 121 Cong. Rec. (1975) (remarks of Rep. Mink) ("handicapped children . . . are denied access to public schools because of a lack of trained personnel").

[14] Similarly, the Senate Report states that it was an "increased awareness of the educational needs of handicapped children and landmark court decisions establishing the right to education for the handicapped children [that] pointed to the necessity of an expanding federal role." S. Rep. No. 94-168, *supra*, at 5. See also H.R. Rep. No. 94-332, *supra*, at 2-3.

[15] The only substantive standard which can be implied from these cases comports with the standard implicit in the Act. *PARC* states that each child must receive "access to free public program of education and training *appropriate to his learning capacities*," 334 F. Supp., at 1258, and that further state action is required when it appears that "the needs of the mentally retarded child are not being adequately served, *id.*, at 1266. (emphasis added.) *Mills* also speaks in terms of "adequate" educational services, 348 F. Supp. at 878, and sets a realistic standard of providing some educational services to each child when every need cannot be met.

"If sufficient funds are not available to finance all of the services and programs that are needed and desirable in the systems then the available funds must be expended equitably in such a manner that no child is entirely excluded from a publicly supported education consistent with his needs and ability to benefit therefrom. The inadequacies of the District of Columbia Public School System, whether occasioned by insufficient funding or administrative inefficiency, certainly cannot be permitted to bear more heavily on the 'exceptional or handicapped child than on the normal child." *Id.*, at 876.

[16] Like the Act, *PARC* required the State to identify, locate [and] evaluate" handicapped children, 334 F. Supp., at 1267, to create for each child an individual educational program, *id.*, 1265, and to hold a hearing "on any change in educational assignment," *id.*, at 1266. *Mills* also required the preparation of an individual educational program for each child. In addition, *Mills* permitted the child's parents to inspect records relevant to the child's education, to obtain an independent educational evaluation of the child, to object to the IEP, and receive a hearing before independent hearing officer, to be represented by counsel at hearing, and to have the right to confront and cross-examine adverse witnesses, all of which are also permitted by the Act. 348 F. Supp., at 879-881. Like the Act, *Mills* also required that the education of handicapped children be conducted pursuant to an overall plan prepared by the District of Columbia, and established a policy of educating handicapped children with nonhandicapped children whenever possible. *Ibid.*

[17] See S. Rep. No. 9-168, *supra*, at 6-7; H.R. Rep. No. 94-332, *supra*, at 3-4.

[18] The 1974 statute 'incorporated the major principles of the right to education, cases, "by adding important new provisions to the Education of the Handicapped Act which require the States to: establish a goal of providing full educational opportunities to all handicapped children; provide procedures for insuring that handicapped children and their parents or guardians are guaranteed procedural safeguards in decisions regarding identification, evaluation, and educational placement of handicapped children; establish procedures to insure that, to the maximum extent appropriate, handicapped children . . . are educated with children who are not handicapped, and establish procedures to insure that testing and evaluation materials and procedures utilized for the for the purposes of classification and placement of handicapped children will be selected and administered so as not to be racially or culturally discriminatory." S.Rep. No. 94-168, *supra*, at 8.

The House Report explains that the Act simply incorporated these purposes of the 1974 statute: the Act was intended "primarily to amend . . . the Education of the Handicapped Act in order to provide permanent authorization and a comprehensive mechanism which will insure that those provisions enacted during the 93rd Congress [the 1974 statute] will result in maximum benefits for handicapped children and their families." H.R. Rep. No. 94-332, *supra*, at 5. Thus, the 1974 statute purposes providing handicapped children access to public education became the purpose of the Act.

[19] These statistics appear repeatedly throughout the legislative history of the Act, demonstrating a virtual consensus among legislators that 3.9 million handicappped children were receiving an appropriate education in 1975. See, e.g. 121 Cong. Rec. 19486 (1975) (remarks of Sen. Williams); 121 Cong. Rec. 19504 (1975) (remarks or Sen. Schweicker); 121 Cong. Rec. 23702 (1975) (remarks of Rep. Madden); 121 Cong. Rec. 23702 (1975) (remarks of Rep. Brademas); 121 Cong. Rec. 23709 (1975) (remarks of Rep. Minish); 121 Cong. Rec. 37024 (1975) (remarks of Rep. Brademas); 121 Cong. Rec. 37027 (1975) (remarks of Sen. Gude); 121 Cong. Rec. 37417 (1975) (remarks of Sen. Javits); 121 Cong. Rec. 37420 (1975) (remarks of Sen. Hathaway).

[20] Senator Randolph stated: "only 55 percent of the school-aged handicapped children and 22 percent of the preschool-aged handicapped children are receiving special educational services." Hearing on S. 6 before the Subcommittee on the Handicapped of the Senate Committee on Labor and Public Welfare, 94th Cong., 1st Sess., 1 (1975). Although the figures differ slightly in various parts of the legislative history, the general thrust of congressional calculations was that roughly one-half of the handicapped children in the United States were not receiving specialized educational services, and thus were not "served." See, e.g., 121 Cong. Rec, 19494 (1975) (remarks of Sen. Javits) ('only 50 percent of the Nation's handicapped children received proper education services"); 121 Cong. Rec. 19504 (1975) (remarks of Sen. Humphrey) ("[a]most 3 million handicapped children, while in school, receive none of the special services that they require in order to make education a meaningful experience"); 121 Cong. Rec. 23706 (1975) (remarks of Rep. Quie) ("only 55 percent [of handicapped children] were receiving a public education"); 121 Cong. Rec. 233709 (1975) (remarks of Rep. Biaggi) ("[o]ver 3 million [handicapped] children in this country are receiving either below par education or none at all").

Statements similar to those appearing in the text, which equate "served" as it appears in the Senate Report to "receiving special education services," appear throughout legislative history. See, e.g., 121 Cong. Rec. 19492 (1975) (remarks of Sen. Williams); 121 Cong. Rec. 19494 (1975) (remarks of Sen. Javits); 121 Cong. Rec. 19496 (1975) (remarks of Sen. Stone); 121 Cong. Rec. 19504-19505 (1975) (remarks of Sen. Humphrey); 121 Cong. Rec. 23703 (1975) (remarks of Rep. Brademas); Hearings on H.R. 7217 before the Subcommittee on Select Education of the Committee on Education and Labor of the House or Representatives, 94th Cong., 1st Sess. 91, 150, 153 (1975); Hearings on H.R. 4199 before the Select Subcommittee on Education of the Committee on Education and Labor of the House of Representatives, 93rd Cong., 1st Sess., 130, 139 (1973). See also 45 CFR 121a.343(b) (1980).

[21] In seeking to read more into the Act that its language or legislative history will permit, the United States focuses upon the word "appropriate,' arguing that "that statutory definitions do not adequately explain what it means." Brief for United States as *Amicus Curiae* 13. Whatever Congress meant by an "appropriate" education, it is clear that it did not mean a potential-maximizing education.

The term as used in reference to educating the handicapped appears to have originated in the *PARC* decision, where the District Court required that handicapped children be provided with "education and training appropriate to [their] learning capacities." 334 F. Supp., at 1258. The word appears again in the *Mills* decision, the District Court at one point referring to the need for an "appropriate educational program," 348 F. Supp., at 879, and at another point speaking of a "suitable publicly-supported education," *id.*, at 878. Both cases also refer to the need for an "adequate" education. See 334 F. Supp., at 1266; 348 F. Supp. at 878.

The use of "appropriate" in the language of the Act, although by no means definitive, suggests that Congress used the word as much to prescribe the settings in which handicapped children should be educated as to prescribe the substantive content or supportive services of their education. For example, 1412(5) requires that handicapped children be educated in classrooms with nonhandicapped children "to the maximum extent appropriate." Similarly, 140(19) provides that "whenever appropriate," handicapped children should attend and participate in the meeting at which their IEP is drafted. In addition, the definition of "free appropriate public education" itself states that instruction given handicapped children should be at an "appropriate preschool, elementary, or secondary school level. 1401(18). The Act's use of the word "appropriate" thus seems to reflect Congress' recognition that some settings simply are not suitable environments for the participation of some handicapped children. At the very least, these statutory uses of the word refute the contention that Congress used "appropriate" as a term of art which concisely expresses the standard found by the lower courts.

[22] See also 121 Cong. Rec. 19492 (1975) (remarks of Sen. Williams); 121 Cong. Rec. 19504 (1975) (remarks of Sen. Humphrey).

[23] This view is supported by the congressional intention, frequently expressed in the legislative history, that handicapped children be enabled to achieve a reasonable degree of self sufficiency. After referring to statistics showing that many handicapped children were excluded from public education, the Senate Report states:

"The long range implications of these statistics are that public agencies and taxpayers will spend billions of dollars over the lifetimes of these individuals to maintain such persons as dependents and in a minimally acceptable lifestyle. With proper education services, many would be able to become productive citizens, contributing to society instead of being forced to remain burdens. Others, through such services, would increase their independence, thus reducing their dependence on society." S. Rep. 94-168, supra, at 9. See also H.R. Rep. No. 94-332, supra, at 11.

Similarly, one of the principal Senate sponsors of the Act stated that "providing appropriate educational services now means that many of these individuals will be able to become a contributing part of our society, and they will not have to depend on subsistence payments form public funds." 121 Cong. Rec. 19492 (1975) (remarks of Sen. Williams). See also 121 Cong. Rec. 25541 (1975) (remarks of Rep. Harkin); 121 Cong. Rec. 37024 -37025 91975) (remarks of Rep. Brademas); 121 Cong. Rec. 37027 (1975) (remarks of Rep. Gude); 121 Cong. Rep. 37410 (1975) (remarks of Sen. Randolph); 121 Cong. Rec. 37416 (1975) (remarks of Sen Williams).

The desire to provide handicapped children with an attainable degree of personal independence obviously anticipated that state educational programs would confer educational benefits upon such children. But at the same time, the goal of achieving some degree of self-sufficiency in most cases is a good deal more modest than the potential-maximizing goal adopted by the lower courts.

Despite its frequent mention, we cannot conclude, as did the dissent in the Court of Appeals, that self-sufficiency was itself the substantive standard which Congress imposed upon the States. Because many mildly handicapped children will achieve self sufficiency without state assistance while personal independence for the severely handicapped may be an unreachable goal, "self sufficiency" as a substantive standard is at once an inadequate protection and an overly demanding requirement. We thus view these references in the legislative history as evidence Congress' intention that the services provided handicapped children be educationally beneficial, whatever the nature or severity of their handicap.

[24] Section 1412(5) of the Act requires that participating States establish "procedures to assure that, to the maximum extent appropriate, handicapped children, including children in public or private institutions or other care facilities, are educated with children who are not handicapped, and that special classes, separate schooling, or other removal of handicapped children from the regular educational environment occurs only when the nature or severity of the handicap is such that education in regular classes with the use of supplementary aids and services cannot be achieved satisfactorily."

[25] We do not hold today that every handicapped child who is advancing from grade to grade in a regular public school system is automatically receiving a "free appropriate public education." In this case, however, we find Amy's academic progress, when considered with the special services and professional consideration accorded by the Furnace Woods school administrators, to be dispositive.

[26] In defending the decisions of the District Court and the Court of Appeals, respondents and United States rely upon isolated statements in the legislative history concerning the achievement of maximum potential, see H.R. Rep. No. 94-332, supra, at 13, as support for the contention that Congress intended to impose greater substantive requirements than we have found. These statements, however, are too thin a reed on which to base an interpretation of the Act which disregards both its language and the balance of its legislative history. "Passing references and isolated phrases are not controlling when analyzing a legislative history." *Department of State v. The Washington Post Co.,*—U.S.—(1982)

Moreover, even were we to agree that these statements evince a congressional intent to maximize each child's potential, we could not hold that Congress has successfully imposed that burden upon the United States.

"Legislation enacted pursuant to the spending power is much in the nature of a contract: in return for federal funds, the States agree to comply with federally imposed conditions. The legitimacy of Congress' power to legislate under the spending power thus rests on whether the State voluntarily and knowingly accepts the terms of the 'contract' . . . Accordingly, if Congress intends to impose a condition on the grant of federal moneys, it must do so unambiguously." *Pennhurst State School v. Halderman,* 451 U.S. 1, 17 (1981). As already demonstrated, the Act and its history impose no requirements on the States like those imposed by the District Court and the Court of Appeal. *A fortiori* Congress has not done so unambiguously, as required in the valid exercise of its spending power.

[27] This inquiry will require a court not only to satisfy itself that the State has adopted the state plan, and assurances required by the Act, but also to determine that the State has created an IEP for the child in question which conforms with the requirements of 1401(19).

[28] When the handicapped child is being educated in the regular classrooms of a public system, the achievement of passing marks and advancement from grade to grade will be one important factor in determining educational benefit. See Part III, supra.

[29] In this case, for example, both the state hearing officer and the District Court were presented with evidence as to the best method for educating the deaf, a question long debated among scholars. See Large, "Special Problems of the Deaf Under Education for All Handicapped Children Act of 1975," *58 Washington U.L.Q.* 213, 229 (1980). The District Court accepted the testimony of respondents' experts that there was "a trend supported by studies showing the greater degree of success of students brought up in deaf households using [method of communication used by the Rowleys]." 483 F. Supp., at 535.

[30] It is clear that Congress was aware of the States' traditional role in the formulation and execution of education policy. "Historically, the States have had the primary responsibility for the education of children at the elementary and secondary level." *121 Cong. Rec.* 19498 (1975) (remarks of Sen. Dole) See also *Epperson v. Arkansas,* 393 U.S. 97, 104 (1968) "by and large, public education in out Nation is committed to the control of state and local authorities."

[31] In addition to providing for extensive parental involvement in the formulation of state and local policies, as well as the preparation of individual educational programs, the Act ensures that States will receive the advice of experts in the field of educating handicapped children. As a condition for receiving federal funds under the Act, States must create "an advisory panel, appointed by the Governor or any official authorized under State law to make such appointments, composed of individuals involved in or concerned with the education of handicapped children, including handicapped individuals, teachers, parents or guardians of handicapped children, State and local education officials, and administrators of programs for handicapped children, which (a) advises the State educational agency of unmet needs within the State in the education of handicapped children, [and] (B) comments publicly on any rules or regulations proposed for issuance by the State regarding the education of handicapped children." 1413(a)(12).

[32] Because the District Court declined to reach respondents' contention that petitioners had failed to comply with the Act's procedural requirements in developing Amy's IEP, 483 F. Supp. at 533, n.8, the case must be remanded for further proceedings consistent with this opinion.

JUSTICE WHITE, with whom JUSTICE BRENNAN and JUSTICE MARSHALL join, **dissenting**.

In order to reach its result in this case, the majority opinion contradicts itself, the language of the statute, and the legislative history. Both the majority's standard for a "free appropriate education" and its standard for judicial review disregard congressional intent.

I

The majority first turns its attention to the meaning of a "free appropriate public education." the Act provides:

> The term "free appropriate public education" means special education and related services which (A) have been provided at public expense, under public supervision and direction, and without charge, (B) meet the standard of the State educational agency, (c) include an appropriate preschool, elementary agency, (D) are provided in conformity with the individualized education program required under section 1414(a)(5) of this title. 20 U.S.C. 1401 (18).

The majority reads this statutory language as establishing a congressional intent limited to bringing "previously excluded handicapped children into the public education systems of the States and requiring the States to adopt procedures which would result in individualized consideration of and instruction for each child." *Ante*, at 12. In its attempt to constrict the definition of "appropriate" and the thrust of the Act, the majority opinion states, "Noticeably absent from the language of the statute is any substantive standard prescribing the level of education to be accorded handicapped children. Certainly the language of the statute contains no requirements like the one imposed by the lower courts-that States commensurate with the opportunity provided to other children." quoting 483, F. Supp. at 534.

I agree that the language of the Act does not contain a substantive standard beyond requiring that the education offered must be "appropriate." However, if there are limits not evident from the face of the statute on what may be considered an "appropriate education," they must be found in the purpose of the statute or its legislative history. The Act itself announces it will provide a "full educational opportunity to all handicapped children." 20 U.S.C. 1412(2)(A) (emphasis added). This goal is repeated throughout the legislative history, in statements too frequent to be "passing references and isolated phrases." 1 Ante, at 27, n. 26, quoting *Department of State v. Washington Post Co.*, —— U.S. —— (1982). These statements elucidate the meaning of "appropriate." According to the Senate Report, for example, the Act does "guarantee that handicapped children are provided equal educational opportunity." S. Rep. No. 94-168, at 9 (1975) (emphasis added). This promise appears throughout the legislative history. See 121 Cong. Rec. 19482-19483 (1975) (remarks of Sen. Randolph); id., at 19504 (Sen. Humphrey); id., at 19505 (Sen. Beall); id., at 23704 (Rep Brademas); id., at 25538 (Rep. Cornell); id., at 25540 (Rep. Grassley); id., at 37025 (Rep. Perkins); id., at 37030 (Rep. Mink); id., at 37412 (Sen. Taft); id., at 37413 (Sen. Williams); id., at 37418-37419 (Sen. Cranston); id., at 37419-37420 (Sen. Beall). Indeed, at times the purpose of the Act was described as tailoring each handicapped child's educational plan to enable the child "to achieve his or her maximum potential." H.R. Rep. No. 94-332, 94th Cong., 1st Sess. 13 19 (1975), See 121 Cong. Rec. 23709 (1975). Sen. Stafford, one of the sponsors of the Act, declared "We can all agree that the education given a handicapped child should be equivalent, at least, to the one those children who are not handicapped receive." 121 Cong. Rec. 19483 (1975). The legislative history thus directly supports the conclusion that the Act intends to give handicapped children an educational opportunity commensurate with that given other children.

The majority opinion announces a different substantive standard, that "Congress did not impose upon the States any greater substantive standard than would be necessary to make such access meaningful." While "meaningful" is no more enlightening than "appropriate," the Court purports to clarify itself. Because Amy was provided with some specialized instruction from which she obtained some benefit and because she passed from grade to grade, she was receiving a meaningful and therefore appropriate education.

This falls far short of what the Act intended. The Act details as specifically as possible the kind of specialized education each handicapped child must receive. It would apparently satisfy the Court's standard of "access to specialized instruction and related services which are individually designed to provide educational benefit to the handicapped child," for a deaf child such as Amy to be given a teacher with a loud voice, for she would benefit from that service. The Act requires more. It defines "special education" to mean "specifically designed instruction, at no cost to parents or guardians, to meet the unique needs of a handicapped child." 1401 (16) (emphasis added). Providing a teacher with a loud voice would not meet Amy's needs and would not satisfy the Act. The basic floor of opportunity is instead, as the courts below recognized, intended to eliminate the effects of the handicap, at least to the extent that the child will be given an equal opportunity to learn if that is reasonably possible. Amy Rowley, without a sign language interpreter, comprehends less than half of what is said in the classroom—less than half of what normal children comprehend. This is hardly an equal opportunity to learn, even if Amy makes passing grades.

Despite its reliance on the use of "appropriate" in the definition of the Act, the majority opinion speculates that "Congress used the word as much described the settings in which the children should be educated as to prescribe the substantive content or supportive services of their education." Of course, the word "appropriate" can be applied in many ways; at times in the Act, Congress used it to recommend mainstreaming handicapped children; at other points, it used the word to refer to the content of the individualized education. The issue before us is what standard the word "appropriate" incorporates when it is used to modify "education." The answer given by the Court is not a satisfactory one.

II

The Court's discussion of the standard for judicial review is as flawed as its discussion of a "free appropriate public education.' According to the Court, a court can ask only whether the State has "complied with the procedures set forth in the Act" and whether the individualized education program is "reasonably calculated to enable the child to receive educational benefit." Both the language of the Act and legislative history, however, demonstrate that Congress intended the courts to conduct a far more searching inquiry.

The majority assigns major significance to the review provision's being found in a section entitled "Procedural Safeguards." But where else would a provision for judicial review belong? The majority does acknowledge that the current language, specifying that a court "shall receive the record of the administrative proceedings, shall hear additional evidence at the request of a party, and basing its decision on the preponderance of the evidence, shall grant such relief as the court determines is appropriate," 1415(e)(2), was substituted at onference for language that would have restricted the role of the reviewing court much more sharply. It is clear enough to me that Congress decided to reduce substantially judicial deference to state administrative decisions.

The legislative history shows that judicial review is not limited to procedural matters and that the state educational agencies are given first, but not final, responsibility for the content of a handicapped child's education. The Conference committee directs courts to make an "independent decision." *S. Conf. Rep. No. 94-455*, at 50. The deliberate change in the review provision is an unusually clear indication that Congress intended courts to undertake substantive review instead of relying on the conclusions of the state agency.

On the floor of the Senate, Senator Williams, the chief sponsor of the bill, committee chairman, and floor manager responsible for the legislation in the Senate, emphasized the breath of the review provisions at both the administrative and judicial levels:

> Any parent or guardian may present a complaint concerning *any matter* regarding the identification, evaluation, or educational placement of the child or the provision of a free appropriate public education to such a child. In this regard, Mr. President, I would like to stress that the language referring to "free appropriate education" has been adopted to make clear that a complaint may involve matters such a questions respecting a child's individualized education program, questions of whether special education and related services are being provided without charge to the parents or guardians, questions relating to whether to the services provided a child meet the standards of the State education agency, *or any other question* within the scope of the definition of "free appropriate public education." In addition, it should be clear that a parent or guardian may present a complaint alleging that a State or local education agency has refused to provide services to which a child may be entitled or alleging that the State or local educational agency has erroneously classified a child as as handicapped child when, in fact, that child is not a handicapped child. 121 Cong. Rec. 37415 (emphasis added).

There is no doubt that the state agency itself must make substantive decisions. The legislative history reveals that the courts are to consider, *de novo*, the same issues. Senator Williams explicitly stated that the civil action permitted under the Act encompasses all matters related to the original complaint. *Id.*, at 37416.

Thus, the Court's limitations on judicial review have no support in either the language of the Act or the legislative history. Congress did not envision that inquiry would end if a showing is made that the child is receiving passing marks and is advancing from grade to grade. Instead, it intended to permit a full and searching inquiry into any aspect of a handicapped child's education. The court's standard, for example, would not permit a challenge to part of the IEP; the legislative history demonstrate beyond doubt that Congress intended such challenge to be possible, even if the plan as developed is reasonably calculated to give the child some benefits.

Parents can challenge the IEP for failing to supply the special education and related services needed by the individual handicapped child. That is what the Rowleys did. As the Government observes, "Courts called upon to review the content of an IEP, in accordance with 20 U.S.C. 1415(e) inevitably are required to make a judgment on the basis of the evidence presented, concerning whether the educational methods proposed by the local school district are 'appropriate' for the handicapped child involved." Brief for United States as Amicus Curiae 13. The courts below, as they were required by the Act, did precisely that.

Under the judicial review provisions of the Act, neither the District Court nor the Court of Appeals was bound by the state's construction of what an "appropriate" education means in general or by what the state authorities considered to be an appropriate education for Amy Rowley. Because the standard of the courts below seems to me to reflect the congressional purpose and because their factual findings are no clearly erroneous, I respectfully dissent.

[1] The Court's opinion relies heavily on the statement, which occurs throughout the legislative history, that, at the time of enactment, one million of the roughly eight million handicapped children in the United States were excluded entirely from the public school system and more than half were receiving an inappropriate education. See, e.g. *ante*, at pp. 11, 18-19. But this statement was often linked to statements urging equal educational opportunity. See, e.g. *121 Cong. Rec.* 19502 (remarks of Sen. Cranston); *id.* at 23702 (remarks of Rep. Brademas). That is, Congress wanted not only to bring handicapped children into schoolhouse, but wanted also to benefit them once they had entered.

[2] As further support of its conclusion, the majority opinion turns to *Pennsylvania Association for Retarded Children v. Commonwalth of Pennsylvania (PARC)*, 334 F. Supp. 1257 (1971), 343 F. Supp. 279 (ED Pa. 1972) and *Mills v. Board of Education of the District of Columbia*, 348 F. Supp. 866 (DDC 1972). That these decisions served as an impetus for the Act does not, however, establish them as the limit of the Act. In any case, the very language that the majority quotes from *Mills* sets a standard not of some education, but of educational opportunity equal to that of non-handicapped children.

Indeed, *Mills*, relying on decisions since called into question by this Court's opinion in *San Antonio School District v. Rodriquez*, 411 U.S. 1 (1973), states:

In *Hobson v. Hansen* [269 F. Supp. 401 (DD,) Judge Wright found that denying poor public school children educational opportunity equal to that available to more affluent public school children was violative of the Due Process Clause of the Fifth Amendment. *A fortiori*, the defendants' conduct here, denying plaintiffs and their class not just an equal publicly supported education while providing such education to other children, is violative of the Due Process Clause." 348 F.Supp., at 875.

Whatever the effect of *Rodriquez* on the validity of this reasoning, the statement exposes the majority's mischaracterization of the opinion and thus of the assumptions of the legislature that passed the Act.

[3] "Related services' are "transportation, and such developmental, corrective, and other supportive services . . . as may be required to assist a handicapped child to benefit from special education." 1401(17).

END OF ROWLEY

Chapter 14

THIS PAGE INTENTIONALLY LEFT BLANK

THE UNITED STATES SUPREME COURT
471 U.S. 359

BURLINGTON SCHOOL COMMITTEE, et.al.,
Petitioners

v.

DEPARTMENT OF EDUCATION
Respondent

> No. 84-433
> Argued March 26, 1985
> Decided April 29, 1985
>
> David Berman, Medford, Mass., for petitioners.
> Ellen L. Janos, Boston, Mass, for the State respondent.
> David W. Rosenberg, Boston, Mass., for respondent Panico.
>
> JUSTICE REHNQUIST delivered the opinion of the court.

The Education of the Handicapped Act (Act), 84 Stat. 175, as amended, 20 U.S.C. § 1401 *et seq.*, requires participating state and local educational agencies "to assure that handicapped children and their parents or guardians are guaranteed procedural safeguards with respect to the provision of free appropriate public education" to such handicapped children. § 1415(a). These procedures include the right of the parents to participate in the development of an "individualized education program" (IEP) for the child and to challenge in administrative and court proceedings a proposed IEP with which they disagree. §§ 1401(19), 1415(b), (d), (e). Where as in the present case review of a contested IEP takes years to run its course–years critical to the child's development–important practical questions arise concerning interim placement of the child an financial responsibility for that placement. This case requires us to address some of those questions.

Michael Panico, the son of respondent Robert Panico, was a first grader in the public school system of petitioner Town of Burlington, Massachusetts, when he began experiencing serious difficulties in school. It later became evident that he had "specific learning disabilities" and thus was "handicapped" within the meaning of the Act, 20 U.S.C. § 1401(1). This entitled him to receive at public expense specially designed instruction to meet his unique needs, as well as related transportation. §§ 1401(16), 1401(17). The negotiations and other proceedings between the Town and the Panicos, thus far spanning more than 8 years, are too involved to relate in full detail; the following are the parts relevant to the issues on which we granted certiorari.

In the spring of 1979, Michael attended the third grade of the Memorial School, a public school in Burlington, Mass., under an IEP calling for individual tutoring by a reading specialist for one hour a day and individual and group counseling. Michael's continued poor performance and the fact that Memorial School encompassed only grades K through 3 led to much discussion between his parents and Town school officials about his difficulties and his future schooling. Apparently the course of these discussions did not run smoothly; the upshot was that the Panicos and the Town agreed that Michael was generally of above average to superior intelligence, but had special educational needs calling for a placement in a school other than Memorial. They disagreed over the source and exact nature of Michael's learning difficulties, the Town believing the source to be emotional and the parents believing it to be neurological.

In late June, the Town presented the Panicos with a proposed IEP for Michael for the 1979-1980 academic year. It called for placing Michael in a highly structured class of six children with special academic and social needs, located at another Town public school, the Pine Glen School. On July 3, Michael's father rejected the proposed IEP and sought review under § 1415(b)(2) by respondent Massachusetts Department of Education's Bureau of Special Education Appeals (BSEA). A hearing was initially scheduled for August 8, but was apparently postponed in favor of a mediation session on August 17. The mediation efforts proved unsuccessful.

Meanwhile, the Panicos received the results of the latest expert evaluation of Michael by specialists at Massachusetts General Hospital, who opined that Michael's "emotional difficulties are secondary to a rather severe learning disorder characterized by perceptual difficulties" and recommended "a highly specialized setting for children with learning handicaps . . . such as the Carroll School," a state approved private school for special education located in Lincoln, Mass. App. 26, 31. Believing that the Town's proposed placement of Michael at the Pine Glen school was inappropriate in light of Michael's needs, Mr. Panico enrolled Michael in the Carroll School in mid-August at his own expense, and Michael started there in September.

The BSEA held several hearings during the fall of 1979, and in January 1980 the hearing officer decided that the Town's proposed placement at the Pine Glen School was inappropriate and that the Carroll School was "the least restrictive adequate program within the record" for Michael's educational needs. The hearing officer ordered the Town to pay for Michael's tuition and transportation to the Carroll School for the 1979-1980 school year, including reimbursement the Panicos for their expenditures on these items for the school year to date.

The Town sought judicial review of the State's administrative decision in the United States District Court for the District of Massachusetts pursuant to 20 U.S.C. § 1415(e)(2) and a parallel state statute, naming Mr. Panico and the State Department of Education as defendants. In November 1980, the District Court granted summary judgment against the Town on the state-law claim under a "substantial evidence" standard or review, entering a final judgment on this claim under Federal Rule of Civil Procedure 54(b). The Court also set the federal claim for future trial. The Court of Appeals vacated the judgment on the state-law claim, holding that review under the state statute was pre-empted by § 1415(e)(2), which establishes a "preponderance of the evidence" standard of review and which permits the reviewing court to hear additional evidence. 655 F.2d. 428 (CA1 1981)

In the meantime, the Town had refused to comply with the BSEA order, the District Court had denied a stay of that order, and the Panicos and the State had moved for preliminary injunctive relief. The State also had threatened outside of the judicial proceedings to freeze all of the Town's special education assistance unless it complied with the BSEA order. Apparently in response to this threat, the Town agreed in February 1981 to pay for Michael's Carroll School placement and related transportation for the 1980-1981 term, none of which had yet been paid, and to continue paying for these expenses until the case was decided. But the Town persisted in refusing to reimburse Mr. Panico for the expenses of the 1979-1980 school year. When the Court of Appeals disposed of the state claim, it also held that under this status quo, none of the parties could show irreparable injury and thus none was entitled to a preliminary injunction. The court reasoned that the Town had not shown that Mr. Panico would not be able to repay the tuition and related costs borne by the Town if he ultimately lost on the merits, and Mr. Panico had not shown that he would be irreparably harmed if not reimbursed immediately for past payments which might ultimately be determined to be the Town's responsibility.

On remand, the District Court entered an extensive pretrial order on the Town's federal claim. In denying the Town summary judgment, it rules that 20 U.S.C. § 1415(e)(3) did not bar reimbursement despite the Town's insistence that the Panicos violated that provision by changing Michael's placement to the Carroll School during the pendency of the administrative proceedings. The court reasoned that § 1415(e)(3) concerned the physical placement of the child and not the right to tuition reimbursement or to procedural review of a contested IEP. The court also dealt with the problem that no IEP had been developed for the 1980-1981 or 1981-1982 school years. It held that its power under § 1415(e)(2) to grant appropriate" relief upon reviewing the contested IEP for the 1979-1980 school year included the power to grant relief for subsequent school years despite the lack of IEPs for those years. In this connection, however, the court interpreted the statute to place the burden of proof on the Town to upset the BSEA decision that the IEP was inappropriate for 1979-1980 and on the Panicos and the State to show that the relief for subsequent terms was appropriate.

After a 4-day trial, the District Court in August 1982 overturned the BSEA decision, holding that the appropriate 1979-1980 placement for Michael was the one proposed by the Town in the IEP and that the parents had failed to show that this placement would not also have been appropriate for subsequent years. Accordingly, the court concluded that the Town was "not responsible for the cost of Michael's education at the Carroll School for the academic years 1979-80 through 1982-82."

In contesting the Town's proposed form of judgment embodying the court's conclusion, Mr. Panico argued that, despite finally losing on the merits of the IEP in August 1982, he should be reimbursed for his expenditures in 1979-1980, that the Town should finish paying for the recently completed 1981-1982 term, and that he should not be required to reimburse the Town for its payments to date, apparently because the school terms in question fell within the pendency of the administrative and judicial review contemplated by § 1415(e)(2). The case was transferred to another District Judge and consolidated with two other cases to resolve similar issues concerning the reimbursement for expenditures during the pendency of review proceedings.

In a decision on the consolidated cases, the court rejected Mr. Panico's argument that the Carroll School was the "current educational placement" during the pendency of the review proceedings and thus that under § 1415(e)(3) the Town was obligated to maintain that placement. *Doe v. Anrig,* 561 F. Supp. 121 (1983). The court reasoned that the Panicos' unilateral action in placing Michael at the Carroll School without the Town's consent could not "confer thereon the imprimatur of continued placement," *id.* at 129, n. 5, even though strictly speaking there was no actual placement in effect during the summer of 1979 because all parties agreed Michael was finished with the Memorial School and the Town itself proposed in the IEP to transfer him to a new school in the fall.

The District Court next rejected an argument, apparently grounded at least in part on a state regulation, that the Panicos were entitled to rely on the BSEA decision upholding their placement contrary to the IEP, regardless of whether that decision were ultimately reversed by a court. With respect to the payments made by the Town after the BSEA decision, under the State's threat to cut off funding, the court criticized the State for resorting to extrajudicial pressure to enforce a decision subject to further review. Because this "was not a case where the town was legally obliged under section § 1415(e)(3) to continue payments preserving the status quo," the State's coercion could not be viewed as "the basis for a final decision on liability" and it could only be "regarded as other than wrongful . . . on the assumption that the payments were to be returned if the order was ultimately reversed." *Id.,* at 130. The court entered a judgment ordering the Panicos to reimburse the Town for its payments for Michael's Carroll placement and related transportation in 1980-1981 and 1981-1982. The Panicos appealed.

In a broad opinion, most of which we do not review, the Court of Appeals for the First Circuit remanded the case a second time. 736 F.2d 773 (1984). The court ruled, among other things, that the District Court erred in conducting a full trial *de novo,* that it gave insufficient weight to the BSEA findings, and that in other respects it did not properly evaluate the IEP. The court also considered several questions about the availability of reimbursement for interim placement. The Town argued that § 1415(e)(3) bars the Panicos from any reimbursement relief, even if on remand they were to prevail on the merits of the IEP, because of their unilateral change of Michael's placement during the pendency of the § 1415(e)(2) proceedings. The court held that such unilateral parental change of placement would not be "a bar to reimbursement of the parents if their actions are held to be appropriate at final judgment." *Id.,* at 799. In dictum, the court suggested, however, that a lack of parental consultation with the Town or "attempt to achieve a negotiated compromise and agreement on a private placement," as contemplated by the Act, "may be taken into account in a district court's computation of an award of equitable reimbursement." *Ibid.* To guide the District Court on remand, the court stated that "whether to order reimbursement, and at what amount, is a question determined by balancing the equities." *Id.,* at 801. The court also held that the Panicos' reliance on the BSEA decision would estop the Town from obtaining reimbursement "for the period of reliance and requires that where parents have paid the bill for the period, they must be reimbursed." *Ibid.*

The town filed a petition for a writ of certiorari in this Court challenging the decision of the Court of Appeals on numerous issues, including the scope of judicial review of the administrative decision and the relevance to the merits of an IEP of violations by local school authorities of the Act's procedural requirements. We granted certiorari, 469 U.S. __ (1984), only to consider the following two issues: whether the potential relief available under § 1415(e)(2) includes reimbursement to parents for private school tuition and related expenses, and whether § 1415(e)(3) bars such reimbursement to parents who reject a proposed IEP and place a child in a private school without the consent of local school authorities. We express no opinion on any of the many other views stated by the Court of Appeals.

Congress stated the purpose of the Act in these words:

> "to assure that all handicapped children have available to them . . . a free appropriate public education which emphasizes special education and related services designed to meet their unique needs [and] to assure that the rights of handicapped children and their parents or guardians are protected." 20 U.S.C. § 1400(c).

The Act defines a "free appropriate public education" to mean:

"special education and related services which (A) have been provided at public expense, under public supervision and direction, and without charge, (B) meet the standards of the State educational agency, (C) include an appropriate preschool, elementary, or secondary school education in the State involved, and (D) are provided in conformity with [an] individualized education program." 20 U.S.C. § 1401(18).

To accomplish this ambitious objective, the Act provides federal money to state and local educational agencies that undertake to implement the substantive and procedural requirements of the Act. See *Hendrick Hudson District Bd. of Education v. Rowley*, 458 U.S. 176, 179-184 (1982).

The *modus operandi* of the Act is the already mentioned "individualized educational program." The IEP is in brief a comprehensive statement of the educational needs of a handicapped child and the specially designed instruction and related services to be employed to meet those needs. § 1401(19). The IEP is to be developed jointly by a school official qualified in special education, the child's teacher, the parents or guardian, and, where appropriate, the child. In several places, the Act emphasizes the participation of the parents in developing the child's educational program and assessing its effectiveness. See §§ 1400(c), 1401(19), 1412(7), 1415(b)(1)(A), (C), (D), (E), and 1415(b)(2); 34 CFR § 300.345 (1984).

Apparently recognizing that this cooperative approach would not always produce a consensus between the school officials and the parents, and that in any disputes the school officials would have a natural advantage, Congress incorporated an elaborate set of what it labeled "procedural safeguards" to insure the full participation of the parents and proper resolution of substantive disagreements. Section 1415(b) entitles the parents "to examine all relevant records with respect to the identification, evaluation, and educational placement of the child," to obtain an independent educational evaluation of the child, to notice of any decision to initiate or change the identification, evaluation, or educational placement of the child, and to present complaints with respect to any of the above. The parents are further entitled to "an impartial due process hearing," which in the instant case was the BSEA hearing, to resolve their complaints.

The Act also provides for judicial review in state or federal court to "[a]ny party aggrieved by the findings and decision" made after the due process hearing. The Act confers on the reviewing court the following authority:

"[T]he court shall receive the records of the administrative proceedings, shall hear additional evidence at the request of a party, and, basing its decision on the preponderance of the evidence, shall grant such relief as the court determines is appropriate." § 1415(e)(2)

The first question on which we granted certiorari requires us to decide whether this grant of authority includes the power to order school authorities to reimburse parents for their expenditures on private special education for a child, if the court ultimately determines that such placement rather than a proposed IEP, is proper under the Act.

We conclude that the Act authorizes such reimbursement. The statute directs the court to "grant such relief as [it] determines is appropriate." The ordinary meaning of these words confers broad discretion on the court. The type of relief is not further specified, except that it must be "appropriate." Absent other reference, the only possible interpretation is that the relief is to be "appropriate" in light of the purpose of the Act. As already noted, this is principally to provide handicapped children with "a free appropriate public education which emphasizes special education and related services designed to meet their unique needs." The Act contemplates that such education will be provided where possible in regular public schools, with the child participating as much as possible in the same activities as nonhandicapped children, but the Act also provides for placement in private schools at public expense where this is not possible. See § 1412(5); 34 CFR §§ 300.132, 300.227, 300.307(b), 300.347 (1984). In a case where a court determines that a private placement desired by the parents was proper under the Act and that an IEP calling for placement in a public school was inappropriate, it seems clear beyond cavil that "appropriate" relief would include a prospective injunction directing the school officials to develop and implement at public expense an IEP placing the child in a private school.

If the administrative and judicial review under the Act could be completed in a matter of weeks, rather than years, it would be difficult to imagine a case in which such prospective injunctive relief would not be sufficient. As this case so vividly demonstrates, however, the review process is ponderous. A final judicial decision on the merits of an IEP will in most instances come a year or more after the school term covered by that IEP has passed. In the meantime, the parents who disagree with the proposed IEP are faced with a choice: go along with the IEP to the detriment of their child if it turns out to be inappropriate or pay for what they consider to be the appropriate placement. If they choose the latter course, which conscientious parents who have adequate means and who are reasonably confident of their assessment normally would, it would be an empty victory to have a court tell them several years later that they were right but that these expenditures could not in a proper case be reimbursed by the school officials. If that were the case, the child's right to a *free* appropriate public education, the parents' right to participate fully in developing a proper IEP, and all of the procedural safeguards would be less than complete. Because Congress undoubtedly did not intend this result, we are confident that by empowering the court to grant "appropriate" relief Congress meant to include retroactive reimbursement to parents as an available remedy in a proper case.

In this Court, the Town repeatedly characterizes reimbursement as "damages," but that simply is not the case. Reimbursement merely requires the Town to belatedly pay expenses that it should have paid all along and would have borne in the first instance had it developed a proper IEP. Such a *post-hoc* determination of financial responsibility was contemplated in the legislative history:

> If a parent contends that he or she has been forced, at that parent's own expense, to seek private schooling for the child because an appropriate program does not exist within the local educational agency responsible for the child's education and the local educational agency disagrees, that disagreement and *the question of who remains financially responsible* is a matter to which the due process procedures established under [the predecessor to § 1415] apply. S. Rep. No. 94-168, p. 32 91975). See 34 CFR § 300.403(b) (1984) (disagreements and question of financial responsibility subject to the due process procedures).

Regardless of the availability of reimbursement as a form of relief in a proper case, the Town maintains that the Panicos have waived any right they otherwise might have to reimbursement because they violated § 1415(e)(3), which provides:

> During the pendency of any proceedings conducted pursuant to [§ 1415], unless the State or local educational agency and the parents or guardian otherwise agree, the child remain in the then current educational placement of such child . . .

We need not resolve the academic question of what Michael's "then current placement" was in the summer of 1979, when both the Town and the parents had agreed that a new school was in order. For the purposes of our decision, we assume that the Pine Glen School, proposed in the IEP, was Michael's current placement and, therefore, that the Panicos did "change" his placement after they had rejected the IEP and had set the administrative review in motion. In so doing, the Panicos contravened the conditional command of § 1415(e)(3) that "the child shall remain in the then current educational placement."

As an initial matter, we note that the section calls for agreement by *either* the *State or* the *local educational agency*. The BSEA's decision in favor of the Panicos and the Carroll School placement would seem to constitute agreement by the State to the change of placement. The decision was issued in January 1980, so from then on the Panicos were no longer in violation of § 1415(e)(3). This conclusion, however, does not entirely resolve the instant dispute because the Panicos are also seeking reimbursement for Michael's expenses during the fall of 1979, prior to the State's concurrence in the Carroll School placement.

We do not agree with the Town that a parental violation of § 1415(e)(3) constitutes a waiver of reimbursement. The provision says nothing about financial responsibility, waiver, or parental right to reimbursement at the conclusion of judicial proceedings. Moreover, if the provision is interpreted to cut off parental rights to reimbursement, the principal purpose of the Act will in many cases be defeated in the same way as if reimbursement were never available. As in this case, parents will often notice a child's learning difficulties while the child is in a regular public school program. If the school officials disagree with the need for special education or the adequacy of the public school's program to meet the child's needs, it is unlikely they will agree to an interim private school placement while the review process runs its course. Thus, under the Town's reading of § 1415(e)(3), the parents are forced to leave the child in what may turn out to be an inappropriate educational placement or to obtain the appropriate placement only by sacrificing any claim for reimbursement. The Act was intended to give handicapped children both an appropriate education and a free one; it should not be interpreted to defeat one or the other of those objectives.

The legislative history supports this interpretation, favoring a proper interim placement pending the resolution of disagreements over the IEP:

> The conferees are cognizant that an impartial due process hearing may be required to assure that the rights of the child have been completely protected. We did feel, however, that the placement, or change of placement should not be unnecessarily delayed while long and tedious administrative appeals were being exhausted. Thus the conference adopted a flexible approach to try to meet the needs of both the child and the State." 121 Cong. Rec. 37412 (1975) (Sen. Stafford).

We think at least one purpose of § 1415(e)(3) was to prevent school officials from removing a child from the regular public school classroom over the parents' objection pending completion of the review proceedings. As we observed in *Rowley*, 458 U.S., at 192, the impetus for the Act came from two federal court decisions, *Pennsylvania Assn. for Retarded Children v. Commonwealth*, 334 F. Supp. 1257 (ED Pa. 1971), and 343 F. Supp. 279 (1972), and *Mills v. Board of Education of District of Columbia*, 348 F. Supp. 866 (DC 1972), which arose from the efforts of parents of handicapped children to prevent the exclusion or expulsion of their children from the public schools. Congress was concerned about the apparently widespread practice of relegating handicapped children to private institutions or warehousing them in special classes. See § 1400(4); 34 CFR § 300.347(a) (1984). We also note that § 1415(e)(3) is located in a section detailing procedural safeguards which are largely for the benefit of the parents and the child.

This is not to say that § 1415(e)(3) has no effect on parents. While we doubt that this provision would authorize a court to order parents to leave their child in a particular placement, we think it operates in such a way that parents who unilaterally change their child's placement during the pendency of review proceedings, without the consent of state or local school officials, do so at their own financial risk. If the courts ultimately determine that the IEP proposed by the school officials was appropriate, the parents would be barred from obtaining reimbursement for any interim period in which their child's placement violated § 1415(e)(3). This conclusion is supported by the agency's interpretation of the Act's application to private placements by the parents:

> (a) If a handicapped child has available a free appropriate public education and the parents choose to place the child in a private school or facility, the public agency is not required by this part to pay for the child's education at the private school or facility . . .
>
> (b) Disagreements between a parent and a public agency regarding the availability of a program appropriate for the child, and the question of financial responsibility, are subject to the due process procedures under [§ 1415]." 34 CFR § 300.403 (1984).

We thus resolve the questions on which we granted certiorari; because the case is here in an interlocutory posture, we do not consider the estoppel ruling below or the specific equitable factors identified by the Court of Appeals for granting relief. We do think that the court was correct in concluding that "such relief as the court determines is appropriate," within the meaning of § 1415(e)(2), means that equitable considerations are relevant in fashioning relief.

The judgment of the Court of Appeals is ***Affirmed.***

END OF BURLINGTON

THE UNITED STATES SUPREME COURT
484 U.S. 305

HONIG, CALIFORNIA SUPERINTENDENT OF PUBLIC INSTRUCTION
Petitioners

V.

DOE, et. al.
Respondents

> No. 86-728
> Argued: November 9, 1987
> Decided: January 20, 1988

> JUSTICE BRENNAN delivered the opinion of the Court as to holdings number 1 and 2, in which Rehnquist, C.J., and White, Marshall, Blackmun, and Stevens, J.J. joined. Rehnquist, C.J., filed a concurring opinion. Scalia J. filed a dissenting opinion in which O'Connor, J. joined.

As a condition of federal financial assistance, the Education of the Handicapped Act requires States to ensure a "free appropriate public education" for all disabled children within their jurisdictions. In aid of this goal, the Act establishes a comprehensive system of procedural safeguards designed to ensure parental participation in decisions concerning the education of their disabled children and to provide administrative and judicial review of any decisions with which those parents disagree. Among these safeguards is the so-called "stay-put" provision, which directs that a disabled child "shall remain in [his or her] then current educational placement" pending completion of any review proceedings, unless the parents and state or local educational agencies otherwise agree. 20 U.S.C. 1415(e)(3). Today we must decide whether, in the face of this statutory proscription, state or local school authorities may nevertheless unilaterally exclude disabled children from the classroom for dangerous or disruptive conduct growing out of their disabilities. In addition, we are called upon to decide whether a district court may, in the exercise of its equitable powers, order a State to provide educational services directly to a disabled child when the local agency fails to do so.

I

In the Education of the Handicapped Act (EHA or the Act), 84 Stat. 175, as amended, 20 U.S.C. 1400 *et. seq.*, Congress sought "to assure that all handicapped children have available to them . . . a free appropriate public education which emphasizes special education and related services designed to meet their unique needs, [and] to assure that the rights of handicapped children and their parents or guardians are protected." § 1400(c). When the law was passed in 1975, Congress had before it ample evidence that such legislative assurances were sorely needed: 21 years after this Court declared education to be "perhaps the most important function of state and local governments," *Brown v. Board of Education*, 347 U.S. 483, 493 (1954), Congressional studies revealed that better than half of the Nation's eight million disabled children were not receiving appropriate educational services. § 1400(b)(3). Indeed, one out of every eight of these children was excluded from the public school system altogether, § 1400(b)(4); many others were simply "warehoused" in special classes or were neglectfully shepherded through the system until they were old enough to drop out. See H. R. Rep. No. 94-332, p. 2 (1975). Among the most poorly served of disabled students were emotionally disturbed children: Congressional statistics revealed that for the school year immediately preceding passage of the Act, the educational needs of 82 percent of all children with emotional disabilities went unmet. See S. Rep. No. 94-168, p. 8 (1975) (hereinafter S. Rep.).

Although these educational failings resulted in part from funding constraints, Congress recognized that the problem reflected more than a lack of financial resources at the state and local levels. Two federal-court decisions, which the Senate Report characterized as "landmark," see *id.* at 6, demonstrated that many disabled children were excluded pursuant to state statutes or local rules and policies, typically without any consultation with, or even notice to, their parents. See *Mills v. Board of Education of District of Columbia*, 348 F. Supp. 866 (DC 1972); *Pennsylvania Assn. for Retarded Children v. Pennsylvania*, 334 F. Supp. 1257 (ED Pa. 1971), and 343 F. Supp. 279 (1972) (*PARC*). Indeed, by the time of the EHA's enactment, parents had brought legal challenges to similar exclusionary practices in 27 other states. See S. Rep., at 6.

In responding to these problems, Congress did not content itself with passage of a simple funding statute. Rather, the EHA confers upon disabled students an enforceable substantive right to public education in participating States, see *Board of Education of Hendrick Hudson Central School Dist. v. Rowley*, 458 U.S. 176 (1982),[1] and conditions federal financial assistance upon a State's compliance with the substantive and procedural goals of the Act. Accordingly, States seeking to qualify for federal funds must develop policies assuring all disabled children the "right to a free appropriate public education," and must file with the Secretary of Education formal plans mapping out in detail the programs, procedures and timetables under which they will effectuate these policies. 20 U.S.C. §§ 1412(1), 1413(a). Such plans must assure that "to the maximum extent appropriate," States will "mainstream" disabled children, i.e., that they will educate them with children who are not disabled, and that they will segregate or otherwise remove such children from the regular classroom setting "only when the nature or severity of the handicap is such that education in regular classes . . . cannot be achieved satisfactorily." § 1412(5).

The primary vehicle for implementing these congressional goals is the "individualized educational program" (IEP) which the EHA mandates for each disabled child. Prepared at meetings between a representative of the local school district, the child's teacher, the parents or guardians, and, whenever appropriate, the disabled child, the IEP sets out the child's present educational performance, establishes annual and short-term objectives for improvements in that performance, and describes the specially designed instruction and services that will enable the child to meet those objectives. § 1401(19). The IEP must be reviewed and, where necessary, revised at least once a year in order to ensure that local agencies tailor the statutorily required "free appropriate public education" to each child's unique needs. § 1414(a)(5).

Envisioning the IEP as the centerpiece of the statute's education delivery system for disabled children, and aware that schools had all too often denied such children appropriate educations without in any way consulting their parents, Congress repeatedly emphasized throughout the Act the importance and indeed the necessity of parental participation in both the development of the IEP and any subsequent assessments of its effectiveness. See §§ 1400 (c), 1401(19), 1412(7), 1415(b)(1)(A), (C), (D), (E), and 1415(b)(2). Accordingly, the Act establishes various procedural safeguards that guarantee parents both an opportunity for meaningful input into all decisions affecting their child's education and the right to seek review of any decisions they think inappropriate. These safeguards include the right to examine all relevant records pertaining to the identification, evaluation and educational placement of their child; prior written notice whenever the responsible educational agency proposes (or refuses) to change the child's placement or program; an opportunity to present complaints concerning any aspect of the local agency's provision of a free appropriate public education; and an opportunity for "an impartial due process hearing" with respect to any such complaints. § 1415(b)(1), (2).

At the conclusion of any such hearing, both the parents and the local educational agency may seek further administrative review and, where that proves unsatisfactory, may file a civil action in any state or federal court. § 1415(c)(e)(2). In addition to reviewing the administrative record, courts are empowered to take additional evidence at the request of either party and to "grant such relief as [they] determine is appropriate." § 1415(e)(2). The "stay-put" provision at issue in this case governs the placement of a child while these often lengthy review procedures run their course. It directs that:

During the pendency of any proceedings conducted pursuant to [1415], unless the State or local educational agency and the parents or guardian otherwise agree, the child shall remain in the then current educational placement of such child. . . . § 1415(e)(3).

The present dispute grows out of the efforts of certain officials of the San Francisco Unified School District (SFUSD) to expel two emotionally disturbed children from school indefinitely for violent and disruptive conduct related to their disabilities. In November 1980, respondent John Doe assaulted another student at the Louise Lombard School, a developmental center for disabled children. Doe's April 1980 IEP identified him as a socially and physically awkward 17 year old who experienced considerable difficulty controlling his impulses and anger. Among the goals set out in his IEP was "[i]mprovement in [his] ability to relate to [his] peers [and to] cope with frustrating situations without resorting to aggressive acts." App. 17. Frustrating situations, however, were an unfortunately prominent feature of Doe's school career: physical abnormalities, speech difficulties, and poor grooming habits had made him the target of teasing and ridicule as early as the first grade, *id.* at

23; his 1980 IEP reflected his continuing difficulties with peers, noting that his social skills had deteriorated and that he could tolerate only minor frustration before exploding. *Id.* at 15-16.

On November 6, 1980, Doe responded to the taunts of a fellow student in precisely the explosive manner anticipated by his IEP: he choked the student with sufficient force to leave abrasions on the child's neck, and kicked out a school window while being escorted to the principal's office afterwards. *Id.*, at 208. Doe admitted his misconduct and the school subsequently suspended him for five days. Thereafter, his principal referred the matter to the SFUSD Student Placement Committee (SPC or Committee) with the recommendation that Doe be expelled. On the day the suspension was to end, the SPC notified Doe's mother that it was proposing to exclude her child permanently from SFUSD and was therefore extending his suspension until such time as the expulsion proceedings were completed.[2] The Committee further advised her that she was entitled to attend the November 25 hearing at which it planned to discuss the proposed expulsion.

After unsuccessfully protesting these actions by letter, Doe brought this suit against a host of local school officials and the state superintendent of public education. Alleging that the suspension and proposed expulsion violated the EHA, he sought a temporary restraining order cancelling the SPC hearing and requiring school officials to convene an IEP meeting. The District Judge granted the requested injunctive relief and further ordered defendants to provide home tutoring for Doe on an interim basis; shortly thereafter, she issued a preliminary injunction directing defendants to return Doe to his then current educational placement at Louise Lombard School pending completion of the IEP review process. Doe re-entered school on December 15, 5 ½ weeks, and 24 school days, after his initial suspension.

Respondent Jack Smith was identified as an emotionally disturbed child by the time he entered the second grade in 1976. School records prepared that year indicated that he was unable "to control verbal or physical outburst[s]" and exhibited a "[s]evere disturbance in relationships with peers and adults." *Id.* at 123. Further evaluations subsequently revealed that he had been physically and emotionally abused as an infant and young child and that, despite above average intelligence, he experienced academic and social difficulties as a result of extreme hyperactivity and low self-esteem. *Id.*, at 136, 139, 155, 176. Of particular concern was Smith's propensity for verbal hostility; one evaluator noted that the child reacted to stress by "attempting to cover his feelings of low self worth through aggressive behavior . . . primarily verbal provocations." *Id.*, at 136.

Based on these evaluations, SFUSD placed Smith in a learning center for emotionally disturbed children. His grandparents, however, believed that his needs would be better served in the public school setting and, in September 1979, the school district acceded to their requests and enrolled him at A. P. Giannini Middle School. His February 1980 IEP recommended placement in a Learning Disability Group, stressing the need for close supervision and a highly structured environment. *Id.*, at 111. Like earlier evaluations, the February 1980 IEP noted that Smith was easily distracted, impulsive, and anxious; it therefore proposed a half-day schedule and suggested that the placement be undertaken on a trial basis. *Id.*, at 112, 115.

At the beginning of the next school year, Smith was assigned to a full-day program; almost immediately thereafter he began misbehaving. School officials met twice with his grandparents in October 1980 to discuss returning him to a half-day program; although the grandparents agreed to the reduction, they apparently were never apprised of their right to challenge the decision through EHA procedures. The school officials also warned them that if the child continued his disruptive behavior—which included stealing, extorting money from fellow students, and making sexual comments to female classmates—they would seek to expel him. On November 14, they made good on this threat, suspending Smith for five days after he made further lewd comments. His principal referred the matter to the SPC, which recommended exclusion from SFUSD. As it did in John Doe's case, the Committee scheduled a hearing and extended the suspension indefinitely pending a final disposition in the matter. On November 28, Smith's counsel protested these actions on grounds essentially identical to those raised by Doe, and the SPC agreed to cancel the hearing and to return Smith to a half-day program at A. P. Giannini or to provide home tutoring. Smith's grandparents chose the latter option and the school began home instruction on December 10; on January 6, 1981, an IEP team convened to discuss alternative placements.

After learning of Doe's action, Smith sought and obtained leave to intervene in the suit. The District Court subsequently entered summary judgment in favor of respondents on their EHA claims and issued a permanent injunction. In a series of decisions, the District Judge found that the proposed expulsions and indefinite suspensions of respondents for conduct attributable to their disabilities deprived them of their congressionally mandated right to a free appropriate public education, as well as their right to have that education provided in accordance with the procedures set out in the EHA. The District Judge therefore permanently enjoined the school district from taking any disciplinary action other than a two- or five-day suspension against any disabled child for disability-related misconduct, or from effecting any other change in the educational placement of any such child without parental consent pending completion of any EHA proceedings. In addition, the judge barred the State from authorizing unilateral placement changes and directed it to establish an EHA compliance-monitoring system or, alternatively, to enact guidelines governing local school responses to disability-related misconduct. Finally, the judge ordered the State to provide services directly to disabled children when, in any individual case, the State determined that the local educational agency was unable or unwilling to do so.

On appeal, the Court of Appeals for the Ninth Circuit affirmed the orders with slight modifications. *Doe v. Maher*, 793 F.2d 1470 (1986). Agreeing with the District Court that an indefinite suspension in aid of expulsion constitutes a prohibited "change in placement" under § 1415(e)(3), the Court of Appeals held that the stay-put provision admitted of no "dangerousness" exception and that the statute therefore rendered invalid those provisions of the California Education Code permitting the indefinite suspension or expulsion of disabled children for misconduct arising out of their disabilities. The court concluded, however, that fixed suspensions of up to 30 school days did not fall within the reach of § 1415(e)(3), and therefore upheld recent amendments to the state education code authorizing such suspensions.[3] Lastly, the court affirmed that portion of the injunction requiring the State to provide services directly to a disabled child when the local educational agency fails to do so.

Petitioner Bill Honig, California Superintendent of Public Instruction,[4] sought review in this Court, claiming that the Court of Appeals' construction of the stay-put provision conflicted with that of several other courts of appeals which had recognized a dangerousness exception, compare *Doe v. Maher*, 793 F. 2d 1470 (1986) (case below), with *Jackson v. Franklin County School Board*, 765 F. 2d 535, 538 (CA5 1985); *Victoria L. v. District School Bd. of Lee County, Fla.*, 741 F.2d 369, 374 (CA 11 1984); *S-1 v. Turlington*, 635 F.2d 342, 348, n. 9 (CA5), cert. denied, 454 U.S. 1030 (1981), and that the direct services ruling placed an intolerable burden on the State. We granted certiorari to resolve these questions, 479 U.S. ___ (1987), and now affirm.

II

At the outset, we address the suggestion, raised for the first time during oral argument, that this case is moot.[5] Under Article III of the Constitution this Court may only adjudicate actual, ongoing controversies. *Nebraska Press Assn v. Stuart*, 427 U.S. 539, 546 (1976); *Preiser v. Newkirk*, 422 U.S. 395, 401 (1975). That the dispute between the parties was very much alive when suit was filed, or at the time the Court of Appeals rendered its judgment, cannot substitute for the actual case or controversy that an exercise of this Court's jurisdiction requires. *Steffel v. Thompson*, 415 U.S. 452, 459, n. 10 (1974); *Roe v. Wade*, 410 U.S. 113, 125 (1973). In the present case, we have jurisdiction if there is a reasonable likelihood that respondents will again suffer the deprivation of EHA-mandated rights that gave rise to this suit. We believe that, at least with respect to respondent Smith, such a possibility does in fact exist and that the case therefore remains justiciable.

Respondent John Doe is now 24 years old and, accordingly, is no longer entitled to the protections and benefits of the EHA, which limits eligibility to disabled children between the ages of three and 21. See 20 U.S.C. Sec. 1412(2)(B). It is clear, therefore, that whatever rights to state educational services he may yet have as a ward of the State, see Tr. of Oral Arg. 23, 26, the Act would not govern the State's provision of those services, and thus the case is moot as to him. Respondent Jack Smith, however, is currently 20 and has not yet completed high school. Although at present he is not faced with any proposed expulsion or suspension proceedings, and indeed no longer even resides within the SFUSD, he remains a resident of California and is entitled to a "free appropriate public education" within that State. His claims under the EHA, therefore, are not moot if the conduct he originally complained of is "'capable of repetition, yet evading review.'" *Murphy v. Hunt*, 455 U.S. 478, 482 (1982). Given Smith's continued eligibility for educational services under the EHA,[6] the nature of his disability, and petitioner's insistence that all local school districts retain residual authority to exclude disabled children for dangerous conduct, we have little difficulty concluding that there is a "reasonable expectation," *ibid.*, that Smith would once again be subjected to a unilateral "change in placement" for conduct growing out of his disabilities were it not for the state-wide injunctive relief issued below.

Our cases reveal that, for purposes of assessing the likelihood that state authorities will re-inflict a given injury, we generally have been unwilling to assume that the party seeking relief will repeat the type of misconduct that would once again place him or her at risk of that injury. See *Los Angeles v. Lyons*, 461 U.S. 95, 105-106 (1983) (no threat that party seeking injunction barring police use of chokeholds would be stopped again for traffic violation or other offense, or would resist arrest if stopped); *Hunt v. Murphy*, supra, at 484 (no reason to believe that party challenging denial of pre-trial bail "will once again be in a position to demand bail"); *O'Shea v. Littleton*, 414 U.S. 488, 497 (1974) (unlikely that parties challenging discriminatory bond-setting, sentencing, and jury-fee practices would again violate valid criminal laws). No such reluctance, however, is warranted here. It is respondent Smith's very inability to conform his conduct to socially acceptable norms that renders him "handicapped" within the meaning of the EHA. See 20 U.S.C. § 1401(1); 34 CFR § 300.5(b)(8) (1987). As noted above, the record is replete with evidence that Smith is unable to govern his aggressive, impulsive behavior—indeed, his notice of suspension acknowledged that "Jack's actions seem beyond his control." App. 152.

In the absence of any suggestion that respondent has overcome his earlier difficulties, it is certainly reasonable to expect, based on his prior history of behavioral problems, that he will again engage in classroom misconduct. Nor is it reasonable to suppose that Smith's future educational placement will so perfectly suit his emotional and academic needs that further disruptions on his part are improbable. Although Justice Scalia suggests in his dissent, post, at 3, that school officials are unlikely to place Smith in a setting where they cannot control his misbehavior, any efforts to ensure such total control must be tempered by the school system's statutory obligations to provide respondent with a free appropriate public education in "the least restrictive environment," 34 CFR § 300.552(d) (1987); to educate him, "to the maximum extent appropriate," with children who are not disabled, 20 U.S.C. § 1412(5); and to consult with his parents or guardians, and presumably with respondent himself, before choosing a placement. §§ 1401(19), 1415(b). Indeed, it is only by ignoring these mandates, as well as Congress' unquestioned desire to wrest from school officials their former unilateral authority to determine the placement of emotionally disturbed children, see *infra*, at 15-16, that the dissent can so readily assume that respondent's future placement will satisfactorily prevent any further dangerous conduct on his part. Overarching these statutory obligations, moreover, is the inescapable fact that the preparation of an IEP, like any other effort at predicting human behavior, is an inexact science at best. Given the unique circumstances and context of this case, therefore, we think it reasonable to expect that respondent will again engage in the type of misconduct that precipitated this suit.

We think it equally probable that, should he do so, respondent will again be subjected to the same unilateral school action for which he initially sought relief. In this regard, it matters not that Smith no longer resides within the SFUSD. While the actions of SFUSD officials first gave rise to this litigation, the District Judge expressly found that the lack of a state policy governing local school responses to disability-related misconduct had led to, and would continue to result in, EHA violations, and she therefore enjoined the state defendant from authorizing, among other things, unilateral placement changes. App. 247-248. She of course also issued injunctions directed at the local defendants, but they did not seek review of those orders in this Court. Only petitioner, the State Superintendent of Public Instruction, has invoked our jurisdiction, and he now urges us to hold that local school districts retain unilateral authority under the EHA to suspend or otherwise remove disabled children for dangerous conduct. Given these representations, we have every reason to believe that were it not for the injunction barring petitioner from authorizing such unilateral action, respondent would be faced with a real and substantial threat of such action in any California school district in which he enrolled. Cf. *Los Angeles v. Lyons*, supra, at 106 (respondent lacked standing to seek injunctive relief because he could not plausibly allege that police officers choked all persons whom they stopped, or that the City "AUTHORIZED police officers to act in such manner" (emphasis added)). Certainly, if the SFUSD's past practice of unilateral exclusions was at odds with state policy and the practice of local school districts generally, petitioner would not now stand before us seeking to defend the right of all local school districts to engage in such aberrant behavior.[7]

We have previously noted that administrative and judicial review under the EHA is often "ponderous," *Burlington School Committee v. Massachusetts Dept. of Education*, 471 U.S. 359, 370 (1985), and this case, which has taken seven years to reach us, amply confirms that observation. For obvious reasons, the misconduct of an emotionally disturbed or otherwise disabled child who has not yet reached adolescence typically will not pose such a serious threat to the well-being of other students that school officials can only ensure classroom safety by excluding the child. Yet, the adolescent student improperly disciplined for misconduct that does pose such a threat will often be finished with school or otherwise ineligible for EHA protections by the time review can be had in this Court. Because we believe that respondent Smith has demonstrated both "a sufficient likelihood that he we will again be wronged in a similar way," *Los Angeles v. Lyons*, 461 U.S., at 111, and that any resulting claim he may have for relief will surely evade our review, we turn to the merits of his case.

III

The language of § 1415(e)(3) is unequivocal. It states plainly that during the pendency of any proceedings initiated under the Act, unless the state or local educational agency and the parents or guardian of a disabled child otherwise agree, "the child ***shall*** remain in the then current educational placement." § 1415(e)(3) (emphasis added). Faced with this clear directive, petitioner asks us to read a "dangerousness" exception into the stay-put provision on the basis of either of two essentially inconsistent assumptions: first, that Congress thought the residual authority of school officials to exclude dangerous students from the classroom too obvious for comment; or second, that Congress inadvertently failed to provide such authority and this Court must therefore remedy the oversight. Because we cannot accept either premise, we decline petitioner's invitation to re-write the statute.

Petitioner's arguments proceed, he suggests, from a simple, common-sense proposition: Congress could not have intended the stay-put provision to be read literally, for such a construction leads to the clearly unintended, and untenable, result that school districts must return violent or dangerous students to school while the often lengthy EHA proceedings run their course. We think it clear, however, that Congress very much meant to strip schools of the **unilateral** authority they had traditionally employed to exclude disabled students, particularly emotionally disturbed students, from school. In so doing, Congress did not leave school administrators powerless to deal with dangerous students; it did, however, deny school officials their former right to "self-help," and directed that in the future the removal of disabled students could be accomplished only with the permission of the parents or, as a last resort, the courts.

As noted above, Congress passed the EHA after finding that school systems across the country had excluded one out of every eight disabled children from classes. In drafting the law, Congress was largely guided by the recent decisions in *Mills v. Board of Education of District of Columbia*, 348 F. Supp. 866 (1972), and *PARC*, 343 F. Supp. 279 (1972), both of which involved the exclusion of hard-to-handle disabled students. *Mills* in particular demonstrated the extent to which schools used disciplinary measures to bar children from the classroom. There, school officials had labeled four of the seven minor plaintiffs "behavioral problems," and had excluded them from classes without providing any alternative education to them or any notice to their parents. 348 F. Supp., at 869-870. After finding that this practice was not limited to the named plaintiffs but affected in one way or another an estimated class of 12,000 to 18,000 disabled students, *id.*, at 868-869, 875, the District Court enjoined future exclusions, suspensions, or expulsions "on grounds of discipline." *Id.*, at 880.

Congress attacked such exclusionary practices in a variety of ways. It required participating States to educate all disabled children, regardless of the severity of their disabilities, 20 U.S.C. § 1412(2)(C), and included within the definition of "handicapped" those children with serious emotional disturbances. § 1401(1). It further provided for meaningful parental participation in all aspects of a child's educational placement, and barred schools, through the stay-put provision, from changing that placement over the parent's objection until all review proceedings were completed. Recognizing that those proceedings might prove long and tedious, the Act's drafters did not intend § 1415(e)(3) to operate inflexibly, see 121 Cong. Rec. 37412 (1975) (remarks of Sen. Stafford), and they therefore allowed for interim placements where parents and school officials are able to agree on one. Conspicuously absent from § 1415(e)(3), however, is any emergency exception for dangerous students. This absence is all the more telling in light of the injunctive decree issued in *PARC*, which permitted school officials unilaterally to remove students in "'extraordinary circumstances.'" 343 F. Supp., at 301. Given the lack of any similar exception in *Mills*, and the close attention Congress devoted to these "landmark" decisions, see S. Rep., at 6, we can only conclude that the omission was intentional; we are therefore not at liberty to engraft onto the statute an exception Congress chose not to create.

Our conclusion that § 1415(e)(3) means what it says does not leave educators hamstrung. The Department of Education has observed that, "while the [child's] placement may not be changed [during any complaint proceeding], this does not preclude the agency from using its normal procedures for dealing with children who are endangering themselves or others." Comment following 34 CFR § 300.513 (1987). Such procedures may include the use of study carrels, time-outs, detention, or the restriction of privileges. More drastically, where a student poses an immediate threat to the safety of others, officials may temporarily suspend him or her for up to 10 school days.[8] This authority, which respondent in no way disputes, not only ensures that school administrators can protect the safety of others by promptly removing the most dangerous of students, it also provides a "cooling down" period during which officials can initiate IEP review and seek to persuade the child's parents to agree to an interim placement. And in those cases in which the parents of a truly dangerous child adamantly refuse to permit any change in placement, the 10-day respite gives school officials an opportunity to invoke the aid of the courts under § 1415(e)(2), which empowers courts to grant any appropriate relief.

Petitioner contends, however, that the availability of judicial relief is more illusory than real, because a party seeking review under § 1415(e)(2) must exhaust time-consuming administrative remedies, and because under the Court of Appeals' construction of § 1415(e)(3), courts are as bound by the stay-put provision's "automatic injunction," 793 F.2d, at 1486, as are schools.[9] It is true that judicial review is normally not available under § 1415(e)(2) until all administrative proceedings are completed, but as we have previously noted, parents may by-pass the administrative process where exhaustion would be futile or inadequate. See *Smith v. Robinson*, 468 U.S. 992, 1014, n. 17 (1984) (citing cases); see also 121 Cong. Rec. 37416 (1975) (remarks of Sen. Williams) ("[E]xhaustion . . . should not be required . . . in cases where such exhaustion would be futile either as a legal or practical matter"). While many of the EHA's procedural safeguards protect the rights of parents and children, schools can and do seek redress through the administrative review process, and we have no reason to believe that Congress meant to require schools alone to exhaust in all cases, no matter how exigent the circumstances. The burden in such cases, of course, rests with the school to demonstrate the futility or inadequacy of administrative review, but nothing in § 1415(e)(2) suggests that schools are completely barred from attempting to make such a showing. Nor do we think that § 1415(e)(3) operates to limit the equitable powers of district courts such that they cannot, in appropriate cases, temporarily enjoin a dangerous disabled child from attending school. As the EHA's legislative history makes clear, one of the evils Congress sought to remedy was the unilateral exclusion of disabled children by *schools*, not courts, and one of the purposes of § 1415(e)(3), therefore, was "to prevent *school* officials from removing a child from the regular public school classroom over the parents' objection pending completion of the review proceedings." *Burlington School Committee v. Massachusetts Dept. of Education*, 471 U.S., at 373 (emphasis added). The stay-put provision in no way purports to limit or pre-empt the authority conferred on courts by 1415(e)(2), see *Doe v. Brookline School Committee*, 722 F.2d 910, 917 (CA1 1983); indeed, it says nothing whatever about judicial power.

In short, then, we believe that school officials are entitled to seek injunctive relief under § 1415(e)(2) in appropriate cases. In any such action, § 1415(e)(3) effectively creates a presumption in favor of the child's current educational placement which school officials can overcome only by showing that maintaining the child in his or her current placement is substantially likely to result in injury either to himself or herself, or to others. In the present case, we are satisfied that the District Court, in enjoining the state and local defendants from indefinitely suspending respondent or otherwise unilaterally altering his then current placement, properly balanced respondent's interest in receiving a free appropriate public education in accordance with the procedures and requirements of the EHA against the interests of the state and local school officials in maintaining a safe learning environment for all their students.[10]

IV

We believe the courts below properly construed and applied § 1415(e)(3), except insofar as the Court of Appeals held that a suspension in excess of 10 school days does not constitute a "change in placement."[11] We therefore affirm the Court of Appeals' judgment on this issue as modified herein. Because we are equally divided on the question whether a court may order a State to provide services directly to a disabled child where the local agency has failed to do so, we affirm the Court of Appeals' judgment on this issue as well.

Affirmed.

Footnotes

[1] Congress' earlier efforts to ensure that disabled students received adequate public education had failed in part because the measures it adopted were largely hortatory. In the 1966 amendments to the Elementary and Secondary Education Act of 1965, Congress established a grant program "for the purpose of assisting the States in the initiation, expansion, and improvement of programs and projects . . . for the education of handicapped children." Pub. L. 89-750, 161, 80 Stat. 1204. It repealed that program four years later and replaced it with the original version of the Education of the Handicapped Act, Pub. L. 91-230, 84 Stat. 175, Part B of which contained a similar grant program. Neither statute, however, provided specific guidance as to how States were to use the funds, nor did they condition the availability of the grants on compliance with any procedural or substantive safeguards. In amending the EHA to its present form, Congress rejected its earlier policy of "merely establishing an unenforceable goal requiring all children to be in school." 121 Cong. Rec. 37417 (1975) (remarks of Sen. Schweiker). Today, all 50 states and the District of Columbia receive funding assistance under the EHA. U.S. Dept. of Education, Ninth Annual Report to Congress on Implementation of Education of the Handicapped Act (1987).

[2] California law at the time empowered school principals to suspend students for no more than five consecutive school days, Cal. Educ. Code Ann. 48903(a) (West 1978), but permitted school districts seeking to expel a suspended student to "extend the suspension until such time as expulsion proceedings were completed; provided, that [it] has determined that the presence of the pupil at the school or in an alternative school placement would cause a danger to persons or property or a threat of disrupting the instructional process." 48903(h). The State subsequently amended the law to permit school districts to impose longer initial periods of suspension. See n. 3, infra.

[3] In 1983, the State amended its Education Code to permit school districts to impose initial suspensions of 20, and in certain circumstances, 30 school days. Cal. Educ. Code Ann. 48912(a), 48903 (West Supp. 1988). The legislature did not alter the indefinite suspension authority which the SPC exercised in this case, but simply incorporated the earlier provision into a new section. See 48911(g).

[4] At the time respondent Doe initiated this suit, Wilson Riles was the California Superintendent of Public Instruction. Petitioner Honig succeeded him in office.

[5] We note that both petitioner and respondents believe that this case presents a live controversy. See Tr. of Oral Arg. 6, 27-31. Only the United States, appearing as amicus curiae, urges that the case is presently nonjusticiable. *Id.*, at 21.

[6] Notwithstanding respondent's undisputed right to a free appropriate public education in California, Justice Scalia argues in dissent that there is no "demonstrated probability" that Smith will actually avail himself of that right because his counsel was unable to state affirmatively during oral argument that her client would seek to re-enter the state school system. See post, at 2. We believe the dissent overstates the stringency of the "capable of repetition" test. Although Justice Scalia equates "reasonable expectation" with "demonstrated probability," the very case he cites for this proposition described these standards in the distinctive, see *Murphy v. Hunt*, 455 U.S., at 482 ("There must be a 'reasonable expectation' OR a 'demonstrated probability' that the same controversy will recur" (emphasis added)), and in numerous cases decided both before and since Hunt we have found controversies capable of repetition based on expectations that, while reasonable, were hardly demonstrably probable. See e.g., *Burlington Northern R. Co. v. Maintenance of Way Employees*, 481 U.S. ___, ___, n. 4 (1987) (parties "reasonably likely" to find themselves in future disputes over collective bargaining agreement); *California Coastal Comm'n v. Granite Rock Co.*, 480 U.S. ___, ___ (1987) (O'Connor, J.) ("likely" that respondent would again submit mining plans that would trigger contested state permit requirement); *Press-Enterprise Co. v. Superior Court of Cal., Riverside County*, 478 U.S. 1, 6 (1986) ("It can reasonably be assumed" that newspaper publisher will be subjected to similar closure order in the future); *Globe Newspaper Co. v. Superior Court of Norfolk County*, 457 U.S. 596, 603 (1982) (same); *United States Parole Comm'n v. Geraghty*, 445 U.S. 388, 398 (1980) (case not moot where litigant "faces some likelihood of becoming involved in same controversy in the future") (dicta). Our concern in these cases, as in all others involving potentially moot claims, was whether the controversy was capable of repetition and not, as the dissent seems to insist, whether the claimant had demonstrated that a recurrence of the dispute was more probable than not. Regardless, then, of whether respondent has established with mathematical precision the likelihood that he will enroll in public school during the next two years, we think there is at the very least a reasonable expectation that he will exercise his rights under the EHA. In this regard, we believe respondent's actions over the course of the last seven years speak louder than his counsel's momentary equivocation during oral argument. Since 1980, he has sought to vindicate his right to an appropriate public education that is not only free of charge, but free from the threat that school officials will unilaterally change his placement or exclude him from class altogether. As a disabled young man, he has as at least as great a need of a high school education and diploma as any of his peers, and his counsel advises us that he is awaiting the outcome of this case to decide whether to pursue his degree. Tr. Oral Arg. 23-24. Under these circumstances, we think it not only counterintuitive but unreasonable to assume that respondent will forgo the exercise of a right that he has for so long sought to defend. Certainly we have as much reason to expect that respondent will re-enter the California school system as we had to assume that Jane Roe would again both have an unwanted pregnancy and wish to exercise her right to an abortion. See *Roe v. Wade*, 410 U.S. 113, 125 (1973).

[7] Petitioner concedes that the school district "made a number of procedural mistakes in its eagerness to protect other students from Doe and Smith." Reply Brief for Petitioner 6. According to petitioner, however, unilaterally excluding respondents from school was not among them; indeed, petitioner insists that the SFUSD acted properly in removing respondents and urges that the stay-put provision "should not be interpreted to require a school district to maintain such dangerous children with other children." *Id.*, at 6-7.

[8] The Department of Education has adopted the position first espoused in 1980 by its Office of Civil Rights that a suspension of up to 10 school days does not amount to a "change in placement" prohibited by 1415(e)(3). U.S. Dept. of Education, Office of Special Education Programs, Policy Letter (Feb. 26, 1987), Ed. for Handicapped L. Rep. 211:437 (1987). The EHA nowhere defines the phrase "change in placement," nor does the statute's structure or legislative history provide any guidance as to how the term applies to fixed suspensions. Given this ambiguity, we defer to the construction adopted by the agency charged with monitoring and enforcing the statute. See *INS v. Cardoza-Fonseca*, 480 U.S. ___, ___ (1987).

Moreover, the agency's position comports fully with the purposes of the statute: Congress sought to prevent schools from permanently and unilaterally excluding disabled children by means of indefinite suspensions and expulsions; the power to impose fixed suspensions of short duration does not carry the potential for total exclusion that Congress found so objectionable. Indeed, despite its broad injunction, the District Court in *Mills v. Board of Education of District of Columbia*, 348 F. Supp. 866 (DC 1972), recognized that school officials could suspend disabled children on a short-term, temporary basis. See *id*, at 880. Cf. *Goss v. Lopez*, 419 U.S. 565, 574-576, (1975) (suspension of 10 school days or more works a sufficient deprivation of property and liberty interests to trigger the protections of the Due Process Clause). Because we believe the agency correctly determined that a suspension in excess of 10 days does constitute a prohibited "change in placement," we conclude that the Court of Appeals erred to the extent it approved suspensions of 20 and 30 days' duration.

[9] Petitioner also notes that in California, schools may not suspend any given student for more than a total of 20, and in certain special circumstances 30, school days in a single year, see Cal. Educ. Code Ann. 48903 (West Supp. 1988); he argues, therefore, that a school district may not have the option of imposing a 10-day suspension when dealing with an obstreperous child whose previous suspensions for the year total 18 or 19 days. The fact remains, however, that state law does not define the scope of 1415(e)(3). There may be cases in which a suspension that is otherwise valid under the stay-put provision would violate local law. The effect of such a violation, however, is a question of state law upon which we express no view.

[10] We therefore reject the United States' contention that the District Judge abused her discretion in enjoining the local school officials from indefinitely suspending respondent pending completion of the expulsion proceedings. Contrary to the Government's suggestion, the District Judge did not view herself bound to enjoin any and all violations of the stay-put provision, but rather, consistent with the analysis we set out above, weighed the relative harms to the parties and found that the balance tipped decidedly in favor of respondent. App. 222-223.

We of course do not sit to review the factual determinations underlying that conclusion. We do note, however, that in balancing the parties' respective interests, the District Judge gave proper consideration to respondent's rights under the EHA. While the Government complains that the District Court indulged an improper presumption of irreparable harm to respondent, we do not believe that school officials can escape the presumptive effect of the stay-put provision simply by violating it and forcing parents to petition for relief. In any suit brought by parents seeking injunctive relief for a violation of 1415(e)(3), the burden rests with the school district to demonstrate that the educational status quo must be altered. 11 See n. 8, supra.

Chief Justice Rehnquist, concurring.

I write separately on the mootness issue in this case to explain why I have joined Part II of the Court's opinion, and why I think reconsideration of our mootness jurisprudence may be in order when dealing with cases decided by this Court.

The present rule in federal cases is that an actual controversy must exist at all stages of appellate review, not merely at the time the complaint is filed. This doctrine was clearly articulated in *United States v. Munsingwear*, 340 U.S. 36 (1950), in which Justice Douglas noted that "the established practice of the Court in dealing with a civil case from a court in the federal system which has become moot while on its way here or pending our decision on the merits is to reverse or vacate the judgment below and remand with a direction to dismiss." *Id.*, at 39. The rule has been followed fairly consistently over the last 30 years. See, e.g., *Preiser v. Newkirk*, 422 U.S. 395 (1975); *SEC v. Medical Committee for Human Rights*, 404 U.S. 403 (1972).

All agree that this case was "very much alive," *ante*, at 10, when the action was filed in the District Court, and very probably when the Court of Appeals decided the case. It is supervening events since the decision of the Court of Appeals which have caused the dispute between the majority and the dissent over whether this case is moot. Therefore, all that the Court actually holds is that these supervening events do not deprive this Court of the authority to hear the case. I agree with that holding, and would go still further in the direction of relaxing the test of mootness where the events giving rise to the claim of mootness have occurred after our decision to grant certiorari or to note probable jurisdiction.

The Court implies in its opinion, and the dissent expressly states, that the mootness doctrine is based upon Art. III of the Constitution. There is no doubt that our recent cases have taken that position. See *Nebraska Press Assn. v. Stuart*, 427 U.S. 539, 546 (1976); *Preiser v. Newkirk*, supra, at 401; *Sibron v. New York*, 392 U.S. 40, 57 (1968); *Liner v. Jafco, Inc.*, 375 U.S. 301, 306, n. 3 (1964). But it seems very doubtful that the earliest case I have found discussing mootness, *Mills v. Green*, 159 U.S. 651 (1895), was premised on constitutional constraints; Justice Gray's opinion in that case nowhere mentions Art. III.

If it were indeed Art. III which—by reason of its requirement of a case or controversy for the exercise of federal judicial power—underlies the mootness doctrine, the "capable of repetition, yet evading review" exception relied upon by the Court in this case would be incomprehensible. Article III extends the judicial power of the United States only to cases and controversies; it does not except from this requirement other lawsuits which are "capable of repetition, yet evading review." If our mootness doctrine were forced upon us by the case or controversy requirement of Art. III itself, we would have no more power to decide lawsuits which are "moot" but which also raise questions which are capable of repetition but evading review than we would to decide cases which are "moot" but raise no such questions.

The exception to mootness for cases which are "capable of repetition, yet evading review," was first stated by this Court in *Southern Pacific Terminal Co. v. ICC*, 219 U.S. 498 (1911). There the Court enunciated the exception in the light of obvious pragmatic considerations, with no mention of Art. III as the principle underlying the mootness doctrine:

The questions involved in the orders of the Interstate Commerce Commission are usually continuing (as are manifestly those in the case at bar) and their consideration ought not to be, as they might be, defeated, by short-term orders, capable of repetition, yet evading review, and at one time the Government and at another time the carriers have their rights determined by the Commission without a chance of redress. *Id.*, at 515.

The exception was explained again in *Moore v. Ogilvie*, 394 U.S. 814, 816 (1969):

The problem is therefore 'capable of repetition, yet evading review.' The need for its resolution thus reflects a continuing controversy in the federal-state area where our 'one man, one vote' decisions have thrust" (citation omitted).

It is also worth noting that *Moore v. Ogilvie* involved a question which had been mooted by an election, just as did *Mills v. Green* some 70 years earlier. But at the time of *Mills*, the case originally enunciating the mootness doctrine, there was no thought of any exception for cases which were "capable of repeition, yet evading review."

The logical conclusion to be drawn from these cases, and from the historical development of the principle of mootness, is that while an unwillingness to decide moot cases may be connected to the case or controversy requirement of Art. III, it is an attenuated connection that may be overridden where there are strong reasons to override it. The "capable of repetition, yet evading review" exception is an example. So too is our refusal to dismiss as moot those cases in which the defendant voluntarily ceases, at some advanced stage of the appellate proceedings, whatever activity prompted the plaintiff to seek an injunction. See, e.g., *City of Mesquite v. Aladdin's Castle, Inc.*, 455 U.S. 283, 289, n. 10 (1982); *United States v. W.T. Grant Co.*, 345 U.S. 629, 632 (1953). I believe that we should adopt an additional exception to our present mootness doctrine for those cases where the events which render the case moot have supervened since our grant of certiorari or noting of probable jurisdiction in the case. Dissents from denial of certiorari in this Court illustrate the proposition that the roughly 150 or 160 cases which we decide each year on the merits are less than the number of cases warranting review by us if we are to remain, as Chief Justice Taft said many years ago, "the last word on every important issue under the Constitution and the statutes of the United States." But these unique resources—the time spent preparing to decide the case by reading briefs, hearing oral argument, and conferring—are squandered in every case in which it becomes apparent after the decisional process is underway that we may not reach the question presented. To me the unique and valuable ability of this Court to decide a case—we are, at present, the only Art. III court which can decide a federal question in which a way as to bind all other courts—is a sufficient reason either to abandon the doctrine of mootness altogether in cases which this Court has decided to review, or at least to relax the doctrine of mootness in such a manner as the dissent accuses the majority of doing here. I would leave the mootness doctrine as established by our cases in full force and effect when applied to the earlier stages of a lawsuit, but I believe that once this Court has undertaken a consideration of a case, an exception to that principle is just as much warranted as where a case is "capable of repetition, yet evading review."

Justice Scalia, with whom Justice O'Connor joins, dissenting.

Without expressing any views on the merits of this case, I respectfully dissent because in my opinion we have no authority to decide it. I think the controversy is moot.

I

The Court correctly acknowledges that we have no power under Art. III of the Constitution to adjudicate a case that no longer presents an actual, ongoing dispute between the named parties. Ante, at 10, citing *Nebraska Press Assn. v. Stuart*, 427 U.S. 539, 546 (1976); *Preiser v. Newkirk*, 422 U.S. 395, 401 (1975). Here, there is obviously no present controversy between the parties, since both respondents are no longer in school and therefore no longer subject to a unilateral "change in placement." The Court concedes mootness with respect to respondent John Doe, who is now too old to receive the benefits of the Education of the Handicapped Act (EHA). *Ante*, at 11. It concludes, however, that the case is not moot as to respondent Jack Smith, who has two more years of eligibility but is no longer in the public schools, because the controversy is "capable of repetition, yet evading review." *Ante*, at 11-16.

Jurisdiction on the basis that a dispute is "capable of repetition, yet evading review" is limited to the "exceptional situation," *Los Angeles v. Lyons*, 461 U.S. 95, 109 (1983), where the following two circumstances simultaneously occur: "'(1) the challenged action [is] in its duration too short to be fully litigated prior to its cessation or expiration, and (2) there [is] a reasonable expectation that the same complaining party would be subjected to the same action again.'" *Murphy v. Hunt*, 455 U.S. 478, 482 (1982) (*per curiam*), quoting *Weinstein v. Bradford*, 423 U.S. 147, 149 (1975) (*per curiam*). The second of these requirements is not met in this case.

For there to be a "reasonable expectation" that Smith will be subjected to the same action again, that event must be a "demonstrated probability." *Murphy v. Hunt, supra,* at 482, 483; *Weinstein v. Bradford, supra,* at 149. I am surprised by the Court's contention, fraught with potential for future mischief, that "reasonable expectation" is satisfied by something less than "demonstrated probability." *Ante,* at 11-12, n. 6. No one expects that to happen which he does not think probable; and his expectation cannot be shown to be reasonable unless the probability is demonstrated. Thus, as the Court notes, our cases recite the two descriptions side by side ("a 'reasonable expectation' or a 'demonstrated probability,'" *Hunt, supra,* at 482). The Court asserts, however, that these standards are "described . . . in the disjunctive," ante, at 11-12, n. 6—evidently believing that the conjunction "or" has no accepted usage except a disjunctive one, i.e., "expressing an alternative, contrast, or opposition," Webster's Third New International Dictionary 651 (1981). In fact, however, the conjunction is often used "to indicate . . . (3) the synonymous, equivalent, or substitutive character of two words or phrases fell over a precipice [or] cliff the off [or] far side lessen [or] abate; (4) correction or greater exactness of phrasing or meaning these essays, [or] rather rough sketches the present king had no children—[or] no legitimate children. . . ." *Id.,* at 1585. It is obvious that in saying "a reasonable expectation or a demonstrated probability" we have used the conjunction in one of the latter, or nondisjunctive, senses. Otherwise (and according to the Court's exegesis), we would have been saying that a controversy is sufficiently likely to recur if either a certain degree of probability exists or a higher degree of probability exists. That is rather like a statute giving the vote to persons who are "18 or 21." A bare six years ago, the author of today's opinion and one other member of the majority plainly understood "reasonable expectation" and "demonstrated probability" to be synonymous. Cf. *Edgar v. MITE Corp.,* 457 U.S. 624, 662, and n. 11 (1982) (Marshall, J., dissenting, joined by Brennan, J.) (using the two terms here at issue interchangeably, and concluding that the case is moot because "there is no DEMONSTRATED PROBABILITY that the State will have occasion to prevent MITE from making a takeover offer for some other corporation") (emphasis added).

The prior holdings cited by the Court in a footnote, see *ante,* at 12, n. 6, offer no support for the novel proposition that less than a probability of recurrence is sufficient to avoid mootness. In *Burlington Northern R. Co. v. Maintenance of Way Employees,* ____ U.S. ____, ____, n. 4 (1987), we found that the same railroad and union were "reasonably likely" to find themselves in a recurring dispute over the same issue. Similarly, in *California Coastal Comm'n v. Granite Rock Co.,* ____ U.S. ____, ____ (1987), we found it "likely" that the plaintiff mining company would submit new plans which the State would seek to subject to its coastal permit requirements. See Webster's Third New International Dictionary 1310 (1981) (defining "likely" as "of such a nature or so circumstanced as to make something probable[] . . . seeming to justify belief or expectation[] . . . in all probability"). In the cases involving exclusion orders issued to prevent the press from attending criminal trials, we found that "[i]t can reasonably be assumed" that a news organization covering the area in which the defendant court sat will again be subjected to that court's closure rules. *Press-Enterprise Co. v. Superior Court of Cal., Riverside County,* ____ U.S. ____, ____ (1986); *Globe Newspaper Co. v. Superior Court of Norfolk County,* 457 U.S. 596, 603 (1982). In these and other cases, one may quarrel, perhaps, with the accuracy of the Court's probability assessment; but there is no doubt that assessment was regarded as necessary to establish jurisdiction.

In *Roe v. Wade,* 410 U.S. 113, 125 (1973), we found that the "human gestation period is so short that the pregnancy will come to term before the usual appellate process is complete," so that "pregnancy litigation seldom will survive much beyond the trial stage, and appellate review will be effectively denied." *Roe,* at least one other abortion case, see *Doe v. Bolton,* 410 U.S. 179, 187 (1973), and some of our election law decisions, see *Rosario v. Rockefeller,* 410 U.S. 752, 756, n. 5 (1973); *Dunn v. Blumstein,* 405 U.S. 330, 333, n. 2 (1972), differ from the body of our mootness jurisprudence not in accepting less than a probability that the issue will recur, in a manner evading review, between the same parties; but in dispensing with the same-party requirement entirely, focusing instead upon the great likelihood that the issue will recur between the defendant and the other members of the public at large without ever reaching us. Arguably those cases have been limited to their facts, or to the narrow areas of abortion and election rights, by our more recent insistence that, at least in the absence of a class action, the "capable of repetition" doctrine applies only where "there [is] a reasonable expectation that the SAME COMPLAINING PARTY would be subjected to the same action again." *Hunt,* 455 U.S., at 482 (emphasis added), quoting *Weinstein,* 423 U.S., at 149; see *Burlington Northern R. Co., supra,* at ____, n. 4; *Illi-*

nois Elections Bd. v. Socialist Workers Party, 440 U.S. 173, 187 (1979). If those earlier cases have not been so limited, however, the conditions for their application do not in any event exist here. There is no extraordinary improbability of the present issue's reaching us as a traditionally live controversy. It would have done so in this very case if Smith had not chosen to leave public school. In sum, on any analysis, the proposition the Court asserts in the present case—that probability need not be shown in order to establish the "same-party-recurrence" exception to mootness—is a significant departure from settled law.

II

If our established mode of analysis were followed, the conclusion that a live controversy exists in the present case would require a demonstrated probability that all of the following events will occur: (1) Smith will return to public school; (2) he will be placed in an educational setting that is unable to tolerate his dangerous behavior; (3) he will again engage in dangerous behavior; and (4) local school officials will again attempt unilaterally to change his placement and the state defendants will fail to prevent such action. The Court spends considerable time establishing that the last two of these events are likely to recur, but relegates to a footnote its discussion of the first event, upon which all others depend, and only briefly alludes to the second. Neither the facts in the record, nor even the extra-record assurances of counsel, establish a demonstrated probability of either of them.

With respect to whether Smith will return to school, at oral argument Smith's counsel forthrightly conceded that she "cannot represent whether in fact either of these students will ask for further education from the Petitioners." Tr. of Oral Arg. 23. Rather, she observed, respondents would "look to [our decision in this case] to find out what will happen after that." Id., at 23-24. When pressed, the most counsel would say was that, in her view, the 20-year-old Smith could seek to return to public school because he has not graduated, he is handicapped, and he has a right to an education. *Id.*, at 27. I do not perceive the principle that would enable us to leap from the proposition that Smith could reenter public school to the conclusion that it is a demonstrated probability he will do so.

The Court nevertheless concludes that "there is at the very least a reasonable expectation" that Smith will return to school. *Ante*, at 12, n. 6. I cannot possibly dispute that on the basis of the Court's terminology. Once it is accepted that a "reasonable expectation" can exist without a demonstrable probability that the event in question will occur, the phrase has been deprived of all meaning, and the Court can give it whatever application it wishes without fear of effective contradiction. It is worth pointing out, however, how slim are the reeds upon which this conclusion of "reasonable expectation" (whatever that means) rests. The Court bases its determination on three observations from the record and oral argument. First, it notes that Smith has been pressing this lawsuit since 1980. It suffices to observe that the equivalent argument can be made in every case that remains active and pending; we have hitherto avoided equating the existence of a case or controversy with the existence of a lawsuit. Second, the Court observes that Smith has "as great a need of a high school education and diploma as any of his peers." *Ibid.*

While this is undoubtedly good advice, it hardly establishes that the 20-year-old Smith is likely to return to high school, much less to public high school. Finally, the Court notes that counsel "advises us that [Smith] is awaiting the outcome of this case to decide whether to pursue his degree." *Ibid.* Not only do I not think this establishes a current case or controversy, I think it a most conclusive indication that no current case or controversy exists. We do not sit to broaden decision-making options, but to adjudicate the lawfulness of acts that have happened or, at most, are about to occur.

The conclusion that the case is moot is reinforced, moreover, when one considers that, even if Smith does return to public school, the controversy will still not recur unless he is again placed in an educational setting that is unable to tolerate his behavior. It seems to me not only not demonstrably probable, but indeed quite unlikely, given what is now known about Smith's behavioral problems, that local school authorities would again place him in an educational setting that could not control his dangerous conduct, causing a suspension that would replicate the legal issues in this suit. The majority dismisses this further contingency by noting that the school authorities have an obligation under the EHA to provide an "appropriate" education in "the least restrictive environment." *Ante*, at 14. This means, however, the least restrictive environment appropriate for the particular child.

The Court observes that "the preparation of an [individualized educational placement]" is "an inexact science at best," ante, at 14, thereby implying that the school authorities are likely to get it wrong. Even accepting this assumption, which seems to me contrary to the premises of the Act, I see no reason further to assume that they will get it wrong by making the same mistake they did last time—assigning Smith to too unrestrictive an environment, from which he will thereafter be suspended—rather than by assigning him to too restrictive an environment. The latter, which seems to me more likely than the former (although both combined are much less likely than a correct placement), might produce a lawsuit, but not a lawsuit involving the issues that we have before us here.

III

The Chief Justice joins the majority opinion on the ground, not that this case is not moot, but that where the events giving rise to the mootness have occurred after we have granted certiorari we may disregard them, since mootness is only a prudential doctrine and not part of the "case or controversy" requirement of Art. III. I do not see how that can be. There is no more reason to intuit that mootness is merely a prudential doctrine than to intuit that initial standing is. Both doctrines have equivalently deep roots in the common-law understanding, and hence the constitutional understanding of what makes a matter appropriate for judicial disposition. See *Flast v. Cohen*, 392 U.S. 83, 95 (1968) (describing mootness and standing as various illustrations of the requirement of "justiciability" in Art. III).

The Chief Justice relies upon the fact that an 1895 case discussing mootness, *Mills v. Green*, 159 U.S. 651 (1895), makes no mention of the Constitution. But there is little doubt that the Court believed the doctrine called into question the Court's power and not merely its prudence, for (in an opinion by the same Justice who wrote Mills) it had said two years earlier:

The court is not EMPOWERED to decide moot questions or abstract propositions, or to declare . . . principles or rules of law which cannot affect the result as to the thing in issue in the case before it. No stipulation of parties or counsel . . . can enlarge the POWER, or affect the duty, of the court in this regard. *California v. San Pablo & Tulare R. Co.*, 149 U.S. 308, 314 (1893) (Gray, J.) (emphasis added).

If it seems peculiar to the modern lawyer that our 19th century mootness cases make no explicit mention of Art. III, that is a peculiarity shared with our 19th century, and even our early 20th century, standing cases. As late as 1919, in dismissing a suit for lack of standing we said simply:

Considerations of propriety, as well as long-established practice, demand that we refrain from passing upon the constitutionality of an act of Congress unless obliged to do so in the proper performance of our judicial function, when the question is raised by a party whose interests entitle him to raise it." *Blaire v. United States*, 250 U.S. 273, 279 (1919).

See also, e.g., *Standard Stock Food Co. v. Wright*, 225 U.S. 540, 550 (1912); *Southern Ry. Co. v. King*, 217 U.S. 524, 534 (1910); *Turpin v. Lemon*, 187 U.S. 51, 60-61 (1902); *Tyler v. Judges of Court of Registration*, 179 U.S. 405, 409 (1900). The same is also true of our early cases dismissing actions lacking truly adverse parties, that is, collusive actions. See, e.g., *Cleveland v. Chamberlain*, 1 Black 419, 425-426 (1862); *Lord v. Veazie*, 8 How. 251, 254-256 (1850). The explanation for this ellipsis is that the courts simply chose to refer directly to the traditional, fundamental limitations upon the powers of common-law courts, rather than referring to Art. III which in turn adopts those limitations through terms ("The judicial Power"; "Cases"; "Controversies") that have virtually no meaning except by reference to that tradition. The ultimate circularity, coming back in the end to tradition, is evident in the statement by Justice Field:

By cases and controversies are intended the claims of litigants brought before the courts for determination by such regular proceedings as are established by law or custom for the protection or enforcement of rights, or the prevention, redress, or punishment of wrongs. Whenever the claim of a party under the constitution, laws, or treaties of the United States takes such a form that the judicial power is capable of acting upon it, then it has become a case. *In re Pacific R. Commn.*, 32 F. 241, 255 (CCND Cal. 1887).

See also 2 M. Farrand, Records of the Federal Convention of 1787, p. 430 (rev. ed. 1966):

Docr. Johnson moved to insert the words 'this Constitution and the' before the word 'laws'

Mr. Madison doubted whether it was not going too far to extend the jurisdiction of the Court generally to cases arising Under the Constitution, & whether it ought not to be limited to cases of a Judiciary Nature. The right of expounding the Constitution in cases not of this nature ought not to be given to that Department.

The motion of Docr. Johnson was agreed to nem: con: it being generally supposed that the jurisdiction given was constructively limited to cases of a Judiciary nature—

In sum, I cannot believe that it is only our prudence, and nothing inherent in the understood nature of "The judicial Power," U.S. Const., Art. III, 1, that restrains us from pronouncing judgment in a case that the parties have settled, or a case involving a nonsurviving claim where the plaintiff has died, or a case where the law has been changed so that the basis of the dispute no longer exists, or a case where conduct sought to be enjoined has ceased and will not recur. Where the conduct has ceased for the time being but there is a demonstrated probability that it will recur, a real-life controversy between parties with a personal stake in the outcome continues to exist, and Art. III is no more violated than it is violated by entertaining a declaratory judgment action. But that is the limit of our power. I agree with The Chief Justice to this extent: the "yet evading review" portion of our "capable of repetition yet evading review" test is prudential; whether or not that criterion is met, a justiciable controversy exists. But the probability of recurrence between the same parties is essential to our jurisdiction as a court, and it is that deficiency which the case before us presents.

* * * *

It is assuredly frustrating to find that a jurisdictional impediment prevents us from reaching the important merits issues that were the reason for our agreeing to hear this case. But we cannot ignore such impediments for purposes of our appellate review without simultaneously affecting the principles that govern district courts in their assertion or retention of original jurisdiction. We thus do substantial harm to a governmental structure designed to restrict the courts to matters that actually affect the litigants before them.

END OF HONIG v. DOE

THE UNITED STATES SUPREME COURT
510 U. S. 7

FLORENCE COUNTY SCHOOL DISTRICT FOUR, et. al.
Petitioners

v.

Shannon CARTER, a minor by and through her father, and next friend, Emory D.
CARTER
Respondent

No. 91-1523

On Writ of Certiorari to the U.S. Court of Appeals for the Fourth Circuit.
November 9, 1993

Counsel for Petitioners: Donald B. Ayer, Esq., Washington, DC.
Counsel for Respondent: Peter W.. D. Wright, Esq., Richmond, VA.
Counsel for the United States, as Amicus Curiae supporting Respondent: Amy L. Wax, Esq., Assistant to
the Solicitor General, Department of Justice, Washington, DC.

Before Rehnquist, C.J., and Blackmun, Stevens, O'Connor, Scalia, Kennedy, Souter, Thomas, and
Ginsburg, JJ.

SANDRA DAY O'CONNOR, Associate Justice.

The Individuals with Disabilities Education Act (IDEA), 84 Stat. 175, as amended, 20 U.S.C. § 1400 *et seq.*
(1988 ed. and Supp. IV), requires States to provide disabled children with a "free appropriate public education,"
§ 1401(a)(18). This case presents the question whether a court may order reimbursement for parents who unilaterally withdraw their child from a public school that provides an inappropriate education under IDEA and
put the child in a private school that provides an education that is otherwise proper under IDEA, but does not
meet all the requirements of § 1401(a)(18). We hold that the court may order such reimbursement, and therefore affirm the judgment of the Court of Appeals.

I

Respondent Shannon Carter was classified as learning disabled in 1985, while a ninth grade student in a
school operated by petitioner Florence County School District Four. School officials met with Shannon's parents to formulate an individualized education program (IEP) for Shannon, as required under IDEA. 20 U.S.C.
§§ 1401(a)(18) and (20), 1414(a)(5) (1988 ed. and Supp. IV). The IEP provided that Shannon would stay in regular classes except for three periods of individualized instruction per week, and established specific goals in
reading and mathematics of four months' progress for the entire school year. Shannon's parents were dissatisfied, and requested a hearing to challenge the appropriateness of the IEP. See § 1415(b)(2). Both the local educational officer and the state educational agency hearing officer rejected Shannon's parents' claim and concluded that the IEP was adequate. In the meantime, Shannon's parents had placed her in Trident Academy, a
private school specializing in educating children with disabilities. Shannon began at Trident in September 1985
and graduated in the spring of 1988.

Shannon's parents filed this suit in July 1986, claiming that the school district had breached its duty under
IDEA to provide Shannon with a "free appropriate public education," § 1401(a)(18), and seeking reimbursement for tuition and other costs incurred at Trident. After a bench trial, the District Court ruled in the parents'

favor. The court held that the school district's proposed educational program and the achievement goals of the IEP "were wholly inadequate" and failed to satisfy the requirements of the Act. App. to Pet. for Cert 27a. The court further held that "although [Trident Academy] did not comply with all the procedures outlined in [IDEA]," the school "provided Shannon an excellent education in substantial compliance with all the substantive requirements" of the statute. *Id.* at 37a. The court found that Trident "evaluated Shannon quarterly, not yearly as mandated in [IDEA], it provided Shannon with low teacher-student ratios, and it developed a plan which allowed Shannon to receive passing marks and progress from grade to grade." *Ibid.* The court also credited the findings of its own expert, who determined that Shannon had made "significant progress" at Trident and that her reading comprehension had risen three grade levels in her three years at the school. *Id.*, at 29a. The District Court concluded that Shannon's education was "appropriate" under IDEA, and that Shannon's parents were entitled to reimbursement of tuition and other costs. *Id.*, at 37a.

The Court of Appeals for the Fourth Circuit affirmed. 950 F.2d 156 (1991). The court agreed that the IEP proposed by the school district was inappropriate under IDEA. It also rejected the school district's argument that reimbursement is never proper when the parents choose a private school that is not approved by the State or that does not comply with all the terms of IDEA. According to the Court of Appeals, neither the text of the Act nor its legislative history imposes a "requirement that the private school be approved by the state in parent-placement reimbursement cases." *Id.*, at 162. To the contrary, the Court of Appeals concluded, IDEA's state-approval requirement applies only when a child is placed in a private school by public school officials. Accordingly, "when a public school system had defaulted on its obligations under the Act, a private school placement is 'proper under the Act' if the education provided by the private school is 'reasonably calculated to enable the child to receive educational benefits.'" *Id.*, at 163, quoting *Board of Ed. of Hendrick Hudson Central School Dist. v. Rowley*, 458 U.S. 176, 207 (1982).

The court below recognized that its holding conflicted with *Tucker v. Bay Shore Union Free School Dist.*, 873 F.2d 563, 568 (1989), in which the Court of Appeals for the Second Circuit held that parental placement in a private school cannot be proper under the Act unless the private school in question meets the standards of the state education agency. We granted certiorari, 507 U.S. __ (1993), to resolve this conflict among the Courts of Appeals.

II

In *School Comm. of Burlington v. Department of Ed. of Mass.*, 471 U.S. 359, 369 (1985), we held that IDEA's grant of equitable authority empowers a court "to order school authorities to reimburse parents for their expenditures on private special education for a child if the court ultimately determines that such placement, rather than a proposed IEP, is proper under the Act." Congress intended that IDEA's promise of a "free appropriate public education" for disabled children would normally be met by an IEP's provision for education in the regular public schools or in private schools chosen jointly by school officials and parents. In cases where cooperation fails, however, "parents who disagree with the proposed IEP are faced with a choice: go along with the IEP to the detriment of their child if it turns out to be inappropriate or pay for what they consider to be the appropriate placement." *Id.*, at 370. For parents willing and able to make the latter choice, "it would be an empty victory to have a court tell them several years later that they were right but that these expenditures could not in a proper case be reimbursed by the school officials." *Ibid.* Because such a result would be contrary to IDEA's guarantee of a "free appropriate public education," we held that "Congress meant to include retroactive reimbursement to parents as an available remedy in a proper case." *Ibid.*

As this case comes to us, two issues are settled: 1) the school district's proposed IEP was inappropriate under IDEA, and 2) although Trident did not meet the § 1401(a)(18) requirements, it provided an education other proper under IDEA. This case presents the narrow question whether Shannon's parents are barred from reimbursement because the private school in which Shannon enrolled did not meet the § 1401(a)(18) definition of a "free appropriate public education."[1] We hold that they are not, because § 1401(a)(18)'s requirements cannot be read as applying to parental placements.

Section 1401(a)(18)(A) requires that the education be "provided at public expense, under public supervision and direction." Similarly, § 1401(a)(18)(D) requires schools to provide an IEP, which must be designated by "a representative of the local educational agency," 20 U.S.C. § 1401(a)(20) (1988 ed., Supp. IV), and must be "established," and "revised" by the agency, § 1414(a)(5). These requirements do not make sense in the context of a parental placement. In this case, as in all *Burlington* reimbursement cases, the parents' rejection of the school district's proposed IEP is the very reason for the parents' decision to put their child in a private school. In such cases, where the private placement has necessarily been made over the school district's objection, the private school education will not be under "public supervision and direction." Accordingly, to read the § 1401(a)(18) requirements as applying to parental placements would effectively eliminate the right of unilateral withdrawal recognized in *Burlington.* Moreover, IDEA was intended to ensure that children with disabilities receive an education that is both appropriate and free. *Burlington,* supra, at 373. To read the provisions of § 1401(a)(18) to bar reimbursement in the circumstances of this case would defeat this statutory purpose.

Nor do we believe that reimbursement is necessarily barred by a private school's failure to meet state education standards. Trident's deficiencies, according to the school district, were that it employed at least two faculty members who were not state-certified and that it did not develop IEPs. As we have noted, however, the § 1401(a)(18) requirements—including the requirement that the school meet the standards of the state educational agency, § 1401(a)(18)(B) –do not apply to private parental placements. Indeed, the school district's emphasis on state standards is somewhat ironic. As the Court of Appeals noted, "it hardly seems consistent with the Act's goals to forbid parents from educating their child at a school that provides an appropriate education simply because that school lacks the stamp of approval of the same public school system that failed to meet the child's needs in the first place." 950 F.2d at 164. Accordingly, we disagree with the Second Circuit's theory that "a parent may not obtain reimbursement for a unilateral placement if that placement was in a school that was not on [the State's] approved list of private" schools. *Tucker,* 873 F.2d, at 568 (internal quotation marks omitted). Parents' failure to select a program known to be approved by the State in favor of an unapproved option is not itself a bar to reimbursement.

Furthermore, although the absence of an approved list of private schools is not essential to our holding, we note that parents in the position of Shannon's have no way of knowing at the time they select a private school whether the school meets state standards. South Carolina keeps no publicly available list of approved private schools, but instead approves private school placements on a case-by-case basis. In fact, although public school officials had previously placed three children with disabilities at Trident, see App. to Pet. for Cert. 28a, Trident had not received blanket approval from the State. South Carolina's case-by-case approval system meant that Shannon's parents needed the cooperation of state officials before they could know whether Trident was state-approved. As we recognized in *Burlington,* such cooperation is unlikely in cases where the school officials disagree with the need for the private placement. 471 U.S., at 372.

III

The school district also claims that allowing reimbursement for parents such as Shannon's puts an unreasonable burden on financially strapped local educational authorities. The school district argues that requiring parents to choose a state-approved private school if they want reimbursement is the only meaningful way to allow States to control costs; otherwise States will have to reimburse dissatisfied parents for any private school that provides an education that is proper under the Act, no matter how expensive it may be.

There is no doubt that Congress has imposed a significant financial burden on States and school districts that participate in IDEA. Yet public educational authorities who want to avoid reimbursing parents for the private education of a disabled child can do one of two things: give the child a free appropriate public education in a public setting, or place the child in an appropriate private setting of the State's choice. This is IDEA's mandate, and school officials who conform to it need not worry about reimbursement claims.

Moreover, parents who, like Shannon's, "unilaterally change their child's placement during the pendency of review proceedings, without the consent of the state or local school officials, do so at their own financial risk." *Burlington,* supra, at 373-374. They are entitled to reimbursement only if a federal court concludes both that the public placement violated IDEA, and that the private school placement was proper under the Act.

Finally, we note that once a court holds that the public placement violated IDEA, it is authorized to "grant such relief as the court determines is appropriate." 20 U.S.C. § 1415(e)(2). Under this provision, "equitable considerations are relevant in fashioning relief," *Burlington,* 471 U.S., at 374, and the court enjoys "broad discretion" in so doing, *id.,* at 369. Courts fashioning discretionary equitable relief under IDEA must consider all relevant factors, including the appropriate and reasonable level of reimbursement that should be required. Total reimbursement will not be appropriate if the court determines that the cost of the private education was unreasonable.

Accordingly, we *affirm* the judgment of the Court of Appeals.

So Ordered.

Footnote

1 Section 1401(a)(18) defines "free appropriate public education" as, special education and related services that
(A) have been provided at public expense, under public supervision and direction, and without charge,
(B) meet the standards of the State educational agency,
(C) include an appropriate preschool, elementary, or secondary school education in the State involved, and
(D) are provided in conformity with the individualized education program . . . .

END OF CARTER

THE UNITED STATES SUPREME COURT
__U.S. __

CEDAR RAPIDS COMMUNITY SCHOOL DISTRICT
Petitioners

v.

GARRET F., a minor, by his mother and next friend, CHARLENE F.
Respondent

> Certiorari to the United States Court of Appeals for the Eighth Circuit
> No. 96-1793.
> Argued: November 4, 1998
> Decided: March 3, 1999
> Counsel for Petitioners: Sue Seitz, Esq., Des Moines, IA.
> Counsel for Respondent: Douglas Oelschlaeger, Esq., Cedar Rapids, IA.
>
> *Stevens, J.*, delivered the opinion of the Court, in which *Rehnquist, C. J.*, and *O'Connor, Scalia, Souter, Ginsburg*, and *Breyer, JJ.*, joined. *Thomas, J.*, filed a dissenting opinion, in which *Kennedy, J.*, joined.
> On Writ of Certiorari to the United States Court of Appeals for the Eighth Circuit
> March 3, 1999

Justice Stevens delivered the opinion of the Court.

The Individuals with Disabilities Education Act (IDEA), 84 Stat. 175, as amended, was enacted, in part, "to assure that all children with disabilities have available to them . . . a free appropriate public education which emphasizes special education and related services designed to meet their unique needs." 20 U. S. C. § 1400(c). Consistent with this purpose, the IDEA authorizes federal financial assistance to States that agree to provide disabled children with special education and "related services." See §§ 1401(a)(18), 1412(1). The question presented in this case is whether the definition of "related services" in § 1401(a)(17)[1] requires a public school district in a participating State to provide a ventilator-dependent student with certain nursing services during school hours.

I

Respondent Garret F. is a friendly, creative, and intelligent young man. When Garret was four years old, his spinal column was severed in a motorcycle accident. Though paralyzed from the neck down, his mental capacities were unaffected. He is able to speak, to control his motorized wheelchair through use of a puff and suck straw, and to operate a computer with a device that responds to head movements. Garret is currently a student in the Cedar Rapids Community School District (District), he attends regular classes in a typical school program, and his academic performance has been a success. Garret is, however, ventilator dependent,[2] and therefore requires a responsible individual nearby to attend to certain physical needs while he is in school.[3]

During Garret's early years at school his family provided for his physical care during the school day. When he was in kindergarten, his 18-year-old aunt attended him; in the next four years, his family used settlement proceeds they received after the accident, their insurance, and other resources to employ a licensed practical nurse. In 1993, Garret's mother requested the District to accept financial responsibility for the health care services that Garret requires during the school day. The District denied the request, believing that it was not legally obligated to provide continuous one-on-one nursing services.

Relying on both the IDEA and Iowa law, Garret's mother requested a hearing before the Iowa Department of Education. An Administrative Law Judge (ALJ) received extensive evidence concerning Garret's special needs, the District's treatment of other disabled students, and the assistance provided to other ventilator-dependent children in other parts of the country. In his 47-page report, the ALJ found that the District has about 17,500 students, of whom approximately 2,200 need some form of special education or special services. Although Garret is the only ventilator-dependent student in the District, most of the health care services that he needs are already provided for some other students. [4] "The primary difference between Garret's situation and that of other students is his dependency on his ventilator for life support." App. to Pet. for Cert. 28a. The ALJ noted that the parties disagreed over the training or licensure required for the care and supervision of such students, and that those providing such care in other parts of the country ranged from non-licensed personnel to registered nurses. However, the District did not contend that only a licensed physician could provide the services in question.

The ALJ explained that federal law requires that children with a variety of health impairments be provided with "special education and related services" when their disabilities adversely affect their academic performance, and that such children should be educated to the maximum extent appropriate with children who are not disabled. In addition, the ALJ explained that applicable federal regulations distinguish between "school health services," which are provided by a "qualified school nurse or other qualified person," and "medical services," which are provided by a licensed physician. See 34 CFR §§ 300.16(a), (b)(4), (b)(11) (1998). The District must provide the former, but need not provide the latter (except, of course, those "medical services" that are for diagnostic or evaluation purposes, § 1401(a)(17)). According to the ALJ, the distinction in the regulations does not just depend on "the title of the person providing the service"; instead, the "medical services" exclusion is limited to services that are "in the special training, knowledge, and judgment of a physician to carry out." App. to Pet. for Cert. 51a. The ALJ thus concluded that the IDEA required the District to bear financial responsibility for all of the services in dispute, including continuous nursing services. [5]

The District challenged the ALJ's decision in Federal District Court, but that Court approved the ALJ's IDEA ruling and granted summary judgment against the District. *Id.*, at 9a, 15a. The Court of Appeals affirmed. 106 F. 3d 822 (CA8 1997). It noted that, as a recipient of federal funds under the IDEA, Iowa has a statutory duty to provide all disabled children a "free appropriate public education," which includes "related services." See *id.*, at 824. The Court of Appeals read our opinion in *Irving Independent School Dist. v. Tatro*, 468 U. S. 883 (1984), to provide a two-step analysis of the "related services" definition in § 1401(a)(17) — asking first, whether the requested services are included within the phrase "supportive services"; and second, whether the services are excluded as "medical services." 106 F. 3d, at 824-825. The Court of Appeals succinctly answered both questions in Garret's favor. The Court found the first step plainly satisfied, since Garret cannot attend school unless the requested services are available during the school day. *Id.*, at 825. As to the second step, the Court reasoned that *Tatro* "established a bright-line test: the services of a physician (other than for diagnostic and evaluation purposes) are subject to the medical services exclusion, but services that can be provided in the school setting by a nurse or qualified layperson are not." *Ibid.*

In its petition for certiorari, the District challenged only the second step of the Court of Appeals' analysis. The District pointed out that some federal courts have not asked whether the requested health services must be delivered by a physician, but instead have applied a multi-factor test that considers, generally speaking, the nature and extent of the services at issue. See, e.g., *Neely v. Rutherford County School*, 68 F. 3d 965, 972-973 (CA6 1995), cert. denied, 517 U. S. 1134 (1996); *Detsel v. Board of Ed. of Auburn Enlarged City School Dist.*, 820 F. 2d 587, 588 (CA2) (*per curiam*), cert. denied, 484 U. S. 981 (1987). We granted the District's petition to resolve this conflict. 523 U. S. __ (1998).

II

The District contends that § 1401(a)(17) does not require it to provide Garret with "continuous one-on-one nursing services" during the school day, even though Garret cannot remain in school without such care. Brief for Petitioner 10. However, the IDEA's definition of "related services," our decision in *Irving Independent School Dist. v. Tatro*, 468 U. S. 883 (1984), and the overall statutory scheme all support the decision of the Court of Appeals.

The text of the "related services" definition, see n. 1, *supra*, broadly encompasses those supportive services that "may be required to assist a child with a disability to benefit from special education." As we have already noted, the District does not challenge the Court of Appeals' conclusion that the in-school services at issue are within the covered category of "supportive services." As a general matter, services that enable a disabled child to remain in school during the day provide the student with "the meaningful access to education that Congress envisioned." *Tatro*, 468 U. S., at 891 (" 'Congress sought primarily to make public education available to handicapped children' and 'to make such access meaningful' " (quoting *Board of Ed. of Hendrick Hudson Central School Dist., Westchester Cty. v. Rowley*, 458 U. S. 176, 192 (1982)).

This general definition of "related services" is illuminated by a parenthetical phrase listing examples of particular services that are included within the statute's coverage. § 1401(a)(17). "Medical services" are enumerated in this list, but such services are limited to those that are "for diagnostic and evaluation purposes." *Ibid*. The statute does not contain a more specific definition of the "medical services" that are excepted from the coverage of § 1401(a)(17).

The scope of the "medical services" exclusion is not a matter of first impression in this Court. In *Tatro* we concluded that the Secretary of Education had reasonably determined that the term "medical services" referred only to services that must be performed by a physician, and not to school health services. 468 U. S., at 892-894. Accordingly, we held that a specific form of health care (clean intermittent catherization) that is often, though not always, performed by a nurse is not an excluded medical service. We referenced the likely cost of the services and the competence of school staff as justifications for drawing a line between physician and other services, ibid., but our endorsement of that line was unmistakable.[6] It is thus settled that the phrase "medical services" in § 1401(a)(17) does not embrace all forms of care that might loosely be described as "medical" in other contexts, such as a claim for an income tax deduction. See 26 U. S. C. § 213(d)(1) (1994 ed. and Supp. II) (defining "medical care").

The District does not ask us to define the term so broadly. Indeed, the District does not argue that any of the items of care that Garret needs, considered individually, could be excluded from the scope of § 1401(a)(17).[7] It could not make such an argument, considering that one of the services Garret needs (catheterization) was at issue in *Tatro*, and the others may be provided competently by a school nurse or other trained personnel. See App. to Pet. for Cert. 15a, 52a. As the ALJ concluded, most of the requested services are already provided by the District to other students, and the in-school care necessitated by Garret's ventilator dependency does not demand the training, knowledge, and judgment of a licensed physician. *Id.*, at 51a-52a. While more extensive, the in-school services Garret needs are no more "medical" than was the care sought in *Tatro*.

Instead, the District points to the combined and continuous character of the required care, and proposes a test under which the outcome in any particular case would "depend upon a series of factors, such as [1] whether the care is continuous or intermittent, [2] whether existing school health personnel can provide the service, [3] the cost of the service, and [4] the potential consequences if the service is not properly performed." Brief for Petitioner 11; see also *id.*, at 34-35.

The District's multi-factor test is not supported by any recognized source of legal authority. The proposed factors can be found in neither the text of the statute nor the regulations that we upheld in *Tatro*. Moreover, the District offers no explanation why these characteristics make one service any more "medical" than another. The continuous character of certain services associated with Garret's ventilator dependency has no apparent relationship to "medical" services, much less a relationship of equivalence. Continuous services may be more costly and may require additional school personnel, but they are not thereby more "medical." Whatever its imperfections, a rule that limits the medical services exemption to physician services is unquestionably a reasonable and generally workable interpretation of the statute. Absent an elaboration of the statutory terms plainly more convincing than that which we reviewed in *Tatro*, there is no good reason to depart from settled law.[8]

Finally, the District raises broader concerns about the financial burden that it must bear to provide the services that Garret needs to stay in school. The problem for the District in providing these services is not that its staff cannot be trained to deliver them; the problem, the District contends, is that the existing school health staff cannot meet all of their responsibilities and provide for Garret at the same time.[9]

Through its multi-factor test, the District seeks to establish a kind of undue-burden exemption primarily based on the cost of the requested services. The first two factors can be seen as examples of cost-based distinctions: intermittent care is often less expensive than continuous care, and the use of existing personnel is cheaper than hiring additional employees. The third factor-the cost of the service-would then encompass the first two. The relevance of the fourth factor is likewise related to cost because extra care may be necessary if potential consequences are especially serious.

The District may have legitimate financial concerns, but our role in this dispute is to interpret existing law. Defining "related services" in a manner that accommodates the cost concerns Congress may have had, cf. *Tatro*, 468 U. S., at 892, is altogether different from using cost itself as the definition. Given that § 1401(a)(17) does not employ cost in its definition of "related services" or excluded "medical services," accepting the District's cost-based standard as the sole test for determining the scope of the provision would require us to engage in judicial lawmaking without any guidance from Congress. It would also create some tension with the purposes of the IDEA. The statute may not require public schools to maximize the potential of disabled students commensurate with the opportunities provided to other children, see *Rowley*, 458 U. S., at 200; and the potential financial burdens imposed on participating States may be relevant to arriving at a sensible construction of the IDEA, see *Tatro*, 468 U. S., at 892. But Congress intended "to open the door of public education" to all qualified children and "require[d] participating States to educate handicapped children with non-handicapped children whenever possible." *Rowley*, 458 U. S., at 192, 202; see id., at 179-181; see also *Honig v. Doe*, 484 U. S. 305, 310-311, 324 (1988); §§ 1412(1), (2)(c), (5)(B).10

This case is about whether meaningful access to the public schools will be assured, not the level of education that a school must finance once access is attained. It is undisputed that the services at issue must be provided if Garret is to remain in school.

Under the statute, our precedent, and the purposes of the IDEA, the District must fund such "related services" in order to help guarantee that students like Garret are integrated into the public schools.

The judgment of the Court of Appeals is accordingly **Affirmed**.

Justice Thomas, with whom Justice Kennedy joins, **dissenting**.

The majority, relying heavily on our decision in *Irving Independent School Dist. v. Tatro*, 468 U. S. 883 (1984), concludes that the Individuals with Disabilities Education Act (IDEA), 20 U. S. C. § 1400 et seq., requires a public school district to fund continuous, one-on-one nursing care for disabled children. Because *Tatro* cannot be squared with the text of IDEA, the Court should not adhere to it in this case. Even assuming that *Tatro* was correct in the first instance, the majority's extension of it is unwarranted and ignores the constitutionally mandated rules of construction applicable to legislation enacted pursuant to Congress' spending power.

I

As the majority recounts, *ante*, at 1, IDEA authorizes the provision of federal financial assistance to States that agree to provide, *inter alia*, "special education and related services" for disabled children. § 1401(a)(18). In *Tatro, supra*, we held that this provision of IDEA required a school district to provide clean intermittent catheterization to a disabled child several times a day. In so holding, we relied on Department of Education regulations, which we concluded had reasonably interpreted IDEA's definition of "related services"[1] to require school districts in participating States to provide "school nursing services" (of which we assumed catheterization was a subcategory) but not "services of a physician." Id., at 892-893. This holding is contrary to the plain text of IDEA and its reliance on the Department of Education's regulations was misplaced.

A

Before we consider whether deference to an agency regulation is appropriate, "we first ask whether Congress has 'directly spoken to the precise question at issue. If the intent of Congress is clear, that is the end of the matter; for the court, as well as the agency, must give effect to the unambiguously expressed intent of Congress.' "*National Credit Union Admin. v. First Nat. Bank & Trust Co.*, 522 U. S. 479, 499-500 (1998) (quoting *Chevron U. S. A. Inc. v. Natural Resources Defense Council, Inc.*, 467 U. S. 837, 842-843 (1984)).

Unfortunately, the Court in *Tatro* failed to consider this necessary antecedent question before turning to the Department of Education's regulations implementing IDEA's related services provision. The Court instead began "with the regulations of the Department of Education, which," it said, "are entitled to deference." *Tatro, supra*, at 891-892. The Court need not have looked beyond the text of IDEA, which expressly indicates that school districts are not required to provide medical services, except for diagnostic and evaluation purposes. 20 U. S. C. § 1401(a)(17). The majority asserts that *Tatro* precludes reading the term "medical services" to include "all forms of care that might loosely be described as 'medical.' " *Ante*, at 8. The majority does not explain, however, why "services" that are "medical" in nature are not "medical services." Not only is the definition that the majority rejects consistent with other uses of the term in federal law,[2] it also avoids the anomalous result of holding that the services at issue in *Tatro* (as well as in this case), while not "medical services," would nonetheless qualify as medical care for federal income tax purposes. *Ante*, at 8.

The primary problem with *Tatro*, and the majority's reliance on it today, is that the Court focused on the provider of the services rather than the services themselves. We do not typically think that automotive services are limited to those provided by a mechanic, for example. Rather, anything done to repair or service a car, no matter who does the work, is thought to fall into that category. Similarly, the term "food service" is not generally thought to be limited to work performed by a chef. The term "medical" similarly does not support *Tatro*'s provider-specific approach, but encompasses services that are "of, *relating to, or concerned with* physicians *or* the practice of medicine." See Webster's Third New International Dictionary 1402 (1986) (emphasis added); see also *id.*, at 1551 (defining "nurse" as "a person skilled in caring for and waiting on the infirm, the injured, or the sick; *specif*: one esp. trained to carry out such duties under the supervision of a physician").

IDEA's structure and purpose reinforce this textual interpretation. Congress enacted IDEA to increase the *educational* opportunities available to disabled children, not to provide medical care for them. See 20 U. S. C. § 1400(c) ("It is the purpose of this chapter to assure that all children with disabilities have . . . a free appropriate public education"); see also § 1412 ("In order to qualify for assistance . . . a State shall demonstrate . . . [that it] has in effect a policy that assures all children with disabilities the right to a free appropriate public education"); *Board of Ed. of Hendrick Hudson Central School Dist., Westchester Cty. v. Rowley*, 458 U. S. 176, 179 (1982) ("The Act represents an ambitious federal effort to promote the education of handicapped children"). As such, where Congress decided to require a supportive service—including speech pathology, occupational therapy, and audiology—that appears "medical" in nature, it took care to do so explicitly. See § 1401(a)(17). Congress specified these services precisely because it recognized that they would otherwise fall under the broad "medical services" exclusion. Indeed, when it crafted the definition of related services, Congress could have, but chose not to, include "nursing services" in this list.

B

Tatro was wrongly decided even if the phrase "medical services" was subject to multiple constructions, and therefore, deference to any reasonable Department of Education regulation was appropriate. The Department of Education has never promulgated regulations defining the scope of IDEA's "medical services" exclusion. One year before *Tatro* was decided, the Secretary of Education issued proposed regulations that defined excluded medical services as "services relating to the practice of medicine." 47 Fed. Reg. 33838 (1982). These regulations, which represent the Department's only attempt to define the disputed term, were never adopted. Instead, "[t]he regulations actually define only those 'medical services' that *are* owed to handicapped children," *Tatro*, 468 U. S., at 892, n. 10) (emphasis in original), not those that *are not*. Now, as when *Tatro* was decided, the regulations require districts to provide services performed " 'by a licensed physician to determine a child's medically related handicapping condition which results in the child's need for special education and related services.' " *Ibid.* (quoting 34 CFR § 300.13(b)(4) (1983), recodified and amended as 34 CFR § 300.16(b)(4) (1998).

Extrapolating from this regulation, the *Tatro* Court presumed that this meant "that 'medical services' not owed under the statute are those 'services by a licensed physician' that serve other purposes." *Tatro*, supra, at 892, n. 10 (emphasis deleted). The Court, therefore, did not defer to the regulation itself, but rather relied on an inference drawn from it to speculate about how a regulation might read if the Department of Education promulgated one. Deference in those circumstances is impermissible. We cannot defer to a regulation that does not exist.[3]

II

Assuming that *Tatro* was correctly decided in the first instance, it does not control the outcome of this case. Because IDEA was enacted pursuant to Congress' spending power, *Rowley*, supra, at 190, n. 11, our analysis of the statute in this case is governed by special rules of construction. We have repeatedly emphasized that, when Congress places conditions on the receipt of federal funds, "it must do so unambiguously." *Pennhurst State School and Hospital v. Halderman*, 451 U. S. 1, 17 (1981). See also *Rowley*, supra, at 190, n. 11; *South Dakota v. Dole*, 483 U. S. 203, 207 (1987); *New York v. United States*, 505 U. S. 144, 158 (1992).

This is because a law that "condition[s] an offer of federal funding on a promise by the recipient ... amounts essentially to a contract between the Government and the recipient of funds." *Gebser v. Lago Vista Independent School Dist.*, 524 U. S. 274, 276 (1998). As such, "[t]he legitimacy of Congress' power to legislate under the spending power . . . rests on whether the State voluntarily and knowingly accepts the terms of the 'contract.' There can, of course, be no knowing acceptance if a State is unaware of the conditions or is unable to ascertain what is expected of it." *Pennhurst*, supra, at 17 (citations omitted). It follows that we must interpret Spending Clause legislation narrowly, in order to avoid saddling the States with obligations that they did not anticipate.

The majority's approach in this case turns this Spending Clause presumption on its head. We have held that, in enacting IDEA, Congress wished to require "States to educate handicapped children with nonhandicapped children whenever possible," *Rowley*, 458 U. S., at 202. Congress, however, also took steps to limit the fiscal burdens that States must bear in attempting to achieve this laudable goal. These steps include requiring States to provide an education that is only "appropriate" rather that requiring them to maximize the potential of disabled students, see 20 U. S. C. § 1400(c) *Rowley, supra,* at 200, recognizing that integration into the public school environment is not always possible, see § 1412(5), and clarifying that, with a few exceptions, public schools need not provide "medical services" for disabled students, §§ 1401(a)(17) and (18).

For this reason, we have previously recognized that Congress did not intend to "impos[e] upon the States a burden of unspecified proportions and weight" in enacting IDEA. *Rowley, supra,* at 176, n. 11. These federalism concerns require us to interpret IDEA's related services provision, consistent with *Tatro,* as follows: Department of Education regulations require districts to provide disabled children with health-related services that school nurses can perform as part of their normal duties. This reading of *Tatro,* although less broad than the majority's, is equally plausible and certainly more consistent with our obligation to interpret Spending Clause legislation narrowly. Before concluding that the district was required to provide clean intermittent catheterization for Amber Tatro, we observed that school nurses in the district were authorized to perform services that were "difficult to distinguish from the provision of [clean intermittent catheterization] to the handicapped." *Tatro,* 468 U. S., at 893. We concluded that "[i]t would be strange indeed if Congress, in attempting to extend special services to handicapped children, were unwilling to guarantee them services of a kind that are routinely provided to the nonhandicapped." *Id.,* at 893-894.

Unlike clean intermittent catheterization, however, a school nurse cannot provide the services that respondent requires, see *ante,* at 3, n. 3, and continue to perform her normal duties. To the contrary, because respondent requires continuous, one-on-one care throughout the entire school day, all agree that the district must hire an additional employee to attend solely to respondent. This will cost a minimum of $18,000 per year. Although the majority recognizes this fact, it nonetheless concludes that the "more extensive" nature of the services that respondent needs is irrelevant to the question whether those services fall under the medical services exclusion. *Ante,* at 9. This approach disregards the constitutionally mandated principles of construction applicable to Spending Clause legislation and blindsides unwary States with fiscal obligations that they could not have anticipated.

For the foregoing reasons, I respectfully dissent.

FOOTNOTES

[1] "The term 'related services' means transportation, and such developmental, corrective, and other supportive services (including speech pathology and audiology, psychological services, physical and occupational therapy, recreation, including therapeutic recreation, social work services, counseling services, including rehabilitation counseling, and medical services, except that such medical services shall be for diagnostic and evaluation purposes only) as may be required to assist a child with a disability to benefit from special education, and includes the early identification and assessment of disabling conditions in children." 20 U. S. C. §1401(a)(17).

Originally, the statute was enacted without a definition of "related services." See Education of the Handicapped Act, 84 Stat. 175. In 1975, Congress added the definition at issue in this case. Education for All Handicapped Children Act of 1975, § 4(a)(4), 89 Stat. 775. Aside from nonsubstantive changes and added examples of included services, see, e.g., Individuals with Disabilities Education Act Amendments of 1997, § 101, 111 Stat. 45; Individuals with Disabilities Education Act Amendments of 1991, § 25(a)(1)(B), 105 Stat. 605; Education of the Handicapped Act Amendments of 1990, § 101(c), 104 Stat. 1103, the relevant language in § 1401(a)(17) has not been amended since 1975. All references to the IDEA herein are to the 1994 version as codified in Title 20 of the United States Code—the version of the statute in effect when this dispute arose.

[2] In his report in this case, the Administrative Law Judge explained that "[b]eing ventilator dependent means that [Garret] breathes only with external aids, usually an electric ventilator, and occasionally by someone else's manual pumping of an air bag attached to his tracheotomy tube when the ventilator is being maintained. This later procedure is called ambu bagging." App. to Pet. for Cert. 19a.

[3] "He needs assistance with urinary bladder catheterization once a day, the suctioning of his tracheotomy tube as needed, but at least once every six hours, with food and drink at lunchtime, in getting into a reclining position for five minutes of each hour, and ambu bagging occasionally as needed when the ventilator is checked for proper functioning. He also needs assistance from someone familiar with his ventilator in the event there is a malfunction or electrical problem, and someone who can perform emergency procedures in the event he experiences autonomic hyperreflexia. Autonomic

hyperreflexia is an uncontrolled visceral reaction to anxiety or a full bladder. Blood pressure increases, heart rate increases, and flushing and sweating may occur.

Garret has not experienced autonomic hyperreflexia frequently in recent years, and it has usually been alleviated by catheterization. He has not ever experienced autonomic hyperreflexia at school. Garret is capable of communicating his needs orally or in another fashion so long as he has not been rendered unable to do so by an extended lack of oxygen." *Id.,* at 20a.

[4] "Included are such services as care for students who need urinary catheterization, food and drink, oxygen supplement positioning, and suctioning." *Id.,* at 28a; see also id., at 53a.

[5] In addition, the ALJ's opinion contains a thorough discussion of "other tests and criteria" pressed by the District, id., at 52a, including the burden on the District and the cost of providing assistance to Garret. Although the ALJ found no legal authority for establishing a cost-based test for determining what related services are required by the statute, he went on to reject the District's arguments on the merits. See *id.,* at 42a-53a. We do not reach the issue here, but the ALJ also found that Garret's in-school needs must be met by the District under an Iowa statute as well as the IDEA. Id., at 54a-55a.

[6] "The regulations define 'related services' for handicapped children to include 'school health services,' 34 CFR § 300.13(a) (1983), which are defined in turn as 'services provided by a qualified school nurse or other qualified person,' § 300.13(b)(10). 'Medical services' are defined as 'services provided by a licensed physician.' § 300.13(b)(4). Thus, the Secretary has [reasonably] determined that the services of a school nurse otherwise qualifying as a 'related service' are not subject to exclusion as a 'medical service,' but that the services of a physician are excludable as such.

" *. . . By limiting the 'medical services' exclusion to the services of a physician or hospital,* both far more expensive, the Secretary has given a permissible construction to the provision." 468 U. S., at 892-893 (emphasis added) (footnote omitted); see also *id.,* at 894 ("[T]he regulations state that school nursing services must be provided only if they can be performed by a nurse or other qualified person, not if they must be performed by a physician").

Based on certain policy letters issued by the Department of Education, it seems that the Secretary's post-*Tatro* view of the statute has not been entirely clear. E.g., App. to Pet. for Cert. 64a. We may assume that the Secretary has authority under the IDEA to adopt regulations that define the "medical services" exclusion by more explicitly taking into account the nature and extent of the requested services; and the Secretary surely has the authority to enumerate the services that are, and are not, fairly included within the scope of § 1407(a)(17). But the Secretary has done neither; and, in this Court, she advocates affirming the judgment of the Court of Appeals. Brief for United States as Amicus Curiae; see also *Auer v. Robbins,* 519 U. S. 452, 462 (1997) (an agency's views as amicus curiae may be entitled to deference). We obviously have no authority to rewrite the regulations, and we see no sufficient reason to revise *Tatro,* either.

[7] See Tr. of Oral Arg. 4-5, 12.

[8] At oral argument, the District suggested that we first consider the nature of the requested service (either "medical" or not); then, if the service is "medical," apply the multi-factor test to determine whether the service is an excluded physician service or an included school nursing service under the Secretary of Education's regulations. See Tr. of Oral Arg. 7, 13-14. Not only does this approach provide no additional guidance for identifying "medical" services, it is also disconnected from both the statutory text and the regulations we upheld in *Irving Independent School Dist. v. Tatro,* 468 U. S. 883 (1984).

"Medical" services are generally excluded from the statute, and the regulations elaborate on that statutory term. No authority cited by the District requires an additional inquiry if the requested service is both "related" and non-"medical." Even if § 1401(a)(17) demanded an additional step, the factors proposed by the District are hardly more useful in identifying "nursing" services than they are in identifying "medical" services; and the District cannot limit educational access simply by pointing to the limitations of existing staff. As we noted in *Tatro,* the IDEA requires schools to hire specially trained personnel to meet disabled student needs. *Id.,* at 893.

[9] See Tr. of Oral Arg. 4-5, 13; Brief for Petitioner 6-7, 9. The District, however, will not necessarily need to hire an additional employee to meet Garret's needs. The District already employs a one-on-one teacher associate (TA) who assists Garret during the school day. See App. to Pet. for Cert. 26a-27a. At one time, Garret's TA was a licensed practical nurse (LPN). In light of the state Board of Nursing's recent ruling that the District's registered nurses may decide to delegate Garret's care to an LPN, see Brief for United States as Amicus Curiae 9-10 (filed Apr. 22, 1998), the dissent's future-cost estimate is speculative. See App. to Pet. for Cert. 28a, 58a-60a (if the District could assign Garret's care to a TA who is also an LPN, there would be "a minimum of additional expense").

[10] The dissent's approach, which seems to be even broader than the District's, is unconvincing. The dissent's rejection of our unanimous decision in *Tatro* comes 15 years too late, see *Patterson v. McLean Credit Union,* 491 U. S. 164, 172-173 (1989) (*stare decisis* has "special force" in statutory interpretation), and it offers nothing constructive in its place. Aside from rejecting a "provider-specific approach," the dissent cites unrelated statutes and offers a circular definition of "medical services." Post, at 3-4 (" 'services' that are 'medical' in 'nature' "). Moreover, the dissent's approach apparently would exclude most ordinary school nursing services of the kind routinely provided to nondisabled children; that anomalous result is not easily attributable to congressional intent. See *Tatro,* 468 U. S., at 893.

In a later discussion the dissent does offer a specific proposal: that we now interpret (or rewrite) the Secretary's regulations so that school districts need only provide disabled children with "health-related services that school nurses can perform as part of their normal duties." Post, at 7. The District does not dispute that its nurses "can perform" the requested services, so the dissent's objection is that District nurses would not be performing their "normal duties" if they met Garret's needs. That is, the District would need an "additional employee." Post, at 8. This proposal is functionally similar to a proposed regulation—ultimately withdrawn—that would have replaced the "school health services" provision. See 47 Fed. Reg. 33838, 33854 (1982) (the statute and regulations may not be read to affect legal obligations to make available to handicapped children services, including school health services, made available to nonhandicapped children). The dissent's suggestion is unacceptable for several reasons. Most important, such revisions of the regulations are better left to the Secretary, and an additional staffing need is generally not a sufficient objection to the requirements of § 1401(a)(17). See n. 8, supra.

FOOTNOTES - Dissent

[1] The Act currently defines "related services" as "transportation and such developmental, corrective, and other supportive services (including speech pathology and audiology, psychological services, physical and occupational therapy, recreation, including therapeutic recreation, social work services, counseling services, including rehabilitation counseling, and medical services, except that such medical services shall be for diagnostic and evaluation purposes only) as may be required to assist a child with a disability to benefit from special education . . . ." 20 U. S. C. § 1401(a)(17) (emphasis added).

[2] See, e.g., 38 U. S. C. § 1701(6) ("The term 'medical services' includes, in addition to medical examination, treatment and rehabilitative services ... surgical services, dental services . . . optometric and podiatric services, . . . preventive health services, . . . [and] such consultation, professional counseling, training, and mental health services as are necessary in connection with the treatment"); § 101(28) ("The term 'nursing home care' means the accommodation of convalescents . . . who require nursing care and related medical services"); 26 U. S. C. § 213(d)(1) ("The term 'medical care' means amounts paid . . . for the diagnosis, cure, mitigation, treatment, or prevention of disease").

[3] Nor do I think that it is appropriate to defer to the Department of Education's litigating position in this case. The agency has had ample opportunity to address this problem but has failed to do so in a formal regulation. Instead, it has maintained conflicting positions about whether the services at issue in this case are required by IDEA. See ante, at 7-8, n. 6. Under these circumstances, we should not assume that the litigating position reflects the "agency's fair and considered judgment." *Auer v. Robbins*, 519 U. S. 452, 462 (1997).

END OF CEDAR RAPIDS

ABOUT THE AUTHORS

Peter W. D. Wright, Esq.

PETER WRIGHT was born and raised in Washington, D.C. In the early 1950's, he was diagnosed with strephosymbolia ("word blindness") and severe hyperkinesis. Today, those labels would be dyslexia, a language learning disability and Attention Deficit Hyperactivity Disorder (ADHD). Pete received intensive daily Orton-Gillingham tutoring from Diana Hanbury King for two years, and attended a residential program for additional remediation of his dyslexia and dysgraphia.

By the end of eleventh grade in Washington D.C. public schools, Pete had a D average. His parents were alarmed about his academic problems and lack of interest in school. They placed him in Moses Brown, a Quaker boarding school in Rhode Island, for two years where he repeated eleventh grade. At Moses Brown, Pete experienced academic success for the first time. He was co-captain of the state championship football team and was selected for the "All-State" and "All New England" football teams.

Pete attended Randolph-Macon College in Ashland Virginia where he majored in psychology. After graduating from college in 1968, he worked in juvenile training schools as a house parent and counselor. Later, he worked as a juvenile probation officer in Richmond, Virginia. He was honored as Virginia's "Juvenile Probation Officer of the Year" in 1972.

During these years, Pete attended graduate school part-time. He completed thirty hours of coursework in psychology. Later, he entered T. C. Williams Law School at the University of Richmond. In December, 1977, he graduated from law school. He is a member of the American Bar Association, American Trial Lawyers Association, and Virginia Trial Lawyers Association.

Pete serves on the boards of several organizations, including the Professional Advisory Board of the Learning Disabilities Association of America (LDAA) and the Council of Parent Attorneys and Advocates (COPPA). He provides special education advocacy training to parents, advocates, and educators, and speaks at legal education seminars around the country about representing children with disabilities.

On October 6, 1993, Pete presented oral argument before the U. S. Supreme Court in *Florence County School District Four v. Shannon Carter*. Thirty-four days later, the Court found for his client, Shannon Carter, in a unanimous landmark decision. Pete is involved in cases around the country and consults with parents in other countries about educational problems.

Pamela Darr Wright, MA, MSW

PAMELA WRIGHT is a psychotherapist who has worked with children and families for more than 30 years. Her training and experience in clinical psychology and clinical social work give her a unique perspective on parent-child-school dynamics, problems, and solutions. She has seen clients in mental health centers, family guidance and psychiatric clinics, correctional institutions, hospitals, and schools.

Pam earned undergraduate and graduate degrees in Psychology from East Carolina University. She worked for ten years as a clinical psychologist in North Carolina before returning to graduate school.

In 1985, she earned a master's degree in clinical social work from Virginia Commonwealth University, graduating *summa cum laude*. Her academic honors include *Who's Who in American Colleges and Universities*.

Pam has written many articles about raising, educating and advocating for children with disabilities. She speaks at conferences around the country on special education advocacy issues.

She designed the Wrightslaw web site at http://www.wrightslaw.com/ and publishes The Special Ed Advocate newsletter.

Index

Turn the page to learn about our Recyling Policy!

ORDER FORM

Quantity	Title	Unit Price	Total
	Subtotal		_____
	Virginia Residents add 4.5% Sales tax		_____
	Shipping ($3.95 for first book; $2.00 each additional)		_____
	TOTAL		_____

Name: __ _____

Address: _____

City, State, ZIP: _____

Phone: _____

For Faster Service, Use Your Credit Card and Our Toll-Free Number (877) LAW IDEA

Toll Free: 1 (877) LAW IDEA. Have your VISA or MasterCard ready.
Toll Free Fax: 800-863-5348
Mail: Harbor House Publications, P. O. Box 480, Hartfield, VA 23071-0480.
E-mail: orders@wrightslaw.com

Payment Method

Check enclosed _____ MasterCard _____ VISA _____

Card Number: _____

Name on card: _____

Exp. date: _____ / _____

Authorizing Signature: _____

Bulk Orders

Harbor House Law Publications are available at discounts for bulk purchases, academic sales or textbook adoptions. For more information, contact Harbor House Law Press, P. O. Box 480, Hartfield VA 23071. Please provide the book title, ISBN number, quantity, how the book will be used, and date needed.
Toll Free Phone Orders: (877) LAW IDEA; Toll Free Fax: 800-863-5348.

SPECIAL OFFER FROM HARBOR HOUSE LAW

Stay Up-to-Date and
Save 25% On Your Next Purchase!

Because law changes and evolves, Wrightslaw: Special Education Law will be revised to reflect current legal information.

When we publish a new edition of Wrightslaw: Special Education Law, you can use our recycling policy to get 25% off the purchase price of the new edition.

Recyling Policy

Remove the cover of this book and send it to us with your order.

We will give you a 25% discount off the retail price of the book when you purchase from us.

For current prices and editions, contact Harbor House Law Press at 1-877-LAW-IDEA.

You can also contact us by email at orders@harborhouselaw.com.

ORDER FORM

Quantity	Title	Unit Price	Total

_____

_____

_____

_____

_____Subtotal _____

_____ Virginia Residents add 4.5% Sales tax   _____

_____ Shipping ($3.95 for first book; $2.00 each additional)   _____

_____ TOTAL _____

Name: _____

Address: _____

City, State, ZIP: _____

Phone: _____

For Faster Service, Use Your Credit Card and Our Toll-Free Number (877) LAW IDEA

Toll Free Phone Orders: 1 (877) LAW IDEA. Have your VISA or MasterCard ready.
Toll Free Fax Orders: 800 863-5348
Mail: Harbor House Publications, P. O. Box 480, Hartfield, VA 23071-0480.
E-mail: orders@wrightslaw.com

Payment Method

Check enclosed _____   MasterCard _____   VISA _____

Card Number: _____

Name on card: _____

Exp. date: _____/_____

Authorizing Signature: _____

Bulk Orders
Harbor House Law Publications are available at discounts for bulk purchases, academic sales or textbook adoptions. For more information, contact Harbor House Law Press, P. O. Box 480, Hartfield VA 23071. Please provide the book title, ISBN number, quantity, how the book will be used, and date needed.
Toll-free Phone Orders: (877) LAW IDEA; Fax   Orders: 800-863-5348.

Wrightslaw: Special Education Law

If you are the parent of a child with a disability or you have a niece, nephew, or grandchild with a disability, Wrightslaw: Special Education Law   is required reading.

If you have a friend or neighbor whose child has a disability, Wrightslaw: Special Education Law should be required reading for the child's parent.

More than five million children with disabilities receive special education services. Unfortunately, few parents understand their children's rights or their parental rights and responsibilities. Ignorance of the law is often as handicapping as the child's disability. Wrightslaw: Special Education Law   is an essential tool for anyone who wants to advocate for a child with a disability.

Wrightslaw: Special Education Law   is the first in a series of special education law and advocacy books and manuals relating to the needs of children with disabilities.

Pete Wright , an attorney with a disability, has represented children with disabilities and their parents for more than 20 years. Pete argued and won a landmark special education case before the U. S. Supreme Court.

Pete and Pam Wright developed Wrightslaw , a compehensive special education advocacy website for parents, attorneys, advocates, and educators.

Wrightslaw: Special Education Law   is an excellent gift for any parent of a child with a disability.

COMING SOON
Wrightslaw: From Emotions to Advocacy

Wrightslaw: From Emotions to Advocacy is the second book in the Wrightslaw series.

In Wrightslaw: From Emotions to Advocacy, Pete and Pam Wright teach parents how to use tactics and strategies to secure quality special education services for children with disabilities. Parents learn how to write appropriate, measureable IEP goals, and how to measure the child's progress in special education. Parents learn about the power of "school culture," the importance of "win-win" solutions, and how to resolve conflict.

If you want to be notified when "Wrightslaw: From Emotions to Advocacy" is available, you should subscribe to The Special Ed Advocate. The Special Ed Advocate is a free online newsletter about special education law and advocacy issues. Newsletter subscribers receive advance information about the status of Wrightslaw books and pre-publication offers.

To subscribe to The Special Ed Advocate, go to the Wrightslaw website at

http://www.wrightslaw.com/

ORDER FORM

Quantity	Title		Unit Price	Total
			Subtotal	
	Virginia Residents add 4.5% Sales tax			
	Shipping ($3.95 for first book; $2.00 each additional)			
			TOTAL	

Name: _____

Address: _____

City, State, ZIP: _____

Phone: _____

For Faster Service, Use Your Credit Card and Our Toll-Free Number
(877) LAW IDEA

Toll Free Phone Orders: (877) LAW IDEA. Have your VISA or MasterCard ready.
Toll Free Fax: 800 863-5348
Mail: Harbor House Law Press, P. O. Box 480, Hartfield, VA 23071-0480.
E-mail: orders@wrightslaw.com

Payment Method

Check enclosed _____ MasterCard _____ VISA _____

Card Number: _____

Name on card: _____

Exp. date: _____ / _____

Authorizing Signature: _____

Bulk Orders

Harbor House Publications   are available at quantity discounts for bulk purchases, academic sales or textbook adoptions. For more information, contact Harbor House Law Press, P. O. Box 480, Hartfield VA 23071. Please provide the book title, ISBN number, quantity, how the book will be used, and date needed.
Toll Free Orders: (877) LAW IDEA